PENGUIN

THE COLLECTED
MARY WOLLSTO

MARY WOLLSTONECRAFT, (1759–97) was an educationalist and miscellaneous writer. She worked at a school at Newington with her sister, and as a governess with Lord Kingsborough. Then she made her living by writing, as a translator, and as a reader for Johnson, a London publisher. She was a member of a group of Radicals which included William Godwin, Tom Paine, Priestley and Fuseli, the painter. Godwin lived with her following her attempted suicide at Putney Bridge, after she had been deserted by her lover. He married her shortly before the birth (which proved fatal) of her daughter, the Mary Wollstonecraft Godwin who became Shelley's second wife and wrote Frankenstein.

JANET TODD is the Francis Hutcheson Professor of English Literature at the University of Glasgow and an Honorary Fellow of Lucy Cavendish College, Cambridge. Her publications include *Women's Friendship in Literature* (1980), *Feminist Literary History* (1988), *The Sign of Angellica: Women, Writing and Fiction 1660–1800* and three biographies, *The Secret Life of Aphra Behn* (1996), *Mary Wollstonecraft: A Revolutionary Life* (2000) and *Rebel Daughters: Rebellion in Ireland 1798* (2003). She has edited *The Collected Letters of Mary Wollstonecraft* (Penguin, 2003) and is the general editor of the Cambridge edition of Jane Austen's works.

The Collected Letters of Mary Wollstonecraft

Edited by JANET TODD

PENGUIN BOOKS

In memory of Ralph M. Wardle,
scholar and editor

PENGUIN BOOKS

Published by the Penguin Group
Penguin Books Ltd, 80 Strand, London WC2R ORL, England
Penguin Group (USA) Inc., 375 Hudson Street, New York, New York 10014, USA
Penguin Books Australia Ltd, 250 Camberwell Road, Camberwell, Victoria 3124, Australia
Penguin Books Canada Ltd, 10 Alcorn Avenue, Toronto, Ontario, Canada M4V 3B2
Penguin Books India (P) Ltd, 11 Community Centre, Panchsheel Park, New Delhi – 110 017, India
Penguin Group (NZ), cnr Airborne and Rosedale Roads, Albany, Auckland 1310, New Zealand
Penguin Books (South Africa) (Pty) Ltd, 24 Sturdee Avenue, Rosebank 2196, South Africa

Penguin Books Ltd, Registered Offices: 80 Strand, London WC2R ORL, England

www.penguin.com

Published by Allen Lane 2003
Published in Penguin Classics 2004
1

Typeset by Rowland Phototypesetting Ltd, Bury St Edmunds, Suffolk
Printed and England by Clays Ltd, St Ives plc

Contents

Acknowledgements

Mary Wollstonecraft's letters are taken from manuscripts where possible and from the first publication where not. I am grateful to the following libraries, art galleries, societies, and owners of collections for permission to reprint letters in their possession: the Lord Abinger Collection at the Bodleian Library, Oxford; the Bancroft Library, University of California; the Royal Watercolour Society at the Bankside Gallery, London; the Beinecke Rare Book and Manuscript Library, Yale University; the Boston Public Library; the Henry W. and Albert A. Berg Collection at the New York Public Library; the Carl H. Pforzheimer Collection at the New York Public Library; the Henry E. Huntington Library and Art Gallery, California; the Historical Society of Pennsylvania; and the Liverpool Central Libraries.

In addition to cooperation from librarians at the British Library and the University Library, Cambridge, I am especially grateful for the help I received from Dr Barker-Benfield at the Bodleian Library, Oxford, Stephen Wagner at the Carl H. Pforzheimer Library, New York, Gayle Barkley at the Huntington Library, California, Simon Fenwick at the Bankside Gallery, London, and Mark Pomeroy at the Royal Academy of Arts. I also appreciate help from Pamela Clemit, Claire Connolly, Seamus Cullen, Robert Cummings, A. L. Gilroy, Rüdiger Görner, Derek Hughes, Sonia Massai, Burton R. Pollin, Gordon Turnbull, W. M. Verhoeven, and Astrid Wilkens. Editing is always a communal enterprise and I owe a debt to many past scholars of Wollstonecraft. In particular I have profited from the work of Kenneth Neill Cameron, W. Clark Durant, and Charles Kegan Paul. My greatest past debt is to Ralph Wardle and his 1979 edition of Wollstonecraft's correspondence, which has been an inspiration for this new edition. My greatest present debt is to my assistant Antje Blank for her dedicated and careful research work. I would also like to thank the British Academy and the University of Glasgow for their financial support.

Introduction[1]

I

Mary Wollstonecraft (1759–1797) is one of the most distinctive letter-writers of the eighteenth century. Her works from her juvenile outpourings as a young girl in the Yorkshire town of Beverley to her final short notes to her husband and future biographer William Godwin are instantly recognizable. Indeed Wollstonecraft's value is as much in letter-writing as in public authorship; often she seems almost to live through her correspondence, expressing within it her numerous roles: child, daughter, companion, friend, teacher, governess, sister, literary hack, woman of letters, lover, wife, rationalist and romantic. She wrote incessantly throughout her life, priding herself on her frank expression and often berating her correspondents for not rising to her expansive standards. She might have said with Amelia Opie, a friend from her final years, 'If writing were an effort to me I should not now be alive . . . and it might have been inserted in the bills of mortality – "dead of letter-writing A. Opie".'[2]

Wollstonecraft's letters were self-aware certainly but they were also dashed off as the overflow sometimes of joy, more often of bitterness, ennui and self-pity. They are occasionally funny, often engaging, but most frequently moving in their self-centred vulnerability. In them Wollstonecraft grows from the awkward child of fourteen to the woman of thirty-eight facing her death in childbirth. One can see

1. A version of the introduction is printed in the *Companion to Mary Wollstonecraft*, ed. Claudia Johnson (Cambridge: Cambridge University Press, 2002).
2. *Amelia: The Tale of a Plain Friend*, by J. Menzies-Wilson and Helen Lloyd (London, 1937), p. v.

where she matured and where she remained entangled in childhood emotions, noting in the swift reading of a lifetime's writing the unity in temperament from beginning to end, the eerie consistency of tone. At different times the letters reveal her wanting to reconcile different irreconcilables – integrity and sexual longing, the needs and duties of a woman, motherhood and intellectual life, fame and domesticity, reason and passion – but all are marked by similar strenuousness, a wish to be true to the complexity she felt. As a result she never seems quite to have said the last word: there are numerous PSs in her letters, mentions of the paper or letter itself and her need to write to its end, to fill in, to dominate her pages. No space should be left empty, no mood untouched by expression: 'I can hardly bid you adieu, till I come to the bottom of my paper,' she wrote. A letter will conclude by promising silence, only to be followed by another begun a few hours later.

Wollstonecraft's letters were not written with half a glance at the public in the manner of some of the Romantic poets like Lord Byron, who expected a place in literary history. At the same time no letter-writer of the time assumed complete one-to-one privacy. Runs of letters were kept, handed around among coteries or colleague groups. When Wollstonecraft asked for her letters back from a correspondent, she was confident that she would receive them intact. Yet inevitably for the modern reader there is a sense of intrusion in reading private writing, even after so long. Those anxious about the tastelessness of the act might look at the words of another friend of her latter years, Mary Hays. Unlike Wollstonecraft, Hays lived long enough to collect her own correspondence, and she wrote, 'Should this book fall into the hands of those who make the human heart their study, they may, it is possible, find some entertainment, should the papers continue legible, in tracing the train of circumstances which have contributed to form a character, in some respects it may be singular and whimsical, yet affording I trust something to imitate, though more to warn and pity.'[3]

Wollstonecraft, like Hays, was aware that she was expressing an inner reality. Inevitably there were outside influences: some letters

3. *Love-Letters of Mary Hays*, ed. A. F. Wedd (London: Methuen, 1925), pp. 13–14.

mentioned reading, usually of improving books, but mostly the modern reader grasps little of the world around – much more appears in her sister Eliza's letters. For Wollstonecraft's response to the great events of her time, the French Revolution and the English reaction, or the deaths of literary and political figures, we must turn to the published writings, to her three polemical works: *A Vindication of the Rights of Men*, *A Vindication of the Rights of Woman* and *An Historical and Moral View of the Origin and Progress of the French Revolution*, or to her journalism with the *Analytical Review*. But she does not, by contrast in her letters, describe a domestic private world outside the public political one; unlike most eighteenth-century letter-writers, especially women, she did not give immense detail of interiors, gardens, consumer objects, dresses and materials. The letters of Jane Austen and Frances Burney are full of muslins, gauzes and hats, as well as of shops and streets they have entered and walked down. Wollstonecraft's letters, often sent from the same fashionable locations, reveal mostly her thoughts, sensations and emotions. In many respects offending the canons of good letter-writing, she was rarely concise, graphic, direct, realistically detailed or detached.

Good letter-writing of the time was described by the Scottish literary critic Hugh Blair, whose popular *Letters on Rhetoric* Wollstonecraft discovered when she was a governess in Ireland in 1786 and 1787. She valued the work but the remarks on letter-writing had little influence on her practice. Blair had expressed the Augustan notion of correspondence as good conversation, sprightly, witty and seemingly natural, above all entertaining, with a constant eye to the recipient. Although she tended to be more open about her feelings with some correspondents than others, these were not always especially appropriate for confidence or especially close in family or friendship. Indeed she seems to have had little concern for the particular effect of her writing on her correspondent; for example, she remarked to an old friend George Blood that he might dread hearing from her if she continued moaning; yet this fear did not inhibit further complaint. She simply did not accept the Augustan advice to calibrate tone and detail according to the recipient. Great letter writers in this tradition such as Horace Walpole took a single event and reported it in different ways for different correspondents. Wollstonecraft was not a leisured and literary letter-writer like this; she did not have Walpole's temperament or his time and space; she was writing on the hoof, in cramped lodgings, on swaying boats, in the wilds of Scandinavia or in freezing Paris before queuing for bread, or between reviewings in London, or indeed before plunging into the Thames to end her life. In such circumstances she was concerned with expressing her emotions as she felt them, not entertaining or worrying about her effect. So she could reveal herself fully to men such as her future publisher Joseph Johnson when she hardly knew him or display her melancholy to a chance acquaintance like the clergyman Henry Gabell.

Perhaps her secret determination to become a writer gave all her communications value in her eyes, however self-obsessed and repetitive they might sound to her correspondent. Just occasionally she sought to entertain – when she replied to her sister Eliza, whom she knew to be gloomy, she tried 'fabricat[ing] a lively epistle' – but this was a rare aim and, if her letters to her other sister are anything to judge by, she soon fell back on her preachy homiletic style or her habit of detailing her moods almost as if conversing with herself rather than another. She was concerned to get herself across to herself as well as to both private recipients and public readership, whatever the cost. As a result of this self-concern there was less distinction than one might have expected between her letters to her lover and those to her sisters or distant friends.

The main impression given by her letters, then, is of self-absorption but not lack of self-awareness; often they seem more like a diary than correspondence, a communion with the self or perhaps a self-created other. Wollstonecraft talked and thought on paper. The strengths of the letters were that, while they were not witty entertainments, they were also not sentimental or exaggeratedly exclamatory in the contemporary feminine mode – letters from Mary Hays or Mary Robinson are examples – nor did they use prepackaged phrases. Instead they sought to dramatize feelings, tease out the meaning from sensations, enacting moods on paper rather than simply describing them. Indeed the letters themselves often formed a large part of the drama of her life. Wollstonecraft would begin to write in one state and end in another or write herself into dramatic misery. Once she portrayed herself awaiting the post, then hearing that nothing had arrived; her fiery brain burnt and she rushed from the room for air. All was captured on paper.

Wollstonecraft's letters create a distinctive world, a sense of inner vitality, revealing a consistent character. Unhappy in Scandinavia, she told her forsaking lover Gilbert Imlay:

> there is such a thing as a broken heart! There are characters whose very energy preys upon them; and who, ever inclined to cherish by reflection some passion, cannot rest satisfied with the common comforts of life. I have endeavoured to fly from myself, and launched into all the dissipation possible here, only to feel keener anguish, when alone with my child.[4]

Her huge sense of the 'I' is always believable and fully present. It is quite unlike the self-image of, for example, Lady Mary Wortley Montagu or the bluestocking writers such as Elizabeth Carter and Catherine Talbot. The bluestockings wrote to each other as friends, but their letters, which seem designed to be passed around among a coterie, have a public quality lacking in Wollstonecraft. Lady Mary Wortley Montagu had a very different temperament from Wollstonecraft, as she disclosed when she wrote her wonderfully sharp and witty letters earlier in the century. Although both struggled for self-mastery – Wollstonecraft through religion in the beginning, then through rationalism – unlike Lady Mary she was not concerned in her letters to discipline her sorrows or to distance her subject matter from herself. She did not try to express herself stoically.[5] Part of the difference lay in their different circumstances. Lady Mary had her aristocratic status to uphold, where Wollstonecraft had little social status but a great deal of valued identity to express.

As her letters indicate, Wollstonecraft believed in getting to truth through investigating her own experience; so her mode of writing was in the main intensely personal. She argued the value of her expression with Godwin, who had been critical of her raw careless style:

4. p. 312.
5. After Wollstonecraft there are other women writers whose private letters reveal a similar intimate self-dramatizing, self-revealing quality: for example, Charlotte Brontë and Virginia Woolf.

I am compelled to think that there is something in my writings more valuable, than in the productions of some people on whom you bestow warm elogiums – I mean more mind – denominate it as you will – more of the observations of my own senses, more of the combining of my own imagination – the effusions of my own feelings and passions than the cold workings of the brain on the materials procured by the senses and imagination of other writers – [6]

Her points remain valid for her public writings or her personal letters.

II

Wollstonecraft's letters survive where someone else wished them to do so. For all his rebuffing, Gilbert Imlay chose to save and then return his lover's letters. His successor, Godwin, read them and found them wonderful and passionate, seductive of the later reader if not of their first recipient; they were in keeping with his image of Wollstonecraft as an author of genius. So, remarkably for the times, he chose to print an intimate record of the intense obsessive love felt by his wife for a former lover as proof of this genius. Perhaps we also owe to Godwin the unflagging intensity of the letters. He liked to see Wollstonecraft as an emotional writer and was less interested in her as a political and economic commentator. Consequently he cut out the sections of the letters from Scandinavia that concerned the business on which Wollstonecraft was travelling (his excisions might also be due to the nature of this business, which was the pursuit of a case arising out of French efforts to circumvent the British blockade during the war between the two countries). As a comparison of these letters with others to her family suggests, he also made them more coherent and corrected the punctuation.

Two other series of letters over which Godwin had control were those between himself and Wollstonecraft and those from Wollstonecraft to her publisher and friend Joseph Johnson. The former he largely kept intact but did not publish, although pencil marks, not in

6. p. 358.

Wollstonecraft's hand, enclosing comments of a personal or possibly sexual nature, might indicate that he once contemplated publication. Many of the interchanges simply consist of notes about quotidian matters, appointments, cold dinners, or arrangements for Wollstonecraft's little daughter by Imlay. Others are longer or more serious, describing the new deep love for Godwin in fleeting voluptuous or tender moments, combined, as always in Wollstonecraft, with moodiness and displays of neediness and self-assertion. The others to Johnson Godwin published together with the Imlay letters in *Posthumous Works* (1798). These also sometimes discuss business – literary assignments and the debts which Wollstonecraft was constantly running up with Johnson – but they also reveal again her troubling mixture of independence and dependence, her conflicting desire to rely on and impress another. Like the Imlay letters, the originals of the Johnson letters were presumably destroyed by Godwin once he had prepared them for publication. There are thus no manuscripts from which to check his editing.

In Godwin's view, the great absence from the letters he was publishing were the extant letters Wollstonecraft wrote to the artist and cultural critic Henry Fuseli, for whom she had had what she described as a 'rational passion' during the early 1790s. They would certainly have been of value since they must have been a record of her mind when she was writing her great polemical works, *A Vindication of the Rights of Men* and *A Vindication of the Rights of Woman*; in addition they would have thrown light on her tortuous efforts to reconcile reason and passion.

When she had been at a low ebb after her suicide attempt in 1795 Wollstonecraft had asked Fuseli as well as Imlay to return her letters. Imlay complied but Fuseli did not. After her death when Godwin was writing his *Memoirs* in loving if undiplomatic remembrance of his wife, he asked Fuseli – whom he knew well but without intimacy – if he might see these letters. Although he had not even opened some of them, so importunate and repetitive had they become in his mind, he had retained them. He showed them in a drawer to Godwin but refused him access; they remained among his papers at his death in 1825. They then became the property of his executor and biographer, John Knowles. Since his subject was Fuseli not Wollstonecraft, Knowles quoted only briefly from them in his 1831 biography.[7] After his death they came into the hands of his son, E. H. Knowles, who announced his possession in 1870.[8] In 1884 E. H. Knowles sold them to Sir Percy Florence Shelley, Mary Shelley's son and Wollstonecraft's grandson. As the child of scandal, brought up to value restraint and propriety, Sir Percy is unlikely to have acquired them for their literary value but rather to stanch the poison of notoriety that seemed to afflict his family – they were after all intense personal letters written from an unmarried woman to a married man. Sir Percy refused Elizabeth Robins Pennell permission to use them for her biography in 1885. Since then they have disappeared and it has long been presumed by scholars that the Shelleys – Sir Percy's wife Jane survived him and was much concerned with the family's legacy – destroyed them.[9]

The letters to Godwin can be explicated through Godwin's own letters, which he also saved; the letters to Imlay have no replies except the fragments quoted within them; the letters to Fuseli exist only in a few quotations by Knowles; one other series of romantic letters surfaces even more shadowly in a newspaper account. Joshua Waterhouse, a clergyman don from St Catherine's College, Cambridge, unmentioned in Wollstonecraft's extant letters, was visiting the fashionable spa of Bath where young Mary was working as a lady's companion. After his murder in 1827 a cache of love-letters was discovered in his possessions: 'Amongst the many fair ones to whom the singular rector of Stukeley paid his addresses was the once-famous Mary Wollstonecraft, distinguished during the period of the French Revolution for her democratical writing. . . . How far the rev. gentleman sped in his wooing with this intellectual amazon we have not been able to ascertain . . .'.[10] The letters have since disappeared.

The greatest gap for our understanding of Wollstonecraft's emotional development is neither the letters to Fuseli nor the supposed ones to Waterhouse but those to Fanny Blood, the main love of her youth. Wollstonecraft was clear about Fanny's significance in a letter

7. *Life and Writings of Henry Fuseli*, 3 vols. (London, 1831).

8. *Notes and Queries*, 19 November 1870, p. 434.

9. See *Letters about Shelley*, ed. Richard Garnett (London: Hodder & Stoughton, 1917).

10. See T. Lovell, *Narrative of the Murder of the late Rev. J. Waterhouse* (1827).

she wrote to Jane Arden: 'I enjoyed the society of a friend, whom I love better than all the world beside, a friend to whom I am bound by every tie of gratitude and inclination: To live with this friend is the height of my ambition . . . her conversation is not more agreeable than improving . . .'. To Godwin Wollstonecraft later described it as 'a friendship so fervent, as for years to have constituted the ruling passion of [my] mind'.[11] Unhappily not a single letter between the pair survives from this period of Wollstonecraft's accelerated emotional and intellectual development.

What does survive is the series of letters to Fanny Blood's younger brother, the enthusiastic George, as well as those to her own youngest sister Everina, these latter perhaps the most revealing of all she wrote since they are rarely inhibited, except about the objects of her affections, and they cover the longest period of her life. Everina held on to these letters until her death in 1843. They were therefore not available to Godwin when he wrote his *Memoirs*, although he had requested them. Everina refused access because she felt she had already suffered enough from her sister's scandalous life – she believed her employment prospects damaged by the relationship. Also she neither liked Godwin nor wished to cooperate on what she regarded as an unwise display of her sister's failings – 'stripping his dead wife naked' as the poet Southey termed it.[12] The counterpart to the Everina letters is the much smaller series to the third sister Eliza Bishop, the most troublesome of the family correspondents and the nearest in temperament and yearnings to Wollstonecraft herself; since Eliza Bishop became thoroughly alienated from her famous sister, even fantasizing her death through several periods of her life, she probably destroyed some of this correspondence; only one letter survives from Wollstonecraft's latter years and it was copied in outrage for her sister Everina to read.

The letters to Everina Wollstonecraft and George Blood have a similar tone; they are often complacent, dominating, dogmatic, frank, complaining and self-assertive: they are deeply interested in the welfare of their recipients but they also blame both for their failures as

---

11. *Memoirs of the Author of A Vindication of the Rights of Woman* (London, 1798), p. 19.
12. Ford K. Brown, *The Life of William Godwin* (London: Dent, 1926), p. 134.

correspondents and occasionally they make it clear that Wollstonecraft regarded herself as their intellectual and temperamental superior. To George Blood she became remarkably close after Fanny Blood's death, before she awkwardly withdrew from what was perhaps more compromising than she had meant. At other times she felt comfortable berating George for his and his family's failings as if she had really been his older sister or mother. On his side he seems to have given unqualified admiration: Wollstonecraft became the 'Princess', a nickname she relished since she referred to it in several of her letters. Without the crucial correspondence with Fanny Blood, this with her brother best charts Wollstonecraft's love affair with the Blood family and her alienation from them as she came to realize their severe limitations (selfishness and fecklessness) and intellectual shortcomings. Poor George, who had been her main comfort through periods of anguish at the loss of Fanny, was later told not to read books above his capacities. The letters to George, like those to her sisters, trail off as Wollstonecraft emotionally outgrew both family and surrogate family.

With her sister Everina, frequently called a 'girl' despite her adult status, Wollstonecraft could be frank and bossy:

your mind certainly requires great attention – you have seldom *resolution* to *think* or *exert* the talents nature, or to speak with more propriety, Providence has given you to be *improved* – our whole life is but an education for eternity – virtue is an *acquirement* – seek for the assistance of Heaven, to enable you *now* to be wise unto Salvation, and regret not the time which is past, which, had others taken the greatest pains to form your mind could only have opened it to instruction – and made you capable of gaining experience – no creatures are so situated but they may obtain His favor from whom *only* TRUE comfort flows *if they seek it*.[13]

While often being dogmatic and homiletic, the letters to her sisters, especially those to Everina, are revelatory and in many ways moving, revealing the transformation of all three of them from vital yearning young girls to sour melancholic women, a character which only Woll-

13. p. 104.

stonecraft escaped with her genius and dramatic action. Depression and self-dramatization marked all the siblings – except the youngest brother Charles – as well perhaps as a certain resilience of which, curiously, Wollstonecraft herself seems to have had the least amount. But the letters reveal more than shared temperament: they also display a family accepting obligations. Each must circulate the last pound when necessary though each is entitled to grumble about his or her generosity. If a brother turns up broke on any sister he will be fed and helped; in return he will leave his dreams with the women who cannot go to sea or speculate in land. When they earn money the younger brothers think of their sisters – as they do again when they lose it. And always there is the parental black hole beneath the tracery of the letters – the father who ruined their childhood and then soaked up whatever money any of them managed to save, the father who with all his vices and faults was not quite repudiated, not even by Mary, who sometimes refused to see him. Johnson rightly emphasized how much Wollstone-craft gave to her siblings and parent – as she did herself. The placing of her letters among those of her family displays how intricate was the network of dependence. Eliza Bishop gave to her father when she herself was almost destitute. Everina sent money to Mary in France as Mary had sent money to her before. In marked contrast, Imlay, outside the blood family, never gave anything to the sisters as a proper husband should have done, nor did he honour the bond for his daughter.[14]

Finally, there are letters to miscellaneous friends and colleagues. The most interesting are a series to her girlhood friend in Beverley, Jane Arden. These letters are a remarkable record of a young girl's hopes and fears, her development and lack of development – for in many ways the bemused, emotional girl of fourteen who begins the series is not much different from the woman of twenty who ends it. At one point in the correspondence Wollstonecraft accused Jane Arden of not valuing her letters. In fact, while Jane Arden's letters have not survived, those from Wollstonecraft were carefully preserved. Later in Wollstonecraft's life other letters went to literary colleagues, a few to liberal men like the United Irishman Archibald Hamilton Rowan or

---

14. I have made this family network a major theme of my biography, *Mary Wollstone-craft: a revolutionary life* (London: Weidenfeld & Nicolson, 2000).

the Liverpool abolitionist, William Roscoe, more to other literary women written in the last years of her life when she was a celebrity and regarded as such by her fellow writers. Her letters to these women were familiar, often bossy. She emerges as both friend and professional, strenuous, formidable, frank and sometimes downright rude. She could be both helpful and haughty towards a fellow writer like Mary Hays whose tone she found irritating, then slightly priggish but affectionate to the quirky, overfamiliar young Amelia Alderson, who she rightly feared held conventional attitudes beneath her modish radicalism.

III

The Arden letters begin in 1773 or early 1774 and address Jane when she is away staying with a friend in Hull; they continue on her return when Mary is hurt and jealous at Jane's attentions to other girls: 'I am a little singular in my thoughts of love and friendship; I must have the first place or none', she wrote. Jane had argued that a person could have many equal friends but Mary doubted it and the girls had quarrelled and refused to speak to each other. So Mary had dashed off her aggrieved note: 'I once thought myself worthy of your friendship; – I thank you for bringing me to a right sense of myself. – When I have been at your house with Miss J—— the greatest respect has been paid to her; every thing handed to her first; – in short, as if she were a superior being; – Your Mama too behaved with more politeness to her.'[15] Such letters with their authentic tone of aggrieved adolescence deliver a prickly, needy but proud girl, eager to prove her value. She was keen to suggest her cultural awareness – her letters were at times a tissue of quotations from writers young people were supposed to read, mingled with doggerel from local poets – as well as her worth as a writer. She might not have the proper pens or have been taught as formally as Jane, but she knew she was expressing authentic 'true' emotion. She also knew that writing was powerful and that she might control others with her words.

15. p. 13.

The youthful letters already indicate her sense of her dysfunctional family. The eldest girl of seven children, she had been caught in her parents' downward social spiral and in her own envy for her eldest brother Ned, who had been singled out by their mother's favour and by their grandfather's excluding will, which left a third of his estate to this one child. By the time the Arden letters commence her family had already moved from London, where her father had been an apprenticed weaver, to a farm in Essex, where he had played gentleman farmer, then to another farm in Beverley. With each move he became more drunken and violent and it was clear to onlookers that he was incapable of flourishing or managing what had once been an adequate inheritance. 'Many people did not scruple to prognosticate the ruin of the whole family, and the way he went on, justified them for so doing.'[16]

The Beverley period ended abruptly in 1775 when Edward Wollstonecraft returned south with his family. The gloom of this move was lightened for his daughter only by her meeting with the engaging Fanny Blood, with whom she soon dreamt of making a life. Her family meanwhile continued its wandering and decline, and it was with relief that she left home at the age of nineteen to become a companion in Bath. There she re-established contact with Jane Arden, now a governess in Norfolk. Her letters, expressing her love for Fanny, revealed continuities with the childhood letters but also a temperamental change. She had become strenuously pious and there was a new depressive strain that would dog her throughout her life:

Pain and disappointment have constantly attended me since I left Beverley. I do not however repine at the dispensations of Providence, for my philosophy, as well as my religion will ever teach me to look on misfortunes as blessings, which like a bitter potion is disagreeable to the palate tho' 'tis grateful to the Stomach. . . . Young people generally set out with romantic and sanguine hopes of happiness, and must receive a great many stings before they are convinced of their mistake, and that they are pursuing a mere phantom; an empty name.[17]

16. p. 23.
17. p. 22.

The sulky demanding girl of Beverley had become a scornful and depressive young lady, a 'spectator' of pleasure, an alienated being marginalized in an uncaring society: 'I wish to retire as much from [the world] as possible – I am particularly sick of genteel life, as it is called; – the unmeaning civilities that I see every day praticed don't agree with my temper; – I long for a little sincerity, and look forward with pleasure to the time when I shall lay aside all restraint.'[18] Yet, despite the moaning, she had kept intact a sense of 'consequence', now expressed as a pride in puritanical austerity and in proper alienation among the trivial.

Wollstonecraft's time as companion was interrupted by family disasters. Her mother was ailing and she returned home to help with nursing. Shortly after Mrs Wollstonecraft's death, the second daughter, Eliza, married Meredith Bishop. Wollstonecraft regarded her as too young for marriage and was unsurprised when, after the birth of a child, Eliza fell into deep melancholy. Wollstonecraft's response was vigorous: she removed her sister from her new husband and baby. The escape was delivered in a series of breathless notes to the third sister, Everina, brilliantly capturing the shifting moods and fears provoked by the drama: 'I knew I should be the . . . *shameful incendiary* in this shocking affair of a woman's leaving her bed-fellow,' Wollstonecraft wrote at one moment; at another, '[Eliza] looks now very wild – Heaven protect us – I almost wish for an husband – for I want some body to support me.'

To help keep Eliza, herself, and in due course her friend Fanny Blood and her sister Everina, she founded a small school in the progressive Dissenting community of Newington Green. The next years are sparsely covered by letters – which is a pity since it was a time of considerable intellectual growth. The period came to an end when Wollstonecraft left for Portugal to be with Fanny Blood during her confinement – consumptive, Fanny had quit the school to be married the year before. After Fanny's death, Wollstonecraft returned to England depressed and lonely; the school collapsed and she accepted a diminished future as governess to the daughters of Lord and Lady Kingsborough in Ireland. The letters during these months and those

18. p. 28.

following, addressed to Fanny's brother George Blood and to Everina Wollstonecraft, primarily describe a prolonged and deep depression, unmitigated by the continuing piety: 'I am here shut out from domestic society – my heart throbs when I see a hand written by any one to whom my affections are attracted,' she lamented. The triviality of life in Mitchelstown Castle and the Dublin townhouse appalled her: 'conversations which have nothing in them' and rituals of dress that consumed time. 'I see Ladies put on rouge without any mauvais honte – and make up their faces for the day – five hours, and who could do it less in – do many – I assure you, spend in dressing – without including preparations for bed. Washing with Milk of roses &c &c.' Her letters, always much concerned with her sensations, now became more specific about her mental and physical ailments: 'Don't smile when I tell you that I am tormented with *spasms* – indeed it is impossible to enumerate the various complaints I am troubled with; and how much my mind is harrassed by them. I know they all arise from disordered nerves, that are injured beyond a *possibility* of receiving *any* aid from medicine – There is no cure for a broken heart!'[19]

During the time in Ireland Wollstonecraft added a new correspondent, Joseph Johnson, the London bookseller who had published her book on education, written on her return from Portugal. He had become a kind of confidant, but he may also have symbolized for her an independent future; so her letters tried to impress him with both her intellect and sensibility. Certainly they eased her forward to a new life which began in 1787 when Lady Kingsborough dismissed her. Declaring herself excitedly to Everina as 'the first of a new genus', Wollstonecraft then went to work for Johnson as an author and reviewer on his new periodical, the *Analytical Review*. The letters to Everina and George Blood became fewer, more aware of growing intellectual distance. They revealed her continuing care for her family and surrogate family, but now mingled with a growing irritation at their failure to flourish independently; her irritation made her franker and more astringent than she had been when she needed their comfort.

One discrete series gives an idea of her developing sense of herself: it was written to Everina during a short vacation in Warminster with

19. pp. 111f.

the clergyman schoolteacher Henry Gabell, whom she had met on her way to Ireland. Now closeted with him and his new wife, she cast a jaundiced eye on the couple's married bliss, revealing in the process her own ambivalent attitude to coupledom and domesticity, as well as her awareness of her own intellectual gifts:

Whenever I read Milton's description of paradise – the happiness, which he so poetically describes fills me with benevolent satisfaction – yet, I cannot help viewing them, I mean the first pair – as if they were my inferiors – inferiors because they could find happiness in a world like this – A feeling of the same kind frequently intrudes on me here – Tell me, does it arise from mistaken pride or conscious dignity which whispering me that my soul is immortal & should have a nobler ambition leads me to cherish it?[20]

Her detailed sense of her intellectual progress during this time was kept primarily for Fuseli, with whom she must have discussed her two polemical triumphs of the early London years, the *Vindications*, both written as sort of public letters in angry reaction to texts by men she considered both powerful and wrong-headed, especially Edmund Burke's *Reflections on the Revolution in France* and Jean-Jacques Rousseau's *Émile*.

Wollstonecraft must have been writing to Fuseli constantly to create the stack of letters Godwin later glimpsed and it was thus a considerable emotional wrench when, repulsed by him and his wife in her efforts to form a *ménage à trois*, she left for France. It was the fourth year of the Revolution and the Jacobin Terror was about to begin. Vulnerable and yearning for old friends, she soon replaced the middle-aged *enfant terrible* Fuseli with a very different man, an American merchant, speculator and liberal author, the tall handsome Gilbert Imlay. Their love burgeoned. When the French grew antagonistic to English well-wishers after the declaration of war between the two countries, Wollstonecraft had to move from Paris to a nearby village. There she began the long series of letters to Imlay which would chart her next few haunted years. They tell a dismal story: of the growth, short flowering and long decline of their relationship through Paris,

20. pp. 179f.

Le Havre, where their child Fanny was born, through a sad reunion in London, through the first suicide attempt, the business trip to Scandinavia, the dreary return and further suicide attempt, to the slow recovery of health and peace.

'Everybody allows that the talent of writing agreeable letters is peculiarly female,' remarked the ironic hero of Austen's *Northanger Abbey*. Letter-writing certainly filled up a good deal of the literate woman's time but the great letter-writers of society were perhaps more men than women, Walpole or Byron rather than the bluestocking ladies. But, when it came to the emotional personal letter, the exemplary exponent was agreed to be the seventeenth-century French Madame de Sévigné, whose love object was her daughter. Only fiction matched this intensity in Wollstonecraft's period and it was the male hero, Werther, in Goethe's *The Sorrows of Young Werther* who had become the standard of passion. In the letters to Imlay Wollstonecraft bears comparison with Madame de Sévigné and Werther.

Indeed the latter parallel was made by Godwin. The Imlay letters contained 'possibly . . . the finest examples of the language of sentiment and passion ever presented to the world'. He went on, 'in the judgement of those best qualified to decide upon the comparison, these Letters will be admitted to have the superiority over the fiction of Goethe. They are the offspring of a glowing imagination, and a heart penetrated with the passion it essays to describe'.[21] The letters were variously crafted, sometimes dashed off and sometimes carefully composed; sometimes they had a literary ring, as though Wollstonecraft were aware of her place among celebrated and passionate female letter-writers such as Ovid's fictional Heroïdes or the medieval nun Héloïse. She was often pleading and abject; at the same time she displayed a very real self-respect: Imlay was berated as lover and failed reader for misunderstanding her message and value. Frequently she broke off in passion, in frustration at her lover's obtuseness and her own desire. Her longings vacillated between neediness and dependence on the one hand and longing for freedom and autonomy on the other. Constantly they grappled with the problem of female sexual desire within society

21. *Works of Mary Wollstonecraft*, ed. Janet Todd and Marilyn Butler (London: Pickering & Chatto, 1989), 6, 367.

and addressed the value, power and seduction of the imagination within human relationships:

Ah! my friend, you know not the ineffable delight, the exquisite pleasure, which arises from a unison of affection and desire, when the whole soul and senses are abandoned to a lively imagination, that renders every emotion delicate and rapturous. Yes; these are emotions, over which satiety has no power, and the recollection of which, even disappointment cannot disenchant; but they do not exist without self-denial. These emotions, more or less strong, appear to me to be the distinctive characteristic of genius, the foundation of taste, and of that exquisite relish for the beauties of nature, of which the common herd of eaters and drinkers and *child-begeters*, certainly have no idea. You will smile at an observation that has just occurred to me: – I consider those minds as the most strong and original, whose imagination acts as the stimulus to their senses.

Well! you will ask, what is the result of all this reasoning? Why I cannot help thinking that it is possible for you, having great strength of mind, to return to nature, and regain a sanity of constitution, and purity of feeling – which would open your heart to me. – I would fain rest there!'[22]

The correspondence with Imlay was returned by him when she requested it; although it must have increased her pain, perhaps when she reread it she realized that letter-writing was her forte, her form. In her final years her works use the epistolary structure repeatedly: for example in her most successful unison of political commentary and personal experience, *Letters from Sweden*, as well as in the fragment 'Letters on the Management of Infants'. A letter also forms the largest part of her unfinished novel, *The Wrongs of Woman*.

Wollstonecraft had met William Godwin when she had been in her robust vindicating phase; he had found her strident and unprepossessing. Now in 1796 they met again and he was impressed with her grief-induced mellowness. They rapidly became close friends and within a few months lovers. Occasionally over the period of courtship and commitment she wrote to him the kind of erotic notes she had earlier addressed to Imlay:

22. p. 297.

Now by these presents let me assure you that you are not only in my heart, but my veins, this morning. I turn from you half abashed – yet you haunt me, and some look, word or touch thrills through my whole frame – yes, at the very moment when I am labouring to think of something, if not somebody, else. Get ye gone Intruder! though I am forced to add dear – which is a call back –

When the heart and reason accord there is no flying from voluptuous sensations, I find, do what a woman can – [23]

On other occasions they read too much into each other's words and ended in emotional tussles. Once Wollstonecraft sent Godwin a fable of a sycamore in which she tried to express her vulnerability and fears about another attachment after the disaster with Imlay; Godwin was obtuse and read the letter as a desire to end the relationship. Or they quarrelled and Godwin would try to remonstrate in a reasoned letter about her extreme irrational spoken words. Mostly, however, they wrote short notes making arrangements, sending over cold dinners, complaining about household duties, or organizing visitors. Both relished a secret life going on below the public meetings, for, until their marriage in March 1797, they kept up a fiction that they were friends but not a couple. Always theirs was a literary relationship, whose intimacy was embodied in the communal bottle of ink. Ever impecunious and distracted by domestic details, Wollstonecraft asked Godwin to send her some ink because she had run out. Later he asked for his bottle back and one can imagine it travelling between the two unconventional households as, now married and about to be parents, they fiercely guarded their independence and signified both their togetherness and separation in their habit of writing rather than speaking – though they saw each other daily and were only a few doors apart.

During the last months of Wollstonecraft's life, two groups of letters are revelatory of her newfound strength yet continuing insecurity and vulnerability to melancholy and suicidal moods. The first concerned her anxiety over Godwin's apparent flirtation with Miss Pinkerton. She remonstrated with him, bringing up the past and reliving her

23. p. 363.

rejections; then she herself wrote the letter of dismissal, leaving Godwin to emend it. The other group arose out of Godwin's visit to the Wedgwoods in Etruria. Godwin had always been self-conscious about his more elaborate letters, for example at the outset of their relationship trying out various forms of love-letter, not always to Wollstonecraft's taste. This time he thought hard about an appropriate style and decided at first on a jocular man-to-man one, varied with more intimate tones, 'Take care of yourself, my love . . .'[24] As the visit progressed, however, he hid the social embarrassments he was suffering in Etruria and adopted a detached tone of travel narrative. It did not suit Wollstonecraft, who regarded his letters less as addressed to her and more of an *aide-mémoire* for himself. She might cajole her readers, but she rarely forgot them altogether, as she accused Godwin of doing. It was epistolary vanity and self-indulgence, she thought.

The letters to Godwin tragically end with the short notes written by Wollstonecraft just hours before the birth which would kill her. Her last recorded writing provides a moving conclusion to her life in its echo of the dying words of her own mother. Mrs Wollstonecraft had declared, 'A little patience, and all will be over!' Her daughter's final written words were, 'Mrs Blenkinsop [the midwife] tells me that I am in the most natural state, and can promise me a safe delivery – But that I must have a little patience[.]'[25]

IV

Wollstonecraft is now mainly delivered as an Enlightenment feminist – as indeed she was. In this role she echoes many of the sentiments of the thinking women of her day, both liberal and conservative. The life and opinions delivered in the letters are more revolutionary and distinctive however. The desultory and experiential form suited her style, allowing for her devotion to candour. So in the letters she grapples with the complexities of woman's lot as she rarely does in the

---

24. *Godwin and Mary: Letters of William Godwin and Mary Wollstonecraft*, ed. Ralph M. Wardle (Lincoln, Nebr.: University of Nebraska Press, 1966), p. 80.
25. p. 437.

published work: their emotional neediness as well as their desire for independence, their anxiety over motherhood as well as their enthusiasm, and their attraction to the romance they might theoretically despise.

The letters sometimes appear melodramatic and self-indulgent but part of this is the fashion of the times, and they need to be judged beside the extreme self-dramatizing of her sister Eliza for example or indeed of her friend Mary Hays, similarly caught up in unrequited love. Taken together they form a remarkable autobiographical document. Unlike a diary or retrospective, they record not a finished or ordered life but the dynamic process of living and experiencing, and inevitably they tell a tale no biography can truly match. They do not reveal the hindsight of commentary, nor do they show the steady progress towards a full articulateness of any vision; instead they reveal flashes of the genius that makes their writer worth recording and reading in the twenty-first century. The novelist Samuel Richardson believed the 'converse of the pen' made distance presence and 'even presence but body, while absence becomes the soul . . .'. At their best, this is the effect of Mary Wollstonecraft's letters.

Janet Todd
University of Glasgow

Editorial Principles

The date and place of writing is given at the top of the letters, moved from the close where Mary Wollstonecraft frequently put the information. Dates and places in square brackets are taken from postmarks, context, or information other than the original manuscript. Conjectural dates and places are explained in the footnotes. Approximate dates are bracketed and preceded by 'c.'; questionable dates are bracketed and preceded by a question mark. Dates and places in the letter headings have been standardized but are kept close to Wollstonecraft's original. Her abbreviations and varying spellings of personal names and places within the manuscripts have been left unchanged, for example 'Mʳ.' and 'Mʳ,' 'Sʳ.' and 'Sʳ,', and 'Mr. J.' and 'Mrs. B'. In the letters first published by Godwin dashes or asterisks are frequently substituted for personal and place names; these names have been filled in within square brackets where the identity is certain; where conjectural, the identity is suggested in a footnote. In letters transcribed from Wollstonecraft's original manuscripts, where names have been abbreviated and might seem obscure to the reader they have been supplied in brackets. Spelling idiosyncrasies and grammatical errors throughout the letters have been left largely as written; square brackets indicate, and endnotes [bracketed numbers] explain, the few editorial changes where Wollstonecraft's original would have confused meaning. Endnotes also register significant differences between the present and earlier published versions of the letters, as well as marks that are not in Wollstonecraft's hand. Brackets around spaces in the text indicate that material has been made illegible mainly through seals or damaged paper.

Some of the dating of the undated letters depends on speculation concerning Wollstonecraft's life. When I have dated according to this criterion I have noted it in the footnotes. For example, one series of letters records her extreme reaction to a proposal of marriage. Ralph Wardle and others have put this fairly late in Wollstonecraft's life, while I believe it reveals an earlier sense of herself as an isolated being with dependence only on God. Throughout the volume the biographical information has been provided on the page so that readers do not have to consult other works or endnotes for the necessary context. If this information is thought intrusive, the letters can be read without reference to the footnotes. My interpretation of Wollstonecraft's life, largely omitted from these notes, is provided in *Mary Wollstonecraft: a revolutionary life* (2000).

Abbreviations

AR	*Analytical Review.*
CL	Ralph Wardle (ed.), *Collected Letters of Mary Wollstone-craft* (Ithaca: Cornell University Press, 1979).
DNB	*Dictionary of National Biography* (Oxford University Press, 1997, CD-rom).
FNL	Benjamin P. Kurtz and Carrie C. Autrey, *Four New Letters of Mary Wollstonecraft and Helen M. Williams* (Berkeley: University of California Press, 1937).
G&M	Ralph Wardle, *Godwin & Mary. The Letters of William Godwin and Mary Wollstonecraft* (London: Constable, 1967).
HF	John Knowles, *The Life and Writings of Henry Fuseli*, 3 vols. (London, 1831).
LI	Mary Wollstonecraft, *Letters to Imlay, with Prefatory Memoir by C. Kegan Paul* (London, 1879).
Memoirs	William Godwin, *Memoirs of the Author of A Vindication of the Rights of Woman* (London, 1798).
OED	*Oxford English Dictionary* (Oxford: Clarendon Press, 1989), 2nd edition.
PW	William Godwin (ed.), *Posthumous Works of the Author of 'A Vindication of the Rights of Woman'*, 4 vols. (London, 1798).
SC	Kenneth Neill Cameron (ed.), *Shelley and his Circle 1773–1822*, 8 vols. (Cambridge, Mass.: Harvard University Press, 1961–7).
Supp.	W. Clark Durant, *'A Supplement' to Memoirs of Mary Wollstonecraft* (London: Constable & Co., 1927).

WG   Charles Kegan Paul, *William Godwin: His Friends and Contemporaries*, 2 vols. (London, 1876).

Works   Janet Todd and Marilyn Butler (eds.), *The Works of Mary Wollstonecraft*, 7 vols. (London: Pickering & Chatto, 1989).

Where possible, footnotes related to Wollstonecraft's quotations refer to eighteenth-century editions.

Yorkshire 1773–1774[1]

1. To Jane Arden[2]

[Beverley] Sunday afternoon, 4 o'clock [c. spring 1773][3]

Dear Miss Arden

According to my promise I sit down to write to you

'My promise and my faith shall be so sure
'As neither age can change, nor art can cure[4]
'Perform thy promise keep within faith's bounds
'Who breaks his word, his reputation wounds.' –

1. Mary's father, Edward Wollstonecraft, had inherited a modest fortune from his father, a substantial master silk weaver in East London. The father had already provided a home and a farm in Epping for his son's family. With his fortune Edward bought a new farm in Essex and set up as a gentleman farmer. When the Essex farm failed he moved to one near Beverley in Yorkshire. When this too failed, the Wollstonecrafts took a house in a square in Beverley. By 1770, with the birth of Charles, the family of seven children was complete. Mary Wollstonecraft, the eldest girl, was just fourteen.

2. Jane Arden (1758–1840) was a friend in Beverley, encountered at the scientific lectures of Jane's father John (1721–1792). The fifteen undated letters to Jane Arden were copied into a volume in the possession of the Carl H. Pforzheimer Library; in CL Wardle assumed that they were in chronological order, but there seems no secure reason to suppose that this is the case.

3. Letters 1–6 can all be dated with reference to performances of Robert Hitchcock's comedy *The Macaroni*, mentioned in the postscript to Letter 2, which played in Beverley on 26 May and 3 June 1773. For further dating of Letters 1–6, see also SC, 2, 940f.

4. Slightly misquoted from John Dryden, *Aeneïs* (1697), bk. 1, ll. 948f. Mary's many quotations in this and subsequent letters to Jane Arden may well have come from an anthology or commonplace book. In her adult life she used and re-used relatively few quotations.

Inclosed you will find 'Sweet Beverley' for meeting with an old copy, and being in a hurry I thought you would excuse the badness of the writing. –

> 'True ease in writing comes from art not chance
> 'As do those move easiest who have learnt to dance'.[5]

I assure you I expect a complimentary letter in return for my staying from church to day. –

I should likewise beg pardon for not beginning sooner so agreeable a correspondence as that I promise myself yours will prove, but from a lady of your singular good nature I promise myself indulgence. –

> 'Indulgence soon meets with a noble mind,
> 'Who can be harsh, that sees another kind?[6]
> 'Goodnature & good sense must ever join.[7]
> 'Mildness of Temper has a force divine.[8]

When you write to Miss G—— pray present my compliments to her, and tell her I should be obliged to her if she would write to me, and inclose it in her letter to you, and I flatter myself you will excuse my asking you to inclose it in your answer to this. – I thought Miss R.——[9] behaved rather oddly on Saturday but I believe I was in the wrong —

> 'I see the right, and I approve it too –
> 'I blame the wrong and yet the wrong pursue.'[10]
> – 'To you good gods I make my last appeal
> 'Or clear my virtues or my crimes reveal
> 'If in the maze of fate I blindly run
> 'And backward tread those paths I ought to shun

---

5. Alexander Pope, *An Essay on Criticism. Written in the Year* 1709 (1711), ll. 364f.
6. Slightly misquoted from William King, *The Art of Love: In Imitation of Ovid De Arte Amandi* (1709), pt. 8, ll. 1f.
7. Alexander Pope, *An Essay on Criticism*, l. 526.
8. Slightly misquoted from William King, *The Art of Love*, pt. 8, l. 12.
9. Probably the Miss Rudd mentioned in Letter 11 and related to Mr Rudd mentioned in Letter 3. The Rudd family lived in the vicinity and one Rudd married an Arden (*SC*, 4, 942).
10. Slightly misquoted from Henry Baker, *However great, whoe'er you are* (1737), ll. 735f.

'Impute my errors to your own decree,
    'My hands are guilty, but my heart is free.'[11]

But however I think it very unpolite in Company if all present are unacquainted with the Cause; – you need not tell Miss R—— or Miss G—— what I have said, but I need not doubt your friendship. –

'A friend should always like a friend indite
'Speak as she thinks, and as she thinks sho.^d write.'

Pray make haste and translate the french Song as I have already made a couple of aenigmas[12] one on Beverley, the other on a friend, and the first time I see you I will shew you them. –

Pray tell Miss C——[13] that if she can get time to write she may inclose it in your letter. –

I wish you may not be as tired[ ] with reading as I am with writing. –

I am, your friend
& humble Servant
Mary Wollstonecraft

P.S. Pray write soon – I have a hundred things to add, but can't get time for my Mama is calling me, so shall reserve them for another letter.

'Sweet Beverley.'

I.
'What nymph so fair as Dolly,
'Smart as Stanhope's polly,[14]

---

11. Slightly misquoted from John Dryden and Nathaniel Lee, *Oedipus* (1679), 3, i, 678f.
12. Riddles.
13. Jane Arden's friend in Hull, possibly Elizabeth-Mary Constable, born in Stepney in June 1760. Jane's father John was a scientific agent for the Catholic landowner William Constable (d. 1791) from Burton Constable Hall in Holderness, Yorkshire; a William Constable had married Mary Holmes in Beverley in August 1756.
14. This poem is a tissue of references to local people and to the fashionable London scene which Beverley supposedly surpasses. Polly was possibly a pet parrot or a girlfriend of one of the Stanhopes, a local family. Girls called Polly featured frequently in eighteenth-century ballads where they were often associated with knowledge, frequently erotic, beyond the family and propriety. See, for example, ballads used by John Gay in *The Beggar's Opera* (1728).

'Should you be seen, with gout or spleen
'They'll cure your melancholy.
'Its Beverley, sweet Beverley, in thee I take delight
'Its' Beverley, sweet Beverley, whose charms I now recite.

2.

'Should you be fond of dancing,
'With steps cotillon[15] prancing
'Our lasses bound,
'In festal round,
'The frolic joy enhancing,
   Its Beverley &.[c] –

3.[d]

'Should noble sports incite you
'The jovial chase invite you
'The Driffield Bards[16]
'With Song and cards
'Will after chase requite you.
   Its Beverley &.[c]

4.th

'Our grave Dons muse and ponder
'Take Snuff, read news and wonder
'And then dear souls —
'They play at Bowls
'Like Jove with all his Thunder
   Its Beverley &.[c]

5.th

'The Dames of ancient Story
'In wisdom placed their glory

---

15. A cotillon is the 'name of several dances, chiefly of French origin, consisting of a variety of steps and figures' (*OED*).

16. A group of poets living at Driffield, about ten miles north of Beverley. They included William Mason (1724–1797), minister at Driffield, playwright and poet, friend and biographer of the poet Thomas Gray. At this stage of his life Mason was a liberal Whig involved in Yorkshire politics. He was a relative by marriage of the scientist and botanical poet Erasmus Darwin (1731–1802).

'Divine Quadrille
'Spadille manille
'Here banish all before you.[17]
       Its Beverley &.[c]

6.th

'If woman's wit can kill you
'With Sappho's[18] numbers chill you
'But they were nought
'In tongue or thought
'To Lady Elizabeth Bielby.
       Its Beverley &.[c]

7.th

'Newmarket boasts its ponies[19]
'Thatch house macaroni's,[20]
'But Thursday's Club
'Would tightly drub
'Such addle pated[21] honies
       It's Beverley &.[c]

8.th –

'But secrets to unlock it
'Avoid my friend the mocket[22]
'Or else his grace

17. Quadrille is a card-game played by four people using forty cards; spadille is the ace of spades in quadrille and manille the second best trump.

18. Greek poet, born c. 612 BC, taken as the type of passionate female poet.

19. Newmarket had become a site of horse-racing from the early seventeenth century. Charles I instituted the first cup-race there and the races were especially patronized by Charles II.

20. The Thatched House Tavern, founded in 1711, was a large tavern with rooms for public meetings. It was a place where noble musicians used sometimes to meet earlier in the century but in the 1770s it was popular with fashionable fops or 'macaronis'. These wore loud and closely fitting clothes, high-heeled shoes, frills and nosegays. They were much mocked as effeminate, foreign and decadent by the respectable press.

21. '[O]ne whose brain cannot distinguish between the objects which are outside it and the imagination within' (*A Dictionary of Slang, Jargon, and Cant*, Ballantyne Press, 1889).

22. *OED* defines a 'mocket' as a bib or handkerchief; the stanza seems to allude to some cheating with a handkerchief either by a card sharper or the owner of the establishment.

'With every ace
'Will jump into your pocket.
        It's Beverley &.ᶜ

                9.ᵗʰ
'Let Jacomb²³ toast piano
'Or squall Italiano
'It would make one huff
'To hear such stuff
'Poor soul he's mad 'tis plaino.
        It's Beverley &.ᶜ

2. *To Jane Arden*

[Beverley, c. spring 1773]

Dear Miss Arden —

As I think ingratitude worse than impertinence I take this opportunity to thank you for your agreeable letter, and likewise for your verses
on the death of H. Bethell Esq²⁴ but you forgot part of your promise
which was to tell me who wrote them. – The most adequate return I
can make, is to send Dʳ. Drake's Satire on 'Sweet Beverley';²⁵ the
Chorus same as the other.

                1.
        'Attend thou great mockpoet
        'Thy verses plainly shew it
        'While in metres rough as thine
        'I describe each hobbling line
        'That all the world may know it
                It's Beverley &.ᶜ

23. Possibly Giacomo or Jacomo, a 'typical' name of an Italian singer (or composer).
24. Hugh Bethell of Rise had become high sheriff of Yorkshire in 1761. He died on
8 May 1772.
25. The author is either Francis Drake (1695–1771) or, more probably, his son of the
same name (1721–1795). The elder Drake, historian of York (*Eburacum*, 1736), lived
in York until 1767 when he came to Beverley to reside with his son, who was vicar of
St Mary's there.

2.

'Slow hand and bold the duty
'To sing of Dolly's beauty
'When such folly and nonsense –
'Cannot claim the least pretence
'To the shadow of her shoe.
        It's Beverley &.ᶜ

3.

'Thy Sappho and thy Lyric
'Disgrace all panegyric
'For wit as thick as Tripes
'It would give a man the gripes
'And make the maids hysteric.
        It's Beverley &.ᶜ

4.

'Such rhymes so rough and teazing
'As sour as Crabs when squeezing
'Like Cleavers on Marrow bones –
'Or rattling of millstones
'Or cart Wheels that want greasing.
        It's Beverley &.ᶜ

5.

'At Whist would you pick his pocket
'His grace would sneer and mock it
'For thy verses are as stale
'As the dregs of muddy ale
'Or candle end when in the Socket
        It's Beverley &.ᶜ

6.

'At bowls on the green when bowling
'It's more music than thy squalling
'For thy singing and thy rhymes
'Are worse a thousand times.
'Than Cats, when catterwauling
        It's Beverley &.

7.

'Then stick to thy fate piano
'And scream Italiano
'Such a Song is out of Season
'That has neither Rhyme nor reason
'Nor of mirth or sense one grain. –
Its Beverley &.ᶜ

It is so long since I wrote the first part of this letter that I don't know how to apologize for my negligence, but by being a more regular correspondent for the future. – My Papa informs me that Miss R—— is gone to York to day: – I wish her an agreeable journey – For my part all animosities have ceased, but I was resolved not to make the first concession. – I hope my not writing sooner, will not prevent your answering it when convenient; – I should indeed then be punished for my neglect. I have just glanced over this letter and find it so ill written that I fear you cannot make out one line of this last page, but you know, my dear, I have not the advantage of a Master as you have, and it is with great difficulty to get my brother to mend my pens:[26] – I am at present in a dilemma, for I have not one pen that will make a stroke, but however I will try to sign myself

Yours sincerely
Mary Wollstonecraft

P.S. I intend going to see the Macaroni if it be performed, and expect a great deal of pleasure.[27]

M. W.

26. Quill pens were difficult to prepare; they quickly became blunt and they had to be sharpened constantly and correctly for the strokes to be elegant. Mary was aware of her lack of formal training in grammar and penmanship beside Jane Arden, who, as an adult, wrote *The Young Ladies' English Grammar* (1799) and *A French Grammar* (1808).
27. Wollstonecraft might already have read the play since, in printed form, *The Macaroni* (York, 1774) lists five subscribers from Beverley.

3. To Jane Arden

[Beverley, c. mid–late 1773]

I have just read your account of the oddest mortal that ever existed, and can't help approving Miss C——'s choice, as the contrast will be very entertaining, – her over-giddiness, and his over-graveness must be superlatively ridiculous; – in short you must allow me to laugh. – I cannot help observing there is not that sympathy of which the poets speak, but you could not more oblige me than by your description of Miss C—— and her lover (lovers you know we are to call them) as it is my greatest pleasure to read odd characters; – her dutifulness too I admire, to parents whose indulgence she has so long experienced; – I cannot help pitying you; a girl of your delicacy must be disgusted with such nonsense; – you may give my compliments to her and inform her that I will go to Hull myself, and set my cap at him, but upon second thoughts the object is too despicable. – I shall inclose you a copy of verses which Mr Rudd[28] has made on the Beverley beauties – I lament, – I am sorry I am not older to have had my name inscribed in such divine poetry. –

I think I have answered all the parts of your letter, except your not dancing with the macaroni at the Concert. – I was in hopes you had left the prude at Beverley by the first part of your letter, but the latter reminds me that you will mend in time. – I have no Beverley news, but that Miss N——s are in mourning for an uncle who has left them a great fortune; – report says that it is £300 a year between them, and a woman of any oeconomy may live very genteelly on £150 a year,[29] but report generally adds. –

We had a very agreeable afternoon at M^{rs} C——'s on Monday; – all the world was there, but there was a want: – I could have been far happier with two persons I could name; – don't be jealous, – the other is not a lady, but more of that by and by. – I won't flatter you so much

28. Possibly related to Miss Rudd or Rud, Jane Arden's friend.
29. Compare Jane Austen's amounts in *Sense and Sensibility* (1811) where £300 is said to make Edward Ferrars comfortable as a bachelor but keep him too poor to marry.

as to inform you how severely I feel your absence, and beg as you love your affectionate friend to return to Beverley as soon as possible. – I beg you will write again. – I am afraid you cannot read this as all the children are plaguing me.

Your's sincerely
Mary Wollstonecraft.

Verses on the Beverley Beauties. –

'Ye tuneful nine and all Apollo's choir,[30]
'With daring thoughts as suppliant bards inspire,
'Nor arms, nor arts employ your Votary's care
'His sole ambition's to oblige the fair
'To paint their virtues with the pen of truth
'The rare the best attendant upon youth.
'To shew their foibles in their truest light,
'Not swayed by prejudice, or Hellborn spite;
'What blooming nymph shall first adorn the lay,
'All knowing muse, divine Thalia[31] say; –
'Amongst the foremost be fair Champion[32] placed
'Champion with sense, with every virtue graced; –
'A form complete in each minutest part,
'A mind enlarged with every useful art;
'From all her sexes faults entirely free,
'From pride, ill nature, and coquetry; –
'In Ward a second Champion we find
'A graceful person and a gen'rous mind
'In temper and in form tis rare to see
'Such perfect union and such Symmetry. –
'To these a contrast, we will now produce

---

30. Apollo, the Greek god of music and poetry, was frequently depicted as the leader of the Nine Muses.

31. Thalia, the Muse of bucolic poetry as well as comedy.

32. The names Champion, Ward, Webb, Smelt, Clubley, Acklom and Stanhope appear in local history, see *SC*, 4, 942; Edward Baines, *History, Directory, and Gazetteer of the County of York* (Leeds, 1823), 2, 165, lists 'Peter Acklam, Esq, North bar street within'; 'Wm Acklam Lieut. East York Militia, Flemingate'; 'Robert Smelt, High Constable, Wednesday market'. See also *Burke's Landed Gentry* for 1837.

'The hints perhaps may be of general use;
'How lovely, how serene did Eve appear
'Till that arch fiend the rebel power drew near
'Till then her mind ne'er knew th'effects of pride
'E'er she had known, happy had she died; –
'A truly noble form in Webb is seen –
'Such as might rival e'en the Cyprian queen,[33]
'But shall there dwell is such a form as this,
'Which seems externally the seat of bliss, –
'That fell destroyer – Pride?
'Beauty alas, a few short years will stay –
'And e'er you know its value fly away; –
'A proper pride's what all the sex should wear
'The badge and ornament of british fair; –
'This guards their virtue from each rude assault
'Inspires their minds with horror at each fault: –
'But self-conceit, ill manners sure disgrace
'The finest person and the fairest face. –
'The growing charms of Helen next rehearse
'Which well deserve the tribute of a verse,
'But oh! fair nymph, your sister's pride avoid
'That pride by which each virtue is destroyed
'Nature and sense in fairest Smelt you see
'With virtue graced, from every foible free: –
'Her sister too, with blooming charms appears
'Each charm encreasing with encreasing years; –
'Oh! happy parents of this lovely pair,
'Still happier he, decreed their love to share; –
'My muse to Clubley now must take its flight
'And paint each beauty in its proper light;
'Happy the man, who shares her mutual love,
'His time one series of true joy will prove; –
'Formed to delight she captivates each eye,
'If scorned by her, the wretch must wish to die! –
'Graceful in form, see lovely Acklom move

33. Venus, goddess of love.

'Attracting nymph, her look commanding love;
'Truth makes me speak, alas! I do't with pain –
'Formed to delight, oh! not to heal a swain: –
'Sweet Stanhope last, not least in love,
'In temper gentle as the Turtle Dove; –
'In beauty too no second part she bears,
'In every pleasing form, she amply shares. –
'Excuse ye fair ones this too faint essay, –
'By truth attended, I've pursued my way. –
'Beauties like powerful princes from their youth
'Are often strangers to the voice of truth; –
'Some praise is his who dares to be sincere
'And wisdom their's who lend a candid ear.' –

4. To Jane Arden

[Beverley, c. mid–late 1773 – November 16th, 1774]

Miss A. – Your behaviour at Miss J——'s hurt me extremely, and your not answering my letter shews that you set little value on my friendship. – If you had sent to ask me, I should have gone to the play, but none of you seemed to want my company. – I have two favors to beg, the one is that you will send me all my letters; – the other that you will never mention some things which I have told you. To avoid idle tell-tale, we may visit ceremoniously, and to keep up appearances, may whisper, when we have nothing to say: – The beaux whisper insignificantly, and nod without meaning. – I beg you will take the trouble to bring the letters yourself, or give them to my sister Betsy.[34] – You never called yesterday; if you wish to be on the least friendly footing, you will call this morning. – If you think it worth while, send an answer by my sister.

M. W.

34. The second Wollstonecraft daughter, Elizabeth (b. 1763), variously called Eliza, Bess and Betsy.

5. To Jane Arden

[Beverley, c. mid–late 1773 – November 16th, 1774]

Miss Arden. – Before I begin I beg pardon for the freedom of my style. – If I did not love you I should not write so; – I have a heart that scorns disguise, and a countenance which will not dissemble: – I have formed romantic notions of friendship. – I have been once disappointed: – I think if I am a second time I shall only want some infidelity in a love affair, to qualify me for an old maid, as then I shall have no idea of either of them. – I am a little singular in my thoughts of love and friendship; I must have the first place or none. – I own your behaviour is more according to the opinion of the world, but I would break such narrow bounds. – I will give you my reasons for what I say; – since Miss C——[35] has been here you have behaved in the coolest manner. – I once hoped our friendship was built on a permanent foundation: – We have all our failings – I have more than usual, but I thought you might mildly have corrected me as I always loved you with true sisterly affection. If I had found any faults I should have told you but a lady possessed of so many accomplishments as Miss A[rden] cannot want for admirers, and who has so many friends cannot find any loss in your humble Servant. – I would not have seen it, but your behaviour the other night I cannot pass over; – when I spoke of sitting with you at Church you made an objection, because I and your sister quarrelled; – I did not think a little raillery would have been taken in such a manner, or that you would have insinuated, that I dared to have prophaned so sacred a place with idle chit-chat.

I once thought myself worthy of your friendship; – I thank you for bringing me to a right sense of myself. – When I have been at your house with Miss J—— the greatest respect has been paid to her; every thing handed to her first; – in short, as if she were a superior being: – Your Mama too behaved with more politeness to her.

I am much obliged to your Papa and Mama and desire you will give them my complimentary thanks, and as I have spent many happy

35. The Hull friend was apparently returning the visit.

hours in your company, shall always have the sincerest esteem for Miss A[rden]. – There is no accounting for the imbecillity of human nature – I might misconstrue your behaviour, but what I have written flows spontaneously from my pen, and this I am sure, I only desire to be done by as I do; – I shall expect a written answer to this, –

and am yours
M. W.

Don't tell C—— to you I have told all my failings; – I would not be so mean as to shew only the bright side of the picture; – I have reason to think you have not been so ingenuous to me. – I cannot bear the reflection that when Miss R—— comes I should have less of your company. – After seeing you yesterday, I thought not to have sent this – (but you desire it) for to see you and be angry, is not in my power. – I long for a walk in my darling Westwood.[36] Adieu.

Mary Wollstonecraft.

6. To Jane Arden

[Beverley, c. mid–late 1773 – November 16th, 1774]

Dear Jenny

I have read some where that vulgar minds will never own they are in the wrong: – I am determined to be above such a prejudice, and give the lie to the poet who says –

> 'Forgiveness to the injured does belong
> 'But they ne'er pardon, who have done the wrong'[37]

and hope my ingenuously owning myself partly in fault to a girl of your good nature will cancel the offence – I have a heart too susceptible for my own peace: – Till Miss C—— came, I had very little of my own; I constantly felt for others; –

36. A rolling common of meadows, woods, windmills and ruins adjacent to Beverley and the racecourse. When Wollstonecraft later remembered the good time at Beverley she mentioned the walks with Jane Arden on Westwood Common.
37. John Dryden, *Conquest of Granada*, Part II (1670), I, ii, 5f.

'I gave to misery all I had, a tear,
  'I gained from heaven, 'twas all I wished, a friend.'[38]

Love and Jealousy are twins. – I would allow Miss R—— the first place, but I could not bear the thought of C——s rivalling me in your love.

As to the affair at Miss J——'s I am certain I can clear myself from the imputation. – I spent part of the night in tears; (I would not meanly make a merit of it.) – I have not time to write fully on the subject, but this I am sure of, if I did not love you,[1] I should not be angry. – I cannot bear a slight from those I love; – I mean no reflection on your papa, I shall always think myself under an obligation for his politeness to me. – I should have called this morning but for a hint in your letter which made me think you have told your Mama and sisters. – I shall take it as a particular favor if you will call this morning, and be assured that however more deserving Miss R—— may be of your favor, she cannot love you better than your humble Servant

Mary Wollstonecraft.

P.S. I keep your letters as a Memorial that you once loved me, but it will be of no consequence to keep mine as you have no regard for the writer. – [39]

There is some part of your letter so cutting, I cannot comment upon it. – I beg you will write another letter on this subject. – Pray send me word by your sister, if you will call this morning. – I inclose the Essay upon friendship[40] which your papa lent me the other day. I have copied

---

38. A variant of the lines from Thomas Gray's *Elegy Written in a Country Churchyard* (1751), ll. 123f. Mary's quotations now appear to reveal wider reading than those in the first letter to Jane Arden. Girls were urged to study, copy and memorize useful quotations.

39. Mary appears not to have kept her friend's letters while Jane Arden preserved Mary's.

40. There were a number of essays on friendship, most famously by Joseph Addison, Oliver Goldsmith and Matthew Prior. Recent ones to which Mary might be referring were the anonymous *Beauty of Love and Friendship* (1745), *On the Delicacy of Friendship* (1755) and *An Essay to F, A Poem* (1767). None has the exact quotation, the nearest being from Mary Deverell's *Sermons on the Following Subjects, viz. Friendship, Gratitude to God, Mercy, etc* (Bristol, 1774). The tone of the quotation seems closest to the sentimental discourse of mid-century novels, educational manuals and magazines.

it for it is beautiful: Many thanks for it. – Friendship founded upon virtue Truth and love; – it sweetens the cares, lessens the sorrows, and adds to the joys of life. – It corrects our foibles and errors, refines the pleasures of sense and improves the faculties of the mind. – It is adapted to all the various changes and exigencies of life, and by a kind of sympathy flowing from mutual sincerity, it bears a part of pain or pleasure as different events affect the mind. – Its pleasures are permanent and increase by reflection, so that a view of the past adds to the enjoyment of the present, opening to the mind the prospect of endless bliss. – Such was the friendship, intended by providence to adorn the most solemn sacred union, displaying itself in all the offices of true affection and esteem. – Happy beyond expression is that pair who are thus united; how rational are their pleasures, how solid their joys, how certain their hopes: – dispositions so excellent are guardian angels to each other, and in a finite degree resemble the harmony above.[41]

7. To Jane Arden

[Beverley] Wednesday noon, November 16th, 1774

Miss Wollstonecraft presents her compliments to Miss J[ane] A[rden] – the book which she would recommend to her particular notice is the Citizen of the World, or letters from a Chinese philosopher residing in London to his friends in the East.[42] —

From my opinion of the Delicacy of your sentiments I am certain it will meet with your approbation. – Pray tell the worthy philosopher,[43]

41. The final description is close to that of marriage in John Milton's *Paradise Lost* (1667), bk. 8, ll. 604f. 'Union of Mind, or in us both one Soule; / Harmonie to behold in wedded pair . . .' Wollstonecraft quoted this book of *Paradise Lost* throughout her life.
42. Oliver Goldsmith's *Citizen of the World* was originally published as *Chinese Letters* in the *Public Ledger* from 24 January 1760, twice weekly throughout 1760 and sporadically in 1761 until 14 August. As *The Citizen of the World* it was published in book form, with a few added letters, on 1 May 1762.
43. John Arden was a 'philosopher' and peripatetic science demonstrator at larger provincial towns in England. He taught a course on electricity, gravitation, magnetism, astronomy, optics and the expansion of metals.

the next time he is so obliging as to give me a lesson on the globes,[44] I hope I shall convince him I am quicker than his daughter at finding out a puzzle, tho' I can't equal her at solving a problem. – I inclose it with my thanks.

Copy of a letter from Dr Clegg to Dr Lathan.[45]

I know you are pleased with any thing curious and uncommon in nature, and if what follows shall appear such, I can assure you, from eye witnesses, of the truth of every particular. –

In a Church at about three miles distance from us, the indecent custom still prevails of burying the dead in the place set apart for the devotion of the living, yet the parish not being very populous, one would scarcely imagine the inhabitants of the grave could be straitened for room, yet it sho.^{d} seem so, for on the last of August several hundred bodies, rose out of the grave in open day in that Church, to the great astonishment and terror of several spectators; – they deserted the Coffin, and arising out of the grave immediately ascended towards heaven, singing in concert all along, as they mounted through the air: – They had no winding-sheets about them, yet did not appear quite naked: – their vesture seemed streaked with gold interlaced with sable, skirted with white, yet thought to be exceedingly light; – by the agility

---

44. Arden had a special portable laboratory of elaborate instruments; his students could use the microscopes and telescopes themselves and learn to read maps and understand globes (the planets). Mary no doubt profited from his teaching and was always sceptical of science that could not be empirically tested.

45. James Clegg (1679–1755), a doctor and Dissenting minister of Chinley, Derbyshire, interested in science and curiosities; he wrote sermons and other works. He visited Beverley in 1740 and married Anne Champion from Edale who may have been connected with the Champions of Beverley. His letter concerning the vision was also published in *The Reliquary* in 1860 by Llewellyn Jewitt and gave rise to a controversy over national credulity or curiosity (see Henry Kirke (ed.), *Extracts from the Diary and Autobiography of the Rev. James Clegg*, London, 1899). Ebenezer Latham (1688–1754) was a Dissenting minister who taught at the academy in Findern, Derbyshire, and wrote on education, ethics and rationalism. The church mentioned in the letter was in Hayfield. It is difficult to gauge Wollstonecraft's connections with Dissenters in her youth but there was a flourishing Independent community in Beverley in her time: an Independent meeting-house near the theatre in Lair-Gate had been built in 1704 and in 1743 a minister's lodgings with garden was purchased (see George Oliver, *The History and Antiquities of the Town & Minster of Beverley*, Beverley, 1829, p. 281).

of their motion and the swiftness of their ascent they left a most fragrant and delicious odour behind them, but were quickly out of sight, and what is become of them, or in what distant region of this vast system, they have fixed their residence, no mortal can tell. –

I.B.

Bath and Windsor 1779–1781

8. To Jane Arden

Milson Street, Bath [?mid 1779][46]

You will, my dear girl, be as much surprised at receiving a letter from me, as I was at hearing, that your family resided at Bath; – I have been at this place two months yet chance never threw your sisters in my way – and if I had not by accident been informed of your father's giving lectures,[47] I might never have met with them. –

As soon as I could enquire out their habitation I seized the first opportunity of paying my compliments to them: – my principal reason

---

46. Godwin recorded that Wollstonecraft left home at nineteen to work as a companion to Mrs Dawson. Sarah Dawson, née Regis (d. 1812), was the widow of William Dawson, a prosperous London merchant, whose son owned the Milson Street house in Bath where his mother was living. The dating of Letters 8–16 is problematic. Wardle in *CL* argues that, since Wollstonecraft states in Letter 10 that her eldest brother, Edward Bland Wollstonecraft, 'has been married . . . and is now a father' and the date of his marriage was 21 June 1778, this and the next three letters must have been written in 1779–80 rather than 1778–79, as the editors of *SC* assumed (2, 959f.). Edward's first recorded child, Elizabeth, was christened on 11 November 1781, which might suggest an even later date, but see note 51 for a discussion. Letter 11 is directed to Jane Arden at the house of Sir Mortdant Martin of Burnham, Norfolk, where she was acting as governess. Letters 8, 9 and 10 were probably also addressed there.

47. Wollstonecraft may have heard of Arden from someone who had come across his name in the *Bath Chronicle* where on 18 February 1779 he advertised his third course of experimental philosophy at an elegant lecture room at his house in St James's Street. In the 26 February issue he was advertising his fourth course of lectures, declaring that he was waiting until he had twenty or more subscribers to begin. Arden had his two daughters Ann and Elizabeth with him.

for so doing, was the hopes of seeing you, tho' I rather wished than expected that pleasure. – I was happy however to hear that you were well and agreeably situated. – I often recollect with pleasure the many agreeable days we spent together when we eagerly told every girlish secret of our hearts – Those were peaceful days; – your's since that period may have been as tranquil, but mine have been far otherwise. – Your sister obligingly offered to send you this in a frank;[48] – and I write it by way of a prelude to a correspondence. –

I would not have you send your answer to this under cover to your own family, but direct to me at W.ᵐ Dawson's Esq. Milson Street, Bath. –

It would be needless again to say that a letter from you, will give sincere pleasure to

Your affectionate friend
Mary Wollstonecraft

9. To Jane Arden

[Bath, ?Christmas 1779][49]

I am happy, my dear girl, to hear from you and should sooner have acknowledged the receipt of your friendly Epistle, if your sister had not told me that her franks were out: – indeed she very obligingly offered to inclose a note, if I could write by the next day; – I accordingly did, but the weather proved so unfavorable, that I was not able to take it to her; – I am exceedingly flattered by your kind remembrance of me; and be assured it will ever give me the sincerest pleasure to be informed of your welfare. There is no prospect of my quitting this place in a hurry, necessity not choice ties me to it, (not but that I receive the greatest civility from this family) yet, I am detained here only by

---

48. The recipient usually paid postage but, if one had access to a frank – a letter or envelope with the signature of someone such as an MP entitled to send letters post free – then this could be avoided.

49. Following the manuscript order Wardle makes this letter the fourth in the sequence to Jane Arden. Its relative formality suggests an earlier position, however; the seasonal greetings indicate Wollstonecraft wrote it around Christmas.

prudential motives, if I was to follow the bent of my inclination I sho^d haste away. – You will not wonder at this, – when you consider I am among Strangers, far from all my former connexions: – The more I see of the world, the more anxious I am to preserve my old friends, for I am now slower than ever in forming friendships; – I would wish to cherish a universal love to all mankind, but the principal part of my heart must be occupied by those who have for years had a place there.

As I ever endeavour to be uniform and constant in my regards, it will not, I assure you be my fault, if our correspondence drops on my leaving Bath, for when that much wished for moment arrives, I shall take care to inform you how you may direct for me, so that it will remain with yourself whether you choose to continue it or not – Bath is remarkably full at present, and nothing is going forward, but Balls & plays without end or number. – I seldom go into public; – I have been but twice at the rooms;[50] – I am quite a piece of still life, not but that I am a friend to mirth and cheerfulness; but I would move in a small circle; – I am fond of domestic pleasures and have not spirit sufficient to bustle about. –

I wish I could write any thing that would entertain you, but I mix so little with the world, that I am at a loss for news, however I shall always be glad to hear about my old School-fellows and acquaintances at Beverley, and any accounts you occasionally send me will be very acceptable.

Pray send me the promised description of the family you are with, and let me hear from you soon. – To the accustomary compliments of the Season, permit me to add my good wishes, and believe me to be

Your most affectionate friend,
Mary Wollstonecraft.

P.S. – My compliments attend your Brother and Sister. – I am sorry for the Miss R——s but I never had a perfect account of their misfortunes. – Tell me, is there any hope of your visiting Bath this spring, for I should not so much regret my being detained here, if I had any prospect of seeing you. – Once more adieu. –

50. The Bath Assembly Rooms used for balls, card-playing, tea-drinking and meeting people.

10. To Jane Arden

[Bath, ?early 1780][51]

I am happy, my dear girl, to find by your letter that you are so agreeably situated; – your mild and amiable temper will always command the love and esteem of those who have the happiness of being well acquainted with you, and I am glad to hear that the family you are with, are of a kind to set a value on merit, for generally speaking to deserve and gain esteem, are two very different things. – I hinted to you in my last that I had not been very happy – indeed, I have been far otherwise: – Pain and disappointment have constantly attended me since I left Beverley. I do not however repine at the dispensations of Providence, for my philosophy, as well as my religion will ever teach me to look on misfortunes as blessings, which like a bitter potion is disagreeable to the palate tho' 'tis grateful to the Stomach – I hope mine have not been thrown away on me, but that I am both the wiser, and better for them. – Tho' I talk so philosophically now, yet I must own, when under the pressure of afflictions, I did not think so rationally; my feelings were then too acute, and it was not 'till the Storm was in some measure blown over, that I could acknowledge the justness of it: – Young people generally set out with romantic and sanguine hopes of happiness, and must receive a great many stings before they are convinced of their mistake, and that they

51. The dating here is difficult because of reference to marriages of both Mary Wollstonecraft's and Jane Arden's brothers. Ned (Edward Bland) Wollstonecraft married Elizabeth Munday at St Botolph's Church, Bishopsgate, on 21 June 1778. They had two recorded children, Elizabeth and Edward. Elizabeth was christened on 11 November 1781 and Edward on 23 November 1783. But the letter cannot have been written after November 1781 for by that time Wollstonecraft was living at home caring for her sick mother. Possibly the implied child is neither Elizabeth nor Edward but a third one who did not survive infancy. Jane Arden's brother is probably John, a physician and apothecary who repeatedly served as mayor of Beverley from 1787 to 1826 (George Pulson, *Beverlac; or, the Antiquities and History of the Town of Beverley*, London, 1829, pp. 401f.). He also became a notable wine merchant in the town (Oliver, *History and Antiquities of Beverley*, p. 398). He married Ann Barker of Cherry Burton, Yorkshire, on 22 September 1779. If the reference is to John, a date for this letter from early 1780 is more likely than Wardle's one of c. May–June 1779.

are pursuing a mere phantom; an empty name. – I think I have said enough by way of preface to an account of myself, tho' I do not intend to be very particular, as the less that is said on a disagreeable subject the better –

It is almost needless to tell you that my father's violent temper and extravagant turn of mind, was the principal cause of my unhappiness and that of the rest of the family. –

The good folks of Beverley (like those of most Country towns) were very ready to find out their Neighbours' faults, and to animadvert on them; – Many people did not scruple to prognosticate the ruin of the whole family, and the way he went on, justified them for so doing: – a pretended scheme of oeconomy induced my father to take us all into Wales,[52] – a most expensive and troublesome journey that answered no one good end. – Business or pleasure took him often to London, and at last obliged him once more to fix there.[53] – I will not say much of his ungovernable temper, tho' that has been the source of much misery[2] to me; – his passions were seldom directed at me,[54] yet I suffered more than any of them – my spirits were weak – in short, a lingering sickness was the consequence of it, and if my constitution had not been very strong, I must have fallen a sacrifice long before this. – as it is, my health is ruined, my spirits broken, and I have a constant pain in my side that is daily gaining ground on me: – My head aches with holding it down, I wrote a long letter before I began to write to you: – I am tired so good night.

12.th – I resume my pen and subject; I have only to add that my father's affairs were so embarrassed by his misconduct that he was

---

52. The Wollstonecraft family had moved from Beverley to Hoxton and then in 1776 to Laugharne in South Wales (without the eldest son Ned, who was pursuing law in London). Mary had been upset by the latter move since she had just met and become enraptured by Fanny Blood (see note 57). William Godwin said her father went to Laugharne for 'agricultural pursuits' (*Memoirs*, p. 23), but it is as likely that he was avoiding creditors and settling his family in a cheap, remote location.

53. According to Godwin, the family moved from Laugharne to Walworth, south of London, so that Mary could be 'near her chosen friend' Fanny in Newington Butts, the Bloods' home (*Memoirs*, p. 24).

54. In *Memoirs* Godwin noted her father's 'cruelty' to Mary (p. 7); in a letter to Joseph Johnson (11 January 1798, Abinger MSS, Dep.b.227/8) he records that Edward hit but did not whip his daughter.

obliged to take the fortune that was settled on us children;[55] I very readily gave up my part; I have therefore nothing to expect, and what is worse depend on a stranger. – I must not forget to tell you that I spent some time with a Clergyman and his lady – a very amiable Couple:[56] – They took some pains to cultivate my understanding (which had been too much neglected) they not only recommended proper books to me, but made me read to them; – I should have lived very happily with them if it had not been for my domestic troubles, and some other painful circumstances, that I wish to bury in oblivion. – At their house too, I enjoyed the society of a friend,[57] whom I love

55. Although the younger Wollstonecraft children were not mentioned in their paternal grandfather's will, which left considerable money to the eldest son Ned, there seems to have been some 'fortune' for them from an additional source, possibly from another member of the Wollstonecrafts or from their mother's relatives, the Irish Dicksons. The legacy taken from the children by their father seems to have been alienated to a Mr Roebuck, possibly the insurance broker in Nicholas Lane (see *Kent's Directory* for 1770s and 1780s, Guildhall microfilms 96917/5). In *The Wrongs of Woman* (1798), which includes several autobiographical details, the heroine mentions 'the settlement made on my mother's children' which the eldest brother manages to set aside so that it can in part be used to keep the impoverished father (*Works*, 1, 140).

56. The Clares lived next door to the Wollstonecraft family during their stay in Queen's Row, Hoxton. Mr Clare 'appears to have been a humourist of a very singular cast. In his person he was deformed and delicate. . . . He had a fondness for poetry, and was not destitute of taste. His manners were expressive of a tenderness and benevolence, the demonstrations of which appeared to have been somewhat too artificially cultivated. His habits were those of a perfect recluse. He seldom went out of his drawing-room. . . . Mary frequently spent days and weeks together, at the house of Mr Clare' (*Memoirs*, pp. 17f.). This may refer to Thomas Clare (b. 1746) from Rugby, who attended St John's College, Oxford, and obtained his Doctorate of Divinity in 1771 (*Alumni Oxonienses 1715–1886*, 1, 253).

57. Wollstonecraft's first mention of Fanny Blood, eldest daughter of Matthew and Caroline Blood (née Roe). Two years Mary's senior, Fanny Blood was a remarkably cultivated young woman who wrote, sang, drew, painted and sewed with much skill. In the first edition of *Memoirs* Godwin described the first meeting in terms of that between the passionate Werther and his beloved Charlotte in Johann Wolfgang von Goethe's popular *Sorrows of Young Werther* (1774): '[Mary] was conducted to the door of a small house, but furnished with peculiar neatness and propriety. The first object that caught her sight, was a young woman of a slender and elegant form, and eighteen years of age, busily employed in feeding and managing some children, born of the same parents, but considerably inferior to her in age. The impression Mary received from this spectacle was indelible; and, before the interview was concluded, she had taken, in her heart, the vows of an eternal friendship' (pp. 20f.).

better than all the world beside, a friend to whom I am bound by every tie of gratitude and inclination: To live with this friend is the height of my ambition, and indeed it is the most rational wish I could make, as her conversation is not more agreeable than improving.[3]

I could dwell for ever more on her praises, and you wo.^d not wonder at it, if you knew the many favors she has conferred on me, and the many valuable qualifications she possesses: – She has a masculine understanding, and sound judgment, yet she has every feminine virtue; – she is now in a bad state of health, and if she should recover, we shall soon be far separated from each other, for she will I believe be obliged to reside in a neighbouring Kingdom.[58] – Tho' this change may probably restore her health, yet I cannot help grieving at it, as I shall then be deprived of my only comfort. – My father has a house near Town, and I hope he will see his error, and act more prudently in future, and then my mother may enjoy some comfort.

– My sisters[59] are at School at Chelsea; – they are both fine girls and Elizabeth in particular is very handsome: – My eldest Brother has been married some time to a very agreeable woman, and is now a father. – Now I think of it, let me congratulate you on a circumstance that I know must have given you great pleasure; I mean your brother's marriage:[60] – I sincerely wish him and his agreeable wife joy, and all the other customary good wishes. – Your sisters are I think very much improved: Elizabeth is exceedingly so, and will I dare say do some execution at Beverley.[61] – As a correspondence will be dull without some swain to talk of, pray tell me when you write, if you have met with an agreeable Norfolk Swain to help to render the Country so delightful: – you had I am sure a little spice of romance in your composition and must before this time have had a predilection in favor of some happy man; – tell me all about it, it will be kind in you, as I

58. Fanny Blood's backward suitor was Hugh Skeys, an Irish merchant who had temporary business involvements in Lisbon and more permanent ones in Dublin. Fanny was already revealing the consumption that would darken the rest of her life; the only known palliative was a sojourn in a warmer climate.

59. Elizabeth and Everina (or Averina) Wollstonecraft. Everina, the youngest sister, was born in 1765.

60. See note 51.

61. Elizabeth (b. 1759) and Ann Arden (b. 1761). Ann was in poor health.

want something to divert my mind – Joking apart – I should be glad to hear that you had met with a sensible worthy man, tho' they are hard to be found. – You never mention your old friend Miss R—— – Send me some account of her – You see I am full of my enquiries, and as I would not wish to confine you to one Sheet of paper, if you have a frank to Mr A[rden] you may inclose your answer to him or your sister, only desire her to keep it, till I call for it. – I have written a vast deal, and shall now only assure you that my best wishes will ever attend you, and that I am yours affectionately

Mary Wollstonecraft.

11. To Jane Arden[62]

Bath, October 17th [?1780]

It is so long since I received your letter – that I am half ashamed to acknowledge the receipt of it. The only thing that I can say by way of excuse, is, that I was just going to Southampton[63] and had no opportunity of writing. After my arrival at that place, I had sufficient leisure; but as I had nothing of consequence to say to you, I put off writing 'till I return'd to Bath, that I might not put you to the expence of postage. So much by way of apology. —

As you kindly interest yourself about me, I know it will give you pleasure to hear, that I have received great benefit from my summer excursion. I was advised by one of the Faculty[64] to bathe in the sea, and, it has been of signal service to me.[65] – Has to the vivacity you talk

---

62. This is the only one of Mary's letters to Jane Arden known to have survived in manuscript. The differences between it and the copybook transcript in the Pforzheimer Library are recorded in *SC*, 2, 969f.

63. Wollstonecraft may have been visiting relatives in Southampton. *The Gentleman's Magazine* for August 1795 records the death of an Edward Bland Wollstonecraft of Gloucester Square, Southampton. This was probably the man earlier listed as first officer of the *Cruttendon*, a merchant ship of which Wollstonecraft's brother had inherited a part share from his grandfather in 1765.

64. Physicians.

65. In the 1770s and 1780s sea-bathing, along with drinking sea-water, was much promoted for health; hence the development of sea resorts such as Southampton.

of – 'tis gone forever – and all I wish for, is a chearful settled frame of mind, which, I use all my endeavors to attain, and hope in time I shall. I never let imaginary troubles disturb me – indeed so many real ones have occurred to harrass my mind and body, that it will require time to bring them into tune again. Tho' I mention this, I would not have you imagine that I repine at what has befalen me – Reason, as well as religion convinces me all has happen'd for the best. This is an old worn-out maxim; but 'tis not the less true – for I am persuaded misfortunes are of the greatest service, as they set things in the light they ought to be view'd in; and gives those that are tried by them, a kind of early old age.

I have spent a very agreeable summer, S[outhampto]n is a very pleasant place, in every sense of the word – The situation is delightful; and, the inhabitants polite, and hospitable. I received so much civility that I left it with regret. I am apt to get attach'd to places – and tho' backward and reserved in forming friendships, yet, I get sometimes so interested in the happiness of mere acquaintances, that it is the source of much pain to me.

I am quite agree with you in admiring Bath, it is a most delightful place – yet, I imagine the prospects did not strike me in the manner they did you. And I will tell you why I think so: you came out of Yorkshire, and out of a part not very beautiful: while on the contrary I had very lately visited Wales – where Nature appears in the most romantic dress – tho' with respect to its natural beauties I think Bath much inferior, yet as to the imbellishments of art, they are not to be compared, for I think the buildings here are the most regular and elegant I have ever seen. I cannot say that I should chuse a large town for my constant residence, if I was my own Mistress, as I am fond of the country; but if I was obliged to fix in one – in point of situation Bath would be as agreeable to me as any.

The family I am with here is a very worthy one, Mrs Dawson – has a very good understanding – and she has seen a great deal of the World, I hope to improve myself by her conversation, and I endeavor to render a circumstance (that at first was disagreeable,) useful to me.

Write to me soon and tell me you are merry and well – and then I will laugh and sing. – The keen blast of adversity has not frozen my heart – so far from it that I cannot be quite miserable while one of my fellow-creatures enjoys some portion of content; that your's may not be a scanty share is the sincere wish of your affectionate Friend

Mary Wollstonecraft

Pray send me some account of your old friend Miss Rud, when you write make my compliments to her. – I am so unwilling to bid you adieu that I have wrote to the bottom of my paper, tho' the watch has long since inform'd me 'tis past twelve o'clock.

12. To Jane Arden

[Windsor, ?April 1781]

Such a variety of things have taken up my attention since I parted with you, that I have not been able to write so soon as I intended.

I cannot lay it all to the charge of my engagements, but I fear I have a kind of indolence growing upon me, that I must endeavour to shake off. – Ceremony you know has long been banished from our correspondence, I shall not therefore multiply apologies, but in a few words assure you, that I have your interest very much at heart, and among the small number of friends in whose memory I wish to live, you hold one of the first places. – To say the truth, I am very indifferent as to the opinion of the world in general; – I wish to retire as much from it as possible – I am particularly sick of genteel life, as it is called; – the unmeaning civilities that I see every day praticed don't agree with my temper; – I long for a little sincerity, and look forward with pleasure to the time when I shall lay aside all restraint.[66] –

This is the gayest of all gay places; – nothing but dress and amusements are going forward; – I am only a spectator – I have lost all my relish for them: – early in life, before misfortune had broken my spirits, I had not the power of partaking of them, and now I am both from

66. The despondency might in part have been due to a failed romance with Joshua Waterhouse, a clergyman don from St Catherine's College, Cambridge. After his murder in 1827 some letters from the 'intellectual amazon' Mary Wollstonecraft were discovered among his numerous 'melting epistles'. He is recorded as a new visitor to Bath in the 17 December 1778 issue of the *Bath Chronicle*.

habit and inclination averse to them. – My wishes and expectations are very moderate. – I don't know which is the worst – to think too little or too much. – 'tis a difficult matter to draw the line, and keep clear of melancholy and thoughtlessness; – I really think it is best sometimes to be deceived – and to expect what we are never likely to meet with; – deluded by false hopes, the time would seem shorter, while we are hastening to a better world, where the follies and weaknesses that disturb us in this, will be no more: – In that abode of peace I hope to meet you, and there our early friendship will be perfected; – You'll think me in a very dull mood, but I am persuaded your good-nature will excuse what arises from ill health & lowness of spirits. – Write me soon, my dearest girl, and tell me how your sister's school goes on.[67] – I want to know, if you have heard of any eligible situation in the country, for I think you would be much more comfortable in a small Town, than a[t] such a large one as Bath: – I have ever approved of your plan, and it would give me great pleasure to find that you and your sister could contrive to live together; – let not small difficulties intimidate you, I beseech you; – struggle with any obstacles rather than go into a state of dependance:[68] – I speak feelingly. – I have felt the

67. In 1780 Jane Arden had left Norfolk to become a governess in Lord and Lady Ilchester's family in Redlynch, Somerset, near enough to Bath for visits to her family and presumably to Wollstonecraft, although the latter had soon moved with her employer to Windsor. Jane was educating the three Ilchester girls aged 7, 4 and 18 months. If she was the predecessor referred to by Agnes Porter, who started her employment at Redlynch in January 1784, the family did not remember her kindly: Mary, one of her pupils, later described her as 'very untrustworthy' and recalled she had taken her to see 'the glassworks in Bristol without permission, when Lady Ilchester was ill at Clifton' (Charlotte Traherne, 'Family Recollections', quoted in *A Governess in the Age of Jane Austen. The Journals and Letters of Agnes Porter*, ed. Joanna Martin, London: The Hambledon Press, 1998, p. 55). Jane Arden's sister had started a school in Catharine Place, Bath, on 9 April 1781, in which venture Jane was thinking of joining her. In 1784 Jane and Ann Arden returned to Beverley where they ran a successful school in Eastgate for many years.

68. In *Thoughts on the Education of Daughters* (1787), Wollstonecraft wrote of the dependence of companioning: 'Few are the modes of earning a subsistence, and those very humiliating. Perhaps to be an humble companion to some rich old cousin, or what is still worse, to live with strangers, who are so intolerably tyrannical, that none of their own relations can bear to live with them, though they should even expect a fortune in reversion. . . . The being dependant on the caprice of a fellow-creature, though certainly very necessary in this state of discipline, is yet a very bitter corrective, which we would fain shrink from' (*Works*, 4, 25).

weight, and wo^d have you by all means avoid it. – Your employm^ts tho a troublesome one, is very necessary, and you have an opportunity of doing much good, by instilling good principles into the young and ignorant, and at the close of life you'll have the pleasure to think that you have not lived in vain, and, believe me, this reflection is worth a life of care. –

I must now go to breakfast, – when I return to finish this, I may have roused up more spirits. –

(Noon). – I had a very pleasant journey to Town [–] the post Coach, is very convenient, and the passengers happened to be agreeable: – They consisted of a Physician and his Son, whose character I was acquaint^d with, and whose conversation was very rational & entertaining: – he has published several things that have been much approved of, and he has travelled thro' the old and new Continent. – We had likewise a civil young woman, – and altogether I should have been very well pleased, if my impatience to reach London had not increased, as I drew nearer to it. – To my great satisfaction, I found Miss Blood in better health than I expected from the accounts I have had of her. – She received me as she ever has done in the most friendly manner, and we passed a comfortable week together, which knew no other alloy than what arose from the thoughts of parting so soon. – The next time we meet, it will be for a longer continuance, and to that period I look, as to the most important one of my life: – this connexion must give the colour to my future days, for I have now given up every expectation and dependance that wo.^d interfere with my determination of spending my time with her. – I know this resolution may appear a little extraordinary, but in forming it I follow the dictates of reason as well as the bent of my inclination; for tho' I am willing to do what good I can in my generation, yet on many accounts I am averse to any matrimonial tie: – If ever you should venture may success attend you; – be not too sanguine in your expectations, and you will have less reason to fear a disappointment; – however it don't much signify what part in life we bear, so as we act with propriety. – Remember me in the kindest manner to your sister, and tell her I would write to her, but I am not willing to put her to the expence of postage: – when I get franks, I shall certainly do myself that pleasure. – My paper admonishes me to bid you adieu, and let me assure you that tho' you may not find the most regular correspondent, you may be sure of the most constant friend in yours &.ᶜ

Mary Wollstonecraft.

13. To Eliza Wollstonecraft

Windsor, August 17ᵗʰ [?1781]⁶⁹

My dear Bess, I this morning received your letter which was truly welcome to me, as I found by it you still remember me; but I must say, I should like to be remembered in a kinder manner, there is an air of irony through your whole epistle that hurts me exceedingly: I would willingly put the most favourable construction on it – yet, still it displeases me – I hate formality and compliments, one affectionate word, would give me more pleasure than all the pretty things that come from the head; but have nothing to say to the heart —

Two or three expressions in your last particularly displeased me, you mention my *condescension*, and early *enquiries* – I know not what to make of those words. – I did not answer my Father's letter because my stay at Bath was so uncertain, and besides, I was not willing a letter from him should come to that place after I had left it; but as soon as I was settled at Windsor I writ to him, and flattered myself I should have be favoured with a line or two in return. – As to Everina's illness my Father only mentioned it in a careless manner to me, and I did not imagine it had been so bad, even now I am ignorant of the nature of her complaint tho' I am very anxious about it –

You don't do me justice in supposing I seldom think of you – the happiness of my family is nearer my heart than you imagine – perhaps, too near for my own health or peace – For my anxiety preys on me, and is of no use to you, – you don't say a word of my mother,⁷⁰ I take it for granted she is well – tho' of late she has not even desired to be remembered to me. – Some time or the other, in this world or a better

69. Wardle places Letter 13 after Letter 14. I have reversed the order since Wollstonecraft mentions in Letter 14 to Jane Arden that she is soon to leave Windsor.
70. It seems likely that Mrs Wollstonecraft was already suffering from the complaint that would shortly kill her.

she may be convinced of my regard – and then may think I deserve not to be thought so harshly of – But enough on this subject, love me but as I love you, and I'll be contented.

I was surprised at your removing – and cannot divine the reason of your taken a house now, when you must pay rent for two 'till Lady-day.[71] I hope Charles continues to improve, I long to see him. –

I have written several letters to Mr Dickson[72] but have had no answers. —

I hear Edward goes on very well, that he is paying of[f] his debts, and that by this time he is again a father.[73] –

I have got no table in my room, and I am obliged to set side-ways to chest of draws on which I endeavour to write. – 'Tis drawing near twelve o'clock – and I must be up soon to dress my hair to go to eight o'clock prayers at the royal chapel, – I have promised to shew a nephew of Mrs Dawson's the way – I must therefore wish you a good night – and assure you that I am in the truest sense of the word your most

Affectionate Sister
Mary Wollstonecraft

Pray make my love and duty acceptable to every part of the family – and beg them all to receive me with smiling faces – for I cannot bear frowns. – or sneers –

71. The Wollstonecrafts had settled in Enfield, a straggling village in Middlesex about ten miles from London. Eliza (Bess) and Everina had been removed from their Chelsea school and were living at home, together with their brother, eleven-year-old Charles, intended for the law with his eldest brother. James had gone to sea. Lady day is 25 March, the Feast of the Annunciation, one of the quarter days used for rent-paying. The poor-rate books for the Town Quarter of Enfield, Middlesex, record the Wollstone-crafts moving within Enfield in 1781 (see Margaret Tims, *Mary Wollstonecraft: A Social Pioneer*, London: Millington, 1976, p. 360n.).

72. Presumably a maternal relative.

73. Since Edward (Ned) had inherited over £3,000 from his grandfather together with a lease on land and a share in a merchant ship it seems likely that, to fall into debt, he had become involved in the elder Edward's collapse. About this time he seems to have taken over the management of their father's finances and to have dealt with the Primrose Street houses, which represented the only remaining part of the original family fortune that went to their father. The reference to Edward's repeated fatherhood strengthens the supposition that Elizabeth, christened in November, was his second child. See note 51.

14. To Jane Arden

[Windsor, ?late summer 1781]

Here I am, quite alone. – M^{rs}. Dawson is gone to pay a visit, and I have the whole house to range in. – I cannot now I have so much time put off answering your last epistle which was truly welcome to me. – I indeed began to wonder at your silence, tho' I hardly deserved a speedy reply, but you used me better than I merited, and I am determined to let you see that I intend to be a regular correspondent. –

Windsor is a most delightful place; – the country about it is charming, and I long to live in the forest every time we ride through it. – The only fault I find is that it is too gay; – I should like a more retired situation. – I go constantly to the Cathedral: – I am very fond of the Service. – I have beside made some visits. – M^{rs}. Dawson has a sister who lives near here; – she is a most pleasant and entertaining woman and behaves to me in the politest manner. – She is rather too fond of dissipation and brings up her daughters in a stile I dont approve of – that is, she seems to wish rather to make them accomplished and fashionable than good and sensible, in the true sense of the word: – In this she follows the crowd, and it is much to be lamented, that the Stream runs so rapidly that way. – You cannot imagine how amazingly they dress here; – It is the important business that takes up great part of the time of both old and young. – I believe I am thought a very poor creature, but to dress violently neither suits my inclination, nor purse.[4] – I told you before, I fancy, that the royal family reside almost constantly here: – The King[74] is quite a domestic man[5] and it is pleasing to see him surrounded by his children: – he is a most affectionate father, but his love seems to be confined to a very narrow circle, at least I am sure his humanity is: – to tell you the truth, he is out of favor with me, and you will not wonder at it when I inform you that he killed three horses the other day riding in a hurry to pay a visit; this has lost him my warm heart; – I cannot bear an unfeeling mortal: –

74. George III (1738–1820) was famously happy in domestic life, unlike his Hanoverian predecessors; he and Queen Charlotte produced nine sons and six daughters.

Indeed I carry my notions on this subject a great way: – I think it murder to put an end to any living thing unless it be necessary for food, or hurtful to us. – If it has pleased the beneficent creator of all to call them into being, we ought to let them enjoy the common blessings of nature, and I declare nothing gives me so much pleasure as to contribute to the happiness of the most insignificant creature: – bound as my power of doing good is, I have sometimes saved the life of a fly, and thought myself of consequence:[75]

– I am running on in a romantic way – to change the subject, let me tell you, that the prince of Wales[76] is the principal beau here; – all the damsels set their caps at him, and you would smile to hear how the poor girls he condescends to take notice of are pulled to pieces: – the withered old maids sagaciously hint their fears, and kindly remark that they always thought them forward things: you would suppose a smile or a look of his had something fatal in it, and that a maid co^d not look at him, and remain pure: – joking apart – you can have no idea of the commotion he throws the good ladies into; he certainly keeps both envy & vanity alive, – but enough of him. – I beg your pardon for not mentioning my family, and thank you for remembering them; – they are all well, and I intend going to them the latter end of this month, and I shall spend as much time with them as I possibly can: – I don't like to think of parting, – it will be a severe trial, but I must submit to it. – We shall leave Windsor very soon and where we next bend our course, is not yet determined: – I shall not therefore expect to hear from you till I write to your sister, and that I intend doing as soon as I am fixed to any place for a time; – Pray make my best compliments to her, or use a more meaning phrase and assure her

75. Wollstonecraft's remark is possibly meant to echo a famous scene in Laurence Sterne's *The Life and Opinions of Tristram Shandy* (1759–67), vol. 2, ch. 12: 'my uncle *Toby* had scarce a heart to retaliate upon a fly. – Go, – says he, one day at dinner, to an over-grown one which had buzz'd about his nose, and tormented him cruelly all dinner-time, – and which, after infinite attempts, he had caught at last, as it flew by him; – I'll not hurt thee, says my uncle *Toby*, rising from his chair, and going a-cross the room, with the fly in his hand, – I'll not hurt a hair of thy head.'

76. George Augustus Frederick (1762–1830), later Prince Regent and George IV. He cut a dashing figure in his youth before he became prodigiously fat and indolent. One of his early mistresses was the young actress Mary Robinson (1758–1800), later a friend of Wollstonecraft.

of my love and good wishes, – the same awaits all your family – What shall I now say to you but that I am your ever affectionate friend

Mary Wollstonecraft.

I have put so much water in my ink, I am afraid you will not be able to read my faint characters, and besides my candle gives such a dreadful light. – I am just going to sup *solus* on a bunch of grapes, and a bread crust; – I'll drink your health in pure water. – I take up my pen again to tell you I have not for a long time been so well as I am at present. – The roses will bloom when there's peace in the breast, and the prospect of living with my fanny gladdens my heart: – You know not how I love her. – I can hardly bid you adieu, till I come to the bottom of my paper.

To hear often from you will give me great pleasure. – God bless you. –

M. W.

London Region 1782–1786

15. To Jane Arden

M^r. Bloods, Walham Green, Fulham, Middlesex
[c. mid – late 1782][77]

I should be quite ashamed, my dear Jane to own that I received your
obliging letter some months ago, if I could not give sufficient reason
for my silence; but at the time it arrived, I was employed in the most
melancholy way; – my poor mother was confined to her room, and
had been so a long while: – her disorder was a dropsy attended with
many other disagreeable complaints, which at last ended in her death.
– I was so fatigued with nursing her, & the many disagreeable circumstances that occurred, that I could not think of writing to you, till I got
a little better spirits. – Your sister was so polite as to write to me, I
believe it was last year, but I have not as yet answered it, and I have
put it off so long, that I don't know how to set about it. – To say the
truth I begin to hate writing, it is grown quite a task to me. – I was
some time before I could rouse myself enough to tell you that I [am]
alive, for I send this merely to convince you that I am in the land of

77. Wardle assigned this undated letter to late 1782 or early 1783; SC dates it January
– May 1781, an impossibility since Mrs Wollstonecraft died on 19 April 1782. Godwin
stated that Wollstonecraft left Mrs Dawson's service after two years. She then seems
to have cared for her mother from about autumn 1781 until her death. After this event,
the family scattered. Edward married a woman called Lydia and returned with her and
his son Charles to Laugharne, while Edward Bland (Ned) and his wife in St Katherine's
Street near the Tower took in Eliza and Everina. Mary joined the Blood family at
1 King's Row, Walham Green, a suburban village west of London.

the living, and still remember you. – I often think of the merry days we spent together at Beverley, when we used to laugh from noon 'till night; – You are a laugher still, but I am a stupid creature, and you would be tired to death of me, if you were to be with me a week. –

I am glad to hear, that you are in every respect so pleasantly situated: – I wish you may continue in it, and that it may be as advantageous as it is agreeable. – I assure you I envy your trip;[78] – of all places in the world, I long to visit Ireland and in particular the dear county of Clare. – The women are all handsome, and the men agreeable; – I honor their hospitality and doat on their freedom and ease, in short they are the people after my own heart. – I like their warmth of Temper, and if I was my own mistress I would spend my life with them: – However, as a friend, I would give you a caution, the men are dreadful flirts, so take care of your heart, and don't leave it in one of the Bogs. – Preserve your cheerful temper, and laugh & dance when a fiddle comes in your way, but beware of the sly collectors; – admire the pretty girls as much as you will, but dont so critically remark the beauty of the men; – you are a good girl – I would therefore have you grow fat, and your good nature, and obliging temper will always ensure you admirers that will have sense enough to prefer such good qualities to a baby face: – For my part – I have already got the wrinkles of old age, and so, like a true woman, rail at what I don't possess. – The inclosed letter is to a friend, I should take it as a favor, if you would forward it to the next post; and I should be happy to hear soon from you. – My stay in England is very uncertain,[79] and I wish to hear from you before I leave it. – Tell me all about your family, and every thing else that gives you pleasure, and believe me to be Yours &.ᶜ

Mary Wollstonecraft

If you can procure a frank of the inclosed, – you would much oblige me. –

78. If Jane Arden were still at Redlynch, she might have been accompanying the Ilchesters to Ireland to visit the family of Lady Ilchester in Co. Limerick. Wollstonecraft had links with Ireland through her mother and she remained in contact with relatives in Cork; Fanny Blood's family also originally came from Ireland and Fanny herself had been sent to Tipperary when family finances demanded her absence. The Bloods dreamt of returning to Ireland when they could afford it. About this time Wollstonecraft seems to have met the Bloods' Irish kinsman, Neptune, with whom she apparently had a flirtation. 79. Wollstonecraft planned to accompany Fanny Blood when she went to marry Hugh Skeys either in Ireland or Portugal.

16. To Jane Arden

[Walham Green, c. late 1782][80]

I congratulate you, my dear Jane, on account of your Sister's wedding, and am happy to find that she is settled to her satisfaction. – I was just going to desire you to wish her joy (to use the common phrase) but I am afraid my good wishes might be unseasonable, as I find by the date of your letter that the honey moon, and the next moon too must be almost over – The joy, and all that,[6] is certainly over by this time, and all the raptures have subsided, and the dear hurry of visiting and figuring away as a bride, and all the rest of the delights of matrimony are past and gone and have left no traces behind them, except disgust: – I hope I am mistaken, but this is the fate of most married pairs. – Solomon says 'there is nothing new under the Sun'[81] for which reason I will not marry, for I dont want to be tied to this nasty world, and old maids are of so little consequence – that 'let them live or die, nobody will laugh or cry.' – It is a happy thing to be a mere blank, and to be able to pursue one's own whims, where they lead, without having a husband and half a hundred children at hand to teaze and controul a poor woman who wishes to be free. – Some may follow Sᵗ Paul's advice 'in doing well,'[82] but I, like a true born Englishwoman, will endeavour to do better. – My sister however has done well, and married a worthy man, whose situation in life is truly eligible.[83] – You remember Bess; she was a mere child when we were together, and it would have hurt our dignity to have admitted her into our parties, but she must now

80. Eliza married on 20 October 1782 and her daughter was born on 10 August 1783; this letter was written between the two events.
81. Ecclesiastes 1:10: 'Nothing under the sun is new.'
82. I Corinthians 7:37–38: 'For he that hath determined being stedfast in his heart, having no necessity, but having power of his own will; and hath judged this in his heart, to keep his virgin, doth well. Therefore both he that giveth his virgin in marriage, doth well; and he that giveth her not, doth better.'
83. Eliza's husband was Meredith Bishop, a friend of Fanny Blood's suitor, Hugh Skeys. Bishop was a well-to-do shipwright from Rotherhithe and owner of a business which built lighters to unload larger cargo ships. Eliza was married at St Katherine's near the Tower; she was given away by her brother Ned.

take place of us, being of the most honorable order of matrons. – I am still in England, and likely to remain here sometime longer, as some unexpected delays have retarded our journey, but I believe we shall certainly go to Lisbon next spring. – I shall expect to hear from you soon; tell me all about your Beverley friends, and tell me you are well and happy. –

Make my good wishes acceptable to your Sister and assure yourself of the love and esteem of

Your ever affectionate
Mary Wollstonecraft.

17. To Everina Wollstonecraft

[Bermondsey] Saturday afternoon [c. late 1783][84]

I expected to have seen you before this – but the extreme coldness of the weather is a sufficient apology – I cannot yet give any certain account of Bess or form a rational conjecture with respect to the termination of her disorder – She has not had a violent fit of phrensy since I saw you – but her mind is in a most unsettled state and attending to the constant fluctuation of of it is far more harassing than the watching of those raving fits that had not the least tincture of reason – Her ideas are all disjointed and a number of wild whims float on her imagination and uncorrected fall from her – something like strange dreams when judgement sleeps and fancy sports at a fine rate – Don't smile at my language – for I am so constantly forced to observe her (lest she runs into mischief) that my thought continual turn on the unaccountable wanderings of her mind – She seems to think she has been very ill used – and in short 'till I see some more favorable symptoms I shall only suppose that her malady has assumed a new

---

84. After the birth of a girl (Elizabeth Mary Frances) on 10 August 1783, Eliza Bishop had suffered a depression and in late 1783 Wollstonecraft moved into the Bishops' house in Bermondsey to care for her. Everina remained with Edward (Ned) and his family. SC (1, 44n.–45n.) dates the letter, together with Letters 18, 20, and 23, a year earlier because they assumed the baby was born in autumn 1782 and that Wollstonecraft moved in with her sister in that year, as Memoirs states (p. 29).

and more *distressing* appearance – Do call some day out of charity to prevent my mind always dwelling on the same th[in]g – 'For that way madness lies'[85] — One thing by way of comfort I must tell you – and it is this – that person[s] who recover from madness are generally in this way before they are perfectly restored – but whether Bess's faculties will ever regain their former *tone* time only will show – At present I am in suspence – — Let me hear from you or see you and believe me to be your's

affectionately, M. W.

Mr D. promised to call last – and I intended sending this by him – We have been out in a coach – but still Bess is *far* from being *well* – Patience – Patience[86] – Farewel – —

Sunday Noon –

18. To Everina Wollstonecraft

[Bermondsey, c. late 1783]

I don't know what to do – Poor Eliza's situation almost turns my brain – I can't stay and see this continual misery – and to leave her to bear it by herself without any one to comfort her is still more distressing – I would do anything to rescue her from her present situation – My head is quite confused with thinking to so little purpose – I should have come over to you if I could have crossed the water – In this case something desperate must be determined on – do you think Edward will receive her   do speak to him – or if you imagine that I should have more enfluence on his mind I will contrive to see you[87] – but you

85. *King Lear*, III, iv, 21f.: 'O! that way madness lies; let me shun that;/No more of that.'
86. Since her mother's final words had, according to Godwin, been 'A little patience, and all will be over!' (*Memoirs*, 28) it is likely that this word was resonating in Wollstonecraft's mind.
87. Wollstonecraft was considering the daring plan of removing her sister from the marital home, but it was unlikely that Edward would receive a runaway wife. According to law the baby, belonging to the father, could not go with her mother.

must caution him against expostulating or even mentioning the affair to Bishop for it would only put him on his g[ua]rd and we should have a storm to encounter that I tremble to think of – I am convinced this is the only expedient to save Bess – and she declare she had rather be a teacher then stay here – I must again repeat it you must be secret nothing can be done till she leaves the house – For his friend Wood very justly said that he was either a 'lion or a spannial' – I have been some time deliberating on this – for I can't help pitying B. but misery must be his portion at any rate till he alters himself – and that would be a miracle – To be at Edward is not desirable but of the two evils she must chuse the least – write me a line by the Bearer or by the post tomorrow don't fail – If you have got the things from Miss Lawrance's send them – The bundle is for Averina[88] who will send for it next saturday and she hopes my sister W.[89] will get the rest of the shirts ready by that time –

I need not urge you to use your endeavors – if I did not see it was absolutely necessary I should not have fixed on it – I tell you she will soon be deprived of reason – B cannot behave properly and those who would attempt to reason with him must be mad or have very little observation – Those who would save Bess must act and not talk[90] –

[Unsigned]

19. To Everina Wollstonecraft

[Bermondsey, c. December 1783][91]

I have nothing to tell that will give you pleasure – Bess is much as usual – she has not slept for any length time this two nights –

D[r] Hawes called here yesterday – He enquired after you and behaved

---

88. Averina or Everina is such an unusual name that this is probably a mistake for Eliza.

89. Probably a reference to her sister-in-law, Elizabeth, Edward's wife.

90. The words 'I will call to night' are written in another hand three lines up from the end of this letter.

91. The date on the MS is not in Wollstonecraft's hand. The letter must have been written before the sisters left Bermondsey early in January 1784.

in such a respectful manner you would have smiled – I did not ask him to see Bess – Skey has not paid us a visit – in short we are much the same as when you saw us last – I am really sorry to observe that you are not well – something I am persuaded preys on your mind besides our poor girl's illness – As you are so secret I leave you to time that sovereign alleviater of all griefs – have a little patience and some remedy will occur or you will cease to want it – I speak from experience – time has blunted the edge of many vexation that I once thought I could never bear – I have no hope nor do I endeavor to attain any thing but composure of mind and that I expect to gain in some degree inspite of the storms and cross winds of life – A fair wind and a gentle stream will waft this and my little charge to you[92] – There's a flourish and a pun –

So good morning —
your's affectionately M W –

Send the child home before it is dark – and write me a line –

20. To Everina Wollstonecraft

[Bermondsey] Monday morning [January 5th, 1784][93]

I have nothing to tell you my dear girl that will give you pleasure – yesterday was a dismal day – long and dreary – Bishop was very ill *&c &c* – He is much better to-day – but Misery haunts this house in one shape or other – How sincerely do I join with you in saying that if a person has *common sense* they cannot make one completely unhappy. But to attempt to lead or govern a weak mind is impossible it will ever press froward to what it wishes regardless of impediments and with a selfish eagerness believe what it desires practicable tho' the contrary is as clear as the noon day – My spirits are hurried with listening to pros and cons and my head is so confused that I sometimes say no when I ought to say yes – My heart is almost broken with listening to B. while

92. Presumably Eliza's baby.
93. Dating follows the postmark, which reads 'JA 8'; 5 January 1784 was a Monday.

he *reasons* the case – I cannot insult him with advise – which he would never have wanted if he was capable of attending to it. May my habitation never be fixed among the tribe that can't look beyond the present gratification – that draw fixed conclution from general rules – that attend to the literal meaning only – and because a thing ought to be expect that it will come to pass – B. has made a confident of Skey and as I can never speak to him in private I suppose his pity may cloud his judgement – If it does I should not either wonder at it or blame him – For I that know and am fixed in my opinion cannot unwaveringly adhere to it – and when I reason am afraid of being unfeeling –

Miracles don't occur now – and only a miracle can alter the minds of some people – They grow old and we can only discover by their countenance that they are so – To the end of the chapter will this misery last – —— I have to request that you will send to Miss Lawrance for the things as I expect Fanny[94] next Thursday and she will stay with us but a few days – Bess desires her love she grows better and of course more sad –

[Unsigned]

21. *To Everina Wollstonecraft*

Church Street, Hackney [c. January 1784]

Here we are Averina – but my trembling hand will scarce let me tell you so – Bess is much more composed then I expected her to be – but to make my trial still more dreadful I was afraid in the coach she was going to have one of her flights for she bit her *wedding ring* to pieces – When I can recollect myself I'll send you particulars but at present my heart beats time with every carriage that rolls by and a knocking at the door almost throws me into a fit – Send the enclosed as soon as possible and if you have the least compassion write directly – I hope B. will not discover us for I could sooner face a Lion – yet the door

94. Fanny Blood's arrival at the house seems to have been essential for the plan of escape since she could help make arrangements, as the next letter indicates.

never opens but I expect to see him panting for breath – ask Ned how
we are to behave if he should find us out for Bess is determined not to
return [–] can he force her – but I'll not suppose it – yet I can think of
nothing else – She is sleepy and going to bed my agitated mind will not
permit me – Don't tell Charles[95] or any creature – Oh! – let me entreat
you to be careful – for Bess does not dread him now as much as I do –
Again let me request you to write as B.['s] behaviour may silence my
fears – you will soon hear from me again – Fanny carried many things
to Lear's brush-maker in the strand – next door to the White Hart

Your's, Mary –

Miss Johnson[96] Mrs Dodd's opposite the Mermaid – Church Street,
Hackney —
    She looks now very wild – Heaven protect us —
    I almost wish for an husband — For I want some body to support
me.

22. To Everina Wollstonecraft

[Hackney] Sunday afternoon [January 11th, 18th or 25th, 1784][97]

Your welcome letter arrived just now – and we thank you for sending
it so soon – Your account of B. does not surprise me as I am convinced
that to gratify the ruling passion he could command all the rest – The
plea of the child occurred to me and it was the most rational thing
he could complain of – I know he will tell a plausible tale and the
generality will pity him and blame me – but however if we can snatch
Bess from extreme wretchedness what reason shall we have to rejoice
– It was indeed a very disagreeable affair and if we had stay'd a day or
two longer I believe it would never have been effected – For Bess's
mind was so harassed with the fear of being discovered and the thought
of leaving the child that she could not have stood it long – I suppose

---

95. Charles, the youngest Wollstonecraft brother, had left his father in Laugharne and
was lodging with Ned, to whom he was to be articled.
96. Wollstonecraft had assumed this name to hide her identity from Bishop.
97. Wardle's dating is 'January 12 or 19' but neither was a Sunday.

B. told you how we escaped – there was full as much good luck as good management in it – as to Bess she was so terrified that she lost all presence of mind and would have done anything – I took a second coach to prevent his tracing us – Well all this may serve to talk about and laugh at when we meet but it was no *laughing* matter at the time — Bess is tolerably well she can't help sighing about little Mary who she tenderly loved – and on this score I both love and pity her – The poor brat it had got a little hold on my affections – some time or other I hope we shall get it – Yesterday we were two languid Ladies – and even now we have pains in all our limbs and are as jaded as if we had taken a long journey – My legs are swelled and I have got a complaint in my stomach &c &c &c but all these disorders will give way to time if it brings a little tranquility with it – and the thought of having assisted to bring about so desirable an event will ever give me pleasure to think of – I hope you sent the letters I enclosed to you as Bess writ a few very proper lines to B. – I am very glad you are in town as I depend on you for keeping Ned firm – B. would make a more determined person flinch – This quiet protends no good he will burst out at last and the calm will end in the usual manner – Tell my brother Bess is fixt in her resolution of never returning let what will be the consequence – and if a separate maintainance[98] is not to be obtained she'll try to earn her own bread – Write to us an account of every thing you can't be too particular – She carried off almost all her cloaths – but we have no linen – I wish you could contrive to send us the first opportunity a few changes – it matters not who they belong to – Bess begs you will lock up all the bundles till we know what to do – and the little trunk need not be opened – we have neither chemise handkerchief or apron so our necessities are pressing –

[Unsigned]

98. As an absconding wife Eliza Bishop had no legal title to a separate maintenance. Private arrangements were sometimes made between estranged spouses but they gave the wife no real security and technically Eliza remained a married woman whose future property could be claimed by a vindictive husband.

23. To Everina Wollstonecraft

[Hackney, c. January 1784]

My dear Girl read the enclosed before you look at this and in it you will find an account of a plan that Bess's melancholy situation retarded – I have maturely considered of it and determined to attempt it – we first thought of a school – but the MONIES did not answer – With economy we can live on a guinea a week and that sum we can with ease earn – The Lady who gave Fanny five guineas for two drawings will assist us and we shall be independant[99] – Now I must tell you I did borrow twenty pounds – and I don't repent – for if I had not the Bloods would [have] been inevitably ruined last Christmas – you may suppose my mind must have been very much distressed before I could submit to this – it added indeed to the misery of that *wretched time* – but there was no resource and he[100] lent it very properly without any parade – yet it made me miserable I saw I was *entangling* myself with an *obligation* — Fanny too was unhappy and when she received the

99. Fanny Blood's reaction to Wollstonecraft's scheme of living with her and Eliza Bishop is contained in a letter to Everina: 'I find [Mary] wrote to her brother informing him that it was our intention to live all together, and earn our bread by painting and needle-work, which gives me great uneasiness, as I am convinced that he will be displeased at his sisters being connected with me; and the forfeiting his favour at this time is of the utmost consequence. – I believe it was I that first proposed the plan – and in my eagerness to enjoy the society of two so dear to me, I did not give myself time to consider that it is utterly impracticable. The very utmost I could earn, one week with another, supposing I had uninterrupted health, is half a guinea a week, which would just pay for furnished lodgings for *three* people to pig together. As for needle-work, it is utterly impossible they could earn more than half a guinea a week between them, supposing they had constant employment, which is of all things the most uncertain. This I can assert from experience. . . . As for what assistance they could give me at the paints, we might be ruined before they could arrive at any proficiency at the art.' Fanny Blood and Mrs Clare came up with an alternative plan: 'no other than keeping a little shop of haberdashery and perfumery, in the neighbourhood of Hoxton, where they may be certain of meeting encouragement. Such a shop may be entirely furnished for fifty pounds, a sum which I should suppose might be raised for them, if it was mentioned to your brother' (Abinger MSS, Dep.b.210/9). Fanny Blood herself would not be involved since her health was poor and Ned disapproved of her.

100. The source of this 'loan' seems, rather surprisingly, to have been Meredith Bishop.

five guineas gave them to me to pay him a part and the rest she is determined to pay as soon as possible As to B's determination 'tis impossible to conjecture what 'twill be – and perhaps when Ned finds that Bess is not to be thrown on his hands he may act with more vigor – At any rate the getting her out of his power is delightful – and compared with that my situation will be comfortable – If Ned makes us a little present of furniture it will be very acceptable but if he is prudent we must try to do without it –

I knew I should be the Mrs *Brown*[101] the *shameful incendiary* in this shocking affair of a woman's leaving her bed-fellow — Skey[7] 'thought the strong affection of a sister *might* apologize for my conduct, but that the scheme was by no means a good one' – In short 'tis contrary to all the rules of conduct that are published for the benefit of new married Ladies[102] by whose advice Mrs Brook was actuated when she with grief of heart gave up my friendship — Mrs Clare too with *cautious words* approves of our conduct – and were she to see B. might advise a reconciliation –

I am sorry but not surprised at your spirits being sunk – Nor do I wonder that the varnish that a sanguine temper gives to every object begins to wear off – The pictures that the imagination draws are so very delightful that we willing let it predominate over reason till experience forces us to see the truth – The mind of man is formed to admire perfection and perhaps our longing after it and the pleasure we take in observing a shadow of it is a *faint line* of that Image that was first stamped on the soul – lost in sensual gratification many think of this world only – and tho' we declare in general terms that there is no such thing as happiness on Earth – yet it requires severe disappointments to make us forbear to seek it and be contented with endeavoring to prepare for a better state – Don't suppose I am preaching when I say uniformity of conduct cannot in any degree be expected from those

---

101. Possibly an allusion to Robert Lloyd's *Chit-Chat* (1762) in which a Mrs Brown mocks husbands.

102. Wollstonecraft was already very much aware that conduct books for women stressed preserving marriage at all costs. The popular *An Unfortunate Mother's Advice to Her Absent Daughters* (1761) by the separated Lady Pennington was particularly clear about the difficulties of falling out of matrimony and the misery of losing one's children.

whose first motive of action is not the pleasing the Suprem Being – and those who humbly rely on Providence will not only be supported in affliction but have a Peace imparted to them that is past all describing – This state is indeed a warfare and we learn little that we don't smart in the attaining – The cant of weak enthusiasts have made the consolations of Religion and the assistance of the Holy Spirit appear to the inconsiderate ridiculous – but it is the only solid foundation of comfort that the weak efforts of reason will be assisted and our hearts and minds corrected and improved till the time arrives when we shall not only see *perfection* but see every creature about us happy —

Bess desires her loves – Her head still continues to ache and she has a troublesome pain in her side – Last night she was very restless and terrified me for when I spoke to her she said she was sufficiently tried – and to day she has been deaf – This was the forerunner of her malady so

[The rest of the letter is missing.]

24. *To Everina Wollstonecraft*

[Hackney] Tuesday night [c. January 1784]

What will be the issue of this affair 'tis impossible to say – but I am cheered with the hope that our poor girl will never again be in this man's power — 'spite of the many vexation that have and still occur – my spirits do not sink supported by conscious rectitude I smile at B's malice and almost thank him for it as it give me fresh strength to pursue what I have begun with vigor – Had he been *only unhappy* I should have felt some pain in acting with firmness (for I hold the marriage vow sacred) – but now I am not much disturbed by compassion —

As to Skey I try to suspend my judgement with respect to his rather unkind behaviour – It would really give me pain to alter my opinion of him – The humane manner in which he exerted himself was not – could not be assumed it raised in my mind gratitude and esteem – and 'till I am convinced of the contrary I must think well of him tho' he is very *prudent* and a little stupid to be the dupe of B. for this is the most favorable construction I can give to his silence – His answer must be directed to you as I did not date my letter from any place – In his last letter he declined speaking much on the subject – but ventured to advise a reconciliation 'that might be productive of perpetual happiness' – This he said tho' a few days before 'he thought the[re] was not the most dista[nt] prospect of comfort' – and 'that she would soon again fall into dispair' – Fanny, who saw, how Bess was agitated at leaving the child, was anxious to gain some intelligence concerning it – and sent George[103] with a note to Skey – His answer was cool and unsatisfactory – He said *poor B.* was puzzling himself to 'bring about a reconciliation' and that he 'hoped' he might succeed as he thought he 'would now endeavor to make Mrs B. happy' – B. has told him a plausible tale and has not adhere to truth – yet still 'tis wonderful he could be so deceived – Dr. S. has been asking us what we intend to do when we are out of B's power, and what is still more, has offered us his advice and assistance – we have been racking our brains and cannot yet fix on any feasible plan – we once thought of going to Ireland & trying to keep a school or a little shop – I wish you would sound Ned but don't hint at the person who [is] to assist us – Something must be done if she can get no allowance – and soon too – The ten guineas came very opportunely[104] – for we had but three between us when we left the *dear spot* – we are good oeconomists – and 'spite of the suspence Bess is more composed then I have seen her since her illness – That look of extreme wretchedness, that hung on her contenance when she was obliged to bear with B., is in some measure dissipated – but she complains of a head ache which may arise from confinement and want of exercise – for we have never stirred out – We thought of Saunders – I am better – tho' I have caught Bishop's complaint and have a little periodical fever that keeps me warm these cold nights — Bess desires her best love. Try to keep Ned firm – I'll write to him if you desire it – or think it necessary –

I forgot to mention to you that M^{rs} C—— the day after she heard of

103. George Blood, Fanny's younger brother, formerly a sailor, but now living at home with his parents.
104. Apparently the source was Hugh Skeys.

our escape – came tho' it rained in a coach to visit us – offered to lend us *money* and has sent us a pye and a bottle of wine – our lodging is comfortable and the people civil – M̠ Blood sent us an invitation to his house – but we did not accept of it – you did not tell me whether you approved of the letter to the Counsellor to want to hear the result – Good Night

[Unsigned]

25. To George Blood[105]

Newington Green, July 3ᵈ [1785]

The pleasure I felt at hearing of your safe arrival was a good deal damp'd by the account you gave of the Captain's brutality – By this time, I hope, all the effects, of so disagreeable a voyage, are gone off – except your being a little weather-beaten or so – and you and I don't think that of much consequence – we have met with so many rough blasts that have sunk *deeper* than the *skin* – you need not have made any apology to me about the old man – when I entreated you, my dear George, to be prudent, I only meant to caution you against throwing your money away on *trifling* gratifications but I did not wish to narrow your heart or desire you to avoid relieving the *present* necessities of your fellow-creatures in order to ward off any *future* ill that might happen to *self* –

I should have answered your letter directly but I waited 'till I could call on M̠ Bibbins who offered of himself to obtain some recommend-

---

105. Wollstonecraft had decided on the option of opening a small school with her sister and Fanny Blood. She was helped financially and practically by Sarah Burgh, a widow from Newington Green whose husband James Burgh (d. 1775) had kept a school there and written several books on education. Wollstonecraft's first attempt, in Islington, failed, but the next, in Newington Green, a village two miles north of London, promised a living and the three women soon had nearly twenty pupils and two families of lodgers. They were joined by Everina; George Blood came to live nearby. He had found a job through the Clares with a wholesale haberdasher called Poole in Cheapside. Soon the group began to disintegrate. Sickly Fanny Blood left for Portugal to be married to Skeys; George Blood departed hurriedly for Ireland fleeing from bailiffs who had come to arrest him on a paternity suit.

atory letters for you – They are to be sent to Betty Delane,[106] and may, perhaps, be of service to you – It would give me great pleasure to hear there was any chance of your getting some employment – In the mean time give way to hope, do your duty and leave the rest to Heaven – forfeit not that *sure* support in the time of trouble – and tho' your want of experience and judgement may betray you into many errors, let not your heart be corrupted by bad example, and then tho' it may be wounded by neglect, and torn by anguish – you will not feel that most acute of all sorrows, a sense of having deserved the miseries that you undergo –

Palmer has been respited – and of course will be pardoned[107] – I have made many enquiries concerning the affair that alarmed us so much – and find that Palmer's Servant has sworn a child to you – and that it was on that account those men came to our house – the girl was waiting at a little ale-house near us – so that if you had stay'd you would have been envolved in a pretty piece of business that your innocence could not have extricated you out of – I suppose the child is P's or many fathers may dispute the honor – Let that be as it will, the recent affair of Mary Ann, would have given this some colour of truth – How troublesome fools are – Mrs Campbell[108] (who has all the constancy that attends on folly – and in whose mind when any prejudice is fixt it remains forever) has long disliked you – this confined ill-humour has at last broken out and she has suf-ficiently railled at your *vices*, and the *encouragement* I have given them – and this to the Morphys, who she is very intimate with – they have repeated her stories to their neighbours – so they have ran all over the Green – and I am assured in a very gross manner – I called on M^rs

106. The daughter of a Dublin merchant, Simon Delane, Betty Delane was a friend of the Bloods and Wollstonecraft. She shared her home at 48 Britain Street with her sister and brother-in-law, Robert Home (d.1834), an English painter.

107. George Blood had been lodging with an attorney called Palmer who was accused of forging documents to indicate that a client, Mrs Jones, was a clergyman's widow whose son was entitled to a pension. Wollstonecraft and George Blood must initially have thought that the bailiffs coming for Blood believed him implicated in Palmer's fraud. Wollstonecraft was quite assured of Blood's innocence on both this charge and the paternity suit.

108. A lodger with the Wollstonecraft sisters; her two sons were enrolled in the school. In Letter 28 Mary refers to her as 'my cousin Campbell'.

Poole[109] she was very rude – as you know the woman you can easily conceive how she would behave – I believe she would have scolded me in the true vulgar female stile – if I had not assumed the Princess[110] – M[r] Carter was full of enquiries and impertinently curious – The Poet[111] was the only one that seemed at all concerned about you – As I find M[r] Poole is returned I shall call on [him] for his sweet *rib*[8] would not settle any thing 'till she saw him – The Clares affected total ignorance and were dreadfully afraid their *good* name should be *sullied* on account of their recommending a person who left his place so hastily – I have been very ill – and gone through the usual physical operations, have been bled and b[l]istered[112] – yet still I am not well – My harrassed mind will in time wear out my body – I have been so hunted down by cares – and see so many that I must encounter that my spirits are quite deprest – I have lost all relish for life – and my almost broken heart is only chear by the prospect of dearth – I may be years a-dying tho', and so I ought to be patient – for at this time to wish myself away would be selfish – your father and mother are well and desire their love – The former has received a letter from Fanny she mentions a packet that she has sent to me, I am afraid it has miscarried for I cannot hear any thing of it – I every day expect another letter in answer to the many I have written – She is much better – but her letters to our father are seldom satisfactory to me – Dr Jeffray[113] who accompanied her to

109. The wife of George Blood's employer. Blood had apparently left without his final wages.
110. Wollstonecraft had been called 'the Princess' by George Blood, a title she obviously enjoyed since she mentioned it more than once.
111. Probably Samuel Rogers (1763–1855), who lived at his father's house on Newington Green, later author of *The Pleasures of Memory* (1792). He left idyllic descriptions of the natural surroundings of the Green.
112. Bleeding, blistering and cupping were current treatments for almost all ailments supposedly related to inflammations: blistering entailed raising blisters through cauterizing or burning the skin and bleeding was the letting of blood, often through applying leeches.
113. In a letter of 30 March 1785 to Everina Wollstonecraft and Eliza Bishop (Abinger MSS, Dep.b.210/9) Fanny Skeys mentioned that she would send a letter by her doctor: 'if you are not carried away by prejudice on the first interview, he will afterwards probably steal into your favour, as he has done into mine. I have given a description of him to Mary; and she is, I hope, already prepared to love him. – He leaves Lisbon in about a week. . . . I shall greatly regret his departure – and the more so, as he spends as much time with me as he possibly can.'

[Lis]bon, brought me a letter the other day – but it was only [an in]troductory one and of [an] earlier date than some I have [received] – He is such a [man] as my fancy has painted [and] my heart longed to meet with – his humane and tender treatment of Fanny made me warm to him and I behaved to him with the freedom of an old friend – I mentioned your father to him – I am still trying to get him a place but my hopes are very faint – Your second letter is just arrived, I will write soon to you again – I sincerely rejoice at your good fortune in meeting with such a kind reception at the Kiernans[114] – you must have patience I think you had best not go Limerick – it would only be going in search of mortifications – for your relation would neglect you   I forgot to tell you that Palmer's Servant says, she followed you one day in Town and raised a mob, but that you ran away – Mrs Jones sent her to us – God Bless you and believe me sincerely and affectionately your friend – I feel that I love you [be]tter than I ever supposed that I did – Adieu [   ] to the village delights. I almost hate the Gre[en which] seems the grave of all my comforts – S[hall I e]ver again see your honest heart danc[ing in] your eyes? —

[Unsigned]

26. To George Blood

Newington Green, July 20th [1785]

I this evening received your letter of the 19th instant – and am really *hurt* that your former one still remains unanswered – I can easily imagine the anxiety my silence must occasion you, and am angry with myself for concurring, with other untowardly circumstances, to vex you – yet I must scold you my dear boy for giving way to *vain* fears – If [a]t any time I am not punctual in writing to you, imagine that I am low spirited, or that I wait for a Lisbon letter (that I may have it in my

114. George Blood was staying at the home of the apothecary George Kiernan, an old family friend. According to *Watson's Almanack for 1785* an apothecary named John Kiernan, possibly a relative, traded at 8 St Anne-Street. George Blood was subsequently hired by a Bride Street linen draper named Hughes (*CL*, p. 92). His mail was addressed through Betty Delane.

power to tell you all about Fanny) – or inshort, suppose any thing, rather then want of affection – I am not so capricious – I value you on account of your goodness of heart, and other qualities that I give you credit for – your letters display them in the fairest point of view – and while I with pleasure observe your refinement of sentiment, and am convinced that the very disappointments that gall you are improving you – can you, for a moment, believe that I am changed? – No, I am not a fair-weather friend – on the contrary, I think, I love most people best when they are in adversity – for pity is one of my prevailing passions[115] – I am not fond of professions – yet once for all, let me assure you, that I have a motherly tenderness for you, and that my heart dances when I make any new discovery of *goodness* in you – It gives me the sincerest satisfaction to find, that you look for comfort where only it is to be met with – and that Being in whom you trust will not desert you! – Be not cast down, while we are struggling with care life slips away, and through the assistance of Divine Grace, we are obtaining habits of virtue that will enable us to relish those joys that we cannot now form any idea of – I feel myself particularly attached to those who are heirs of the promises, and travel on in the thorny path with the same *Christian hopes* that render my severe trials a cause of thankfulness – when I *can* think[116] –

I am glad to hear that your friends still continue constant – tho' I hope you will not long stand in need of their assistance – you have been but a short time in Dublin, some thing may occur when you least expect it – your intention with respect to your father and mother does you honour and gives me pleasure – They are both well, and have not yet felt the *gripe* of poverty – I believe in a few days your father will

115. In the late eighteenth century some people still held an old psychological belief that each individual mind was affected or acted upon by particular passions such as ambition, avarice, desire, love or hatred and that these passions became overpowering and gave colour to the whole mind, cf. Alexander Pope, *Of the Use of Riches, an Epistle to the Right Honourable Allen Lord Bathurst* (1732), l. 156: 'The ruling Passion conquers Reason still.'

116. Wollstonecraft had been nominally raised an Anglican but seems to have had little pious example at home. Her renewed faith during the early years of her adulthood may have been influenced by her surrogate parents, the Clares of Hoxton, and by her new society in Newington Green; the village housed a famous community of Dissenters including the preacher, political commentator and scientist Dr Richard Price.

get the employment in the India house, that has been so long talked of
– Friendly Church[117] told him so to day – He was very much mortified
at not having obtained it sooner – your father is now very well satisfied
with the place, as he finds on enquiry, it is far from being laborious –
On every account I wish him to be employed for your mother will be
much more comfortable when he is out part of the day – I often see
them – they desire to be remembered to you in the kindest manner –
and intirely acquit you you of the crime that is laid to your charge, as
do the girls[118] – The Hewletts[119] have been in the country this vacation,
so that it is some time since I saw them – Sowerby[120] is full of business
– [He did] a picture for Dr Lettsome[121] that has [done grea]t service to
him – you know he is [one] of [the few] good creatures – He sometimes
visits the *deserted village*[122] and I try to smile – but some how or other,
my spirits are fled, and I am incapable of joy – Nothing interest me –
yes, I forgot, *humane* rational Church can please me – but business
and many other things prevents his calling often, and when he does, I
seldom enjoy his company, we have so many tattling females – I have
no creature to be unreserved to, Eliza & Averina are so different, that
I could as soon fly as open my heart to them – How my social comforts
have dropped away[123] – Fanny first – and then you went over the hills
and far away – I am resigned to my fate but 'tis that gloomy kind of

117. Mrs Burgh's nephew.
118. Presumably her sisters Eliza and Everina; Wollstonecraft tended to refer to them
as 'the girls' well into their adulthood.
119. The Revd. John Hewlett (1762–1844), a teacher and Anglican clergyman from
Magdalene College, Cambridge, became the author of textbooks, sermons and an
annotated edition of the Bible, all published by the liberal London publisher and
bookseller Joseph Johnson.
120. James Sowerby (1757–1822) of Stoke Newington was a naturalist later famous
for the 2,592 plates he made for Sir Edward Smith's *English Botany* (13 vols., 1790–
1814) and for his own *Coloured Figures of English Fungi* (1797–1815); connected
with this work, he also made more than 200 models of British fungi (*DNB*).
121. John Coakley Lettsome (1744–1815), a fellow of the Royal Society and a Quaker
physician. He used his private fortune and considerable medical income to support
philanthropic ventures as well as a museum, library, and botanical garden on his estate
of Grove Hill in Camberwell.
122. Newington Green without Fanny and George Blood. The reference is to Goldsmith's famous poem *The Deserted Village* (1769).
123. Samuel Johnson, *On the Death of Dr Robert Levet* (1783), l. 4: 'Our social
comforts drop away'.

resignation that is akin to dispair – My heart – my affection cannot fix here and without some one to love this world is a desart to me – Perhaps tenderness weaken the mind, and is not fit for a state of trial – I am very uneasy on account of Fanny's silence indeed that was the reason I did not write sooner as I expected every day to hear from her – When I do I'll answer Betty Delane's letter – I will not write to you both at the same time – by which means you will hear oftener from me – give my love to the Delanes. We have lost Miss Mason[124] – She is a good girl and I was sorry to loose her – The rest of the family remain much the same as when you left them – Eliza still turns up her nose and ridicules and as to Averina I can neither *love* or *hate* her – or to use softer her word, be indifferent to her – I shall speak to your father about Ellis – Remember me to Lucas[125] – I think the fewer people you make confidents of,[126] the better – I shall tell Fanny how you go on – Write often to me, for your letters give pleasure to your truly affection-ate friend

Mary

Your mother was wi[shing to] hear some news from Tipperary[127] [in p]articular where your aunt Collis [   ] – and how they live —

124. This helper at the school seems to have made a deep impression on Wollstonecraft since she used the name for the virtuous governess in *Original Stories from Real Life* (1788). Miss Mason might have been an old Beverley connection since she shares her name with William Mason of Driffield (see note 16).
125. Wardle speculates that this might be a cousin of George and Fanny Blood, whose paternal grandmother's maiden name was Lucas (*CL*, p. 94).
126. Wollstonecraft frequently had to warn George Blood to be more reticent if he wished to impress people. Presumably she was advising him not to reveal the paternity charge.
127. Probably a reference to the family of Archdeacon Baillie in Tipperary, the uncle of Fanny and George Blood. Mrs Baillie seems to have been Mrs Blood's sister; when she later visited them, Wollstonecraft remarked on the resemblance.

27. To George Blood

Newington Green, July 25th [1785]

My dear George

I have at last received the long expected packet. The person to whose care it was intrusted, knew it was not a letter of *business*, and so detain[ed] it a month, 'till she could conveniently deliver it – I expect every day to hear that another packet is arrived, when it does I will write to Betty Delane – The account Fanny gives of her health is far from pleasing me, tho' I imagine that her complaints arise from a *new cause* that you can easily guess[128] – Skeys is quite delighted with the prospect; but Fanny is out of spirits, and tired with contending with sickness and care – She has received several of our letters – and read in the papers an account of Palmer – which made her very uneasy lest your name should be mention'd which would have been an *effectual* bar to your settling in Lisbon,[129] she has not even told Skeys of your living with P. as it would have *lowered* you in his esteem – I wish you had not writ to her about being introduced to his brother – I know pride predominates in his composition and that it easily takes fire – His nephew is now provided for – and he intends being very assiduous in looking out for an employment for you, and in all probability will succeed, in a short time so keep up your spirits – better day will come – I am certain Fanny will keep this whole affair a secret – do you be cautious that it may not get wind, and be communicated to Skeys by some other hand – I really believe it will not be long before you are sent for to Lisbon – yet I would not have you remit your endeavours to get into some place in Dublin tho' I would have this hope chear you under any disappointment – If you have any time to yourself look over your french grammer   a little knowledge of that language, would be of great use to you – Do try my dear boy to encourage hope – without this pleasing delusion life is dull indeed – and no undertaking is carried

128. Fanny's pregnancy was soon confirmed; it was unfortunate given her poor state of health.
129. Skeys was to help bring George Blood to Lisbon when he had found an opening for him. Involvement in Palmer's fraud would have destroyed any prospects.

on with vigour – as to any little expence that you may be to George K.[130] you ought not to be uneasy about it – He can very well afford it – I don't mean to lessen the favor – but this consideration makes your situation much more easy – Skeys has received congratulatory letters from most of his friends and relations in Ireland and he now regrets that he did not marry sooner – all his mighty fears had no foundation – so that if he had had courage to have braved the worlds dread laugh and ventured to have acted for himself he might have spared Fanny many griefs the *scars* of which will *never* be obliterated – nay more, if she had gone a year or two ago her health might have been *perfectly* restored which I do not now think will ever be the case – Before true passion, I am convinced, every thing but a sense of duty moves, True love is warmest when the object is absent – How Hugh could let Fanny languish in England while he was throwing money away at Lisbon is to me inexplicable if he had a passion that did not require the *fuel* of seeing the object – I much fear that he values her not for the qualities that re[nder] her dear to my heart – Her tenderness and delicacy is not even conceived by a man who would be satisfied with the *fondness* of [com]mon (I mean one of the general run) of women – If he did not exert himself for her how can you expect that he will for you – keep up your own dignity – and do not be so familiar with Skeys as to let him discover your weaknesses – He has too high an opinion of his own cleverness and [is] so little conversant with his own heart, and of course so little acquainted with human nature – that he can't make allowance for the infirmities that are often found in the best characters – He has formed to himself a picture of a perfect creature – The principal features may be just – but the little minute things sensibility can only feel and teach – refinement of sentiment and the general notion of goodness is very different – according to the vulgar phrase the one may assist them to escape Hell but the other is wanted to give a relish for those pure joys that we cannot form a conception of in our present imperfect state – or to speak more like a Christian that Being who is gone before to prepare a mansion for us must cleanse our hearts and make us fit for it – Betty Delane is a good girl and has your interest at heart tho' she does not profess much – call often on her – Her

130. See note 114.

conversation will improve you – 'Tis so short a time since I writ I have nothing new to tell you with respect to the family at I.[131] or myself – I was determined to write soon again to make amends for my former silence – for I would not *even* have you *suppose* that your are neglected by your ever affectio[nate] friend Mary

28. To George Blood

Newington Green, August 14th [1785]

I received your truly welcome letter, my dear George, soon after I writ you a voluntary[132] so I did not think it necessary to answer it, 'till I had some account to send you of Fanny's health – I have heard several times from her – but I wait in vain for good news – She is still very ill and low spirited, a poor solitary creature – and here I am tied by the leg and cannot go to her – I hope however you will soon be sent for – I know you would be a great comfort to her – and that being so would make you very happy – I enclose you a letter which was written before she was informed of your departure from England, indeed I have not had a packet since; my letters are a long time before they reach her, on account of their being sent by private hand – From every account I think you may reasonably expect to visit Lisbon before the year expires – and if possible, I would have you save money enough to defray the expence of the voyage – I have from time to time sent Fanny accounts of you – for I know she is deeply interested in every thing that concerns you – I was quite delighted with George K.'s goodness – and I would have you try to take advantage of it and learn french. – He must be a good creature and I shall ever respect him – Remember me to him. I was never in a worse humour to write 'tis quite a task to me – I have nothing to say that will give you any pleasure – your father is still out of employment – and I am anxious about many things – I wish to hear often from you – but hate to write myself when my spirits are low – you may perceive by what I have already written how confused my

---

131. Islington; the remainder of the Blood family had moved there.
132. Her previous letter had not been in answer to one of George Blood's.

thoughts are – I write one word for another – and yet I cannot think of missing this opportunity lest you should for a moment suppose that I forget you or would not contrive to write to you – you are often in my thoughts – my dear boy, and every dawning of goodness, that I observe in you, gives me pleasure – ——

Our family is still the same – but my 'social comforts drop away' – for I now seldom see Church or any other rational creature who I can love – Labour and sorrow fill up my time, and so I toil through this vale of tears – and all this leads to an end which will be happy if I faint not – Mrs Roebuck[133] behave much better than she did, as to my cousin Campbell – she is still the same in every sense of the word – and as to the girls they teaze and please me by turns – I am particularly anxious

[Here four lines have been crossed out.][134]

– I have paid your Taylor – he and the Pooles behaved very rude, but they are vulgar and ignorant, so it is not to be wondered at – I will attempt to write to Betty Delane tho' I dislike it at this time; but I am not willing to put her to the expence of postage when I can avoid it – Sowerby is gone into the country – He has been very fortunate, Dr Lettsome has introduced him to several pe[ople] who have had their pictures drawn – He de[sires] to be remembered to [you] – The girls speak of you with kindness, and wish you well —— I shall write to you as soon as I see Mr John Skeys[135] who is now on his way to London – I expect he'll bring me a large packet.

Adieu

your ever affectionate friend [Signature cut away][136]

---

133. Presumably the wife of the man who would soon be involved in the lawsuit with the Wollstonecrafts over their alienated legacy (see Letter 43).

134. The first of the passages in letters to George Blood which were defaced with a blunt pen. Judging from what can be deciphered elsewhere, they seem to criticize family members harshly. The most likely person to have defaced the letters was Everina who, according to SC, 1, 50, kept her sister's letters. The defacing might also have been done by George Blood, or Sir Percy and Lady Shelley, who received the letters after Everina's death in 1843.

135. Hugh Skeys's brother and partner.

136. The practice of cutting away signatures to paste into autograph books has led to many unascribed letters.

This letter is a proof of my affection to you for spite of langour and sickness of heart I have forced myself to write

I ought to apologize for opening Fanny's letter but you'll excuse as I was not actuated by curiosity[137]—.

29. To George Blood

Newington Green, September 4th [1785]

By this time my dear George, I suppose you have received Fanny's letter, inform[ing] you that your fortune has at last taken a turn – I only heard of it yesterday, and I most sincerely rejoice, as I earnestly wish to hear of your arrival at Lisbon[138] on Fanny's account as well as well as your own – I hope too to see you before the year is out, as I am determined to be with her on a certain occasion, if I can possibly contrive it – I have many difficulties to overcome – yet I am not intimidated tho' worried almost to death – your father is still [un]provided for; but I shall endeavor so to manage matters that they may not feel any distress during my absence – for return I must to this delight[ful] spot – My spirits are very much harried – vexations and disappointments have as usual continual occurred – Church tell me I shall never thrive in the world – and I believe he is right – I every day grow more and more a proficient in that kind of knowlege which renders the world distasteful to me – well, well, but we'll meet in Lisbon and talk over all our past griefs – I wish I had fairly weathered the storms that I have to encounter on shore, I would willing compound for one at sea. Mrs Campbell left us today – we have lost a good lodger and been disappointed with respect to one that we had reason to expect to fill her place – our affairs here do not wear the most smiling aspect – But some how or other Prov[idence w]ill, I trust enable us to struggle through – Averina is grown indefatigable in her endeavors to improve herself – and altogether she assists me very much in the school and

137. Wollstonecraft wrote this on the cover of her letter.
138. Hugh Skeys had found an opening for George Blood in the consulate at St Obes, near Lisbon.

house – I have been plagued with bad servants added to the other cares that attend the management of a family – All these things, I hope, will tend to improve my temper and regulate my mind – I am grown quite meek and forbearing —

Your mother is well, and your good prospects have delighted her, she desires her love to you as does your father, who has not been well of late but he is now better – Palmer has hatched up some story to my discredit in order to be revenged on me for opening M^{rs} D's[139] eyes to his vilanies – He is still in prison – [ ]eiled to Mrs Jones[140] – I believe I forgot to tell you that the girl swore the child to him when she could get no one else to father it – The Clares are not by any means reconciled to your journey or satisfied with the odium that was thrown on *their* recommendation — I intend writing to Betty Delane very soon – Give my love to her – and accept the same with additional fervour from

your ever affectionate friend
Mary Wollstonecraft

I shall expect a letter before you set off – your long silence surprizes me – 5[th September] I have been teazed to death this morning – Mrs Cockburn[141] has taken it into her head to oppose my going to Lisbon, and Mrs Burgh has so warmly espoused my cause they have almost quarrelled about it – I shall ever have the most grateful sense of this good old woman's kindness to me, indeed I feel an affection for her – Mrs C. carries it so far as to say she'll prevent our having three very advantageous lodgers (which I expected to have) if I do not promise to stay – I am not to be governed in this way – I should have been sorry to have acted contrary to M^{rs} B's judgement, because I esteem

[The rest of the letter is missing.]

---

139. Probably Mrs Disney, a boarder with the Wollstonecrafts; her three children were pupils in the school. The Disneys may have been relatives of the prominent Dissenting family one of whose members, Dr John Disney (1746–1816) of Essex Street Chapel, was associated with Wollstonecraft's later friend Mary Hays.
140. The woman for whom Palmer had forged documents.
141. A neighbour in Newington Green who, like the Wollstonecrafts, took lodgers.

30. *To Eliza Bishop*[142]

[Lisbon, c. late November 1785]

My dear Girls

I am now beginning to awake out of a terrifying dream – for in that light does the transactions of these two or three last days appear – Before I say any more let me tell you that when I arrived here Fanny was in labour and that four hours after she was delivered of a boy – The child is alive and well and considering the *very very* low state Fanny was reduced to she is better than could be expected I am now watching her and the child, my active spirits has not been much at rest ever since I left England. I could not write to you on shipboard the sea was so rough – and we had such hard gales of wind the Capᵗ, was afraid we should be dismasted – I cannot write to-night or collect my scattered thoughts – My mind is quite unsettled – Fanny is so worn out her recovery would be almost a resurrection – and my reason will scarce allow me to think 'tis possible – I *labour* to be resigned and by the time I am a little so some *faint* hope sets my thoughts again a float – and for a moment I look forward to days, that will, alas! I fear, never come – I will try tomorrow to give you some little regular account of my journey – tho' I am almost afraid to look beyond the present moment. – was not my arrival Providential? I can scarce be persuaded that I am here and that so many things have happened in so short a time – My head grows light with thinking of it —

Wednesday night. Friday morning

Fanny has been so exceedingly ill since I wrote the above I intirely gave her up – and yet *I could not* write and tell you so, it seemed like signing her death warrant – yesterday afternoon some of the most alarming symptoms a little abated and she had a comfortable night – yet I rejoice with trembling lips – and am afraid to indulge hope, she is very low –

142. Following the intention described in the previous letter, Wollstonecraft had abandoned the school to travel to Lisbon to be with Fanny Skeys during her confinement. Mrs Burgh had 'supplied her with money, which however she always believed came from Dr Price' (*Memoirs*, p. 45).

Her stomach is so weak it will scarce bear to receive the lightest nourishment – in short if I was to tell you all her complaints you would not wonder at my fears – The child tho' a puny one is well I have got a wet nurse for it – The packet[143] does not sail 'till the latter end of next week, I send this by a ship, I shall write by every opportunity – I [arr]iv[ed] last monday – we were only thirteen days at sea – The wind was so high and the sea so bosterous the water came in at the cabin windows, and the ship rolled about in such a manner it was dangerous to stir – The woman was sea-sick the whole time, and the poor invalid so opprest by his complaints I never expected he would live to see Lisbon – I have supported him hours together gasping for breath, and at night if I had been inclined to sleep his *dreadful* cough would have kept me awake – you may suppose I have not rested much since I came here – yet I am tolerably well – and calmer than I could expect to be – Could I not have turn for comfort where only 'tis to be found, I should have been mad before this – but I feel that I am supported by that Being – who alone can heal a wounded spirit – May He Bless you both –

Yours
Mary[144]

31. To George Blood[145]

Newington Green, February 4th [1786]

I write to you my dear George, lest my silence should make you uneasy – yet what have I to say that will not have the same effect? Things do

143. The mailboat.

144. Fanny Skeys died on 29 November 1785. After the death Wollstonecraft stayed on in Portugal for a few weeks until about 20 December 1785: descriptions of expatriates and of Portuguese culture occur in her novel *Mary, a Fiction* (1788) and in reviews, especially of Arthur William Costigan's *Sketches of Society and Manners in Portugal* (*Works*, 7, 29).

145. Wollstonecraft returned to England to find that 'her school had suffered considerably in her absence' (*Memoirs*, p. 50). George Blood had reached Lisbon after his sister's death. Something went wrong with his proposed employment and he returned to Dublin, once more to be unemployed. He received this letter care of Betty Delane's brother-in-law, Robert Home.

not go well with me – and my spirits seem forever flown. I was a month on my passage, and the weather was so tempestuous, we were several times in imminent danger – I did not expect ever to have reached land – If it had pleased Heaven to have called me home – what a world of cares I should have missed. I have lost all relish for pleasure – and life seems a burthen almost too heavy to be endured – My head is stupid, and my heart sick and exhausted – But why should I worry you? and yet if I don't tell you my vexations what can I write about —

Your mother and father are tolerably well, and enquire most affectionately concerning you, they do not suspect that you have left Lisbon – and I do not intend informing them of it till you are provided for – I am very unhappy on their account, for tho' I am determined they shall share my last shilling, yet I have every reason to apprehend extreme distress, and of course they must be envolved in it – The school dwindleds to nothing, and we shall soon loose our last boarder, Mrs Disney – She and the girls quarrelled, while I was away; which contributes to make the house very disagreeable – Her sons are to be whole boarders at Mrs Cockburn's – Let me turn my eyes on which side I will, I can only anticipate misery – Are such prospects as these calculated to heal an almost broken heart – The loss of Fanny was sufficient of itself to have thrown a cloud over my brightest days – What effect then must it have, when I am bereft of every other comfort – I have too many debts – I can not think of remaining any longer in this house, the rent is so enormous, and where to go, without money or friends, who can point out[146] – My eyes are very bad and my memory gone, I am not fit for any situation and as to Eliza I don't know what will become of her – My constitution is so impaired, I hope, I shan't live long – yet I may be a tedious time dying — Well, I am too impatient – The Will of Heaven be done! – I will labour to be resigned – 'The spirit is willing but the flesh is weak'[147] I scarce know what I write – yet my writing at all, when my mind is so disturbed, is a proof to you that I can never be lost so intirely in misery as to forget those I love – I long

146. Although the school ultimately collapsed, it had had a longer life than many such ventures: it had sustained four women for two and a half years. Godwin is therefore just in declaring that 'No person was ever better formed for the business of education' than Wollstonecraft (*Memoirs*, p. 41).

147. Matthew 26:41: 'The spirit indeed is willing, but the flesh weak.'

to hear that you are settled – 'tis the only quarter from which I can reasonably expect any pleasure – I have received a very short unsatisfactory letter from Lisbon[148] – it was written to apologize for not sending the money to your father which he promised – It would have been particularly acceptable to them at this time – but he is prudent and will not run any hazard to serve a friend – indeed, delicacy made me conceal from him my dismal situation, but he must know th[at I] am embarrassed – Write to me soon, and give my love to Betty Delane and the rest of the family – I am very low-spirited, so of course my letter is very dull – I will not lengthen it out in the same strain – but conclude with, what alone will be acceptable, an assurance of love and regard – believe me to be ever your sincere and affec^te friend

Mary Wollstonecraft

32. To George Blood

Newington Green, February 27th [1786]

Your letter my dear George gave me the sincerest pleasure, not only on account of your unexpected success;[149] but as it displayed to me the goodness of your heart. I am indeed very much distressed at present, and my future prospects are still more gloomy – yet nothing should induce me to fly from England – My creditors have a right to do what they please with me, should I not be able to satisfy their demands. I am almost afraid to look forward, tho' I am convinced that the same Providence that brought me through past difficulties, will still continue to protect me. Should our present plan fail, I cannot even guess, what the girls will do. My brother, I am sure, will not receive them, and they are not calculated to struggle with the world – Eliza in particular, is very helpless – Their situation has made [me] very uneasy, – and as to your father and mother they have been a continual weight on my spirits – you have removed part of the load, for I now hope you would

148. From Hugh Skeys.
149. George Blood had found work as an assistant in the shop of Brabazon Noble, a Dublin wine merchant; *Wilson's Dublin Directory, For the Year 1787* lists Noble as trading at 96 Britain Street, to which subsequent letters to Blood were addressed.

be able to keep them from perishing, should my affairs grow desperate, – and this hope, has made me very grateful – for often when I have thought of death as the only end of my sorrows and cares, I earnestly wished to see them settled before I went to *rest* – Indeed I am very far from being well, I have a pain in my side, and a whole train of nervous complaints, which render me very uncomfortable – My spirits are very very low, and am so opprest by continually anxiety 'tis a labour to me to any thing – my former employments are quite irksome to me – If something decisive was to happen I should be better; but 'tis this suspence, this dread of I cannot tell what, which harasses me.

I have something to tell you which you'll rejoice at, your father has taken a quite serious turn, and our mother[150] never lived so comfortably with him in her life – Caroline[151] has left them, I am glad of it, they are much better without her – your mother enjoys tolerable health, but I suppose she has told you every thing – I have not yet been able to pay their last quarter's rent – Well, we must all have patience – I was in hopes Skeys would have sent them some trifle before this, at present it would be very acceptable to them – He has no consideration – He writ me two letters and one to Eliza at the same time, all but one was quite unnecessary – for two of them only informed me that the other was coming – of course the postage was thrown away – Will[m152] was very well, and thriving apace – M[rs] S.[153] had taken him to her house – He complains of his brother's neglect, I believe he has been very ill used – yet I am certain a few pounds would not make any difference in his affairs – yet why should I be surprised – did he not neglect Fanny – I am quite pleased with the Delanes and Homes – remember me to them in the kindest style – I almost wish a school was feasible in Dublin –

Sowerby is married, I have not yet seen the bride – I will write to Betty Delane very soon – Adieu –

yours affectionately
Mary Wollstonecraft

---

150. Although not always made (see Letter 34), this distinction between the Blood parents – Mrs Blood referred to as 'our mother' and Mr Blood as 'your father' – is a common one in Wollstonecraft's writing.
151. Sister of Fanny and George Blood.
152. The baby of Fanny and Hugh Skeys. He died shortly after.
153. Probably John Skeys's wife, the baby's aunt.

33. To George Blood

Newington Green, May 1ˢᵗ [1786]

I would not have, my dear George, suppose that I mean either to forget
or neglect him – He knows me too well to suspect that[; he] should,
and can make due allowance for my silence – yet I would not wish
on any account to give you uneasiness, though I cannot send you any
satisfactory answer to your enquiries concerning my affairs. They wear
at present a most gloomy aspect – and 'spite of all the fortitude I endeavour to muster up, I dread the *crisis* — yet I am convinced a state of
suspence is far worse than the certainty of any misfortune, for the continual fluctuation between hope and fear prevents the mind's exerting itself
– and why should I give way to fear? have I not a recent mercy to be
thankful for? – the being able to send your father and mother to Dublin
was a most Providencial thing,[154] and an answer to my fervent prayers.
You will think so when you hear all – They are very happy to return
to their native country – and I hope your mother has some comforts
to enjoy there. Your father seems an altered man try to deepen the
serious impression my poor girl's death made on him. You have not
yet forgot her? She was indeed George my best earthly comfort – and
my poor heart still throbs with *selfish* anguish – it is formed for
friendship and confidance – yet how often is it wounded –

[Here sixteen lines have been crossed out.]

I am however melancholy rather than unhappy now my hopes of
happiness are extinct – I am only anxious to improve myself and so
run my race that I may met my poor girl where sorrow and sighing
shall be no more. Your mother will tell you every circumstance which
relates to us – I am so blind I can scarcely see to write – In a very short
time I shall plunge again into some new scene of life – 'tis only when

154. Despite her depression Wollstonecraft had managed to write her first work,
Thoughts on the Education of Daughters, its title echoing James Burgh's *Thoughts on
Education* (1747) and John Locke's *Some Thoughts Concerning Education* (1693).
Her book was to be published by Joseph Johnson. The money he paid her was used to
send the Blood parents to Ireland.

my spirits are low that I dread it – My debts too haunt me like furies
– Well, well I tell thee I do not dispond, on the contrary am convince
that virtue is acquired in this thorny path – I would not shrink from the
trials, or avoid the chastisement – tho' I think them grievous – I am too
apt to be attached with a degree of warmth that is not consistent with a
probationary state, I have leaned on earth and have been *sorely hurt*.
Yet let me not forget to mention to you an act of disinterested kindness
– Mr Hewlett[155] exerted himself to obtain the money for your father in a
way that has insured him my esteem – you never saw a creature happier
then he was when he returned to tell me the success of his commission –
the sensibility and goodness that appeared in his countenance made
me love the man. How I love to receive acts of kindness from my
fellow-creatures – My heart would fain hold all the human race, and
every new affection would add to its comfort but for the bitter alloy
which will mix itself with every thing here –

    Adieu, I am labouring for patience – write to me soon – and believe
me to be your truly affectionate friend and sister

Mary Wollstonecraft —

I have not heard from Skeys.

34. To George Blood

Newington Green, May 22^d [1786]

By this time, my dear George, I hope your father and mother have
reached Dublin; I long to hear of their safe arrival. A few days after
they set sail I received a letter from Skeys, – he laments his inability to
assist them, and dwell on his own embarrassments. How glad I am
they are gone! My affairs are hastening to a crisis – The money that is
due to me on account of the Disneys, would, very nearly, have discharged all my debts; but I have little hopes of getting it – and this
disappointment distresses me beyond measure, as some of my creditors
cannot well afford to wait for their money – as to leaving England in
debts I am determined not to do it – The Will of Heaven be done! I am

---

155. John Hewlett had recommended Wollstonecraft's work to Johnson.

now grown quite patient – Tell your father and mother, the scheme with respect to Cork, is not practicable. Averina, and Eliza, are both endeavoring to go out into the world, the one as a companion, and the other as a teacher – and I believe I shall continue some time on the Green. I intend taking a little cheap lodging, and living without a servant, and the few scholars I have will maintain me, I have done with all worldly pursuits, or wishes I only desire to subsist, without being dependant on the caprice of an fellow-creature, I shall have many solitary hours; but I have not much to hope for in life, and so it would be absurd to give way to fear. Besides, I try to look on the best side, and not to dispond. While I am trying to do my duty in that station in which Providence has placed [me], I shall enjoy some tranquil moments – and the pleasures I have the greatest relish for, are not intirely out of my reach. I am just going to write to Mrs Prior,[156] about Eliza, if I could get her recommended to some eligible situation it would be a great weight of[f] my mind. She could not give up the world or live in the style I intend to do, if it was possible, to earn a scanty subsistence together – I have been trying to muster up my fortitude, and labouring for patience to bear my many trials – surely when I could determine to survive Fanny, I can endure poverty and all the lesser ills of life. I dreaded – Oh! how I dreaded this time – and now it is arrived I am calmer than I expected to be – I have been very unwell my constitution is very much impaired – the prison walls are decaying – and the prisoner will ere long get free[157] – I am not however impatient – I wish both to practise and feel resignate [– we] are by imperceptible degrees prepared for things – My present plan would have made me shudder some years ago, and now it does not terrify me, – I cannot bear to think of bustling forever with the world in an extensive way – and a little peace is all I desire. I have not been very punctual in answering your letters. my mind has been so disturbed yet you should not neglect me, as your correspondence affords me great

---

156. Wife of Mr Prior, assistant master at Eton and later fellow of King's College, Cambridge. Kegan Paul records that he was the grandson of a porter (WG, 1, 181). The contact was apparently made through Mrs Burgh.

157. For a religious use of 'prisoner' cf. Alexander Pope, Elegy on an Unfortunate Lady (1717), ll. 17f.: 'Most souls, 'tis true, but peep out once an age / Dull sullen pris'ners in the body's cage.'

pleasure. I shall write to you soon again – and hope to be settled – if my creditors can be prevailed on to have patience – if not, I know the worst and am prepared to brave it – I shall sell all my furniture – and what other things I can muster up —

Remember me in the kindest manner to our father and mother – and remember too – that I am your truly affectionate

friend and sister
Mary Wollstonecraft

Be very particular in your account of your situation, and Betty Delane's reception of your father and mother –

35. To George Blood

Newington Green, June 18th [1786]

My dear George

I have received your's and your father's letter; but you both forgot my determination of not leaving England 'till my debts are paid.[158] And to treat you with sincerity my dear boy I must be independant and earn my own subsistence, or be very uncomfortable – I could not live with your father, or condescend to practise those *arts* which are *necessary* to keep him in temper – and as to being *under obligations to him* it would never do, perhaps, it is not in the power of any human creature to render such a situation easy – and a selfish person, I am, sure could not – Besides, how you could think I could sit all day with the family, when you know we could not find conversation, surprises me; but I can account for it your eagerness to have me with you made you overlook every obstacle – and I dwell on them to you to reconcile you to my determination – The confinement of two little rooms would not be *solitude*, on the contrary I should from the nature of the society always be envolved in *insignificant* cares, which would worry me out of my life – I love your mother but she would not be a companion for

158. The Blood parents and George had both suggested that Wollstonecraft try to set up a school somewhere in Ireland or come to live with them, reneging on her debts.

me, any more than she was for Fanny – As to a school my want of knowledge with respect to the french language would be an impediment, and if I did not succeed I should have no recourse – The affectionate and warm interest you take in my affairs gives me pleasure – and I take the *will* for the *deed*, if you support your father and mother it will be a great thing – and will raise you higher in my opinion than any exertion in my favour – I am to remove to Mrs Blackburn's this week[–]Eliza must still remain with me, Averina will return to my brother's – I shall part with our servant and adopt the most rigid oeconomy – If Eliza leaves me, I think a day school would maintain me in lodgings and I have no objection to living alone now. Providence by imperceptible degrees prepares us for every change, and my want of domestic comfort will render solitude acceptable to me – I am indeed a sociable creature; but I must curb my affections which are too apt to run into extremes, and rivet me to earth – I took up a small sheet of paper as I found my spirits low – I wish not to dwell on evils which do not admit of [a] remedy – My prospects are gloomy – I dreamt the other night I saw my poor Fanny, and she told me I should soon follow her – I am sick of the world, ''tis an unweeded garden'[159] – I have a number of nervous complaints – I want a friend I am now *alone* and my heart not expanded by the usual affection prey on itself. I can scarcely find a name for the apathy that has seized on me – I am sick of every thing under the sun – for verily every thing is grievous to me – all our pursuits are vain only the end which they brings us to is of consequence[160] Give my love to *your*[9] mother – but do not give her my letters to read – as it would restrain my pen – I shall write soon again – remember me to your father and poor Betty delane. I shall answer her letter the first opportunity – I should not have written to you now but I thought you would be full of anxiety on my account – Caroline called on me the other day, I hope your father has wrote to Dalton, he complained of his neglect – Let me hear frequently from you and believe me to be your sincere friend

Mary

159. *Hamlet*, I, ii, 135f.: 'Fie on't! O fie! 'tis an unweeded garden, / That grows to seed; things rank and gross in nature / Possess it merely.'
160. Wollstonecraft was given to echoing biblical language during this period of intense melancholy.

36. To George Blood

Newington Green, July 6th [1786]

What can I say to you my dear George, I am afraid you are too sanguine, and that your desire to have me with you blinds your judgement. I must again repeat to you I am determined to earn my own subsistence, nay, more, I hope to save money to pay my debts, which worry me beyond measure – Here, I am afraid, I never shall be able – and I am exposed to insults which my unprotected situation naturally produces – yesterday one of my creditors behaved to me with great rudeness – but 'tis vain to talk of it – I must have patience – and yet the loss of Mrs Disney's money is a very severe blow, for it would *almost* have paid all I owe and removed from my mind a weight of anxiety which sinks my spirits and renders me unfit to bustle or enter on any new undertaking – you may mention these things to Mrs Shirley – and tell her am afraid a school would not succeed (and this fear arises from experience) without I could take a house and set off in a genteel style – Poverty will oftener raise contempt than pity – and my fate at Newington Green too plainly proves to me that to gain the respect of the vulgar, (a term which I with propriety apply to the generality however weighty their purses) – you must dazzle their senses – and even not appear to want their assistance if you expect to have it – a favorite author of your's, says, 'That pity is the most short-lived passion and that a speech di[c]tated by wisdom herself, would not be atten[d]ed to, if the person who delivered it was poor.' The drapery is what catches the superficial eye – and the necessary appendage – wealth, will go much farther than the most shining abilities to make a person respected[161] – In Ireland I know they are particularly attentive to appearances; and the first impression is of the utmost consequence. I will own to you that if 'twas feasible such a plan would be very

---

161. Samuel Johnson, *The Rambler no. 166* (19 October 1751): 'There are natural reasons why poverty does not easily conciliate affection. . . . The grossness of vulgar habits obstructs the efficacy of virtue, as impurity and harshness of stile impairs the force of reason, and rugged numbers turn off the mind from artifice of disposition, and fertility of invention.'

agreeable to me – much more so than any one I am likely to fix on. I have had two offers of being received as a governess in reputable families – The one in Wales and the other in Ireland – and this last appears so advantageous *duty* impels me to consider about it and not too hastily to reject it – and yet only duty would influence me if accept of it – It is Lady Kingsborough[162] who has written on the subject to Mrs Prior – and I wait for farther particulars before I give my final answer. Forty pounds a year[163] was the terms mentioned to me – and half of that sum I could spare to discharge my debts, and afterwards to assist Eliza. This is a certainty which I could dwell on to my creditors; but if I embarked in so precarious a scheme, as establishing a school, I could not promise any thing. I by no means like the proposal of being a governess – I should be shut out from society – and be debarred the *imperfect* pleasures of friendship – as I should on every side be surrounded by *unequals* – To live only on terms of civility and common benevolence without any interchange of little acts of kindness and tenderness would be to me extremely irksome – but I touch on too tender a string.[164] I said just now friendship – *even* friendship the medicine the *cordial* of life was imperfect and so is every thing in a world which is [only] to educate us for a better – Here we have no resting place nor any stable comfort but what arises from our resig- nation to the Will of Heaven and our firm reliance on those gracious promises delivered to us by Him who brought light and immortality into the world – He has told us not only that we *may inherit* eternal life; but that *we* shall be *changed* if we do not perversely reject the

162. Caroline King, Lady Kingsborough (1754–1823), was the daughter of Colonel Richard Fitzgerald and his first wife, Margaret King, heiress of Mitchelstown (d. 1763). As a great heiress Caroline was married at the age of fifteen to her young cousin Robert King, Viscount Kingsborough, later second Earl of Kingston. They lived frequently on Lady Kingsborough's inherited estate of Mitchelstown in Co. Cork and had seven sons and five daughters.

163. This was a reasonable sum for a governess; a highly educated lady might have commanded more, but Wollstonecraft's lack of proficiency in French no doubt dimin- ished her value.

164. In a chapter in *Thoughts* entitled 'The Benefits which arise from Disappointments', Wollstonecraft had described the contempt meted out to the teacher, companion and governess, and gloomily anticipated her own future employed by unappreciative, vain parents (see note 68).

offerred Grace.[165] Your letters my dear boy afford me great pleasure – and if mine are not always written in an *equal* style of affection impute it to the right cause, lowness of spirits – I am often with myself at war – and forget the *shews* of love to other's – nay I cannot always feel alike – my heart sometimes overflows with tenderness – and at others seems quite exhausted and incapable of being warmly interested about any one – my regards carried beyond the pitch which wisdom prescribes – often throw me into apathy; but though I cannot answer for my feelings – I can promise my understanding will ever approve of you while you adhere to your present line of conduct – I should have no objection to receive any favour from you – because I esteem you – yet I would have you seriously consider of what consequence the next step I take is to my future comfort – could I provide for my sisters it would give great pleasure. Give my love to your father and mother – and you may give the same to Neptune,[166] I have done with all resentments – and perhaps I was as much to blame in expecting too much as he in doing too little – I looked for what was not to be found – Your's

Mary

37. To George Blood

Newington Green, August 25th [1786]

Your silence, my dear George, I must own made me very uneasy – though I attributed it to the right cause, and should have written to you, if I had not waited till I was relieved out of a disagreeable state of suspence – with respect to the time of my departure; but it is still

165. Wollstonecraft thought about religion all her life, but in this period there was more emphasis on grace and redemption than at any other; possibly this was a residual influence of the Clares. See Letter 10.

166. Presumably Neptune Blood. Several members of the Blood family had the name, which derived from an ancestor born at sea. This Neptune is probably the one born in Ireland about 1750 to Mark Blood and a mother with the maiden name of O'Neill. Wardle speculates that Neptune was a second cousin of Fanny and George Blood (*CL*, p. 111). In 1800 George married Deborah, another name that recurs in the Blood genealogy. Deborah was born c. 1780, sister of a Neptune and daughter of Neptune Blood of Ballyshean and Miss O'Neill.

unsettled – and so is the law-suit about the childrens money[167] – If I possibly can I will not leave the Kingdom 'till that affair is determined – To tell you the truth, I *could not* contrive to buy a few things – which I am in great need of, and which I cannot do without – if this money is not paid – and I have very little reason to expect that I shall ever get it – and how shall I be able to satisfy my creditors, I cannot even guess, and it harrasses me beyond measure – I owe near eighty or ninety pounds – and some of the debts I would give the world to pay – I did expect Skeys would have made me some present which would have enabled me to have paid a part – but I will not dwell on his behaviour it has been *uniform* throughout – If you could immediately send me a few yards to match a gown, the pattern of which your mother has, it would be of essential service to me as I cannot afford to buy one – Skeys was to have sent me one which was in the custom house when I was at Lisbon – I therefore think it my own – and it would at this time have been very acceptable. –

I am now intirely alone – Averina has been for some time at St Katherine's[168] and Mrs Burgh, has recommended Eliza to a boarding school in Leicestershire[169] – She has been there some time –

[Here nine lines have been crossed out.]

is now fully employed – I am now writing in the school with the children – whom I now intirely manage myself – and I have eleven of

167. Another reference to the Wollstonecraft legacy, apparently alienated to Roebuck: see note 55. The suit went in the Wollstonecrafts' favour but letters suggest that Edward Bland Wollstonecraft failed to give his sister what she regarded as her fair share. For further speculation see *SC*, 1, 85f.

168. The home of her brother and sister-in-law, 1 St Katherine's Street, Tower Hill.

169. It is not clear whether Eliza Bishop was in part a parlour boarder (see note 387) or a teacher at Mrs Sampel's School in Market Harborough, Leicestershire. When she arrived, she was horrified to find her companions strict Presbyterians who damned books and plays and attended four services on a Sunday. In turn they were shocked by her anomalous marital status. She wrote to Everina, 'Oh! How my heart pants to be free – I can no longer indulge the delusions of fancy, and the phantoms of hope are for ever, ever flown ... praying is their only amusement, not forgetting eating, and *Marr[y]ing*, and so on – The idea of parting from a *husband*, one could never make them *comprehend*, I could much sooner persuade them, that a stone might speak' (Abinger MSS, Dep.b.210/7). All subsequent letters from Eliza Bishop quoted in the footnotes are from this source.

my old flock — Besides I have paid great attention to french — which will be absolutely necessary in my new situation – I have made a great proficiency and have a most excellent master – I am to have forty guineas a year, half of which I could save to pay off my debts – and could I borrow the whole sum of one person it would make me very easy – but I have no friends who are both able and willing to assist me – and so must wait 'till the time arrives without being able to determine on any particular mode of conduct – My spirits are a little hurry but my heart is never so ingrossed by its own cares as not to be anxiously concerned about you indeed my dea[r] boy – I have a very great affection for you and when I am settled you shall find me a more punctual correspondent   We will then talk of our poor lost friend and cherish the melancholy pleasure – *even* in my present hurrying life her image continually obtrudes itself – and when I rejoice at her release – I cannot forget that I am a poor forlorn wretch without her – The children tease me so – I can hardly tell what I write, I will inform you immediately I know myself, when and how I am to come to Ireland – I have been very much pressed to accept of a situation in wales – indeed I have had several offers – Adieu God Bless and preserve you give my kind love to our mother – I am sorry to hear – what expect to hear with respect to your father

> Believe me to be your
> affectionate sister
> Mary

38. To Eliza Bishop

Newington Green, September 23ᵈ [1786]

I have put off writing to you, my dear Girl, 'till the last moment, as I expected to hear from you – I am at present literally speaking on the wing – as I have received a letter from Mʳˢ Prior to desire me to be in readiness as she shall send for me as soon as the children arrive – I wish the time had been fixed – as I hate this state of suspence – Poor Mason has been with me this day or two – I do not know what I should have done without her – I could not have made a great coat or have done any thing which required thought.[170] I have settled my affairs much better than I could have expected – Mrs Burgh has been as anxious about me as if I had been her daughter – I have paid all my trifling debts and bought all the things I think absolutely necessary – Mrs Price died the other day – and Dr P. intends soon leaving the Green – He has been uncommonly friendly to me.[171] I have the greatest reason to be thankful – for my difficulties appeared insurmontable – This is the last letter I shall write to you from this Island – and indeed I never was in a worse humour for writing – I thought I had half an hundred things to tell you; but I know not how to collect them together. Edward behaved very rude to me – and has not assisted me in the smallest degree — Mr Jackson has never answered my letter – he is gone on a *pleasure jant* – 'Is this the world'? Yet though many have disappointed me other[s] have gone beyond my hope or expectation – I wish to remember it – for I like to encourish an affection for all mankind – and the unkindness of some individuals now and then, made me turn, sick, from all social affections. I long to hear what kind of a woman the new governess is.

Septr 28th I was interrupted last week, and as I could not send the box, I left my letter unfinis[hed]. Since that I have received the parcel and your very affectionate epistle – which was a cordial to me, when my worn-out spirits, required a very potent one – Indeed my dear girl I felt a glow of tenderness which I cannot describe – I could have clasped you to my breast as I did in days of yore, when I was your nurse – you know I doat on disinterested acts of kindness – and that it gives me the sincerest pleasure to receive favours from those I love – I was pleased to find you endeavor to make the best of your situation, and try to improve yourself – You have not many comforts it is true – yet you *might* have been in a much more disagreeable predicament at present – but it is not the evils that we escape which we dwell on – *I*

170. Probably the same Mason as the one who had been described as leaving in Letter 26.

171. In his last years at Newington Green Richard Price had devoted himself to his childless, invalid wife. In the eighteenth century the sympathetic male mentor role was popular: Samuel Johnson and Samuel Richardson had had coteries of bluestocking ladies for whom they became nurturing father figures. For Wollstonecraft, Richard Price appears in part to have played this role.

feel the truth of this observation – and can scarcely offer you a comfort which I do not lay-hold of myself – Life glides away – and we should be careful not to let it pass without leaving some useful traces behind it – I could go on moralizing for half an hour – and yet nature will prevail – and reason cannot remove the oppression I feel at my heart – I intend making enquiries concerning the route I am to take and if I can *possibly* contrive it – will certainly call on you – at any rate I will write on the road – and bid you dieu before I leave my native shore — I shall not expect to hear from you again – as my departure is so uncertain, and must of course be soon – Mr Hewlett – desired me to give his *love* to poor Mrs Bishop – he would have said compliments if his wife had been by – He has [been] very unwel – Poor tender friendly soul how he is yoked![172] You can have no conception of Mrs Burgh's kindness – we are to dine with her to-morrow – She has enabled me to pay Hinxman[173] and the rest of my creditors – but I told you so before – –

Adieu my dear girl
and believe me to be your
affectionate friend & sister
Mary Wollstonecraft

39. To Everina Wollstonecraft

Eton, Sunday, October 9th [1786]

The children are not yet arrived; but we hourly expect them; as the Priors have received an account of their being actually on the road.[174] I wish they had not hurried me in the manner they did, the time I spend here, appears lost, while I remained in England I would fain have been near those I love – In my present state, I cannot bear to be hampered

---

172. Hewlett had married Mary Anderson on 24 November 1785. Wollstonecraft made several disparaging remarks about the new wife.
173. A local musician who was not well off; hence Wollstonecraft's eagerness to repay him.
174. Wollstonecraft had moved to Eton to stay with the Priors and meet up with 'the children', possibly the King boys, who, as their father had done, were studying at Eton.

with forms, which at any time would not be pleasing to me – In short I could not live the life they lead at Eton[175] – nothing but dress and ridicule going forward – and I really believe their fondness for ridicule tends to make them affected – the women in their manners, and the men in their conversation – for witlings abound – and *puns* fly about like crackers, tho' you would scarcely guess they had any meaning in them, if you did not hear the noise they create – So much company without any socibility, would be to me an insurportable fatigue – I am, 'tis true quite alone in a crowd – yet cannot help reflecting on the scene around me, and my thoughts harrass me – Vanity in one shape or other reigns triumphant – and has banished love in all its modifications – and without it what is society? A false kind of politeness throws a varnish over every character – neither the heart nor sentiments appear in their true colours. Few indeed are eccentrick – one universal attraction prevails – and all move in the same round and do not fly off to any other sphere – or seek any new *lights* – Engrossed by these reflections which force themselves upon me – how grateful to me was you[r] tender unaffected letter – I wept over it – for I am in a melting mood – and should have answered it directly; but I was so very unwel – I waited till, I could give a better account of myself – A whole train of nervous disorders have taken possession of me – and they appear to arise so much from the mind – I have little hopes of being better – You will be surprised to hear that a disappointment with respect to your visit made me almost faint – last friday – Miss F.[176] will stay with Mrs P. some time longer, and she is very much mortified at not being able to receive you; but she will strain every nerve to get you into an eligible situation, and will write to you – I was so full of your affairs – I for a

175. The most famous of England's public schools for boys, Eton was widely criticized. A visiting private tutor noted that the masters were 'all so rich, so purse-proud and so much addicted to allow consequence to a man only in proportion to his rank in the Church. . . . The question there is not "What are his attainments? Is he ingenuous?" but "Is he an Etonian? Is he entered at King's College? What views of preferment has he?"' (*Etoniana* 44/691; Richard Ollard, *An English Education. A Perspective of Eton*, London: Collins, 1982, p. 43).
176. Possibly a relative of Lady Kingsborough. She had three half-sisters (Maria, Harriet, and Margaret Fitzgerald), one of whom, Wardle speculates, might be referred to here (*CL*, p. 120). However, they appear too young for the reference; later Wollstonecraft describes them as too 'silly' to be good company (see Letter 55).

while forgot myself – but when I was roused all my cares and vexations rushed back with additional violence for having been for a while suspended – and I was indeed very ill – Mrs P. was very attentive to me, and Miss F's more judicious tenderness soothed me – In a tete a tete she is a charming woman – why with so much sense is she such a slave to the world? I am more than ever convinced that neither great virtues nor abilities will appear where refinement has gone beyond a certain pitch – selfishness gains ground and all the generous impulses, and warm affections are smothered – I like to see starts of affection and humanity – and on many occasions would have people consult their own heart only and if conscience does not check them act with vigor and dignity – as St Paul would advise, and not be conformed to the world.[177] I long to set off – I find I shall be more alone in my new situation than I even supposed, as I shall often be left at the country seat with the younger children, as they do not spend the winters with their mother in Dublin[178] – From what I can gather – Lady K. must be a good kind of woman – and not a very happy one – for his Lordship has been very extravagant[179] – and the children neglected and left to the management of servants – She says, in one of her letters to Mrs P. that those who have hitherto had the care of them have neglected their minds and only attended to the ornamental part of their education, which she thinks ought ever to be a secondary consideration – These sentiments prejudice me in her favor – more than any thing I have

177. Cf. Romans 12:2: 'And be not conformed to this world; but be ye reformed in the newness of your mind: that you may prove what is the good, and the acceptable, and the perfect will of God.'

178. Wealthy landed families spent the winter season from about November to March in Dublin.

179. Major landlords had to be very extravagant to get through their large income. The rent roll in 1799 recorded that the premier Irish peer, the Duke of Leinster, received £20,000 and Lord Kingston (formerly Lord Kingsborough) £18,000 (*The Complete Peerage*, London, 1916, 4, Appendix C). Lord Kingsborough, although chronically in debt, was not as frivolous as Wollstonecraft makes him sound: he was interested in new farming methods and had hired the agricultural theorist Arthur Young to help him put his farms on a better footing. Young supported his employer in his efforts to let the lands directly to the occupying farmers, thus ridding himself of middlemen. See *Arthur Young's Tour in Ireland (1776–1779)*, ed. Arthur Wollaston Hutton (London, 1892), 1, 459, and *The Autobiography of Arthur Young*, ed. M. Betham-Edwards (London, 1898), p. 78.

heard of her – for I cannot venture to depend on the opinion of people who are dazzled by her superior station in life – I am not however very anxious, I will endeavor to act up to the best of my judgment and leave the rest to heaven. They do reside near Cork – at Mitchelson – where Lord K. has established a manufactory.[180] The first letter you write may be directed to me – The right Honble Lord Kingsborough's Dublin[181] and it will be forward with his letters – when I am settled – I shall know what to desire you to do in future – I am to travel all the way in a post-chaise – and to regulate the journey myself – we do not go through Northampton – Eliza must have made some mistake – as the route is quite in the south direction – we are to go to Holy-head[182] – as it is the best and shortest passage – I shall stay a day in Dublin – and afterwards I have about a hundred and seventy miles to go before I reach my destined home – *home*, delightful word – but what a different one, that will be – how unlike the one I have in my 'mind's eye.' When shall we meet? your image haunts me – and I could take my poor timid girl to my bosom and shield her from the keen winds – and if possible save her from the contagion of folly – or the inroads of sorrow! My thoughts and wishes tend to that land where the God of love will wipe away all tears from our eyes – where sencerity and truth will flourish – and the imagination will not dwell on pleasing illusions – which vanish like dreams, when experience forces us to see things as they really are – with what delight do I anticipate the time – when neither death nor accidents of any kind will interpose to separate me from those I love – A mind that has once felt the pleasure of loving and being beloved cannot rest satisfied with any inferior gratifications. —

180. The Kingsboroughs had knocked down the old town and built a new model one for their workers and tenants in Mitchelstown. Over the years they tried to establish various industries, including a silk one, for which they ordered the planting of mulberry trees.

181. When in Dublin the Kingsboroughs stayed at their spacious townhouse, originally owned by Lord Kingsborough's father, the Earl of Kingston, 15–16 Henrietta Street, near the current Law Library in north Dublin. It had become Robert's on his marriage. Viscountess Kingsborough is listed as living at this address in *A List of the Proprietors of Licenses on Private Sedan Chairs, At 25th March, 1787, Alphabetically ranged, with their respective residences* . . . (Dublin, 1787).

182. On the island of Anglesey in North Wales, the beginning of the main crossing to Ireland.

That Poor wretch Barton – I do not wonder you were shocked – Ned acted in character[183] – How earnestly I wish you out of his house? If you possibly can, try to exert yourself – or you will fall a prey to melancholy – you require kindness and look round for domestic comfort and congenial souls – but those you are with are the merest earth worms – Try to cultivate a taste for religion – read the scriptures and you will soon relish them – and in the hour of distress your thoughts will involuntarily turn to that Being who can, in a way not [to] be described, convey consolation to a broken spirit – and raise it above the world[184] – I am writing almost a volume – I shall tire you – and yet I am not in a scribbling vein – For I have had so many new ideas of late, I can scar[c]ely arrange them – I am lost in a *sea* of thoughts – Well – Well — I shall write soon again – do not answer this – for I think, and hope, I shall not remain in this land many days longer —

Give my love to Mason – and when you visit the Green – be very particular in your enquiries concerning all matters there – I should be glad to hear Mrs Morphy[185] had settled her account. —

Adieu believe me to be your

affectionate friend and sister
Mary Wollstonecraft

---

183. Apart from keeping the money which Wollstonecraft believed should be hers, her brother Edward Bland had damned himself in her eyes by spreading rumours of Everina's misbehaviour with a view to getting rid of her.

184. Wollstonecraft's sisters shared her melancholy temperament but revealed little of the piety that supported her during this period.

185. See Letter 25; a gossiping friend of Mrs Campbell, who had lodged with the Wollstonecrafts. It is possible that the Morphys were also lodgers at some point.

Ireland 1786–1787

40. To Everina Wollstonecraft

The castle Mitchelstown, October 30th [1786]

Well my dear Girl – I am at length arrived at my journey's end – I sigh when I say so – but it matters not   I must labor for content and try to reconcile myself to a state which is contrary to every feeling of my soul – I can scar[c]ely persuade myself that I am awake – my whole life appears like a frightful vision and equally disjointed – I have been so very low spirited for some days passed, I could not write – all the moments I could spend in solitude were lost in sorrow – and unavailing tears. There was such a solemn kind of stupidity about this place as froze my very blood – I entered the great gates with the same kind of feeling as I should if I was going into the Bastile[186] – you can make allowance for feelings which the general[it]y would term ridiculous, or artificial – I found I was to encounter a *host* of females – my Lady – her step mother, and three sisters[187] – and M^{rse's} and *Misses* without number – who of course, would examine me with the most minute attention. I cannot attempt to give you a description of the family – I

186. Before its destruction in the French Revolution a few years on, the Bastille had become a symbol of tyrannical oppression. Mitchelstown Castle, situated near the Galtee Mountains in north Cork, was a fashionable, large, square, winged Palladian house incorporating two towers from the old structure. It had classically designed gardens, statued terraces, conservatories, vineyards, and woods spreading for 1,200 acres.

187. Lady Kingsborough's stepmother, Mary Fitzgerald (née Mary Mercer of Louth), heiress and second wife, now widow of Colonel Richard Fitzgerald. She and her children stayed for long periods at Mitchelstown.

am so low, I will only mention some of the things which particularly worry me – I am sure much more is expected from me than I am equal to – with respect to french, I am certain Mr P. has mislead them and I expect, in consequence of it, to be very much mortified – Lady K. is a shrewd clever woman a great talker – I have not seen much of her as she is confined to her room by a sore thoart – but I have seen half dozen of her companions – I mean not her children, but her dogs[188] – To see a woman without any softness in her manners caressing animals, and using infantine expression – is you may conceive very absurd and ludicrous – but a fine Lady is new species to me of animals. I am however treated like a gentlewoman by every part of the family – but the forms and parade of high life suit not my mind – I am in a land of strangers – I am too worried about fancy works &c &c[189] [–] you may perceive how unwel I am by my confused style I cannot collect my thoughts, I hope soon to be more composed – when I will write to poor Bess – I do not mean to neglect her and yet I do not wish to set a bad precedent and my pen is not easily restrained – you must be content to hear that I am alive,[10] and wait a few days for more particular intelligence, I am so fatigued with the labors of the day – the endeavor to conquer the dislike I feel – that I must soon sink into a state of insensibility – and then I shall wake to all the cares I have left behind. I hear a fiddle below   the servant are dancing – and the rest of the family diverting themselves – I only am melancholy and alone – To tell the truth I hope part of my misery arises from disordered nerves,[190] for I would fain believe my mind is not so very weak. The

188. This passion for dogs marks the portrait of the trivial mother in *Mary, A Fiction* (ch. 1) and the unmaternal fashionable lady in *A Vindication of the Rights of Woman* (ch. 12).

189. The relative lack of formal education of the Wollstonecraft sisters is revealed in their inadequate skill in French and fancy needlework, necessary accomplishments for a governess of high status.

190. Nerves had become a common diagnosis for many ailments in the eighteenth century, especially of women. The diagnosis stressed the power of the body over the mind. See George Cheyne's *The English Malady* (London, 1733), William Cullen's *First Lines of the Practice of Physic* (Edinburgh, 1784), and Robert Whytt's *Observations on the Nature, Causes and Cure of those Disorders which have been commonly Called Nervous, Hypochondriac, or Hysteric* (Edinburgh, 1765).

children[191] are literally speaking wild Irish, unformed and not very pleasing – but you shall have a full and true account, my dear girl, in a few days – I hate to send this unconnected scrawl – and yet as the post does not go out for a few days again – I am not willing to throw it into the fire and put off writing 'till then, for it is not certain that I shall be in a better mood to morrow – or the day after – or the day after that – I cannot write to Mrs B. to night she would have no patience with me[192] – The man is just now playing dismal tune – I must listen to it – well and what has music done you will say? not roused me – I assure you – nor inspired me – I shall then only add what does not require any new inspiration, that

I am your affectionate Sister and sincere friend

Mary Wollstonecraft

41. To Eliza Bishop

Mitchelstown, November 5th [1786]

I hope, my dear Bess, has made some excuse to herself for my silence – Believe me my dear girl, it did not proceed from forgetfulness or negligence – nor altogether from want of time – but distraction of thought – and a something like *forgetting* myself. From the date of this you will perceive that I am arrived at the end of my journey. If I had not dwelt on the *end* of it – I should have enjoyed it – as the weather was fin[e] the prospects delightful, and what was of still more consequence, I had an agreeable companion – a young Clergyman,[193] who

---

191. Wollstonecraft had been hired as governess to the three eldest daughters: Margaret, Caroline, and Mary, between the ages of fourteen and eight. Despite this poor impression (see also Letter 41), the eldest girl Margaret soon became a firm favourite.
192. According to Letter 41 Eliza Bishop had 'a *sneaking* kindness... for people of quality'.
193. The Revd. Henry Dyson Gabell had received his BA from New College, Oxford, in 1786 and become a fellow. He later corresponded with Wollstonecraft and visited her in Dublin. At this point he was going briefly to join the household of John O'Neill at Shane's Castle, Co. Antrim, where, Wollstonecraft suggests, he would act as tutor to O'Neill's sons. In 1788 Gabell received the living of St Lawrence in Winchester. In Robert Hope's *A History of the Lord Weymouth School* (Bradford, 1961), p. 61, he is described as tall with 'bold, handsome features'.

was going to settle in Ireland, in the same capacity as myself. He was intelligent and had that kind of politeness, which arises from sensibility. My conductor, was beyond measure civil and attentive to me, he is a good sort of a man, I was, at first, at a loss to guess what department he filled in the family; but I find now he is the Butler, and his wife the house-keeper. I spent a few days in Dublin, George and his mother, you may suppose, were glad to see me, and so was Betty Delane – She is just the same lively creature, though by no means in a comfortable situation, when I am more at ease, I will give you a particular account of the family; but at present I think you will be in haste to hear all about the one I am to reside in – before I talk of them let me tell you that old Blood is now settled in a very eligible place, the income of which will enable him to live very comfortably[194] This is a weight of[f] my mind. – and now to introduce the *castle* to you and all its inhabitants – a numerous tribe, I assure you. The castle is very pleasantly situated – and commands the kind of prospects I most admire – Near the house, literally speaking is a cloud-capt hill – and altogether the country is pleasant, and would please me when any thing of the kind could rouse my attention – But my spirits have been in continual agitation – and when they will be at rest, heaven only knows! I fear I am not equal to the tasks I have been persuaded to undertake – and this fear worries me – Lady K. is a *clever* woman – and a well[-]meaning one; but not of the order of being, that I could love – His Lordship, I have had little conversation with – but his countenance does not promise much more than good humour, and a little *fun* not refined – another face in the house appears to me more interesting – a pale one – no other than the author of 'Shepherds I have lost my love.'[195] His wife is with him a gentle pleasing creature, and

194. Matthew Blood had found a position in the Prerogative Court of the Church of Ireland. He died in 1794.

195. George Ogle (1742–1814) of Bellevue, Co. Wexford, a wealthy member of the Irish House of Commons, and probably a relative of Lady Kingsborough. Godwin reported that Wollstonecraft 'held his talents in very high estimation; she was strongly prepossessed in favour of the goodness of his heart; and she always spoke of him as the most perfect gentleman she had ever known'. Godwin added that she 'felt the regret of a disappointed friend, at the part he has lately taken in the politics of Ireland' (*Memoirs*, p. 58), possibly alluding to his spearheading of opposition to Roman Catholic emancipation in 1795 – although his ultra-Protestant stance had been much the same in 1786.

her sister, a beauty, and a sensible woman into the bargain.[196] Besides them, and casual visitors, we have resident here Lady K's step-mother and her three daughters – fine girls, just going to market, as their brother, says. – I have committed to my care three girls – the eldest fourteen – by no means handsome – yet a sweet girl – She has a wonderful capacity but she has such a multiplicity of employments it has not room to expand itself – and in all probability will be lost in a heap of rubbish miss-called accomplishments, I am grieved at being obliged to continue so wrong a system – She is very much afraid of her mother – that such a creature should be ruled with a rod of iron, when tenderness would lead her any where – She is to be always with me – I have just promised to send her love to my sister – So pray receive it. Lady K. is very civil, nay, kind – yet – I cannot help fearing her – She has a some thing in her person and manner which puts me in mind of Mrs Hewlett – and her turn of thinking seems similar. All the rest of the females labor to be civil to me; but we move in so different a sphere, I feel grateful for their attention; but not amused. I have scarcely a moment to myself to collect my thought and *reason* sorrow away – when I am alone I endeavour to study the french – and this unwearied application to business undermines my health. I am treated like a gentlewoman[197] – but I cannot easily forget my inferior station — and this something betwixt and between is rather aukward – it pushes me forward too notice – I will finish this letter tomorrow – I am sleepy –

(6,th) I am very anxious to hear from you my dear girl – do let me

---

Others were less favourable about his abilities: 'His sources of information are not very copious, but he has a lively imagination, a good understanding, and a fine person; his arguments are more shewy than solid, and have more surface than depth' (*Sketches of Irish Political Characters*, London, 1799, pp. 199f.). The song Wollstonecraft refers to is *Banna's Bank*, a popular anthology work beginning: 'Shepherds, I have lost my love! / Have you seen my Anna? / Pride of ev'ry shady grove, / Upon the banks of Banna!'

196. Ogle's wife was the former Elizabeth Moore; her sister was Mary Moore. It was thought erroneously that his most famous ballad, *Molly Asthore*, was written for Elizabeth, see Henry Grattan, *Memoirs of the Life and Times of the Rt. Hon. Henry Grattan* (London, 1841), 3, 42f.

197. This was important for a governess who wished to be distinguished from the servants.

entreat you to write to me directly and direct to me – The Rt. Honble Lord Kingsborough's Mitchelstown. Ireland. My sweet little girl is now playing and singing to me – she has a good ear and some taste and feeling – I have been interrupted several times since I began this last side – I was going to tell you that my pupils are left to intirely my management – only her Ladyship sometimes condescends to give her opinion – The eldest my favorite has great faults, which I am almost afraid I shall never conquer – The other two are more in a middling way – But you [have] a *sneaking* kindness you say for people of quality – and I almost forgot to tell you that I was in company with a Lord Fingal[198] in the packet – Shall I try to remember the titles of all the Lords and Viscounts I am in company with not forgetting the clever things they say – I would sooner tell you a tale of some humbler creatures   Intend visiting the poor cabbins   as Miss K. is allowed to assist the poor I shall make a point of finding them out.

> Adieu my dear girl,
> yours affectionately
> Mary Wollstonecraft

42. To George Blood

Mitchelstown, November 7th [1786]

I shall not attempt to apologize to my dear George for my silence – though it may have appeared unkind – yet it was not the case – I often thought of him but could not sufficiently compose my mind to write – and indeed I am scarcely ever alone – what with the necessary business of my new situation – and the visits I daily receive from the different females of this family – my time is fully occupied, and my thoughts still more so – I am endeavoring to conquer myself – I am trying to be

198. Arthur James Plunkett, seventh earl of Fingall (1731–1793), a prominent Catholic peer who supported moderate concessions to Irish Catholics but opposed the movement for independence from Westminster. Wollstonecraft's scorn for titles and her dislike of Catholicism perhaps obscured any interest in Fingall's politics. '[S]*neaking* kindness' echoes Richardson's *Clarissa*, 3, Letter 56, where Anna Howe remarks of Hickman: 'I believe I have a sneaking kindness for the sneaking fellow.'

resigned to my fate – and yet I have no reason to complain with respect to the treatment I meet with. Every part of the family behave with civility – nay, even with kindness – but when I am in better spirits you shall have a full and true account – I [d]o begin to know the inhabitants of my new place of residence – Give my love to *our* Mother and write directly – you may soon expect a long letter from me adieu believe me to be yours sincerely

Mary

43. To Everina Wollstonecraft

Mitchelstown, November 17th [1786]

Your letter my dear Girl tended to increase the gloom which is daily stealing on me – write to me often – and directly, and if possible rouse me out of this dispondency – oh! my Everina my heart is almost broken – However I rejoice that Roebuck's money is to be paid it would hurt me to die before I had discharged my debts.[199] Life has lost its relish, all my faculties languish – I try to be patient; but only fatigue my spirits – and yet according to the general notion of things – I have no reason to complain – mine, at present, might be termed comparative rather than positive misery – let it be called what it will – I am grown a poor melancholy wretch – I have intended for this week past to write you a particular account of this Castle and its inhabitants; but the few moments, I could call my own, have been spent in a way you would not think very philosophic – I long for my eternal rest – My nerves are so impaired I suffer much more than I supposed I should do, I want the tender soothings of friendship – I want – but I will be resigned – if I was stronger, if my health was not so much impaired, I should have more power over myself, as it is I am quite unstrung – you must read my heart[, see] my situation, to judge of it – it is not to be described – even the good humoured attention of the silly girls worry me – I am

---

199. The apparently successful suit against Roebuck had persuaded Wollstonecraft that she would soon receive money with which to reimburse Mrs Burgh. This was not the case and the debt to Mrs Burgh remained unpaid.

an exile – and in a new world – If my vanity could be flattered, by the respect of people, whose judgement I do not care a fig for – why in this place it has sufficient food – though rather of the grosser kind; but I hate to talk all myself, and only make the ignorant wonder and admire. Confined to the society of a set of silly females, I have no social converse – and their boisterous spirits and unmeaning laughter exhausts me, not forgetting, hourly domestic bickerings – The topics of matrimony and dress take their turns – Not in a very *sentimental* style – alas poor sentiment it has no residence here – I almost wish the girls were novels readers and romantic, I declare false refinement is better than none, at all; but these girls understand several languages, and have read *cart*-loads of history, for their mother was a prudent woman – Lady K's animal passion fills up the hours which are not spent in dressing. All her children have been ill – very disagreeable fevers – Her Ladyship visited them in a *formal* way – though their situation called forth my tenderness – and I endeavored to amuse them while she lavished awkward fondness on her dogs – I think now I hear her infantine lisp – She rouges – and in short is a fine Lady without fancy or sensibility. I am almost tormented to death by dogs – But you will perceive I am not under the influence of my darling passion pity; it is not always so, I make allowance – and *adapt* myself – talk of getting husbands for the *Ladies* – and the *dogs* – and am wonderfully entertaining and then I retire to my room, form figures in the fire, listen to the wind or view the Galties a fine range of mountains near us – and so does time *waste* away in apathy or misery – I would not write thus to Eliza – she cannot discriminate; but to you I *cannot* be reserved – and I hope the dreadful contagion will not infect you – I am thought to have an angelick temper, 'Tis true sorrow has taught me forbearance, I am often grieved but seldom provoked – indolent and indifferent my voice is never heard in a contending strain – and so low am I, that if any one would attempt to smite one cheeck – I should be apt to turn the other. I will write to you soon again. And direct your letters to Brab^t Noble's Esqr, Dublin,[200] and George will get franks and forward them to me. I am drinking ass's milk, but do not find it of any service[201] – I

200. See note 149.
201. Frederick Hoffman's *Treatise of the Extraordinary Virtues and Effects of Asses Milk* (London, 1754), p. 9, recommended asses' milk for consumptive, hypochondriac and hysteric disorders. One difficulty was its availability and William Buchan in his

am really very ill and so low spirited – my tears flow in torrents almost insensibly – I struggle with myself – but I hope my Heavenly Father will not be extreme to mark my weakness – and that he will have compassion on a poor *bruised reed*,[202] & pity a miserable wretch whose sorrows he only knows! I am resigned, but my content is the result of duty – and when I beg the assistance of heaven – I almost wish my warfare was over – One part of your letter particularly pleased me, you can *guess which*.

[Unsigned]

44. *To George Blood*

[Mitchelstown] 12 o'clock night, December 4ᵗʰ [1786]

I received your letter, to-day, my dear George, and am determined to answer it directly; but it requires an exertion to take up my pen, which you can scarcely conceive – I am indeed very unwell, a kind of melancholy langour consumes me – all my active spirits are fled – every thing is tasteless – and uninteresting – I am grown beyond measure indolent, and neglect the few comforts, which are within my reach – I find exercise fatiguing and irksome – Inshort my nerves have been so much injured I am afraid I shall never be tolerably well – These disorders are particularly distressing as they seem intirely to arise from the mind – and that an exertion of the reasoning faculties would banish them and bring it to a proper tone – but slackened nerves are not to be braced by arguments   physical as well as mental causes have contributed to reduce me to my present weak state – Believe me my dear brother you are as dear to me as ever you were – and yet I appear

Domestic Medicine (London, 8th edn., 1784), p. 199, noted that people generally took the milk in too small quantities, 'whereas, to produce any effects, it ought to make a considerable part of the patient's diet'.

202. Matthew 12:20: 'The bruised reed he shall not break, and smoaking flax he shall not extinguish: till he send forth judgment unto victory.' 'Bruised reed' was a common phrase in eighteenth-century hymns, e.g. 'The bruised reed he never breaks, / Nor scorns the meanest name', Isaac Watts, *Hymn 125. Christ's Compassion to the weak and tempted*, l. 19; John and Charles Wesley, *Another. My God, (if I may call thee mine)*, l. 7; *Written in Stress of Temptation*, l. 65; and *A Thought in Affliction*, l. 8.

to neglect you – I would, and could, any day command an hour to write to you – if I could as easily collect my scattered thoughts, or conquer the lassitude which is creeping over me – I frequently sit, at night an hour or two lost in thought – About this time last year I closed my poor Fanny's eyes – I have been reviewing my past life – and the ghost of my former joys, and vanished hopes, haunted me continually – pity me – and excuse my silence – do not reproach me – for at this time I require the most friendly treatment – With respect to my situation I have no just cause for complaint. – the whol family make a point of paying me the greatest attention – and some part of it treat me with a degree of tenderness which I have seldom met with from strangers – It is true sick and low spirited I may sometimes long for the bosom of a friend – and fondly dwell on scenes which will obtrude themselves on me, bitter recollections wound my poor heart which cannot be filled by mere common placed affections – yet every thing which humanity dictates is thought of for me – and if I was not a strange being I should be contented from feeling satisfied – and not from reflecting that it is my duty in 'whatsoever state I am, therewith to be contented'[203] This warfare will in time be over – and my soul will not vainly pant after happiness – or doubt in what it consists – I have fostered too great a refinement of mind, and given a keener edge to the sensibility nature gave me – so that I do not relish the pleasures most people pursue – nor am I disturbed by their trifling cares – yet it would be well if I had any hope to gild my prospect – any thing to animate me in my race besides the desire of reaching the goal –

you will not be very desirous of hearing from me if I write in this way; but I will try to be a more punctual and more chearful correspondent. Give my love to your mother, and make up the *chemises* in a parcel well packed – and send them to Lord K.'s house in Dublin directed to me to be forward to Mitchelstown. I received Averina's letter – and I have intended mentioning it to you – but I am good for nothing. I assure you, post after post, I have reproached myself for not writing to you – yet still could not rouse my dormant spirits or call off my thoughts from the train of reflection which have taken possession of

203. Philippians 4:11: 'I speak not as it were for want. For I have learned, in whatsoever state I am, to be content therewith.'

me – Do write often to me – and though I am almost afraid to promise any thing – I will try what I can do — In the mean while believe me to be your affectionate and sincere Friend Mary

Mrs Fitz Gerald, is to have a parcel sent her, very soon, I find – you may then over the paper directed to me – write a direction – To Mrs Fitz Gerald – Mitchelstown – and take it the first opportunity to N° 15 Merion Square[204] —

I have been riding out – and I met Mrs Thornhill and her mother Mrs Bunbury – I remembered often to have heard Fanny talk of them[205] – these reflections did not tend to make me enjoy my airing – I do not know how it is my heart is broken – I cannot rouse myself from this painful state – God Bless you —

45. To Joseph Johnson[206]

Mitchelstown, December 5th [1786]

Sir

When I had the pleasure of seeing you, if I mistake not, you men-

204. By this method Wollstonecraft would avoid the cost of postage. Mrs Fitzgerald and her children lived in 15 Merrion Square when they were in Dublin. It was a fashionable square, one side of which was occupied by the Duke of Leinster's townhouse.
205. During family financial crises Fanny Blood had spent some time with the Baillies, her relatives in Tipperary. There she probably became acquainted with Mrs Thornhill, wife of Major James Badham Thornhill of Thornhill Lawn, one of the middlemen on the Mitchelstown estate. The Thornhills' position had been threatened by the reforms of Arthur Young, who called Mrs Thornhill 'an artful and designing woman, ever on the watch to injure those who stood in her husband's way'; she falsely 'impressed into his Lordship's mind that [Young] was in love with Lady K.' and thus contributed to his sacking (see *Autobiography of Arthur Young*, pp. 78f.).
206. Joseph Johnson (1738–1809), radical bookseller, whose bookshop was at 72 St Paul's Churchyard, London. He published many famous authors such as William Cowper (1731–1800), Joseph Priestley (1733–1804) and Erasmus Darwin (1731–1802) and served as patron to others such as the painter Henry Fuseli (1741–1825). Wollstonecraft kept this letter over a month before posting it, perhaps, as *SC* argues, because of some 'feeling of diffidence over writing to Johnson, or hope that she would hear from him first' (1, 72).

tioned to me, that Mrs Barbauld[207] intended undertaking a new plan of education. I wish to hear some particulars about it, and knew not any person, whom I could apply to, for the necessary information; but yourself. Mrs Fitz Gerald, Lady Kingsborough's stepmother, has an only Son,[208] of course a great favourite. She has deliberated so long about the method she should adopt for his education, the season is almost passed away. Some place must then be determined on immediately; and she has requested me to make some enquiries for her. A public school is objected to – nor would she wish him to reside in London, on account of the air, which country people lay great stress on. Money is not an object, as he has an independant fortune. She would give a hundred, or even more, a year, if he could be placed in a respectable family, a Clergyman's would be preferred. I will just describe the kind of situation she wishes for. A well regulated family, and a few other pupils; but above all that her son might frequently be in company with his tutor, as his temper is violent and his mind not cultivated – she is a good sort of woman, and more anxious about his heart than head – and particularly desirous that sentiments of religion should be fixed in his mind. Mr Hewlett, I know had some intention of undertaking a similar plan; but I have not heard any thing of it. I should be much obliged to you, if you would inform me directly, if Mrs Barbauld, or Mr Hewlett, have actually carried their plans into execution[209] –. and I should be very glad if you would, as soon as convenient, send me a dozen of Mr Hewlett's spelling-books, for Lady

207. Anna Laetitia Barbauld, née Aikin (1743–1825), well-educated daughter of a Dissenting clergyman, became a poet, celebrated teacher and writer of educational works, published by Johnson. She was married to the Revd Rochemont Barbauld.

208. [Henry] Gerald Fitzgerald b. 1772. Wollstonecraft makes no mention of Henry Gerald Fitzgerald, Viscountess Kingsborough's cousin, who appears also to have been resident at the castle and who was later the lover of her pupil Mary King. The two young men were frequently confused.

209. From before 27 September 1788 when Godwin called on him, Hewlett ran a school in Shacklewell near Hackney, to which Godwin sent his cousin and ward Thomas Cooper. The Barbaulds had a school at Palgrave, Suffolk, from 1774 to 1785; in spring 1787 they moved to No. 8 Church Row, Hampstead, where Rochemont Barbauld served as pastor to the Dissenting community. They did not establish a school there but regularly took in a few pupils.

K., His Sermons,[210] and Charlotte Smith's poems,[211] and a few copies of my little book,[212] if it is published. Let them be directed to me at Viscount Kingsborough's Dublin.

As I mentioned to you, previous to my departure, that I entered on my new way of life with extreme regret[213] – I am vain enough to imagine you wish to hear how I like my situation. A state of dependance must ever be irksome to me, and I have *many* vexations to encounter, which some people would term trifling – I have most of the [n]ative comforts of life – yet when weighed with liberty they are of little value – In a christian sense I am resigned – and contented; but it is with pleasure that I observe my declining health, and cherish the hope that I am hastening to the Land where all these cares will be forgotten.

I am Sir
yours Respectfully
Mary Wollstonecraft

46. To Eliza Bishop[214]

Mitchelstown, December 22ᵈ [1786]

I received your letter my dear Girl, and though I did not answer it directly – I have not forgot you – I cannot now write a very long letter as I am confined to a sick chamber – My poor little favourite[215] has

210. Johnson published Hewlett's *An Introduction to Reading and Spelling, Written on a New Plan, and Designed for the Use of Schools* and *Sermons on Different Subjects* in 1786.

211. Charlotte Smith, née Turner (1749–1806), was the author of the very popular *Elegiac Sonnets and Other Essays*; it reached its third edition early in 1786.

212. Johnson published *Thoughts on the Education of Daughters* in late January or early February 1787.

213. Johnson can have been in little doubt of Wollstonecraft's sentiments before reading this, since *Thoughts* frequently alluded to the misery of the intelligent but poor woman forced to depend on coarse employers: 'The mind must then sink into meanness, and accommodate itself to its new state, or dare to be unhappy' (*Works*, 4, 26).

214. The letter is addressed to Mrs Bishop at Mrs Tew's, Market Harborough in Leicestershire, which suggests that Eliza Bishop had changed employers and was probably acting as part companion, part lodger, while continuing to teach.

215. The eldest girl, Margaret King.

had a violent fever – and can scarcely bear to have me a moment out of her sight – her life was dispaired of – and this illness has produced an intimacy in the family which a course of years might not have brought about. Your situation has made me very uneasy – but I did not dwell on it when I saw no remedy – now I have an offer to make you, will you come to Dublin, if I can get you into a reputable school? Lady K. has authorised me to tell you she is sure she should succeed if she tried, and I can get money to defray the expences of the journey – or you could come over with the Mr Kings[216] next summer – I intend, if Averina has no objection to have her here too – and should have it in my power to be very useful to you – The holidays we might be together – as I think you would be invited here, but this is a conjecture – at any rate we should often meet and I could render your situation in some degree easy – Pray write to me directly – This plan delights me, do not raise any objection – and try in the intrim to perfect yourself in english and fancy works – I am not very well and I have many things to tell you – but the hope of seeing you has driven them out of my mind – I am anticipating the social conversations we shall have – in short you must come to Ireland – I am a GREAT favorite in this family – and am certain you would please them – Do not scold if I do not fill this sheet – I will soon write a long letter – but would not delay sending you this pleasing intelligence. We are to go to Dublin the beginning of Feb.ʸ you may therefore in future direct to me Viscount Kingsborough's Dublin, and let me be w[h]ere I will – they will forward the letters to me – I long to hear from you, though from my silence you may not suppose it. Adieu yours sincerely and affectionately

Mary Wollstonecraft

216. George and Robert, eldest sons of Lord and Lady Kingsborough, presumably returning to Ireland from school at Eton.

47. To Everina Wollstonecraft

[Mitchelstown, c. January 15th, 1787]

I am not angry with you, my dear Girl though if you knew the pleasure your letters give me, you would be more punctual – I am here shut out from domestic society – my heart throbs when I see a hand written by any one to whom my affections are attracted – I am some times so low spirited, I think anything *like* pleasure will never revisit me – I go to the nursery – *something like* maternal fondness fills my bosom – The children cluster about me – one catches a kiss, another, lisps my long name – while, a sweet little boy, who is conscious that he is a favorite, calls himself my son – At the sight of their mother they tremble and run to me for protection – this renders them dear to me – and I discover the kind of happiness I was formed to enjoy – I am harrassed with company – and conversations which have nothing in them – I go but slowly on with my french – I have read a novel or two – the narrative assists me – Caroline de Lichtfield[217] is one of the prettiest things I have ever read – Some letters on education, too, written by the author of the tales of the castle[218] – I think wonderfully clever – I wish you would try to read them – but I know you[r] very disagreeable situation, and how incapable the minds is of attending to any thing when worried

217. *Caroline de Lichtfield. Par madame de* *** was a sentimental novel by Baroness de Montolieu, with echoes of Jean-Jacques Rousseau's *Julie ou la Nouvelle Héloïse* (1761). The plot centres on Caroline, married at sixteen to an older, deformed man; she falls in love with a young baron who, she discovers, has caused her husband's deformity. He undertakes to make her appreciate the older man's noble virtue, which she comes to do. The novel's interest lies in the psychological conflict between the husband's desire for Caroline and his honourable intention to grant her as much freedom as possible, and in the depiction of the early, giddy Caroline hoping for a pretty, dancing husband. The novel was translated into English in 1786 by Thomas Holcroft (1745–1809).

218. *Adèle et Théodore, ou Lettres sur l'éducation: contenant tous les principes relatifs aux trois différens plans d'éducation des princes, des jeunes personnes, & des hommes* by Stéphanie de Genlis, marchioness de Sillery, the most popular educational writer of the day; the second edition came out in London in 1784. She was also the author of a volume of educational stories, *Tales of the Castle*, translated by Thomas Holcroft in the same year.

and disgusted – Poor Charles![219] Give my love to him – and tell him, I intend writing to him very soon – and tell my father I wrote to him a few posts ago – and say something civil to him, and Mrs W.,[220] if it will not blister your tongue – I enclose you a letter for Eliza – She speaks of your attention with great gratitude – Tell me something of Mason?[221] and send me a direction to her, I ought to have written to her before – Do pray make a point of writing frequently to me – and be very minute in your account of the few people I esteem – I am a sojourner in a strange land – and like to be reminded that I still live in the remembrance of those, whose very names fills me with tenderness – Tell me more about Mrs Morphy – and Hewlett – and give a very particular account of your health, and state of mind – I cannot help pitying Hinxman – such power have the *graces* – Remember me to Sowerby – and tell Mrs Cockburn – if I make any conquests in Ireland it will be owing to the *blue hat* – which is the first phenomenon of the kind, that has made its appearance in this hemisphere[222] – There is a period for you! – worthy of an author whose work is just ushered into the world – Well, Everina – am I not merry? My poor Charles, I cannot help thinking of him, make him write to me – I am very anxious to know how the affair will turn out – with respect to Roebuck's money – and I am sure you will send me the earliest intelligence. Have you ever seen Millington – or heard anything of Baillis or Mrs Disney – Her follies were only copies of high-life and not by any means despicable daubings – I see Ladies put on rouge without any mauvais honte – and make up their faces for the day – five hours, and who could do it less in – do many – I assure you, spend in dressing – without including preparations for bed. Washing with Milk of roses[223] &c &c — I am [wri]ting in a great hurry as this letter must go off [in t]he morning – Did you ever enquire at Mrs Blackburn's if any

---

219. The youngest brother, Charles Wollstonecraft, was lodging with his eldest brother Edward Bland, to whom he was articled.

220. Presumably their father Edward and his second wife Lydia had come to stay with Edward Bland in London.

221. See note 124.

222. Mrs Cockburn, the Newington Green friend, had obviously forgiven Wollstonecraft her trip to Lisbon.

223. According to newspaper advertisements milk of roses, suitable for ladies of the nobility and gentry, cost 10/6d for a large bottle. It was a potion to cleanse, soften and preserve the skin.

one had ever been to look for me?[224] – Have you seen poor Mrs Long? – I feel for her this bitter weather – Lady K is really charitable – and the poor about here [ ] bless her – I have just been putting

[The rest of the letter is missing.]

48. To George Blood

[Mitchelstown, c. January 1787]

My dear George

I know will be glad to hear that in the course of a fortnight, or three weeks, at farthest, he will again see his friend, and Sister, Mary.[225] In my way to Dublin I intend spending a few days in Tipperary[226] – I earnestly wish to see your uncle Baillie, to see the Place, my poor Fanny was so attached to – I shall lay in a stock of news for our mother. Her sister Collis, I am informed, is gone to France, I shall enquire about her – and you will hear all from me. Is Neptune[227] still in Dublin? –

Let me hear from you directly – this is the last letter I intend writing, if nothing occurs to retard our journey. I know you will be angry if I bid you adieu without mentioning my health — and yet what can I say – I am good for nothing – life is but a frightful dream – I long to go to sleep – with my friend in the house appointed for all living! – I cannot write any more —

your's sincerely
Mary

224. Wollstonecraft had lodged with Mrs Blackburn in Newington Green after the collapse of her school.
225. The Kingsboroughs were about to move to Dublin. They were late in arriving for the main winter season but there was often an influx into the capital after Christmas, with social activity peaking in early spring. Contrary to her original expectations, Wollstonecraft and the girls in her charge were to be of the party, the changed regime perhaps revealing Lady Kingsborough's desire for her governess's company.
226. Wollstonecraft may have been travelling to Tipperary solely to see Archdeacon Baillie and his family in Tipperary, not far from Mitchelstown (see notes 127 and 205) or she may also have been accompanying one of the Kings since the family held estates in Co. Limerick and Co. Tipperary as well as Co. Cork.
227. Presumably Neptune Blood; see notes 78 and 166.

49. *To Everina Wollstonecraft*

Dublin, February 10th 17[87][11]

Your silence surprises me, my dear Girl, – I had a letter yesterday from Eliza – in her usual pensive strain – and, among other things, she mentions, not having heard from you, for some time past. I wish you would *try* to be a more punctual correspondent – need I repeat to you – that your letters afford me comfort, & that when you *neglect* me, my busy imagination conjures up a thousand vexatious cares, which haunt me. Mrs Burgh has written to inform me of the payment of Roebuck's money; and to enquire how she is to act? I suppose Ned will send it to her – If he does not I shall desire her to write to him – I do not like to write to him myself. She mentions Hewlett, in very illiberal terms. Have you seen him? Sowerby has written to me a long letter; which I found no easy matter to decypher – it was, however, very friendly, the heart appeared better than the head –

I arrived here a few days ago. Previous to my departure from Mitchelstown I spent a few days in Tipperary where I was received in a most hospitable manner. I found the elder Mr Baillie a rational man – in his conversation, judgment was much more conspicuous than genius – *coldly* correct in his behaviour, and style; and intirely devoid of elegance. His wife resembles Mrs Blood – I need say no more – His daughter is *quiet*; her understanding – such as it is – highly cultivated – nay, foreign plants are *forced* to grow – and wonder how they came there – yet she sometimes put me in mind of my poor Fanny – His Son is so like *your* friend Mr Thompson – I almost imagined myself in his company – when he was trying to make himself agreeable. The Town – I mean, the inhabitants, resembled the Beverley society. This visit and the journey hurried my spirits, I have been teased with a violent pain in my side, which affected my breath. I *must* attend to french and Italian – We are to have an *inundation* of Masters. The children and I came to Town first – To-morrow the rest of the family is expected – and then the *hurly burly* will begin. We have had some visitors – The Ogles[228]

228. The Ogles lived in Merrion Square near Mrs Fitzgerald.

came – and greeted me kindly. And this evening Betty Delane came, and her lively conversation diverted – nay, charmed my little Margaret – I have much more convenient apartments here. A fine school room – The use of one of the drawing rooms where the Harpsichord is – and a parlour to receive my *Male* visitors in – Here is no medium! – The last poor Governess – was treated like a servant. Betty Delane is still the same – only rather in better spirits than usual – as Mr Home [h]as met with uncommon success lately[229] – He has been in the North some time – I have not yet seen him. Good Night my dear Sister – I am not well I will go to bed – I wish I knew how you were employ'd, & how it fares with you in every particular —

(11th) Mrs Burgh mentioned her having half a dozen of my books – I wish her to give you three, and request you to send one to Mrs Prior by the Windsor stage as soon as you can. You write so seldom – our separation is really *like* death – I wish to hear every *minute* particular concerning you – but you put it off from time to time, and then in a *hurry* to write take up a *small* sheet of paper – and have done with it – as a *disagreeable* task – Is it not so? – I know you are sometimes unwell – but you have oftener not resolution to exert yourself – The most trifling amusement – (I use your own words) will take up your attention – and detach your thoughts from your situation – and yet, your affections are not sufficiently warm, or lasting, to enable you to keep up a regular correspondence, which would *improve* you, afford me *great* comfort, and turn your thoughts from the present scene. ' 'Tis deeds of kindness shew the heart'[230] – Can I suppose that I am loved, when I am not *told* that I am *remembered*. I am not angry – but *hurt*

---

229. Betty Delane's brother-in-law, Robert Home, son of a London apothecary, studied art under Angelica Kauffmann. Despite Wollstonecraft's reference to his temporary good fortune, he failed as a portrait painter in Ireland. He achieved more lasting success after his move to London in 1789, and India shortly after. As chief artist to the King of Oude he amassed a fortune with his sumptuous and detailed paintings of court figures and ceremonials. He died in Cawnpore in 1834.

230. cf. William Dodd, *Thoughts in Prison. Commenced Sunday Evening, Eight O'Clock February 23, 1777*, ll. 398f.: 'That heart hath in thy love known thorough peace! ... And sought occasions to display its warmth / By deeds of kindness, mild humanity', and *Clarissa*, 2, Letter 27, Anna Howe to Clarissa: '. . . I have heard you say, it is a good rule to *give* WORDS *the hearing, but to form our judgments of men and things by* DEEDS ONLY'.

and disappointed. Here I feel myself *alone* – dead to most pleasures – I wish to live in the remembrance of a few – and it would cheer my heart to receive little tokens of tenderness.

Adieu –
Your affectionate Sister
Mary Wollstonecraft

Give my love to Charles —

50. To the Reverend Henry Dyson Gabell

[Dublin] Friday morning, two o'clock [c. early 1787][231]

My dear Sir,

I thought it would be uncivil to send the promised little book, without a line – yet be it know to thee – I am both sick and sleepy – it being past the *witching time of night*[232] – and I have been thinking 'how stale, flat, and unprofitable'[233] this world is grown to me – you'll say – I am always running on in the same strain – and, perhaps, tell me, as a friend once before did, alluding to music, that I mistook a *flat* for a *natural*.

Good night – or good morning

yours sincerely
Mary Wollstonecraft

---

231. The approximate date is suggested by the reference to Wollstonecraft's 'little book', *Thoughts on the Education of Daughters*, published in late January or early February 1787.

232. *Hamlet*, III, ii, 413f.: ' 'Tis now the very witching time of night, / When church-yards yawn and hell itself breathes out / Contagion to this world.'

233. *Hamlet*, I, ii, 133f.: 'How weary, stale, flat, and unprofitable / Seem to me all the uses of this world.' Wollstonecraft again used this quotation in Letters 55 and 189.

51. To Everina Wollstonecraft

Dublin, February 12th, 17[87][12]

I have just sent off a letter to Eliza, though I had nothing material to say to her – yet as I thought some new subjects might for a little while divert her, I tried to fabricate a lively epistle. George sent me to-day your letter – the sight of the *large* paper gave me pleasure – disinterested pleasure, as I am always glad to see you roused from indolence by anything but bodily riotous pursuits, your mind certainly requires great attention – you have seldom *resolution* to *think* or *exert* the talents nature, or to speak with more propriety, Providence has given you to be *improved* – our whole life is but an education for eternity – virtue is an *acquirement* – seek for the assistance of Heaven, to enable you *now* to be wise unto Salvation, and regret not the time which is past, which, had others taken the greatest pains to form your mind could only have opened it to instruction – and made you capable of gaining experience – no creatures are so situated but they may obtain His favor from whom *only* TRUE comfort flows *if they seek it.* I am not well – yet, repeat it, scarcely know what to do with myself – Last sunday I went to church, the service discomposed – hurried, my spirits – Lady K. sat me down at M[r] Home's[234] when I got into the house I fell into such a violent fit of trembling as terrified Betty Delane – and it continued in a lesser degree all day – I very frequently am very near fainting and have almost always a rising in my throat, which I know to be a nervous affection – I am however satisfied to bear these disorders – (though as they seem to attack the mind, they are doubly distressing) if I can fulfil the duties of my station. I am more comfortable here than I was at Mitch[n], as I have more time to myself – that is I have only the children with me. The hours I have spent with L.K. could not have been very pleasant – now she must visit – and my spirits are spared this weight – and as to the Fitz Geralds, they are preparing cloaths for the Castle[235] – I have

234. Wollstonecraft had been taken to Betty Delane at her brother-in-law's house.
235. Elaborate dressing for presentation to the lord lieutenant at Dublin Castle was an emotive issue. As Irish manufactures declined owing to English restrictions and a failure to develop cheaper production methods, it became the custom for invitations

not seen them since my arrival – I am then tranquil – I commune with my own spirit – and am detached from the world – I have plenty of books. I am now reading some philosophical lectures, and metaphysical sermons – for my own *private* improvement. I lately met with Blairs lectures on genius taste &c &c[236] – and found them an intellectual feast. I have, too, met with a french book, which pleased me – Mon bonnet de nuit[237] – –

M^r and Mrs Home are still in the country – Betty D. has spent two evenings with me and her conversation is so much superior, to what I meet with in general, it is quite a treat to me – George is still the *same* – His understanding soon arrived at maturity. He has made me a very acceptable present Shakespear's plays, the new edition.[238] Old Blood's place is likely to turn out much more advantageous than he at first supposed it would. I have not yet seen them, the days I intended going

---

to official events to request that Irish fabrics be worn. Newspapers urged ladies to buy 'Irish stuff' to help poor Irish weavers and avoid foreign silks and brocades; none the less much fancy material was still imported from Paris for court occasions. As so often in Ireland, Wollstonecraft makes no comment on the sort of problems which would later strike her when contemplating countries with large social distinctions.

236. Hugh Blair's popular *Lectures on Rhetoric and Belles Lettres* (1783) was an important document in the development of literary and historical studies. Blair's opinions that moral virtue was the foundation of genius and appreciation and that art needed impassioned observation greatly influenced Wollstonecraft's views.

237. A four-volume collection of fables published in 1784 and 1785 by Louis Sebastien Mercier (1740–1814). Excerpts were printed in *Walker's Hibernian Magazine* in May 1786 and February and March 1787. Wollstonecraft may in particular have been influenced in this letter by one item entitled 'On Old Age' (May 1786) which includes a graphic description of physical decline followed by a portrayal of death as a release from the process. In 'Tableau de Paris' Mercier supported Wollstonecraft's views expressed in Letter 43 that romance-reading might be useful: 'Romances, which the proud men of letters think frivolous, and which they cannot make, are more useful than histories. The human heart seems analised, painted in all its forms, the variety of characters and events; all this is an inexhaustible source of pleasure and reflection' (pp. 230f.).

238. The publisher J. Bell was bringing out two new editions of Shakespeare in 1787: one in twelve volumes (1785–1787) with text edited by Samuel Johnson and George Steevens and another in sixteen volumes (1786–1788) with the addition of Johnson and Steevens's notes. Wardle comments that, despite Wollstonecraft's mention of a 'new' edition, George Blood's gift would probably have been more modest than these – perhaps the first edition in a single octavo volume edited by S. Ayscough and published by J. Stockdale in 1784 (*CL*, p. 139).

turned out wet, and I am obliged to be careful. My little pupil, is still delicate, tomorrow the physician is to pays us a visit – Lady K. I believe, intends consulting him about me, though I have requested her not, as I am sure it would answer no good end. I shall write to Mason directly, and M^{rs}, B.[239] – I owe M^{rs}, Prior a letter too. In future direct to me at Viscount Kingsborough's Dublin, I thought I had desired you to do so before; but perhaps, I only intended it. I hope very soon, some inquiries will be made to accelerate our plan. I really pity poor Eliza her situation is indeed *very* disagreeable – I am glad you sent her some books. Do you go often to the theatre? we have got Wroughton[240] and Mrs Crawford[241] here, I intend going to see them. Young Walker too has delivered his astronomical lectures;[242] but I have not seen any body who attended them. I am glad you have met with a rational acquaintance – Do you ever see Hinxman? – It was not talking of rationality that made me remember him. – I am sorry for poor Hewlett – Betty Delane read his sermons with great pleasure – Little Johnson[243] sent them to Cork[244] for me, and at the same time Cowper's

239. Mrs Burgh, to whom Wollstonecraft owed a large sum of money and who had fallen out of favour owing to her alleged conventional attitudes.

240. Despite being an ugly man with a disagreeable voice, Richard Wroughton (1748–1822) was yet a creditable and unaffected actor. Having been at Covent Garden for eighteen years he was about to transfer to Drury Lane, where he remained for twenty-eight years. He was probably in Dublin in the 1786–7 season since at that time he disappeared from the London bills. He acted in both comedy and tragedy, one of his best parts being as Douglas in Hannah More's *Percy*.

241. Ann Crawford, née Street (1734–1801), rival to Sarah Siddons as tragic actress, had a long career in Covent Garden and Drury Lane, London, as well as in Dublin. Her tempestuous private life included three marriages. She had an intimate association with the Crow-Street Theatre, Dublin, two of whose owner-managers she had married consecutively.

242. Adam Walker (1731?–1821), inventor and lecturer on natural philosophy who 'devised engines for raising water, carriages to go by wind and steam, a road mill, a machine for watering land, and a dibbling plough' (*DNB*). His eldest son William Walker (1767?–1816) assisted him in his lectures. The lecture referred to by Wollstonecraft might have been *An Account of the Eidouranion, or transparent orrery, invented by A. Walker as lectured on by his own son, W. Walker*; in the printed version it had reached ten editions by 1793.

243. The poet William Blake (1757–1827) described Joseph Johnson as a 'squat, little' man; see Thomas Wright, *The Life of William Blake* (Olney, 1929), 1, 20.

244. Wollstonecraft had relatives in Cork, probably Dickson kin of her mother.

Powems[245] – and a very civil note. I have since written to him for some books for this family; and to make some enquiries concerning a school, which Mrs Fitz Gerald wished to send her son to. I want to hear if you have seen Mrs Morphy? As I have now more time to myself; I shall write oftener to you – Adieu George desired his love –

Your's sincerely
Mary Wollstonecraft

By this time, I hope, M^{rs}. Burgh has received Roebuck's money –

52. To Everina Wollstonecraft

Dublin, March 3^d [1787]

I am a little surprised and disappointed at not receiving an answer to my two or three last letters; but I ought *not* to have expected from *you* that kind of affection, which only can gratify *my* heart, of course, my disappointment arises from myself – I too frequently, willing to indulge a delightful tenderness, forget the convictions of reason, and give way to chimerical hopes, which are as illusive, as they are pleasant. I know very well friendship can only take root in a cultivated mind – and that it is the result of reason and sensibility, *warm starts* of *tenderness*, do not deserve that name – they are the *mere ornaments* of it, and may adorn the language but do not influence the conduct – yet like other ornaments they first catch the eye. You have a great many agreeable qualities – but I will have done with the subject. I am not well, the Physician who attends this family, thinks I have a constant nervous fever on me – and I am sure he is right. Many things contribute to increase it. When I wrote last, I believe, I mentioned Miss King's illness, the fever was prematurely stopped, and it was of so malignant a nature, the remnant of it still lurks in her blood, and produces very disagreeable effects.[246]

245. William Cowper's *Poems*, 2 vols. The first edition of each volume was issued separately, the first in 1782 and the second in 1785; the 1785 publication included *The Task*.

246. Wollstonecraft was sceptical of much conventional medical intervention. She was impressed, however, with nerve theory, which for a time seemed to explain to her the

My anxiety on her account is very much augmented by her Mother's improper treatment – as I fear she will hurry her into a consumption – and, I dread it the more, as it is a disorder incident to the family.

When I first came to Dublin, Lady K. was so much out, I hoped to enjoy a little quietness in my own apartments; but it was a vain hope! We have had nothing but hurry and confusion here – and all about the mighty important business of preparing wreaths of roses for a birth day dress – Well, it was finished; but next week the same work, or something similar, will occur, for there is to be a Ball at the Castle – and a masquerade[247] – and as it is impossible for a fine Lady to fix, in time, on her dress, when the day arrives many necessaries are wanted and the whole house from the kitchen maid to the governess are obliged to assist, and the children forced to neglect their employments. You know, I never liked Lady K., but I find her still more haughty and disagreeable now she is not under M[rs], FitzGerald's eye. Indeed, she behaved so improperly to me once, or twice, in the Drawing room, I determined never to go into it again. I could not bear to stalk in to be stared at, and her *proud* condescension added to my embarrassment, I begged to be excused in a civil way – but she would not allow me to absent myself – I had too, another reason, the expence of hair-dressing, and millinery, would have exceeded the sum, I chuse to spend in those things.[248] I was determined – just at this juncture she offered me a

---

mixture of mental and physical ailments from which she suffered. See note 190. As an adult Margaret wrote on the medical treatment of children and leaned towards her governess's more natural approach rather than to her mother's interventionist one. See *Advice to Young Mothers on the Physical Education of Children* (1823).

247. Since the Hanoverian succession, the lord lieutenant who administered Ireland had been 'an English nobleman of high rank': John Gamble, *Sketches of History, Politics and Manners, Taken in Dublin, and the north of Ireland, in the Autumn of 1810* (London, 1811), p. 49. When he was in Dublin for the parliamentary season there was an elaborate round of entertainments at Dublin Castle attended by the Anglo-Irish elite. Royal birthdays and anniversaries were marked to signal the connection of England and Ireland. Much patronized by the nobility, masquerades were a favourite pastime in Dublin from 1773 onwards. It was the fashion on masquerade nights for masqueraders to parade through public apartments in the houses of the noble and rich such as the Duke of Leinster.

248. Hair-dressing in high society was expensive, especially with Dublin hair-dressers who declared knowledge of Paris and London fashions and supported various 'ethnic' styles. It was almost impossible to do one's hair oneself since it had to be shaped into

present, a poplin gown and petticoat, I refused it, and explained myself – she was very angry; but Mrs F., who was consulted on the occasion, took my part, and made her ask my pardon, and consent to let me stay always in my own room – Since that she has endeavored to treat me with more propriety, and I believe she does do so to the best of her knowledge. She is very proud, and ready to take fire on the slightest occasion – her temper is violent, and anger intirely predominantes in her mind – now, and then, I have seen a momentary start of tenderness – sufficient to convince me she might have been a more tolerable companion, had her temper been properly managed; as to her understanding, it could never have been made to rise above mediocrity. I pity her, but I am deprived of all society, and when I do sit with her, she worries me with prejudices, and complaints. I am very well persuaded that to make any great advance in morality genius is necessary – a peculiar kind of genius which is not to be described, and cannot be conceived by those who do not possess it – you might as well expect a man born blind to have just notions of the beauty arising from varied rays of light. I am very uneasy about Roebuck's money as I suppose Ned has not paid it or you would have informed me of it. I have neglected writing to M^{rs}, Burgh expecting every day a letter from you. You may direct to me at Viscount K's – now I am in Dublin my letters need not go first to George; it would occasion a delay, and not save any postage. He complains of your silence, I seldom see him. Adieu yours sincerely

Mary Wollstonecraft

53. To Everina Wollstonecraft

Dublin, March 4th [1787]

Your last letter my dear Girl has made me very uneasy – and I have drawn an inference from Edward's conduct, which did not occur to

---

height with help of rolls, cushions, wire and extra lengths of other hair. Powder, especially costly after 1786 when a tax was placed on it, was sprinkled over the whole, which was then often surmounted with caps and feathers.

you – He wishes to get you out of the house before Lucy Dickson[249] arrives, I am persuaded this motive made him invent the shameful story you mention – I am really full of indignation, the reputation of a young person is not to be trifled with. As to his delaying to pay the money, I expected it, and did not doubt but he would hatch some story to exculpate himself and gain time – yet I did not imagine, when on the verge of the grave, that he would have done a *friendless* sister an irreparable injury. I very much approve of your intention of leaving his house, and shall wait with impatience for your next letter. I have had some conversation with M^rs, F.[250] she has been disappointed in a situation she wished to obtain for you. I know not what to say about it – I do not like Ireland. The family pride which reigns here produces the worst effects –[251] They are ingeneral proud and mean, the servile respect that is universally paid to people of quality disgusts me, and the minute attention to propriety stops the growth of virtue. As a nation, I do not *admire* the Irish, I never before felt what it was to love my country; but now I have a value for it built on rational grounds, and my feelings [c]oncur to fix it, I never see an English face without feeling tenderness. In short I should not chuse this Kingdom for my residence, if I could subsist any where else. Miss Burney's account of high life was *very* just – I have seen the *supercilious* and been pestered to death by the *volubles*.[252] Oh! for quietness! I have been thinking of you ever since I received your last – and am worried beyond measure. If you go to Newington Green do not explain the affair to M^rs, Burgh,

---

249. Presumably a maternal relative of the Wollstonecrafts. If the legacy behind 'Roebuck's money' was from the Dicksons, then Edward Bland might not have wished Everina to meet this relative and describe his ungenerous dealings. From subsequent letters it is clear that Everina received a small annuity at some point.
250. Mrs Fitzgerald.
251. Like the Welsh the Irish were noted for their interest in genealogy and ancient history. The aspect is stressed in Sydney Owenson's *The Wild Irish Girl* (1806).
252. In *Cecilia, or Memoirs of an Heiress* (1782), Frances Burney satirizes London fashionable life through Mr Gosport: 'The TON misses, as they are called, who now infest the town, are in two divisions, the SUPERCILIOUS, and the VOLUBLE. The SUPERCILIOUS, like Miss Leeson, are silent, scornful, languid, and affected ... the VOLUBLE, like Miss Larolles, are flirting, communicative, restless, and familiar, and attack without the smallest ceremony, every one they think worthy of their notice' (vol. 1, bk. 1, ch. 5).

the best natured people, generally speaking, imagine there is always some foundation for reports similar to this, and it is too humiliating to be forced to vindicate ones conduct from such gross assertions. You'll find by my last letter, that I perfectly coincide with you in opinion relative to M^rs, B. I hope to send her a remittance very soon. I don't know how it is but my mind is unhinged – I cannot write about comparatively indifferent matters, and I do not like to delay writing at this juncture. Pray write immediately and summon up all your fortitude. With your letter I got a melancholy one from poor Mason. Her situation is truly deplorable. She speaks of you with great affection.

Lady K. has been in the country some time I yesterday received a long letter from her, and could perceive that she labored to write not only in a polite but a friendly style. You were [   ] as well as myself, Miss K's education is by no means comp[   ] 'spite of her abilities – she harrasses my spirits [   ] colt is not easily broke – I cannot write m[y] spir[its] are almost worn out.

Adieu believe me to be yo[ur]
sincere and constant friend
Mary Wollstonecraft

54. To Everina Wollstonecraft

Dublin, March 14th [1787]

Mr Skeys[253] has at last delivered your letter &c The mistake you made in directing it, occasioned the delay, and I wonder he ever found me out. I have too received two other letters from you, one of a prior, and the other of a latter date, no, I am wrong, they were both written since. If lowness of spirits were a sufficient apology for not writing I should very very seldom take up my pen. I am very well convinced that body and mind both contribute to weaken each other. Don't smile when I tell you that I am tormented with *spasms* – indeed it is impossible to enumerate the various complaints I am troubled with; and how much my mind is harrassed by them. I know they all arise from disordered

---

253. Hugh Skeys, Fanny's widower. He was now residing in Dublin.

nerves, that are injured beyond a *possibility* of receiving *any* aid from medicine – There is no cure for a broken heart! It is true, it may languidly perform its *animal* functions – but it can no longer be *inflated* with hope. The nervous fever, I am subject to, has increased my natural sensibility to such a degree – I may with reason complain of the irritability of my nervous. I want a tender nurse – I want – but it matters not – the Will of Heaven be done – I am resigned. I do not imagine that any of my complaints promise a hasty dissolution – though they render me very uncomfortable; the constant bustle I am in tends to increase them. By this time, I hope, Ned has paid the money. While I remember, let me desire you, not to seal your letters at the sides, for I have paid double for most of them, and so did George. I shall answer Skey's letter. And when you have an opportunity, I wish you would inform M^r, Church,[254] that I intend mentioning his demand myself but if he chuses to write, do you give him a direction and you may add, too, that I consider *myself* in his debt, *and shall not forget it.* —

I am very weak to day; but I can account for it. The day before yesterday there was a masquerade, in the course of conversation, some time before, I happened to wish to go to it. Lady K. offered me two tickets, for myself and Miss Delane, to accompany me, I refused them on account of the expence of dressing properly, she then to obviate that objection lent me a black domino.[255] I was out of spirits – and thought of another excuse; but she proposed, to take me and Betty Delane, to the houses of several people of fashion who saw masques. We went to a great number, and were a tolerable, nay, a much admired group. Lady K. went in a domino, with a smart cockade   Miss Moore dressed in the habit, of one of the females, of the new discovered Islands,[256] Betty D. as a forsaken shepherdess – and your sister Mary

254. Mrs Burgh's nephew, from whom Wollstonecraft had earlier borrowed money.
255. A domino was a large cape that covered and disguised the whole body.
256. The costume of George Ogle's sister-in-law was topical. The Pacific islands were being explored in the 1770s and '80s. See *Voyage to the Pacific Ocean, undertaken by the command of his Majesty, for making Discoveries in the Northern Hemisphere, and performed under the Direction of Captains Cook, Clerke, and Gore* ... Extracts in *Walker's Hibernian Magazine*, Appendix for 1785, describe the dress of the Sandwich Island women. 'The "pan" is [a] dress very frequently worn by the younger part of the

in a black domino. As it was taken for granted, the stranger who was just arrived, could not speak the language, I was to be her interpreter, which afforded me an ample field for satire. I happened to be very melancholy in the morning – as I am every morning almost; but at night my fever gives me *false* spirits – this night the lights the novelty of the scene, and every things together contributed to make me *more* than half mad – I gave full scope to a satyrical vein – and suppose

[The rest of the letter is missing.]

55. To Everina Wollstonecraft

Dublin, March 24ᵗʰ [1787]

I begin to grow very uneasy – Surely Edward will not attempt to keep the money! This suspense worries me; but I must have patience. I am, at present, rather melancholy than unhappy – the things of this world appear *flat*, *stale* and *unprofitable* to me, and, sometimes, I am perhaps, too impatient to leave the *unweeded* garden.[257] I do not now complain, a listless kind of dispair has taken possession of me, which I cannot shake off; however, I am satisfied, and will try contentedly to travel through the *solitary* path, fate has thrown me into. As to employments, I have sufficient; but confined to the society of Children, books are my only relaxation, yet, I do not read much – I think, and think, and these reveries do not tend to fit me for enjoying the *common* pleasures of this world – what does it signify? I am going home! well, what shall I write about? what passes in my mind is of too abstracted a nature to amuse – and as to my heart, He only who made it can *account* for, and compassionate its numerous weaknesses, why then should I display them to those who would, perhaps, rather dispise than pity me – yet so frequently do they force themselves on my view – and so lively

sex. It is made of the thinnest and finest sort of cloth, wrapt several times round the waist, and descending to the legs. . . . Their necklaces are made of shells, or of a hard, shining, red berry. Besides which, they wear wreaths of dried flowers of the Indian mallow' (February 1786, p. 79).

257. See note 159. Wollstonecraft also referred to this quotation in Letter 136 to Imlay.

are the emotions I wish to analyze – they too often tincture my conver[s]ation and letters – These dark tinges occur continually they want *relief* – I am only alive to *attendrissement* – Certainly I must be in love – for I am grown 'thin and lean, pale and wan.'[258] —

(29th) The other day I received a letter from M^{rs}, Burgh, advising me to write to my brother, in a very *humble* style &c &c So the money is still in his hands – I do not intend to follow her advice, and suppose she will be displeased. I know she expected that I should make my fortune here – and to pecuniary considerations, she thinks, every thing ought to give way; but it matters not, yet it is by no means pleasant to be under obligations to a person, with whose opinions I can so seldom coincide. I have often wished to hear something concerning Mrs Morphy. Do you ever see her? —

Lady K left Dublin last week, she is to be absent a fortnight – you may suppose I am not very much grieved, though we are on tolerable terms. Her conversation is ever irksome to me as she has neither sense nor feeling; besides she torments the children. She took a poor little girl with her, who was so much afraid of being alone with her mother, she wept herself sick. Mrs Fitz-Gerald has given us a general invitation; but I seldom avail myself of it – the girls are so silly, and the rest of her acquaintance so very fashionable and insipid they *annoy* me; to use the phrase of the ton. She has not forgot to interest herself about you but she has not yet succeeded. I have put off writing to Eliza hoping to have some agreeable intelligence to communicate to her; but I must not delay any longer. Betty Delane often visits me – we talk of Fanny, and this topic is ever interesting and dear to me, I love her for shedding tears when she recollects the time they spent together – if she weeps – what should I do? I believe I told you before, that as a nation I do not admire the Irish. and as to the great world and its frivolous ceremonies – I *cannot* away with them they fatigue me – I thank Heaven that I was not so unfortunate as to be born a Lady of quality. I am now reading Rousseau's Emile, and love his paradoxes. He chuses a *common* capacity to educate – and gives, as a reason, that a genius will educate

258. Possibly referring to William Broome, *A Dialogue between a Lady and her Looking-glass* (1739), l. 20: 'Tis true, you're meagre, pale, and wan, / The Reason is you're sick for Man.' See also Sir John Suckling's song *Why so pale and wan, fond Lover?* (1646).

itself [259] – however he rambles into that [   ] *chimerical* world in which I have too often [wand]ered – and draws the usual conclusion, that all is vanity and vexation of spirit. He was a strange inconsistent unhappy clever creature – yet he possessed an uncommon portion of sensibility and penetration. You know my *concatenation* of ideas – talking of Rousseau, I think of his confessions [260] and they bring poor Hewlett into my mind – Poor H! I am sorry to find he has entangled himself in worldly affairs – apropos, have you seen Le Sage? [261] I shall never mention your writing again Adieu

Yours sincerely Mary –

Give my love to Charles. I went to the play the other night to see M^rs, Crawford perform Lady R. [262] and have scarcely got the better of the fatigue. They have a most excellent comedian here – I think him superior to Edwin [263] as he has more native humour. The Theatre is not

259. A reference to Book 2 of *Émile* (1762) by Jean-Jacques Rousseau, the French philosopher with whom Wollstonecraft was often in dialogue throughout her life. Rousseau's idea of the self-education of the boy formed the motto for her first novel, *Mary, A Fiction*. She was less charmed by the education of the girl as it was described in Book 5; see ch. 5, section 1, of *A Vindication of the Rights of Woman*.

260. Rousseau's posthumously published *Confessions* came out in 1781 and 1788. Wollstonecraft would later review the English translation of the second part for the April 1790 issue of *AR*, see *Works*, 7, 228f.

261. Possibly a reference to Samuel Foote's play, *The Devil upon Two Sticks* (1768), based on Alain-René LeSage's *Le diable boiteux*; it was being performed in Covent Garden between February and June 1787. The play is primarily a satire on the medical profession, with passing swipes at the Irish, with their passion for genealogy, and at greedy preachers, including Methodists, who aim at the purses of their congregation.

262. Lady Randolph in John Home's famous tragedy *Douglas* (1756). Mrs Crawford and Mrs Siddons played the role almost simultaneously, Crawford at Covent Garden from 13 November 1783, Mrs Siddons making her debut on Monday, 22 December 1783 at Drury Lane. The pair were frequently compared. The *Public Advertiser* for 24 December commented, 'The Siddons, younger and more rich in natural Gifts, certainly offers much to the Mind, and yet much more to the Eye. The Crawford, by some means or other, offers more to the Heart.' The actresses especially competed in their portrayal of the mother at last hearing news of a lost child. (Charles Beecher Hogan *et al.*, *London Stage*, 5, 1776–1800, p. cxiv)

263. Probably Andrew Cherry, who started his career in Belfast. In 1787 he was engaged at Smock-Alley in Dublin, where he became a favourite comedian and was known as 'Little Cherry'. His first role there was Darby in O'Keeffe's *Poor Soldier*

a good one.[264] Inshort Dublin is not like a Metropolis, there are only two ranks of people.

I am like a *lilly* drooping – Is it not a sad pity that so sweet a flower should waste its sweetness on the *Desart* air,[265] or that the Grave should receive its *untouched* charms, Yours an Old Maid — ' 'Tis true a pity and 'tis pity tis true'[266] — Alas!!!!!!!!

56. To Everina Wollstonecraft

Dublin, March 25th [1787]

I was just now – that is a few hours ago, going to answer your letter – and I was in a melancholy mood – when Miss Moore and M[rs] Ogle paid me a visit – and her Ladyship followed – Her father-in-law[267] had dined with her, and she repeatedly requested me to come down to the drawing-room to see him – and Miss M. tried all she could to prevail on me – I at last consented – and could perceive that she had a guard over herself – For to tell you a secret she is afraid of me – Why she wishes to keep me I cannot guess – for she cannot bear that any one should take notice of me. Nay would you believe it she used several arts to get me out of the room before the gentlemen came up – one of them I really wanted to see Mr Ogle – He is between forty and fifty – a *genius*, and *unhappy* – Such a man, you may suppose would catch your sister's eye – As he has the name of being a man of sense Lady K. has chosen him for her *flirt* – don't mistake me – her flirtations are very harmless and she can neither understand nor relish his conversation. But she wishes to be taken particular notice of by a man of

(1783). John Edwin the Elder (1749–1790) was a popular comedian; he was playing Dr Last in Foote's comedy.

264. A surprising remark since Dublin was famed for its theatres at Smock-Alley and Crow-Street, which had both been invigorated after Ireland's partial legislative independence in 1782–3.

265. Gray's *Elegy*, ll. 55f.: 'Full many a flower is born to blush unseen / And waste its sweetness on the desert air'. Above the word '*Desart*' Wollstonecraft wrote '*Dublin*'.

266. *Hamlet*, II, ii, 97f.: 'That he is mad, 'tis true; 'tis true 'tis pity, / And pity 'tis 'tis true.'

267. Edward King, first Earl of Kingston (1726–1797).

acknowledged cleverness. As he had not seen me lately he came and seated himself by me – indeed his sensibility has ever lead him to pay attention to a poor forlorn stranger – He paid me some *fanciful* compliments – and lent me some very pretty stanzas – melancholy one, you may suppose, as he thought they would accord with my feelings. Lord K. came up – and was surprised at seeing me there – he bowed respectfully – a *contatenation* of thoughts made me out *blush* her Ladyship's rouge.[268] Did I ever tell you she is very *pretty* – and *always* pretty. Such is the style I live in – I went into the steward's room, the other day, and felt something like a sensation of envy – I am a something betwixt and between – Well, my dear Girl – I am very uneasy about you, and still more anxiously do I feel for Eliza – I think I hear her gloomy sing-song – I am afraid it is not as easy, as I supposed, to get her into a school in this country, as M^{rs}, F. has not yet heard of any eligible situation, though I am certain she has exerted herself. I believe, I could have interest enough to recommend her or you as a Governess – but I scarcely know how to persuade you to enter on such an arduous and uncertain undertaking – besides *what* could Eliza undertake? I know not what to say – or advise. My next half-year stipend will discharge the rest of my debts, if Ned ever pays the money. – By this time George has left London – I long to see him – to hear every particular concerning you. I really rejoice to hear that you endeavor to improve yourself – 'tis a pity your faculties should lie dormant – I have written this letter by such bits and scraps I forget what I intended to say when I sat down to answer your letter. Lady K. and the Miss[es] FitzGerald have just been with me – Those Girls worry me – they are such nothings – I spent a cheerful hour, with the female part of the Ogle family, this morning, and I supped with them the night before last – and the moments glided away enlivened by *wit* and rational conversation – and at midnight I came home to recline on my sopha – and think — I dread going to Mitchelstown; I feel

---

268. Although there is nothing in her letters to suggest any intimacy, gossip later linked Wollstonecraft and Lord Kingsborough. In a letter of 14 May 1798 to his wife, Bishop Percy of Dromore observed that 'Lady K. is said to have discharged the Governess after one year's trial, because she wanted to discharge the Marriage Duties, with that Lady's husband. – Such is the report –' (BL add. MS 32.335).

myself tempted to transcribe a short definition of genius, written by Mr Ogle.

What do you say to this? do you coincide with the author- If I had remembered it I would have sent you, some of his poems by George; they have really great merit. [ ] –

Genius! 'tis th' ethereal Beam, –
'Tis sweet Willy Shakespear's dream, –
'Tis the muse upon the wing, –
'Tis wild Fancy's magic ring, –
'Tis the Phrenzy of the mind, –
'Tis the eye that ne'er is blind, –
'Tis the Prophet's holy fire,
'Tis music of the lyre
'Tis th' enthusiast's frantic bliss –
'Tis anything – alas – but this.[269]

I have just been interrupted again, my l[ittle gi]rl is gone to the play with her mother and her Ladyship with great civility desired me to send for Miss Delane or take the little ones out with me – They are all about me entreating to go to Mrs Moore's – a sister of Mrs Ogles – I must indulge them though I had intended spending a quiet evening. Adieu – write soon –

and believe me to be your
affectionate friend and sister
Mary Wollstonecraft

57. To Joseph Johnson[270]

Dublin, April 14th [1787]

Dear sir,

I am still an invalid – and begin to believe that I ought never to expect to enjoy health. My mind preys on my body – and, when I

269. Possibly *bouts rimés*, a game in which specific rhymes have to be used. Ogle contributed some examples to *Poetical Amusements at a Villa near Bath* (Bath, 1775).
270. In *P W* Godwin published and numbered Wollstonecraft's letters to Johnson; this was Letter 1 in the series. Presumably he then destroyed the manuscripts. In *CL* Wardle

endeavour to be useful, I grow too much interested for my own peace. Confined almost entirely to the society of children, I am anxiously solicitous for their future welfare, and mortified beyond measure, when counteracted in my endeavours to improve them. – I feel all a mother's fears for the swarm of little ones which surround me, and observe disorders, without having power to apply the proper remedies. How can I be reconciled to life, when it is always a painful warfare, and when I am deprived of all the pleasures I relish? – I allude to rational conversations, and domestic affections. Here, alone, a poor solitary individual in a strange land, tied to one spot, and subject to the caprice of another, can I be contented? I am desirous to convince you that I have *some* cause for sorrow – and am not without reason detached from life. I shall hope to hear that you are well, and am yours sincerely

Mary Wollstonecraft.

58. To the Reverend Henry Dyson Gabell

Dublin, April 16th [1787]

My dear friend

The evening I received your letter I intended answering it; but was prevented; and since that vexations which I cannot banish, have not allowed me leisure to consider abstruse speculations. I am of opinion that much may be said on both sides of the question – and yet cannot intirely coincide with you.[271] It appears to me self-evident, that an

---

changed the sequence to cover a range of years from 1787 to late 1795 primarily on the assumption that the changes of mood argued their composition over a long period. I have kept to Godwin's order except where external references make it inappropriate since I find nothing improbable in Wollstonecraft's varying attitudes.

271. Gabell held latitudinarian ideas on doctrine and church government, considering that God was not prescriptive in all matters and expected people to make the best of their world. See his letters to Dr Parr in J. Johnstone, L.P. (ed.), *The Works of Samuel Parr*, 8 vols. (London, 1828). In politics he tended towards conservatism and an association of religion and state far from Wollstonecraft's developing views; see *A Discourse Delivered on the Fast-Day in February 1799, in the Church of St Lawrence, Winchester* (London, 1799).

All-wise and good Being created nothing in vain. He cannot be mistaken, or cause *needless* pain. Ignorance would be desirable if all our attainments had a reference only to our present mode of existence. Man would then disquiet himself in vain – and enlarge his mind, for no other purpose; but to extend the dominion of sorrow, and sharpen the arrows of affliction. A *good* understanding prevents a person's enjoying the common pleasures of this life – if it does not prepare him for a better it is a *curse*.[272] Why have we implanted in us an irresistible desire to think – if thinking is not in some measure necessary to make us wise unto salvation. Indeed intellectual and moral improvement seem to me so connected – I cannot, even in thought separate them. Employing the understanding purifies the heart, gives dignity to the affections, by allowing the mind to analyze them – and they who can assign a reason for loving their fellow-creatures – will endeavor to serve The Great Spirit[273] *rationally* – they will see the *beauty* of holiness,[274] and be drawn by the cords of love. How can the mind govern the body if it is not exercised – Dr Johnson, has said, that the most trivial occupations, such as collecting shells, &c &c are of use, and even, promote the cause of virtue, as some time is stolen from sensual pursuits.[275] I agree with him – and think if we were more perfect the

272. Perhaps an echo of Mercier, who in 'Optimism: A Dream' told of a man of feeling who even in sleep was tremblingly alive to the suffering of others. Seeing injustice, crimes, and tyranny, he starts to question Providence; suddenly he is swept up to Heaven where an angel tells him he will learn 'that if Providence sometimes ordains the good man to be unhappy, it is to lead him more certainly to happiness' and that 'Virtue often suffers, because it would cease to be virtue if it had no struggles' (*Walker's Hibernian Magazine*, February 1787, p. 75).

273. A common phrase in seventeenth- and eighteenth-century hymns and religious poetry, e.g. Sir Richard Blackmore, *A Hymn to the Sacred Spirit*, l. 76; Christopher Smart, *Hymn XI. Easter Day*, l. 67; and Samuel Wesley, the elder, *Marlborough, or, the Fate of Europe*, l. 369.

274. Often used in the Bible and hymns, e.g. Psalms 29:2; 96:9; and 110:13; Isaac Watts, *Psalm 96. As the 113th Psalm. The God of the Gentiles*, l. 23; *Psalm 110. First Part Christ exalted, and Multitudes converted; or, the Success of the Gospel*, l. 12.

275. See *The Rambler*, no. 83 (1 January, 1751): 'Between men of different studies and professions, may be observed a constant reciprocation of reproaches. The collector of shells and stones, derides the folly of him who pastes leaves and flowers upon paper . . . There are, indeed, many subjects of study which seem but remotely allied to useful knowledge, and of little importance to happiness or virtue. . . . It is impossible to determine the limits of enquiry, or to foresee what consequences a new discovery may

single desire of pleasing the Author of all good might be sufficient to make us virtuous – but we are so framed that we want continual variety – and the appetites will rule if the mind is *vacant*. It is true our reasonings are often fallacious – and our knowledge mostly conjectural – yet these flights into an obscure region open the faculties of the soul. St. Paul says, 'we *see* through a glass *darkly*'[276] – but he does not assert that we are *blind*. Besides if animals have souls, I should not suppose that when they leave the body they will be on a par with man – on the contrary, I *imagine* they must be an inferior link in the great chain[277] – in which man, I should *conjecture*, does not hold a very high place. In short the more I reflect, the less apt am I to concur with you – if I did, I should envy *comfortable* folly – 'Fat contented ignorance'![278] Well are you almost tired – I promised you a sermon, and behold I have written one – yet I have not done with the subject. The main hinge on which my argument turns, is this, refinement genius – and those charming talents which my soul instinctively loves, produce misery in this world – abundantly more pain than pleasure. Why then do they at all unfold themselves *here*? if useless, would not the Searcher of hearts, the tender Father, have shut them up till they could bloom in a more favorable climate; where no keen blasts could blight the opening flower. Besides sensibility renders the path of duty more

produce.' In the same essay, however, Johnson warns, 'The virtuoso . . . cannot be said to be wholly useless; but perhaps he may be sometimes culpable for confining himself to business below his genius, and losing in petty speculations, those hours by which if he had spent them in nobler studies, he might have given new light to the intellectual world.'

276. I Corinthians 13:12: 'We see now through a glass, darkly: but then face to face. Now I know in part: but then I shall know even as I am known.'

277. The Great Chain of Being, a favourite eighteenth-century notion expressed poetically by Pope: 'Vast chain of being! which from God began, / Natures aethereal, human, angel, man, / Beast, bird, fish, insect, what no eye can see, / No glass can reach; from infinite to thee, / From thee to nothing. . . . / . . . one step broken, the great scale's destroy'd (*Epistle I Of The Nature And State Of Man With Respect To The Universe*, 1732, ll. 229f.).

278. Laurence Sterne, *A Sentimental Journey through France and Italy* (1768), vol. 1, ch. 3, describing a benevolent monk: 'It was one of those heads, which Guido has often painted – mild, pale – penetrating, free from all common-place ideas of fat contented ignorance looking downwards upon the earth – it look'd forwards; but look'd, as if it look'd at something beyond this world.'

intricate – and the warfare *much* more severe – Surely *peculiar* wretchedness has something to balance it! I was pleased with you manner of treating the subject – and beg you to continue to write to me in this way. We generally conclude from ou[r] own partial experience, my reason has been too far stretched, and tottered almost on the brink of madness – no wonder then, if I humbly hope, that the ordeal trial answered some end, and that I have not suffered in vain. Pray write soon under cover to Lord K. you are enjoying the sweets of spring – while I scarcely know how vegetation advances.

Adieu, your affectionate

Sister

Mary

Whether intellect.[1] acquirem.[ts] gained here are of any service or pleasure hereafter? Aff.[n]

59. To Everina Wollstonecraft

Dublin, May 11th, 1787

Your silence, and George's long absence[279] makes me very uneasy – though I take it for granted he is to bring me half a hundred letters – I hope to hear that the money is paid – To hear how you look – and – but it matters not – I am afraid to anticipate any good lest I add bitterness to disappointment. Is Bess to be with you the approaching vacation? She has not answered my last two letters – I suppose she was displeased at my long silence – She had no occasion – I do not forget her. I *rack* my mind to think of some expedient to relieve her out of her present uncomfortable situation; but no feasible method has yet occurred. What do you intend doing with yourself? Do pray write oftener – Suspense wears me away –

'That vivacity which encreases with age is not far from madness.'

---

279. George Blood had been visiting London, where he met and became attached to Everina Wollstonecraft, still living unhappily with her brother Edward Bland.

Says Rochefoucault,[280] [–] I then am mad – deprived of the only comforts I can relish, I give way to whim – and yet when the most sprightly sallies burst from me the tear frequently trembles in my eye and the long drawn sigh eases my full heart – so my eyes roll in the wild way you have *seen* them. a deadly paleness overspreads my countenance – and yet so weak am I a sudden thought or any *recollected* emotion of tenderness will occasion the most painful suffusion. You know not my dear Girl of what materials, this strange inconsistency heart of mine, is formed and how alive it is to tenderness and misery. Since I have been here I have turned over severy pages in the vast volume of human nature, and what is the amount? Vanity and vexation of spirit[281] – and yet I am *tied* to my fellow-creatures by partaking of their weaknesses – I rail at a fault – sicken at the sight – and find it stirring within me – new sympathies and feelings *start* up – I know not myself – [']'Tis these whims' Mʳ Ogle tells me, 'render me interesting' and Mʳˢ Ogle with a placid smile quotes some of my own sentiments – while I cry the physici[an] *cannot* heal himself – This man has *great* faults and his wife *little* ones – They vex me – yet he say a witty thing and genius and sensibility lights his eyes – tenderness illumines her's, and her face is dressed in smiles of benignity – I forget reason – the present pleasing *impulse* rules the moment and it *flies* – We have had a commemoration of Handel.[282] Lady Kingsborough took me both days, and I was very much obliged to her. The first day's performance was fine – but they made a blunder the second. Lady K. and I are on much better terms than ever we were – To tell the truth she is afraid of me, 'tis not pleasant to be forced to view folly and lament the consequence of it – and yet feel a sort of *mortal* yearning. I love peace

280. Seventeenth-century *Maximes* of the duc de la Rochefoucauld; cf. Maxim 416: 'La vivacité qui augmente en viellissant ne va pas loin de la folie.'

281. Ecclesiastes 1:14: 'I have seen all things, that are done under the sun, and behold all is vanity, and vexation of spirit.'

282. Some 300 performers including the amateurs Lady Portarlington (see note 288) and Sir Hercules Langrishe presented a concert sponsored by the Irish Musical Fund at the fashionable St Werburgh's Church, Dublin, on 3 May 1787, commemorating the recitals Handel had given in Dublin in 1741–1742, which included the first performance of *The Messiah*. The *Daily Universal Register* for Saturday, 12 May 1787 quoted a letter: 'A more elegant or brilliant auditory never appeared to honour the memory of that great musical genius. The church could with difficulty accommodate the numbers . . .'

– and though the conversation of this female cannot amuse me I try to entertain her – and the result of my endeavors worries *me* for I have more of her company. She however keeps in her temper surprisingly before me and really labors to be civil – The defect is in her nature – She is devoid of sensibility – of course, *vanity only* inspires her immoderate love of praise – and *selfishness* her *traffick* of civility – and the fulsome untruths, with all their train of strong expressions without any ideas annexed to them. But I must not forget to tell you that Neptune[283] enquired after me – yet could not find time to visit me. At the Rotunda,[284] where Lady K. took me one evening, he was coming up to speak to me – I was in the *party* of a Lady *quality* – and he wished to speak to me – but I *would* not see him – and from the corner of my eye he might have caught a look of ineffable contempt – if he *could* have felt it. I saw him too last night in the Green-room[285] at the play-house – but he did not attempt to speak to me. He has never called on Mrs Blood.

My little Girls have been in bed these many hours – I sit up very late. 'Tis the only time I *live*, in the morning I am a poor melancholy wretch – and at night *half* mad, a p[re]tty account I give of myself – Margaret is really a fine girl and so much attached to me I govern her completely[286] –

283. See notes 78 and 166.

284. The Rotunda Hospital on Great Britain Street was a lying-in hospital with a round assembly hall and gardens laid out like Vauxhall. Both hall and gardens were used for concerts, masquerades and card-parties, which raised funds for the hospital. The most fashionable time to visit the Rotunda was on Sunday evening.

285. The room in the theatre where actors rested when not on stage; the *OED* speculates that it was probably so called because originally painted green. *SC* states that in 1787 the room must have been at Crow-Street since Smock-Alley had been closed in 1786, but La Tourette Stockwell in *Dublin Theatres and Theatre Customs* (Kingsport, 1938), p.156, declares that the company moved from Smock-Alley to Crow-Street only in June 1787. The Smock-Alley theatre, which had its green rooms on the opposite side from the vice-regal box, was a little less sophisticated than Crow-Street. Both theatres were fashionable places to be seen, although both were also disturbed by riots and brawling from time to time.

286. There is much evidence of Wollstonecraft's influence over the young girl. In her short autobiography Margaret (by then the Countess of Mount Cashell) describes how she contracted 'a premature disgust to the follies of dress, equipage & the other usual objects of female vanity' (Pforzheimer MSS). In later life Lady Mount Cashell abandoned her husband and called herself Mrs Mason, the name of the governess in Wollstonecraft's *Original Stories*; she lived for many years with George Tighe in Italy and became a friend of Percy Bysshe and Mary Shelley, Wollstonecraft's second daughter.

yet her violence of temper teases me though I myself never feel the effects of it – she sees her mother's faults – and sometimes ridicules them – I try to curb her, but fear she will launch out when out of my sight. Good night! I'll finish this to-morrow – for 'tis the very *witching* hour of night!!!!!! —

(12) I scarcely know where we shall spend the summer. I am trying to persuade Lady K to go to the Continent but am afraid she will not. I wish to take in some *quite* new objects.[287] You cannot conceive my dear Girl the dissipated lives the woman of quality lead – When I am in spirits I will give you a faithful picture. In many respects the *Great* and *little* vulgar resemble and in none more than the motives which induce them to marry. They look not for a companion and are seldom alone together but in bed – The husband, perhaps drunk and the wife's head full of the *pretty* compliment that some creature, that Nature designed for a Man – paid her at the card table. The Irish men are reckoned terrible heart stealers – but I do not find them so very formidable – on the contrary their manners do not please me. The women are very pretty I have been pleased with many – yet cannot dwell on one as particularly charming – They catch the senses – 'tis beauty's province – but sensibility can only reach the heart – attractive genius – I bow before thee – and instinctively love thee. A Lady Portarlington who sung at the commemoration [de]lighted me – but she is married to a *nonentity*.[288] Have you ever by any chance met Jackson – or heard any thing of him – Poor dear Hewlett – do you ever go to hear him? How does Mrs C. do without him? Has he succeeded in his school – Give my love to Charles and Mason and believe me to be yours sincerely

Mary Wollstonecraft

287. Clearly Wollstonecraft was persuasive since a later letter indicates that the Kingsboroughs were planning a European trip, taking the governess with them.
288. Caroline Dawson (née Stuart), Countess of Portarlington, daughter of the third Earl of Bute and granddaughter of Lady Mary Wortley Montagu, was a talented painter and musician. When Lord Portarlington came courting Lady Caroline, Mrs Delany found him 'a man of fashion – tall, genteel, not handsome, *rather serious*, but seems *very sincerely* attached to her'. In her adverse opinion Wollstonecraft may have echoed Lady Kingsborough, who was acquainted with the family.

Tell me do they charge you double postage – on account of the size of the sheet

60. To Everina Wollstonecraft

Dublin, May 15th [1787]

Yesterday I received your long letter – you know very well that it contained many things, which of course *must* worry me. As to the money matter[289] I endeavor not to think of it – it is so severe a disappointment – more so than you can imagine – as 'till my debts are paid I cannot take any *active* step to make myself useful to those I am most interested about. I cannot be more explicit or explain schemes which are only in embryo.[290] I shall be glad to hear that you are out of Ned's house – Let you go where you will. I approve of Eliza's conduct in refusing to come to Town – but regret that you cannot pass the vacation together. Write to me *immediately* and let me know what the expence of your going down and living there will amount to – and I will if possible muster it up – but M[rs] B.[291] *must* not know anything about it. – I have been considering – a journey would be of great use to you – and your presence of the most essential service to Bess – I can raise the money – four guineas, I imagine will be sufficient and I will enclose it. You will try to manage the affair that I may not appear in it. The account you sent about Henry[292] has hurried my spirits – and altogether I am not in a writing mood. – and should not have written to-day but on account of sending it by a private hand. Mr Barry, the

289. Presumably the money from Roebuck which her brother Edward Bland Wollstonecraft was not disbursing.
290. By now Wollstonecraft was seriously entertaining the idea of becoming a professional writer.
291. Mrs Burgh, to whom Wollstonecraft still owed a great debt and who would expect to be paid out of any spare money.
292. Possibly a reference to Wollstonecraft's second brother Henry Woodstock, who had been apprenticed in 1775 to an apothecary-surgeon in Beverley but who had thereafter been absent from any of the extant family letters. Emily Sunstein has convincingly suggested that he may have ended in a lunatic asylum in London (*A Different Face: The Life of Mary Wollstonecraft*, New York, 1975, pp. 36f.).

little Clergyman, who will deliver it to you is the private Tutor of Lord K's younger children. He is a *good sort* of a man – and I request you would pay him particular attention. And I have a commission for you – which I could not avoid promising that you would execute. It is to buy Lady K. six worked aprons. Two of them are to be fine handsome ones. She would go to a guinea and a half a piece for them – and the other four are not to exceed a guinea – if you can get them cheaper so much the better – but be particular in your choice – *as it is an affair of consequence*. Mr Barry will give you the money. I am not in a humor to write – and yet must try to fabricate a letter to M*rs* Burgh – alias the Green – and Eliza too, I cannot avoid addressing a few lines to – Poor Girl! Do you not perceive what a miscellaneous epistle I am writing. I shall write by the post very soon. Pray remember me in the most affectionate manner to Hewlett – 'Tis a pity that *such* a man should be thrown away!!! — I must not forget to tell you that you have rivalled *the princess*[293] – George talks continually of you and *blushes* when he mentions your name – Betty Delane drank tea with me yesterday – He dined with her, and you were the burthen of his song. I find Church is still the same *prudent* creature. I have mentioned his demand to Skeys. You may tell him so – *that* subject he will find interesting. I will not close this 'till I have finished the rest, I may

[The rest of the letter is missing.]

293. See note 110.

England 1787–1792

61. To Eliza Bishop

Bristol,[294] June 27th [1787]

I have just received your letter, and write in a hurry to request you or Everina, if you can *possibly* contrive it, to pay Gibbons the money I owe him – Give him two guineas. If I knew how to convey it to you I could send it directly. I have *every* reason to think I shall be able to pay my debts before I again leave the Kingdom. *A friend* whose name I am not *permitted* to mention has insisted on lending me the money[295] – I shall certainly borrow it – and as I shall then reckon myself rich, I hope to contrive for you and Averina to spend the winter-vacation together, as the only alleviation I can devise to render your confinement tolerable. With respect to this money matter you must not enquire, or expect any other explanation – yet let me tell you dear Girls, the manner in which this favor has been conferred on my *greatly* enhanced the obligation – I could have no scruple – and I rejoiced to meet with a fellow-creature whom I could admire for doing a *disinterested* act of kindness – In short it is a present; but I would not have it mention to

294. The Kingsboroughs had crossed the Irish Sea at the beginning of June and were now in Bristol Hot-Wells to sample the medicinal waters before embarking on their Continental tour. Like Bath, Bristol Hot-Wells was primarily a fashionable resort for the rich, leisured and ailing. After the Hot-Wells and before the crossing to France it had been decided that Wollstonecraft should take a short holiday with her sisters.
295. This might have been Joseph Johnson, although there would then have been no need for secrecy. Another possibility is Lord Kingsborough or some other person with whom she was acquainted in Dublin.

any creature – The lending it was first mentioned as the most delicate way of reconciling me to it. I intend paying Sowerby – and every body; and as Lady K. is in my debt I shall be able to afford to visit you and Everina. You will no doubt be surprised – so am I; but while I praise an *earthly* benefactor I do not forget that Gracious Being who has delivered me out of so many troubles, and allowed me to receive his mercies through the medium of my fellow-creatures whom I ardently wish to love.

Margaret is very far from being well, and I am anxious about her, she often puts me in mind of Everina, whom she resembles in mind and temper – I have many things to worry me, poor dear Bess Delane used to pity me, when she saw the difficult card I had to play. I really feel very lonely without her – I received the other day a truly elegant friendly epistle from her – She has one of the best hearts in the world and a most excellent temper. I have not heard from Mrs Burgh a long time, I suppose she puts off writing on account of the delay of payment. I intend discharging the pecuniary obligation I am under to Church. My nerves daily grow worse and worse – yet I strive to occupy my mind even when duty does not force me to do it – in a trifling way I net purses, and intend having two smart ones to present to you and Everina – and when I have more strength I read Philosophy – and write – I *hope* you have not forgot that I am an Author,[296] yet many are the hours that are loaden with cares – I shake my head but it remains heavy – and I *ruminate* without digesting. I have several neighbors; but none of them please me. Lords are not the sort of beings who afford me amusement – nor in the nature of things can they – poor half-mad Mr Ogle was the only Rt. Honorable I was ever pleased with – and I pity him – I am sorry to hear a man of sensibility and cleverness *talking* of sentiment sink into sensuality – such will ever I fear be the case with the inconsistent human heart when there are no *principles* to restrain and direct the wayward impulses of it. I have lately been reading a book which I wish Everina to peruse. It is called Paley's philosophy. The definition of virtue I particularly admire – it is short.

296. *Thoughts on the Education of Daughters* had now been out some time and Godwin records that at Bristol Hot-Wells Wollstonecraft composed her second work and first novel, *Mary, A Fiction*, much of it loosely based on the events of her friendship with Fanny Blood and on her experience with the Kingsboroughs.

'Virtue is the doing good to mankind, in obedience to the *will* of God, and for the sake of everlasting happiness.'[297]

How do you contrive to live with Mrs Tew,[298] now you have no school employments? You are not, I hope, confined to her society. The weather has been intolerably bad in this part of the Island, I am sorry for it, as the comfort of invalids depend in great meas[ure] on it. If I had the wings of a Dove I would fly a[way] though I might not find rest.[299] Pray recollect all the news you can – Did Everina ever visit poor unfortunate Mrs Morphy? – or see *your* Goldsmith! *All* diamonds do not prove Bristol stones![300] Hinxman[301] the gentlest of his kind what is become of him where does he wan[   ]

together an [   ]

begin ha[   ]

sides, th[   ]

The[   ]

[   ]

I sit down for a moment to write a few lines in order to recruit my worn-out spirits I have been lost in stupidity, listening to the chat of some people of quality, and wished *even* for vulgar humor to have seasoned it – My way of being introduced into company is very unpleasant – and particularly so now Mrs Fitz-Gerald is not one of the party – My cheeks too frequently are flushed by a *decent* pride – My spirit rises and assumes its native dignity and feels itself superior to the *little souls* clothed with adventitious

---

297. William Paley, *Principles of Moral and Political Philosophy* (London, 1785), p. 35. Paley, a kind of theological utilitarian, put morality within life and supported women's education and independence. He became a favourite author of Wollstonecraft's pupil, Margaret King.

298. The owner of the house where Eliza Wollstonecraft lived as lodger and/or companion. From her time with Mrs Dawson in Bath, Wollstonecraft was very much aware of the horror of being an inferior condemned to the society of one person.

299. Psalms 54:7: 'And I said: Who will give me wings like a dove, and I will fly and be at rest.'

300. Bright transparent rock crystal found in the limestone at Clifton, Bristol.

301. The musician from whom Wollstonecraft had borrowed money when in Newington Green; he proved to be mean and graceless when Eliza later met him in Bath.

[   ] has never
[   ] the honor of
[   ] tempt, 'till
[   ] this train
[   ] is not
[   ] ptibly
[   ] – I
[   ] possess.

[The rest of the letter is missing.]

62. *To George Blood*[302]

Henley, September 11th [1787]

My dear George,

I have received both your letters, though from the date of my letter you may suppose I am on the wing. In few days I set off for Leicestershire, to visit Eliza, and intend to remain there about a fortnight. Everina, who is now teaching the young ideas how to shoot, talks of adding a postscript to this epistle; but lest she should not have time to explain matters to you I will.[303] The plan you mention, my dear boy, is not feasible.[304] – In the first place, my brother has not paid the money nor do I expect he ever will; and if he had, and could my sisters through your *kind* assistance raise the necessary sum, to deal

302. By September Wollstonecraft had been dismissed by the Kingsboroughs, who had removed to London. She had met Joseph Johnson, her publisher, and been encouraged to try to earn her living as a writer. Before she settled in London, she visited her two sisters but without telling them of her plans. She was writing to George Blood from Henley, where Everina Wollstonecraft was working as a teacher at Miss Rowden's school.

303. Everina supplied a postscript of just over half a page apologizing to George Blood for her silence and declaring that she had little time for writing. She described herself as 'disagreeably situated': she had not smiled in Henley until her sister came.

304. George Blood frequently tried to persuade the Wollstonecraft sisters to come to Ireland, both because he wished to repay Mary's kindness to his family and because he was now in love with Everina. His latest plan was that the sisters should set up a school in Dublin, using Mary's contacts from her time with the Kingsboroughs.

ingenuously with you, I do not think them calculated to carry on such an undertaking. Eliza wants activity, [here two words have been defaced]; and Everina's vivacity, would by the injudicious, be termed giddiness: – her youth too would furnish another pretext for doubting her abilities; and besides, they could not pretend to teach french, and without a knowledge of that language it is vain to attempt any thing in the school line. Your exertions, I *know* would be great; but consider in what a *strange* sea of vexations they would enter, I am not so inexperienced as to imagine that my irish connexions would be of much use to them; vague professions of friendship are not to be relied on, especially when made to an inferior, in point of rank[;] self-interest, or vanity, is the cement of *worldly* friendships; two Girls without a fortune, or a *consequential* name, could not expect to be supported *merely* because related to one who is, perhaps, forgotten. Dublin too has not the advantages which result from residing in London; every one's conduct is canvassed, and the least deviation from a ridiculous rule of propriety (which might arise from conscious rectitude) would endanger their precarious subsistence. Everina and I have discussed this subject, and perfectly coincide in opinion; but while we knock down your fabric, we are not able to raise a better – I am afraid they must remain in their present *situations* 'till circumstances point out the steps they ought to take, – Everina's is very unpleasant, I shall let her describe the companion, the only companion, she has to converse with after the labors of the school have rendered a little relaxation necessary: the inhabitants are vulgar, and would they condescend to take notice of a Teacher, their acquaintance would not be very desirable.[305] The ink and pens are so bad, I can scrarcely write intelligibly. –

Give my love to your mother, and Betty Delane, and tell the latter,

---

305. Little is known of Miss Rowden. Frances Ann Kemble in *Record of a Girlhood* (London, 1878), 1, 76ff., mentions as her headmistress a Mrs Rowden, who in the late 1790s had run a successful school at 22 Hans Place in London and then went on to open a prosperous school in Paris primarily for English pupils. Kemble notes that, while during her London years Mrs Rowden had admired the theatre, she later turned 'Methodistical'. It is possible that the strict headmistress referred to by Kemble was once Everina's employer (she would have adopted the title Mrs as she became more established), or that she was Miss Rowden's niece.

I have received her letter and shall answer it very soon. Remember me to M^r. Roe, and your uncle Baillie; have you written to him lately? Everina, I know, intends making many apologies for leaving your letter so long unanswered but really she has full employment, and when she can steal a moment, she has not always sufficient resolution to collect her thoughts and sit down to converse with the absent; as she is not fond of writing it requires a stronger effort. – Now I am here she cannot prevail on herself to give up the few hours we have to spend together to any other occupation, even that of writing to a *beau*, and what is more a friendly creature; but entre nous, my good George, you pay her many fine compliments, I have *observed* them – well *pure* friendship is a rare commodity! adieu, I must leave room for the postscript; but first let me assure you of my *simple* friendship without any alloy; it has more solidity than brightness, and therefore will not wear out or dazzle.

Mary Wollstonecraft.

63. To Joseph Johnson

Henley, Thursday, September 13th [1787]

My dear sir,

Since I saw you, I have, literally speaking, *enjoyed* solitude. My sister could not accompany me in my rambles; I therefore wandered alone, by the side of the Thames, and in the neighbouring beautiful fields and pleasure grounds: the prospects were of such a placid kind, I *caught* tranquillity while I surveyed them – my mind was *still*, though active. Were I to give you an account how I have spent my time, you would smile. – I found an old French bible here, and amused myself with comparing it with our English translation; then I would listen to the falling leaves, or observe the various tints the autumn gave to them – At other times, the singing of a robin, or the noise of a water-mill, engaged my attention – partial attention –, for I was, at the same time perhaps discussing some knotty point, or straying from this *tiny* world to new systems. After these excursions, I returned to the family meals, told the children stories (they think me *vastly* agreeable), and my sister was amused. – Well, will you allow me to call this way of passing my days pleasant?

I was just going to mend my pen; but I believe it will enable me to say all I have to add to this epistle. Have you yet heard of an habitation for me?[306] I often think of my new plan of life; and, lest my sister should try to prevail on me to alter it, I have avoided mentioning it to her. I am determined! – Your sex generally laugh at female determinations; but let me tell you, I never yet resolved to do, any thing of consequence, that I did not adhere resolutely to it, till I had accomplished my purpose, improbable as it might have appeared to a more timid mind. In the course of near nine-and-twenty years, I have gathered some experience, and felt many *severe* disappointments – and what is the amount? I long for a little peace and *independence*! Every obligation we receive from our fellow-creatures is a new shackle, takes from our native freedom, and debases the mind, makes us mere earthworms – I am not fond of grovelling!

I am, sir, yours, &c.
Mary Wollstonecraft.

64. To the Reverend Henry Dyson Gabell[307]

Henley, September 13th [1787]

My dear Sir,

It is a long time since I wrote to you; but I think you would excuse me did you guess how *many* cares harrass my mind. I left Bristol to visit my friend,[308] and am now with a favorite sister, whose situation is very unpleasant; my anxiety and affection has made me strain every nerve to alter it; but I have continually been disappointed. I dare say you have gathered from my conversation, that I have been in every respect very unfortunate: indeed from my infancy I have drank of the

306. Johnson was going to be Wollstonecraft's patron and employer; in addition he was planning to find lodgings for her and set her up with a servant.
307. The clergyman and teacher Wollstonecraft had enjoyed meeting on her voyage to Ireland.
308. Probably a reference to Joseph Johnson.

bitter cup, my fortune has not been chequered, on the contrary one color has prevailed, and given its tincture to my frame of my mind – the *tone* of melancholy you observed on our first acquaintance. You have read my sentiments relative to those unfortunate females who are left by inconsiderate parents to struggle with the world, and whose cultivation of mind renders the endeavor doubly painful – I felt what I wrote! – were I to give you an account of *all* my misfortunes, and vexations, I should write a volume instead of a letter – I will only dwell on one which at present presses *sorely* on my spirit. If you have any curiosity to know more about me I will, when I write again, be more explicit, I should, when we parted, had I imagined it was for so long a time. The extravagance of a Father, and his second marriage has left my sisters friendless; I would fain be their mother and protector; but I am not formed to obtain the good things of this world – on their account they would be valuable. The sister I am at present anxious about, a fine girl, is now a Teacher in a vulgar school, and she wastes her youth in wishing for some of the pleasures of the world, which she just tasted, and acquired a relish for; she has fine spirits, I grieve to see them broken so soon; nor do I desire to pour premature knowledge into her mind – if it was *possible* for me to persuade her that the pleasures she sighs for would prove fallacious when attained. She has a small annuity,[309] and I wish to place her in a Gentlemans family 'till fortune smiles on me – or she gains experience; I could often have placed her in a situation similar to my own, but she [c]ould not undertake it[310] – If you do not think there would be a *great* impropriety in it – you could oblige me, nay, essential serve me, by mention her to M^rs O'Neill,[311] and requesting her to exert herself in her f[avo]r – I mentioned before that I had be[en] disap[poi]nted in several attempt which wore [an] aspect more promising than the present, indeed it is

309. It is not clear where this annuity came from or why Everina alone of the Wollstone-craft sisters seems to have had one. See notes 55, 167 and 249.

310. According to earlier letters Wollstonecraft had not found it easy to place her sister in a comparable situation to herself in Ireland, despite the occasional encouragement of Lady Kingsborough and her stepmother, Mrs Fitzgerald.

311. Henrietta, wife of John O'Neill of Shanes Castle, Henry Gabell's employer. She was a friend of the poet and novelist Charlotte Smith, whose work Wollstonecraft was reading in Ireland. Smith included Henrietta O'Neill's poem *Ode to the Poppy* in her novel *Desmond* (1792).

so wild it looks like the *forlorn* hope – need I apologize to you? – I *think* not. I am still on the ramble,[312] if you write soon direct to me at Mʳ Johnson's Bookseller, Sᵗ, Paul's Church-yard, London, at any rate, send your letter there, it will be forwarded to me. I suppose *your own Ann*[313] – has informed you that I wrote to her. I intended visiting her; but it was not convenient. My head is in such a confused state I scarcely know what I am writing – Adieu Mon cher ami

Mary Wollstonecraft

When do you visit England? Are you perfectly recovered? 'Spite of my vexations, I have lately written, a fiction[314] which I intend to give to the world; it is a tale, to illustrate an opinion of mine, that a genius will educate itself.[315]

I have drawn from Nature.

65. To Joseph Johnson

Market Harborough, September 20ᵗʰ [1787][316]

My dear sir,

You left me with three opulent tradesmen; their conversation was not calculated to beguile the way, when the sable curtain concealed the

---

312. Wollstonecraft seems to be hinting at her dismissal by the Kingsboroughs while not making this entirely clear.

313. Ann Gage, Gabell's fiancée.

314. *Mary, A Fiction*, which Wollstonecraft wrote during the summer of 1787 in Bristol Hot-Wells and possibly earlier in Ireland. Joseph Johnson published it early in 1788. For its connection with Wollstonecraft's earlier life see Todd, *Mary Wollstonecraft*, pp. 111f.

315. In her 'Advertisement' to *Mary, A Fiction* Wollstonecraft declared her aim to display a woman with 'thinking powers ... whose grandeur is derived from the operations of its own faculties, not subjugated to opinion; but drawn by the individual from the original source' (*Works*, 1, 5). Her title page quoted Rousseau, 'L'exercice des plus sublimes vertus éleve et nourrit le génie', *Lettres de deux Amants* (1761), 2, xxvii, 202. The sentence was quoted in *Les Pensées de J. J. Rousseau* (1763), of which Wollstonecraft later reviewed two translations in *AR* (*Works*, 7, 49).

316. Wollstonecraft was visiting her sister Eliza Bishop at Mrs Tew's in Market Harborough, Leicestershire.

beauties of nature. I listened to the tricks of trade – and shrunk away, without wishing to grow rich; even the novelty of the subjects did not render them pleasing; fond as I am of tracing the passions in all their different forms – I was not surprised by any glimpse of the sublime, or beautiful – though one of them imagined I should be a useful partner in a good *firm*. I was very much fatigued, and have scarcely recovered myself. I do not expect to enjoy the same tranquil pleasures Henley afforded: I meet with new objects to employ my mind; but many painful emotions are complicated with the reflections they give rise to.

I do not intend to enter on the *old* topic, yet hope to hear from you – and am yours, &c.

Mary Wollstonecraft.

66. *To the Reverend Henry Dyson Gabell*

[London, October 9th–19th, 1787][317]

My dear Sir

I have received both your letters, and would wish to write many things in answer to them; but an ugly giddiness in my head; – and eyes that will scarcely lend me their assistance, renders writing, at present, a task. I will then confine myself to th[e] subject I am most interested about [and] treat of other matters when I am m[ore] at ease – When the body is *whole*; and the mind needs not a physician.

I think my sister would be desirous to live in a genteel family as a *companion*. I cannot describe the kind of situation; but imagine M^{rs} O'Neill would not be at a loss to guess, when you inform her, that you interest yourself in the fate of an unfortunate gentlewoman, who has a small stipend, and wishes to make herself *useful* and agreeable, in return for board and protection. If I cannot settle my sister in this way, I *must* try to remove her to a more comfortable abode, as a Teacher in

---

317. By October Wollstonecraft had moved into her new London house south of the river, 49 George Street (now Dolben Street), which Johnson had found for her. He had also acquired a relative from the country as her servant. The new situation, although exciting, was stressful and Wollstonecraft was anxious about her and her sisters' futures. The dating of this letter follows the postmark which reads 'OC 1[ ] 87'.

a reputable [sch]ool; perhaps M^{rs}. O. might hear of [one]; but do not omit to mention, that she does not pretend to be mistress of the Frenhc language, though I am sure she soon would. Pray write immediately. I cannot lengthen this letter – a universal langor pervades my relaxed system.

Yours sincerely
Mary Wollstonecraft

Your exertions will gratify me even though they should have no effect; but should they be successful – What a weight of anxiety you would relieve me from!
[   ]. Direct to me at M^{r}. Johnson's &c

67. To Everina Wollstonecraft

London, November 7th [1787]

Though I am persuaded my silence must have given rise to various conjectures in your mind, my dear Girl, yet I am *certain* you have already imagined that it was not the effect of negligence, or want of affection. – Far indeed from it! Two letters have passed between Gabell and me, relative to you, part of the last I will transcribe; and then speak of myself.

'I have confer'd with O'Neill on the subject of your last, and he fears, with me, that what you wish for, will not easily be found. Nevertheless he has engaged to write to a Mr Jackson, his brother-in-law, and a widower, with an only daughter about 15 years of age, on the subject. There seems to be a chance of success here, if any where; but don't be sanguine. Nor must you expect any account yet awhile of the result of this application; for O'Neill is naturally languid in all his motions.'

What do you think of this – and how do [you] go on? If you love me write immediately – I want comfort! I take it for granted my brother has not paid the money – I have sent M^{rs}. Burgh twenty pounds[318] –

---

318. Probably the half wages with which Wollstonecraft would have been dismissed by the Kingsboroughs.

and I was on [e]*very* account sorry to part with it, as I am afraid I shall not be able to contrive to pay Sowerby[319] and enable Eliza to spend her Holidays in Town. I am my dear Girl once more thrown on the world; I *have* left Lord K's and they return next week to Mitchelstown. I long since imagined that my departure would be sudden. I *have not seen* M^{rs}. Burgh; but I have informed her of this circumstance, and at the same time, mentioned to her, that I was *determined* not to see any of my friends 'till I am in away to earn my own subsistence. And to this determination I *will* adhere. You can conceive how disagreeable pity and advice would be at this juncture – I have too, other cogent reasons. Before I go on will you pause – and if after deliberating you will promise not to mention to *any one* what you know of my designs (*though you may think my requesting you to conceal them unreasonable*) I will trust to your honor – and proceed. Mr Johnson, whose uncommon kindness, I believe, has saved me from despair, and vexations I shrink back from – and *feared* to encounter; assures me that if I exert my talents in writing I may support myself in a comfortable way. I am then going to be the first of a new genus – I tremble at the attempt yet if I fail – I *only* suffer – and should I succeed, my dear Girls will ever in sickness have a home – and a refuge where for a few months in the year, they may forget the cares that disturb the rest. I shall strain every nerve to procure a situation for Eliza, nearer Town. In short I am once more envolved in schemes – Heaven only knows whether they will answer! yet while they are pursued life slips away. I would not on any account inform my father or Edward of my designs – you and Eliza are the only part of the family I am interested about – I wish to be a mother to you both. My undertaking would subject me to ridicule – and an *inundation* of *friendly* advice, to which I cannot listen – I must be independent. I wish to introduce you to Mr Johnson – you would respect him; and his sensible conversation would soon wear away the impression, that a formality – or rather stiffness of manners, first makes to his disadvantage – I am sure you would love him did you know with what *tenderness* and humanity he has behaved to me. I before requested you to write

319. James Sowerby had recently married Ann De Carle. Wollstonecraft was eager to pay back her loan to him.

directly to me, at M^r. Johnson's Bookseller, N^o, 72 S^t, Paul's Church-Yard, London.

I cannot now write more explicitly. I have *indeed* been very much harrassed – But Providence has been very kind to me – and when I reflect on past mercies with respect to the future I am not without hope – And freedom, *even* uncertain freedom – is dear. I shall watch for the post – I should have written before but I wait till I was determined what course to pursue; if I had had any good to communicate, I should not have been so tardy. This project has *long* floated in my mind. You know I am not born to tread in the beaten track – the peculiar bent of my nature pushes me on. Have you heard from George? Adieu believe ever your

sincere friend and affec^{te} sister
Mary Wollstonecraft

Seas will not now divide us; or years elapse before we see each other.

68. *To Everina Wollstonecraft*

[London, c. mid November 1787]^{320}

I was just going to write to Eliza, and so I shall to-day; but an organ under my window has been playing *for tenderness framed* – and *welladay my poor heart*^{321} – my spectacles are *dim* – the present sprightly strain seems impertinent – I cannot keep time with it! – I will now give an account of myself. The regret Margaret shewed, when I

---

320. This undated letter appears to follow soon after the previous dated one of 7 November.

321. Probably *For Tenderness Framed*, a song adapted by Linley Sen. from *Saper Bramate* in Giovanni Paisiello's *Il Barbiere di Siviglia*, and first performed in John Burgoyne's sentimental comedy *The Heiress* (1786): 'For tenderness framed in life's earliest day, / A parent's soft sorrows to mine led the way; / The lesson of pity was caught from her eye, / And ere words were my own, I spoke in a sigh . . .' *Ah, Well-a-day, my Poor Heart!* is by Thomas Holcroft and William Shield and was sung in the character of a page by Mrs Martyr in Holcroft's *The Follies of a Day; or, the Marriage of Figaro*, acted at Covent Garden in 1784: 'To the winds, to the waves, to the woods I complain, / Ah, well-a-day, my poor heart! They hear not my sighs, and they heed not my pain.'

left her for a short time, was Lady K's pretext for parting with me, they had violent quarrels and the consequence was this determination – it disconcerted me at first; but I will not discribe *what* I suffered – though I long expected something of the kind would happen. I informed M[r]. Johnson of my situation; he insisted on my coming to his house, and contrived to detain me there a long time – you can *scarcely* conceive how warmly, and delicately he has interested himself in my fate. He has now settled me in a little house, in a street near Black-Friars-Bridge, and he *assures* me I may earn a comfortable maintainance if I exert myself. I have given him *Mary* – and before your vacation, I shall finish another book for young people,[322] which I think has some merit. I live alone, I mean I have only a servant, a relation of M[r]. Johnson's, sent to me, out of the country. All this will appear to you like a dream; whenever I am tired of solitude, I go to M[r]. Johnson's, and there I met the kind of company *I* find most pleasure in – the *standing* dishes I will introduce to you when I am in better spirits. I spent a day at M[rs] Trimmer's,[323] and found her a truly respect-able woman. I intend to try to get Bess a situation near me – and before the summer vacation, hope to succeed, at any rate, she shall spend the approaching one in my house, M[r]. J. knows that next to obtaining the means of life, I wish to mitigate her's, and your fate. – I have *done* with the delusion of fancy – I only live to be useful – benevolence must fill every void in *my* heart. I have a room but not furniture. J. offered you both a bed at his house;[324] but that would not be pleasant; I believe I must try to purchase a bed, which I shall reserve for my poor girls while I have a house. If you pay any visits you will comply with my whim, and not mention my place of abode or mode of life. I shall have

---

322. *Original Stories from Real Life; with Conversations, Calculated to Regulate the Affections, and Form the Mind to Truth and Goodness* was published in April 1788.

323. Sarah Trimmer (1741–1810), author of books for children. She had just published her popular animal stories, *Fabulous Stories* (1786), which included her best-known tale, *Story of the Robins*. In *Fabulous Stories* a female authority-figure, Mrs Benson, interpreted the world for her charges, teaching them to respond critically; the device probably influenced Wollstonecraft in her creation of the exemplary tutor Mrs Mason in *Original Stories*. With numerous children to raise, Trimmer did not much move in London literary circles and so did not often meet Wollstonecraft.

324. Apart from his bookshop at 72 St Paul's Churchyard and the house leased behind it, Johnson also had a country house at Purser's Cross, Fulham.

a spur to push me forward, the desire of rendering two months in the year, a little pleasanter than they would other wise be, to you and poor uncomfortable Bess. If I do, my struggles and misery will have answered a good end. I shall pay M^{rs}. B.[325] and Sowerby, and then shall only have to provide for the *passing* day. Eliza could sleep with me; but I wish to have *you* too with me. Charles[326] wrote me an angry letter, I have answered it, and if he behaves properly, I shall desire him to call at M^r. Johnson's, where I will meet him. I am thankful to Providence for these prospects indeed I am. But you my dear Girl have never felt the violent

[The rest of the letter is missing.]

69. To Joseph Johnson

[London] Friday night [c. late 1787 – early 1788][327]

My dear sir,

Though your remarks are generally judicious – I cannot *now* concur with you, I mean with respect to the preface,[328] and have not altered it. I hate the usual smooth way of exhibiting proud humility. A general rule *only* extends to the majority – and, believe me, the few judicious parents who may peruse my book, will not feel themselves

325. Mrs Burgh.
326. The youngest brother, still lodging at St Katherine's Street with their eldest brother, to whom he was articled. Presumably the anger was directed towards Edward Bland Wollstonecraft, with whom their father also was irritated because of the handling of his finances; no doubt he encouraged Charles's resentment.
327. The date comes from Wollstonecraft's references to the preface of *Original Stories*, published in 1788.
328. 'To *Original Stories*' (Godwin's note). Wollstonecraft had provided a stern preface in which she declared children should be taught by example rather than precept. She added, 'But to wish that parents would, themselves, mould the ductile passions, is a chimerical wish, for the present generation have their own passions to combat with and fastidious pleasures to pursue, neglecting those pointed out by nature: we must therefore pour premature knowledge into the succeeding one; and, teaching virtue, explain the nature of vice. Cruel necessity' (*Works*, 4, 359).

hurt – and the weak are too vain to mind what is said in a book intended for children.

I return you the Italian MS.[329] – but do not hastily imagine that I am indolent. I would not spare any labour to do my duty – and, after the most laborious day, that single thought would solace me more than any pleasures the senses could enjoy. I find I could not translate the MS. well. If it was not a MS, I should not be so easily intimidated; but the hand, and errors in orthography, or abbreviations, are a stumbling-block at the first setting out. – I cannot bear to do any thing I cannot do well – and I should lose time in the vain attempt.

I had, the other day, the satisfaction of again receiving a letter from my poor, dear Margaret.[330] – With all a mother's fondness I could transcribe a part of it – She says, every day her affection to me, and dependence on heaven increase, &c. – I miss her innocent caresses – and sometimes indulge a pleasing hope, that she may be allowed to cheer my childless age – if I am to live to be old. – At any rate, I may hear of the virtues I may not contemplate – and my reason may permit me to love a female. – I now allude to ——. I have received another letter from her, and her childish complaints vex me – indeed they do – As usual, good-night.

Mary.

If parents attended to their children, I would not have written the stories; for, what are books – compared to conversations which affection inforces! –

329. The confidence with which Wollstonecraft aimed to translate while knowing only the rudiments of a language is impressive to modern readers. Obviously she thought better of her scheme with Italian, which she seems to have begun studying in Ireland.
330. Her former pupil Margaret King; she corresponded clandestinely for a short time with Wollstonecraft through George Blood.

70. To George Blood[331]

London, January 1st [1788]

My dear George,

I received your letter, and should not so long have delayed answering it, if I could have avoided mentioning a circumstance which has occasioned me some vexation. Last week Mrs Burgh wrote to me, to inform me, that the parish officers of Islington had been with her to enquire where your father resided that they might *pass* Caroline[332] to him. She was taken up in a *dreadful* situation – and they now permit her to remain in the workhouse,[333] on conditions *I* pay them half a crown a week, 'till I write to her father. What is to be done my dear boy? I cannot allow them again to turn her out – nor will I see her, if she knew where I lived, she would come to me, and be a burden I could *not* bear. Your father, I know, lost in the most *selfish* sensuality, only cares for his own ease, I should not wish to screen him from any vexations – if you and our mother were not with him – an indignant blush suffuses my cheeks when I think of him. Write to me directly – I was obliged to force my self to mention a circumstance that I knew would vex your worthy heart. Your behavior with respect to the Homes[334] – I admire

---

331. Wollstonecraft was writing from her house in George Street, where her sisters were staying for the Christmas vacation. Everina had left her position in Henley.

332. The younger sister of Fanny and George Blood, who according to Letter 32 had earlier moved from their parents' home.

333. 'The parish workhouse stands at a little distance from the Back road, nearly opposite Barnesbury-street. It is a commodious building of brick, and was erected in the year 1777. . . . It has a spacious garden attached, from which a considerable portion of the vegetables used in the house are supplied. . . . The number of poor in the workhouse generally averages about 200 . . .' The rules, laid down at a meeting in 1798, were as follows: during wintertime everyone had to be up, washed and dressed by 7 in the morning, and work from 8 until 4 in the afternoon; there were prayers after supper, and everyone had to be in bed by 8 in the evening. John Nelson, *The History, Topography, and Antiquities of the Parish of St Mary Islington* (London, 1811), pp. 84f.

334. It sounds as though George Blood had lent money to Betty Delane's sister and brother-in-law, who was not doing well as an artist in Dublin. George Blood was still with the wine merchant Brabazon Noble in 96 Britain Street.

– suffer not the seeds of virtue in your bosom to lie dormant or to be choked by a mistaken fondness for present gratifications – but you are not selfish – and the striking example you always have before your eyes, will be more efficacious to deter you than a thousand precepts though dictated by the warmest friendship. My Sisters are now both with me, Everina complains of your silence, yet desires her love. She has left Miss Rowden, and her future situation is not yet determined on. You may suppose that their unsettled state harrasses me, in particular I am uneasy about Eliza, I cannot support her, or even recommend her to a more comfortable school – yet I shall go on trying – and leave the rest to Heaven – My own situation is much the same as when I wrote last – I labor for tranquillity of mind – and that patient fortitude which will enable me to bear what I cannot ward off.

Give my love to Bess Delane, and the remembrances, you think most acceptable, to the rest of the good folks who enquire about me – The ringing of the bells reminds me that the new year this day begins – need I send you a formal complimentary wish – instead of it, let me tell you, that I am in tolerable health, and your affectionate

Friend
Mary

I shall write to Bess D. tomorrow or next day –

71. To George Blood

London, January 17th [1788]

My dear George,

I have been considering, and as I would willingly spare you and our mother the uneasiness Caroline's presence will of course produce; I will try to board her at the work-house, and buy her a few clothes to cover her, if your father will contrive to send me ten pounds.[335] My plan is to deposite part of it with Mrs Burgh and to prevail on her to

---

335. The rule of the workhouse was that 'every poor person have a shirt or a shift once in every week' and that 'the mistress deliver out the soap, and see all the linen of the house brought into the wash-house, washed, got up, and properly mended': Nelson, *History of St Mary Islington*, p. 90.

undertake the business, if this scheme is not feasible, I must send her to you. I agree with you she had best remain here till your father's death delivers your mother from one torment – poor woman! After that she might manage her, and I think she ought to try. I highly approve of your intention of living alone, and am sure you will not be carried away by the *Irish* vain desire of *making* a *figure*; and attaining respect from so ignoble a source. Those who know your heart will not require this trivial support of their esteem, on the contrary, your not being very eager about youthful pleasures, and your self-denial to enable you to fulfil your unpleasant duties has [merited] my regard. My sister Bishop returns reluctantly to Harbro: next week; but before the ensuing vacation, I have reason to hope I shall be able to procure her a more eligible situation, I regret that I cannot immediately place her in a more comfortable habitation, and it is this reflection

[Here one line has been defaced]

which grieves me. Everina has left Henley, and I believe I shall contrive for her to spend a few months in France, could she catch the French accent I could easily procure her a reputable abode.[336] They both desire to be remembered to you, and Everina will write as soon as we are out of suspense.

Pray write soon, and mention Bess Delane when you do – I want to know whether *you* think they will be able to leave Ireland – tell me all about them. and give my love to Bess, and our mother. I have not heard from Mr Arbuckle, I hope he is well. I am going on as usual, except being in better health than I have enjoyed for some years. I had rather you would not read Dr Price's sermons,[337] as they would lead

336. Wollstonecraft was aided in her effort by Johnson's friend Henry Fuseli, who had written to Paris, 'A young woman, who purposes to become a teacher of French in a school here and who is already somewhat familiar with the language, wishes to live in Paris for six months *En pension* with a good family. Let me know whether 15 Guineas will cover her *board* and *lodging* for this period. She is not rich —'. The letter in German is in the Zentralbibliothek, Zurich, and is translated by D. H. Weinglass in 'Henry Fuseli's Letter of Enquiry to Paris on Behalf of Mary Wollstonecraft's Sister Everina', *Blake: An Illustrated Quarterly*, Spring 1988, pp. 144f.
337. *Sermons on the Christian Doctrine, as Received by the Different Denominations of Christians, To Which are Added Sermons on the Security and Happiness of a Virtuous Course, etc.* (London, 1787). The difficulty for George Blood would have

you into controversial disputes, and your limited range of books would not afford you a clue – the Dissertations[338] are less entangled with controverted points, and contain useful truths – coming warm from the heart they find the direct road to it; but the sermons require more profound thinking, are not calculated to improve the generality.

Farewell – yours affectionately
Mary

72. *To Joseph Johnson*

[London, ?early 1788][339]

My dear sir,

Remember you are to settle *my account*, as I want to know how much I am in your debt – but do not suppose that I feel any uneasiness

---

been in the detailed discussions of different theological positions, e.g. Sermon 1 is 'Of the Christian Doctrine as held by all Christians', but Sermon 2 is 'Of the Christian Doctrine as held by *Trinitarians* and *Calvinists*', and the following 'Of the Christian Doctrine as held by *Unitarians* and *Socinians*'. Price goes into detailed descriptions, e.g. from Sermon 2, p. 53: 'In the doctrine of *predestination* some include *reprobation* as well as *election*; while others make *reprobation* to be only *preterition*: That is, not an *appointment* to damnation, but an *abandonment* of all the non-elected posterity of Adam by which they are left necessarily to perish. According to some, the eternal decree of predestination respected men as *fallen* beings; and this class of divines have been distinguished under the name of *sub*-lapsarians. But according to other divines (called *supra*-lapsarians) predestination was an arbitrary decree which respected men merely as *creatures* . . .'.

338. *Four Dissertations*, 'I. On PROVIDENCE.', 'II. On PRAYER.', 'III. On the REASONS for Expecting that Virtuous Men shall meet after Death in a State of Happiness.', and 'IV. On the Importance of CHRISTIANITY, the Nature of HISTORICAL EVIDENCE, and MIRACLES' (London, 1767). Some of the 'truths – coming warm from the heart' which Wollstonecraft might have enjoyed: 'Let us labour earnestly to bring our minds into that temper which the doctrine of Providence requires. Let us follow implicitly wherever it leads us, and make an absolute surrender of our wills to God's will . . . Oh! joyful reflection! God reigns and all is well. Eternal wisdom and benevolence are present every where, and govern all things. Welcome then every event. Welcome disappointment, sickness or death' (pp. 192f.); and 'Let us resolve to cultivate friendships only with those whom we may hope to be happy with *for ever*' (pp. 347f.).

339. The letter implies that Wollstonecraft was still repaying the debts she had incurred with Johnson by moving to London.

on that score. The generality of people in trade would not be much obliged to me for a like civility, *but you were a man* before you were a bookseller – so I am your sincere friend,

Mary.

73. To George Blood

London, March 3^{d} [1788]

My dear George

How goes the world with you? are you removed to your new habitation? I am again a solitary being, Everina has been in France about three weeks;[340] but I suppose she will soon write to you, I have already received two long letters from her, full of accounts, of disasters and difficulties, which must necessarily occur in a strange country. So much the better, it is proper that some people should be roused or they would be devoted to pleasure; but this entre nous. I have lately been a little too studious, and the consequence is the return of some of my old nervous complaints. I will try to shake them off as the spring advances – I do not take sufficient exercise I know, I am eager to catch at any excuse for staying at home, and I blame myself, without correcting the fault. Even now I am suffering; a nervous head-ache torments me, and I am ready to throw down my pen – almost unable to direct it – my thoughts are frozen – I cannot thaw them – or force them to flow glibly from my pen – I shall write nothing but tautology – well – well – Nature will sometimes prevail, 'spite of reason, and the thick blood lagging in the veins, give melancholy power to harass the mind; or produce a listlessness which destroys every active purpose of the soul.[341] – I am

340. In early February Everina had gone to Paris to lodge with Mademoiselle Henry, rue de Tournon, between the Luxembourg Gardens and the Church of Saint-Suplice in Faubourg Saint-Germain.
341. The general humorous belief was that blood was connected with melancholia, e.g. in *Practice of Physic* Cullen wrote of melancholia: 'it may be observed, that in it there is a degree of torpor in the motion of the nervous power, both with respect to sensation and volition; that there is a general rigidity of the simple solids; and that the balance of the sanguiferous system is upon the side of the veins' (4, 181). There was much discussion over whether melancholy came from thick or thin blood. *Boerhaave's*

not however going to complain; for I have abundant reason to be thankful to Providence for the many comforts I at present enjoy, and the evils I have escaped. I hope I shall be able to procure Eliza a more eligible situation, her present one is indeed very disagreeable. My good friend, Mr Johnson, every day displays more goodness of heart, and I often visit his hospitable mansion – where I meet some sensible men, at any rate my worthy friend – who bears with my infirmities. Yesterday I heard your favorite Hewlett[342] preach a sermon, which he wrote to oblige me, on the recognition of our friends in a future state; the subject was affecting, and rendered more so by his tremulous voice; he appears to me not to be in a good state of health, the cares of the world, and domestic vexations prey on him – Such is the world! – A good one, when considered as a road – but no abiding place for those that feel – From Hewlett – it is a great transition to my brother Charles – whose warm youthful blood paints joy on his cheeks, and dances in his eyes – I very frequently see him, and labour to fix some principles in him to counteract the bad examples he has ever before his eyes, I think him improved in every respect, he desires to be remembered to you.[343] I have seen Sowerby this afternoon, he is one of the invariables in every sense of the word – and Mrs S. is sunk into a mere nurse; her little stock of beauty not vivified by a soul, is flown – flown with the childish vavicity, which animated her youthful face, and inspired her *animal*

Aphorisms Concerning the Knowledge and Cure of Diseases. Translated from the last Edition Printed in Latin at Leyden, 1722 (London, 1724), p. 312, declared it derived from 'Malignancy of the Blood and Humors'; the blood became 'thick, black, fat and earthy'. Nicholas Robinson, *A New System of the Spleen, Vapours and Hypochondriack Melancholy* (London, 1779), p. 198, wrote, 'the blood, in all Splenetick Cases is thick, heavy, and what we call Melancholy Blood. . . . In some Cases of the Spleen, the Impulse of the Nerves is made so faintly on the seat of the common Sensorium as scarce to awaken the Soul into a Sensibility of Being.' Whytt in *Observations* stated the opposite: 'A third general occasional cause of nervous disorders may be, the want of a sufficient quantity of blood, or of blood of a proper density' (p. 183). In *The Elements of Medicine: or, A Translation of the Elementa Medicinae Brunonis* (London, 1788), CXXXIV, John Brown observed: '. . . it is not the quality of the blood, but its quantity, which is to be found fault with' (p. 118).

342. In his *Sermons on Different Subjects* (London, 1786) Hewlett was identified as 'Lecturer of the United Parishes of St Verdant, Foster – Lane, and St Michael le Queme'.

343. Her brothers Charles and Edward Bland Wollstonecraft had quarrelled and Mary had found Charles a new attorney for his articles.

gambols – the sporting of lambs, and kittens, is pleasing, when it does not occur too of[ten]. She is entirely the mother – I mean a fo[oli]sh one – and the child of course is not properly managed:[344] I have once seen Curtis, his new work answers, and he enters more than ever into the pleasures of the world[345] – He has not any drawbacks – for nature gave him a little taste, but forgot his heart – *his blood* is separated without it, and adds flesh to his ribs – for he has now a goodly appearance. – I enclose you a letter for my dear Margaret King – but be very careful to not let any body see it – and keep it till she *sends* to Mr Noble's for it. Give my love to our mother – and believe me to be your affectionate friend

Mary

When you write why don't give me some account of Roe &c and the books you read. Have you written to Skeys? You ought not to neglect it, I told you so before, you appear ungrateful, and give up a connexion which might perhaps be useful to our mother – for I still believe he *intends* some time or other to do as he promised.

I shall soon take a parcel to Daltons for you, and will write a long letter – if I can – but long or short I am ever yours sincerely

Mary Wollstonecraft

---

344. James and Ann Sowerby's baby, James de Carle Sowerby, was born on 5 June 1787 in Stoke Newington.
345. Presumably William Curtis for whose *Flora Londinensis* Fanny Blood had provided illustrations. The new work was either part of *The Botanical Magazine or Flower Garden displayed in which the most ornamental foreign plants will be accurately represented in their natural colours*, vols. 1–14 (London, 1787–1800) or *A Companion to the Botanical Magazine or a Familiar Introduction to the study of botany, being the substance of a lecture . . . in the form of a dialogue betwixt a pupil and his preceptor* (London, 1788).

74. To Everina Wollstonecraft

[London] March 22[d] [1788]

I believe it is now near three weeks since I wrote you a very long letter, and made up in a packet with it three others, from Crystall,[346] Eliza, and Charles; but I found last sunday, that M[r]. Edwards had not had an opportunity of forwarding it to you, and I hastily wrote another sheet, to swell the packet, and to express my surprise and uneasiness on account of your silence. Mr. J.[347] and myself went to the Inn, where the Paris delegance[348] sets off from, with it, and some others papers, I suppose M. Laurent[349] has received before this; but the sealed letters were objected to, and they now rest quietly till M[r]. J. hears of a private hand. I am thus particular as I do not wish to appear negligent, and to convince you that the few who love you have not forgot you. I will very soon write you one of my long epistles, and now can only cursorily touch on the subjects I wish to mention. Well then, to write methodically, I rejoice to find that you have such an opportunity of improvement, when the desire is, I hope, *more* than a start, I was apprehensive you might catch vulgar French, but now you are secure, and when you have acquired a little knowledge of the language, you will yourself be able to discriminate. Pray enquire of the *literary* man about some particulars, relative to M. Necker, the late Minister which I shall mention. He has written a book entitled De l'importance des opinions Religeuses, it pleases me, and I want to know the character of the man, in domestic life and public estimation &c and the opinion the French have of his literary abilities.[350] Indeed you would oblige me, by

346. Probably Anne Cristall (b. 1769), a teacher and poet living in Blackheath; or, less likely, her brother, the future watercolourist, Joshua Cristall (1767-1847). The Cristalls were friends both of the Wollstonecraft siblings and of the Blood family.
347. Joseph Johnson.
348. A diligence was a public stage-coach.
349. A bookseller in Paris, whose bookshop was frequented by the upper orders. He was apparently a business connection of Joseph Johnson; Everina Wollstonecraft made contact with him in Paris.
350. Jacques Necker (1732-1804) was controller-general of French finance from 1776 to 1781. He was a prolific writer, especially on finance. At this time he was out of

gathering together all the news you can, with respect to literature, and send it to me – for I am almost as deeply immersed in study as the Baron himself. Many motives impel me besides sheer love of knowledge, which, however has ever been a predominate mover in my little world, it is the only way to destroy the worm that will gnaw the core – and make that being an isolé, whom nature made too susceptible of affections, which stray beyond the bounds, reason prescribes. I am studying French, and wish I had an opportunity of conversing indeed, if I have ever any money to spare to gratify myself, I will certainly visit France, it has long been a desire floating in my brain, that even hope has not given *consistency* to; and yet it does not evaporate. I wish you would take Bark, or bathe in a cold bath, I am sure either would be of use to your eyes[351] &c and I wish you could point out a way in which I could be useful to young Laurent, now resident in London, as the behavior of his parents to a stranger, has procured them my esteem, and I should be glad to do more than express gratitude for it. I forgot the hour, and must close my letter in a hurry, but my next shall amply compensate, and I will repeat what I have written before, if the packet should still be detained. –

(I write now, principally, to enclose a letter for M. Necker, which I request you *immediately*, without delay, to deliver yourself to M. Laurent, he will of course recollect the late Minister, the letter is to be forward with some papers sent last sunday, by the coach, should they already have been delivered, it may follow them; but do not lose time.) I entreat you, write to Eliza, your letters would amuse her, and poor Girl, she wants amusement. Take care of your health, improve yourself, and contentedly bear trifling vexations. I shall more particular answer

---

office and had just written *De l'importance des opinions religieuses* (1788), which Wollstonecraft was to translate as *Of the Importance of Religious Opinions*, published by Joseph Johnson late in 1788. Neither the work nor its author retained her good opinion; in *The Origin and Progress of the French Revolution* she called the book 'various metaphysical shreds of arguments' in a style as 'inflated and confused as the thoughts were far-fetched and unconnected' (*Works*, 6, 42).

351. According to Buchan's *Domestic Medicine*, p. 291, bathing one's eyes in cold water and a little brandy would strengthen them after an inflammation. Bark refers either to the willow or to the Peruvian bark, a source of quinine; the latter was called Jesuit's bark since it was allegedly brought to Europe by Jesuit missionaries. Both sorts of bark were prescribed for fevers and inflammation.

some parts of your two letters, when I write again. Farewell – believe me

[Signature cut out]

Give your letters always to M.L.[352] (to be conveyd to [D] post office) as your silence really made very uneasy.[353]

75. To George Blood

London, May 16th [1788]

My dear George,

Yesterday Mr Johnson sent a parcel to Dublin; the name of the bookseller, to whose care your books &c, are consigned, is Gilbert, you will of course enquire about them; M^r. Johnson intended troubling you with a commission, and I mentioned it, in the letter in the parcel; but he changed his mind. Before you give *Mary* to Bess Delane &c, alter two mistakes the printers have made. Page 47, the fifth line, put in *as* between and the bruises, & P. 178. line 17. alter returned to *relumed*, or the passage would be absolute nonsense.[354] I did not perceive these mistakes till after the parcel was packed up. I have lately being very busy translating a work of importance, and have made a very advantageous contract for another[355] besides, I have had a variety

---

352. Probably Monsieur Laurent.

353. Joseph Johnson appended a postscript: 'Your sister told me I might add a postscript & you see what room she has left me, not to make love surely! only to express my good wishes for your happiness / JJ.' The previous instruction about the letters is also in Johnson's handwriting.

354. Ch. 7 of *Mary, A Fiction* initially read: 'Her father was thrown from his horse, when his blood was in a very inflammatory state, and the bruises were very dangerous'; ch. 29: 'the spreading film retired, and love returned them', *Works*, 1, 23 and 70.

355. Presumably a reference to the Necker translation. The new contract returned Wollstonecraft to the juvenile market: Christian Salzmann's *Moralisches Elementarbuch*, translated as *Elements of Morality, for the Use of Children; with an Introductory Address to Parents* was published by Johnson in three volumes between October 1790 and March 1791. Wollstonecraft corresponded with Salzmann: see Thomas Sadler, *Diary, Reminiscences, and Correspondence of Henry Crabb Robinson* (London, 1869), 1, 206f. She approved his educational principles, which were described by Crabb

of other employments, in short, my dear Boy, I succeed beyond my most sanguine hopes, and really believe I shall clear above two hundred pounds this year, which will supply amply all *my* wants and enable me defray the Expences of Everina's journey, and let her remain at Paris longer than I at first intended.[356] I am thankful to Heaven for enabling me to be useful, and this consideration, sweetens my toil, for I have been very diligent. Tell Bess D. and you may whisper the same to yourself that she ought not to wait for my answers, when she knows what pleasure her letters afford me; and I am sure she would not wonder at my silence, if she knew how much I have lately written[357] – I have had some difficulties at the onset which imperc[ep]tibly melt away as I encounter them – and I daily earn more money with less trouble. You would love M^r. Johnson, if you knew how *very* friendly he has been to the *princess*.[358] In both my books you will find some trifling errors of the press, which you *may* correct; but those two material ones you will not forget. Everina has had some things to tease her since she left England besides ill health so that she has neglected every body, on this side the water, except myself; but now she is grown more tranquil, I am *sure* she will write to you. Eliza I am laboring to remove from H.[359] I have determined on one thing, *never* to have my Sisters to live with me, my solitary manner of living would not suit them, nor *could* I pursue my studies if forced to conform. I have taken more exercise lately and *snuffed* the fragrant gale of spring; and am

Robinson in 1804 after a visit to Salzmann's seminary at Schnepfenthal: Salzmann paid much attention to 'the gymnastical part of education', disliked too much discipline, never struck the boys, and let them wander off, climb trees, skate, swim and jump over hedges. Crabb Robinson saw that the pupils 'were healthy, happy, and courageous' and that they had received 'liberty' without developing 'licentiousness', but he feared Salzmann neglected 'solid learning' and he judged his institution was not without 'affectation' and that it even showed signs of 'quackery'.

356. Wollstonecraft was too sanguine about her earning power; consequently she overspent on her siblings. Johnson reported of her years in London, 'She could not during this time I think expend less than £200 upon her brothers & sisters' (Johnson to Godwin, Abinger MSS, Dep.b.210/3).

357. In May Johnson and Thomas Christie (1761–1796) had begun a radical magazine review, the *Analytical Review*, consisting of unsigned book reviews with copious quotations. Wollstonecraft began her reviewing career with women's fiction.

358. See note 110.

359. Market Harborough.

then *excellently* well, entre nous, have you lost your theatrical *manie* – why do you not write all about yourself?

I will write to Bess, very soon again, that is when I can breathe, and entreat her to write to me. As I am almost alone in a crowd I have not any news to send you. Give my love to our mother, and remember me to Roe, as to sending a remembrance to Bess it would be formal, so farewell, and believe me to be your sincere friend

Mary Wollstonecraft

I anticipate the comfort I shall receive from Bess's society – tell me when they expect to visit our shore? I believe I mentioned to you that your just and serious reflections gave me pleasure – go on in the same track improve your mind, and practice virtue, and you will every day gain more dominion over your passions, according to an old proverb, resist the *Devil* and he will fly from you[360] – our passions are a *legion*

76. *To George Blood*

[London] May 26th or 27th [1788]

My dear George, as I do not now know how to direct to Bess, I of course write to you; your letter, which I received this afternoon made me write in such haste – *you can* imagine the interest I take in whatever concerns that truly respectable tender hearted girl – I am sure, I feel most for her disappointment – but it is a severe blow to myself – for I had anticipated comforts, and encouraged hopes I know not how to dismiss. I thought I had answered at least one of your letters, but I have been so hurried, that I might easily have forgot it, as no disagreeable circumstance reminded me that a letter was necessary. Do write as soon as you receive the books, and be more particular in your account of Bess, I cannot help thinking Mr H.[361] has been very ungrateful – he knows not how to value a treasure. I cannot write about indifferent subjects or connect what I do say – You may soon look for an epistle

360. James 4:7: 'Be subject therefore to God, but resist the devil, and he will fly from you.'
361. Probably Betty Delane's brother-in-law, Robert Home.

from Everina as she is now more comfortably – and my dear friend never suspect my friendship because I do not repeat continually my assurances of regard. I am with respect to circumstances comfortable – but this *event* does *not* make amends for my former cares – and deep rooted sorrows – I dread – I sicken at the thought, the bare thought, of encountering Skeys – the smiles of fortune I should have hailed – *when* – but *now* they only shut out care – and do not introduce pleasure – and many solitary hours are spent brooding over past tumultuous scenes of woe – thinking of that dear friend – whom I shall love while memory holds its seat[362] – I am weaker tonight than usual; the disappointment with respect to Bess – and the name of Skeys, has conjured up many sorrows – adieu – love your sincere friend Mary.

Have you delivered – or rather has my letter to M: K.[363] been called for? – And where are my books? I have received another letter from that dear girl – I scarcely knew how much I loved her till I was torn from her – so do my comforts drop away. —

Give my love to our mother –
Farewel —

77. To Joseph Johnson

[London, c. July 1788][364]

I send you *all* the books I had to review except Dr. J——'s Sermons, which I have begun. If you wish me to look over any more trash this month – you must send it directly. I have been so low-spirited since I saw you – I was quite glad, last night, to feel myself affected by some passages in Dr. J——'s sermon on the death of his wife[365] – I seemed

---

362. *Hamlet*, I, v, 96f.: 'Ay, thou poor ghost, while memory holds a seat / In this distracted globe. Remember thee!' Wollstonecraft was still lamenting Fanny Blood.
363. Margaret King.
364. Wollstonecraft's review of Samuel Johnson's *Sermons* appeared in the *AR* for August 1788.
365. *A Sermon Written by the late Samuel Johnson, LL.D., for the Funeral of His Wife* had been composed in 1752 but published only after his death in 1784. Wollstonecraft had written, 'We read this sermon deliberately, and paused at some passages to reflect, with a kind of gloomy satisfaction, that the heart which dictated those pathetic effusions

(suddenly) to *find* my *soul* again – It has been for some time I cannot tell where. Send me the Speaker[366] – and *Mary*, I want one – and I shall soon want some paper – you may as well send it at the same time – for I am trying to brace my nerves that I may be industrious. – I am afraid reason is not a good bracer – for I have been reasoning a long time with my untoward spirits – and yet my hand trembles. – I could finish a period very *prettily* now, by saying that it ought to be steady when I add that I am yours sincerely,

Mary.

If you do not like the manner in which I reviewed Dr. J——'s s—— on his wife, be it known unto you – I *will* not do it any other way – I felt some pleasure in paying a just tribute of respect to the memory of a man – who, spite of his faults, I have an affection for – I say *have*, for I believe he is somewhere – *where* my soul has been gadding perhaps; – but *you* do not live on conjectures.

78. To Joseph Johnson

[London, ?late 1788 – early 1789]

As I am become a reviewer, I think it right, in the way of business, to consider the subject. You have alarmed the editor of the Critical, as the advertisement prefixed to the Appendix plainly shows.[367] The

---

of real anguish now ceased to throb, and that the mind we had often received instruction from, was no longer disquieted by vain fears.' She was so moved that she abrogated judgement, 'After the emotions these reflections raised we *cannot* criticise; trifling remarks appear impertinent, when we tread as it were, on a grave recently closed, before the clods have formed one common mass.'

366. *The Speaker; or, Miscellaneous Pieces*, a popular anthology by Dr William Enfield (1741–1797), rector of the Warrington Dissenting Academy; published by Johnson, it aimed to prepare boys for careers of useful public speaking. Wollstonecraft's *The Female Reader; or Miscellaneous Pieces in Prose and Verse . . . for the Improvement of Young Women* (London, 1789) adapted Enfield's form for girls in private life and added devotional pieces.

367. The *Advertisement* to volume 65 of the *Critical Review* (January–June 1788) seems to be a reply to the first edition of the *AR* published in May 1788, which included a manifesto-like address 'TO THE PUBLIC'. This attacked journals for reviewing too

Critical appears to me to be a timid, mean production, and its success is a reflection on the taste and judgment of the public; but, as a body, who ever gave it credit for much? The voice of the people is only the voice of truth, when some man of abilities has had time to get fast hold of the GREAT NOSE of the monster. Of course, local fame is generally a clamour, and dies away. The Appendix to the Monthly afforded me more amusement, though every article almost wants energy and a *cant* of virtue and liberality is strewed over it; always tame, and eager to pay court to established fame. The account of Necker is one unvaried tone of admiration.[368] Surely men were born only to provide for the sustenance of the body by enfeebling the mind!

Mary.

79. To Joseph Johnson

[London, ?late 1788 – early 1789][369]

My dear sir, I send you a chapter which I am pleased with, now I see it in one point of view – and, as I have made free with the author, I hope you will not have often to say – what does this mean?

---

many 'trifling' books and insufficiently noting 'foreign Literature' and for delaying reviews. The *Critical* defended itself against these general charges, pointing out that, in particular, English scientific books were more numerous than Continental and should have priority. Johnson had circulated his plan for a new journal a few months before his first publication.

368. The Appendix to volume 78 (January–June 1788) of the *Monthly Review* contained an eight-page article with the title *De l'importance des opinions religeuses*. It gave unqualified praise for both book and author, 'a virtuous man' whose 'destiny' it was to 'arrive at eminence in every line that he has pursued'. Wollstonecraft's ironic remark about 'enfeebling the mind' probably refers to the passage in the review devaluing rational philosophy: '[Necker] points out with precision the various kinds of happiness of which mankind are deprived by that dismal philosophy, which derives *intelligence, reason, mind*, and all the sublime harmony of nature, from (those words without a meaning) a fortuitous combination of mechanical principles.'

369. Wardle dated this letter to mid 1788 because of its connection with Letter 72 also mentioning her account, and which he dated to mid 1788, since he assumed Wollstonecraft would still be repaying debts relating to her move to London. The dating also depends on 'the author' with whom she has made free. As Durant pointed out in *Supp.*, p. 181, this could refer to Edmund Burke, whom she answered in *A*

You forgot you were to make out my account – I am, of course, over head and ears in debt; but I have not that kind of pride, which makes some dislike to be obliged to those they respect. – On the contrary, when I involuntarily lament that I have not a father or brother, I thankfully recollect that I have received unexpected kindness from you and a few others. – So reason allows, what nature impels me to – for I cannot live without loving my fellow-creatures – nor can I love them, without discovering some virtue.

Mary.

80. To Joseph Johnson

[London] Monday morning [?early 1789][370]

I really want a German grammar, as I intend to attempt to learn that language – and I will tell you the reason why. – While I live, I am persuaded, I must exert my understanding to procure an independence, and render myself useful. To make the task easier, I ought to store my mind with knowledge – The seed-time is passing away. I see the necessity of labouring now – and of that necessity I do not complain; on the contrary, I am thankful that I have more than common incentives to pursue knowledge, and draw my pleasures from the employments that are within my reach. You perceive this is not a gloomy day – I feel at this moment particularly grateful to you – without your humane and *delicate* assistance, how many obstacles should I not have had to encounter – too often should I have been out of patience with my

---

Vindication of the Rights of Men in 1790, but it is perhaps more applicable to an author she was translating. The Necker translation is the likeliest candidate since Wollstonecraft made free with Salzmann throughout and the book was addressed to children. Alternatively the phrase could refer to an abridgement of a French version of Johann Caspar Lavater's *Physiognomische Fragmente* (1775–8) which she made but did not publish, probably because Thomas Holcroft's complete edition, *Essays on Physiognomy Written in German by J. C. Lavater*, appeared in 1789.

370. Wardle dated this letter to late 1789 or early 1790 because he assumed Wollstonecraft wanted the German grammar to help her work with the translation of Salzmann's *Moralisches Elementarbuch*. I am assuming that she would want to 'attempt to learn the language' some time before she began translating.

fellow-creatures, whom I wish to love! – Allow me to love you, my dear sir, and call friend a being I respect. – Adieu!

Mary W.

81. To George Blood

London, February 28th [1789]

Dear George,

I am sorry you were made uneasy by M[r]. Arbuckle's[371] mistake – I never suspected you of negligence therefore was the more surprised; yet I think you might contrive to write oftener to me, whole months roll away before you answer my letters. I am really vexed to find M[r] Noble[372] takes advantage of your desire to please, and forces you to exert yourself beyond your strength. I have not your last letter by me but I recollect it left a painful impression on my mind. – *Why* did you entangle yourself again in M[r]. Home's affairs?[373] I thought you had paid for your experience – how could you be so inconsiderate! I shall anxiously expect to hear from you in answer to this and do not forget to tell me the true state of your health and circumstances. Did you ever receive a letter from Everina? She enclosed one for you in a packet to me, and I gave it to Skeys, when I supposed he was to set off in a few days for Dublin, after his route was changed I forgot the letter, so I suppose it has never found its way to you. She is still in France –

[Here nine lines have been crossed out.]

Tell Bess Delane I will not allow her to find fault with the language I am learning in which I am told the sweetest verses are written, and the

371. Possibly a common friend of Wollstonecraft and George Blood, through whom the latter sent his letter since Arbuckle appears to have been about to leave Dublin for England.
372. See note 149.
373. Betty Delane's brother-in-law, the painter Robert Home, had just moved from Dublin to London to seek more employment – probably without repaying what he owed George Blood.

people have still that simplicity of manners, I dote fondly on[374] – What an association of idea! – talking of indolence – I instantly reverted to my present labours – Blessed be that Power who gave me an active mind! if it does not smooth it enables me to jump over the rough places in life. I had had a number of draw-backs on my spirits and purse; but I still I cry avaunt despair – and I push forward. I will soon send you some books – and mean time let us talk of business. I find Caroline is very well and so industrious she is mentioned as a pattern by the mistress of the house. You must recollect that it is now above a twelvemonth since your father remitted me ten pounds – if he had any sense of honour he would not wait to be reminded, but I must beg you to get it, and take it to M[rs] Fitz-Gerald. For to tell you [a] secret, I borrowed ten pounds, I mean Guineas, of her, to lend Bess D. it was swallowed in the quicksand, but I do not forget it – and wish to get it out of my mind. Do not tell your father, for his notion of justice are so lax, he would call honesty romance. You shall soon see what I have been doing – so I need not dwell on that subject. I have not visited M[rs]. H.[375] very lately – she seems very near her time, and he is apparently attentive – I cannot warm to him – I see the snake in the grass – Give my love to our mother – and give Bess a still kinder assurance of my affection I shall write to her when I have seen susan, and believe me to be your sincere and affec[te]

Friend
M.W.

Let me entreat you, if you value my friendship, not to be so long in future without writing to me.

Tell M[rs] Fitz-Gerald that I am well, and enjoy more worldly comfort than ever I did – you may add, that I should have written to her if she had asked me, as it would really give me pleasure to hear some times of her welfare – enquire about my Margaret &c

374. Presumably the German language mentioned in Letter 80.
375. Susanna Home, Robert Home's wife and eldest sister of Betty Delane.

82. *To George Blood*

[London] April 16th [1789]

Dear George,

I know you will be sorry to hear that I am envoled in numberless difficulties – but Heaven grant me patience – and I will labour to overcome them all – Before you receive this, or very soon after, you will see Charles[376] – he will tell you some of my vexations – those *very* severe ones he has brought on me I suppose he will throw into the shade; but I will not prejudice you against him though he has wound a heart that was full of anxiety on his account – and disappointed hopes, which my benevolence makes me regret, more than reason can justify. Let me now request you to have an eye on his conduct, and if you can get him into any employment you will relieve me from a heavy weight of care. *Pray* write soon – I am so agitated now, and so unwell, I cannot write – I shall expect from you faithful account of him – I would fain have made him a virtuous character and have improved his understanding at the same time – had I succeed I should have been amply reward – but he has disappointed me – disappointed me, when various cares pressed sorely on me – when I was searching for a little remnant of comfort. My hand trembles – I will write again as soon as I can calm my mind – I beg you if you have any love for me – try to make him exert himself – try to fix him in a situation or heaven knows into what vices he may sink! You may tell him that I feel more sorrow than resentment – say that I forgive him – yet think he must be devoid of all feeling if he can forgive himself —

Yours affectionately
Mary Wollstonecraft

I know he will plunge into pleasure while he has a farthing left – for God endeavour to save him from ruin by employing him!

---

376. Charles Wollstonecraft had been dismissed by his new attorney, presumably for squandering or even pilfering his employer's money, and he seems to have become a heavy drinker. He had recently left for Ireland.

83. To George Blood

London, September 15th [1789]

I cannot help saying, my still dear George, that I think you very unkind in not contriving to write to me, you know how anxious I am to hear a just and particular account of Charles, to be informed what company he keeps and in what manner he spends his time &c, and you will not afford me that satisfaction.

I am afraid [   ]; for if a spark of gratitude or affection remained in his heart he would not [reason] in his present thoughtless[13] style, and neglect a friend who would fain have been a mother to him; but I will not repine, the ways of Heaven are often dark; yet ever just. I suppose you have heard of – and even suffered from Home's hasty departure; why do you not write circumstantially, you know – you must know, the interest I take in your welfare, and that your late embarrassments made me very uneasy; yet you will not tell me how you have extricated yourself. I have not answered Bess Delane's last letter, and I shall wait 'till I hear again from Susan;[377] perhaps, when we meet in Wales,[378] you may be able to steal a week or two from business and sail over the channel to shake hands with an old friend – need I tell you that it would give me pleasure.

The week before last I heard, that the man, whom I sent you an order on, had paid the money   I was disappointed at not receiving the information from you, because I wish when I transact any business for M[r]. Johnson to observe a certain degree of punctuality. Charles often vexed me by disappointing me, the few times, 'spite of painful experience, I ventured to trust to him; however I am convinced it is vain to attempt to teach some people to be punctual; but as I thought that you were scrupulously so your silence alarms me. Pray write immediately and borrow one half hour from sleep to tell me where you are, and what you intend to do. I hope your father is not to give up his place, I never could

377. Presumably Susanna Home: see note 375.
378. Wollstonecraft appears to have been planning a visit to Wales, perhaps to see her father in Laugharne.

understand your future plan, the account I have received has been such a lame one.[379] – If he is to live in sensual idleness, I totally disapprove of your change of situation, and think your blind obedience weakness; but I forbear to censure till I know on what ground to rest, yet being so well acquainted, as I am, with the principal defect in your temper, I cannot banish all apprehension; I dread lest that artful selfish man should take advantage of it and make you his slave while he lives.

I am so fatigued with poring over a German book,[380] I scarcely can collect my thoughts or even spell English words, of course, you must not expect any chat, indeed I have nothing new to talk about, my Sisters are well, I take it for granted that they write to you. Remember me to your Mother, Bess D. &c

And believe me your sincere,
though neglected Friend
Mary Wollstonecraft

When did M[r]. Arbuckle leave Dublin?

84. To George Blood

[London] November 19th [1789]

I received your letter and the enclosed bill the 15th, and I must own the letter surprised me – I cannot comprehend what you intended to say to account for (an excuse was out of the question), your strange unfriendly conduct – nor can I conceive that my letters, or silence, could affect you, in the manner you mention, after your unaccountable neglect of a friend who placed the most unreserved confidence in your affection and goodness of heart – all this appears inexplicable – I *cannot* understand it – I am not easily offended with those I love – I force myself to have patience, but if once my good opinion, the foundation of my esteem, is shaken – I cannot in a moment forget a calm conclusion of reason, and allow vague expressions of sorrow to work

---

379. George Blood was apparently intending to move back in with his parents and even to work with his father in some capacity.

380. Probably Salzmann's *Moralisches Elementarbuch*, which Wollstonecraft was translating and which took many months to appear in instalments.

on me like a charm. – talking of forgiveness is childish – and while your silence appears to me in the light it now does, it would be vain for me to attempt to think of you as I formerly did. – I am not unreasonable you might have written to me a few lines to account for your conduct – you were not shut up in the Bastile – and as, for the pretext of business, I shall not admit it, an hour might have been stolen from sleep without injuring your health – in short, you have obliged me to alter my opinion of you – recollect that it is above three months since you ought to have written to me, if I had only been a respectable acquaintance. Had you in a frank manly manner sent me a true account of your situation – Heaven knows, I would have put myself to any inconvenience rather than have added to your vexations – Betty D. desired me to suspend my judgment I could not suspend it when facts starred me full in the face. If I were to write to a volume, I should only repeat the same things – I cannot use my India rubber to obliterate the traces of sorrow and disappointed affection your behaviour has left on my memory. I sincerely wish you happy, and shall be glad to hear that you have extricated yourself out of your pecuniar difficulties, but I do not think it probable that I shall ever be able to respect and trust you as I habitually did, some month ago – I loved you, because I gave you credit for more substantial virtues then I now think you possess – of course, I am obliged to recollect that I am writing to Fanny's brother – and this reflected affection will prevent my coldly subscribing myself a well wisher, in the style humanity dictates – for while I remember the friend of my youth I shall ever be particularly interested about you – and therefore shall add that I am

yours affectionately
Mary Wollstonecraft

The money you sent for Caroline was quite sufficient but, if you had not forgotten my former letters, you would have paid it to M^{rs}. Fitz-Gerald, instead of sending it to me. I wrote to you repeatedly about Charles, requesting you to

[Here one line has been defaced.]

for it; but though you must suppose that I am still anxious to hear how he goes on – *you have not time* to satisfy me.

85. To Joseph Johnson

[London, ?1790][381]

You made me very low-spirited last night, by your manner of talking. – You are my only friend – the only person I am *intimate* with. – I never had a father, or a brother – you have been both to me, ever since I knew you – yet I have sometimes been very petulant. – I have been thinking of those instances of ill-humour and quickness, and they appeared like crimes.

Yours sincerely
Mary.

86. To George Blood

London, March 10th [1790]

I am a little surprised and hurt at your silence George – why have you not answered my two last letters? I really wish to have an account of your future prospects from yourself – are you to be in the office with your father? or are you to be in partnership with Skeys?[382] you see how I conjecture – pray send me a clue! It is so long since you have written to me, that I *cannot* talk of myself – when you ask me any questions I will answer them – till then I shall only assure you that I am your sincere Friend

Mary Wollstonecraft

I have sent you another bill to receive for M[r]. Johnson, if M[r] Skeys is still in Dublin he will take charge of it – I mean of the money – I send

---

381. Wardle places this letter after Letter 79 because of the repetition of the phrase about not having a father or brother. This however might argue a gap between the two letters rather than proximity.
382. George Blood wrote in his memoir that he was employed by Brabazon Noble from 1786 to 1794, but from this letter he appears to have worked for a short time in 1790 for his brother-in-law Hugh Skeys. See *CL*, p. 187n.

it to you that you may not think that I keep up a foolish kind of resentment on account of your first want of punctuality.

87. To Joshua Cristall

London, March 19th [?1790][383]

I was a little angry with you for sending a copy of M[r] Bloods letter to Charles; but I will lett my resentment subside for the present and only write about your own affairs. I think you ingenious — yet I am afraid that you are too sanguine in your expectation of succeeding as an artist. — Besides abilities a happy concurrence of circumstances is necessary to enable a painter to earn a *livelihood* — and many years of anxiety and painful industry must be passed before a man of superior talents can look with any certainty for to morrows subsistence, you admired M[r] Homes pictures, yet he was obliged to leave the kingdom, because he could not get employment — and M[r] F. with his original genius and uncommon diligence had a very precarious support until the Shakespearian plans commenced[384] — in short I could mention

383. The letter to Joshua Cristall, Anne's brother, gives no year. Durant in *Supp.*, p. 187, suggested 1789; I have followed *CL* in assuming 1790 after Charles Wollstonecraft's dismissal by the London attorney. John Tisdall in his biography *Joshua Cristall 1768–1847. In Search of Arcadia* (Lapridge Publications, 1996), p. 28, also suggests that this and Letter 98 were written in 1790 when Cristall was twenty-two and recently employed at Thomas Turner's porcelain factory at Caughley, near Ironbridge, Shropshire (introducer of the Blue Willow and Brosely Blue Dragon patterns to British consumers). John Lewis Roget, *A History of the 'Old Water-colour Society'* (London, 1891), gives no exact date for this employment but presumably it followed the death of Mr Ewson, Aldgate, his former employer, 'who did a good business in china and glass' (I, 181). The *DNB* entry for Anne Batten Cristall states that their father suffered a paralytic stroke in the early 1790s, which indicates a date for the two letters before then, since Wollstonecraft refers to Cristall senior without commenting on his state.

384. Henry Fuseli (1741–1825), a Swiss-born painter, translator and writer who settled in London in the late 1770s. His nightmarish paintings reflected his interest in the supernatural and extremes of human passions. In social circles he was equally admired and feared for his wit and intense moods, but the poet William Blake praised him as 'The only man that e'er I knew / Who did not make me almost spew'. Fuseli was one of Johnson's oldest friends and a frequenter of his dinners. In 1786 he had married a former model, Sophia Rawlins, and, after years of struggling, he at last achieved some

manny other instances, but it appears unnecessary — for you will not put yourself on a par with Mr Home I am sure — however my arguments are not brought forward to discourage you f[ro]m following in some degree your bent — I only wish to caution you against the headstrong ardour of youth. Pursue your studies, practice as much as you can, but do not think of depending on painting for a subsistence before you know the first rudiments of the art — I know that you earnestly wi[s]h to be the friend and protector of your amiable sister and hope no inconsiderate act or thoughtless mode of conduct will add to her cares — for her comfort very much depends on you. I find M^r. Turner intends to send you to travel for him very soon, this will in every respect be a great advantage to you, you will see the country, form connexions and have more leisure to improve.[385] Pray let me hear from you soon, and tell me what you intend to do and I will candidly give you my opinion and as I have had more experience than you it may be useful to you. I now write in a hurry — because the post is going out, but I wish I could forcibly represent to you the necessity of following your inclinations with caution — A manly character is of the greatest importance in any line — and if you determine to leave M^r. Turner when your time expires I hope you will be careful not to quarrel with him — Charles is now at Cork eating the bread of idleness — and living on the kindness of relations who do not respect him.[386] His example ought to impress you — it is a great disadvantage to a young man to be thought unsettled. How do you come on with your Music & drawing. — You scarcely know what industry is required to arrive at a degre[e] of perfection in the fine arts and how dreadful it is

fame in 1788 with his exhibition of Shakespeare illustrations for Alderman Boydell's *Shakespeare Gallery*. Since she had arrived in London Wollstonecraft had become increasingly fascinated by Fuseli. See note 229 for Home.

385. Cristall was so eager to be an artist that, although employed as a travelling salesman, he spent time sketching sights: 'the late Dr Percy in his MS Catalogue, now at the BM, states that he saw in 1881, at Sir John St Aubyn's, at Mount's Bay, Cornwall, some large drawings of that county signed 'J. Cristall', with a date about 1790 or somewhat later, "very carefully done and of a prevailing blue colour"' (Roget, *A History*, 1, 189). Roget states that Cristall 'entered on his favourite occupation' only after the death of his father, who had opposed his plans to become a painter (1, 187).

386. Possibly the people to whom Johnson had sent books for Wollstonecraft (Letter 51).

to plunge into the world without friends or acknow[led]ged abilities. I have lately made some enquiries — and I think that it would be next to madness for you to launch out before you made any preparatory steps. — London is not now paved with gold and a false step in the beginning of life frequently throws a gloomy cloud over the fairest hopes — If your determine to endeavour to become a painter — declare your intentions to your Master father and friends in a manly manner, when you have courage to do so, and act with firmness instead of rashness I shall begin to think that you have some chance to succeed — a w[eak] man may be rash — but only a strong understanding may enable a youth to act with firmness — should I perceive such strength of mind in you I shall suppose that you follow the impulse of nature and are not lead away by unprincipled wishes — wild disires which nature [makes] you selfishly forgot your sisters peace of mind — and your own future advantage. virtue is self-denial — if you cannot bear some present inconvenience you are a common man and will never arise to any degree of eminence in any thing you undertake. I am yours M W

88. To Joseph Johnson

[London] Friday morning [?early 1790][387]

I am sick with vexation – and wish I could knock my foolish head against the wall, that bodily pain might make me feel less anguish from self-reproach! To say the truth, I was never more displeased with

---

387. Wardle dates this to c. mid summer 1790 owing to the asterisks and reference to her sister. Godwin uses asterisks to hide a name and Wardle speculates that they correspond to letters since he routinely substituted five asterisks for Imlay's name and four for Mary's – as opposed to the dash used for others. So the six asterisks here probably indicate Fuseli. There is, however, no need to assume a date when Fuseli had become an obsessive object for Wollstonecraft; he was already known to her in 1788 and had helped arrange her sister's trip to Paris. The sister referred to here is probably Eliza Bishop who, with Wollstonecraft's financial help, had moved from her teaching position in Market Harborough to Mrs Bregantz's Boarding School in Putney, where she was a parlour boarder (a lady paying for her own keep while lodging in a school and perhaps learning some skills and helping with teaching). When she returned from Paris at the end of the year Everina would join Eliza in Putney.

myself, and I will tell you the cause. – You may recollect that I did not mention to you the circumstance of —— having a fortune left to him; nor did a hint of it drop from me when I conversed with my sister; because I knew he had a sufficient motive for concealing it. Last Sunday, when his character was aspersed, as I thought, unjustly, in the heat of vindication I informed ****** that he was now independent; but, at the same time, desired him not to repeat my information to B——; yet, last Tuesday, he told him all – and the boy at B——'s gave Mrs. —— an account of it. As Mr. —— knew he had only made a confident of me (I blush to think of it!) he guessed the channel of intelligence, and this morning came (not to reproach me, I wish he had!) but to point out the injury I have done him. – Let what will be the consequence, I will reimburse him, if I deny myself the necessaries of life – and even then my folly will sting me. – Perhaps you can scarcely conceive the misery I at this moment endure – that I, whose power of doing good is so limited, should do harm, galls my very soul. ****** may laugh at these qualms – but, supposing Mr. —— to be unworthy, I am not the less to blame. Surely it is hell to despise one's self! – I did not want this additional vexation – at this time I have many that hang heavily on my spirits. I shall not call on you this month – nor stir out. – My stomach has been so suddenly and violently affected, I am unable to lean over the desk.

Mary Wollstonecraft.

89. To Eliza Bishop

[London] Thursday noon [c. mid 1790]

Dear Bess

I should have written to you before; but I waited 'till I could send some money and have not been able. The painter *dunned* me every day – I was at last obliged to apply to Johnson – and when I had discharged his bill, and another little demand, I was pennyless – The man from Primrose Street never brought the rent[388] and I am afraid to

---

388. Influenced by her own distrust of her brother Edward Bland and her father's sense that he was being cheated out of the remittances from his properties in Primrose Street,

be importunate – however I must again apply to Johnson, yet I shall do it with great reluctance because I have done so little for him. Heaven grant me patience! I hope it is my body which thus weighs me down, but I know not what to do with myself, or how to shake off the fever which consumes me[389] – as I did not receive immediate benefit from bathing I left it off because it was so expensive – in short, I never was in the state, I am at present, for such a length of time – I really do every thing which reason suggests – and still have this dreadful complicated, lingering illness. Perhaps when the weather grows cooler I shall be better, it is not of illness I complain I could bear it, but I am very unhappy at being thus idle. I called on the Homes last week – their affairs were still unsettled – yet I believe she is determined to return to Ireland – for I hinted to her that it would be the ruin of Mrs B.[390] if she was kept long out of her money – he intends to take the greater part of what he gets with him. I have not heard from them since, of course suppose that they have given up all thoughts of Putney – I will however call again. – I am a little disappointed – because they spoke to Mrs B. nay, they seemed fixed – he is sly – without a certainty of the board being paid I coolly determined to prevent her coming – she is so foolish – Well so much for that bubble! The man who sent you the letter came to Johnson's for a direction and insisted on your having a son, the name is a common one and the mistake might easily have been made; but why they directed to you at Sr Paul's – I cannot guess, some trifling circumstance, I suppose, occasioned an incident, which puzzled you. My head is now very bad – and I scarcely know what I write. I shall send the money the moment I can get it, and the book Everina is to translate for me &c with the [   ] answer of the Homes, but I think you had better hint to Mrs B. your doubts – I am sorry they ever mentioned it. I have not heard from Ireland – and I have been teased

---

Wollstonecraft had persuaded Johnson to help her take over and handle her father's finances. Johnson reluctantly agreed: 'she had the care of her father's estate, which was attended with no little trouble to both of us,' he wrote (Johnson to Godwin, Abinger MSS, Dep.b.210/3).

389. Johnson later blamed this period of inactivity on Wollstonecraft's growing obsession with Fuseli, to whom she was writing copious letters.

390. Mrs Bregantz, Eliza Bishop's and Everina Wollstonecraft's headmistress; apparently the Homeses had considered taking lodgings with her also.

with dreams about Charles being in distress – and lossing his watch
&c – this was one effect of my slow fever – but it harassed me –

Yours affectionately

M. W.

How do you go on in the school &c —

90. To Joseph Johnson

[London, ?summer 1790][391]

I thought you *very* unkind, nay, very unfeeling, last night. My cares
and vexations – I will say what I allow myself to think – do me honour,
as they arise from my disinterestedness and *unbending* principles; nor
can that mode of conduct be a reflection on my understanding, which
enables me to bear misery, rather than selfishly live for myself alone. I
am not the only character deserving of respect, that has had to struggle
with various sorrows – while inferior minds have enjoyed local fame
and present comfort. – Dr. Johnson's cares almost drove him mad –
but, I suppose, you would quietly have told him, he was a fool for not
being calm, and that wise men striving against the stream, can yet

---

391. 'This [letter] alludes to a foolish proposal of marriage for mercenary considerations, which the gentleman here mentioned thought proper to recommend to her.
The two letters which immediately follow, are addressed to the gentleman himself'
(Godwin's note). Wardle placed this and the next two undated letters in 1795 assuming
that Wollstonecraft's 'almost hysterical reaction' suggested that the proposal was
intended to cover up the Imlay affair and the illegitimate child. William St Clair placed
the incident and therefore the letters even later, in 1797 when Wollstonecraft found
herself pregnant again by Godwin and before he offered marriage: *The Godwins and
the Shelleys* (London, 1989), p. 170. He speculated that the 'source of perfection' might
have been Godwin. However it seems more likely to refer to God, a felt presence in
the period before Wollstonecraft went to France. If the proposal had belonged to the
Godwin period, it seems probable that it would have had more repercussions on the
relationship. Also, after Wollstonecraft returned from France, she was passing as
married; if the gentleman had been told by Johnson that she was not married, then she
might have been expected to berate Johnson for this failure of confidence. I have dated
the letters to summer 1790 when debts and family demands made Wollstonecraft feel
poor and before the success of *A Vindication of the Rights of Men*, which turned her
into a relatively famous author.

be in good humour. I have done with insensible human wisdom, – 'indifference cold in wisdom's guise,'[392] – and turn to the source of perfection – who perhaps never disregarded an almost broken heart, especially when a respect, a practical respect, for virtue, sharpened the wounds of adversity. I am ill – I stayed in bed this morning till eleven o'clock, only thinking of getting money to extricate myself out of some of my difficulties – The struggle is now over. I will condescend to try to obtain some in a disagreeable way.

Mr. —— called on me just now – pray did you know his motive for calling? – I think him impertinently officious. – He had left the house before it occurred to me in the strong light it does now, or I should have told him so – My poverty makes me proud – I will not be insulted by a superficial puppy. – His intimacy with Miss —— gave him a privilege, which he should not have assumed with me – a proposal might be made to his cousin, a milliner's girl, which should not have been mentioned to me. Pray tell him that I am offended – and do not wish to see him again! – When I meet him at your house, I shall leave the room, since I cannot pull him by the nose. I can force my spirit to leave my body – but it shall never bend to support that body – God of heaven, save thy child from this living death! – I scarcely know what I write. My hand trembles – I am very sick – sick at heart. –

Mary.

91. To ——[393]

[London] Tuesday evening [?summer 1790]

Sir,

When you left me this morning, and I reflected a moment – your *officious* message, which at first appeared to me a joke – looked so

---

392. Jonathan Swift, *Verses on the Death of Dr Swift* (1739), 211: 'Indiff'rence clad in wisdom's guise.'

393. This and the following letter are clearly addressed to the man who acted as go-between for the marriage proposal. Presumably Wollstonecraft sent copies to Johnson who kept them with the letters addressed to him and they were printed by Godwin as 'Letters to Mr Johnson' XII and XIII.

very like an insult – I cannot forget it – To prevent then the necessity of forcing a smile – when I chance to meet you – I take the earliest opportunity of informing you of my real sentiments.

Mary Wollstonecraft.

92. To ——

[London] Wednesday, 3 o'clock [?summer 1790]

Sir,

It is inexpressibly disagreeable to me to be obliged to enter again on a subject, that has already raised a tumult of *indignant* emotions in my bosom, which I was labouring to suppress when I received your letter. I shall now *condescend* to answer your epistle; but let me first tell you, that, in my *unprotected* situation, I make a point of never forgiving a *deliberate insult* – and in that light I consider your late officious conduct. It is not according to my nature to mince matters – I will then tell you in plain terms, what I think. I have ever considered you in the light of a *civil* acquaintance – on the word friend I lay a peculiar emphasis – and, as a mere acquaintance, you were rude and *cruel*, to step forward to insult a woman, whose conduct and misfortunes demand respect. If my friend, Mr. Johnson, had made the proposal – I should have been severely hurt – have thought him unkind and unfeeling, but not *impertinent*. – The privilege of intimacy you had no claim to – and should have referred the man to myself – if you had not sufficient discernment to quash it at once. I am, sir, poor and destitute. – Yet I have a spirit that will never bend, or take indirect methods, to obtain the consequence I despise; nay, if to support life it was necessary to act contrary to my principles, the struggle would soon be over. I can bear any thing but my own contempt.

In a few words, what I call an insult, is the bare supposition that I could for a moment think of *prostituting* my person for a maintenance; for in that point of view does such a marriage appear to me, who consider right and wrong in the abstract, and never by words and local opinions shield myself from the reproaches of my own heart and understanding.

It is needless to say more – Only you must excuse me when I add, that I wish never to see, but as a perfect stranger, a person who could so grossly mistake my character. An apology is not necessary – if you were inclined to make one – nor any further expostulations. – I again repeat, I cannot overlook an affront; few indeed have sufficient delicacy to respect poverty, even where it gives lustre to a character – and I tell you sir, I am POOR – yet can live without your benevolent exertions.

Mary Wollstonecraft.

93. To Everina Wollstonecraft[394]

The Revd Mr Gabell's, Warminster, Wiltshire, Saturday morning
[August 21st, 1790][395]

My journey to Salisbury was *tolerably* pleasant where I met M^rs. Gabell and a younger brother of M^r. Gabell's, and if the stage had not been detained on the road by a trifling accident, which happened to the wheel, we might have reached Warminster the very day I left town: – as it was we breakfasted with the master of this house in very good time next morning. I did not find Ann the kind of woman that my imagination had sketched – She has it is true light full eyes with scarcely any eye-brows, a fair complexion and soft brown hair; yet she is rather a fine than a pretty woman – and has an expression of bluntness instead of the gentleness which I expected to see in her countenance. Her person is large and well proportioned – She made me think of a Doric pillar, for proportion without beauty – symmetry without grace, appears in her person, and activity and ease in her gestures. Indeed her activity is quite exemplary and she manages her large family[396] with a

394. Seeing Wollstonecraft's misery over Fuseli, Johnson had suggested a country break; she had gone to stay with the Revd Henry Gabell in Warminster, near Salisbury, where he was acting as master of the Warminster School. After Ireland he had visited France, where he was present at the storming of the Bastille; he returned to England and in January 1790 married Ann Gage, daughter of an Oxfordshire clergyman. The pair lived in the School House. Wollstonecraft was writing to Everina in Putney.
395. The dating of the letter follows the postmark, which reads 23 August; 21 August was a Saturday.
396. The pupils at the school.

degree of cleverness that surprises me, considering how little experience she has had; but her hearts and thoughts are at home. The town does not contain many desirable neighbours – and after the various employments of the day they find most pleasure in each others society – of which Milton has given a description, when he speaks of the first pair[397] – M[rs]. B.[398] may smile; but still I must tell her, that in this House she would find domestic felicity, and see caresses as pure as those her botanic friend[399] lavishes on his favourites – *Much of a muchness.*[400] – You can scarcely imagine *how much* happiness and innocent fondness constantly illumines the eyes of this good couple – so that I am never disgusted by the frequent *bodily* display of it – they seem inshort just to have sufficient refinement to make them happy without ever straying so far from common life as to wish for what life never affords – or only for a moment. The quietness of the scene and a view of their innocent pleasures have calmed my mind and gratified my heart more than you can conceive – yet I caught myself wishing this morning for a sight of my little room, and a ramble to St, Paul's-Church-yard. This wish was as involuntary as it was unreasonable – for I am perfectly mistress of my room and time and find Ann and Henry anxious to please me whenever I appear – to say the truth they try with the most unaffected good nature to make my situation agreeable. His conversation is superior to what one can generally meet with, and she has great rectitude of mind and common sense though the circle of her thoughts seldom extends beyond her family and never enters into the labyrinths of sentiment and taste. She sometimes makes me think of M[rs]. Brooks and sometimes of Mason – her voice is harsh and a blunt laugh often disconcerts me – in [other] words, she has tenderness

---

397. Adam and Eve express their happiness: '. . . let us ever praise him, and extoll / His bountie, following our delightful task / To prune these growing Plants, and tend these Flours, / Which were it toilsom, yet with thee were sweet', *Paradise Lost*, 4, 436f.
398. Eliza Bishop.
399. Erasmus Darwin, whose *Loves of the Plants*, Part 2 of *The Botanic Garden*, was published in 1789 by Johnson. It made poetry out of Linnaeus's classification of plants. Some found the foregrounding of sexuality shocking, but Wollstonecraft had no problem with this aspect.
400. Sir John Vanbrugh and Colley Cibber, *The Provoked Husband*, 1, 575f.: '*Manly.* I hope at least, you and your good woman agree still. / *John Moody.* Aye, aye, much of a muchness.'

without sensibility clearness of judgment without comprehension of thought. This country does not afford the prospects I am fondest of; but I have enjoyed many pleasant walks – and now my eyes rest on green fields, which please without given any colour to my thoughts. Can you understand my account of myself and the worthy family I am with? Give my love to M^{rs}. B. I shall write to her soon; but I thought that you were entitled to the first letter – let me hear from you and believe me yours affectionately

M W.

94. *To Everina Wollstonecraft*

[Warminster] Saturday night, September 4th [17]90

I this day received a letter from the Frenchman; how long it laid at my house before it was forwarded to me I cannot say, for it has no date – I will transcribe the part of his letter which I wish you to be immediately acquainted with. 'A nobleman's family in the country wants a governess for two young Ladies of 16 & 14 years old. She ought to be born in England, to understand French grammatically & needlework – is to be treated like a child of the house – and to receive 25 guineas a-year and some presents. After the education will be finished it might be found a useful connexion to the person chosen. If this should please Miss W. you will be so kind as to apply at the gentleman's, to whom I will enclose a direction, in the name of M^{r}. Satis. M^{r}. Willis at MM Scaife and Willis Man's-Mercers, Fleet Street – near Mr Butts and Downer.['] – I have not troubled myself to correct his English as the account is intelligible – Satis I know is a French master in many good families. If it was worth enquiring about – it is probably now too late – however, were I in your place I would call at the house in Fleet Street – it could do no harm – but you will judge for yourself you know as much of the matter as I do – If there should be any thing in it I would not have you be precipitate in engaging yourself – I shall expect to hear from you – If you come to Town, call at George Street, and see how the house stands – I think of returning in the course of a fortnight – Tell Eliza that my visit to Warminster has convinced me, that in the distribution of human happiness there is some *apparent* disproportion, that clashes with a few of my opinions, which she has no great respect for – but we'll talk of these matters when I open my budget. The weather has been very unfavourable lately & at home I cannot help, sometimes, feeling like an intruder – my die is cast! – I could not now resign intellectual pursuits for domestic comforts – and yet I think I could form an idea of more *elegant* felicity – where mind chastens sensation, and rational converse gave a little dignity to fondness – I can scarcely make my pen mark though I press with all my might and main. I am besides quite weary for I brushed the dew off the hill soon after the sun rose this morning – and conversing with my own fancy, if I may so express myself, I exhausted my spirits; and having my feet wet so long has given me a head ache, which I hope to leave on my pillow – I have been very industrious during the last week – that is some comfort! I have had a letter from M[rs]. S.[401] which you shall see when I return – as part of it is addressed to you two. – She gives too good a [r]easo[n] for her silence – I am afraid, by her account, poor M[rs]. Home is in the last stage of a consumption. This account gave me some pain; but did not surprise me.

Comparisons, the vulgar tell us, are odious – will you think me saucy when I say, that you and Eliza appear to me to *very* clever, and *most* agreeable women, when compared with the Goddess of this place. Now we are at a distance I long to see you both – though M[rs]. B. was on stilts when we parted.

yours affectionately
M. W.

I wish you would send me Cristall's[402] direction, to Black-Heath, I am afraid I have hurt her by my silence.

---

401. Hugh Skeys's second wife was the former Betty Delane. The marriage took place at St James, Dublin, on 1 July 1790. Later Skeys declared he had married two penniless women. Mrs Susanna Home was Mrs Skeys's sister.
402. Their friend Anne Cristall; see note 346.

95. To Everina Wollstonecraft

[Warminster] Friday, September 10th [17]90

Dear Everina,

I thank you for your caution respecting M[r]. Satis; but in the present instance it is unnecessary – I saw M[r]. Satis since he heard my name and I mentioned you to him. I had a sufficient reason for not chusing to mention my name to him before – and it was only necessary for me to hold my tongue – however I may approve of passive, I do not like active steps to keep a secret. It is needless after this preface to allow you to tell M[r] W.[14] that I know M[r] Satis. Thank Eliza for her consideration, I expected to have heard from her. I perfectly agree with you that the the Frenchman's would not be a very respectable recommendation – nor would it be the real one – for Satis is the man who interested himself – I shall call on him, when I come to Town – and make some enquiries concerning the family, at the same time I thank him. I could almost wish you not to take a decided step before I obtain some account of the family – which would not be difficult, when we once know its name – the salary appears to be low – and I do not like to see meanness on the face of an offer, and promises to veil it. I thought of returning to Town the later end of next week or the beginning of the following one; but, if you wish me to come sooner, lay aside all false delicacy – and to say the truth the sacrifice would not be very great – for I am grown a little weary too, and my heart and thoughts turn towards home. I write in a hurry that I may not miss the returning post – I want to caution you not to accept the offered situation, if any disagreeable conditions are annexed – for if you determine to exert yourself I am certain you have no reason to fear, but that an eligible one will occur before or after Christmas – and I rather wish you could be placed in a family that, at least, spent their winters in Town. I did intend to have mentioned your situation to the good folks here – but I have changed my mind – *happiness* is not a softener of the heart – and from them I should always expect little acts of kindness and grateful civilities – but never any great exertion, which might disturb, for a moment, the even tenor of their loves and lives. Whenever I read

Milton's description of paradise – the happiness, which he so poetically describes fills me with benevolent satisfaction – yet, I cannot help viewing them, I mean the first pair – as if they were my inferiors – inferiors because they could find happiness in a world like this[403] – A feeling of the same kind frequently intrudes on me here – Tell me, does it arise from mistaken pride or conscious dignity which whispering me that my soul is immortal & should have a nobler ambition leads me to cherish it?[404]

Yours affectionately M. W.

If you should come to Town again before my return – enquire whether any thing has been done to cure my chimney –

96. To Eliza Bishop

[London] Thursday night [?autumn 1790][405]

Dear Bess

Poor Cristall, as the enclosed notes will inform you, was greatly disappointed, I am really sorry she was not of the party, and could I

403. *Paradise Lost*, 4, 412f.: 'needs must the power / That made us, and for us this ample World / Be infinitely good, and of his good / As liberal and free as infinite, / That rais'd us from the dust and plac't us here / In all this happiness'.

404. Some of Wollstonecraft's new dissatisfaction with Gabell may have stemmed from political differences. She was about to write *A Vindication of the Rights of Men* while he may already have been holding views similar to those he would express on political rights in *A Discourse Delivered on the Fast-Day in February 1799, in the Church of St Lawrence, Winchester* (London, 1799): 'History will record, for the instruction of future ages, and the everlasting disgrace of the present, that Europe, at the close of the eighteenth century, in all the pride and presumption of superior wisdom, was betrayed into a philosophy, the wildest and maddest, to say nothing of its wickedness, that ever imposed on the credulity of the human understanding . . . The tacticks of the Rights of Man furnish them with stratagems adapted to every age, temper, or condition. To the indigent, they promise plunder; to the ambitious, power; to the envious, the fall of greatness: honour, to the traitor; to the assassin, if the blood spilled be royal, immortal glory; to the wicked in general, release from all moral obligation here, and beyond the grave, impunity and everlasting sleep . . .' (p. 15n.).

405. This undated letter must have been written between late 1788, when Eliza Bishop went to Putney, and early 1792, when the school was disbanded. *CL* placed it in autumn

afford it I would fix on another day – but I cannot, so I can only write a friendly letter to her – I do not like to give pain to such a tender affectionate heart. I am rather low spirited to night, I was harassed by the account you gave of Mrs Bregantz, when I reflected on it – and some other things contributed to sink me. I met Mr Curtis to-day when I returned from Ned's[406] school; he said he was glad to see me look *tolerably* well – for his brother, had informed him that I looked wretchedly ill – when my heart's vigour appears to be flown – and my reason is clouded, I grow fanciful, and imagine that I shall not live long – that I am wearing away – and so on. – I will not write any more in this strain, tell Everina I wish she would make a point of taking three doses of salts,[407] I am sure it is necessary and would relieve her eyes, and I rather think it would be useful to you, considering – that ugly spots sometimes appear on your fair face. Good Night – I am very cold – and have a painful sensation of *loneliness* which to-morrow's sun perhaps may dissipate –

yours
Mary W——

97. To Eliza Bishop

[London] Saturday [c. late 1790][408]

By this time, I suppose you have received the letter I wrote yesterday morning – yours, which I this moment received, explains the matter more fully – you treated me as I deserved – had you behaved with

1790 because Wollstonecraft's concern about Anne Cristall echoes that expressed in the postscript to Letter 94.
406. Probably a reference to her nephew Edward, son of her eldest brother Edward Bland. He would have been seven in 1790.
407. Epsom salts were used as a purgative. In his *Practice of Physic*, 1, 267, Cullen wrote, 'Besides blood-letting, purging, as a remedy suited to inflammation in general, has been considered as peculiarly adapted to inflammations in any of the parts of the head, and therefore to Ophthalmia', though he himself doubted the efficacy, remarking it 'does not prove useful in any degree in proportion to the evacuation excited'.
408. This undated letter must have been written during the latter part of 1790 when both Eliza and Everina were living at Mrs Bregantz's school.

more greatness of mind, especially as Ann[409] informed you, before my return, that I had been vexed the foregoing night, I should have admired you – now I only beg your pardon. Had you been alone, I am certain you would not have let me go out of the house, after I had informed you that I was harassed by a fear compared to which your distress was trivial. On Wednesday evening I received Mr Briggs packet when I was sitting tranquilly at work – I was disconcerted and hastened to St Pauls to ask poor J's advice, by some accident or other, I have not lately had any private conversation with him – After supper he seriously told me that some alarming symptoms in his head and arm, made him apprehend the approach of a paralytic stroke – a few years ago he had a very alarming fit – and he added, with composure, that he was settling his affairs that they might not be left in confusion. I am not ashamed to own that this conversation threw me into a fever & one of my agitated nights ensued – I stayed late in bed, and in the morning was so languid I was glad of the excuse of getting the money to pay Briggs, that I might not sit alone – Business after dinner called J. away – and I still sat alone brooding over my vexations – and thinking of the arguments I should use to persuade him to go to Dr F.[410] the next day – I wished for supper time to have an opportunity to speak to him – I therefore was vexed at being called away – but I did not think of this when I hastily left J. I supposed something dreadful had happened – however as I came along I recollected that the only anguish I had ever seen Everina in had been on account of money or bodily fatigue – I knew that the strongest expressions had before been culled on occasions which appeared to me trivial – my mind was off its poize I grew unreasonable and out of humour and behaved in a manner to you I blush to recollect. I own you had not that day entered my head nor was this *very* extraordinary – Before I came to Putney I had been

---

409. Wollstonecraft had taken into her house a seven-year-old girl, identified by Godwin as the niece of Hugh Skeys's second wife, Betty Delane (*Memoirs*, p. 71). However, an American friend of Wollstonecraft in London, Mrs Mark Leavenworth, declared the child to be 'an orphan Girl, which the dying mother of the Child an East Indian gave her to bring up, and which she is educating she says as a child of nature, aet.11', *The Literary Diary of Ezra Stiles* (New York, 1901), 3, 502f.

410. Dr George Fordyce, FRS (1736–1802), the Scottish lecturer-physician from St Thomas Hospital, author of medical texts, and a close friend of Johnson.

very uneasy; but after Miss B. left Town, I gave way to the hope, that respecting you I should have a little peace – and for *some* years I have not had this satisfactory feeling – indeed this hope had had a good effect on my mind – I mentioned in one of my letters that I was in better health and till Wednesday evening my employments engrossed my attention, I dismissed you from my thoughts, but not before I had promised myself more comfort than usual from the holiday – because I took it for granted that James[411] would be with us, and I own he rises in my esteem. I know you would have explained the affair in the evening if things had appeared to you in this light. But I was to blame I ought have had more presence of mind, in future I shall shut up all my private sorrows in my own breast. In the morning I must own Everina's brutal manner of stopping you, when you were going to explain the the matter did provoke me – if I had not cared for my sisters who certainly do not adore me – the two last years of my life might have passed tranquilly not embittered by pecuniar cares – and if I had lost my friend, who has been a father and brother to me ever since I knew him – I should not have been left involved in debts – but my circumstances do not alarm me – I have hitherto struggled through great [difficul]ties – I have now more experience – and can exert myself with fresh vigour when it is necessary. [I] am prepared for every thing of that kind which can happen and not anxious about it – I shall live independent or not live at all, besides, my late acquirement renders me more independent – It [is] then the prospect of death that makes me very sad – death has appeared to stalk abroad of late — I should be deprived of a tender friend who bore with my faults – who was ever anxious to serve me – and solitary would my life be, the only friend[412] who would exert himself to comfort me, is so peculiarly circumstanced he cannot – and he too is sick – yet I know while he lives I shall never want an indulgent warm friend – but his society I cannot enjoy.

Adieu yours affectionately
Mary.

411. Their brother, James Wollstonecraft, who had been a sailor since the age of twelve although not much liking the sea. Believing he needed formal training to advance, Wollstonecraft was paying for him to be taught at the Military Academy, Woolwich, by John Bonnycastle, a celebrated mathematician and friend of Johnson.
412. Presumably a reference to the married Henry Fuseli.

98. To Joshua Cristall

[London] December 9th [?1790][413]

Your sister has, I hope long since informed you that my silence was
not an intentional slight, but the natural consequence of various circumstances, my time is fully employed, and when I cannot attend to the
pursuits, which on every account occupy my mind, I am not in a humour
to write, I want air and exercise; indeed I am grown a wretched correspondent, when neither duty nor business impels me – I am sorry to hear
that you are yet unsettled, halting between two opinions, you ought
resolutely to determine on the part you mean to act in life, and adhere to
your determination   if you waver much longer you will spend your
most vigourous days in childish wishes, and, instead of being useful to
your Sisters, become a burthen to yourself. Determine like a man
whether Drawing is to be the business or amusement of your future
life and banish vain regrets, if you ever intend to make a respectable
figure in the world. – With respect to music, I would by all means have
you cultivate your taste, when nature gives a propensity, it ought not
to be neglected and every accomplishment you acquire will render you
a more agreeable companion, and furnish you with an innocent source
of pleasure when you are alone, and every innocent relaxation is a
support to virtue – for I respect the good old proverb that idleness is
the mother of vice. and I am persuaded that our greatest comforts
must arise from employments – But I need not tell you so for you are
always active and eager to improve yourself and make a proper use of
your time – I am afraid Charles tainted your mind and unhinged you;
had you not met with him I do not think you would have spent more

413. This letter is copied from a transcript made by Joseph John Jenkins, secretary of the
Society of Painters in Water Colours, and now in possession of the archives of the Royal
Watercolour Society at the Bankside Gallery, London. Roget, who excerpted it in *A
History of the 'Old Water-Colour Society'*, stated that the date assigned to this and the
previous Cristall letter was '1793, or thereabouts' but considered it more likely that the
letters were written three or four years earlier (1, 182). Although this letter could come
from 1791 I have surmised the dating of 1790 because the strictures on Charles suggest
that it refers to a time when Wollstonecraft was most irritated at her brother; by late 1791
she was trying hard to do something for him and was seemingly less critical.

money than you could afford, nor have run into a gross vice which equally injures the mind and body – You were and I fear are too partial to him – I can depend on the veracity of my Friends in Ireland and I find Charles behaved himself very ill when he first arrived, in short I have little hopes of his amendment and to speak in the softest terms I think him a selfish weak being who only lives to gratify his appetites – You should beware of encouraging that lax kind of Candour which shades Virtue into Vice, and gives the mild name of thoughtlessness to depravity; but I will not dwell any longer on the ungrateful subject –

I have seldom seen your Sister since you left town   I fear her situation is still very uncomfortable I wish she could obtain a little more strength of mind   I am afraid she gives way to her feelings more than she ought to do – If I were to give a short definition of virtue I should call it fortitude

Adieu believe me your friend

Mary Wollstonecraft

99. To *Catherine Macaulay*[414]

[London] Thursday morning [December 1790]

Madam

Now I venture to send you [*A Vindication of the Rights of Men*][415] with a name utterly unknown to you in the title page, it is necessary

414. Catherine Macaulay (1731–1791), republican writer and pamphleteer associated with the radical political aims of John Wilkes. She published a Whig interpretation of the Civil War in *History of England* (1767–83), opposed Edmund Burke's position in two pamphlets in 1770 and 1791, and influenced Wollstonecraft with her feminist *Letters on Education* (1790), which asserted that the only difference in the sexes was physical. In 1778 Macaulay scandalized her contemporaries when she married a man nearly thirty years her junior.

415. The title *A Vindication of the Rights of Men* has been cut from the letter. In 1790 Edmund Burke published his *Reflections on the Revolution in France*, which included an attack on Wollstonecraft's old mentor from Newington Green, Richard Price, and defended the British constitution against the liberal demands for reform. She replied with *A Vindication of the Rights of Men* (1790), the first of at least forty-five answers to Burke written in the year following publication. The first edition was printed anonymously, the second carried her name.

to apologize for thus intruding on you – but instead of an apology shall I tell you the truth? You are the only female writer who I coincide in opinion with respecting the rank our sex ought to endeavour to attain in the world. I respect Mrs Maculay Graham because she contends for laurels whilst most of her sex only seek for flowers.

I am Madam,
Yours Respectfully
Mary Wollstonecraft[416]

100. To George Blood

London, February 4th [17]91

My Dear George,

I should have answered your letter before, but cares and employments, as usual, have of late very much engaged my attention – I am still in the most anxious state of suspense respecting the settlement of my father's affairs – and that is a serious business – however, we will not now talk of the cares which I see in perspective, which time may ward off or lessen – for poor Susan[417] has been haunting me ever since I read your letter to Eliza – I only received it this morning, and I have not been able to drive her image from my mind, though I do not think

416. Catherine Macaulay's reply of 30 December 1790, accompanied by her own answer to Burke 'in a letter to Earl Stanhope', is copied in a different hand on the second sheet of Wollstonecraft's letter: 'The receipt of your letter with one of the copies of the second edition of your excellent pamphlet in vindication of the rights of men gave me a pleasure derived from a variety of causes. I was pleased at the attention of the public to your animated observations, pleased with the flattering compliment you paid me in a second remembrance, and still more highly pleased that this publication which I have so greatly admired from its pathos & sentiment should have been written by a woman and thus to see my opinion of the powers and talents of the sex in your person so early verified.

Believe me Dear Madam I shall ever be happy in your valuable correspondence, and when opportunity offers shall with great pleasure avail myself of it for changing the lesser satisfaction of a correspondence by letters to that of a personal acquaintance.' Macaulay died in June 1791.
417. Susanna Home was dying of consumption.

that her death should be regretted on account of her children, for she would never have been an active mother – and they may be as well taken care of, putting blind tenderness out[15] of the question, as if their mother was still alive. I shall write to Bess[418] by this post, for I know the tenderness of her heart. –

Now my dear George let me more particularly allude to your own affairs – I ought to have done it sooner, but there was an awkwardness in the business which made me shrink back. We have all my good friend a sisterly affection for you – and this very morning Everina declared to me that she had more affection for you than for either of her brothers – Edward is, of course out of the question; but accustomed to consider you in that light she cannot view you in any other – let us then be on the old footing – love us as we love you – but give your heart to some worthy girl, and do not cherish an affection which may interfer with your prospects when there is no reason to suppose that it will ever be returned. Everina does not seem to think of marriage, she has no particular attachment – yet she was anxious, when I spoke explicitly to her, to speak to you in the same terms that she might correspond with you, as she has ever done, with sisterly freedom and affection. – Let us have done with this subject; but I still persist to advise you not to marry merely to settle, for I am convinced that your known probity would secure you from dependence; nay, procure you a comfortable situation if you should ever determine to leave Skeys[419] – Have you ever spoken to M^r. Noble – or has he had any conversation with you? Do not forget to tell me when you write. – I cannot help wishing to hear that you were settled permanently though, considering all things, your situation is a comfortable one – some thing must be borne with [in] every society – this is a trite remark – but it is not the less true. Pray write soon, I shall write again when I can give you a satisfactory account of my own affairs   mean while believe me your affectionate Friend

Mary Wollstonecraft

418. Although Eliza Bishop was frequently referred to as 'Bess', this reference is clearly to Betty Skeys, formerly Delane.
419. George Blood was working for Hugh Skeys in Dublin at his shop at 125 Great Britain Street; Wollstonecraft favoured his return to Brabazon Noble. See note 382.

M^r. Johnson has requested me to ask you whether the parcel for M^r. Baker, which he requested M^r. Skeys to enquire after is found, for he is very uneasy about it — Do not neglect to enquire concerning it – and tell me the result. —

101. To George Blood

New Store Street, October 6th [17]91[420]

Dear George,

Though I so seldom hear from you I still consider you as my friend – and write now to ask you to do me a kindness – if perfectly convenient. I have lately been actually tormented by pecuniary cares – so many things occurred at once to oppress me, I am now, I hope, overcoming them; but I have two or three trifling debts that plague me, at present, and I have lately applyed to M^r. Johnson so frequently (to fit Everina out, for her journey &c &c)[421] that I would fain wait a little while before I ask for any more. [Ex]cepting[16] M^r. J. I do not owe twenty pounds, this winter I shall *try hard* to lessen *the pounds* that stand against me in his books – but *these trifles* buzz continually in my ears, and ten pounds, in particular, I have *promised* to pay the 19,th of this month. – It is about this ten pounds that I now write to you, could you let me have it – you would do me an essential service by calming my mind – at any rate let me hear from you. I do not wish Skeys to know

420. At Michaelmas, Wollstonecraft had moved from George Street to more spacious lodgings in Store Street, north-east of Bedford Square, close to the present British Museum. In *HF*, 1, 163f., Fuseli's friend and biographer, John Knowles, ascribed the move to Wollstonecraft's desire to please Fuseli: '[She] moulded herself upon what she thought would be most agreeable to him. Change of manners, of dress, and of habitation were the consequences; for she now paid more than ordinary attention to her person, dressed fashionably, and introduced furniture somewhat elegant into commodious apartments, which she took for that purpose.' The change may also have responded to her growing fame.

421. Mrs Bregantz's school had collapsed and Eliza Bishop and Everina Wollstonecraft had to find governess positions as soon as possible. The latter had accepted one in the family of Samuel Boyse of Bishop's Hall, near Waterford in southern Ireland. According to Eliza Bishop, it would include dealing with 'brawling brats' and living a life 'imbittered by sideboards, folly and superstition!'.

any thing of this application. – The desire of making a shew, in some minds, swallows up every friendly feeling – When Everina went I found little Ann, at first, very troublesome; but now I manage her better, she is, as usual, in great spirits – in fact, her spirits sometimes oppress me, though I would not for the world damp them. She is an affectionate, artless child. James sailed last week;[422] but Charles is still unprovided for – this is my present blister.[423] Yet, George, I do not complain, I have some reason to hope that I shall overcome all these difficulties – and whilst I struggle I catch some gleams of sunshine – tranquillity does not fly from my quiet study, and the pictures, which fancy traces on the walls, have often the most glowing colours. Now the girls[424] have both left Town you must write to me immediately – for I can receive no indirect intelligence of you. – Pray tell me all about yourself – and tell me whether there is any chance of the Child's[425] ever making its appearance? – The Snaggs and I have had some jokes on that score.

> Adieu, believe me
> your's affectionately
> M. Wollstonecraft

Direct to me at M^r. Johnson's.

Tell Bess[426] that the Cups are on the way to her – *I hope* they will come in time. Tell her also that now I have, in some degree, recovered

422. Despite his new training James Wollstonecraft had failed to secure a commission in the Royal Navy; to Mary's dissatisfaction he had signed up as an officer on a merchantman. He had promised to share with his sisters any prize money he might make. A letter to Everina Wollstonecraft summed up Eliza Bishop's views on Mary's present attitudes: she was 'in good spirits, and . . . brimful of her friend, Fuseli, a visible pleasure at her brother's departure is expressed'.

423. Despite her disgust with Charles Wollstonecraft's behaviour in London, Mary was still trying to improve his fortunes. He had returned from Ireland to his father in Laugharne where the pair were on bad terms. According to Eliza Bishop her brother was running around 'half naked' but drinking 'never any thing but water'; he thought to list 'for a soldier' but 'if he does, there is an end of him'.

424. Her usual term for her sisters. In spring 1791 Eliza Bishop had taken a position as governess at Upton Castle, Pembrokeshire, owned by a nabob called Tasker. She received £40 per annum (the amount her sister had earned with the Kingsboroughs) to look after three teenaged girls. She judged the family uncultivated and vulgar.

425. The Skeyses expected a baby.

426. Betty Skeys, formerly Delane.

my spirits, I do not find the child[427] so troublesome as I did when I wrote last to her.

You must try George to get me some subscribers for *The Milton*[428] – for I am one of its warmest friends.

102. *To William Roscoe*[429]

[London] October 6th [17]91

Be it known unto you, my dear Sir, that I am actually sitting for the picture[430] and that it will be shortly *forthcoming*. I do not imagine that it will be a very striking likeness; but, if you do not find me in it, I will send you a more faithful sketch — a book that I am now writing, in which *I* myself, for I cannot *yet* attain to Homer's dignity, shall certainly appear, head and heart — but this between ourselves — pray respect a woman's secret![431]

Milton is, at present, the word, I did not answer your last letter respecting it, because I waited till the plan was shaped into proposals[432]

---

427. Her ward Ann, who might have been Betty's niece. See note 409.

428. Fuseli was working on a project of forty paintings based on Milton's work. Originally Johnson proposed a new edition of the poems edited by William Cowper to be illustrated with engravings from these paintings but the work was not published. The 'Milton Gallery', begun in 1790, was exhibited at the Royal Academy Rooms on 20 May 1799 with no great success.

429. William Roscoe (1753–1831), a Liverpool lawyer with interest in literature and the arts, was a supporter of the French Revolution and of the abolition of the slave trade, for which cause he had written many poems and pamphlets. He was a friend of Johnson, through whom he had met Wollstonecraft in London following the publication of her *Vindication of the Rights of Men*.

430. Roscoe so admired Wollstonecraft and her work that he commissioned the first portrait of her, now in the Walker Art Gallery in Liverpool.

431. It was a critical commonplace that Homer, in contrast to Milton, did not intrude himself into his epics; see Johnson, 'Milton', in *The Lives of the English Poets* (1781): 'who does not wish that the author of the *Iliad* had gratified succeeding ages with a little knowledge of himself?' According to Godwin *A Vindication of the Rights of Woman* (1792) took six weeks to complete. It asserted the potential intellectual equality of the sexes and pleaded for equal educational opportunities.

432. See note 428.

— and now you have received the proposal let me hear what you think of it.

I am now going to ask a favour of you — when I ask it I take it for granted that you would be glad to serve me, so you need not hesitate to say no — if you cannot say yes. But first let me tell you that the annuitant has the houses[433] entirely in his possession, and I am glad of it — for I now know what I am about — my two Sisters are settled very comfortably, and one of my brother's, who threw some money away to dance after preferment, when the fleet last paraded at Portsmouth, has, at last, condescended to take the command of a trading vessel; but, observe, it is a voyage of speculation. My present care, or rather blister, is a younger brother (he is just of age) and loitering away his time in Wales. He was bound to my eldest brother; but my father took him away, when the dispute about the property commenced — since which he has been unsettled. He was with me some time. He is a thoughtless youth with common abilities, a tolerable person, some warmth of heart, and a turn for humour. If he remains much longer idle, he will, of course, grow vicious. His boiling blood could only be cooled by employment and I cannot procure him a situation. I have been repeatedly disappointed in my endeavours to get him an appointment in the East India service — and I write to you as a forlorn hope, because I do not know what step to take. I should be glad to place him in any situation, were it but a temporary one, to employ him till something better occurred. Could you procure him any station in a counting-house, at Liverpool? I should wish him not to be left too much to himself.[434]

Yours Sincerely
M. Wollstonecraft

I have lately removed[435] — but you direct to me at Mr Johnson's. —

433. The increasingly dilapidated Primrose Street Houses, still owned by her father Edward Wollstonecraft and administered by Mary Wollstonecraft and Johnson.
434. Despite Wollstonecraft's lukewarm testimonial, Roscoe found a position for Charles, possibly in the law.
435. See note 420.

103. To George Blood

[London] January 2ᵈ[17]92

Dear George,

I am sorry to find that you are still unsettled; but coincide with you in opinion that you have little to expect from Skeys and that a connexion with the house would not, now *especially*, be desirable. I think you ought to endeavour to make a friend of Mʳ. Noble by frankly telling him your situation and views; for he is certainly humane and rich, and from Mʳ. Arbuckle's account, I should suppose friendly; besides, it is always best to act, as the vulgar say, above board. Our friend Bess[436] has an affectionate heart; but I always thought her too much attached to the world, and her conduct since her marriage proves to me that I read her right. I have indeed, been particularly hurt by her neglect of the Snaggs to whom a small present would have been a proper testimony of regard that might have enlivened their whole winter; for their income generally falls short towards the end of the quarter. Let me tell you it has often been a great mortification to me that I could not make them comfortable by affording them this trifling relief. But, various circumstances still keep me down. I do hope and believe that the girls are tolerably settled for the present. I have not heard very lately from Everina; but I am far from being uneasy on that account, for she is very apt to forget the absent when amused by the present. Charles is my care just now, and I have been repeatedly disappointed in my endeavours to obtain him an appointment in India – Unless I can procure him a situation I do not know what will become of him – and it is not easy to procure a situation for a young man who has nothing to recommend him.[17] This is a constant weight on my mind, and respecting my father I live in continual fear of having him thrown upon me for his whole support; for though E.[437] is once more in business; and even in a flourishing way, I am told, yet he is going on in the old track, and it does not require great foresight to say what must

436. Betty Skeys, formerly Delane.
437. Her eldest brother Edward Bland Wollstonecraft.

be the consequence, however, I do not disturb myself by anticipating an evil, which no forethought can ward off. I write now in a hurry; and, do not think me unkind! with my head full of some thing else; but, believe me, my dear George, I am ever interested about your welfare and ever

> Yours Sincerely
> M. Wollstonecraft

I have not inquired about Caroline lately for a very good reason, because, when I call, I must pay for her board; and nearly the ten pounds is due, which you have remitted. I always thought you wrong in not obliging your father to pay for her board, now he can afford it – but it is needless to make any further comments on his selfishness, remember me to your Mother, and let me hear from you soon again. Tell Ellis that had I know of his situation before I would have endeavoured to have procured him the sole reception of subscriptions for the Milton, now he can be only one of the receivers, if he thinks fit, because M^r. Johnson spoke to Mr Archer himself when he was in London, and printed his name to some of the proposals.

I thought of sending you my new book; but the last sheet is still at the press.[438]

104. To William Roscoe

Store Street, January 3^d [17]92

Dear Sir,

I should have written to you sooner, not only to have thanked you for so speedily answering my letter, but for your affectionate *remembrances* in Mr Fuseli's, had I not been very much engrossed by writing and printing my vindication of the Rights of Woman, and by a standing-dish of family cares. I shall give the last sheet to the printer to day; and, I am dissatisfied with myself for not having done justice to the subject. — Do not suspect me of false modesty — I mean to say,

---

438. Referring to the publication of *A Vindication of the Rights of Woman*.

that had I allowed myself more time I could have written a better book, in every sense of the word, the length of the Errata vexes me — as you are gentleman author[439] you can make some allowance for a little ill humour at seeing such a blur, which would only make those, who have never dabbled in ink, smile. I intend to finish the next volume before I begin to print, for it is not pleasant to have the Devil[440] coming for the conclusion of a sheet before it is written.[441] Well, I have said enough of this said book — more than is civil, and not sufficient to carry off the fumes of ill humour which make me quarrel with myself. —

And now, not to affront your authorship, I must tell you that I like some lines in your Revolution song, and some stanzas in your ballad.[442] — Our friend Fuseli is going on with more than usual spirit — like Milton he seems quite at home in hell — his Devil will be the hero of the poetic series; for, *entre nous*, I rather doubt whether he will produce an Eve to please me in any of the situations, which he has selected, unless it be after the fall.[443] When I am in a better humour I will give

439. Roscoe had written many political poems and pamphlets, e.g. *Ode. On the Institution of a Society in Liverpool for the encouragement of designing, drawing, painting, etc., read before the society, December 17th, 1773* (1777); *The Wrongs of Africa, a poem* (London, 1787; 2nd part 1788); *A General View of the African Slave-Trade, demonstrating its injustice and impolicy: with hints towards a bill for its abolition* (London, 1788); *Ode to the People of France; imitated from a Canzone of Petrarch: with the Italian original* (Liverpool, 1789); and *Millions be free. A new song* (?1790).

440. Runner of errands in a printing office.

441. Polemical works and many novels were frequently printed as they were being written. In the middle of *A Vindication of the Rights of Men* Wollstonecraft had wished to stop writing. Johnson had offered to destroy what he had already printed.

442. At a meeting held on 14 July 1790 Roscoe had written 'Song' to celebrate the taking of the Bastille; the last stanza begins: 'France! We share in the rapture thy bosom that fills, / When the Spirit of Liberty bounds o'er thy Hills'. The following year he wrote 'O'er the Vine-Covered Hills' to be recited on 14 August 1791; it included the line: 'Let Burke like a bat from its splendour retire'. He continued the theme with *The Life, Death, and Wonderful Atchievements of Edmund Burke* (1792) in which he described Wollstonecraft's *Rights of Men* in three stanzas, beginning: 'And lo! an Amazon stept out, / One WOLSTONECRAFT her name, / Resolv'd to stop his mad career, / Whatever chance became . . .' Paine is described as an even 'fiercer foe'. *Poetical Works of William Roscoe* (London, 1857).

443. In her *Rights of Woman* Wollstonecraft mocked the male vision of Eve before the fall. Rousseau restored 'the rib' and made 'one moral being of a man and woman; not forgetting to give her all the ' "submissive charms" ', a reference to *Paradise Lost*, 4,

you an account of those already sketched — but had you not better come and see them? — We have all an individual way of feeling grandeur and sublimity.

My brother, the brother, whom I mention[ed] to you, is now in Town,[444] and I have been repeatedly disappointed in my attempts to procure him an appointment in the service of the East-India Company; or, indeed, to procure him any situation — This is a serious vexation. I did not take advantage of what you offered, because I doubted about his professional knowledge, but I was not the less obliged to you for endeavouring to serve me — It is now time to bid you adieu — for after suffering a transient gust of sourish gall to flow over, I must not harp on a string that is constantly out of tune.

Yours Sincerely
Mary Wollstonecraft

105. To William Roscoe

Store Street, Bedford Square, February 14th [17]92

Dear Sir,

I am not a very punctual answerer of letters; but I write now to inform you of a circumstance that has afford'd me great satisfaction, and to request some professional advice. I have, at last, settled my brother, or rather put him in the way to be settled just as I could wish. He is to accompany a Mr. & Mrs. Barlow[445] to America who will

---

497f.: 'he in delight / Both of her beauty and submissive charms / Smiles with superior love'.

444. Charles had left Laugharne and returned to his eldest brother's house in London. Underestimating Wollstonecraft's concern, Eliza Bishop at first suggested he avoid his sister but soon the pair met and Wollstonecraft continued planning his future.

445. The American Joel Barlow (1754–1812) had been a chaplain, editor and poet; he was now a pamphleteer and businessman. He married Ruth Baldwin in 1781, went to Paris to sell American land, then moved to London. Ruth (1756–1818) was the daughter of a Connecticut blacksmith. The couple were intending to return to America but Barlow was fascinated by the politics and business possibilities of revolutionary France. He had started out poor but, unknown to Wollstonecraft, was becoming deeply involved in lucrative capitalist enterprises.

endeavour to place him in a farm to obtain a little experience till he can purchase some land for himself. M^r. B. has lately published a sensible political pamphlet,[446] which you will like, it has prejudised me in his favour, and Mr Paine[447] assures me that he could not be recommended to a more worthy man, and that there is not a doubt of his earning a respectable livelihood if he will exert himself — I want now to ask you in what manner he must empower me to take possession of and sell for him the little property which he will be entitled to when my father dies, whose state of health is very precarious, and how, for I once was very much provoked by the unjust conduct of a person[448] with respect to a *lapsed legacy*, he could leave it to his sisters, should he chance to die before he received intelligence of my father's death — you will readily perceive that my dear-bought experience makes me anxious to guard against contigencies lest by some quirk of the law my eldest brother, *the Attorney*, should snap at the last morsel.

Well, now to talk of something else — schemes for printing works *embellished* with prints have lately been started with *catch-penny* eagerness, and such an inundation, to borrow a fashional cant word, has damped my hopes with respect to the success of our friend's.[449] I love the man and admire the artist, and am sorry to find that subscribers come in very slowly. This I mention to you in confidence and make light of it to him, for on this work the comfort of his life, in every sense of the word, seems to depend. Mr Johnson[,] the world contains not a more friendly heart, [has] many employments and could not condescend to use the mean arts, had he leisure, which the promoters of other plans, of a similar nature, avail themselves of, in this puffing age, and I still think, I speak without reserve, that it would have been carried on with more spirit had there been a partner or two with

446. *Advice to the Privileged Orders*, another reply to Burke's *Reflections*, published by Johnson on 4 February 1792.
447. Thomas Paine (1737–1809), revolutionary writer and activist, friend of Johnson and Wollstonecraft, was the son of a staymaker from Thetford. He became a powerful propagandist in the American Revolution and was now agitating for reform in England. Part 1 of his answer to Burke, *The Rights of Man*, had been published in 1791; the more radical and inflammatory Part 2 appeared on 16 February 1792, with four other printings within the next two weeks.
448. Reference to her eldest brother Edward Bland and the 'Roebuck' legacy.
449. See note 428.

money to speculate with. The first number most probably will have considerable effect towards filling the subscription; but till then I am sorry M^r. F. has not more encouragement, for I should be vext to see his fancy spent in brooding over disappointments. Remember me kindly to M^rs. Roscoe and her fine brood,[450] and believe me yours sincerely

Mary Wollstonecraft

Direct to me immediately. M^r. J. tells me that you make the liverpool women read my book. —

106. To Everina Wollstonecraft

[London] February 23^d [1792]

Since I wrote to you last I have seen and heard more of Mr Barlow, and think Charles' prospect a most promising one indeed – I shrewdly suspect that Mr B. has some thoughts of keeping him in his own family; but he waits till he sees more of him before he avows his intention. Such a situation would be a most desirable one, for he has a sound understanding with great mildness of temper. I mean rather a regulated temper than natural good humour. The other day he clapped C., in his dry way, on the knee and said — 'that as his wife and he could never contrive to make any boys they must try what they could do with one ready brought up to their hands.'[451] I am particularly anxious that C. should behave properly for unless he forgets himself I have not the least doubt of his doing *very* well. He is in great spirits and I think very much improved.[452] Did I tell you that Fuseli insisted on making Charles a present of ten pounds, because he liked the scheme.

I am sorry to give you bad account of Ann after my late praise; but a few days ago I discovered that she has been stealing sugar out of my

---

450. Roscoe was married to Jane Griffies, with whom he had seven sons and three daughters.

451. Joel and Ruth Barlow had no children of either sex.

452. Wollstonecraft had placed her brother on a farm in Leatherhead to study agriculture; she bought him suitable farming clothes.

closet constantly, and the artful way she managed it, not to mention the lies, really vexes me – She is undoubtedly very much improved and my visitors think her a fine girl – yet I have long been convinced that she will never be the kind of child I should love with all my heart. She has great *animal* spirits and quick feelings, but I shall be much mistaken if she have any considerable portion of sensibility when she grows up.

Mr. Opie, who frequently calls upon me has introduced me to his wife.[453] – She is really a pretty easy woman, too much of a flirt to be a proper companion for him, yet though they do not appear to see *many* things in the same light they concur in shewing me uncommon civility. And be it know unto you that my book &c &c has afforded me an opportunity of settling *very* advantageous in the matrimonial line, with a new acquaintance; but entre nous – a handsome house and a proper man did not tempt me; yet I may as well appear before you with the feather stuck in my cap. I have not lately heard from George, but coincide in opinion with you that he has not been used well – M^rs. S.[454] has, at last, brought forth a *little* girl. Do you ever hear any thing of Bushe?[455] I neglected to answer his last letter for some time, and it is now a long time since I *did* write – Still I have received no letter – Make some inquiries about him and the thoughtless ungrateful Lady Mount C[456] Is not M^r. Ogle Member for Waterford?[457] Do you ever hear how his affairs are settled or likely to be settled?

I do not recollect the M^rs. Johnson, whom you mention, but I will

453. John Opie (1761–1807), portrait painter from Cornwall, was married to Mary Bunn.

454. Mrs Betty Skeys.

455. The word is unclear but is very likely 'Bushe'. Possibly this is a reference to Charles Kendal Bushe (1767–1843), son of the first chaplain of Kingston College, Mitchelstown. He was an acquaintance of the Kingsboroughs, including Margaret, and since 1790 a Dublin lawyer. Wardle conjectures a reference to Meredith Bishop, Eliza's husband, but the juxtaposition with her other Irish acquaintances suggests another Irishman.

456. Margaret King, Wollstonecraft's old pupil, had married the second earl of Mount Cashell on 12 September 1791. She held her governess's liberal political principles and it is unclear how she might have offended, except in marrying ill-advisedly and too young.

457. George Ogle, the poet who had impressed Wollstonecraft in Ireland, had been an Irish MP since 1768 but for Wexford not Waterford. See note 195.

ask Paine.[458] Charles has written to you and will write soon again – If you can spare the twenty pounds it will be particularly acceptable at this time –

yours affectionately M. W.

107. To William Roscoe

[London, c. 1792]

Dear Sir,

M^r. Johnson tells me that he has a frank for you, and that I *ought* to write to you — I am not in a mood to chat on paper — I had rather not talk *all* myself — yet, it is a shame to be so indolently fond of my own *reveries* when I have to thank you for the kindnesses that were not lost on me. — I felt them — and that I may still continue to remember them I *will not* thank you — Debts of this kind rest lightly on my pillow, and sweeten instead of disturbing my slumbers — I love to sip the milk of human kindness, when I can, to make the bitter pill of life go down.

[The rest of the letter is missing.]

108. To Everina Wollstonecraft

London, June 20th [17]92

I have put off writing to you from day to day expecting to see M^r. B.[459] who has now been absent above nine weeks, though he only talked of staying ten days or a fortnight, when he left England. These delays vex me, yet I really believe they will have no other bad consequence,

458. Paine was still in London; he would leave abruptly for Paris after the publication of *The Rights of Man*, Part 2, when William Blake warned him his life was in danger.
459. Barlow was staying in Paris rather than going to America, as previously planned. Wollstonecraft was unaware that he had become less interested in politics than commerce and was now busy amassing a great deal of money.

but that of continuing a heavy expence, the keeping Charles at the farm-house. The Barlows are, indeed, very worthy people, and she has been gratified by my attention to her during her husbands absence. I do hope that he will soon return and then I shall be able to form some judgment respecting their future plans. M^{rs}. B. has a very benevolent, affectionate heart, and a tolerable understanding, a little warped it is true by romance; but she is not the less friendly on that account. Delighted with some of her husband's letters, she has exultingly shewn them to me; and, though I took care not to let her see it, I was almost disgusted with the *tender* passages which afforded her so much satisfaction, because they were turned so prettily that they looked more like the cold ingenuity of the head than the warm overflowings of the heart – However, she did not perceive that the head and heart were gadding far away, when he calls 'her arms his heaven', in search of fame on this same dirty earth – so all was well. – I have described your situation to her and shewn her some parts of your letters, and she is continually saying how well you might be settled in America. European women, very absurdly, are particularly respected in America, and she confidently asserts that you and Eliza might live, by taken a few young people under your care, and be respected by the first families; nay, marry well, but this entre nous. She has even said that you might come and live with her, and Eliza keep Charles's house, till you could look about you – I almost wish that you would begin a correspondence with her, it might be of use to Charles.

I have delayed writing also on another account, for I have been considering what you say respecting Eliza's residence in France. For some time past M^r. & M^{rs}. Fuseli, M^r. Johnson and myself have talked of a summer excursion to Paris; it is now determined on and we think of going in about six weeks. I shall be introduced to many people, my book has been translated[460] and praised in some popular prints; and, Fuseli, of course, is well known; it is then very probable that I shall hear of some situation for Eliza, and I shall be on the watch.[461] We

---

460. *The Rights of Woman* was translated as *Défense des droits des femmes* and published at Paris and Lyons in 1792.
461. As her letters make clear Eliza Bishop was eager to leave Upton and go to France to learn French. She vacillated between immense faith in her eldest sister's ability to rescue her and envy at her fame and more exciting life. She became embittered when

intend to be absent only six weeks, if then I fix on an eligible situation for her she may avoid the Welsh winter. This journey will not lead me into any extraordinary expence, or I should put it off till a more convenient season, for I am not, as you may suppose, very flush of money, and Charles is wearing out the clothes, which were provided for his voyage, still I am glad that he has acquired a little practical knowledge of farming – as I do begin to hope that his indolence has received a shove.

I lately received a few lines from James, brought by a man of war from one of the Cape de Verd Island,[462] He writes in tolerable spirits, desires to be affectionately remembered to you all, and says that she[18] shall probably return towards Christmas.

I wonder Charles has not written to you, he promised to write frequently to you from Leatherhead – I shall remind him and remain

yours affectionately M. W.

---

she learnt through Everina Wollstonecraft of Mary's proposed travel plans: she wrote, 'So the author of the rights of Woman is going to France I dare say, her chief motive is to promote her poor Bess's Comfort! or thine my girl or at least I think she will thus reason – Well, in spite of *Reason* when Mrs W reaches the Continent she will be but a woman! I Cannot help painting her in the height of all her wishes, at the very summit of happiness, for will not ambition fill every Chink of her Great Soul? (for such I really think her's) that is not occupied by *Love*? After having drawn this sketch, you can hardly suppose me so sanguine as to expect my pretty face will be thought of when matters of State are in agitation.'

462. The Cape Verde archipelago of ten volcanic islands had been Portuguese since the fifteenth century. It served as a convict colony but also collected salt and grew crops such as coffee and sugar cane; its main prosperity came from the transatlantic slave trade. Porto Inglez on Maio was occupied until the end of the eighteenth century by the British, who based their claim on the marriage treaty between Charles II and Catharine of Braganza. Smuggling and piracy were rife in the area.

109. To Mary Hays[463]

Store Street, Bedford Square, August 11th [1792]

Madam,

Intending to call upon you I put off answering your letter from time to time till, as is usually the case, it became a task and I could not recollect what I thought of saying when I first read it. I will then simply acknowledge the receipt of your testimony of esteem[464] merely to have an opportunity of telling you that when I return to Town[465] I shall be glad to see you. I should, indeed, have invited you, if convenient, to have visited me before my departure; but some family cares, among the rest the settling a brother in life, drove secondary objects out of my mind.

I am Madam Your's &c
[Mary Wollstonecraft][19]

110. To Everina Wollstonecraft

London, September 14th [17]92

Dear Everina,

I arrived in Town the day before yesterday[466] and found Charles well and happy – and, what was still more satisfactory, heard that he

---

463. Mary Hays (1760–1843), novelist and polemical writer from a Dissenting family. She had been engaged to marry John Eccles, who died before the wedding, and she was now living with her mother in Gainsford Street, Southwark. She had been intending to write on the subject of women when she read Wollstonecraft's *A Vindication of the Rights of Woman*, which she greatly admired.

464. Hays had written a letter to Wollstonecraft complimenting her on *A Vindication of the Rights of Woman* and on her 'spirited support of the just and natural rights of her sex'.

465. Wollstonecraft refers to the proposed trip to Paris with Johnson and the Fuselis.

466. Wollstonecraft, Johnson and the Fuselis had gone as far as Dover but then cancelled their trip because of the worsening political situation in Paris. On 10 August the Tuileries, Louis XVI's palace, had been assaulted and his Swiss guard assassinated; then between 2 and 6 September 1,400 priests, prisoners and aristocrats were massacred.

had been very industrious during my absence. He has regained M[r].
J's[467] good opinion by the propriety of his behaviour, and the habit of
order which he is acquiring, by attending to business will, to use M[r].
Paine's phrase, 'do him no harm in America'; besides, the company he
mixes with at this social table opens his mind. I cannot yet get a
decided answer from M[r]. Barlow, he is a worthy man, but devoured
by ambition. – His thoughts are turned towards France and till the
present commotions are over, I am much mistaken if he do not find
some excuse every month to make to *himself* for staying in Europe –
Lingering amidst alarms instead of returning to the peaceable shades
of America, because, may I moralize? rest is the rack of active minds,
and life loses its zest when we find that there is nothing worth wishing
for, nothing to detain the thoughts in the present scene, but what
quickly grows stale, rendering the soul torpid or uneasy. But I began
with an intention of answering the letter you wrote to Charles. –

M[rs]. Brégantz[468] called upon me some time ago to tell me that she
was removed to Kensington with M[rs]. Cooksey, her new partner and
that Aline[469] was married – She did not stop there, but informed me
that Amée was shortly to be married also still more advantageously
than her sister in point of fortune. Before I left Town I dined with her
and she gave me some letters to her daughters, who were then in Paris.
M[rs]. Cooksey is a shewy agreeable woman, Miss Marshall has left
them, at least, for some months, to visit yorkshire, she called on me
several times with Mrs Barber, who came to invite me to her house.
Poor Miss Brégantz has obtained by some means a situation, but as
she seldom writes to M[rs]. B. I could learn nothing more. Miss Meyer
after spending fifty pounds, and attempting to drown herself set out
for her own country – Miss Steward is married to a rich old man. I
pity M[rs]. Cooksey, the school will scarcely answer, but she has good
spirits. I think I have now given you the desired information – Let me
hear from you soon and believe me yours affectionately

Mary Wollstonecraft.

---

467. Joseph Johnson's.
468. Wollstonecraft adds an accent to the name of the former Putney headmistress
here and in Letter 118 but nowhere else.
469. Mrs Bregantz's daughter had married M. Filliettaz; she was now living in a grand
house, 22 rue Meslée, near the present Place de la République.

111. To William Roscoe

London, October 2ᵈ [17]92

Dear Sir,

I have put off writing to you till the noon of the day of my brother's departure[470] and I find my spirits so low that I shall not attempt to lengthen out this introductory letter; or rather I have desired my brother to call upon you as a proof of my respect, for his stay will be so short he cannot avail himself of the civilities which I know you would shew him. One word more, pray do not wait for an *excuse* when your spirit (or your heart) let Mʳˢ. Roscoe see this parenthesis, moves you to write to me, for I shall always be glad to hear from you, though I cannot promise to be, what I have never yet been, a punctual correspondent.

Yours Sincerely
Mary Wollstonecraft

112. To Henry Fuseli[471]

[speculative reconstruction]

[London, ?late 1792]

[For some years before our acquaintance, I] read no book for mere amusement, not even poetry, but studied those works only which are addressed to the understanding; [I] scarcely tasted animal food, or allowed [myself] the necessaries of life that [I] might be able to pursue some romantic schemes of benevolence; seldom went to

---

470. Wollstonecraft had learnt that Barlow was not planning to leave France soon; therefore Charles must go alone to America, which he was now doing. He would be leaving from the port of Liverpool, near where Roscoe lived.
471. Knowles printed brief excerpts from Wollstonecraft's many letters to the Fuselis (originals now lost) in his *HF*, 1, 163f., see 'Sources', pp. 439f.; all are undated but were probably written late in 1792. This is a collection of these fragments.

any amusements (being resident chiefly at Bath, and in the midst of pleasure), and [my] clothes were scarcely decent in [my] situation of life . . .

[I have never before known a man] possessed of those noble qualities, that grandeur of soul, that quickness of comprehension, and lively sympathy [essential to my happiness] . . . For I always catch something from the rich torrent of [your] conversation, worth treasuring up in my memory, to exercise my understanding . . .

[I] hope to unite [myself] to [your] mind . . . [I] was designed to rise superior to [my] earthly habitation, . . . [I] always thought, with some degree of horror, of falling a sacrifice to a passion which may have a mixture of dross in it . . . If I thought my passion criminal, I would conquer it, or die in the attempt. For immodesty, in my eyes, is ugliness; my soul turns with disgust from pleasure tricked out in charms which shun the light of heaven . . .

113. To Joseph Johnson

[London] Saturday night [?October 1792][472]

I am a mere animal, and instinctive emotions too often silence the suggestions of reason. Your note – I can scarcely tell why, hurt me – and produced a kind of winterly smile, which diffuses a beam of despondent tranquillity over the features. I have been very ill – Heaven knows it was more than fancy – After some sleepless, wearisome nights, towards the morning I have grown delirious. – Last Thursday, in particular, I imagined —— was thrown into great distress by his folly; and I, unable to assist him, was in an agony. My nerves were in such a painful state of irritation – I suffered more than I can express – Society was necessary – and might have diverted me till I gained more

472. Wardle has dated this letter to late 1792 because of the long dash in the fifth sentence. He thought it was probably substituted by Godwin for Fuseli's name; he also assumed that Wollstonecraft was berating herself for her proposal to live with the Fuselis. While Godwin's usual mode is asterisks, as in Letter 88, and Wollstonecraft may have experienced many moments of misery during her months of infatuation with Fuseli, this placing in autumn or winter 1792 yet seems the most plausible.

strength; but I blushed when I recollected how often I had teazed you with childish complaints, and the reveries of a disordered imagination. I even *imagined* that I intruded on you, because you never called on me – though you perceived that I was not well. – I have nourished a sickly kind of delicacy, which gives me many unnecessary pangs. – I acknowledge that life is but a jest – and often a frightful dream – yet catch myself every day searching for something serious – and feel real misery from the disappointment. I am a strange compound of weakness and resolution! However, if I must suffer, I will endeavour to suffer in silence. There is certainly a great defect in my mind – my wayward heart creates its own misery – Why I am made thus I cannot tell; and, till I can form some idea of the whole of my existence, I must be content to weep and dance like a child – long for a toy, and be tired of it as soon as I get it.

We must each of us wear a fool's cap; but mine, alas! has lost its bells, and is grown so heavy, I find it intolerably troublesome. – Good-night! I have been pursuing a number of strange thoughts since I began to write, and have actually both wept and laughed immoderately – Surely I am a fool –

Mary W.

114. To William Roscoe

London, November 12th [17]92

My Dear Sir,

For your most friendly behaviour to my brother receive my sincere thanks, it is pleasant not to find oneself mistaken in a character — or rather, I am glad to hear that absence has not cooled the little kindness you felt for me when we met, for the first and last time, in Town. — When do you think of again visiting the metropolis? Not very soon, I hope, for I intend no longer to struggle with a rational desire,[473] so have determined to set out for Paris in the course of a fortnight or

---

473. Reference to Wollstonecraft's affection for Fuseli, about which, as a close friend of the latter's, Roscoe seems to have known.

three weeks;[474] and I shall not now halt at Dover, I promise you; for as I go alone neck or nothing is the word.[475] During my stay I shall not forget my friends; but I will tell you so when I am really there. Mean time let me beg you not to mix with the shallow herd who throw an odium on immutable principles, because some of the mere instrument of the revolution were too sharp.[476] — Children of any growth will do mischief when they meddle with edged tools.[477] It is to be lamented that *as yet* the billows of public opinion are only to be moved forward by the strong wind, the squally gusts of passion; but if nations be educated by their governments it is vain to expect much reason till the system of education becomes more reasonable. You are employed, however, to exhibit the glossy side of aristocracy,[478] yet I hope you

474. Knowles described the precipitating events: see 'Sources', pp. 439f. A later friend, the Silesian count Christoph Georg Gustav von Schlabrendorf (1750–1824), described Wollstonecraft's love more sympathetically: 'During that time in London (between 1787 and 1790) she saw much of Fuseli. She was attracted by his genius, and only by that. Fuseli, an admirer of Rousseau, despised anything cultured and civilised, he believed only in the power of genius. His wit and sarcasm gave something crude to his manner and views. Mary attached herself to Fuseli with all her soul, a feeling she allowed herself to indulge in, because she knew he was married, and was sure of her own pure and undemanding nature. Soon after, however, their relationship began to seem unsatisfactory to her and tormented her. She realised a growing tendency for passion in herself and withdrew.' Schlabrendorf's notes, which he wrote in the margins of his edition of Godwin's *Memoirs*, are cited in Heinrich Zschokke, *Carl Gustav Jochmann's, von Pernau, Reliquien. Aus seinen nachgelassenen Papieren* (Hechingen, 1836), p. 196.

475. In Paris Wollstonecraft would find some of her old associates, especially Paine and Thomas Christie, the founder with Johnson of *AR*. Christie had moved to Paris in late 1789; in 1793 he was the agent for Turnbull Forbes & Co.

476. The news of the September massacres revolted the English, also influenced by the Pitt government's anti-French propaganda. Roscoe found his radicalism making him unpopular among the once-sympathetic property-owners of Liverpool.

477. Possibly an echo of Lord Chesterfield's famous remark in *Letters written by the Late Honourable Philip Dormer Stanhope, Earl of Chesterfield, to His Son* (London, 1774), I, pp. 330f.: 'Women, then, are only children of a larger growth', itself a reworking of John Dryden's 'Men are but children of another growth', *All for Love*, IV, i, 43.

478. Roscoe had long been writing a cultural biography of the Florentine Renaissance leader, Lorenzo de' Medici, depicting him as a republican spirit, epitome of the true patriot and patron. In 1791 he published privately an edition of Lorenzo de' Medici entitled *Smaller Collections. Poesie . . . tratte da testi a penna della libreria Mediceo-Laurenziana, e finora inedite* (regular edition Liverpool, 1795). William Hazlitt's

have not quite forgot the *order* of the day, or I shall think your praises of Liberty mere headwork; and laugh as I once saucily did when even in rhyme you talked of *declining* a transport[479] — But for the sake of the jingle, I know the same breath must blow hot and cold, so *beauty* must forgive the affront.

Our friend Johnson is well — I am told the world, to talk big, married m[e] to him whilst we were away;[480] but you [?guess] that I am still a Spinster on the wing. At Paris, indeed, I might take a husband for the time being, and get divorced when my truant heart longed again to nestle with its old friends;[481] but this speculation has not yet entered into my plan.

Remember me to M^rs. Roscoe and believe me Yours Sincerely

Mary Wollstonecraft.

memoir of Roscoe preceding *Life of Lorenzo de' Medici called the Magnificent* (London, 1883) recorded that Roscoe sent the first sheets of this work to the press in autumn 1793, with full publication occurring in February 1796 at the author's expense – he then sold the copyright to Cadell & Davies for £1,200. Wollstonecraft distrusted Roscoe's fascination with Lorenzo, whom she saw as a prince rather than a patriot.

479. In his 'Song [Written for the Purpose of Being Recited on the Anniversary of the 14 of August, 1791]' Roscoe had written: 'When the bosom of Beauty the throbbing heart meets, / Ah who can the transport decline?'

480. After the aborted earlier trip, Wollstonecraft and Johnson may have spent a short time out of London together.

481. On 20 September 1792 the French Legislative Assembly had made divorce available to women.

115. To Mary Hays[482]

Store Street, November 25th [17]92

Dear Madam

I yesterday mentioned to M[r]. Johnson your request and he assented desiring that the title page might be sent to him[483] – I, therefore, can say nothing more, for trifles of this kind I have always left to him to settle; and, you must be aware, Madam, that the *honour* of publishing, the phrase on which you have laid a stress, is the cant of both trade and sex: for if really equality should ever take place in society the man who is employed and gives a just equivalent for the money he receives will not behave with the servile obsequiousness of a servant.

I am now going to treat you with still greater frankness – I do not approve of your preface[484] – and I will tell you why. If your work should

---

482. Since writing her last letter Hays had persuaded Joseph Johnson to arrange a breakfast meeting with Wollstonecraft, after which Hays called at Store Street: 'I was extremely gratified by this interview. This lady appears to me to possess the sort of genius which Lavater calls the one to ten million. Her conversation, like her writings, is brilliant, forcible, instructive and entertaining. She is the true disciple of her own system, and commands at once fear and reverence, admiration and esteem' (*The Love-Letters of Mary Hays*, ed. A. F. Wedd, London: Methuen, 1925, p. 5). Both Wollstonecraft and Hays were much influenced by Lavater's *Essays on Physiognomy*, which argued the correspondence of inner and outer appearance.

483. Since Christie went to France, Wollstonecraft had taken on a more editorial role on the *AR*. Johnson and Wollstonecraft were presumably helping Hays with publication since her *Letters and Essays* (with two tales by her sister Elizabeth) were in fact published by another publisher. Probably Hays had sent in the preface and title page for an opinion; they came with a covering letter declaring her 'honour' at acceptance.

484. Presumably the original was highly effusive; the final version read: 'It is observed by the sensible vindicator of female rights – "that as society is at present constituted, the little knowledge, which even women of stronger minds attain, is of too desultory a nature, and pursued in too secondary a manner to give vigour to the faculties, or clearness to the judgment". I feel the truth of this observation with a mixture of indignation and regret: and this is the only apology I shall make to the critical reader, who may be inclined to censure as unconnected, or inconclusive, any of the subsequent remarks.'

deserve attention it is a blur on the very face of it. – Disadvantages of education &c ought, in my opinion, never to be pleaded (with the public) in excuse for defects of any importance, because if the writer has not sufficient strenght of mind to overcome the common difficulties which lie in his way, nature seems to command him, with a very audible voice, to leave the task of instructing others to those who can. This kind of vain humility has ever disgusted me – and I should say to an author, who humbly sued for forbearance, 'if you have not a tolerably good opinion of your own production, why intrude it on the public? we have plenty of bad books already, that have just gasped for breath and died.'

The last paragraph I particularly object to, it is so full of vanity. your male friends will still treat you like a woman – and many a man, for instance D^r. Johnson, Lord Littelton, and even D^r, Priestley, have insensibly been led to utter warm elogiums in private that they would be sorry openly to avow without some cooling explanatory ifs.[485] An author, especially a woman, should be cautious lest she too hastily swallows the crude praises which partial friend and polite acquaintance bestow thoughtlessly when the supplicating eye looks for them. In short, it requires great resolution to try rather to be useful than to please. With this remark in your head I must beg you to pardon my freedom whilst you consider the purport of what I am going to add. – Rest, on yourself – if your essays have merit they will stand alone, if not the *shouldering up* of D^r this or that will not long keep them from falling to the ground. The vulgar have a pertinent proverb – 'Too many cooks spoil the broth', and let me remind you that when weakness claims indulgence it seems to justify the despotism of

---

485. The letter suggests that Wollstonecraft had heard such men. When she was teaching at Newington Green, her friend Hewlett had introduced her to Samuel Johnson (see *Memoirs*, p. 45) and she might well have met the famous Unitarian scientist Joseph Priestley (1733–1804) in the circles of Price or Johnson. It is hard to imagine her meeting George Lyttelton, first baron Lyttelton (1709–1773); perhaps she was alluding to Johnson's remark (in his sketch of Lyttelton in *Lives of the English Poets*) that, after the *Critical Review* praised *Dialogues of the Dead*, 'poor Lyttelton with humble gratitude returned, in a note which I have read, acknowledgements which can never be proper, since they must be paid either for flattery or for justice' (4, 446). See *CL*, p. 220.

strength.[486] Indeed the preface, and even your pamphlet, is too full of yourself – Inquiries ought to be made before they are answered; and till a work strongly interests the public true modesty should keep the author in the back ground – for it is only about the character and life of a *good* author that curiosity is active – A blossom is but a blossom.

I am Madam

yours &c

Mary Wollstonecraft

S[t], Paul's[487] As you seemed uneasy when you wrote, contrary to my first intention I have just now spoken to M[r]. J. who desires me to tell you that he very willingly waves the privilege of seniority, though as it is an impropriety, I should think his name might as well be omitted.[488] –

116. To Mary Hays

Store Street, Saturday morning [c. late 1792]

Dear Madam,

I have just cast my eye over your sensible little pamphlet,[489] and found fewer of the superlatives, exquisite, fascinating, &c, all of the feminine gender, than I expected. Some of the sentiments, it is true, are rather obscurely expressed; but if you continue to write you will imperceptibly correct this fault and learn to think with more clearness,

486. A major theme of *The Rights of Woman*, in which women as well as men were urged to change their sexual attitudes.

487. Wollstonecraft was writing a postscript from Johnson's shop in St Paul's Churchyard.

488. *Letters and Essays* was published in March 1793 by T. Knott, publisher of Hays's earlier *Cursory Remarks* and a friend of her supporter John Disney, to whom the work was inscribed as 'an unaffected tribute of esteem'.

489. Given Wollstonecraft's previous remarks on the preface to *Letters and Essays*, this may possibly refer to Hays's controversial pamphlet of 1791 arguing the need for public religious ceremonies: *Cursory Remarks on an Enquiry into the Expediency and Propriety of Public or Social Worship by Eusebia*. It responded to Gilbert Wakefield's attack on Dissenting practices in his *Enquiry into the Expediency and Propriety of Public or Social Worship* (1791), in which he argued that enforced public worship was corrupt and that religion was essentially private.

and consequently avoid the errours naturally produced by confusion of thought.

As you wish to have your proofs quickly returned, I should think that you had better desire the printer's boy to bring them to me and wait for them, for I will read them immediately, unless I should happen to be particularly engaged. I shall use a pencil so you may adopt or erase my corrections without much trouble.

I thank you for recollecting the inquiries which I requested you to make, respecting my brother; but since I saw you I have received a letter from him.

I shall not forget your message to M^r. Johnson and remain yours Sincerely

Mary Wollstonecraft

117. *To Everina Wollstonecraft*

[London, c. early December 1792][490]

Dear Everina,

On Saturday I actually set out once more for Dover – yet in going I seem to strive against fate, for had I not taken my place I should have put off the journey again on account of the present posture of affairs at home,[491] which are really rather alarming. My spirits even sink; but I go – yet should any accident happen to my dear and worthy friend Johnson during my absence I should never forgive myself for leaving him – These are vapourish fears – still they fasten on me and press home most feelingly a long comment on the vanity of human wishes. But to answer your letter. As soon as I arrive at Madame Filliettaz, late Aline Bregantz,[492] I will write to you and Eliza – and when her situation is once fixt I would have you enclose the thirty pounds in a

490. The letter was undated but the postmark is either 'DE 9' or 'DE 10'.
491. Apart from anxiety over Johnson, Wollstonecraft was worrying over the international crisis; England and France declared war a few weeks later, on 1 February 1793.
492. Wollstonecraft was planning to lodge with Mrs Bregantz's daughter, Aline Filliettaz.

letter to M^r. Johnson on whom I can draw from Paris.[493] All I know of the Gentleman is that he is a man of respectable character, not young, and that he did not wish to have a young woman – But, when I write I can tell you all, for I shall be on the spot. As you have seen M^rs. Irwin I think you have acted right and the situation will probably be more comfortable than your present one;[494] indeed, it can scarcely fail to be so as you will have friends near you, with whom you can mix on equal terms. You tell me nothing of your health. You remember Dr Fordyce,[495] I lately dined at his house, and I have seldom been in company with more intelligent pleasing women than his two daughters. There education has been attend[ed] to, I may say with emphasis; and there father is now rewarded for his care.

I shall expect to receive a long letter soon after my arrival, you forgot to mention little Ann[496] or George, be more explicit when you write next. By this time you have got my letter enclosing James's[497] curious epistle – and you share my vexation – I hope I shall not see him, for he tries my patience.

[The rest of the letter is missing.]

493. Wollstonecraft had asked her sisters to contribute money through drafts on Johnson (see Letters 122 and 127). Presumably in Everina's case this reflected her earlier support in Paris and, in Eliza Bishop's, Wollstonecraft's plan to find her sister a position. The money featured much in Eliza Bishop's letters: in the early ones she doubted that her sister would do anything for her, but later came to believe that Wollstonecraft was actively working for her and on 30 January 1793 she wrote to Everina Wollstonecraft: '. . . let me beg of you to send your twenty to Johnson and she will *immediately* draw on him – I told her I had thirty pounds from you, counting what I have had: and she of course says, she will draw on J. for that sum.' On 24 April she wrote: '. . . I am truly glad we sent the money, as it must be very acceptable at this juncture . . .'

494. The 'Gentleman' was probably a prospective employer of Everina Wollstonecraft or Eliza Bishop in France. When she left Waterford, Everina went to work for the Irwins of Fortick's Grove near Dublin; she was thus near the Bloods and the Skeyses.

495. Dr George Fordyce, a close friend of Johnson.

496. Wollstonecraft's ward Ann had presumably been sent to Everina or Betty Skeys to be looked after in Ireland.

497. James Wollstonecraft was alternately trying to leave the sea and take money from his sisters to equip himself for naval promotion. Eliza Bishop greatly lamented the money already spent on his training.

France 1792–1795

118. To Everina Wollstonecraft

Monsr. Filliettaz, Rue Meslée N°. 22, Paris, December 24th [17]92

I should have written to you immediately after my arrival had I found Madame F.[498] at home, but not having it in my power to obtain any intelligence respecting the situation which I mentioned to you previous to my departure, I put off writing till I received a letter and the purport of it you already know. I am a little vext at the disappointment especially as I cannot immediately determine what advice to give to Eliza; but in the course of a month I shall be able to look about me and hope to make some acquaintance that will point out a proper situation in France, for Geneva is not now, by M^{rs}. Brégantz's account, desirable on the score of cheapness. I will write to Eliza the moment I can speak decidedly   mean time will you desire her to keep up her spirits, for I shall not leave Paris till I have settled her. I suppose M^{rs}. B[regantz?] informed you that I came to an empty Hôtel – and you will easily imagine how awkwardly I behaved unable to utter a word and almost stunned by the flying sounds. I caught a violent cold on the road, and still have a very troublesome cough. To morrow I expect to see Aline, during her absence the servants endeavoured to render the house, a most excellent one, comfortable to me; but as I wish to acquire the language as fast as I can I was sorry to be obliged to remain so much alone. I apply so closely to the language, and labour so continually to understand what I hear that I never go to bed without a head ache –

---

498. Aline Filliettaz. Her home in the rue Meslée was situated in the Marais district.

and my spirits are fatigued with endeavouring to form a just opinion of public affairs – The day after to morrow I expect to see the king at the bar – and the consequences that will follow I am almost afraid to anticipate.[499]

I have seen very little of Paris the streets are so dirty, and I wait till I can make myself understood before I call upon Madame Laurent[500] &c. Miss Williams[501] has behaved very civilly to me and I shall visit her frequently, because I *rather* like her, and I meet french company at her house. Her manners are affected, yet the *simple* goodness of her heart continually breaks through the varnish, so that one would be more inclined, at least I should, to love than admire her. – Authorship is a heavy weight for female shoulders especially in the sunshine of prosperity. Of the french I will not speak till I know more of them. They seem the people of all others for a stranger to come amongst; yet sometimes when I have given a commission, which was eagerly asked for – it has not been executed – and when I ask for an explanation, I allude to the servant maid a quick girl, whom, [and] please you, has been a Teacher in an English boarding-school, dust is thrown up with a self-sufficient air, and I am obliged to appear to see her meaning clearly, though she puzzles herself, that I may not make her feel her ignorance; but you must have experienced the same thing.

I will write to you soon again – mean time let me hear from you, and believe me yours

sincerely and affectionately,

M. W.

---

499. Wollstonecraft did indeed watch the king passing through the streets to his trial on 26 December: see next letter.

500. The wife of a bookseller who had befriended Everina when she had stayed in Paris. He was a business associate of Johnson.

501. Helen Maria Williams (1761/2–1827), poet, novelist and chronicler. Publishing poems and a novel, she became popular in liberal bluestocking and Dissenting circles before going to France in 1790. She returned to publish the pro-revolutionary *Letters Written in France in the Summer of 1790*, which was very widely read in Britain. She then went back to France with her mother and sisters and wrote further chronicles of the Revolution. When Wollstonecraft met her she was associated with the married radical author, publisher and businessman John Hurford Stone; she held a salon on the rue Helvétius, where French revolutionary leaders mixed with expatriate British and German well-wishers. Her affectation was much noted.

119. To Joseph Johnson[502]

Paris, December 26th, 1792

I should immediately on the receipt of your letter, my dear friend, have thanked you for your punctuality, for it highly gratified me, had I not wished to wait till I could tell you that this day was not stained with blood. Indeed the prudent precautions taken by the National Convention to prevent a tumult, made me suppose that the dogs of faction would not dare to bark, much less to bite, however true to their scent; and I was not mistaken; for the citizens, who were all called out, are returning home with composed countenances, shouldering their arms.[503] About nine o'clock this morning, the king passed by my window, moving silently along (excepting now and then a few strokes on the drum, which rendered the stillness more awful) through empty streets, surrounded by the national guards, who, clustering round the carriage, seemed to deserve their name. The inhabitants flocked to their windows, but the casements were all shut, not a voice was heard, nor did I see any thing like an insulting gesture. – For the first time since I entered France, I bowed to the majesty of the people, and respected the propriety of behaviour so perfectly in unison with my own feelings. I can scarcely tell you why, but an association of ideas made the tears flow insensibly from my eyes, when I saw Louis sitting, with more dignity than I expected from his character, in a hackney coach, going to meet death, where so many of his race have triumphed. My fancy instantly brought Louis XIV before me, entering the capital with all his pomp, after one of the victories most flattering to his pride, only to see the sunshine of prosperity overshadowed by the sublime

---

502. The last of the letters to Johnson printed by Godwin in *PW*.

503. France had been defeated by Austria and Prussia, and internal subversives including the king, Louis XVI, were blamed; he was tried for treason on 26 December. Louis was being held in the King's Prison at the Temple close to Wollstonecraft's lodgings. It remains unclear how she could have seen the procession from the house on rue Meslée but Richard Holmes speculated that she might have been watching from the high attic (*Footsteps. Adventures of a Romantic Biographer*, London, 1985, pp. 99f.).

gloom of misery.[504] I have been alone ever since; and, though my mind is calm, I cannot dismiss the lively images that have filled my imagination all the day. – Nay, do not smile, but pity me; for, once or twice, lifting my eyes from the paper, I have seen eyes glare through a glass-door opposite my chair, and bloody hands shook at me. Not the distant sound of a footstep can I hear. – My apartments are remote from those of the servants, the only persons who sleep with me in an immense hotel, one folding door opening after another. – I wish I had even kept the cat with me! – I want to see something alive; death in so many frightful shapes has taken hold of my fancy. – I am going to bed – and, for the first time in my life, I cannot put out the candle.

M. W.

120. To Eliza Bishop[505]

[Paris] January 20th [1793]

I have put off writing to you day after day, because I waited till I could write in a satisfactory manner; but I have met with several disappointments with respect to you, yet, I do not despair, nay, I repeat the promise, which I made to Everina, I will not leave P. till you are settled, so let the hope, or rather the moral certainty, keep you warm this cold weather   Indeed you can live on hope better than most people   I am hurt by George's behavior, yet you are not to blame [For]get it as fast as you can, and only remember the pleasure [ ] to keep you from almost hating your fellow [creatures.] The unsettled state of public affairs, in this kingdom, and the season makes me less regret that I have not procured you a situation immediately – only

504. In *The French Revolution*, Wollstonecraft wrote: '. . . the imposing pomp and false grandeur of the reign of the haughty and inflated Louis 14th; which, by introducing a taste for majestic frivolity, accelerated the perfection of that species of civilization, which consists in the refining of the senses at the expence of the heart . . . The glory of France, a bubble raised by the heated breath of the king, was the pretext for undermining happiness; whilst politeness took place of humanity . . .' (*Works*, 6, 24)
505. This letter survives only in a transcript made by Eliza Bishop in a letter to her sister Everina dated 30 January 1793.

remember that this is not the only string to my bow – I have just received a letter from James to inform me that he is now in London wishing to put himself into the way of promotion, but utterly at a loss how to equip himself – I would willingly most willingly, forward any plan that would lead him to sea again;[506] yet how can I apply to J[ohnson] continually you will readily guess my vexation & reluctance – Still I must for were he once a Lieu[t] he would have an annuity for life   I can only now write about family affairs.[507] I highly approve of Everina's conduct with respect to M[r] [Ervin][508] and I am persuaded that she will find that situation more comfortable – I wish she would soon remit the money which she has saved for you to Johnson and I will immediately draw for it because the exchange is greatly in favor of the English, & the thirty pound will now go as far as forty or fifty at any other time. I like Mons[r] Filliettaz, and you would like him for without being what is termed a polite man he has great softness of manners which you find so fascinating – He resembles M[r] Edridge & [   ] I have not any reason to alter the opinion which I formed of the french from reading their history & memoirs yet I must make one observation to you for it has forcible struck me – those who wish to live for themselves without close friendship, or wa[rm] affection ought to live in Paris for they have the pleasantest way of *whiling away time* – and their urbanity, like their furniture is *tres commode* Yet I have even met with affection in P.;[509]

---

506. Eliza Bishop was less charitable. She wrote to Everina Wollstonecraft, 'This Philosopher, I own has dreadfully disappointed me – you *know*, I *looked* forward with hope, to the time when he would return; and be happy to pay M., what his extravagance has extorted from her . . . how finely are my hopes crushed, on hearing he is returned to London; and again applied for *Money* . . . why do I dwell on James? who I own I feel a great contempt for.'

507. French military reverses were making even sympathetic foreigners unpopular in Paris. The Jacobins headed by Robespierre (1758–1794) and Danton (1759–1794) were especially suspicious of British liberals who tended to support their opponents, the Girondins.

508. Probably this should have been 'Irwin', the name of the family to whom Everina would soon move when she left the Boyses.

509. *CL* speculates that this is the first mention of the man who would become Wollstonecraft's lover in France, the American businessman and author, Gilbert Imlay. This is possible if, as I think is the case, Wollstonecraft met him before April, the usual date given for the beginning of their friendship (see *Memoirs*, p. 103, where Godwin follows I. B. Johnson, one of Wollstonecraft's acquaintances in Paris, from whom he had requested information on his wife's past life. Johnson said he met Wollstonecraft

but it is not of french women I am going to speak, nor am I now introducing my favorite Mrs Schweizer to your notice Lavater's neice[510] Pray write soon & believe me your affectionate sister

M. W.

---

in April and that she and Imlay had been 'lately introduced', *SC*, 1, 125f.). Imlay was known to be in London on 2 February 1793 when he dated a letter from there to Harry Toulmin, who appended it to his *A Description of Kentucky, in North America* (1792). It is however possible that Imlay, who was trying to involve France and the US in a scheme for capturing Louisiana from the Spanish, was in Paris before that date as well as after – he was recommended by J.-P. Brissot (1754–93), the Girondin leader, to the French Foreign Office on 26 March 1793. The affair with Imlay must have been sufficiently well advanced by 19 April 1793 for Wollstonecraft to reveal her new emotions to Joel Barlow, who wrote home to Ruth on that date, 'Between you and me – you must not hint it to her or to J[ohnson] or to anyone else – I believe [Mary] has got a sweetheart – and that she will finish by going with him to Am[eric]a a wife. he is of Kentucky & a very sensible man' (Joel Barlow to Ruth, Houghton Library, Harvard; quoted in Eleanor Flexner, *Mary Wollstonecraft: A Biography*, New York, 1972, p. 181).

510. Madeleine Schweizer (1751–1814), formerly Anna Magdalena Hess of Zurich. She was not Lavater's niece but Lavater was the step-uncle (and guardian) of her husband, Johann Caspar Schweizer (b. December 1754), a Swiss banker of revolutionary leanings; the couple lived and entertained at their luxurious house in the Chaussée d'Antin (see David Hess, *Johann Caspar Schweizer und seine Gattin Anna Magdalena Hess, Eine biographische Skizze in 50 freien Umrissen*, 1822, pp. 4f.). When Fuseli had been passionately in love with Anna Landolt vom Rech, he had also flirted with Anna Magdalena Hess. In Ostend waiting for his passage to England, he sketched the portrait of Anna Magdalena Hess, at the back of which he wrote the love poem to Anna Landolt, 'To Nanna's Eye' (Gert Schiff, *Johann Heinrich Füssli, 1741–1825*, Zürich, 1973, p. 85). Fuseli painted several portraits of the three Hess sisters, especially Martha, who died of consumption shortly after his departure to England. According to the Hess biography, p. 19, Madeleine Schweizer dressed rather unconventionally in toga fashion after ancient classical paintings, liked to flirt and declared 'Je dois être libre comme l'air' to be her motto. She was still in contact with Fuseli at the time she met Wollstonecraft: a letter written on 12 September 1792 details the political terror and depicts her own sufferings through her sensibility and the illness of her husband. Madame Schweizer seems to have returned Wollstonecraft's regard although she was sometimes repulsed by her new friend's opinionated manner; see her journal, quoted in *Supp.*, p. 247, and *Athenaeum*, 3011, 11, July 1885.

121. To Ruth Barlow

Rue Meslée, Paris, February [1ˢᵗ–14ᵗʰ, 1793][511]

My Dear Madam,

I can scarcely tell you how much I was gratified by your kind letter – yes, it was very kind to write immediately, and I ought to have told you so sooner and intended to do so, yet I have put it off from day to day I know not why, tho' I should wish rather to talk to you than write to you I acknowledge, especially as I have not seen Mʳ B.[512] or heard any tidings of him. Mʳˢ Blackden[513] called on me the other day; but I happened to be out and I have not had an opportunity since of returning her visit, for the weather is very bad and I half ruin myself in coach-hire. The streets of Paris are certainly very disagreeable, so that it is impossible to walk for air, and I always want air. I am endeavouring to acquire the language, I mean that I should not be content to speak as many of the English speak, who talk away with an unblushing face, and I am exceedingly fatigued by my constant attention to words, particularly as I cannot yet get rid of a foolish bashfulness which stops my mouth when I am most desirous to make myself understood, besides when my heart sinks or flies to England to hover round those I most love all the fine French phrases, ready cut and dry for use, fly away the Lord know where. A Gentleman the other day, to whom I frequently replied, oui, oui, when my thoughts were far away, told me that I was acquiring in France a bad custom, for that I might chance to say oui, when I did not intend it, *par habitude*.

I am afraid that I have a strange spirit of contradiction in me physically and morally, for though the air is pure I am not well, and

---

511. The dating is from *SC*, 4, 870, where editors argue that, since Louis XVI had been executed on 21 January and the new constitution was to be presented to the Paris Convention on 15 February, Wollstonecraft would have written the letter between 1 February (the declaration of war between England and France possibly prompted the gentleman's offer of a place in his coach) and 14 February.

512. Although Joel Barlow was in Paris, Ruth had remained in London. After war broke out British distrust of French sympathizers burgeoned and Ruth left England to join Joel in Paris.

513. The wife of Colonel Blackden, an American speculator in land.

the vivacity that should amuse me fatigue me more than you can conceive. All the affection I have for the French is for the whole nation, and it seems to be a little honey spread over all the bread I eat in their land.[514] Yesterday a Gentleman offered me a place in his carriage to return to England and I knew not how to say no, yet I think it would be foolish to return when I have been at so much trouble to master a difficulty, when I am just turning the corner, and I am, besides, writing a plan of education for the Committee appointed to consider that subject.[515]

I will not now advert to public news excepting to tell you that the new constitution will soon make its appearance, and that Paris has remained perfectly tranquil ever since the death of the King.[516]

I write as usual in haste; but let me beg you to write to me soon, very soon; and tell me what you know and what you think. I am almost overwhelmed with civility here, and have even met with more than civility, still I long to return to my study, where I should be very glad to breakfast with you again – say, Amen! and believe me yours Sincerely.

M. W.

I hope you do not forget to employ Ann.[517] –

---

514. Eliza Bishop noted the strain of melancholy in her sister's letters. 'I am *convinced* M. has met with some great disappointment lately,' she told Everina, 'her letters are not in the same strain as when she was in London; she complains of lowness of Spirits ... Mary seems rather *disgusted* with the French in general yet I am sure there [is] a Cause.'

515. This invitation probably came through Paine or Condorcet, a member of the committee on public education. Condorcet (1743-1794) was sympathetic to Wollstonecraft's views; see his *Premier Mémoire*, where he wrote: 'L'instruction doit être la même pour les femmes et pour les hommes'. All women could attend primary classes and those with an aptitude for learning should not be prevented from continuing. Sciences were suitable for women, especially those branches that depended on minute observations (*Condorcet: cinq mémoires sur l'instruction publique*, ed. Charles Coutel and Catherine Kintzler, Paris, 1994, pp. 96f.).

516. Paine and Condorcet were members of the committee preparing the new constitution. Louis XVI had been executed on 21 January 1793.

517. It seems that Wollstonecraft's ward Ann was now with friends in London; this was the last mention of her in the extant letters.

122. To Joseph Johnson

Paris, May 2ᵈ, 1793

Sir,

On demand pay to Messʳ, Turnbull, Forbes and Coᵒ⁵¹⁸ Thirty pounds Sterling for value which I have received here of Mʳ. Christie and place it to my account, provided you have not already paid a similar order of the same date as this one

Mary Wollstonecraft

123. To Gilbert Imlay⁵¹⁹

[?Paris] Wednesday morning [c. April/May 1793]⁵²⁰

You have often called me, dear girl, but you would now say good, did you know how very attentive I have been to the —— ever since I came

518. Christie was the Paris agent for Turnbull Forbes & Co. Imlay had an agreement with this London firm, which in 1792 still had a contract with the city of Paris to deliver corn: see Per Nyström's *Mary Wollstonecraft's Scandinavian Journey* (Göteborg: Acta Regiae Societatis Scientiarum et Litterarum Gothoburgensis, 17, 1979), p. 20.

519. Wollstonecraft met Gilbert Imlay at the Christies' house, where he 'appeared to pay her more than common attention' (*SC*, 1, 125). He came from a prosperous mercantile and farming family of Scottish descent which had moved to Monmouth Co., New Jersey. He called himself Captain Imlay though there is no evidence he rose above the rank of lieutenant during the War of Independence. He claimed wrongly that he had grown up in the Western territories. Imlay speculated in land in Kentucky, where he had become a deputy land surveyor; he was heavily in debt by the time he left America. In Europe he published *A Topographical Description of the Western Territory of North America* (London, 1792) and *The Emigrants* (London, 1793). He was now associating with Barlow in the sale of American land to European settlers. In *Memoirs*, ch. 7, Godwin described Wollstonecraft's growing love for Imlay: 'She nourished an affection, which she saw no necessity of subjecting to restraint; and a heart like her's was not formed to nourish affection by halves. Her confidence was entire. Now, for the first time in her life, she gave a loose to all the sensibilities of her nature.'

520. The dating of this letter is problematic. Godwin places it undated before Letter 130 and after Letter 128 (Letters IV and II in the sequence to Imlay). *LI* and *CL* date it to August 1793. I have put it earlier, at the beginning of the relationship. In 'Imlay's

to Paris. I am not however going to trouble you with the account, because I like to see your eyes praise me; and, Milton insinuates, that, during such recitals, there are interruptions, not ungrateful to the heart, when the honey that drops from the lips is not merely words.[521]

Yet, I shall not (let me tell you before these people enter, to force me to huddle away my letter) be content with only a kiss of DUTY – you *must* be glad to see me – because you are glad – or I will make love to the *shade* of Mirabeau,[522] to whom my heart continually turned,

---

"Ghost": Wollstonecraft's Authorship of 'The Emigrants', in *Eighteenth-Century Women: Studies in Their Lives, Work, and Culture*, ed. Linda V. Troost (New York: AMS Press, 2001), pp. 263–98, John R. Cole has suggested an even earlier dating, arguing that the attentiveness mentioned here is proof of Wollstonecraft's ghosting of Imlay's only novel, *The Emigrants*, listed in *AR*, 16 (May–August 1793), p. 541, as published in the first half of the year, a claim earlier put forward more diffidently by Robert O. Hare in his edition of *The Emigrants* (Gainesville, Fla, 1964). It can certainly be argued that, were the dates to fit, Wollstonecraft seems a suitable source for some of the polemical passages on the victimization of women by the English marriage laws, as well as for those expressing sympathy for George III's miserable sister Caroline Matilda (also mentioned in *Letters from Sweden*) and those seeming to echo the married dilemma of her sister Eliza Bishop. On the other side, Imlay was both a fairly skilled writer (though not novelist) and an opportunist who mixed with radical thinkers in England where he could have picked up this kind of material (he was in London for at least part of February and could also have seen that radical polemical novels were becoming fashionable there). Wollstonecraft's complete authorship argued by Cole seems improbable since *The Emigrants* calls on a North American landscape, promotes a physiocratic ideology alien to Wollstonecraft's thinking, and celebrates an American commercial empire in the making; it also provides romantic conclusions to female dilemmas of the sort she never countenanced in her fiction and presents sentimental visions of ladies needing gallant male protection – for example, 'I pronounce that man a paltroon who would suffer any consideration under heaven, to weigh with him, when the feelings of an unprotected woman have been violated' (*The Emigrants*, ed. W. M. Verhoeven and Amanda Gilroy, London, 1998, p. 88). Finally neither Wollstonecraft nor Godwin ever attributed the novel to her.

521. *Paradise Lost*, 8, 54f. '. . . hee, she knew, would intermix / Grateful digressions, and solve high dispute / With conjugal Caresses, from his Lip / Not Words alone pleas'd her.' Wollstonecraft alluded to this vision of domestic and sexual intimacy more than once in her letters.

522. Honoré Gabriel Victor Riqueti, comte de Mirabeau (1749–1791), the fiery orator and revolutionary leader who favoured constitutional monarchy and was elected president of the French National Assembly. Wollstonecraft showed some political admiration for him in her *French Revolution*: 'Mirabeau . . . seems to have had from nature a strong perception of a dignified propriety of conduct; and truth appearing to give earnestness to his arguments, his hearers were compelled to agree with him out of respect to themselves'

whilst I was talking with Madame ——, forcibly telling me, that it will ever have sufficient warmth to love, whether I will or not, sentiment, though I so highly respect principle. —

Not that I think Mirabeau utterly devoid of principles – Far from it – and, if I had not begun to form a new theory respecting men, I should, in the vanity of my heart, have *imagined* that *I* could have made something of his – it was composed of such materials – Hush! here they come – and love flies away in the twinkling of an eye, leaving a little brush of his wing on my pale cheeks.

I hope to see Dr. —— this morning; I am going to Mr. ——'s to meet him. ——, and some others, are invited to dine with us to-day; and to-morrow I am to spend the day with ——.

I shall probably not be able to return to —— ——[523] to-morrow; but it is no matter, because I must take a carriage, I have so many books, that I immediately want, to take with me. – On Friday then I shall expect you to dine with me – and, if you come a little before dinner, it is so long since I have seen you, you will not be scolded by yours affectionately

[Mary].[524]

124. To Gilbert Imlay

[Neuilly-sur-Seine] Two o'clock [c. June 1793][525]

My dear love, after making my arrangements for our snug dinner to-day, I have been taken by storm, and obliged to promise to dine, at

(*Works*, 6, 124). The reference here suggests Wollstonecraft had been reading Mirabeau's published love-letters: *Lettres originales de Mirabeau, écrites du Donjon de Vincennes, pendant les années 1777, 78, 79, et 80; contenant tous les détails sur sa vie privée, ses malheurs, et ses amours avec Sophie Ruffei, marquise de Monnier* (1792).

523. *LI* here adds *Saint Germain*, the section of Paris where Imlay was presumably living.

524. In *PW* Godwin substituted four asterisks for the signature in this and later letters to Imlay. In *CL* and *LI* and in Roger Ingpen's *The Love Letters of Mary Wollstonecraft to Gilbert Imlay* (London, 1908), the name Mary has been restored, as here.

525. In May the revolutionary faction of the Girondins, with whom most of the expatriate British were associated, were defeated by the Jacobins. Robespierre proposed

an early hour, with the Miss ———s,[526] the *only* day they intend to pass
here. I shall however leave the key in the door, and hope to find you
at my fire-side when I return, about eight o'clock. Will you not wait
for poor Joan? – whom you will find better, and till then think very
affectionately of her.

Yours, truly,

[Mary].

I am sitting down to dinner; so do not send an answer.

125. To Eliza Bishop[527]

[Neuilly-sur-Seine] June 13th [1793]

My dear *Bess*!

I can scarcely tell you how very uneasy I have been on your account
ever since the communication with England has been stoped[528] and I
have been convinced that it was next to impossible to obtain a passport,
or an eligible situation for you here till things were settled and peace
in view. But, do not be discouraged, I am not apt to give false hopes;
yet I will venture to *promise* that brighter days are in store for you. I
cannot explain myself excepting just to tell you that I have a plan in
my head, it may prove abortive, in which you and Everina are included,
if you find it good, that I contemplate with pleasure as a mode of bringing

---

that all foreigners should be expelled. Fearing to compromise the Filliettazes, Wollstonecraft moved with their help from Paris to the nearby village of Neuilly-sur-Seine,
close to the Longchamp tollgate of the city, north of the Bois de Boulogne. The house
and garden were tended by the old Filliettaz gardener. This letter, as first published in
PW, has no date. Kegan Paul in *LI* supplied in brackets the date 'June ?1793'; it seems
that the letter was written about the time of the next dated one.

526. Probably Helen Maria Williams, her sister Cecilia and half-sister Persis Williams.

527. This letter and the next survive in transcripts made by Eliza Bishop in a letter to
Everina from Upton Castle, Wales, dated 14 July 1793.

528. Conventional postal services between Britain and France had ceased with the
declaration of war. Probably Wollstonecraft's letter, no doubt one of many written,
arrived in Wales through Barlow's American business associates in London.

us all together again.[529] I have been endeavouring to obtain a passport a long time and did not get it till after I had determined to take a lodging in the country — for I could not think of staying any longer at Madame F's   I am now at the house of an old Gardener writing a great book;[530] and in better health and spirits than I have ever enjoyed since I came to France, whilst you, it always disturbs me when I think of it, are desponding – But do not despair, my dear girl, once more breathe on the ashes of hope; I mean not to pun on the word, and I will render your fate more tolerable, unless *my* hopes deceive me. I have lately received a letter from James, but written two months ago – I have also heard of you and Everina, by the way of Ireland; but from M^r. Johnson it is, indeed, a long time since I have received a line   I write with *reserve* because all the letters are opened; but with earnestness I request you to write to me immediately and to keep up your spirits. I shall soon have an opportunity to write you by the same conveyance, meantime this will assure you that I am alive and most affectionately yours

Mary.

I shall write to E. under cover to Mrs Skeys.

126. To Eliza Bishop

Neuilly-sur-Seine, June 24th [1793]

My *dear Bess*!

   Fearing that my last letter may not have reached you, I write again with the same depressing uncertainty, only to tell you of any unavailing endeavours to settle you here and the vexation the continual disappointments have cost me. At present, indeed, it would be madness

---

529. Imlay had suggested to Wollstonecraft that he earn money in France so that they might settle together on a farm in America. In addition he had become involved with Barlow in a French scheme to take Louisiana for revolutionary France with the tacit approval of the new US government, which feared a British takeover.
530. Wollstonecraft had begun the work which would be called *An Historical and Moral View of the Origin and Progress of the French Revolution; and the Effect It Has*

to think of it; yet I do not give up the prospect should peace and order ever be established in this distracted Land – And, mean time, I carry my eye still further, and have actually a plan in my head which promises to render the evening of your life more comfortable. I cannot explain myself in a clearer manner, and knowing how sanguine you are I am almost afraid to set your imagination to work and lead you to rekindle hope with all your might and main, whilst you are talking in heroics of despair[531] – I am now hard at work in the country, for I could not return to England without proofs that I have not been idle. Last week I received two letters from Ireland; but I have not had a line from Everina or M[r]. Johnson so long that I am next to certain my letters must have miscarried. Let me beg of you, my dear Girl, if you receive any of my letters, to write immediately, for I feel quite lonely here now the communication is shut; and, as absence renders my friends more dear to me my heart bounds, when I think of you with the emotions of youthful fondness

Yours &c
Mary

Do not touch on politics —

127. To Joseph Johnson

Paris, July 13th, 1792

Dear Sir

Please to pay to M[r]. Thomas Christie, or order, twenty pounds for value received by me.

Mary Wollstonecraft.[20]

£20.0.0

Produced in Europe, Volume the First, dealing with the first months of the Revolution. Johnson published it in 1794.

531. Eliza Bishop had been writing to Everina that she was so miserable in Upton that her body was wasting away and her hair falling out in 'handfuls'; she was 'on the rack'. Her response to Wollstonecraft's unusually elated letter was further suspicion: she wished 'Mary would not write from the feelings of the moment – for it awakens feelings I wish not to rouse'. When she had copied out the letters for Everina, she exclaimed: 'What say you Everina now to the *Continental air*. – Or is it A *Love*? Ambition or Pity? That has wrought the Miracle?' (14 July, 1793).

128. To Gilbert Imlay

[Neuilly-sur-Seine] Monday night, past twelve o'clock
[c. August 1793][532]

I obey an emotion of my heart, which made me think of wishing thee, my love, good-night! before I go to rest, with more tenderness than I can to-morrow, when writing a hasty line or two under Colonel ——'s eye.[533] You can scarcely imagine with what pleasure I anticipate the day, when we are to begin almost to live together; and you would smile to hear how many plans of employment I have in my head, now that I am confident my heart has found peace in your bosom. – Cherish me with that dignified tenderness, which I have only found in you; and your own dear girl will try to keep under a quickness of feeling, that has sometimes given you pain – Yes, I will be *good*, that I may deserve to be happy; and whilst you love me, I cannot again fall into the miserable state, which rendered life a burthen almost too heavy to be borne.

But, good-night! – God bless you! Sterne says, that is equal to a kiss[534] – yet I would rather give you the kiss into the bargain, glowing with gratitude to Heaven, and affection to you. I like the word affection, because it signifies something habitual; and we are soon to meet, to try whether we have mind enough to keep our hearts warm.

[Mary]

I will be at the barrier[535] a little after ten o'clock to-morrow. – Yours –

532. Date supplied in brackets by Godwin.
533. As an American, Imlay could still reside in Paris. He was an associate of Colonel Blackden, possibly alluded to here, who may have been serving as postman to the pair.
534. Yorick, the hero in Sterne's *Sentimental Journey*, observed that 'in Paris, as none kiss each other but the men, I did what amounted to the same thing – I bid God bless her' (vol. 2, ch. 1).
535. One of the fifty-four tollgates or customs posts in the Paris city wall, where Wollstonecraft and Imlay met.

129. To Ruth Barlow[536]

[?Neuilly-sur-Seine] Friday afternoon [c. mid 1793][537]

My Dear friend,

A word or two, which dropt from you, when I last *saw* you, for circumstances scarcely allowed me to speak to you, have run in my head ever since – Why cannot we meet and breakfast together, *quite alone*, as in days of yore? I will tell you how – will you meet me at the Bath about 8 O'clock either monday or tuesday? – I will come on monday unless it should rain, or you write to forbid me – we may then breakfast in your favourite place and chat as long as we please before we part to return to our respective homes, for I do not wish to spend a whole day in Paris for a little time to come and when I do I must visit Madame Schweizer.

Yours affectionately
M. Wollstonecraft

Remember the *pills*!! —
and, do not forget, to ask Mrs Stone[538] what is become of Mr. Schlabberndorf[539] – give my love to M^rs, Blackden –

536. Like Imlay, the American Barlows could remain in Paris. Wollstonecraft was writing to Ruth as Citoyenne Barlow at Hôtel de la Grande Bretagne in rue Jacob, Faubourg St-Germain.
537. *CL* gives the address for this and the next letter as Paris. This is possible but assumes that Wollstonecraft moved back into the city alone before the registration by Imlay. Yet by mid to late summer the French government was actively persecuting British subjects in Paris. When Durant first printed this letter in *Supp.*, p. 265, he dated it late in 1794. But, as *CL* argued, it was obviously written at a time when Wollstonecraft and Ruth Barlow were living in or near Paris, therefore between June 1793, when the latter arrived in Paris, and January 1794, when Wollstonecraft left for Le Havre.
538. Rachel (Coope) Stone, wife of John Hurford Stone, the radical author and businessman, now the companion of Helen Maria Williams.
539. Graf von Schlabrendorf, an enthusiastic revolutionary who was living 'on almost nothing' to avoid adverse comment on his wealth (*Henry Crabb Robinson's Diary*, 1, 299), had fallen in love with Wollstonecraft. In his notes he enthused, 'The authoress of the right of woman [*sic*] believed, loved and lived, according to what she wrote. This was the cause of her unhappiness, why she was scorned by her own sex. She wanted to restore women's human rights in a bourgeois world; rights which had been denied to women, in all countries, by men's power, despotism, and legislation. And even when

130. To Gilbert Imlay[540]

[Paris] Friday morning [c. September 1793][541]

A man, whom a letter from Mr. —— previously announced, called here yesterday for the payment of a draft; and, as he seemed disappointed at

---

she could not restore these injured, withheld rights through her persuasive writings, at least she would not have them taken from herself. And in doing so she overstepped the boundaries of social prejudices and superstition, and the opinion of the world turned against this unhappy woman. And still Mary was the most noble, virtuous, sensuous female creature, that I ever met.' In Durant's translation of this passage Wollstonecraft became 'the noblest, purest and most intelligent woman I have ever met' (*Supp.*, p. 251), while Emma Rauschenbusch-Clough, *A Study of Mary Wollstonecraft and The Rights of Woman* (London, 1898), pp. 201f., translated the German word *sinnvollste* as 'thoughtful', although in the eighteenth century *sinnvoll* meant *sinnesvoll*, denoting 'sensuous, sensual'. Schlabrendorf continued: 'Mary was, without being a dazzling beauty, full of grace and charm. Her soulful face was more than regular beauty. Enchantment lay in her look, voice, and movement. She often visited me in prison. She captivated me more and more. Only after she had left Paris did I realize that I loved her. Her unhappy union with Imlay hindered a closer relationship with her' (cited in Zschokke, *Jochmann's Reliquien*, pp. 193f.).

540. On 28 August the British fleet overcame the French garrison at Toulon and news reached Paris on 2 September. In xenophobic reaction, on 17 September the French National Convention passed the Law of Suspects threatening all British expatriates in France with imprisonment until the war ended; Imlay therefore registered Wollstonecraft at the American Embassy as his wife although they did not marry. The registration left her free to quit Neuilly. From now on she would openly be linked with Imlay, to whose apartment in Saint-Germain-des-Prés she probably moved.

541. Godwin, who supplied the bracketed date in *PW*, inserted this note: 'This and the thirteen following letters appear to have been written during a separation of several months; the date, Paris.' Godwin called this series 'the offspring of a glowing imagination, and a heart penetrated with the passion it essays to describe' (*PW*, 3, 7). Wollstonecraft was alone in Paris since, shortly after her arrival, Imlay left for Le Havre on business. The Food Commission (Commission des Subsistances) was about to be established and placed under the direct supervision of the Committee of Public Safety. Their authority extended to all sectors of the economy and they oversaw foreign purchases. The sea blockade had reduced foreign trade without interrupting it altogether and the Commission responded by opening French ports to neutral shipping, for example from Sweden and the US. It provided these ships with luxury goods exempted from price controls and expected grain and armaments in return. From spring 1794, the volume of exports increased considerably. See Marc Bouloiseau, *The Jacobin Republic 1792–94*, tr. Jonathan Mandelbaum (Cambridge, 1983), pp. 107f.

not finding you at home, I sent him to Mr. ——. I have since seen him, and he tells me that he has settled the business.

So much for business! – May I venture to talk a little longer about less weighty affairs? – How are you? – I have been following you all along the road this comfortless weather; for, when I am absent from those I love, my imagination is as lively, as if my senses had never been gratified by their presence – I was going to say caresses – and why should I not? I have found out that I have more mind than you, in one respect; because I can, without any violent effort of reason, find food for love in the same object, much longer than you can. – The way to my senses is through my heart; but, forgive me! I think there is sometimes a shorter cut to yours.

With ninety-nine men out of a hundred, a very sufficient dash of folly is necessary to render a woman *piquante*, a soft word for desirable; and, beyond these casual ebullitions of sympathy, few look for enjoyment by fostering a passion in their hearts. One reason, in short, why I wish my whole sex to become wiser, is, that the foolish ones may not, by their pretty folly, rob those whose sensibility keeps down their vanity, of the few roses that afford them some solace in the thorny road of life.

I do not know how I fell into these reflections, excepting one thought produced it – that these continual separations were necessary to warm your affection. – Of late, we are always separating. – Crack! – crack! – and away you go. – This joke wears the sallow cast of thought;[542] for, though I began to write cheerfully, some melancholy tears have found their way into my eyes, that linger there, whilst a glow of tenderness at my heart whispers that you are one of the best creatures in the world. – Pardon then the vagaries of a mind, that has been

Along with Joel Barlow, who had direct contact with the Commission, and a Swedish merchant with French connections, Elias Backman, Imlay was involved in one of the schemes to evade the British blockade and import grain, soap and iron; he would export Bourbon silver in return. Barlow negotiated with the purchasing agents in Paris; Imlay handled the incoming shipments in Le Havre; and Backman set up headquarters in Gothenburg. See James Woodress, *A Yankee's Odyssey* (New York, 1958). Backman carried on a large shipping business with England, France, and Spain and dealt in grain, steel, wood, naval stores, and potash.

542. *Hamlet*, III, i, 84f.: 'And thus the native hue of resolution / Is sicklied o'er with the pale cast of thought.'

almost 'crazed by care,' as well as 'crossed in hapless love,'[543] and bear with me a *little* longer! – When we are settled in the country together, more duties will open before me, and my heart, which now, trembling into peace, is agitated by every emotion that awakens the remembrance of old griefs, will learn to rest on yours, with that dignity your character, not to talk of my own, demands.

Take care of yourself – and write soon to your own girl (you may add dear, if you please) who sincerely loves you, and will try to convince you of it, by becoming happier.

[Mary]

131. To Gilbert Imlay[544]

[Paris] Sunday night [c. November 1793][545]

I have just received your letter, and feel as if I could not go to bed tranquilly without saying a few words in reply – merely to tell you, that my mind is serene, and my heart affectionate.

Ever since you last saw me inclined to faint, I have felt some gentle twitches, which make me begin to think, that I am nourishing a creature

543. Gray's *Elegy*, l. 108: 'craz'd with care, or cross'd in hopeless love.'
544. Imlay had visited Paris at the end of October. Between 10 and 14 October, about 250 British subjects had been taken to the Luxembourg, including Stone and Williams; Schlabrendorf had also been imprisoned. Later in the month the Terror began: on 31 October the twenty-one Girondin deputies were guillotined, among them their leader and Imlay's associate, J.-P. Brissot. Wollstonecraft fainted when she heard the news, as Amelia Alderson reported in a letter to her friend Mrs Taylor: 'Mrs Imlay tells me, no words can describe the feelings which the scenes she witnessed in France gave birth to continually – it was a sort of indefinite terror. She was sitting alone, when Imlay came in and said, "I suppose you have not heard the sad news of to-day?" "What is it? is Brissot guillotined?" "Not only Brissot, but the *one-and-twenty* are." Amongst them she could immediately conjure up the faces of some lately endeared acquaintances, and before she was conscious of the effect of the picture, she sunk lifeless on the floor: and Mrs Imlay is not a fine lady – if any mind could be unmoved at such things hers would; but a series of horrors must have a very weakening tendency' (Cecilia Lucy Brightwell, *Memorials of the Life of Amelia Opie, Selected and Arranged from Her Letters, Diaries, and Other Manuscripts*, 2nd edn., Norwich and London, 1854, pp. 58f.).
545. Date supplied by Kegan Paul in *LI*.

who will soon be sensible of my care. – This thought has not only produced an overflowing of tenderness to you, but made me very attentive to calm my mind and take exercise, lest I should destroy an object, in whom we are to have a mutual interest, you know. Yesterday – do not smile! – finding that I had hurt myself by lifting precipitately a large log of wood, I sat down in an agony, till I felt those said twitches again.

Are you very busy?

[In *P W* Godwin here indicated the omission of 5 lines.][546]

So you may reckon on its being finished soon, though not before you come home, unless you are detained longer than I now allow myself to believe you will.[547]

Be that as it may, write to me, my best love, and bid me be patient – kindly – and the expressions of kindness will again beguile the time, as sweetly as they have done to-night. – Tell me also over and over again, that your happiness (and you deserve to be happy!) is closely connected with mine, and I will try to dissipate, as they rise, the fumes of former discontent, that have too often clouded the sunshine, which you have endeavoured to diffuse through my mind. God bless you! Take care of yourself, and remember with tenderness your affectionate

[Mary]

I am going to rest very happy, and you have made me so. – This is the kindest good-night I can utter.

132. To Gilbert Imlay

[Paris] Friday morning [c. December 1793][548]

I am glad to find that other people can be unreasonable, as well as myself – for be it known to thee, that I answered thy *first* letter, the

---

546. *CL* notes that these omitted lines appear to concern Imlay's business affairs.
547. Imlay had declared he was going to Le Havre only for a short time. Wollstone-craft's anxiety mounted as his stay lengthened.
548. Date supplied by Kegan Paul in *LI*.

very night it reached me (Sunday), though thou couldst not receive it before Wednesday, because it was not sent off till the next day. – There is a full, true, and particular account. –

Yet I am not angry with thee, my love, for I think that it is a proof of stupidity, and likewise of a milk-and-water affection, which comes to the same thing, when the temper is governed by a square and compass. – There is nothing picturesque in this straight-lined equality, and the passions always give grace to the actions.

Recollection now makes my heart bound to thee; but, it is not to thy money-getting face, though I cannot be seriously displeased with the exertion which increases my esteem, or rather is what I should have expected from thy character. – No; I have thy honest countenance before me – Pop – relaxed by tenderness; a little – little wounded by my whims; and thy eyes glistening with sympathy. – Thy lips then feel softer than soft – and I rest my cheek on thine, forgetting all the world. – I have not left the hue of love out of the picture – the rosy glow; and fancy has spread it over my own cheeks, I believe, for I feel them burning, whilst a delicious tear trembles in my eye, that would be all your own, if a grateful emotion directed to the Father of nature, who has made me thus alive to happiness, did not give more warmth to the sentiment it divides – I must pause a moment.

Need I tell you that I am tranquil after writing thus? – I do not know why, but I have more confidence in your affection, when absent, than present; nay, I think that you must love me, for, in the sincerity of my heart let me say it, I believe I deserve your tenderness, because I am true, and have a degree of sensibility that you can see and relish.

Yours sincerely

[Mary]

133. To Gilbert Imlay

[Paris] Sunday morning [December 29th, 1793][549]

You seem to have taken up your abode at H[avre]. Pray sir! when do you think of coming home? or, to write very considerately, when will business permit you? I shall expect (as the country people say in England) that you will make a *power* of money to indemnify me for your absence.

[In *PW* Godwin indicated the omission of 7 lines.]

Well! but, my love, to the old story – am I to see you this week, or this month? – I do not know what you are about – for, as you did not tell me, I would not ask Mr. ——, who is generally pretty communicative.

  I long to see Mrs. ——; not to hear from you, so do not give yourself airs, but to get a letter from Mr. ——. And I am half angry with you for not informing me whether she had brought one with her or not. – On this score I will cork up some of the kind things that were ready to drop from my pen, which has never been dipt in gall when addressing you; or, will only suffer an exclamation – "The creature!" or a kind look, to escape me, when I pass the slippers – which I could not remove from my *salle* door, though they are not the handsomest of their kind.

  Be not too anxious to get money! – for nothing worth having is to be purchased. God bless you.

Yours affectionately
[Mary]

---

549. Godwin's dating in *PW*.

134. To Gilbert Imlay

[Paris] Monday night [December 30th, 1793][550]

My best love, your letter to-night was particularly grateful to my heart, depressed by the letters I received by ——, for he brought me several, and the parcel of books directed to Mr. —— was for me. Mr. ——'s letter was very long and very affectionate; but the account he gives me of his own affairs, though he obviously makes the best of them, has vexed me.[551]

A melancholy letter from my sister has also harrassed my mind[552] – that from my brother[553] would have given me sincere pleasure; but for

[In *P W* Godwin indicated the omission of 9 lines.]

There is a spirit of independence in his letter, that will please you; and you shall see it, when we are once more over the fire together. – I think that you would hail him as a brother, with one of your tender looks, when your heart not only gives a lustre to your eye, but a dance of playfulness, that he would meet with a glow half made up of bashfulness, and a desire to please the —— where shall I find a word to express the relationship which subsists between us? – Shall I ask the little twitcher? – But I have dropt half the sentence that was to tell you how much he would be inclined to love the man loved by his sister. I have been fancying my-self sitting between you, ever since I began to write, and my heart has leaped at the thought! – You see how I chat to you.

I did not receive your letter till I came home; and I did not expect it, for the post came in much later than usual. It was a cordial to me – and I wanted one.

550. Godwin's dating in *P W*.

551. The books were probably from Johnson in London, perhaps to help with the writing of *The French Revolution*.

552. Probably from Eliza Bishop. Wollstonecraft later mentioned a letter from Eliza that had been back and forth to France; I have assumed that this is the letter. Ignorant of the marriage manoeuvre, Eliza Bishop responded to reports in London papers that her sister had been arrested with other British residents.

553. Charles Wollstonecraft, now settled in America.

Mr. ——[554] tells me that he has written again and again. – Love him a little! – It would be a kind of separation, if you did not love those I love.

There was so much considerate tenderness in your epistle to-night, that, if it has not made you dearer to me, it has made me forcibly feel how very dear you are to me, by charming away half my cares.

Yours affectionately
[Mary]

135. To Gilbert Imlay

[Paris] Tuesday morning [December 31st, 1793][555]

Though I have just sent a letter off, yet, as captain —— offers to take one, I am not willing to let him go without a kind greeting, because trifles of this sort, without having any effect on my mind, damp my spirits: – and you, with all your struggles to be manly, have some of this same sensibility. – Do not bid it begone, for I love to see it striving to master your features; besides, these kind of sympathies are the life of affection: and why, in cultivating our understandings, should we try to dry up these springs of pleasure, which gush out to give a freshness to days browned by care!

The books sent to me are such as we may read together; so I shall not look into them till you return; when you shall read, whilst I mend my stockings.

Yours truly
[Mary]

554. Probably Joseph Johnson. When in London, Imlay had not been part of Johnson's circle.
555. Godwin's dating in *P W*.

136. To Gilbert Imlay

[Paris] Wednesday night [January 1st, 1794][556]

As I have been, you tell me, three days without writing, I ought not to complain of two: yet, as I expected to receive a letter this afternoon, I am hurt; and why should I, by concealing it, affect the heroism I do not feel?

I hate commerce. How differently must ——'s head and heart be organized from mine! You will tell me, that exertions are necessary: I am weary of them! The face of things, public and private, vexes me.[557] The 'peace' and clemency which seemed to be dawning a few days ago, disappear again. 'I am fallen,' as Milton said, 'on evil days;'[558] for I really believe that Europe will be in a state of convulsion, during half a century at least. Life is but a labour of patience: it is always rolling a great stone up a hill; for, before a person can find a resting-place, imagining it is lodged, down it comes again, and all the work is to be done over anew!

Should I attempt to write any more, I could not change the strain. My head aches, and my heart is heavy. The world appears an 'unweeded garden,' where 'things rank and vile' flourish best.[559]

If you do not return soon – or, which is no such mighty matter, talk of it – I will throw your slippers out at window, and be off – nobody knows where.[560]

[Mary]

Finding that I was observed, I told the good women, the two Mrs. ——s, simply that I was with child: and let them stare! and ——, and

556. Godwin's dating in *PW*.
557. The Terror continued unabated but, with Williams and Stone recently released, Wollstonecraft now had some acquaintances in Paris.
558. *Paradise Lost*, 7, 25f., where Milton seems to lament his grim situation, personal and political, after the failure of the republic and the restoration of the monarchy: '... though fall'n on evil dayes, / On evil dayes though fall'n, and evil tongues.'
559. *Hamlet*, I, ii, 135f.; Wollstonecraft had referred to this passage earlier, in Letter 35 to George Blood and Letter 55 to Everina.
560. One of Imlay's business partners had confirmed her suspicion that Imlay always expected to remain in Le Havre for a further three months.

——, nay, all the world, may know it for aught I care! – Yet I wish to avoid ——'s coarse jokes.

Considering the care and anxiety a woman must have about a child before it comes into the world, it seems to me, by a *natural right*, to belong to her. When men get immersed in the world, they seem to lose all sensations, excepting those necessary to continue or produce life! – Are these the privileges of reason? Amongst the feathered race, whilst the hen keeps the young warm, her mate stays by to cheer her; but it is sufficient for man to condescend to get a child, in order to claim it. – A man is a tyrant!

You may now tell me, that, if it were not for me, you would be laughing away with some honest fellows in L[ondo]n. The casual exercise of social sympathy would not be sufficient for me – I should not think such an heartless life worth preserving. – It is necessary to be in good-humour with you, to be pleased with the world.[561]

Thursday Morning

I was very low-spirited last night, ready to quarrel with your cheerful temper, which makes absence easy to you. – And, why should I mince the matter? I was offended at your not even mentioning it. – I do not want to be loved like a goddess; but I wish to be necessary to you. God bless you!

137. To Gilbert Imlay

[Paris] Monday night [January 6th, 1794][562]

I have just received your kind and rational letter, and would fain hide my face, glowing with shame for my folly. – I would hide it in your

---

561. Godwin added the note: 'Some further letters, written during the remainder of the week, in a similar strain to the preceding, appear to have been destroyed by the person to whom they were addressed.'

562. *FNL*, p. 56, established Friday, 17 January 1794 as the date of Wollstonecraft's arrival in Le Havre and dated Letters 137–143 to Imlay (Godwin's XI–XVII) accordingly.

bosom, if you would again open it to me, and nestle closely till you bade my fluttering heart be still, by saying that you forgave me. With eyes overflowing with tears, and in the humblest attitude, I intreat you. – Do not turn from me, for indeed I love you fondly, and have been very wretched, since the night I was so cruelly hurt by thinking that you had no confidence in me –

It is time for me to grow more reasonable, a few more of these caprices of sensibility would destroy me. I have, in fact, been very much indisposed for a few days past, and the notion that I was tormenting, or perhaps killing, a poor little animal, about whom I am grown anxious and tender, now I feel it alive, made me worse.[563] My bowels have been dreadfully disordered, and every thing I ate or drank disagreed with my stomach; still I feel intimations of its existence, though they have been fainter.

Do you think that the creature goes regularly to sleep? I am ready to ask as many questions as Voltaire's Man of Forty Crowns.[564] Ah! do not continue to be angry with me! You perceive that I am already smiling through my tears – You have lightened my heart, and my frozen spirits are melting into playfulness.

Write the moment you receive this. I shall count the minutes. But drop not an angry word – I cannot now bear it. Yet, if you think I deserve a scolding (it does not admit of a question, I grant), wait till you come back – and then, if you are angry one day, I shall be sure of seeing you the next.

563. It was commonly believed that the maternal body transmitted harmful emotions to the foetus. In *Essays on Physiognomy*, tr. Thomas Holcroft (London, 1789), 3, 161, J. C. Lavater, whose work Wollstonecraft also in part translated, wrote: 'Could a woman keep an accurate register of what happened, in all the powerful moments of imagination, during her state of pregnancy, she then might, probably, be able to foretell the chief incidents, philosophical, moral, intellectual, and physiognomonical, which should happen to her child. Imagination actuated by desire, love, or hatred, may, with more than lightning-swiftness, kill or enliven, enlarge, diminish, or impregnate, the organized foetus.'

564. Voltaire's *L'Homme aux quarante écus* (1768) is a dialogue concerning taxation and economic policy. The Man of Forty Crowns repeatedly asks questions of a Geometrician. He concludes by declaring, 'We pass our lives in hope, and die hoping to the last. Adieu, Sir, you have enlightened me, but my heart is grieved.' The Geometrician replies, 'That is often the fruit of knowledge' (*The Man of Forty Crowns. Translated from the French of M. de Voltaire*, Dublin, 1770, p. 39).

—— did not write to you, I suppose, because he talked of going to H[avre]. Hearing that I was ill, he called very kindly on me, not dreaming that it was some words that he incautiously let fall, which rendered me so.

God bless you, my love; do not shut your heart against a return of tenderness; and, as I now in fancy cling to you, be more than ever my support. – Feel but as affectionate when you read this letter, as I did writing it, and you will make happy, your

[Mary]

138. To Gilbert Imlay

[Paris] Wednesday morning [January 8th, 1794]

I will never, if I am not entirely cured of quarrelling, begin to encourage 'quick-coming fancies,'[565] when we are separated. Yesterday, my love, I could not open your letter for some time; and, though it was not half as severe as I merited, it threw me into such a fit of trembling, as seriously alarmed me. I did not, as you may suppose, care for a little pain on my own account; but all the fears which I have had for a few days past, returned with fresh force. This morning I am better; will you not be glad to hear it? You perceive that sorrow has almost made a child of me, and that I want to be soothed to peace.

One thing you mistake in my character, and imagine that to be coldness which is just the contrary. For, when I am hurt by the person most dear to me, I must let out a whole torrent of emotions, in which tenderness would be uppermost, or stifle them altogether; and it appears to me almost a duty to stifle them, when I imagine *that I am treated with coldness*.

I am afraid that I have vexed you, my own ——. I know the quickness of your feelings – and let me, in the sincerity of my heart, assure you, there is nothing I would not suffer to make you happy. My own happiness wholly depends on you – and, knowing you, when my

565. *Macbeth*, V, iii, 38f.: 'she is troubled with thick-coming fancies, / That keep her from her rest.'

reason is not clouded, I look forward to a rational prospect of as much felicity as the earth affords – with a little dash of rapture into the bargain, if you will look at me, when we meet again, as you have sometimes greeted, your humbled, yet most affectionate

[Mary]

139. To Gilbert Imlay

[Paris] Thursday night [January 9th, 1794]

I have been wishing the time away, my kind love, unable to rest till I knew that my penitential letter had reached your hand – and this afternoon, when your tender epistle of Tuesday gave such exquisite pleasure to your poor sick girl, her heart smote her to think that you were still to receive another cold one. – Burn it also, my ——; yet do not forget that even those letters were full of love; and I shall ever recollect, that you did not wait to be mollified by my penitence, before you took me again to your heart.

I have been unwell, and would not, now I am recovering, take a journey, because I have been seriously alarmed and angry with myself, dreading continually the fatal consequence of my folly. – But, should you think it right to remain at H[avre], I shall find some opportunity, in the course of a fortnight, or less perhaps, to come to you, and before then I shall be strong again. – Yet do not be uneasy! I am really better, and never took such care of myself, as I have done since you restored my peace of mind. The girl is come to warm my bed – so I will tenderly say, good night! and write a line or two in the morning.

Morning

I wish you were here to walk with me this fine morning! yet your absence shall not prevent me. I have stayed at home too much; though, when I was so dreadfully out of spirits, I was careless of every thing.

I will now sally forth (you will go with me in my heart) and try whether this fine bracing air will not give the vigour to the poor babe, it had, before I so inconsiderately gave way to the grief that deranged my bowels, and gave a turn to my whole system.[566]

Yours truly
[Mary Imlay][567]

140. To Gilbert Imlay

[Paris] Saturday morning [January 11th, 1794]

The two or three letters, which I have written to you lately, my love, will serve as an answer to your explanatory one. I cannot but respect your motives and conduct. I always respected them; and was only hurt, by what seemed to me a want of confidence, and consequently affection. – I thought also, that if you were obliged to stay three months at H[avre], I might as well have been with you. – Well! well, what signifies what I brooded over – Let us now be friends!

I shall probably receive a letter from you to-day, sealing my pardon – and I will be careful not to torment you with my querulous humours, at least, till I see you again. Act as circumstances direct, and I will not enquire when they will permit you to return, convinced that you will hasten to your [Mary],[568] when you have attained (or lost sight of) the object of your journey.

What a picture you have sketched of our fire-side! Yes, my love, my fancy was instantly at work, and I found my head on your shoulder, whilst my eyes were fixed on the little creatures that were clinging about your knees. I did not absolutely determine that there should be six – if you have not set your heart on this round number.

I am going to dine with Mrs. ——. I have not been to visit her since the first day she came to Paris. I wish indeed to be out in the air as

566. Women often remained as inactive as possible through pregnancy but the latest medical opinion, even in France, urged exercise. Cf. Dr Nicolas, *Le cri de la Nature en Faveur des Enfants Nouveau-nés* (Paris, 1775).
567. In *PW* the signature is given as **** *****. Since Godwin was careful with his asterisks, it seems that Wollstonecraft was now using the name Mary Imlay in certain circumstances.
568. Godwin substitutes ****.

much as I can, for the exercise I have taken these two or three days past, has been of such service to me, that I hope shortly to tell you, that I am quite well. I have scarcely slept before last night, and then not much. – The two Mrs. ——s have been very anxious and tender.

Yours truly

[Mary]

I need not desire you to give the colonel[569] a good bottle of wine.

141. To Gilbert Imlay

[Paris] Sunday morning [January 12th, 1794]

I wrote to you yesterday, my ——; but, finding that the colonel is still detained (for his passport was forgotten at the office yesterday) I am not willing to let so many days elapse without your hearing from me, after having talked of illness and apprehensions.

I cannot boast of being quite recovered, yet I am (I must use my Yorkshire phrase;[570] for, when my heart is warm, pop come the expressions of childhood into my head) so *lightsome*, that I think it will not *go badly with me*. – And nothing shall be wanting on my part, I assure you; for I am urged on, not only by an enlivened affection for you, but by a new-born tenderness that plays cheerly round my dilating heart.

I was therefore, in defiance of cold and dirt, out in the air the greater part of yesterday; and, if I get over this evening without a return of the fever that has tormented me, I shall talk no more of illness. I have promised the little creature, that its mother, who ought to cherish it, will not again plague it, and begged it to pardon me; and, since I could not hug either it or you to my breast, I have to my heart. – I am afraid to read over this prattle – but it is only for your eye.

I have been seriously vexed, to find that, whilst you were harrassed by impediments in your undertakings, I was giving you additional uneasi-

569. Possibly the man who took letters between them, perhaps Colonel Blackden, whose drunkenness is commented on in Letter 149.
570. Wollstonecraft had spent much of her youth in Beverley, Yorkshire.

ness. – If you can make any of your plans answer – it is well, I do not think a *little* money inconvenient; but, should they fail, we will struggle cheerfully together – drawn closer by the pinching blasts of poverty.

Adieu, my love! Write often to your poor girl, and write long letters; for I not only like them for being longer, but because more heart steals into them; and I am happy to catch your heart whenever I can.

Yours sincerely

[Mary]

142. To Gilbert Imlay

[Paris] Tuesday morning [January 14th, 1794]

I seize this opportunity to inform you, that I am to set out on Thursday with Mr. ——, and hope to tell you soon (on your lips) how glad I shall be to see you.[571] I have just got my passport, so I do not foresee any impediment to my reaching H[avre], to bid you good-night next Friday in my new apartment[572] – where I am to meet you and love, in spite of care, to smile me to sleep – for I have not caught much rest since we parted.

You have, by your tenderness and worth, twisted yourself more artfully round my heart, than I supposed possible. – Let me indulge the thought, that I have thrown out some tendrils to cling to the elm by which I wish to be supported. – This is talking a new language for me![573] – But, knowing that I am not a parasite-plant, I am willing to receive the proofs of affection, that every pulse replies to, when I think of being once more in the same house with you. – God bless you!

Yours truly

[Mary]

---

571. Wollstonecraft had been worrying about the effect of the winter journey on her unborn child; none the less she was now determined to join Imlay in Le Havre.
572. Imlay rented a spacious house, owned by John Wheatcroft, an English soap merchant, near the harbour on the rue de Corderie in the Section des Sans-Culottes.
573. Wollstonecraft had mocked this sort of language and attitude in *The Rights of Woman*: 'To see a mortal adorn an object with imaginary charms, and then fall down and worship the idol which he had himself set up – how ridiculous!' (*Works*, 5, 180).

143. To Gilbert Imlay

[Paris] Wednesday morning [c. January 15th, 1794]

I only send this as an *avant-coureur*, without jack-boots,[574] to tell you, that I am again on the wing, and hope to be with you a few hours after you receive it. I shall find you well, and composed, I am sure; or, more properly speaking, cheerful. – What is the reason that my spirits are not as manageable as yours? Yet, now I think of it, I will not allow that your temper is even, though I have promised myself, in order to obtain my own forgiveness, that I will not ruffle it for a long, long time – I am afraid to say never.

Farewell for a moment! – Do not forget that I am driving towards you in person! My mind, unfettered, has flown to you long since, or rather has never left you.

I am well, and have no apprehension that I shall find the journey too fatiguing, when I follow the lead of my heart. – With my face turned to H[avre] my spirits will not sink – and my mind has always hitherto enabled my body to do whatever I wished.

Yours affectionately

[Mary]

144. To Ruth Barlow

[?Le Havre] February 3^d [1794][575]

My Dear Friend,

Why do I not hear from you — or rather, why do I not see you? I begin to be uneasy on your account, and to think that disappointment

---

574. A messenger herald; jack-boots were strong boots, the top of which stretched over the knee.
575. Another hand has written Paris on the manuscript, crossed it out and inserted Neuilly. *CL* placed this in Le Havre following the dating (also in another hand) of 1794.

pursues you. The little time I had to chat with M^r L——,[576] was, almost all, spent in questions concerning your affairs, to which I did not receive very satisfactory answers. — Pray tell me, and soon, what is your opinion.

I have been closely employed ever since I came here preparing a part of my M.S.[577] to send by M^r. Codman,[578] and the untowardly circumstances, which detain him, will enable me to give him a tolerable quantity. My lodgings are pleasantly situated, and I have hired a maid servant, so that I am very comfortably settled, and shall remain so, if the high price of all the necessaries of life, do not ruin US.

Mr Leavenworth will pay you the livres you advanced for me,[579] and I should be much obliged to M^r. Barlow, if he would get me the debates and decrees,[580] from the commencement of that publication and order them to be sent to me here, in future, by the post – for I never see a paper. Tell him that I am now more seriously at *work* than I have ever been yet, and that I daily feel the want of my *poor Books* — M^r. Imlay laughs at my still retaining any hopes of getting them; but I send you my signature on the other side, above which an order might be written – to make a last effort. I am quite out of the world,

576. Probably the American Mark Leavenworth (1752–1812) mentioned in the third paragraph. He was a business partner of Joel Barlow and involved with him and Imlay in the Louisiana scheme (see note 529 and Woodress, *A Yankee's Odyssey*, 144f.). His and Barlow's proposal to make a contract for seizing Louisiana for the French in the winter of 1793–94 is dated 'November 23, 1793, at the maison de Bretagne, Paris' (*Archives des Affaires Etrangères, Espagne*, vol. 636, fol. 391). Wollstonecraft knew the Leavenworths from 1793 or before (see *Ezra Stiles*, 3, 502f.) and Mark often acted as a go-between between her and the Barlows.

577. Her *Origin and Progress of the French Revolution*.

578. Richard Codman (d. 1806), Harvard graduate and Boston merchant (Woodress, p. 201), took the first part of Wollstonecraft's *Origin and Progress of the French Revolution* from France to Johnson in London through the blockade of the French coast.

579. Presumably Ruth Barlow had lent money for the journey to Le Havre. Wollstonecraft seems to have had no obvious source of income at this time.

580. *Journal des débats et des décrets* published by the National Assembly. Wollstonecraft used the work, especially the first three volumes, for her *Origin and Progress of the French Revolution*; she also depended heavily on the English *Annual Register* and was later criticized for doing so.

bid M^rs. B.[581] and your husband write to me – remember me kindly to them, and believe me yours truly

Mary Imlay

145. To Everina Wollstonecraft

[Le] Havre, March 10th [17]94

My Dear Girl,

It is extremely uncomfortable to write to you thus without expecting, or even daring to ask for an answer, lest I should involve others in my difficulties, and make them suffer for protecting me. The French are, at present, so full of suspicion that had a letter of James's, improvidently sent to me, been opened, I would not have answered for the consequence. I have just sent off great part of my M.S. which Miss William would fain have had [m]e[211] burn, following her example.[582] – And to tell you the truth, – my life, would not have been worth much, had it been found.[583] It is impossible for you to have any idea of the impression the sad scenes I have been a witness to, have left on my mind. The climate of France is uncommonly fine, the country

---

581. Possibly Mrs Blackden; see Letter 121.

582. Helen Maria Williams had been entrusted with manuscripts by both Madame Roland and Madame de Genlis. She destroyed them as well as her own writing when she was in danger. See *Souvenirs de la Révolution Française; par Héléna Maria Williams, traduit de l'Anglais*, Paris, 1827, pp. 80f. (Williams's last work was published only in a French translation by her nephew Charles Coquerel): '[Un] inspecteur dans la police de Robespierre, . . . nous offrit de renvoyer la garde, et nous dit de plus de ne pas nous presser, et qu'il attendrait volontiers quelques heures jusqu'à ce que nous fussions prêtes. Je compris sur-le-champ l'étendue de cette proposition. L'inspecteur se mit à dormir sur un sofa, et, pendant ce temps, je m'empressai de brûler dans la chambre voisine des tas énormes de papiers, dont la découverte nous eût été funeste; des billets de Mme Roland, des lettres de Lasource et autres correspondans *conspirateurs*. L'inspecteur eut l'attention réellement délicate et généreuse de ne se réveiller que lorsque la combustion des papiers fut entièrement terminée; ensuite il nous reconduisit dans la nouvelle prison, au couvent des Anglaises, rue de Charenton, et ne nous quitta qu'après nous y avoir vu écrouer.'

583. Wollstonecraft was writing only about events before the Jacobins came to power; none the less she deplored the 'ferocity of the parisians' and declared the recent bloody events a betrayal of the principles of the Revolution.

pleasant, and there is a degree of ease, and even simplicity, in the manners of the common people, which attaches me to them – Still death and misery, in every shape of terrour, haunts this devoted country – I certainly am glad that I came to France, because I never could have had else a just opinion of the most extraordinary event that has ever been recorded – and I have met with some uncommon instances of friendship, which my heart will ever grate[ful]ly store up, and call to mind when the remembrance is keen of the anguish it has endured for its fellow creatures, at large – for the unfortunate beings cut off around me – and the still more unfortunate survivors. If any, of the many letters I have written, have come to your hands, or Eliza's, you know that I am safe, through the protection of an American. A most worthy man, who joins to uncommon tenderness of heart and quickness of feeling, a soundness of understanding, and reasonableness of temper, rarely to be met with – Having also been brought up in the interiour parts of America, he is a most natural, unaffected creature. I am with him now at Havre, and shall remain there, till circumstances point out what it is necessary for me to do. Before I left Paris I attempted to find the Laurents,[584] whom I had several times previously sought for; but to no purpose – and I am apt to think that it was very prudent in them to leave a shop that had been the resort of the nobility. Where is poor Eliza? from a letter I received many, many months after it was written and travelled to France and back again to [ ] I suppose, she is in Ireland[585] – Will you write to tell her that I most affectionately remember her, and still have in my mind some plans for her future comfort. Are you well? But, why do I ask, you cannot reply to me – This thought throw a damp on my spirits, whilst I write; and makes my letter rather an act of duty than a present satisfaction – God bless you! I will write by every opportunity and am yours sincerely and affectionately Mary.

584. Mr Laurent was the Parisian bookseller, friend of Joseph Johnson and Everina Wollstonecraft when she had been learning French in Paris.
585. Eliza Bishop had mentioned her inclination to work near Everina in Ireland, but she was far more eager to go to Paris. At this time she was still in Wales, hoping desperately that Mary would rescue her.

146. To Gilbert Imlay

[Le] H[avre], Thursday morning, March [13th, 1794][586]

We are such creatures of habit, my love, that, though I cannot say I was sorry, childishly so, for your going,[587] when I knew that you were to stay such a short time, and I had a plan of employment; yet I could not sleep. – I turned to your side of the bed, and tried to make the most of the comfort of the pillow, which you used to tell me I was churlish about; but all would not do. – I took nevertheless my walk before breakfast, though the weather was not very inviting – and here I am, wishing you a finer day, and seeing you peep over my shoulder, as I write, with one of your kindest looks – when your eyes glisten, and a suffusion creeps over your relaxing features.

But I do not mean to dally with you this morning – So God bless you! Take care of yourself – and sometimes fold to your heart your affectionate

[Mary]

147. To Gilbert Imlay

[Le Havre, c. March 1794][588]

Do not call me stupid, for leaving on the table the little bit of paper I was to inclose. – This comes of being in love at the fag-end of a letter of business. – You know, you say, they will not chime together. – I had got you by the fire-side, with the *gigot*[589] smoking on the board, to lard your poor bare ribs, – and behold, I closed my letter without taking the paper up, that was directly under my eyes! – What had I got

---

586. Kurtz and Autrey point out that, although Wollstonecraft dated the letter 'Thursday Morning, March 12', 12 March 1794 was actually a Wednesday. They consider that she was more likely to mistake the date than the day of the week: see *FNL*, p. 56n.
587. Imlay had returned to Paris for a brief visit.
588. Date suggested by Kegan Paul in *LI*.
589. Leg of mutton.

in them to render me blind? – I give you leave to answer the question, if you will not scold; for I am

Yours most affectionately

[Mary]

148. To Ruth Barlow

[Le] Havre, April 27th [17]94

My Dear Friend,

I wrote to Mr. B.[590] by post the other day telling him that I indulge the expectation of success, in which you are included, with great pleasure — and I do hope that he will not suffer his sore mind to be hurt, sufficiently to damp his exertions, by any impediments or disappointments, which may, at first cloud his views or darken his prospect — Teasing hinderance of one kind or other continually occur to *us* here — you perceive that I am acquiring the matrimonial phraseology without having clogged my soul by promising obedience &c &c — — Still we do not despair — Let but the first ground be secured — and in the course of the summer we may, perhaps celebrate our good luck, not forgetting good management, together. — There has been some plague about the shipping of the goods, which Mr. Imlay will doubtless fully explain — but the delay is not of much consequence as I hope to hear that Mr. B. enters fully into the whole interest. You will be civil to the Danish Cap[t],[591] who will take charge of this, he is a worthy unassuming man — but, if you see proper to send me any thing, I mean a little dimity, white calico, or a light-coloured printed calico, for a morning gown, do not send a stinted pattern, you had

590. It seems that Joel Barlow had left for Hamburg where he would engage in business; Ruth was still in Paris but would soon join him.

591. Presumably the young Norwegian shipmaster Peder Ellefsen, in whose name Imlay had purchased a French cargo ship called *La Liberté*, renamed it *Maria and Margaretha*, and certified it as Norwegian. Ellefsen was to sail it from Le Havre to Norway under a Danish flag, thus evading the British blockade. For details of the transaction see Nyström's *Scandinavian Journey*.

better give them to Clough.[592] I have found some linen for Shirts for Mr. I. so do not want any — As I am not absolutely in want of the other articles do not purchase them should they be extravagantly dear — you will, however, judge, and I need not trouble you with directions.

I am still very well; but imagine it cannot be long before this lively animal pops on us — and now the history is finished and every thing arranged I do not care how soon.

Let me hear from you — Give me an account of your health situation — I mean how you are lodged, and whether you have any acquaintance. I shall have frequent opportunities of writing to you and shall avail myself of them — Believe me yours

affectionately
Mary

Give my Love to M^r. Barlow. —

149. To Ruth Barlow

[Le] Havre, May 20th [17]94

Here I am, my Dear Friend, and so well, that were it not for the inundation of milk, which for the moment incommodes me, I could forget the pain I endured six days ago.[593] — Yet nothing could be more natural or easy than my labour — still it is not smooth work — I dwell on these circumstances not only as I know it will give you pleasure; but to prove that this struggle of nature is rendered much more cruel by the ignorance and affectation of women.[594] My nurse has been

592. The word may be a variant spelling of Clô. Hess in *Johann Caspar Schweizer*, pp. 58 and 170f., mentions an Italian bookseller Angelo Clô, who was by 1801 married to Victoire Frescarode, a friend of Mme Schweizer. Dimity is strong cotton cloth with raised stripes or figures, usually used undyed; calico is plain unprinted cotton cloth.

593. The baby was born at two o'clock in the afternoon on 14 May 1794 (25 Floréal in the revolutionary calendar, which divided the year into ten rather than twelve units); she was registered as legitimate under the name Françoise Imlay in the Maison Commune of Havre-Marat (Le Havre's revolutionary name). The English landlord John Wheatcroft and his wife were witnesses.

594. Wollstonecraft was a devotee of natural childbirth, wanting as little interference as possible from doctors, whom she always distrusted.

twenty years in this employment, and she tells me, she never knew a woman so well — adding, Frenchwoman like, that I ought to make children for the Republic, since I treat it so slightly[595] — It is true, at first, she was convinced that I should kill myself and my child; but since we are alive and so astonishingly well, she begins to think that the *Bon Dieu* takes care of those who take no care of themselves. But, while I think of it, as your correspondent said, let me tell you that I have got a vigorous little Girl, and you were so out in your calculation respecting the quantity of brains she was to have, and the skull it would require to contain them, that you made almost all the caps so small I cannot use them; but it is of little consequence for she will soon have hair enough to do without any. – I feel great pleasure at being a mother — and the constant tenderness of my most affectionate companion makes me regard a fresh tie as a blessing. There — have I not talked sufficiently of myself and my child — and the *all about it* — as Richardson would have made Lovelace say.[596] —

Mr Imlay has been rendered almost impatient by the continual hinderances, which circumstances and the mismanagement of some the people intrusted with the concerns of the party — not to talk of the constant embarrassments occasioned by those whipping embargos, that slip off and on, before you know where you are. —

Poor Blackden[597] sailed 7 or 8 days ago in the mo[st] comfortable ship, with a Gentlemanlike Captain, for Lisbon in his way home — I was exceedingly glad to have him leave Havre for during the last weeks he began to seek for comfort in the old way — and was actually drunk when he was carried on board.

595. Others were not so kind. According to Schlabrendorf, 'The women in Havre called her an uncaring mother; yet the child prospered, grew up strong and beautiful. When I asked her what the women made of that, she replied: "They all say I do not deserve to have such a child." ' See Schlabrendorf's notes quoted in Zschokke, *Carl Gustav Jochmann's Reliquien*, p. 197.

596. Letter 21 of the third edition of Samuel Richardson's novel *Clarissa*: 'After her haughty treatment of me, I am resolved she *shall* speak out. . . . I'll tell thee beforehand, how it will be with my Charmer in this case – She will be about it, and about it, several times: But I will not understand her: At last, after half a dozen hem-ings, she will be obliged to speak out – ' (*Clarissa*, London, 1751, 4, 108).

597. Imlay's business associate from Paris. Presumably he was returning to America through Le Havre. See note 569.

I shall write a line or two to your husband to extort an answer; and I shall soon have another opportunity to assure of my regard and affection

Mary —

23^d, The vessel being detained I add a line to say that I am now, the 10th, day, as well as I ever was in my life – In defiance of the dangers of the ninth day, I know not what they are, entre nous, I took a little walk out on the eighth — and intend to lengthen it to day. —

My little Girl begins to suck so *manfully* that her father reckons saucily on her writing the second part of the R–ts of Woman

once more yours —

150. To Ruth Barlow

[Le] Havre, July 8th [17]94

My Dear friend,

I received but the other day your letter of May the 6th, and since then I have written to you or M^r. B. several times. Yesterday, I find, by a letter from Mr. B. that he wrote to me by the Dane, enclosing one from Charles — It would have given me great pleasure to have received this letter, but, as I fear I shall never see it, I must beg you, or Mr. B. to endeavour to recollect the substance of it, for I long to hear *how* Charles has succeeded — tell me likewise, at the same time, what Mr J.[598] says, for I cannot get a line from him.

I am very well, and my little Girl not only uncommonly healthy, but already, as sagacious as a child of five or six months old, which I rather attribute to my good, that is natural, manner of nursing her, than to any extraordinary strength of faculties. She has not tasted any thing, but my milk,[599] of which I have abundance, since her birth, yet, as I intend to

598. Joseph Johnson in London.
599. There was a growing movement in England and France against once fashionable wet-nursing. Rousseau had advocated maternal breast-feeding as good for the child and Wollstonecraft had favourably reviewed Ben Lara's *Essay on the Injurious Custom of Mothers not suckling their own Children*, which argued that not to breast feed was bad

begin to teach her to eat in a month or two, I must beg you to send me, if possible some more of those fine biscuits, for the bread commonly made here is worse than ever, and I get no more of the good.

I am glad to find that you are pleasantly situated, and hope to hear that you are again become fat and well likened. Mrs Swan popt on me about a fortnight ago, instead of surprising you, which was her intention – she was delighted with the reception and pleasures of England, not forgetting the delight of travelling in a Coach and four on the Bristol Road &c – Entre nous, I believe she was glad to get rid of M^{rs}. Blackden. She return to France in consequence of the information she received of the precarious state of her husband's health.

Mr. Imlay has not been well for some weeks past, and during the last few days he has [been] seriously feverish. His mind has been harass by continual disappointments — Sh[ips] do not return, and the government is perpetually throwing impediments in the way of business. I cannot help sharing his disquietude, because the fulfilling of engagements appears to me of more importance than the making a fortune. Of the state of things here, and the decree against the English[600] I will not speak — The French will carry all before them — but, my God, how many victims fall beneath the sword and the Guillotine![601] — My blood runs cold, and I sicken at thoughts of a Revolution which costs so much blood and bitter tears.

Adieu!
yours Sincerely
Mary

---

for the *mother's* health (*Works*, 7, 385f.). Breast-feeding was especially enjoined on revolutionary mothers.

600. The decree of 27 Germinal (16 April) had expelled foreigners from Paris. Anxieties about the increasing number of war prisoners contributed to the decision of 7 Prairial (26 May) that no British prisoners be taken – though the army, fearing reciprocal treatment, did not always obey the decree (Bouloiseau, *Jacobin Republic*, pp. 206f.).

601. The law of Prairial had accepted that political crimes were worse than common crimes because they threatened society. Henceforth anyone denounced for slandering patriotism, sapping revolutionary energy or spreading false news could be brought before the Revolutionary Tribunal which could either acquit or kill. To expedite revolutionary justice, no witnesses would be allowed and the accused would have no defence counsel. Consequently executions greatly accelerated from an average of five a day in Germinal to twenty-six in Messidor (19 June–18 July); this was the final stage of bloodletting under Robespierre and the Jacobins.

Remember me to your husband. –

I will send you a new vial by the first opportunity — Removing to another house the papers where disordered and I have not now time to regulate them. —

Mr. I. has just desired me not to send the papers lest they should endanger. I will forward them by Clough.

151. To Gilbert Imlay[602]

[Le Havre] Sunday, August 17ᵗʰ [1794]

[In *P W* Godwin indicated the omission of 3 lines.]

I have promised —— to go with him to his country-house, where he is now permitted to dine – I, and the little darling, to be sure – whom I cannot help kissing with more fondness, since you left us. I think I shall enjoy the fine prospect, and that it will rather enliven, than satiate my imagination.

I have called on Mrs. ——. She has the manners of a gentlewoman, with a dash of the easy French coquetry, which renders her *piquante*. – But *Monsieur* her husband, whom nature never dreamed of casting in either the mould of a gentleman or lover, makes but an aukward figure in the foreground of the picture.

The H——s are very ugly, without doubt – and the house smelt of commerce from top to toe – so that his abortive attempt to display taste, only proved it to be one of the things not to be bought with gold. I was in a room a moment alone, and my attention was attracted by the *pendule* – A nymph was offering up her vows before a smoking altar, to a fat-bottomed Cupid (saving your presence), who was kicking his heels in the air. – Ah! kick on, thought I; for the demon of traffic will ever fright away the loves and graces, that streak with the rosy

602. There is a gap here of over a month. Robespierre fell on 28 July 1794 after the coup of 9 Thermidor. In August Ellefsen sailed from Le Havre on the *Maria and Margaretha*. Imlay had no further need to remain in Le Havre and presumably wished to make contact with the new people in power; he therefore left Wollstonecraft and baby Fanny and returned to Paris.

beams of infant fancy the *sombre* day of life – whilst the imagination, not allowing us to see things as they are, enables us to catch a hasty draught of the running stream of delight, the thirst for which seems to be given only to tantalize us.

But I am philosophizing; nay, perhaps you will call me severe, and bid me let the square-headed money-getters alone. – Peace to them! though none of the social sprites (and there are not a few of different descriptions, who sport about the various inlets to my heart) gave me a twitch to restrain my pen.

I have been writing on, expecting poor —— to come; for, when I began, I merely thought of business; and, as this is the idea that most naturally associates with your image, I wonder I stumbled on any other.

Yet, as common life, in my opinion, is scarcely worth having, even with a *gigot* every day, and a pudding added thereunto, I will allow you to cultivate my judgment, if you will permit me to keep alive the sentiments in your heart, which may be termed romantic, because, the offspring of the senses and the imagination, they resemble the mother more than the father,[603] when they produce the suffusion I admire. – In spite of icy age, I hope still to see it, if you have not determined only to eat and drink, and be stupidly useful to the stupid –

Yours
[Mary]

152. To Gilbert Imlay

[Le] H[avre], Tuesday, August 19th [1794]

I received both your letters to-day – I had reckoned on hearing from you yesterday, therefore was disappointed, though I imputed your silence to the right cause. I intended answering your kind letter immediately, that you might have felt the pleasure it gave me; but —— came

---

603. Godwin noted that Wollstonecraft meant 'the latter more than the former'. This is a touchstone of sentimental doctrine, cf. especially Rousseau's *La Nouvelle Héloïse* (1761) and Henry Mackenzie's *Julia de Roubigné* (1777) where the imaginary is seen to have greater effect than ordinary reality.

in, and some other things interrupted me; so that the fine vapour has evaporated – yet, leaving a sweet scent behind, I have only to tell you, what is sufficiently obvious, that the earnest desire I have shown to keep my place, or gain more ground in your heart, is a sure proof how necessary your affection is to my happiness. – Still I do not think it false delicacy, or foolish pride, to wish that your attention to my happiness should arise *as much* from love, which is always rather a selfish passion, as reason – that is, I want you to promote my felicity, by seeking your own. – For, whatever pleasure it may give me to discover your generosity of soul, I would not be dependent for your affection on the very quality I most admire. No; there are qualities in your heart, which demand my affection; but, unless the attachment appears to me clearly mutual, I shall labour only to esteem your character, instead of cherishing a tenderness for your person.

I write in a hurry, because the little one, who has been sleeping a long time, begins to call for me. Poor thing! when I am sad, I lament that all my affections grow on me, till they become too strong for my peace, though they all afford me snatches of exquisite enjoyment – This for our little girl was at first very reasonable – more the effect of reason, a sense of duty, than feeling[604] – now, she has got into my heart and imagination, and when I walk out without her, her little figure is ever dancing before me.

You too have somehow clung round my heart – I found I could not eat my dinner in the great room – and, when I took up the large knife to carve for myself, tears rushed into my eyes. – Do not however suppose that I am melancholy – for, when you are from me, I not only wonder how I can find fault with you – but how I can doubt your affection.

I will not mix any comments on the inclosed (it roused my indignation) with the effusion of tenderness, with which I assure you, that you are the friend of my bosom, and the prop of my heart.

[Mary]

604. In *The Rights of Woman* Wollstonecraft had argued, 'Natural affection, as it is termed, I believe to be a very faint tie, affections must grow out of the habitual exercise of a mutual sympathy' (*Works*, 5, 223).

153. To Gilbert Imlay

[Le] H[avre], August 20ᵗʰ [1794]

I want to know what steps you have taken respecting ——. Knavery always rouses my indignation – I should be gratified to hear that the law had chastised —— severely; but I do not wish you to see him, because the business does not now admit of peaceful discussion, and I do not exactly know how you would express your contempt.

Pray ask some questions about Tallien[605] – I am still pleased with the dignity of his conduct. – The other day, in the cause of humanity, he made use of a degree of address, which I admire – and mean to point out to you, as one of the few instances of address which do credit to the abilities of the man, without taking away from that confidence in his openness of heart, which is the true basis of both public and private friendship.[606]

Do not suppose that I mean to allude to a little reserve of temper in you, of which I have sometimes complained! You have been used to a

605. Jean Lambert Tallien (1767–1820) had been a corrupt and often cruel official who ordered the deaths of many Bordeaux merchants whose money he then confiscated. Now, however, he was instrumental in stopping the Terror, which he called the weapon of tyranny. After helping topple Robespierre three weeks earlier, he suppressed the Revolutionary Tribunal and closed the Jacobin Club. The new political climate allowed Wollstonecraft to contemplate continuing her history of the French Revolution into the violent phase which she had witnessed. She later claimed she had written a 'considerable part' of two or three further volumes but Godwin states that 'No part of the proposed continuation of this work, has been found among the papers of the author' (*Memoirs*, p. 105n.).

606. Wollstonecraft is possibly referring to Tallien's speech on the freedom of the press delivered at the Jacobin Club on 1 Fructidor and repeated before the Convention the following day: 'Without the adoption of this motto, *Freedom of the press or death*, without its full execution, we are no more than abject slaves of the whims and despotic moods of the first man who, invested with authority, can turn it against us with impunity, and use it to crush us. . . . It is only by guaranteeing this precious liberty that you will be able to find a secure shelter against all the blows of arbitrary authority' (Aulard, *Société des Jacobins*, vol. 6, pp. 354f., cited in Bronislaw Baczko, *Ending the Terror. The French Revolution after Robespierre*, tr. Michel Petheram, Cambridge, 1994, p. 80).

cunning woman,[607] and you almost look for cunning – Nay, in *managing* my happiness, you now and then wounded my sensibility, concealing yourself, till honest sympathy, giving you to me without disguise, lets me look into a heart, which my half-broken one wishes to creep into, to be revived and cherished. – You have frankness of heart, but not often exactly that overflowing (*épanchement de coeur*[608]), which becoming almost childish, appears a weakness only to the weak.

But I have left poor Tallien. I wanted you to enquire likewise whether, as a member declared in the convention, Robespierre really maintained a *number* of mistresses.[609] – Should it prove so, I suspect that they rather flattered his vanity than his senses.

607. In the preface to his edition of the Imlay letters, p. xv, Roger Ingpen speculated that Helen Maria Williams had been Imlay's mistress but I have found no evidence in the writings of Williams or Wollstonecraft that this is the case; Williams had been involved with the political activist and merchant John Hurford Stone for some time and seems to have visited Wollstonecraft in Neuilly when the latter's affair with Imlay had begun. 'Cunning is a natural gift of woman,' noted Rousseau in his description of the ideal woman, *Emile* tr. Barbara Foxley (London, 1974), p. 334.

608. Outpourings of the heart. Diderot and D'Alembert's *Encyclopédie* (Paris, 1755) defined 'épanchement' medically: 'Ce terme est employé à-peu-près dans le même sens qu'*éffusion, extravasation*; il semble cependant plus particulierement affecté pour exprimer l'écoulement considérable d'un fluide, dans quelqu'espace du corps humain qui n'est pas destiné à en contenir, comme lorsque la sérosité du sang sort de ses vaisseaux, et se répand dans la cavité du bas-ventre: d'où résulte une hydropisie ascite . . .' (5, 744).

609. Robespierre was famously austere in his domestic life. William Augustus Miles to Pye, 1 March, 1791, cited in J. M. Thompson, *Robespierre* (Oxford, 1988), p. 142f.: 'He is a stern man, rigid in his principles, plain, unaffected in his manners, no foppery in his dress, certainly above corruption, despising wealth, and with nothing of the volatility of a Frenchman in his character.' 'Robespierre jugé par le médecin Souberbielle', in Louis Jacob, *Robespierre vu par ses contemporains* (Paris, 1938), p. 204: 'On répète dans toutes les histories qu'il était l'amant de la fille Duplay. Comme commensal habituel de cette maison, dont j'étais le médecin, je fais le serment que c'est une calomnie. Ils s'aimaient beaucoup, leur mariage était arrêté; mais il ne s'est rien passé entre eux qui pût faire rougir une vierge. Sans affectation et sans pruderie, Robespierre évitait, arrêtait même, les conversations libres. Ses mœurs étaient pures.' Yet after his execution there were widespread rumours about his licentiousness. Galart de Montjoye's *Historie de la conjuration de Maximilien Robespierre* (1796) represented him taking part in orgies with prostitutes, while Abbé Proyart's *La Vie et les crimes de Maximilien Robespierre* (Augsburg, 1795) depicted him drinking the blood of his victims, eating the roasted flesh of priests and sending their skins to the tanneries to make shoes for the *sans-culottes*.

Here is a chatting, desultory epistle! But do not suppose that I mean to close it without mentioning the little damsel – who has been almost springing out of my arm – she certainly looks very like you – but I do not love her the less for that, whether I am angry or pleased with you. –

Yours affectionately

[Mary]

154. To Everina Wollstonecraft[610]

Paris, September 20th [1794]

As you must, my dear Girl, have received several letters from me, especially one I sent to London by M[r] Imlay, I avail myself of this opportunity just to tell you that I am well and my child, and to request you to write by this occasion – I do, indeed, long to hear from you and Eliza, I have, at last got some tidings of Charles – and as they must have reached you I need not tell you what sincere satisfaction they afforded me – I have also heard from James, he too talks of success, but in a querulous strain[611] – What are you doing? Where is Eliza? You have, perhaps answered these questions in answer to the letters I gave in charge to M[r] I – but fearing that some fatality might have prevented their reaching you let me repeat that I have written to you and to Eliza, at least, half a score times, pointing out different ways for you to write to me, still have received no answers.

---

610. Business took Imlay to London from Paris and he apparently visited Wollstone-craft in Le Havre *en route*. She then returned with the baby to Paris. Williams and Stone were now in Switzerland, the Barlows in Hamburg, and Paine still in prison. Other friends were available, however, including a friendly German lady and Schlabrendorf. Probably this letter, sent through Miss Moore and Co., Finsbury Square, was being forwarded through Imlay's business associates. Thomas Christie, with whom Imlay also did business, lived with his wife Rebecca in Finsbury Square.

611. According to Eliza Bishop's letters to Everina Wollstonecraft, Charles claimed he had become a 'speculator' in Pennsylvania, bought land, and was contemplating a company to buy 300,000 acres for a settlement of English emigrants. Within a year he expected all to be flourishing and 'Then Eliza will give up romantic plans; and resolve to leave England – she will find not only a home but a brother in America'. James had returned to sea and was in line for bounty.

I have again and again given you an account of my present situation and introduced Mr Imlay to you as a brother you would love and respect – I hope the time is not very distant when we shall all meet – do be very particular in your account of yourself and if you have not time to procure me a letter from her tell me all about her – Tell me too what is become of George &c &c I only write to ask questions and to assure you that I am most affectionately

yours
Mary Imlay[612]

Should peace take place this winter what say you to a voyage in the Spring, if not to see your old acquaintance to see Paris, which I think you did not do justice to – I want you to see my little girl, who is more like a boy – She is ready to fly away with spirits – and has eloquent health in her cheeks and eyes – She does not promise to be a beauty; but appears *wonderfully* intelligent; and, though I am sure she has her father's quick temper and feelings, her good humour runs away with all the credit of my good nursing – I managed myself so well that my lying-in scarcely deserved the name; I only rested, through persuasion, in bed one day and was out a walking the eight. She is now only four months old – She caught the small-pox at Havre where they treat th[at] dreadful disorder very improperly – I, however, determined to follow the suggestions of my own reason, and saved her much pain, probably her life, for she was very full, by putting her twice a day into a warm bath[613] – Once more Adieu! the letter not being sent

612. Eliza Bishop had been slow to believe in her sister's marriage: she wrote in August to Everina, 'Mary cannot be *Married*!! It is mere *report*. It is natural to conclude her protector is her *Husband* – Nay, on reading Charles's letter, *I* for an *instant* believed it true — I would, my Everina we were out of suspense for all at present is uncertainty; and the most cruel suspense[.] Still Johnson does not repeat things at random and that the very same tale should have crossed the Atlantic makes me almost believe that the *once* M. is now Mrs Imlay, and a mother – Are we ever to see this *Mother and Her Babe*[?]' In October Eliza heard through Everina that Wollstonecraft was indeed married, as the signature here implies.

613. Smallpox was a serious disease for anyone, especially young children. Earlier in the century Lady Mary Wortley Montagu had popularized the eastern idea of giving children weak doses to inoculate them against more serious versions, and Wollstonecraft's pupil Margaret King had been inoculated in Ireland as a baby. The practice was lengthy and dangerous, requiring much supervision of the child, but, had she been in

for as soon as I expected gave me an opportunity to add this prattling postscript – you will see the last vol: I have written, it is the commence of a considerable work – Tell Mrs Skeys, who could not fulfil her promise respecting her portrait, that it was written during my pregnancy – —

155. To Gilbert Imlay

[Paris] September 22^d [1794]

I have just written two letters, that are going by other conveyances, and which I reckon on your receiving long before this. I therefore merely write, because I know I should be disappointed at seeing any one who had left you, if you did not send a letter, were it ever so short, to tell me why you did not write a longer – and you will want to be told, over and over again, that our little Hercules is quite recovered.

Besides looking at me, there are three other things, which delight her – to ride in a coach, to look at a scarlet waistcoat, and hear loud music – yesterday, at the *fête*,[614] she enjoyed the two latter; but, to honour J. J. Rousseau,[615] I intend to give her a sash, the first she has ever had round her – and why not? – for I have always been half in love with him.

Well, this you will say is trifling – shall I talk about alum or soap?[616] There is nothing picturesque in your present pursuits; my imagination

Britain, Wollstonecraft would probably have had Fanny inoculated. Johnson had printed John Haygarth's *An Inquiry How to Prevent Small-Pox* (1784), a work advocating inoculation, and in 1794 his sequel, *A Sketch of a Plan to Exterminate the Casual Small-Pox from Great Britain*.

614. 21 September 1794 was a holiday to celebrate the replacing in the Panthéon of Mirabeau's body with that of the more radical revolutionary leader Marat. Jacobins still controlled parts of the city but would not do so for long; consequently the body of Marat was removed four months later.

615. Rousseau's body was also in the Panthéon.

616. Two of the products Imlay and his business associates were importing into France. Alum was a mineral salt taken from shale and used in the leather industry and as a mordant or binder in dyeing.

then rather chuses to ramble back to the barrier[617] with you, or to see you coming to meet me, and my basket of grapes. – With what pleasure do I recollect your looks and words, when I have been sitting on the window, regarding the waving corn!

Believe me, sage sir, you have not sufficient respect for the imagination – I could prove to you in a trice that it is the mother of sentiment, the great distinction of our nature, the only purifier of the passions – animals have a portion of reason, and equal, if not more exquisite, senses; but no trace of imagination, or her offspring taste, appears in any of their actions.[618] The impulse of the senses, passions, if you will, and the conclusions of reason, draw men together; but the imagination is the true fire, stolen from heaven, to animate this cold creature of clay, producing all those fine sympathies that lead to rapture, rendering men social by expanding their hearts, instead of leaving them leisure to calculate how many comforts society affords.[619]

If you call these observations romantic, a phrase in this place which would be tantamount to nonsensical, I shall be apt to retort, that you are embruted by trade and the vulgar enjoyments of life – Bring me then back your barrier-face, or you shall have nothing to say to my

617. The Paris gate where Wollstonecraft and Imlay used to meet when the former lived in Neuilly and where she assumed Fanny had been conceived.

618. Cf. *Original Stories from Real Life*, ch. 2: 'Animals have not the affections which arise from reason, nor can they do good, or acquire virtue. Every affection, and impulse, which I have observed in them, are like our inferior emotions, which do not depend entirely on our will, but are involuntary ... we neither see imagination nor wisdom in them; and, what principally exalts man, friendship and devotion, they seem incapable of forming the least idea of' (*Works*, 4, 372). In *Discourse on the Method* (1637), pt. 5, Descartes includes an argument based on language which relegated animals to mechanical automata devoid of anything that could qualify as consciousness.

619. A common sentiment since the early eighteenth century, e.g. Samuel Colliber, *Free Thoughts concerning Souls: In Four Essays* (London, 1734), pp. 60f.: '*Imagination* or *Phantasie*, gives us likewise, in some respects, a considerable Advantage over the most perfect of Brutes. This, when directed by Reason, works in a surprizing manner on the Ideas furnished by Memory ... such is the Beauty of the Scenes and Images which Human Imagination presents, that, like some curious Pieces of Painting, they seem to excel even Nature itself; and the Pleasures they give have actually more of Rapture, tho' far less of Solidity, than those that proceed from the Discovery of Reason.'

barrier-girl; and I shall fly from you, to cherish the remembrances that will ever be dear to me; for I am yours truly

[Mary].

156. To Gilbert Imlay

[Paris] Evening, September 23^d [1794]

I have been playing and laughing with the little girl so long, that I cannot take up my pen to address you without emotion. Pressing her to my bosom, she looked so like you (*entre nous*, your best looks, for I do not admire your commercial face) every nerve seemed to vibrate to the touch, and I began to think that there was something in the assertion of man and wife being one[620] – for you seemed to pervade my whole frame, quickening the beat of my heart, and lending me the sympathetic tears you excited.

Have I any thing more to say to you? No; not for the present – the rest is all flown away; and, indulging tenderness for you, I cannot now complain of some people here, who have ruffled my temper for two or three days past.

Morning

Yesterday B—— sent to me for my packet of letters. He called on me before; and I like him better than I did – that is, I have the same opinion of his understanding, but I think with you, he has more tenderness and real delicacy of feeling with respect to women, than are commonly to be met with. His manner too of speaking of his little girl, about the age of mine, interested me. I gave him a letter for my sister, and requested him to see her.

I have been interrupted. Mr. —— I suppose will write about business. Public affairs I do not descant on, except to tell you that they

620. In *The Rights of Woman*, Wollstonecraft had mocked the idea when expressed in a legal context: 'The laws respecting woman ... make an absurd unit of a man and his wife; and then, by the easy transition of only considering him as responsible, she is reduced to a mere cypher' (*Works*, 5, 215).

write now with great freedom and truth, and this liberty of the press[621] will overthrow the Jacobins,[622] I plainly perceive.

I hope you take care of your health. I have got a habit of restlessness at night, which arises, I believe, from activity of mind; for, when I am alone, that is, not near one to whom I can open my heart, I sink into reveries and trains of thinking, which agitate and fatigue me.

This is my third letter; when am I to hear from you? I need not tell you, I suppose, that I am now writing with somebody in the room with me, and —— is waiting to carry this to Mr. ——'s. I will then kiss the girl for you, and bid you adieu.

I desired you, in one of my other letters, to bring back to me your barrier-face – or that you should not be loved by my barrier-girl. I know that you will love her more and more, for she is a little affectionate, intelligent creature, with as much vivacity, I should think, as you could wish for.

I was going to tell you of two or three things which displease me here; but they are not of sufficient consequence to interrupt pleasing sensations. I have received a letter from Mr. ——. I want you to bring —— with you. Madame S——[623] is by me, reading a German translation of your letters[624] – she desires me to give her love to you, on account of what you say of the negroes.[625]

Yours most affectionately,
[Mary]

621. The Constitution of 1793 had confirmed the freedom of the press, but the Jacobins undermined it and executed many for their writings. Now, although there were no specific acts restoring freedom, speeches before the Convention by Tallien on 2 Fructidor and by Fréron on 9 Fructidor sparked a prolonged debate that began to shift public opinion (see note 606).

622. The remaining Jacobins interpreted the debate on the freedom of the press as an attack on their politics, suspecting that Fréron and Tallien wished to give aristocrats and royalists the opportunity to speak; they believed that undefined press freedom must destroy the Republic since it was incompatible with revolutionary government. Opinion did indeed move to the right and in spring 1795 the Convention tried to legislate to control it.

623. Probably Madeleine Schweizer, with whom Wollstonecraft had been friendly when first in Paris.

624. *A Topographical Description of the Western Territory of North America* (1792) written as eleven letters. A German translation by L. A. W. Zimmermann, *Nachrichten von dem Westlichen Lande*, was published in Berlin in 1793.

625. The abolition of slavery was a popular cause among European liberals. Much of Imlay's book supported it, proposing gradual emancipation and the possibility of intermarriage between races.

157. *To Gilbert Imlay*

Paris, September 28th [1794]

I have written to you three or four letters; but different causes have prevented my sending them by the persons who promised to take or forward them. The inclosed is one I wrote to go by B——; yet, finding that he will not arrive, before I hope, and believe, you will have set out on your return, I inclose it to you, and shall give it in charge to ——, as Mr. —— is detained, to whom also I gave a letter.

I cannot help being anxious to hear from you; but I shall not harrass you with accounts of inquietudes, or of cares that arise from peculiar circumstances. – I have had so many little plagues here, that I have almost lamented that I left H[avre]. ——,[626] who is at best a most helpless creature, is now, on account of her pregnancy, more trouble than use to me, so that I still continue to be almost a slave to the child. – She indeed rewards me, for she is a sweet little creature; for, setting aside a mother's fondness (which, by the bye, is growing on me, her little intelligent smiles sinking into my heart), she has an astonishing degree of sensibility and observation. The other day by B——'s child, a fine one, she looked like a little sp[ri]te. – She is all life and motion, and her eyes are not the eyes of a fool – I will swear.

I slept at St. German's, in the very room (if you have not forgot) in which you pressed me very tenderly to your heart. – I did not forget to fold my darling to mine, with sensations that are almost too sacred to be alluded to.

Adieu, my love! Take care of yourself, if you wish to be the protector of your child, and the comfort of her mother.

I have received, for you, letters from ——.[627] I want to hear how that affair finishes, though I do not know whether I have most contempt for his folly or knavery.

Your own
[Mary]

---

626. The maidservant brought from Le Havre.
627. Possibly allusion to Ellefsen and the ship the *Maria and Margaretha*, which seems by now to have been missing, along with its valuable cargo of silver.

158. To Gilbert Imlay

[Paris] October 1st [1794]

It is a heartless task to write letters, without knowing whether they will ever reach you. – I have given two to ――, who has been a-going, a-going, every day, for a week past; and three others, which were written in a low-spirited strain, a little querulous or so, I have not been able to forward by the opportunities that were mentioned to me. *Tant mieux!* you will say, and I will not say nay; for I should be sorry that the contents of a letter, when you are so far away, should damp the pleasure that the sight of it would afford – judging of your feelings by my own. I just now stumbled on one of the kind letters, which you wrote during your last absence. You are then a dear affectionate creature, and I will not plague you. The letter which you chance to receive, when the absence is so long, ought to bring only tears of tenderness, without any bitter alloy, into your eyes.

After your return I hope indeed, that you will not be so immersed in business, as during the last three or four months past – for even money, taking into account all the future comforts it is to procure, may be gained at too dear a rate, if painful impressions are left on the mind. – These impressions were much more lively, soon after you went away, than at present – for a thousand tender recollections efface the melancholy traces they left on my mind – and every emotion is on the same side as my reason, which always was on yours. – Separated, it would be almost impious to dwell on real or imaginary imperfections of character. – I feel that I love you; and, if I cannot be happy with you, I will seek it no where else.

My little darling grows every day more dear to me – and she often has a kiss, when we are alone together, which I give her for you, with all my heart.

I have been interrupted – and must send off my letter. The liberty of the press will produce a great effect here – the *cry of blood will not be vain*! – Some more monsters will perish – and the Jacobins are conquered. – Yet I almost fear the last flap of the tail of the beast.[628]

I have had several trifling teazing inconveniences here, which I shall not now trouble you with a detail of. – I am sending —— back; her pregnancy rendered her useless. The girl I have got has more vivacity, which is better for the child.[629]

I long to hear from you. – Bring a copy of —— and —— with you.

—— is still here: he is a lost man. – He really loves his wife, and is anxious about his children; but his indiscriminate hospitality and social feelings have given him an inveterate habit of drinking, that destroys his health, as well as renders his person disgusting. – If his wife had more sense, or delicacy, she might restrain him: as it is, nothing will save him.

Yours most truly and affectionately
[Mary]

159. To Gilbert Imlay

[Paris] October 26th [1794]

My dear love, I began to wish so earnestly to hear from you, that the sight of your letters occasioned such pleasurable emotions, I was obliged to throw them aside till the little girl and I were alone together; and this said little girl, our darling, is become a most intelligent little creature, and as gay as a lark, and that in the morning too, which I do not find quite so convenient. I once told you, that the sensations before she was born, and when she is sucking, were pleasant; but they do not deserve to be compared to the emotions I feel, when she stops to smile upon me, or laughs outright on meeting me unexpectedly in the street, or after a short absence. She has now the advantage of having two

---

628. Several Jacobins were still influential, for example Collot d'Herbois (1749–1796), while Jean-Baptiste Carrier (1756–1794) remained one of the most militant and active members in the Society.

629. The new vivacious maidservant was probably Marguerite Fourneé, who remained with Wollstonecraft for the rest of the latter's life.

good nurses, and I am at present able to discharge my duty to her, without being the slave of it.

I have therefore employed and amused myself since I got rid of ——, and am making a progress in the language amongst other things. I have also made some new acquaintance. I have almost *charmed* a judge of the tribunal, R——,[630] who, though I should not have thought it possible, has humanity, if not *beaucoup d'esprit*. But let me tell you, if you do not make haste back, I shall be half in love with the author of the *Marseillaise*, who is a handsome man, a little too broad-faced or so, and plays sweetly on the violin.[631]

What do you say to this threat? – why, *entre nous*, I like to give way to a sprightly vein when writing to you, that is, when I am pleased with you. 'The devil,' you know, is proverbially said to be 'in a good humour, when he is pleased.'[632] Will you not then be a good boy, and come back quickly to play with your girls? but I shall not allow you to love the new-comer best.

[In *P W* Godwin indicated the omission of 4 lines.]

My heart longs for your return, my love, and only looks for, and seeks happiness with you; yet do not imagine that I childishly wish you to come back, before you have arranged things in such a manner,

630. The Revolutionary Tribunal underwent complete reorganization after the fall and execution of Robespierre. James Logan Godfrey, 'Revolutionary Justice. A Study of the Organization, Personnel, and Procedure of the Paris Tribunal, 1793–1795', in *James Sprunt Studies in Historical and Political Science* (1951), 33, p. 48, mentions only one member of the Tribunal with a name beginning with R: Rudler, a judge at Colmar, from the Basses-Alpes.

631. Claude Joseph Rouget de l'Isle (1760–1836), composer and soldier, was the son of royalist parents and a member of the Constitutional party; he opposed the abolition of the monarchy and had been imprisoned until the fall of Robespierre. In *Letters Containing A Sketch of the Politics of France From the Thirty-first of May 1793, till the Twenty-eighth of July 1794* (London, 1796), 4, 160f., Helen Maria Williams also described conversations with him; he told her affecting stories of his command of the republican column at Quiberon when the émigrés surrendered. In Christiane Laroque's *Rouget de Lisle. De la Marseillaise à l'Oublie* (Paris, 1999), p. 153f., he is described as receiving a gift of a violin taken from an émigré in honour of his composition of the national song.

632. An old proverb with many variants, the most common form being 'The devil is good when he is pleased.'

that it will not be necessary for you to leave us soon again, or to make exertions which injure your constitution.

Yours most truly and tenderly
[Mary]

P.S. You would oblige me by delivering the inclosed to Mr. —— and pray call for an answer. – It is for a person uncomfortably situated.

160. To Gilbert Imlay[633]

[Paris] December 26th [1794]

I have been, my love, for some days tormented by fears, that I would not allow to assume a form – I had been expecting you daily – and I heard that many vessels had been driven on shore during the late gale. – Well, I now see your letter – and find that you are safe; I will not regret then that your exertions have hitherto been so unavailing.

[In *PW* Godwin indicated the omission of 3 lines.]

Be that as it may, return to me when you have arranged the other matters, which —— has been crowding on you. I want to be sure that you are safe – and not separated from me by a sea that must be passed. For, feeling that I am happier than I ever was, do you wonder at my sometimes dreading that fate has not done persecuting me? Come to me, my dearest friend, husband, father of my child! – All these fond ties glow at my heart at this moment, and dim my eyes. – With you an independence is desirable; and it is always within our reach, if affluence escapes us – without you the world again appears empty to me. But I am recurring to some of the melancholy thoughts that have flitted across my mind for some days past, and haunted my dreams.

My little darling is indeed a sweet child; and I am sorry that you are not here, to see her little mind unfold itself. You talk of 'dalliance'; but

633. Godwin recorded that Imlay had intended returning to Paris about this time. He reached Ramsgate when 'he was recalled, as it should seem, to London, by the further pressure of business now accumulated upon him' (*PW*, 3, 91).

certainly no lover was ever more attached to his mistress, than she is to me. Her eyes follow me every where, and by affection I have the most despotic power over her. She is all vivacity or softness – yes; I love her more than I thought I should. When I have been hurt at your stay, I have embraced her as my only comfort – when pleased with you, for looking and laughing like you; nay, I cannot, I find, long be angry with you, whilst I am kissing her for resembling you. But there would be no end to these details. Fold us both to your heart; for I am truly and affectionately

Yours
[Mary]

161. To Gilbert Imlay

[Paris] December 28th [1794]

[In P W Godwin indicated the omission of 3 lines.]

I do, my love, indeed sincerely sympathize with you in all your dis-appointments. – Yet, knowing that you are well, and think of me with affection, I only lament other disappointments, because I am sorry that you should thus exert yourself in vain, and that you are kept from me.

——,[634] I know, urges you to stay, and is continually branching out into new projects, because he has the idle desire to amass a large fortune, rather an immense one, merely to have the credit of having made it. But we who are governed by other motives, ought not to be led on by him. When we meet, we will discuss this subject. – You will listen to reason, and it has probably occurred to you, that it will be better, in future, to pursue some sober plan, which may demand more time, and still enable you to arrive at the same end. It appears to me absurd to waste life in preparing to live.

Would it not now be possible to arrange your business in such a

634. The American business associate of Imlay through whom Wollstonecraft was to receive money and send and receive letters; she quickly saw him as her enemy and rival for control of Imlay.

manner as to avoid the inquietudes, of which I have had my share since your departure? Is it not possible to enter into business, as an employment necessary to keep the faculties awake, and (to sink a little in the expressions) the pot boiling, without suffering what must ever be considered as a secondary object, to engross the mind, and drive sentiment and affection out of the heart?

I am in a hurry to give this letter to the person who has promised to forward it with ——'s. I wish then to counteract, in some measure, what he had doubtless recommended most warmly.

Stay, my friend, whilst it is *absolutely* necessary. – I will give you no tenderer name, though it glows at my heart, unless you come the moment the settling the *present* objects permit. – *I do not consent* to your taking any other journey – or the little woman and I will be off, the Lord knows where. But, as I had rather owe every thing to your affection, and, I may add, to your reason, (for this immoderate desire of wealth, which makes —— so eager to have you remain, is contrary to your principles of action), I will not importune you. – I will only tell you, that I long to see you – and, being at peace with you, I shall be hurt, rather than made angry, by delays. – Having suffered so much in life, do not be surprised if I sometimes, when left to myself, grow gloomy, and suppose that it was all a dream, and that my happiness is not to last. I say happiness, because remembrance retrenches all the dark shades of the picture.

My little one begins to show her teeth, and use her legs. – She wants you to bear your part in the nursing business, for I am fatigued with dancing her, and yet she is not satisfied – she wants you to thank her mother for taking such care of her, as you only can.

Yours truly
[Mary]

162. To Gilbert Imlay

[Paris] December 29th [1794]

Though I suppose you have later intelligence, yet, as —— has just informed me that he has an opportunity of sending immediately to you, I take advantage of it to inclose you

[In *P W* Godwin indicated the omission of 1 line.]

How I hate this crooked business! This intercourse with the world, which obliges one to see the worst side of human nature! Why cannot you be content with the object you had first in view, when you entered into this wearisome labyrinth? – I know very well that you have imperceptibly been drawn on; yet why does one project, successful or abortive, only give place to two others? Is it not sufficient to avoid poverty? – I am contented to do my part; and, even here, sufficient to escape from wretchedness is not difficult to obtain. And, let me tell you, I have my project also – and, if you do not soon return, the little girl and I will take care of ourselves; we will not accept any of your cold kindness – your distant civilities – no; not we.

This is but half jesting, for I am really tormented by the desire which —— manifests to have you remain where you are. – Yet why do I talk to you? – If he can persuade you – let him! – for, if you are not happier with me, and your own wishes do not make you throw aside these eternal projects, I am above using any arguments, though reason as well as affection seems to offer them – if our affection be mutual, they will occur to you – and you will act accordingly.

Since my arrival here, I have found the German lady, of whom you have heard me speak. Her first child died in the month; but she has another, about the age of my [Fanny], a fine little creature. They are still but contriving to live – earning their daily bread – yet, though they are but just above poverty, I envy them. – She is a tender, affectionate mother – fatigued even by her attention. – However she has an affectionate husband in her turn, to render her care light, and to share her pleasure.

I will own to you that, feeling extreme tenderness for my little girl,

I grow sad very often when I am playing with her, that you are not here, to observe with me how her mind unfolds, and her little heart becomes attached! – These appear to me to be true pleasures – and still you suffer them to escape you, in search of what we may never enjoy. – It is your own maxim to 'live in the present moment.' – *If you do* – stay, for God's sake; but tell me the truth – if not, tell me when I may expect to see you, and let me not be always vainly looking for you, till I grow sick at heart.

Adieu! I am a little hurt – I must take my darling to my bosom to comfort me.

[Mary]

163. To Gilbert Imlay

[Paris] December 30th [1794]

Should you receive three or four of the letters at once which I have written lately, do not think of Sir John Brute,[635] for I do not mean to wife you. I only take advantage of every occasion, that one out of three of my epistles may reach your hands, and inform you that I am not of ——'s opinion, who talks till he makes me angry, of the necessity of your staying two or three months longer. I do not like this life of continual inquietude – and, *entre nous*, I am determined to try to earn some money here myself, in order to convince you that, if you chuse to run about the world to get a fortune, it is for yourself – for the little girl and I will live without your assistance, unless you are with us. I may be termed proud – Be it so – but I will never abandon certain principles of action.

The common run of men have such an ignoble way of thinking, that, if they debauch their hearts, and prostitute their persons, following perhaps a gust of inebriation, they suppose the wife, slave rather, whom they maintain, has no right to complain, and ought to receive the sultan, whenever he deigns to return, with open arms, though his

635. A character in Sir John Vanbrugh's comedy *The Provok'd Wife* (1697) who was both bored and disillusioned by the demands of matrimony.

have been polluted by half an hundred promiscuous amours during his absence.

I consider fidelity and constancy as two distinct things; yet the former is necessary, to give life to the other – and such a degree of respect do I think due to myself, that, if only probity, which is a good thing in its place, brings you back, never return! – for, if a wandering of the heart, or even a caprice of the imagination detains you – there is an end of all my hopes of happiness – I could not forgive it, if I would.

I have gotten into a melancholy mood, you perceive. You know my opinion of men in general; you know that I think them systematic tyrants, and that it is the rarest thing in the world, to meet with a man with sufficient delicacy of feeling to govern desire. When I am thus sad, I lament that my little darling, fondly as I doat on her, is a girl. – I am sorry to have a tie to a world that for me is ever sown with thorns.

You will call this an ill-humoured letter, when, in fact, it is the strongest proof of affection I can give, to dread to lose you. —— has taken such pains to convince me that you must and ought to stay, that it has inconceivably depressed my spirits – You have always known my opinion – I have ever declared, that two people, who mean to live together, ought not to be long separated. – If certain things are more necessary to you than me – search for them – Say but one word, and you shall never hear of me more. – If not – for God's sake, let us struggle with poverty – with any evil, but these continual inquietudes of business, which I have been told were to last but a few months, though every day the end appears more distant! This is the first letter in this strain that I have determined to forward to you; the rest lie by, because I was unwilling to give you pain, and I should not now write if I did not think that there would be no conclusion to the schemes, which demand, as I am told, your presence.

[Mary]

164. To Gilbert Imlay

[Paris] January 9th [1795]

I just now received one of your hasty *notes*; for business so entirely occupies you, that you have not time, or sufficient command of thought, to write letters. Beware! you seem to be got into a whirl of projects and schemes, which are drawing you into a gulph, that, if it do not absorb your happiness, will infallibly destroy mine.

Fatigued during my youth by the most arduous struggles, not only to obtain independence, but to render myself useful, not merely pleasure, for which I had the most lively taste, I mean the simple pleasures that flow from passion and affection, escaped me, but the most melancholy views of life were impressed by a disappointed heart on my mind. Since I knew you, I have been endeavouring to go back to my former nature, and have allowed some time to glide away, winged with the delight which only spontaneous enjoyment can give. – Why have you so soon dissolved the charm?

I am really unable to bear the continual inquietude which your and ——'s never-ending plans produce. This you may term want of firmness – but you are mistaken – I have still sufficient firmness to pursue my principle of action. The present misery, I cannot find a softer word to do justice to my feelings, appears to me unnecessary – and therefore I have not firmness to support it as you may think I ought. I should have been content, and still wish, to retire with you to a farm – My God! any thing, but these continual anxieties – any thing but commerce, which debases the mind, and roots out affection from the heart.

I do not mean to complain of subordinate inconveniences – yet I will simply observe, that, led to expect you every week, I did not make the arrangements required by the present circumstances, to procure the necessaries of life.[636] In order to have them, a servant, for that

636. The new regime had liberalized commerce and removed some controls on imports and prices established by the revolutionary Commission des Subsistances. Consequently prices had soared. There was still bread and meat rationing but the former had been cut while meat had become difficult to obtain. There was also a severe shortage

purpose only, is indispensible – The want of wood, has made me catch the most violent cold I ever had; and my head is so disturbed by continual coughing, that I am unable to write without stopping frequently to recollect myself. – This however is one of the common evils which must be borne with – bodily pain does not touch the heart, though it fatigues the spirits.

Still as you talk of your return, even in February, doubtingly, I have determined, the moment the weather changes, to wean my child.[637] – It is too soon for her to begin to divide sorrow! – And as one has well said, 'despair is a freeman,'[638] we will go and seek our fortune together.

This is not a caprice of the moment – for your absence has given new weight to some conclusions, that I was very reluctantly forming before you left me. – I do not chuse to be a secondary object. – If your feelings were in unison with mine, you would not sacrifice so much to visionary prospects of future advantage.

[Mary]

165. To Gilbert Imlay

[Paris] January 15th [1795]

I was just going to begin my letter with the fag end of a song, which would only have told you, what I may as well say simply, that it is pleasant to forgive those we love. I have received your two letters, dated the 26th and 28th of December, and my anger died away. You can scarcely conceive the effect some of your letters have produced on me. After longing to hear from you during a tedious interval of suspense, I have seen a superscription written by you. – Promising myself pleasure, and feeling emotion, I have laid it by me, till the person who brought it, left the room – when, behold! on opening it, I have found

---

of firewood, which Wollstonecraft felt acutely since 1794–5 was the coldest winter of the century in France. The Seine and all the Paris water fountains froze.

637. Wollstonecraft had been breast-feeding for about eight months; the usual period was closer to eighteen to twenty-four months.

638. Quoting the Arab proverb, 'Despair is a freeman, Hope is a slave'.

only half a dozen hasty lines, that have damped all the rising affection of my soul.

Well, now for business –

[In *P W* Godwin indicated the omission of 3 lines.]

My animal is well; I have not yet taught her to eat, but nature is doing the business. I gave her a crust to assist the cutting of her teeth; and now she has two, she makes good use of them to gnaw a crust, biscuit, &c. You would laugh to see her; she is just like a little squirrel; she will guard a crust for two hours; and, after fixing her eye on an object for some time, dart on it with an aim as sure as a bird of prey – nothing can equal her life and spirits. I suffer from a cold; but it does not affect her. Adieu! do not forget to love us – and come soon to tell us that you do.

[Mary]

166. To Gilbert Imlay

[Paris] January 30th [1795]

From the purport of your last letters, I should suppose that this will scarcely reach you; and I have already written so many letters, that you have either not received, or neglected to acknowledge, I do not find it pleasant, or rather I have no inclination, to go over the same ground again. If you have received them, and are still detained by new projects, it is useless for me to say any more on the subject. I have done with it for ever; yet I ought to remind you that your pecuniary interest suffers by your absence.

[In *P W* Godwin indicated the omission of 3 lines.]

For my part, my head is turned giddy, by only hearing of plans to make money, and my contemptuous feelings have sometimes burst out. I therefore was glad that a violent cold gave me a pretext to stay at home, lest I should have uttered unseasonable truths.

My child is well, and the spring will perhaps restore me to myself. – I have endured many inconveniences this winter, which I should be ashamed to mention, if they had been unavoidable. 'The secondary pleasures of life,' you say, 'are very necessary to my comfort:' it may be so; but I have ever considered them as secondary. If therefore you accuse me of wanting the resolution necessary to bear the *common*[639] evils of life; I should answer, that I have not fashioned my mind to sustain them, because I would avoid them, cost what it would –

Adieu!

[Mary]

167. To Gilbert Imlay

[Paris] February 9th [1795]

The melancholy presentiment has for some time hung on my spirits, that we were parted for ever; and the letters I received this day, by M[r]. ——, convince me that it was not without foundation. You allude to some other letters, which I suppose have miscarried; for most of those I have got, were only a few hasty lines, calculated to wound the tenderness the sight of the superscriptions excited.

I mean not however to complain; yet so many feelings are struggling for utterance, and agitating a heart almost bursting with anguish, that I find it very difficult to write with any degree of coherence.

You left me indisposed, though you have taken no notice of it; and the most fatiguing journey I ever had, contributed to continue it. However, I recovered my health; but a neglected cold, and continual inquietude during the last two months, have reduced me to a state of weakness I never before experienced. Those who did not know that the canker-worm was at work at the core, cautioned me about suckling my child too long. – God preserve this poor child, and render her happier than her mother!

But I am wandering from my subject: indeed my head turns giddy, when I think that all the confidence I have had in the affection of others

639. Godwin noted: 'This probably alludes to some expression of the person to whom the letters are addressed, in which he treated as common evils, things upon which the letter writer was disposed to bestow a different application' (*PW*, 3, 100).

is come to this. – I did not expect this blow from you. I have done my duty to you and my child; and if I am not to have any return of affection to reward me, I have the sad consolation of knowing that I deserved a better fate. My soul is weary – I am sick at heart; and, but for this little darling, I would cease to care about a life, which is now stripped of every charm.

You see how stupid I am, uttering declamation, when I meant simply to tell you, that I consider your requesting me to come to you, as merely dictated by honour. – Indeed I scarcely understand you. – You request me to come, and then tell me, that you have not given up all thoughts of returning to this place.

When I determined to live with you, I was only governed by affection. – I would share poverty with you, but I turn with affright from the sea of trouble on which you are entering. – I have certain principles of action: I know what I look for to found my happiness on. – It is not money. – With you I wished for sufficient to procure the comforts of life – as it is, less will do. – I can still exert myself to obtain the necessaries of life for my child, and she does not want more at present. – I have two or three plans in my head to earn our subsistence; for do not suppose that, neglected by you, I will lie under obligations of a pecuniary kind to you! – No; I would sooner submit to menial service. I wanted the support of your affection – that gone, all is over! – I did not think, when I complained of ——'s contemptible avidity to accumulate money, that he would have dragged you into his schemes.

I cannot write. – I inclose a fragment of a letter, written soon after your departure, and another which tenderness made me keep back when it was written. – You will see then the sentiments of a calmer, though not a more determined, moment. – Do not insult me by saying, that 'our being together is paramount to every other consideration!' Were it, you would not be running after a bubble, at the expence of my peace of mind.

Perhaps this is the last letter you will ever receive from me.

[Mary].

168. To Gilbert Imlay

[Paris] February 10th [1795]

You talk of 'permanent views and future comfort' – not for me, for I am dead to hope. The inquietudes of the last winter have finished the business, and my heart is not only broken, but my constitution destroyed. I conceive myself in a galloping consumption, and the continual anxiety I feel at the thought of leaving my child, feeds the fever that nightly devours me. It is on her account that I again write to you, to conjure you, by all that you hold sacred, to leave her here with the German lady you may have heard me mention! She has a child of the same age, and they may be brought up together, as I wish her to be brought up. I shall write more fully on the subject. To facilitate this, I shall give up my present lodgings, and go into the same house. I can live much cheaper there, which is now become an object. I have had 3000 livres from ——,[640] and I shall take one more, to pay my servant's wages, &c. and then I shall endeavour to procure what I want by my own exertions. I shall entirely give up the acquaintance of the Americans.

—— and I have not been on good terms a long time. Yesterday he very unmanlily exulted over me, on account of your determination to stay. I had provoked it, it is true, by some asperities against commerce, which have dropped from me, when we have argued about the propriety of your remaining where you are; and it is no matter, I have drunk too deep of the bitter cup to care about trifles.

When you first entered into these plans, you bounded your views to the gaining of a thousand pounds. It was sufficient to have procured a farm in America, which would have been an independence. You find now that you did not know yourself, and that a certain situation in life is more necessary to you than you imagined – more necessary than an uncorrupted heart – For a year or two, you may procure yourself

640. According to the calculation table in Arthur Young's *Travels in France, During the Years 1787, 1788, and 1789* (London, 1792), p. viii, 3,000 livres amounted to £131 5s.

what you call pleasure; eating, drinking, and women; but, in the solitude of declining life, I shall be remembered with regret – I was going to say with remorse, but checked my pen.

As I have never concealed the nature of my connection with you, your reputation will not suffer. I shall never have a confident: I am content with the approbation of my own mind; and, if there be a searcher of hearts, mine will not be despised. Reading what you have written relative to the desertion of women, I have often wondered how theory and practice could be so different, till I recollected, that the sentiments of passion, and the resolves of reason, are very distinct.[641] As to my sisters, as you are so continually hurried with business, you need not write to them – I shall, when my mind is calmer. God bless you! Adieu!

[Mary]

This has been such a period of barbarity and misery, I ought not to complain of having my share. I wish one moment that I had never heard of the cruelties that have been practised here, and the next envy the mothers who have been killed with their children. Surely I had suffered enough in life, not to be cursed with a fondness, that burns up the vital stream I am imparting. You will think me mad: I would I were so, that I could forget my misery – so that my head or heart would be still. –

641. If this is a reference to *The Emigrants* rather than missing personal letters, then it appears to prove Imlay's sole authorship of that novel. There are several appropriate passages including the following: '[Women's] tenderness entitles them to our protection and utmost care ... who can help feeling the most exquisite anguish, when they recollect that the ingenuous heart of an amiable woman, who is formed for the soft endearments of domestic felicity, should be first imposed upon by a base and cowardly being, who ought to have been her guardian and protector, and who after having shocked her delicacy, and sullied her honour by his unmanly aspersions, should be condemned to eternal disgrace?' (pp. 32 and 132).

169. To Gilbert Imlay

[Paris] February 19th [1795]

When I first received your letter, putting off your return to an indefinite time, I felt so hurt, that I know not what I wrote. I am now calmer, though it was not the kind of wound over which time has the quickest effect; on the contrary, the more I think, the sadder I grow. Society fatigues me inexpressibly – So much so, that finding fault with every one, I have only reason enough, to discover that the fault is in myself. My child alone interests me, and, but for her, I should not take any pains to recover my health.

As it is, I shall wean her, and try if by that step (to which I feel a repugnance, for it is my only solace) I can get rid of my cough. Physicians talk much of the danger attending any complaint on the lungs, after a woman has suckled for some months. They lay a stress also on the necessity of keeping the mind tranquil – and, my God! how has mine been harrassed! But whilst the caprices of other women are gratified, 'the wind of heaven not suffered to visit them too rudely,'[642] I have not found a guardian angel, in heaven or on earth, to ward off sorrow or care from my bosom.

What sacrifices have you not made for a woman you did not respect! – But I will not go over this ground – I want to tell you that I do not understand you. You say that you have not given up all thoughts of returning here – and I know that it will be necessary – nay, is. I cannot explain myself; but if you have not lost your memory, you will easily divine my meaning. What! is our life then only to be made up of separations? and am I only to return to a country, that has not merely lost all charms for me, but for which I feel a repugnance that almost amounts to horror, only to be left there a prey to it!

Why is it so necessary that I should return? – brought up here, my girl would be freer. Indeed, expecting you to join us, I had formed

642. *Hamlet*, I, ii, 141f.: 'That he might not beteem the winds of heaven / Visit her face too roughly.'

some plans of usefulness that have now vanished with my hopes of happiness.

In the bitterness of my heart, I could complain with reason, that I am left here dependent on a man, whose avidity to acquire a fortune has rendered him callous to every sentiment connected with social or affectionate emotions – With a brutal insensibility, he cannot help displaying the pleasure your determination to stay gives him, in spite of the effect it is visible it has had on me.

Till I can earn money, I shall endeavour to borrow some, for I want to avoid asking him continually for the sum necessary to maintain me – Do not mistake me, I have never been refused. – Yet I have gone half a dozen times to the house to ask for it, and come away without speaking – you must guess why – Besides, I wish to avoid hearing of the eternal projects to which you have sacrificed my peace – not remembering – but I will be silent for ever –

[Unsigned]

170. To Gilbert Imlay

[Le Havre] April 7th [1795]

Here I am at H[avre], on the wing towards you,[643] and I write now, only to tell you, that you may expect me in the course of three or four days: for I shall not attempt to give vent to the different emotions which agitate my heart – You may term a feeling, which appears to me to be a degree of delicacy that naturally arises from sensibility, pride – Still I cannot indulge the very affectionate tenderness which glows in my bosom, without trembling, till I see, by your eyes that it is mutual.

I sit, lost in thought, looking at the sea – and tears rush into my eyes,

643. As the previous letter suggests, for some time Imlay had been urging Wollstonecraft to come to England; she had at first been fearful but, according to Letter 213, Imlay had written: 'Come to any port, and I will fly down to my two dear girls with a heart all their own.' She was now *en route* through Le Havre, staying in the house she and Imlay had rented from Wheatcroft; she had with her Fanny, Marguerite the maid, and a child she was escorting to England.

when I find that I am cherishing any fond expectations – I have indeed been so unhappy this winter, I find it as difficult to acquire fresh hopes, as to regain tranquillity. – Enough of this – lie still, foolish heart! – But for the little girl, I could almost wish that it should cease to beat, to be no more alive to the anguish of disappointment.

Sweet little creature! I deprived myself of my only pleasure, when I weaned her, about ten days ago – I am however glad I conquered my repugnance – It was necessary it should be done soon, and I did not wish to embitter the renewal of your acquaintance with her, by putting it off till we met. – It was a painful exertion to me, and I thought it best to throw this inquietude with the rest, into the sack that I would fain throw over my shoulder. – I wished to endure it alone, in short – Yet, after sending her to sleep in the next room for three or four nights, you cannot think with what joy I took her back again to sleep in my bosom!

I suppose I shall find you, when I arrive, for I do not see any necessity for your coming to me. – Pray inform Mr. ——, that I have his little friend with me. – My wishing to oblige him, made me put myself to some inconvenience – and delay my departure; which was irksome to me, who have not quite as much philosophy, I would not for the world say indifference, as you. God bless you!

Yours truly
[Mary]

171. To Archibald Hamilton Rowan[644]

[Le Havre] April 9th [1795]

My dear Sir

Going off at an hours notice I have scarcely a moment at command

---

644. Archibald Hamilton Rowan (1751–1834) was a rich lawyer and member of the Dublin United Irishmen, a radical Irish group aiming at the separation of Ireland from Britain; he had recently escaped to France from a Dublin prison where he had been held for circulating rebellious propaganda. He received this letter under his alias 'J. Thomson'. Wollstonecraft had met him at the fête for Marat on 21 September 1794 (see Letter 155); they became good friends but Rowan had initially been shocked at

to wish you well and to express my regret that I have not had the pleasure of seeing you again. I have left you a few things in a closet – and believe me it will give me sincere pleasure to see you once more – Pray let me hear from you – God Bless you remember that I wish to be number amongst your friend – I ought to be for I feel that I am sorry to say Adieu and that I shall think of you with affection

M. IMLAY

Germinal[645]

172. To Archibald Hamilton Rowan[646]

[Le] Havre, April, 1795

My dear Sir

I wrote a few hasty lines to you just now, before we entered the Vessel, and after hurrying myself out of breath – for, as I do not like exaggerated phrases, I would not say *to death* – the awkward pilot ran us aground – so here we are in an empty house; and with the heart and imagination on the wing you may suppose that the slow march of time is felt very painfully. – I seem to be counting the ticking of a Clock, and there is no clock here. – For these few days I have been busy preparing, now all is done, and we cannot go. – If you were to pop in

---

her situation: ' "What!" said I within myself, "this is Miss Mary Wollstonecraft, parading about with a child at her heels, with as little ceremony as if it were a watch she had just bought at the jeweller's. So much for the rights of women," thought I. But upon farther inquiry, I found that she had, very fortunately for her, married an American gentleman a short time before the passing of that decree which indiscriminately incarcerated all the British subjects who were at that moment in this country. My society, which before this time was entirely male, was now most agreeably increased, and I got a dish of tea and an hour's rational conversation, whenever I called on her' (*The Autobiography of Archibald Hamilton Rowan, Esq.*, Dublin, 1840, pp. 253f.). Wollstonecraft was allowing Rowan to use her house during his journey to America.

645. Germinal stretched from 21 March until 19 April.

646. This and Letter 246 exist in two transcripts, one in *The Autobiography of Archibald Hamilton Rowan*, pp. 249f., and the other in MS copies in the Abinger collection. I have followed the fuller version in Abinger. Significant discrepancies between the two versions are recorded in the endnotes.

I should be glad, for in spite of my impatience to see a friend who deserves all tenderness, I still have a corner in my heart, where I will allow you a place, if you have *no objection*. – It would give me sincere pleasure to meet you at any future period, and to be introduced to your Wife.[647] – Pray take care of yourself, and when you arrive let me hear from you. – Direct to me at M^r. Johnson's S^t. Paul's Church yard London, and wherever I may be the letter will not fail to reach me.[22] – You will not find a very comfortable house; but I have left a little store of provisions in a closet, and the Girl who assisted in our kitchen, and who has been well paid, has promised to do every thing for you. – M^r. Wheatcroft has all your packages, and will[23] give you all the information and assistance he can – I believe I told you that I offered M^r. Russell's[648] family my house; but since I arrived I find there is some chance of letting it – Will you then, when Mr Wheatcroft informs in what manner he has settled it, write the particulars to them. – I imagine that the house will be empty for a short time to come at any rate; but I find it necessary to take my linen with me, and the good people here sold my kitchen furniture for me. – Still I think, as they have many necessaries, they will find this house much more comfortable than an Inn. – Perhaps I may visit[24] – if so, I shall not forget to tell your Wife that I call yourself my friend.[649] – I neither like to say or write *adieu* – If you see my brother Charles, pray assure him that I most affectionately remember him.[650] – Take any precaution to avoid danger.

Yours sincerely
Mary Imlay

647. Wollstonecraft was carrying back to Britain a watch to be given to 'G.M' from Rowan. See *Supp.*, p. 255. Rowan also used Wollstonecraft to send a letter to his wife in Ireland dated 20 March 1795, enclosed in one of Wollstonecraft's for her sister Everina.
648. Possibly Thomas Russell (1767–1803), another United Irishman involved with both Rowan and a United Irish leader, Wolfe Tone. Russell was arrested for subversive activities in September 1796, so he might, before that date, have been planning to flee to France, as Rowan had done.
649. After her death an unwise phrase in Godwin's *Memoirs*, that Wollstonecraft had derived 'particular gratification' (p. 122) from Rowan, led to the assumption in conservative periodicals like the *Anti-Jacobin Review* that the pair had been lovers.
650. Rowan met Charles Wollstonecraft in America. Subsequently Charles worked for Rowan in his calico printing factory in Wilmington, Delaware.

England 1795

173. To Gilbert Imlay

Brighthelmstone,[651] Saturday, April 11th [1795]

Here we are, my love, and mean to set out early in the morning; and, if I can find you, I hope to dine with you to-morrow. – I shall drive to ——'s hotel, where —— tells me you have been – and, if you have left it, I hope you will take care to be there to receive us.

I have brought with me Mr. ——'s little friend, and a girl whom I like to take care of our little darling – not on the way, for that fell to my share.[652] – But why do I write about trifles? – or any thing? – Are we not to meet soon? – What does your heart say!

Yours truly
[Mary]

I have weaned my [Fanny], and she is now eating away at the white bread.

---

651. The earlier name for Brighton, used in the Domesday Book.
652. The maid Marguerite suffered from seasickness.

174. To Eliza Bishop[653]

N° 26 Charlotte S^r, Rathbone Place, London [c. April 23^d, 1795][654]

I arrived in Town near a fortnight ago, my dear Girl, but having previously weaned my child on account of a cough I found myself extremely weak. I have intended writing to you, every day; but have been prevented by the impossibility of determining in what way I can be of essential service to you. When Mr Imlay and I united our fate together he was without fortune; since that there is a prospect of his obtaining a considerable one; but though the hope appears to be well founded I cannot yet act as if it were a certainty   He is the most generous creature in the world and if he succeed, as I have the greatest reason to think he will, he will, in proportion to his acquirement of property, enable me to be useful to you and Everina – I wish you and her could adopt any plan in which five or six hundred pounds could be of use. As to myself I cannot yet say where I shall live for a continuance it would give me the sincerest pleasure to be situated near you – I know you will think me unkind – and it was this reflection that has prevented my writing to you sooner, not to invite you to come and live with me – But Eliza it is my opinion, not a newly formed one, the presence of a third person interrupts or destroys domestic happiness – Accepting this sacrifice there is nothing I would not do to promote your comfort – I am hurt at being obliged to be thus explicit and do indeed severely feel for the disappointments which you have meet with in Life – I have not heard from Charles nor can I guess what he is about – What was done with the fifty pounds he speaks of having sent to England?[655] – Do pray write to me immediately and do justice to

653. The letter survives in a transcript made by Eliza Bishop and enclosed in a letter to Everina Wollstonecraft sent from Pembroke and dated 29 April 1795.
654. Wollstonecraft and Imlay re-met in London and tried briefly to live together. In *Memoirs*, Godwin reported that Imlay was having an affair with 'a young actress from a strolling company of players' (p. 124). Imlay lodged Wollstonecraft and Fanny in a furnished house in Charlotte Street. The dating follows the previous letter and Wollstonecraft's remark that she had been in London almost two weeks.
655. Charles had become a 'Speculator' in Pennsylvania and for a time believed himself rich. He had promised to send money to his sisters and pay their passage to America.

my heart I do not wish to endanger my own peace without a certainty of securing yours – Yet I am still your most sincere and affectionate

Friend Mary.[656]

M.[rs] Imlay

175. To Everina Wollstonecraft[657]

N° 26 Charlotte Street, Rathbone Place, April 27th [1795]

When you hear, my dear Everina that I have been in London near a fortnight without writing to you or Eliza you will, perhaps accuse me of insensibility – for I shall not lay any stress on my not being well in consequence of a violent cold I caught during the time I was nursing; but tell you that I put off writing because I was at a loss what I could do to render Eliza's situation more comfortable. I instantly gave James[25] ten pounds to send, for a very obvious reason, in his own name to my father,[658] and I could send her a trifle of this kind

---

Despite suspecting he was 'too sanguine' Eliza put some trust in his promises and was deeply disappointed when they proved untrue: 'I own I never expected from this brother – not even after all that happened in days of yore —.'

656. Eliza Bishop's reaction to this letter was extreme, in part because of her own precarious situation. Desperate to be invited to France by Mary, she had left her governess position in Upton and was learning French in Pembroke from an émigré priest. The letter signalled the end of her hopes and she wrote to Everina Wollstonecraft, 'Good God what a letter! how have I merited such pointed cruelty? I may say *insolence*[.] When did I ask to live with her at what time wish for a moment, to interrupt *their Domestic* happiness? Was ever a present offered in so humiliating a style – ought the poorest domestick to be thus insulted – Are your Eyes opened, at last, Everina? – What do you now say to our goodly prospects.' To Mary she simply wrote, 'Mrs B. has never received any money from America.' In fact, while Eliza assumed Mary cared nothing for her, Mary was still urging Imlay to send money to her sisters even when she had refused it for herself.

657. The letter was addressed to Everina at Hugh Skeys's address. According to the *Wilson's Dublin Directory, For the Year 1795*, Skeys traded with his brother John at 125 Great Britain Street. By now Wollstonecraft did not know that Everina, having left the Boyses of Waterford, had moved to the Irwins at Fortick's Grove near Dublin, and then to the Maunsells of Hume Street, Dublin. See also Letter 125.

658. Like Charles, James had promised to give something to his sisters when he had his prize money, but, despite the recent expensive training Wollstonecraft had given

immediately were a temporary assistance necessary. I believe I told you that M^r. Imlay had not a fortune when I first knew him   since that he has entered into very extensive plans which promise a degree of success, though not equal to the first prospect – When a sufficient sum is actually realized I know he will give me for you and Eliza five or six hundred pounds, or more, if he can – In what way could this be of the most use to you? – I am above concealing my sentiments though I have boggled at uttering them – It would give me sincere pleasure to be situated near you both, I cannot yet say where I shall determine to spend the rest of my life; but I do not wish to have a third person in the house with me – my domestic happiness would perhaps be interrupted without my being of much use to Eliza – This is not a hastily formed opinion, nor is it in consequence of my present attachment, yet I am obliged now to express it, because it appears to me that you have formed some such expectation for Eliza – you may wound me by remarking on my determination   still I know on what principle I act and therefore you can only judge for yourself. I have not heard from Charles a great while – By writing to me immediately you would relieve me from considerable anxiety –

Yours sincerely
Mary
M^{rs}. Imlay

176. To Gilbert Imlay[659]

London, Friday, May 22^d [1795]

I have just received your affectionate letter, and am distressed to think that I have added to your embarrassments at this troublesome juncture, when the exertion of all the faculties of your mind appears to be necessary, to extricate you out of your pecuniary difficulties. I suppose

---

him, he declared he could not conquer his 'aversion to the sea' and instead wanted to go to France to live cheaply. He therefore had no spare money for his father or sisters.
659. Shortly before this letter Wollstonecraft had decided to kill herself. According to Godwin: 'It was perhaps owing to [Imlay's] activity and representations, that her life was, at this time, saved. She determined to continue to exist' (*Memoirs*, p. 127).

it was something relative to the circumstance you have mentioned, which made —— request to see me to-day, to *converse about a matter of great importance*. Be that as it may, his letter (such is the state of my spirits) inconceivably alarmed me, and rendered the last night as distressing, as the two former had been.

I have laboured to calm my mind since you left me – Still I find that tranquillity is not to be obtained by exertion; it is a feeling so different from the resignation of despair! – I am however no longer angry with you – nor will I ever utter another complaint – there are arguments which convince the reason, whilst they carry death to the heart. – We have had too many cruel explanations, that not only cloud every future prospect; but embitter the remembrances which alone give life to affection. – Let the subject never be revived!

It seems to me that I have not only lost the hope, but the power of being happy. – Every emotion is now sharpened by anguish. – My soul has been shook, and my tone of feelings destroyed. – I have gone out – and sought for dissipation, if not amusement, merely to fatigue still more, I find, my irritable nerves –

My friend – my dear friend – examine yourself well – I am out of the question; for, alas! I am nothing – and discover what you wish to do – what will render you most comfortable – or, to be more explicit – whether you desire to live with me, or part for ever? When you can once ascertain it, tell me frankly, I conjure you! – for, believe me, I have very involuntarily interrupted your peace.

I shall expect you to dinner on Monday, and will endeavour to assume a cheerful face to greet you – at any rate I will avoid conversations, which only tend to harrass your feelings, because I am most affectionately yours,

[Mary]

177. To Gilbert Imlay

[London] Wednesday [May 27th, 1795][660]

I inclose you the letter,[661] which you desired me to forward, and I am tempted very laconically to wish you a good morning – not because I am angry, or have nothing to say; but to keep down a wounded spirit. – I shall make every effort to calm my mind – yet a strong conviction seems to whirl round in the very centre of my brain, which, like the fiat of fate, emphatically assures me, that grief has a firm hold of my heart.

God bless you!

Yours sincerely
[Mary]

660. Date supplied by Kegan Paul in *LI*.
661. Perhaps one of the explanatory letters which Wollstonecraft intended to leave behind when she committed suicide. Later she declared that she had destroyed others. See note 665.

178. To Gilbert Imlay[662]

[Hull] Wednesday, two o'clock [June 10th, 1795][663]

We arrived here about an hour ago. I am extremely fatigued with the child, who would not rest quiet with any body but me, during the night – and now we are here in a comfortless, damp room, in a sort of tomb-like house. This however I shall quickly remedy, for, when I have finished this letter, (which I must do immediately, because the post goes out early), I shall sally forth, and enquire about a vessel and an inn.

I will not distress you by talking of the depression of my spirits, or the struggle I had to keep alive my dying heart. – It is even now too full to allow me to write with composure. – [Imlay], – dear [Imlay], – am I always to be tossed about thus? – shall I never find an asylum to rest *contented* in? How can you love to fly about continually – dropping down, as it were, in a new world – cold and strange! – every other day? Why do you not attach those tender emotions round the idea of home, which even now dim my eyes? – This alone is affection – every thing else is only humanity, electrified by sympathy.

662. Imlay was sending Wollstonecraft to Scandinavia on his behalf to pursue the lawsuit which he and his business associate Backman had begun against the Norwegian captain Ellefsen, who, they believed, had stolen their ship and its cargo of silver worth £3,500 (see Nyström's *Scandinavian Journey*, pp. 18f.). Imlay promised to meet Wollstonecraft in Basle in Switzerland at the end of her journey. So that she could act as his agent he had provided her with a document declaring her 'Mary Imlay my best friend and wife' and authorizing her 'to take the sole management and direction of all my affairs and business which I had placed in the hands of Mr Elias Backman negotiant Gottenburg or in those of Messrs Myburg & Co. Copenhagen' and to collect the sum awarded in a suit against Ellefsen for violation of trust. As his 'dear beloved friend and companion' she was given his complete confidence (Abinger MSS, Dep.b.210/4). Wollstonecraft was accompanied by Fanny and the French maid Marguerite; all three had gone to Hull to catch a boat to Norway.

663. Some of the nine letters Wollstonecraft wrote in Hull were dated, some had only the weekday. *LI* dated the first two 27 and 28 May while Wollstonecraft herself dated the third as Friday 12 June. Yet, as *CL* points out, this last was obviously written only a few days after Wollstonecraft's arrival at Hull and refers to Imlay's letter 'dated the 9th' and 'Your second letter'. The *LI* dating suggests Imlay waited two weeks or so before writing to Wollstonecraft; this seems unlikely.

I will write to you again to-morrow, when I know how long I am to be detained – and hope to get a letter quickly from you, to cheer yours sincerely and affectionately

[Mary]

[Fanny] is playing near me in high spirits. She was so pleased with the noise of the mail-horn, she has been continually imitating it. – Adieu!

179. To Gilbert Imlay

[Hull] Thursday [June 11th, 1795]

A lady[664] has just sent to offer to take me to ——. I have then only a moment to exclaim against the vague manner in which people give information

[In *PW* Godwin indicated the omission of 5 lines.]

But why talk of inconveniences, which are in fact trifling, when compared with the sinking of the heart I have felt! I did not intend to touch this painful string – God bless you!

Yours truly,
[Mary]

180. To Gilbert Imlay

[Hull] Friday, June 12th [1795]

I have just received yours dated the 9th, which I suppose was a mistake, for it could scarcely have loitered so long on the road. The general observations which apply to the state of your own mind, appear to me just, as far as they go; and I shall always consider it as one of the most serious misfortunes of my life, that I did not meet you, before satiety had rendered your senses so fastidious, as almost to close up every

664. The wife of a physician in Hull to whom Wollstonecraft had an introduction.

tender avenue of sentiment and affection that leads to your sympathetic heart. You have a heart, my friend, yet, hurried away by the impetuosity of inferior feelings, you have sought in vulgar excesses, for that gratification which only the heart can bestow.

The common run of men, I know, with strong health and gross appetites, must have variety to banish *ennui*, because the imagination never lends its magic wand to convert appetite into love, cemented by according reason. – Ah! my friend, you know not the ineffable delight, the exquisite pleasure, which arises from a unison of affection and desire, when the whole soul and senses are abandoned to a lively imagination, that renders every emotion delicate and rapturous. Yes; these are emotions, over which satiety has no power, and the recollection of which, even disappointment cannot disenchant; but they do not exist without self-denial. These emotions, more or less strong, appear to me to be the distinctive characteristic of genius, the foundation of taste, and of that exquisite relish for the beauties of nature, of which the common herd of eaters and drinkers and *child-begeters*, certainly have no idea. You will smile at an observation that has just occurred to me: – I consider those minds as the most strong and original, whose imagination acts as the stimulus to their senses.

Well! you will ask, what is the result of all this reasoning? Why I cannot help thinking that it is possible for you, having great strength of mind, to return to nature, and regain a sanity of constitution, and purity of feeling – which would open your heart to me. – I would fain rest there!

Yet, convinced more than ever of the sincerity and tenderness of my attachment to you, the involuntary hopes, which a determination to live has revived, are not sufficiently strong to dissipate the cloud, that despair has spread over futurity. I have looked at the sea, and at my child, hardly daring to own to myself the secret wish, that it might become our tomb; and that the heart, still so alive to anguish, might there be quieted by death. At this moment ten thousand complicated sentiments press for utterance, weigh on my heart, and obscure my sight.

Are we ever to meet again? and will you endeavour to render that meeting happier than the last? Will you endeavour to restrain your caprices, in order to give vigour to affection, and to give play to the checked sentiments that nature intended should expand your heart? I cannot indeed, without agony, think of your bosom's being continually contaminated; and bitter are the tears which exhaust my eyes, when I recollect why my child and I are forced to stray from the asylum, in which, after so many storms, I had hoped to rest, smiling at angry fate. – These are not common sorrows; nor can you perhaps conceive, how much active fortitude it requires to labour perpetually to blunt the shafts of disappointment.

Examine now yourself, and ascertain whether you can live in something like a settled stile. Let our confidence in future be unbounded; consider whether you find it necessary to sacrifice me to what you term the 'zest of life;' and, when you have once a clear view of your own motives, of your own incentive to action, do not deceive me!

The train of thoughts which the writing of this epistle awoke, makes me so wretched, that I must take a walk, to rouse and calm my mind. But first, let me tell you, that, if you really wish to promote my happiness, you will endeavour to give me as much as you can of yourself. You have great mental energy; and your judgment seems to me so just, that it is only the dupe of your inclination in discussing one subject.

The post does not go out to-day. To-morrow I may write more tranquilly. I cannot yet say when the vessel will sail in which I have determined to depart.

Saturday Morning.

Your second letter reached me about an hour ago. You were certainly wrong, in supposing that I did not mention you with respect; though, without my being conscious of it, some sparks of resentment may have animated the gloom of despair – Yes; with less affection, I should have been more respectful. However the regard which I have for you, is so unequivocal to myself, I imagine that it must be sufficiently obvious to every body else. Besides, the only letter I intended for the public eye was to ——, and that I destroyed from delicacy before you saw them, because it was only written (of course warmly in your praise) to prevent any odium being thrown on you.[665]

---

665. Godwin added the note: 'This passage refers to letters written under a purpose of suicide, and not intended to be opened till after the catastrophe.'

I am harrassed by your embarrassments, and shall certainly use all my efforts, to make the business terminate to your satisfaction in which I am engaged.

My friend – my dearest friend – I feel my fate united to yours by the most sacred principles of my soul, and the yearns of – yes I will say it – a true, unsophisticated heart.

Yours most truly
[Mary]

If the wind be fair, the captain talks of sailing on Monday; but I am afraid I shall be detained some days longer. At any rate, continue to write (I want this support) till you are sure I am where I cannot expect a letter; and, if any should arrive after my departure, a gentleman (not Mr. ——'s friend, I promise you) from whom I have received great civilities, will send them after me.

Do write by every occasion! I am anxious to hear how your affairs go on; and, still more, to be convinced that you are not separating yourself from us. For my little darling is calling papa, and adding her parrot word – Come, Come! And will you not come, and let us exert ourselves? – I shall recover all my energy, when I am convinced that my exertions will draw us more closely together. One more adieu!

181. To Gilbert Imlay

[Hull] Sunday, June 14th [1795]

I rather expected to hear from you to-day – I wish you would not fail to write to me for a little time, because I am not quite well – Whether I have any good sleep or not, I wake in the morning in violent fits of trembling – and, in spite of all my efforts, the child – every thing – fatigues me, in which I seek for solace or amusement.

Mr. —— forced on me a letter to a physician of this place; it was fortunate, for I should otherwise have had some difficulty to obtain the necessary information. His wife is a pretty woman (I can admire, you know, a pretty woman, when I am alone,) and he an intelligent and rather interesting man – They have behaved to me with great hospitality; and poor [Fanny] was never so happy in her life, as amongst their young brood.

They took me in their carriage to [Beverley], and I ran over my favourite walks, with a vivacity that would have astonished you. – The town did not please me quite so well as formerly – It appeared so diminutive; and, when I found that many of the inhabitants had lived in the same houses ever since I left it, I could not help wondering how they could thus have vegetated, whilst I was running over a world of sorrow, snatching at pleasure, and throwing off prejudices.[666] The place where I at present am, is much improved; but it is astonishing what strides aristocracy and fanaticism[667] have made, since I resided in this country.

The wind does not appear inclined to change, so I am still forced to linger – When do you think that you shall be able to set out for France? I do not entirely like the aspect of your affairs, and still less your connections on either side of the water. Often do I sigh, when I think of your entanglements in business, and your extreme restlessness of mind. – Even now I am almost afraid to ask you, whether the pleasure of being free, does not overbalance the pain you felt at parting with me? Sometimes I indulge the hope that you will feel me necessary to you – or why should we meet again? – but, the moment after, despair damps my rising spirits, aggravated by the emotions of tenderness, which ought to soften the cares of life. – God bless you!

Yours sincerely and affectionately

[Mary]

666. Her childhood friend Jane Arden was still living in Beverley and running a school.
667. The word 'fanaticism' could be used for political conservatism as well as religious zeal and Methodism, e.g. when Eliza Wollstonecraft remarked that she was 'buried' among fanatics in Upton in 1794. In *Cursory Remarks* (London, 1792, 2nd edn.), postscript, Mary Hays uses the word to suggest irrationality: 'supposing these ideas tinctured with fanaticism, an Enthusiast on whom the "club of argument" makes no impression, will rarely be corrected by the "shafts of ridicule".'

182. To Gilbert Imlay

[Hull] June 15th [1795]

I want to know how you have settled with respect to ——. In short, be very particular in your account of all your affairs – let our confidence, my dear, be unbounded. – The last time we were separated, was a separation indeed on your part – Now you have acted more ingenuously, let the most affectionate interchange of sentiments fill up the aching void of disappointment. I almost dread that your plans will prove abortive – yet should the most unlucky turn send you home to us, convinced that a true friend is a treasure, I should not much mind having to struggle with the world again. Accuse me not of pride – yet sometimes, when nature has opened my heart to its author, I have wondered that you did not set a higher value on my heart.

Receive a kiss from [Fanny], I was going to add, if you will not take one from me, and believe me yours

Sincerely
[Mary]

The wind still continues in the same quarter.

183. To Gilbert Imlay

[Hull] Tuesday morning [June 16th, 1795]

The captain has just sent to inform me, that I must be on board in the course of a few hours. – I wished to have stayed till to-morrow. It would have been a comfort to me to have received another letter from you – Should one arrive, it will be sent after me.

My spirits are agitated, I scarcely know why – The quitting England seems to be a fresh parting. – Surely you will not forget me. – A thousand weak forebodings assault my soul, and the state of my health renders me sensible to every thing. It is surprising that in London, in a continual conflict of mind, I was still growing better – whilst here, bowed down by the despotic hand of fate, forced into resignation by despair, I seem to be fading away – perishing beneath a cruel blight, that withers up all my faculties.

The child is perfectly well. My hand seems unwilling to add adieu! I know not why this inexpressible sadness has taken possession of me. – It is not a presentiment of ill. Yet, having been so perpetually the sport of disappointment, – having a heart that has been as it were a mark for misery, I dread to meet wretchedness in some new shape. – Well, let it come – I care not! – what have I to dread, who have so little to hope for! God bless you – I am most affectionately and sincerely yours

[Mary]

184. To Gilbert Imlay

[Hull] Wednesday morning [June 17th, 1795]

I was hurried on board yesterday about three o'clock, the wind having changed. But before evening it veered round to the old point; and here we are, in the midst of mists and water, only taking advantage of the tide to advance a few miles.

You will scarcely suppose that I left the town with reluctance – yet it was even so – for I wished to receive another letter from you, and I felt pain at parting, for ever perhaps, from the amiable family, who had treated me with so much hospitality and kindness. They will probably send me your letter, if it arrives this morning; for here we are likely to remain, I am afraid to think how long.

The vessel is very commodious, and the captain a civil, open-hearted, kind of man. There being no other passengers, I have the cabin to myself, which is pleasant; and I have brought a few books with me to beguile weariness; but I seem inclined, rather to employ the dead moments of suspense in writing some effusions, than in reading.

What are you about? How are your affairs going on? It may be a long time before you answer these questions. My dear friend, my heart sinks within me! Why am I forced thus to struggle continually with my affections and feelings? – Ah! why are those affections and feelings the source of so much misery, when they seem to have been given to vivify my heart, and extend my usefulness! But I must not dwell on this subject. – Will you not endeavour to cherish all the affection you can for me? What am I saying? – Rather forget me, if you can – if other gratifications are dearer to you. – How is every remembrance of mine embittered by disappointment? What a world is this! – They only seem happy, who never look beyond sensual or artificial enjoyments. – Adieu!

[Fanny] begins to play with the cabin-boy, and is as gay as a lark. – I will labour to be tranquil; and am in every mood,

Yours sincerely
[Mary]

185. To Gilbert Imlay

[Hull] Thursday [June 18ᵗʰ, 1795]

Here I am still – and I have just received your letter of Monday by the pilot, who promised to bring it to me, if we were detained, as he expected, by the wind. – It is indeed wearisome to be thus tossed about without going forward. – I have a violent head-ache – yet I am obliged to take care of the child, who is a little tormented by her teeth, because [Marguerite] is unable to do any thing, she is rendered so sick by the motion of the ship, as we ride at anchor.

These are however trifling inconveniences, compared with anguish of mind – compared with the sinking of a broken heart. – To tell you the truth, I never suffered in my life so much from depression of spirits – from despair. – I do not sleep – or, if I close my eyes, it is to have the most terrifying dreams, in which I often meet you with different casts of countenance.

I will not, my dear [Imlay] torment you by dwelling on my sufferings – and will use all my efforts to calm my mind, instead of deadening it – at present it is most painfully active. I find I am not equal to these continual struggles – yet your letter this morning has afforded me some comfort – and I will try to revive hope. One thing let me tell you – when we meet again – surely we are to meet! – it must be to part no more. I mean not to have seas between us – it is more than I can support.

The pilot is hurrying me – God bless you.

In spite of the commodiousness of the vessel, every thing here would disgust my senses, had I nothing else to think of – 'When the mind's free, the body's delicate';[668] – mine has been too much hurt to regard trifles.

Yours most truly

[Mary]

186. To Gilbert Imlay

[Hull] Saturday [June 20th, 1795]

This is the fifth dreary day I have been imprisoned by the wind, with every outward object to disgust the senses, and unable to banish the remembrances that sadden my heart.

How am I altered by disappointment! – When going to [Lisbon], ten years ago, the elasticity of my mind was sufficient to ward off weariness – and the imagination still could dip her brush in the rainbow of fancy, and sketch futurity in smiling colours. Now I am going towards the North in search of sunbeams! – Will any ever warm this desolated heart? All nature seems to frown – or rather mourn with me. – Every thing is cold – cold as my expectations! Before I left the shore, tormented, as I now am, by these North-east *chillers*, I could not help exclaiming – Give me, gracious Heaven! at least, genial weather, if I am never to meet the genial affection that still warms this agitated bosom – compelling life to linger there.

I am now going on shore with the captain, though the weather be rough, to seek for milk, &c. at a little village, and to take a walk – after which I hope to sleep – for, confined here, surrounded by disagreeable smells, I have lost the little appetite I had; and I lie awake, till thinking almost drives me to the brink of madness – only to the brink, for I never forget, even in the feverish slumbers I sometimes fall into, the

---

668. *King Lear*, III, iv, 8ff.: 'But where the greater malady is fix'd, / The lesser is scarce felt. . . . When the mind's free / The body's delicate; the tempest in my mind / Doth from my senses take all feeling else, / Save what beats there.'

misery I am labouring to blunt the sense of, by every exertion in my power.

Poor [Marguerite] still continues sick, and [Fanny] grows weary when the weather will not allow her to remain on deck.

I hope this will be the last letter I shall write from England to you – are you not tired of this lingering adieu?

Yours truly

[Mary]

187. To Gilbert Imlay

[Hull] Sunday morning [June 21st, 1795]

The captain last night, after I had written my letter to you intended to be left at a little village, offered to go to —— to pass to-day. We had a troublesome sail – and now I must hurry on board again, for the wind has changed.

I half expected to find a letter from you here. Had you written one hap-hazard, it would have been kind and considerate – you might have known, had you thought, that the wind would not permit me to depart. These are attentions, more grateful to the heart than offers of service – But why do I foolishly continue to look for them?

Adieu! adieu! My friend – your friendship is very cold – you see I am hurt. – God bless you! I may perhaps be, some time or other, independent in every sense of the word – Ah! there is but one sense of it of consequence. I will break or bend this weak heart – yet even now it is full.

Yours sincerely

[Mary]

The child is well; I did not leave her on board.

Scandinavia 1795

188. To Gilbert Imlay[669]

[Gothenburg] Saturday, June 27th [1795]

I arrived in [Gothenburg] this afternoon, after vainly attempting to land at [Arendal]. I have now but a moment, before the post goes out, to inform you we have got here; though not without considerable difficulty, for we were set ashore in a boat about twenty miles below.[670]

What I suffered in the vessel I will not now descant upon – nor mention the pleasure I received from the sight of the rocky coast. – This morning however, walking to join the carriage that was to transport us to this place, I fell, without any previous warning, senseless on the rocks – and how I escaped with life I can scarcely guess. I was in a stupour for a quarter of an hour; the suffusion of blood at last restored me to my senses – the contusion is great, and my brain confused. The child is well.

669. Wollstonecraft's journey through Scandinavia can be followed through the travelogue she published with Joseph Johnson in 1796, *Letters Written During a Short Residence in Sweden, Norway, and Denmark*. Her first duty had been to meet Imlay's business partner in Gothenburg, Elias Backman. From there she went on to Norway, travelling to the fortress of Frederiksten; then from Risör on the south coast of Norway she made her way back to Kristiana (now Oslo), Gothenburg and Copenhagen, returning to England via Hamburg.
670. Wollstonecraft and her party had been rowed ashore by sailors from the English ship. After considerable journeying along the almost empty shoreline they were met by a lieutenant who entertained Wollstonecraft, Marguerite and Fanny at his house on the Onsala peninsula while the sailors returned to their ship. He then organized their journey to Gothenburg, where Backman invited them to stay in his house.

Twenty miles ride in the rain, after my accident, has sufficiently deranged me – and here I could not get a fire to warm me, or any thing warm to eat; the inns are mere stables – I must nevertheless go to bed. For God's sake, let me hear from you immediately, my friend! I am not well, and yet you see I cannot die.

Yours sincerely
[Mary]

189. To Gilbert Imlay

[Gothenburg] June 29th [1795]

I wrote to you by the last post, to inform you of my arrival; and I believe I alluded to the extreme fatigue I endured on ship-board, owing to ——'s illness,[671] and the roughness of the weather – I likewise mentioned to you my fall, the effects of which I still feel, though I do not think it will have any serious consequences.

[Backman] will go with me, if I find it necessary to go to [Copenhagen].[672] The inns here are so bad, I was forced to accept of an apartment in his house. I am overwhelmed with civilities on all sides, and fatigued with the endeavours to amuse me, from which I cannot escape.

My friend – my friend, I am not well – a deadly weight of sorrow lies heavily on my heart. I am again tossed on the troubled billows of life; and obliged to cope with difficulties, without being buoyed up by the hopes that alone render them bearable. 'How flat, dull, and unprofitable,'[673] appears to me all the bustle into which I see people here so eagerly enter! I long every night to go to bed, to hide my melancholy face in my pillow; but there is a canker-worm in my bosom that never sleeps.

[Mary]

671. Either Marguerite, who suffered from sea-sickness, or Fanny, who was teething.
672. The Supreme Court for Norway and Denmark was in Copenhagen. It was also the place where, in January 1795, the Danish government had set up the Royal Commission which was to hear the case and deliver judgment on Ellefsen.
673. *Hamlet*, I, ii. 133f.; Wollstonecraft also referred to this passage in Letter 50 to Gabell and Letter 55 to Everina.

190. To Gilbert Imlay

[Gothenburg] July 1st [1795]

I labour in vain to calm my mind – my soul has been overwhelmed by sorrow and disappointment. Every thing fatigues me – this is a life that cannot last long. It is you who must determine with respect to futurity – and, when you have, I will act accordingly – I mean, we must either resolve to live together, or part for ever, I cannot bear these continual struggles – But I wish you to examine carefully your own heart and mind; and, if you perceive the least chance of being happier without me than with me, or if your inclination leans capriciously to that side, do not dissemble; but tell me frankly that you will never see me more. I will then adopt the plan I mentioned to you – for we must either live together, or I will be entirely independent.

My heart is so oppressed, I cannot write with precision – You know however that what I so imperfectly express, are not the crude sentiments of the moment – You can only contribute to my comfort (it is the consolation I am in need of) by being with me – and, if the tenderest friendship is of any value, why will you not look to me for a degree of satisfaction that heartless affection cannot bestow?

Tell me then, will you determine to meet me at Basle? – I shall, I should imagine, be at [Hamburg?] before the close of August; and, after you settle your affairs at Paris, could we not meet there?

God bless you!

Yours truly
[Mary]

Poor [Fanny] has suffered during the journey with her teeth.

191. To Gilbert Imlay

[Gothenburg] July 3ᵈ [1795]

There was a gloominess diffused through your last letter, the impression of which still rests on my mind – though, recollecting how quickly you throw off the forcible feelings of the moment, I flatter myself it has long since given place to your usual cheerfulness.

Believe me (and my eyes fill with tears of tenderness as I assure you) there is nothing I would not endure in the way of privation, rather than disturb your tranquility. – If I am fated to be unhappy, I will labour to hide my sorrows in my own bosom; and you shall always find me a faithful, affectionate friend.

I grow more and more attached to my little girl – and I cherish this affection without fear, because it must be a long time before it can become bitterness of soul. – She is an interesting creature. – On ship-board, how often as I gazed at the sea, have I longed to bury my troubled bosom in the less troubled deep; asserting with Brutus, 'that the virtue I had followed too far, was merely an empty name!'[674] and nothing but the sight of her – her playful smiles, which seemed to cling and twine round my heart – could have stopped me.

What peculiar misery has fallen to my share! To act up to my principles, I have laid the strictest restraint on my very thoughts – yes; not to sully the delicacy of my feelings, I have reined in my imagination; and started with affright from every sensation, (I allude to ——) that stealing with balmy sweetness into my soul, led me to scent from afar the fragrance of reviving nature.

My friend, I have dearly paid for one conviction. – Love, in some minds, is an affair of sentiment, arising from the same delicacy of perception (or taste) as renders them alive to the beauties of

---

674. Cf. Lucius Annaeus Florus, *Epitome of Roman History*, bk. 2, ch. 17: 'Et quam verum est, quod moriens [Brutus] efflavit, non in re, sed in vero tantum esse virtutem!' Wollstonecraft was probably quoting Brutus's words as reported in the *Spectator*, no. 293 (5 February 1712): 'O *Virtue, I have worshiped thee as a Substantial Good, but I find thou art an Empty Name.*'

nature, poetry, &c, alive to the charms of those evanescent graces that are, as it were, impalpable – they must be felt, they cannot be described.

Love is a want of my heart. I have examined myself lately with more care than formerly, and find, that to deaden is not to calm the mind – Aiming at tranquillity, I have almost destroyed all the energy of my soul – almost rooted out what renders it estimable – Yes, I have damped that enthusiasm of character, which converts the grossest materials into a fuel, that imperceptibly feeds hopes, which aspire above common enjoyment. Despair, since the birth of my child, has rendered me stupid – soul and body seemed to be fading away before the withering touch of disappointment.

I am now endeavouring to recover myself – and such is the elasticity of my constitution, and the purity of the atmosphere here, that health unsought for, begins to reanimate my countenance.

I have the sincerest esteem and affection for you – but the desire of regaining peace, (do you understand me?) has made me forget the respect due to my own emotions – sacred emotions, that are the sure harbingers of the delights I was formed to enjoy – and shall enjoy, for nothing can extinguish the heavenly spark

Still, when we meet again, I will not torment you, I promise you. I blush when I recollect my former conduct – and will not in future confound myself with the beings whom I feel to be my inferiors. – I will listen to delicacy, or pride.

[Unsigned]

192. To Gilbert Imlay

[Gothenburg] July 4th [1795]

I hope to hear from you by to-morrow's mail. My dearest friend! I cannot tear my affections from you – and, though every remembrance stings me to the soul, I think of you, till I make allowance for the very defects of character, that have given such a cruel stab to my peace.

Still however I am more alive, than you have seen me for a long,

long time.[675] I have a degree of vivacity, even in my grief, which is preferable to the benumbing stupour that, for the last year, has frozen up all my faculties. – Perhaps this change is more owing to returning health, than to the vigour of my reason – for, in spite of sadness (and surely I have had my share), the purity of this air, and the being continually out in it, for I sleep in the country every night, has made an alteration in my appearance that really surprises me. – The rosy fingers of health already streak my cheeks – and I have seen a *physical* life in my eyes, after I have been climbing the rocks, that resembled the fond, credulous hopes of youth.

With what a cruel sigh have I recollected that I had forgotten to hope! – Reason, or rather experience, does not thus cruelly damp poor [Fanny]'s pleasures; she plays all day in the garden with [Backman]'s children, and makes friends for herself.

Do not tell me, that you are happier without us – Will you not come to us in Switzerland? Ah, why do not you love us with more sentiment? – why are you a creature of such sympathy, that the warmth of your feelings, or rather quickness of your senses, hardens your heart? It is my misfortune, that my imagination is perpetually shading your defects, and lending you charms, whilst the grossness of your senses makes you (call me not vain) overlook graces in me, that only dignity of mind, and the sensibility of an expanded heart can give. – God bless you! Adieu.

[Unsigned]

193. To Gilbert Imlay

[Strömstad] July 7th [1795]

I could not help feeling extremely mortified last post, at not receiving a letter from you. My being at [Strömstad][676] was but a chance, and you might have hazarded it; and would a year ago.

675. *Letters from Sweden* indicates that Wollstonecraft was sightseeing in and around Gothenburg and being entertained by the rich merchants of the town.
676. Imlay's agent Christoffer Nordberg and the judge A. J. Unger, two of the judges on the Board of Inquiry set up to look into the Ellefsen affair, lived in Strömstad close

I shall not however complain – There are misfortunes so great, as to silence the usual expressions of sorrow – Believe me, there is such a thing as a broken heart! There are characters whose very energy preys upon them; and who, ever inclined to cherish by reflection some passion, cannot rest satisfied with the common comforts of life. I have endeavoured to fly from myself, and launched into all the dissipation possible here, only to feel keener anguish, when alone with my child.

Still, could any thing please me – had not disappointment cut me off from life, this romantic country, these fine evenings, would interest me. – My God! can any thing? and am I ever to feel alive only to painful sensations? – But it cannot – it shall not last long.

The post is again arrived; I have sent to seek for letters, only to be wounded to the soul by a negative. – My brain seems on fire. I must go into the air.

[Mary]

194. To Gilbert Imlay[677]

[Larvik] July 14th [1795]

I am now on my journey to [Tönsberg]. I felt more at leaving my child, than I thought I should – and, whilst at night I imagined every instant that I heard the half-formed sounds of her voice, – I asked myself how I could think of parting with her for ever, of leaving her thus helpless?

Poor lamb! It may run very well in a tale, that 'God will temper the

---

to the Norwegian border. Wollstonecraft travelled there with Fanny and Marguerite through 'the most uncultivated part of the country' (*Works*, 6, 260).

677. Wollstonecraft had left Strömstad and was on her way to Tönsberg in Norway to interview Backman's former agent, Jacob Wulfsberg, who had been on the original inquiry and was now one of the commissioners appointed to the Ellefsen case. The journey between Strömstad and Tönsberg was difficult and Wollstonecraft had left Fanny behind with Marguerite. She began by going alone by boat to Larvik, which she hated: even its best-known home, the grand seventeenth-century mansion of Herregarden where the Danish governors lived, displeased her as showy. She proceeded on her journey by cabriolet with a half drunk driver (*Works*, 6, 268ff.).

winds to the shorn lamb!'[678] but how can I expect that she will be shielded, when my naked bosom has had to brave continually the pitiless storm? Yes; I could add, with poor Lear – What is the war of elements to the pangs of disappointed affection, and the horror arising from a discovery of a breach of confidence, that snaps every social tie![679]

All is not right somewhere! – When you first knew me, I was not thus lost. I could still confide – for I opened my heart to you – of this only comfort you have deprived me, whilst my happiness, you tell me, was your first object. Strange want of judgment!

I will not complain; but, from the soundness of your understanding, I am convinced, if you give yourself leave to reflect, you will also feel, that your conduct to me, so far from being generous, has not been just. – I mean not to allude to factitious principles of morality; but to the simple basis of all rectitude. – However I did not intend to argue – Your not writing is cruel – and my reason is perhaps disturbed by constant wretchedness.

Poor [Marguerite] would fain have accompanied me, out of tenderness; for my fainting, or rather convulsion, when I landed, and my sudden changes of countenance since, have alarmed her so much, that she is perpetually afraid of some accident – But it would have injured the child this warm season, as she is cutting her teeth.

I hear not of your having written to me at [Gothenburg?]. Very well! Act as you please – there is nothing I fear or care for! When I see whether I can, or cannot obtain the money I am come here about, I will not trouble you with letters to which you do not reply.

[Unsigned]

678. In Sterne's *Sentimental Journey*, vol. 2, ch. 27, mad Maria told Yorick that she had 'stray'd as far as Rome, and walk'd round St Peter's once – and return'd back – that she found her way alone across the Appenines . . . how she had borne it, and how she had got supported, she could not tell – but *God tempers the wind*, said Maria, to the shorn lamb. Shorn indeed! and to the quick, said I.' Maria was quoting a Languedoc proverb, cf. Ferrar, *Illustrations of Sterne* (London, 1798).

679. *King Lear*, III, iv, 28ff.: 'Poor naked wretches, whereso'er you are, / That bide the pelting of this pitiless storm, / How shall your houseless heads and unfed sides, / . . . defend you / From seasons such as these?'; III, ii, 1ff.: 'Blow winds and crack your cheeks! . . . / I tax not you, you elements, with unkindness; / I never gave you kingdom, called you children'.

195. To Gilbert Imlay

[Tönsberg] July 18ᵗʰ [1795]

I am here in [Tönsberg], separated from my child – and here I must remain a month at least, or I might as well never have come.[680]

[In *PW* Godwin indicated the omission of 3 lines.]

I have begun ——[681] which will, I hope, discharge all my obligations of a pecuniary kind. – I am lowered in my own eyes, on account of my not having done it sooner.

I shall make no further comments on your silence. God bless you!

[Mary]

196. To Gilbert Imlay

[Tönsberg] July 30ᵗʰ [1795]

I have just received two of your letters, dated the 26th and 30th of June; and you must have received several from me, informing you of my detention, and how much I was hurt by your silence.

[In *PW* Godwin indicated the omission of 3 lines.]

Write to me then, my friend, and write explicitly. I have suffered, God knows, since I left you. Ah! you have never felt this kind of sickness of heart! – My mind however is at present painfully active, and the sympathy I feel almost rises to agony. But this is not a subject

---

680. Wollstonecraft found some tranquillity in Tönsberg, with its brightly painted wooden houses and friendly people. She went to dinners at Rossegarden, where the wealthiest merchants lived, and through Wulfsberg, the town mayor, she was invited to the Danish Earl of Jarlsberg's red wooden mansion. By now she realized she would need to go on to Oslo to pursue her business.

681. *CL* suggests that this refers to the work that would become *Letters from Sweden*; alternatively Wollstonecraft may have been doing French translation for Joseph Johnson.

of complaint, it has afforded me pleasure, – and reflected pleasure is all I have to hope for – if a spark of hope be yet alive in my forlorn bosom.

I will try to write with a degree of composure. I wish for us to live together, because I want you to acquire an habitual tenderness for my poor girl. I cannot bear to think of leaving her alone in the world, or that she should only be protected by your sense of duty. Next to preserving her, my most earnest wish is not to disturb your peace. I have nothing to expect, and little to fear, in life – There are wounds that can never be healed – but they may be allowed to fester in silence without wincing.

When we meet again, you shall be convinced that I have more resolution than you give me credit for. I will not torment you. If I am destined always to be disappointed and unhappy, I will conceal the anguish I cannot dissipate; and the tightened cord of life or reason will at last snap, and set me free.

Yes; I shall be happy – This heart is worthy of the bliss its feelings anticipate – and I cannot even persuade myself, wretched as they have made me, that my principles and sentiments are not founded in nature and truth. But to have done with these subjects.

[In *P W* Godwin indicated the omission of 3 lines.]

I have been seriously employed in this way since I came to [Tönsberg]; yet I never was so much in the air. – I walk, I ride on horseback – row, bathe, and even sleep in the fields; my health is consequently improved. The child, —— [682] informs me, is well. I long to be with her.

Write to me immediately – were I only to think of myself, I could wish you to return to me, poor, with the simplicity of character, part of which you seem lately to have lost, that first attached to you.

Yours most affectionately
[Mary Imlay]

I have been subscribing other letters – so I mechanically did the same to yours.

---

682. Possibly Marguerite or Backman.

197. To Gilbert Imlay

[Tönsberg] August 5th [1795]

Employment and exercise have been of great service to me; and I have entirely recovered the strength and activity I lost during the time of my nursing. I have seldom been in better health; and my mind, though trembling to the touch of anguish, is calmer – yet still the same.[683] – I have, it is true, enjoyed some tranquillity, and more happiness here, than for a long – long time past. – (I say happiness, for I can give no other appellation to the exquisite delight this wild country and fine summer have afforded me.) – Still, on examining my heart, I find that it is so constituted, I cannot live without some particular affection – I am afraid not without a passion – and I feel the want of it more in society, than in solitude. –

[In *P W* Godwin indicated the omission of 3 lines.]

Writing to you, whenever an affectionate epithet occurs – my eyes fill with tears, and my trembling hand stops – you may then depend on my resolution, when with you. If I am doomed to be unhappy, I will confine my anguish in my own bosom – tenderness, rather than passion, has made me sometimes overlook delicacy – the same tenderness will in future restrain me.

God bless you!

[Unsigned]

683. In Sterne's *Sentimental Journey*, when the hero Yorick meets Maria, he already knows her sad story. As he takes out his handkerchief, she notices 'that it was steep'd too much already to be of use, would needs go wash it in the stream – And where will you dry it, Maria? said I – I'll dry it in my bosom, said she – 'twill do me good. And is your heart still so warm, Maria? said I' (vol. 2, ch. 27).

198. To Gilbert Imlay

[Tönsberg] August 7th [1795]

Air, exercise, and bathing, have restored me to health, braced my muscles, and covered my ribs, even whilst I have recovered my former activity. – I cannot tell you that my mind is calm, though I have snatched some moments of exquisite delight, wandering through the woods, and resting on the rocks.

This state of suspense, my friend, is intolerable; we must determine on something – and soon; – we must meet shortly, or part for ever. I am sensible that I acted foolishly – but I was wretched – when we were together – Expecting too much, I let the pleasure I might have caught, slip from me. I cannot live with you – I ought not – if you form another attachment. But I promise you, mine shall not be intruded on you. Little reason have I to expect a shadow of happiness, after the cruel disappointments that have rent my heart; but that of my child seems to depend on our being together. Still I do not wish you to sacrifice a chance of enjoyment for an uncertain good. I feel a conviction, that I can provide for her, and it shall be my object – if we are indeed to part to meet no more. Her affection must not be divided. She must be a comfort to me – if I am to have no other – and only know me as her support. I feel that I cannot endure the anguish of corresponding with you – if we are only to correspond. – No; if you seek for happiness elsewhere, my letters shall not interrupt your repose. I will be dead to you. I cannot express to you what pain it gives me to write about an eternal separation. – You must determine – examine yourself – But, for God's sake! spare me the anxiety of uncertainty! – I may sink under the trial; but I will not complain.

Adieu! If I had any thing more to say to you, it is all flown, and absorbed by the most tormenting apprehensions; yet I scarcely know what new form of misery I have to dread.

I ought to beg your pardon for having sometimes written peevishly; but you will impute it to affection, if you understand any thing of the heart of

Yours truly
[Mary]

199. To Gilbert Imlay

[Tönsberg] August 9th [1795]

Five of your letters have been sent after me from ——.[684] One, dated the 14th of July, was written in a style which I may have merited, but did not expect from you. However this is not a time to reply to it, except to assure you that you shall not be tormented with any more complaints. I am disgusted with myself for having so long importuned you with my affection. –

My child is very well. We shall soon meet, to part no more, I hope – I mean, I and my girl. – I shall wait with some degree of anxiety till I am informed how your affairs terminate.

Yours sincerely
[Mary]

200. To Gilbert Imlay[685]

[Gothenburg] August 26th [1795]

I arrived here last night, and with the most exquisite delight, once more pressed my babe to my heart. We shall part no more. You perhaps cannot conceive the pleasure it gave me, to see her run about, and play alone. Her increasing intelligence attaches me more and more to her. I have promised her that I will fulfil my duty to her; and nothing in future shall make me forget it. I will also exert myself to obtain an independence for her; but I will not be too anxious on this head.

I have already told you, that I have recovered my health. Vigour, and even vivacity of mind, have returned with a renovated constitution.

---

684. Probably Gothenburg or Strömstad.
685. Wollstonecraft had travelled from Tönsberg back to Larvik to meet Imlay's lawyers, who proved unsatisfactory. She then went to East Risör possibly to see Ellefsen, commenting on the town, 'To be born here, was to be bastilled by nature' (Works, 6, 295). She returned to Tönsberg and from there went on to Oslo. Finally she reached Gothenburg and Fanny, from whom she had been absent for six weeks.

As for peace, we will not talk of it. I was not made, perhaps, to enjoy the calm contentment so termed. –

[In *PW* Godwin indicated the omission of 3 lines.]

You tell me that my letters torture you; I will not describe the effect yours have on me. I received three this morning, the last dated the 7th of this month. I mean not to give vent to the emotions they produced. – Certainly you are right; our minds are not congenial. I have lived in an ideal world, and fostered sentiments that you do not comprehend – or you would not treat me thus. I am not, I will not be, merely an object of compassion – a clog, however light, to teize you. Forget that I exist: I will never remind you. Something emphatical whispers me to put an end to these struggles. Be free – I will not torment, when I cannot please. I can take care of my child; you need not continually tell me that our fortune is inseparable, *that you will try to cherish tenderness* for me. Do no violence to yourself! When we are separated, our interest, since you give so much weight to pecuniary considerations, will be entirely divided. I want not protection without affection; and support I need not, whilst my faculties are undisturbed. I had a dislike to living in England; but painful feelings must give way to superior considerations. I may not be able to acquire the sum necessary to maintain my child and self elsewhere. It is too late to go to Switzerland. I shall not remain at ——,[686] living expensively. But be not alarmed! I shall not force myself on you any more.

Adieu! I am agitated – my whole frame is convulsed – my lips tremble, as if shook by cold, though fire seems to be circulating in my veins.

God bless you.

[Mary]

686. Perhaps Charlotte Street, where Wollstonecraft had been lodging before her Scandinavian travels.

201. To Gilbert Imlay[687]

[Copenhagen] September 6th [1795]

I received just now your letter of the 20th. I had written you a letter last night, into which imperceptibly slipt some of my bitterness of soul. I will copy the part relative to business. I am not sufficiently vain to imagine that I can, for more than a moment, cloud your enjoyment of life – to prevent even that, you had better never hear from me – and repose on the idea that I am happy.

Gracious God! It is impossible for me to stifle something like resentment, when I receive fresh proofs of your indifference. What I have suffered this last year, is not to be forgotten! I have not that happy substitute for wisdom, insensibility – and the lively sympathies which bind me to my fellow-creatures, are all of a painful kind. – They are the agonies of a broken heart – pleasure and I have shaken hands.

I see here nothing but heaps of ruins, and only converse with people immersed in trade and sensuality.

I am weary of travelling – yet seem to have no home – no resting place to look to. – I am strangely cast off. – How often, passing through the rocks, I have thought, 'But for this child, I would lay my head on one of them, and never open my eyes again!' With a heart feelingly alive to all the affections of my nature – I have never met with one, softer than the stone that I would fain take for my last pillow. I once thought I had, but it was all a delusion. I meet with families continually, who are bound together by affection or principle – and, when I am conscious that I have fulfilled the duties of my station, almost to a forgetfulness of myself, I am ready to demand, in a murmuring tone, of Heaven, 'Why am I thus abandoned?'

You say now

[In *P W* Godwin indicated the omission of 2 lines.]

687. With Fanny and Marguerite, Wollstonecraft had travelled through Sweden, then across the water to Elsinore and on to Copenhagen, where she pursued her legal business by meeting Count Bernstorff, the 'real sovereign' of Denmark and Norway as she expressed it.

I do not understand you. It is necessary for you to write more explicitly – and determine on some mode of conduct. – I cannot endure this suspense – Decide – Do you fear to strike another blow? We live together, or eternally part! – I shall not write to you again, till I receive an answer to this. I must compose my tortured soul, before I write on indifferent subjects.

[In *PW* Godwin indicated the omission of 2 lines.]

I do not know whether I write intelligibly, for my head is disturbed. – But this you ought to pardon – for it is with difficulty frequently that I make out what you mean to say – You write, I suppose, at Mr.——'s after dinner, when your head is not the clearest – and as for your heart, if you have one, I see nothing like the dictates of affection, unless a glimpse when you mention the child. – Adieu!

[Unsigned]

202. To Gilbert Imlay[688]

[Hamburg] September 25th [1795]

[Hamburg] September 25th [1795]

I have just finished a letter, to be given in charge to captain ——. In that I complained of your silence, and expressed my surprise that three mails should have arrived without bringing a line for me. Since I closed it, I hear of another, and still no letter. – I am labouring to write calmly – this silence is a refinement on cruelty. Had captain —— remained a few days longer, I would have returned with him to England. What have I to do here? I have repeatedly written to you fully. Do you do

---

688. Wollstonecraft had sometimes hoped that Imlay would meet her in Hamburg. Switzerland, the original place of planned rendezvous, was probably now inappropriate given the progress of the French armies in Europe. By early 1795 they had conquered Belgium, the Dutch Republic, and the left bank of the Rhine, leaving only the fortresses of Luxemburg and Mainz in the hands of the allied and royalist armies. Wollstonecraft, Marguerite and Fanny had travelled from Denmark across the Great Belt and Little Belt and into the duchies of Schleswig and Holstein. They arrived in the free city of Hamburg, spent one uncomfortable night there, then moved to more expensive, more appropriate lodgings in nearby Altona.

the same – and quickly. Do not leave me in suspense. I have not deserved this of you. I cannot write, my mind is so distressed. Adieu!

[Mary]

203. *To Gilbert Imlay*

[Hamburg] September 27th [1795]

When you receive this, I shall either have landed, or be hovering on the British coast – your letter of the 18th decided me.

By what criterion of principle or affection, you term my questions extraordinary and unnecessary, I cannot determine. – You desire me to decide – I had decided. You must have had long ago two letters of mine, from ——, to the same purport, to consider. – In these, God knows! there was but too much affection, and the agonies of a distracted mind were but too faithfully pourtrayed! – What more then had I to say? – The negative was to come from you. – You had perpetually recurred to your promise of meeting me in the autumn – Was it extraordinary that I should demand a yes, or no? – Your letter is written with extreme harshness, coldness I am accustomed to, in it I find not a trace of the tenderness of humanity, much less of friendship. – I only see a desire to heave a load off your shoulders.

I am above disputing about words. – It matters not in what terms you decide.

The tremendous power who formed this heart, must have foreseen that, in a world in which self-interest, in various shapes, is the principal mobile, I had little chance of escaping misery. – To the fiat of fate I submit. – I am content to be wretched; but I will not be contemptible. – Of me you have no cause to complain, but for having had too much regard for you – for having expected a degree of permanent happiness, when you only sought for a momentary gratification.

I am strangely deficient in sagacity. – Uniting myself to you, your tenderness seemed to make me amends for all my former misfortunes. – On this tenderness and affection with what confidence did I rest! – but I leaned on a spear, that has pierced me to the heart. – You have thrown off a faithful friend, to pursue the caprices of the moment. –

We certainly are differently organized; for even now, when conviction has been stamped on my soul by sorrow, I can scarcely believe it possible. It depends at present on you, whether you will see me or not. – I shall take no step, till I see or hear from you.

Preparing myself for the worst – I have determined, if your next letter be like the last, to write to Mr. [Johnson?] to procure me an obscure lodging, and not to inform any body of my arrival. – There I will endeavour in a few months to obtain the sum necessary to take me to France – from you I will not receive any more. – I am not yet sufficiently humbled to depend on your beneficence.

Some people, whom my unhappiness has interested, though they know not the extent of it, will assist me to attain the object I have in view, the independence of my child. Should a peace take place,[689] ready money will go a great way in France – and I will borrow a sum, which my industry *shall* enable me to pay at my leisure, to purchase a small estate for my girl. – The assistance I shall find necessary to complete her education, I can get at an easy rate at Paris – I can introduce her to such society as she will like – and thus, securing for her all the chance for happiness, which depends on me, I shall die in peace, persuaded that the felicity which has hitherto cheated my expectation, will not always elude my grasp. No poor tempest-tossed mariner ever more earnestly longed to arrive at his port.

[Mary]

I shall not come up in the vessel all the way, because I have no place to go to. Captain —— will inform you where I am. It is needless to add, that I am not in a state of mind to bear suspense – and that I wish to see you, though it be for the last time.

689. In the summer of 1795 the French Directory was known to be economically hard pressed and William Pitt constantly told the British public that the French could not hold out much longer. However, actual attempts at peace negotiations seem not to have taken place until 1796.

204. To Gilbert Imlay

[Dover] Sunday, October 4th [1795]

I wrote to you by the packet, to inform you, that your letter of the 18th of last month, had determined me to set out with captain ——; but, as we sailed very quick, I take it for granted, that you have not yet received it.

You say, I must decide for myself. – I had decided, that it was most for the interest of my little girl, and for my own comfort, little as I expect, for us to live together; and I even thought that you would be glad, some years hence, when the tumult of business was over, to repose in the society of an affectionate friend, and mark the progress of our interesting child,[690] whilst endeavouring to be of use in the circle you at last resolved to rest in; for you cannot run about for ever.

From the tenour of your last letter however, I am led to imagine, that you have formed some new attachment. – If it be so, let me earnestly request you to see me once more, and immediately. This is the only proof I require of the friendship you profess for me. I will then decide, since you boggle about a mere form.

I am labouring to write with calmness – but the extreme anguish I feel, at landing without having any friend to receive me, and even to be conscious that the friend whom I most wish to see, will feel a disagreeable sensation at being informed of my arrival, does not come under the description of common misery. Every emotion yields to an overwhelming flood of sorrow – and the playfulness of my child distresses me. – On her account, I wished to remain a few days here, comfortless as is my situation. – Besides, I did not wish to surprise you. You have told me, that you would make any sacrifice to promote my happiness – and, even in your last unkind letter, you talk of the ties which bind you to me and my child. – Tell me, that you wish it, and I will cut this Gordian knot.

I now most earnestly intreat you to write to me, without fail, by the

690. Since spring 1795 the only reference to Fanny as 'our' rather than 'the' or 'my' child.

return of the post. Direct your letter to be left at the post-office, and tell me whether you will come to me here, or where you will meet me. I can receive your letter on Wednesday morning.

Do not keep me in suspense. – I expect nothing from you, or any human being: my die is cast! – I have fortitude enough to determine to do my duty; yet I cannot raise my depressed spirits, or calm my trembling heart. – That being who moulded it thus, knows that I am unable to tear up by the roots the propensity to affection which has been the torment of my life – but life will have an end!

Should you come here (a few months ago I could not have doubted it) you will find me at ——. If you prefer meeting me on the road, tell me where.

Yours affectionately
[Mary]

London 1795–1797

205. To Gilbert Imlay

[London, c. October 10ᵗʰ, 1795][691]

I write you now on my knees; imploring you to send my child and the maid with ——, to Paris, to be consigned to the care of Madame ——,[692] rue ——, section de ——. Should they be removed, —— can give their direction.

Let the maid have all my clothes, without distinction.

Pray pay the cook her wages, and do not mention the confession which I forced from her – a little sooner or later is of no consequence. Nothing but my extreme stupidity could have rendered me blind so long. Yet, whilst you assured me that you had no attachment, I thought we might still have lived together.

I shall make no comments on your conduct; or any appeal to the world. Let my wrongs sleep with me! Soon, very soon, shall I be at peace. When you receive this, my burning head will be cold.

I would encounter a thousand deaths, rather than a night like the last. Your treatment has thrown my mind into a state of chaos; yet I am serene. I go to find comfort, and my only fear is, that my poor

691. On her return to England Wollstonecraft had met Imlay in London where he took lodgings for her. She sensed his withdrawal and questioned the cook he had hired for her. Thus she learnt that he had a new mistress. She confronted him, then resolved to kill herself. The dating of this letter comes from a notice in *The Times* for October 1795 which most likely refers to Wollstonecraft's suicide attempt on 10 October.
692. Probably the German lady in Paris to whom Wollstonecraft had earlier proposed to entrust Fanny in case of her early death.

body will be insulted by an endeavour to recal my hated existence. But I shall plunge into the Thames where there is the least chance of my being snatched from the death I seek.

God bless you! May you never know by experience what you have made me endure. Should your sensibility ever awake, remorse will find its way to your heart; and, in the midst of business and sensual pleasure, I shall appear before you, the victim of your deviation from rectitude.

[Mary]

206. To Gilbert Imlay

[London] Sunday morning [c. October 1795][693]

I have only to lament, that, when the bitterness of death was past, I was inhumanly brought back to life and misery. But a fixed determination is not to be baffled by disappointment; nor will I allow that to be a frantic attempt, which was one of the calmest acts of reason.[694] In this respect, I am only accountable to myself. Did I care for what is termed reputation, it is by other circumstances that I should be dishonoured.

You say, 'that you know not how to extricate ourselves out of the wretchedness into which we have been plunged.' You are extricated long since. – But I forbear to comment. – If I am condemned to live longer, it is a living death.

693. Wollstonecraft first went to Battersea Bridge to drown herself but found it too public for a suicide attempt. Then she hired a boatman to row her to Putney Bridge in Fulham, near Walham Green where she had lived with Fanny Blood's family after her mother died. There, after drenching her clothes in the rain, she jumped from the bridge. She was rescued unconscious by fishermen and carried to the Duke's Head Tavern. According to *The Times* account, she gave her place of abode and added that the cause of her 'second act of desperation' was the brutal behaviour of her husband. She was taken home, then persuaded to go to the Christies' house in Finsbury Square to recuperate. *LI* and *CL* assign this and the subsequent three letters (excluding 207) to November 1795. It seems more likely that Letters 206, 207 and 208 were written in October close to the suicide attempt.

694. In the mid and late eighteenth century there was much discussion over the rational right to suicide, for example in the works of Rousseau, Hume and Godwin. Wollstonecraft had encountered many 'rational' suicides among politicians during the French Revolution.

It appears to me, that you lay much more stress on delicacy, than on principle; for I am unable to discover what sentiment of delicacy would have been violated, by your visiting a wretched friend – if indeed you have any friendship for me. – But since your new attachment is the only thing sacred in your eyes, I am silent – Be happy! My complaints shall never more damp your enjoyment – perhaps I am mistaken in supposing that even my death could, for more than a moment. – This is what you call magnanimity. – It is happy for yourself, that you possess this quality in the highest degree.

Your continually asserting, that you will do all in your power to contribute to my comfort (when you only allude to pecuniary assistance), appears to me a flagrant breach of delicacy. – I want not such vulgar comfort, nor will I accept it. I never wanted but your heart – That gone, you have nothing more to give. Had I only poverty to fear, I should not shrink from life. – Forgive me then, if I say, that I shall consider any direct or indirect attempt to supply my necessities, as an insult which I have not merited – and as rather done out of tenderness for your own reputation, than for me. Do not mistake me; I do not think that you value money (therefore I will not accept what you do not care for) though I do much less, because certain privations are not painful to me. When I am dead, respect for yourself will make you take care of the child.

I write with difficulty – probably I shall never write to you again. – Adieu!

God bless you!

[Mary]

207. To Gilbert Imlay[695]

[speculative reconstruction]

[London, c. October 1795]

If we are ever to live together again, it must be now. We meet now, or we part for ever. You say, You cannot abruptly break off the connection you have formed. It is unworthy of my courage and character, to wait the uncertain issue of that connection. I am determined to come to a decision. I consent then, for the present, to live with you, and the woman to whom you have associated yourself. I think it important that you should learn habitually to feel for your child the affection of a father. But, if you reject this proposal, here we end. You are now free. We will correspond no more. We will have no intercourse of any kind. I will be to you as a person that is dead.

208. To Gilbert Imlay

[London] Monday morning [c. October 1795]

I am compelled at last to say that you treat me ungenerously. I agree with you, that

[In *PW* Godwin indicated the omission of 4½ lines.]

But let the obliquity now fall on me. – I fear neither poverty nor infamy. I am unequal to the task of writing – and explanations are not necessary.

[In *PW* Godwin indicated the omission of 2 lines.]

695. Quoted in *Memoirs*, ch. 8, and prefaced by Godwin: 'The language she employed, was, in effect, as follows'. The passage may paraphrase conversations reported by Wollstonecraft or a letter omitted from the sequence because used in *Memoirs* (in *PW*, Letter LXXII is missing). Wollstonecraft had proposed living together in a house with Fanny, Imlay, and his new mistress.

My child may have to blush for her mother's want to prudence – and may lament that the rectitude of my heart made me above vulgar precautions; but she shall not despise me for meanness. – You are now perfectly free. – God bless you!

[Mary]

209. *To Gilbert Imlay*

[London] Saturday night [c. November 1795][696]

I have been hurt by indirect enquiries, which appear to me not to be dictated by any tenderness to me. – You ask 'If I am well or tranquil?' – They who think me so, must want a heart to estimate my feelings by. – I chuse then to be the organ of my own sentiments.

I must tell you, that I am very much mortified by your continually offering me pecuniary assistance – and, considering your going to the new house,[697] as an open avowal that you abandon me, let me tell you that I will sooner perish than receive any thing from you[698] – and I say this at the moment when I am disappointed in my first attempt to obtain a temporary supply.[699] But this even pleases me; an accumulation of disappointments and misfortunes seems to suit the habit of my mind. –

Have but a little patience, and I will remove myself where it will not be necessary for you to talk – of course, not to think of me. But let me see, written by yourself – for I will not receive it through any other medium – that the affair is finished. – It is an insult to me to suppose,

696. This letter is LXXIII in Godwin's sequence, although it followed the previous one, numbered LXXI by Godwin. See note 695.

697. The plan of a *ménage à trois* had been dropped and Imlay had moved into the new house with his mistress alone.

698. In the end Wollstonecraft was persuaded to take a bond for Fanny but it was never honoured. After her death Imlay demanded the trust deed back and Godwin returned it. Imlay was clearly ashamed of his conduct and asked Joseph Johnson not to spread news of it abroad.

699. Probably Wollstonecraft's attempt to write a comedy which would include serious descriptions of her life. She presented a draft to two publishers, who rejected it. Godwin burnt the manuscript, deeming it in too 'crude and imperfect a state'.

that I can be reconciled, or recover my spirits; but, if you hear nothing of me, it will be the same thing to you.

[Mary]

Even your seeing me, has been to oblige other people, and not to sooth my distracted mind.

210. To Gilbert Imlay

[London] Thursday afternoon [c. November 1795]

Mr. —— having forgot to desire you to send the things of mine which were left at the house, I have to request you to let —— bring them [t]o ——.

I shall go this evening to the lodging;[700] so you need not be restrained from coming here to transact your business. – And, whatever I may think, and feel – you need not fear that I shall publicly complain. – No! If I have any criterion to judge of right and wrong, I have been most ungenerously treated: but, wishing now only to hide myself, I shall be silent as the grave in which I long to forget myself. I shall protect and provide for my child. – I only mean by this to say, that you have nothing to fear from my desperation.

Farewel.

[Mary]

700. In part so that Imlay could continue to visit the Christies, both his friends and business colleagues, Wollstonecraft was moving from their house into her own lodgings near by at 16 Finsbury Place. She left her furniture in store since she still intended returning to Paris.

211. To Gilbert Imlay

London, November 27th [1795]

The letter, without an address, which you put up with the letters you returned,[701] did not meet my eyes till just now. – I had thrown the letters aside – I did not wish to look over a register of sorrow.

My not having seen it, will account for my having written to you with anger – under the impression your departure, without even a line left for me, made on me, even after your late conduct, which could not lead me to expect much attention to my sufferings.

In fact, 'the decided conduct, which appeared to me so unfeeling,' has almost overturned my reason; my mind is injured – I scarcely know where I am, or what I do. – The grief I cannot conquer (for some cruel recollections never quit me, banishing almost every other) I labour to conceal in total solitude. – My life therefore is but an exercise of fortitude – continually on the stretch – and hope never gleams in this tomb, where I am buried alive.

But I meant to reason with you, and not to complain. – You tell me, 'that I shall judge more coolly of your mode of acting, some time hence.' But is it not possible that *passion* clouds your reason, as much as it does mine? – and ought you not to doubt, whether those principles are so 'exalted,' as you term them, which only lead to your own gratification? In other words, whether it be just to have no principle of action, but that of following your inclination, trampling on the affection you have fostered, and the expectations you have excited?

My affection for you is rooted in my heart. – I know you are not what you now seem – nor will you always act, or feel, as you now do, though I may never be comforted by the change. – Even at Paris, my image will haunt you. – You will see my pale face – and sometimes the tears of anguish will drop on your heart, which you have forced from mine.

701. Wollstonecraft had asked Imlay to return her letters. He did so, enclosing a note, then set off to Paris with his mistress. Wollstonecraft's letter was intended to catch him in Dover.

I cannot write. I thought I could quickly have refuted all your *ingenious* arguments; but my head is confused. – Right or wrong, I am miserable!

It seems to me, that my conduct has always been governed by the strictest principles of justice and truth. – Yet, how wretched have my social feelings, and delicacy of sentiment rendered me! – I have loved with my whole soul, only to discover that I had no chance of a return – and that existence is a burthen without it.

I do not perfectly understand you. – If, by the offer of your friendship, you still only mean pecuniary support – I must again reject it. – Trifling are the ills of poverty in the scale of my misfortunes. – God bless you!

[Mary]

I have been treated ungenerously – if I understand what is generosity. – You seem to me only to have been anxious to shake me off – regardless whether you dashed me to atoms by the fall. – In truth I have been rudely handled. *Do you judge coolly*, and I trust you will not continue to call those capricious feelings 'the most refined,' which would undermine not only the most sacred principles, but the affections which unite mankind. – You would render mothers unnatural – and there would be no such things as a father! – If your theory of morals is the most 'exalted,' it is certainly the most easy. – It does not require much magnanimity, to determine to please ourselves for the moment, let others suffer what they will!

Excuse me for again tormenting you, my heart thirsts for justice from you – and whilst I recollect that you approved Miss ——'s conduct – I am convinced you will not always justify your own.

Beware of the deceptions of passion! It will not always banish from your mind, that you have acted ignobly – and condescended to subterfuge to gloss over the conduct you could not excuse. – Do truth and principle require such sacrifices?

212. *To Gilbert Imlay*

London, December 8th [1795]

Having just been informed that —— is to return immediately to Paris, I would not miss a sure opportunity of writing, because I am not certain that my last, by Dover has reached you.

Resentment, and even anger, are momentary emotions with me – and I wished to tell you so, that if you ever think of me, it may not be in the light of an enemy.

That I have not been used *well* I must ever feel; perhaps, not always with the keen anguish I do at present – for I began even now to write calmly, and I cannot restrain my tears.

I am stunned! – Your late conduct still appears to me a frightful dream. – Ah! ask yourself if you have not condescended to employ a little address, I could almost say cunning, unworthy of you? – Principles are sacred things – and we never play with truth, with impunity.

The expectation (I have too fondly nourished it) of regaining your affection, every day grows fainter and fainter. – Indeed, it seems to me, when I am more sad than usual, that I shall never see you more. – Yet you will not always forget me. – You will feel something like remorse, for having lived only for yourself – and sacrificed my peace to inferior gratifications. In a comfortless old age, you will remember that you had one disinterested friend, whose heart you wounded to the quick. The hour of recollection will come – and you will not be satisfied to act the part of a boy, till you fall into that of a dotard. I know that your mind, your heart, and your principles of action, are all superior to your present conduct. You do, you must, respect me – and you will be sorry to forfeit my esteem.

You know best whether I am still preserving the remembrance of an imaginary being. – I once thought that I knew you thoroughly – but now I am obliged to leave some doubts that involuntarily press on me, to be cleared up by time.

You may render me unhappy; but cannot make me contemptible in my own eyes. – I shall still be able to support my child, though I am disappointed in some other plans of usefulness, which I once believed would have afforded you equal pleasure.

Whilst I was with you, I restrained my natural generosity, because I thought your property in jeopardy. – When I went to [Scandinavia], I requested you, *if you could conveniently*, not to forget my father, sisters, and some other people, whom I was interested about. – Money was lavished away, yet not only my requests were neglected, but some trifling debts were not discharged, that now come on me. – Was this friendship – or generosity? Will you not grant you have forgotten yourself? Still I have an affection for you. – God bless you.

[Mary]

213. To Gilbert Imlay

[London, c. December 1795][702]

As the parting from you for ever is the most serious event of my life, I will once expostulate with you, and call not the language of truth and feeling ingenuity!

I know the soundness of your understanding – and know that it is impossible for you always to confound the caprices of every wayward inclination with manly dictates of principle.

You tell me 'that I torment you.' – Why do I? – Because you cannot estrange your heart entirely from me – and you feel that justice is on my side. You urge, 'that your conduct was unequivocal.' – It was not. – When your coolness has hurt me, with what tenderness have you endeavoured to remove the impression! – and even before I returned to England, you took great pains to convince me, that all my uneasiness was occasioned by the effect of a worn-out constitution – and you concluded your letter with these words, 'Business alone has kept me from you. – Come to any port, and I will fly down to my two dear girls with a heart all their own.'

With these assurances, is it extraordinary that I should believe what I wished? I might – and did think that you had a struggle with old propensities; but I still thought that I and virtue should at last prevail. I still thought that you had a magnanimity of character, which would enable you to conquer yourself.

702. Date supplied by Kegan Paul in *LI*.

[Imlay], believe me, it is not romance, you have acknowledged to me feelings of this kind. – You could restore me to life and hope, and the satisfaction you would feel, would amply repay you.

In tearing myself from you, it is my own heart I pierce – and the time will come, when you will lament that you have thrown away a heart, that, even in the moment of passion, you cannot despise. – I would owe every thing to your generosity – but, for God's sake, keep me no longer in suspense! – Let me see you once more! –

[Unsigned]

214. To Henry Fuseli

[London] Monday morning [c. late 1795]

When I returned from France, I visited you, Sir, but finding myself after my late journey in a very different situation, I vainly imagined you would have called upon me. I simply tell you what I thought, yet I write not, at present, to comment on your conduct or expostulate. I have long ceased to expect kindness or affection from any human creature, and would fain tear from my heart its treacherous sympathies. I am alone. The injustice, without alluding to hopes blasted in the bud, which I have endured, wounding my bosom, have set my thoughts adrift into an ocean of painful conjectures. I ask impatiently what – and where is truth? I have been treated brutally; but I daily labour to remember that I still have the duty of a mother to fulfil.

I have written more than I intended, – for I only meant to request you to return my letters: I wish to have them, and it must be the same to you.[703] Adieu!

Mary

To Mr. Fuseli.

703. Unlike Imlay, Fuseli did not return the letters, and he denied Godwin their use for his *Memoirs*. They were found in 1825 among his papers and quoted by Knowles in *HF*. It seems that Knowles's son sold the letters to Sir Percy Florence Shelley, Wollstonecraft's grandson. They appear to have been destroyed since they are not with the Abinger papers.

215. To Mary Hays

[London] Saturday evening [c. late 1795]

I have promised to dine with M^r. Johnson to morrow, and he requested me to invite you. If you have no previous engagement, I will call on you about half after four, as the dining hour is five.

yours truly
Mary

Send me your exact direction though I do not think that I shall often have occasion to write by the post, now we are so near.[704]

216. To Archibald Hamilton Rowan

London, January 26th [1796]

My dear Sir,

Though I have not heard from you I should have written to you, convinced of your friendship,[705] could I have told you any thing of myself that that would have afforded you pleasure – But what can I say to you – I am unhappy – I have been treated with unkindness and even cruelty, by the person, from whom I had every reason to expect affection – I write to you with an agitated hand – I cannot be more explicit – I value your good opinion – and you know how to feel for me – I looked for some thing like happiness – *happiness*! in the discharge of my relative duties – and the heart on which I leaned has peirced mine to the quick – I have not been used well – and I live, but

704. According to *Love-Letters of Mary Hays*, p. 8, 'during the year 1795, Mary [Hays] had ... begun writing for the "Critical Review" ... Being thus rendered independent, she remov[ed] from her mother's new home in Surrey Road, to solitary lodgings at 30, Kirby Street, Hatton Garden.' This was near to Wollstonecraft in Finsbury Place.

705. Rowan later claimed he had not written because of his own miseries in North America at being separated from his family and exiled from Ireland.

for my child – for am weary of myself – When I am more composed I will write to you again. Mean time let me hear from you – and tell me some thing of Charles – I avoid writing to him, because I hate to explain myself – I still think of settling in France, because I wish to leave my little Girl there – I have been very ill – Have taken some desperate steps – But now I am writing for independence – I wish I had no other evil to complain of than the necessity of providing for myself and child – do not mistake me – Mr. Imlay would be glad to supply all my pecuniar wants; but, unless he returns to himself, I would perish first – Pardon the incoherence of my style, I have put off writing to you from time to time, because I could not write calmly. It would afford me the sincerest satisfaction to hear that you were reunited to your family, for I am your affectionate

and sincere friend
Mary Imlay

Pray write to me – I will not fail, I was going to say when I have any thing good to tell you – But for me there is nothing good in store, my heart is broken. adieu! God bless you! —

If you can be of any service to the bearer you will oblige me – He is an industrious young man – He was a clerk to Mr. Imlay – and – I should think might get into a better situation in America than in England – The state of public affairs here[706] are not in a posture[26] to assuage private sorrow. – [27]

217. To Gilbert Imlay

[London, c. March 1796]

You must do as you please with respect to the child. – I could wish that it might be done soon, that my name may be no more mentioned to you. It is now finished. – Convinced that you have neither regard

---

706. Following an attack on the king's coach on 29 October 1795, the British government had rushed in the Sedition and Treason Bills, giving them powers to suppress political meetings and publications.

nor friendship, I disdain to utter a reproach, though I have had reason to think, that the 'forbearance' talked of, has not been very delicate. – It is however of no consequence. – I am glad you are satisfied with your own conduct.

I now solemnly assure you, that this is an eternal farewell. – Yet I flinch not from the duties which tie me to life.

That there is 'sophistry' on one side or other, is certain; but now it matters not on which. On my part it has not been a question of words. Yet your understanding or mine must be strangely warped – for what you term 'delicacy,' appears to me to be exactly the contrary. I have no criterion for morality, and have thought in vain, if the sensations which lead you to follow an ancle or step, be the sacred foundation of principle and affection. Mine has been of a very different nature, or it would not have stood the brunt of your sarcasms.

The sentiment in me is still sacred. If there be any part of me that will survive the sense of my misfortunes, it is the purity of my affections. The impetuosity of your senses, may have led you to term mere animal desire, the source of principle; and it may give zest to some years to come. – Whether you will always think so, I shall never know.

It is strange that, in spite of all you do, something like conviction forces me to believe, that you are not what you appear to be.

I part with you in peace.

[Unsigned]

218. To Mary Hays?[707]

[speculative reconstruction]

[London, c. April – May 1796]

[I went to France] to lose in public happiness the sense of private misery . . .[708]

Love, dear, delusive love! . . . rigorous reason had forced [me] to resign; and now [my] rational prospects were blasted, just as [I] had learned to be contented with rational enjoyments[709] . . .

[I was] existing . . . in a living tomb, and [my] life [was] but an exercise of fortitude, continually on the stretch. . . . During [Imlay's] absence, affection had led [me] to make numberless excuses for his conduct [but when I desired to see him once more] he returned no other answer, except declaring, with unjustifiable passion, that he would not see [me].[710]

It was not for the world . . . that I complied with this request [of retaining the name of Imlay], but I was unwilling to cut the gordian knot, or tear myself away in appearance, when I could not in reality.[711]

707. These fragments of retrospective analysis after the final meeting with Imlay come from Mary Hays's entry on Wollstonecraft written for *The Annual Necrology, for 1797–8* (London, 1800), pp. 411f., and from Godwin's *Memoirs*, ch. 8, where some are said to be from 'a letter to a friend', most probably Hays. Hays frequently used her friends' letters verbatim in her published work, for example *Memoirs of Emma Courtney*. I have dated these fragments to around March 1796, the time of the break with Imlay and presumably assessment of the relationship. See 'Sources' for original material.

708. *Annual Necrology*, p. 424, referring to Wollstonecraft's infatuation with Fuseli.

709. *Memoirs*, ch. 8, referring to the period just before the first suicide attempt, in late May 1795.

710. *Memoirs*, ch. 8.

711. *Annual Necrology*, p. 451. *Memoirs*, ch. 8, quotes a variation of this passage.

219. To Gustav, Graf von Schlabrendorf[712]

London, May 13th, 1796

I wrote to you, dear Sir, some months ago and I think you would have answered my letter, had you received it – for I wrote you in quest of your comfort and I am sure you would not have neglected a wounded spirits. I felt inclined to adress you because I thaught there was some similarity in our feelings. – The attention of friendship is a moral want that torments us both. I was led to expect that I had found it only to be cruelly disceived. . . . The man on whom I relied with the utmost affection and confidence has betrayed me, used me ill,[28] dishonorably – and ceasing to esteem him I have almost learnt to hate mankind – yet I will live for my child.[29] – This explanation is entre nous . . . I wish to leave England for ever yet have not determined where to direct my weared feet – what Place can please when we are tired of ourselves? Philosophy cannot fill though it may in a degree calm an affectionate heart. – If the calmness does not rather deserve the name of despair – which flows from such a cruel disappointment.

Yours sincerly
Mary Imlay.

712. The letter fragment survives only in the partial transcript printed in Karl Faehler's dissertation, University of Jena, the first chapter of which was published as *Studien zum Lebensbild eines Deutschen Weltbürgers, des Grafen von Schlabrendorf* (Munich, 1909), pp. 17n.–18n. Schlabrendorf's papers were destroyed during the Second World War. Wollstonecraft seems also to have written for comfort to Ruth Barlow, since Joel wrote to his wife from Algiers on 8 July, 1796: 'Mary ——, poor girl! You know her worth, her virtues, and her talents; and I am sure you will not fail to keep yourself informed of her circumstances. She has friends, or at least had them, more able than you will be to yield her assistance in case of need. But they may forsake her for reasons which, to your enlightened and benevolent mind, would rather be an additional inducement to contribute to her happiness': cited in C. B. Todd, *Life and Letters of Joel Barlow* (New York, 1886), p. 300.

220. To William Godwin[713]

[London] July 1st, 1796

I send you the last volume of 'Héloïse,'[714] because, if you have it not, you may chance to wish for it. You may perceive by this remark that I do not give you credit for as much philosophy as our friend, and I want besides to remind you, when you write to me in *verse*, not to choose the easiest task, my perfections, but to dwell on your own feelings – that is to say, give me a bird's-eye view of your heart. Do

713. This letter, quoted in F. K. Brown's *Life of William Godwin* (London, 1926), p. 116, the first in a long series to Godwin, is not in the Abinger MSS. Probably it is one of the nine missing ones. The remaining 151 letters exchanged between Wollstonecraft and Godwin, arranged in chronological order and numbered in Godwin's hand, survive in the Abinger MSS and have been previously published by Wardle in *G&M*. As he records in *Memoirs*, Godwin had met Wollstonecraft in November 1790 at one of Johnson's weekly dinners, soon after publication of *The Rights of Men*. He found her overbearing and shallow and each criticized the other. He re-met her at Hays's lodgings on 8 January 1796. In his diary he recorded that in mid January he spent three days reading *Letters from Sweden* and realized how much Wollstonecraft had softened: 'She speaks of her sorrows, in a way that fills us with melancholy, and dissolves us in tenderness, at the same time that she displays a genius which commands our admiration' (*Memoirs*, p. 129). In mid February 1796 Godwin called at the Christies' house expecting to find Wollstonecraft, but she was in Berkshire with her friend Mrs Cotton. When she returned, she moved from Finsbury Place to 1 Cumming Street, just off the Pentonville Road. In mid April she called at Godwin's lodgings near by, 25 Chalton Street, and thereafter she featured regularly in his diary. By the summer the pair were intimate and Godwin had tried to woo Wollstonecraft in verse (the verse does not survive). According to his diary, on the date of this letter Godwin called on Wollstonecraft, then left for Norfolk. In Norwich he met Dr Alderson and his diary recorded 'Propose to Alderson' (Abinger MSS, Dep.e.203). Commentators including Wardle have assumed that this was a marriage proposal to Amelia Alderson, the doctor's young daughter whom Godwin much admired. St Clair has argued that it refers to her father and that Godwin was by now seriously involved only with Wollstonecraft (*The Godwins and the Shelleys*, p. 164).

714. *Julie; ou, La Nouvelle Héloïse*, by Rousseau, referred to as 'our friend' here. Despite her irritation at Rousseau's presentation of women in *Émile* (see *The Rights of Woman*, ch. 5), Wollstonecraft was fascinated by *Héloïse*'s depiction of female emotion and sexual attraction.

not make me a desk 'to write upon,'[715] I humbly pray – unless you honestly acknowledge yourself *bewitched*.

Of that I shall judge by the style in which the eulogiums flow, for I think I have observed that you compliment without rhyme or reason, when you are almost at a loss what to say.

221. *To William Godwin*

Judd Place West, Thursday [July 21st, 1796][716]

I send you, as requested, the altered M.S.[717] Had you called upon me yesterday I should have thanked you for your letter – and – perhaps, have told you that the sentence I *liked* best was the concluding one, where you tell me, that you were coming home, to depart *no more*[718] – But now I am out of humour I mean to bottle up my kindness, unless

---

715. Samuel Butler, *Hudibras* (1664), Part 2, Canto 1, ll. 591. 'Shee that with *Poetry* is won / Is but a *Desk* to write upon'; Godwin had written, 'Well then, what shall be my subject. Shall I send you an eulogium of your beauty, your talents & your virtues?' (*G&M*, p. 8).

716. While Godwin was away in Norfolk Wollstonecraft took her furniture out of storage and moved to 16 Judd Place West on the edge of Somers Town, close to Godwin's lodgings. Most of her notes to him were delivered by a servant and were without address and postmark. The exceptions are Letters 221, 294, 326, and 329. Wollstonecraft and Godwin provided the day of the week, sometimes the time of day when they wrote, but rarely the dates; these were later supplied by Godwin, presumably with reference to his diary, and are printed here in brackets.

717. Possibly this suggests that Wollstonecraft was working again for Joseph Johnson on something that also concerned Godwin or it might be a first reference to the novel she had begun, *The Wrongs of Woman; or, Maria*, left unfinished at her death. She was much concerned with readers' attitudes to this work, which she had some difficulty in composing.

718. Godwin had written in a facetious style: 'Now, I take all my Gods to witness . . . that your company infinitely delights me, that I love your imagination, your delicate epicurism, the malicious leer of your eye, in short every thing that constitutes the bewitching tout ensemble of the celebrated Mary. . . . Shall I write a love letter? May Lucifer fly away with me, if I do!' He ended by asking Wollstonecraft to let Marguerite tell his janitor he was returning in a week, 'to depart no more' (*G&M*, pp. 8f.). Wollstonecraft expected Godwin's return on 20 July but was disappointed when he reached London later, on the 24th.

something in your countenance, when I do see you, should make the cork fly out – whether I will or not. –

Mary —

222. *To William Godwin*

[London] Tuesday [July 26th, 1796]

The weather not allowing me to go out about business to day, as I intended, if you are disengaged, I and my *habit* are at your service, in spite of wind or weather —

Mary[719] —

223. *To Mary Hays*[720]

[London] Sunday morning [1796]

Pray do not make any more allusion to painful feelings, past and gone – I have been most hurt at your not *labouring* to acquire more contentment; for true it is wisdom, I believe, to extract as much happiness, as we can, out of the various ills of life – for who has not cause to be miserable, if they will allow themselves to think so?

Yours Sincerely
Mary

---

719. 'Mrs Robinson's' is added in pencil in Wollstonecraft's hand just above her signature. Mary Robinson, née Darby (1758–1800), former actress, called 'Perdita' because in that role she had charmed the seventeen-year-old Prince of Wales, whose mistress she became. In 1782 she entered a relationship with the soldier, politician and gambler, Banastre Tarleton; she had a miscarriage, became crippled with arthritis, and was now making a living with poetry and novels. She was a close friend of Godwin and more recently of Wollstonecraft.

720. This letter is a fragment; the top half of the sheet has been torn away. While Wollstonecraft was grieving over Imlay, Mary Hays was lamenting over a failed relationship with the leading radical Unitarian, William Frend (1757–1841). She had poured out her sorrows in a series of love letters, some versions of which were published within her novel *Memoirs of Emma Courtney* (1796); she had also been corresponding with Godwin about her predicament as an intelligent sexual and single woman.

224. *To William Godwin*

[London, August 2ᵈ, 1796]

From the style of the note, in which your epistle was enveloped, Miss Hays seems *plus triste que ordinaire*. Have you seen her?

I suppose you mean to drink tea with me, *one* of these day – How can you find in your heart to let me pass so many evenings alone – you may saucily ask, why I do not send for Mʳ. Twiss[721] – but I shall reply with dignity – No; there will be more dignity in silence – so mum.

I did not wish to see you this evening, because you have been dining, I suppose, with Mʳˢ. Perfection,[722] and comparison are odious

[Unsigned]

225. *To William Godwin*

[London, August 4ᵗʰ, 1796]

I spent the evening with Mademoiselle Alderson[723] – you, I'm told, were ready to devour her – in your little parlour. Elle est trés jolie – n'est pas? I was making a question yesterday, as I talked to myself,

---

721. The scholar and teacher Francis Twiss (1760–1827) had made an important verbal index of Shakespeare revealing new shades of meaning in his words (see James Boaden, *Memoirs of Mrs Siddons*, London, 1827, 2, 102). Twiss had married Frances Kemble, sister of the actress Sarah Siddons. In later life he and his wife kept a school at Bath.

722. Elizabeth Inchbald (1753–1821), dramatist, actress and author of the novels *A Simple Story* (1791) and *Nature and Art* (1796). Godwin was a great admirer of her conversation and beauty, and she and Wollstonecraft had become rivals for his attentions. She had obtained the nickname 'Mrs Perfection' through her superlative praise of Godwin's novel *Caleb Williams* (1794).

723. Amelia Alderson (1769–1853), from a Unitarian family in Norwich. She had visited London in 1794 and become a friend of Godwin, Holcroft, and Inchbald. Godwin introduced her to Wollstonecraft at this time and the two women became friends.

whether Cymons of forty could be *informed*[724] – Perhaps, after last nights electrical shock, you can resolve me —

[Unsigned]

226. *To William Godwin*[725]

[London, August 6th, 1796]

Miss Alderson, was wondering, this morning whether you *ever* kissed a maiden fair – As you do not like to solve problems, *on paper*, TELL her *before* you part – She will tell *me* next – year —

[Unsigned]

227. *To William Godwin*

[London, August 7th, 1796]

I supped in company with Mrs. Siddons,[726] last night. When shall I tell you what I think of her? —

[Unsigned]

---

724. In Boccaccio's *Decameron, or Ten Days of Entertainment* (Fifth Day, First Novel) the crude Cimon, 'a perfect natural', is transformed into a genteel, educated man after seeing and falling in love with the beautiful Ephigenia. In 'a very short time he not only got over the first rudiments of learning, but attained to some knowledge in philosophy. Afterwards, his love for *Ephigenia* being the sole cause of it, his rude and rustick speech was changed into a tone more agreeable and civilized ... In short ... before the expiration of his fourth year from his being first in love, he turned out the most accomplished young gentleman in every respect that ever *Cyprus* could boast of.' Wollstonecraft was probably referring to Dryden's version of the tale in his *Fables ancient and modern* (1700).

725. Wollstonecraft addressed this note 'To Willm *Godwin Philosopher*' adding: 'Not to be opened 'till the Philosopher has been an hour, at least, in Miss Alderson's company, cheek by jowl.'

726. Sarah (Kemble) Siddons (1755–1831), the most famous actress of her day, celebrated in a poem of 1783 as the 'Tragic Muse'. Siddons complemented her risqué theatrical cross-dressing – she played Hamlet for example – with a much-vaunted maternity and virtue in private life. Wollstonecraft had met her through Godwin.

228. To William Godwin.

[London, August 11ᵗʰ, 1796]

Won'tee, as Fannikin would say, come and see me to day? and I will
go home with you to hear your essays, should you chance to be
awake.[727] I called on you yesterday, in my way to dinner, not for
Mary – but, *to bring* Mary[728] – Is it necessary to tell your sapient
Philosophership that I mean myself —

[Unsigned]

229. To William Godwin

[London, August 16ᵗʰ, 1796]

I send the new[sp]aper before the hour, because I suppose you will go
out earlier than usual today.

Give Churchhill[729] to Fanny if you can spare him, and, you may kiss
her, if you please.

727. The MS of *The Enquirer*, a collection of essays that Godwin published early in
1797. *CL* notes that, in a letter to John Rickman (16 September 1801), Charles Lamb
remarked on Godwin's tendency to fall asleep if he remained out in company after
11 p.m.: 'He lays down his spectacles, as if in scorn, & takes 'em up again from
necessity, and winks that she may'nt see he gets sleepy about eleven oClock' (*The
Letters of Charles and Mary Anne Lamb*, ed. Edwin W. Marrs, Jr., Ithaca: Cornell
University Press, 1975-8, 2, 22).
728. Wollstonecraft's early novel *Mary, A Fiction*, which, as entries in his diary reveal,
Godwin had been reading during the previous week. He esteemed the novel but
Wollstonecraft no longer cared for it and called it a 'crude production' (see Letter 314).
729. There are many possibilities for this reference. It might refer to Junius Churchill,
Esq., *Liverpool Odes, Or, Affectionate Epistles, for the Year 1793* (London, 1793),
which satirized as mean and greedy Clayton Tarleton, mayor of Liverpool in 1792 and
brother of Mary Robinson's lover and Godwin's friend, Banastre. Or it might refer to
a publication of Charles Churchill (1731–1764), author of the satiric *Rosciad, The
Prophecy of Famine*, and other poems. *The Political Works of Charles Churchill* had
been republished in four volumes in 1791. A third possibility is Thomas O. Churchill,
who could at the time have been translating Johann Gottfried von Herder's *Ideen zur
Philosophie der Menschheit* (1784–91); the translation, *Outlines of a Philosophy of*

Entre nous – did you feel very lonely last night?[730]

Mary

230. *To William Godwin*

[London] Wednesday morning [August 17th, 1796]

I have not lately passed so painful a night as the last.[731] I feel that I cannot speak clearly on the subject to you; let me then briefly explain myself now I am alone. Yet, struggling as I have been a long time to attain peace of mind (or apathy) I am afraid to trace emotions to their source, which border on agony.

Is it not sufficient to tell you that I am thoroughly out of humour with myself? Mortified and humbled, I scarcely know why – still, despising false delicacy I almost fear that I have lost sight of the true. Could a wish have transported me to France or Italy, last night, I should have caught up my Fanny and been off in a twinkle, though convinced that it is my mind, not the place, which requires changing. My imagination is for ever betraying me into fresh misery, and I perceive that I shall be a child to the end of the chapter. You talk of

---

the History of Man, was published by Johnson in 1800. Churchill had help with Herder's difficult German and, though the assistant was never named, circumstantial evidence points firmly to Fuseli, friend of both Godwin and Wollstonecraft. The preface, dated 15 November 1799, acknowledges 'the encouragement of one, who can appreciate the merits of Herder; who happily unites a critical knowledge of the English language with that of the german; and to whose kindness I am indebted for the explanation of many passages, and the improvement of many expressions, as well as some notes distinguished by the signiture "F".'

730. Godwin seems to have first declared his love at Wollstonecraft's lodgings; his diary entries for 15 and 16 August include the notation 'chez moi', which, with 'chez elle', he used to record his assignations with Wollstonecraft. After one meeting in which the pair appear to have become physically intimate but not complete lovers, Godwin failed to call on Wollstonecraft and she tried to rally him with this note.

731. In a letter dated 16 August, Godwin had written, 'I have been very unwell all night. You did not consider me enough in that way yesterday, & therefore unintentionally impressed upon me a mortifying sensation. When you see me next; will you condescend to take me for better for worse, that is, be prepared to find me, as it shall happen, full of gaiety & life, or a puny valetudinarian?' (*G&M*, p. 14).

the roses which grow profusely in every path of life – I catch at them; but only encounter the thorns. —

I would not be unjust for the world – I can only say that you appear to me to have acted injudiciously; and that full of your own feelings, little as I comprehend them, you forgot mine – or do not understand my character. It is my turn to have a fever to day – I am not well – I am hurt – But I mean not to hurt you. Consider what has past as a fever of your imagination; one of the slight mortal shakes to which you are liable – and I – will become again a *Solitary Walker.*[732] Adieu! I was going to add God bless you! —

[Unsigned]

231. *To William Godwin*

[London] Two o'clock [August 17th, 1796]

I like your last – may I call it *love* letter?[733] better than the first – and can I give you a higher proof of my esteem than to tell you, the style of my letter will whether I will or no, that it has calmed my mind – a mind that had been painfully active all the morning, haunted by old sorrows that seemed to come forward with new force to sharpen the present anguish – Well! well – it is almost gone – I mean all my

732. A reference to Rousseau's autobiographical *Les Reveries du Promeneur Solitaire* in which the author described himself as once social but now solitary and misunderstood.

733. Godwin had responded to Letter 230: 'You do not know how honest I am. I swear to you that I told you nothing but the strict & literal truth, when I described to you the manner in which you set my imagination on fire on Saturday. For six & thirty hours I could think of nothing else. I longed inexpressibly to have you in my arms. Why did not I come to you? I am a fool. . . . I see nothing in you but what I respect & adore. . . . Do not cast me off. Do not become again a *solitary walker*. Be just to me, & then, though you will discover in me much that is foolish and censurable, yet a woman of your understanding will still regard me with some partiality . . .' (*G&M*, pp. 16f.). Two hours after he delivered the letter he wrote again, 'Intent upon an idea I had formed in my own mind of furtive pleasure, I was altogether stupid & without intelligence as to your plan of staying, which it was morally impossible should not have given life to the dead. . . . I have now only left to apologize for my absurdity . . .' (*G&M*, pp. 19f.).

unreasonable fears – and a whole train of tormenters, which you have routed – I can scarcely describe to you their ugly shapes so quickly do they vanish – and let them go, we will not bring them back by talking of them. You may see me when you please. I shall take this letter, just before dinner time, to ask you to come and dine with me, and Fanny, whom I have shut out to day. Should you be engaged come in the evening. Miss H—— seldom stays late, never to supper[734] – or to morrow – as you wish – I shall be content – you say you want soothing – will it sooth you to tell you the truth? I cannot hate you – I do not think you deserve it. Nay, more I cannot withhold my friendship from you, and will try to merit yours, that *necessity* may bind you to me.

One word of my ONLY fault[735] – our imaginations have been rather differently employed – I am more of a painter than you – I like to tell the truth, my taste for the picturesque has been more cultivated – I delight to view the grand scenes of nature and the various changes of the human countenance – Beautiful as they are animated by intelligence or sympathy – My affections have been more exercised than yours, I believe, and my senses are quick, without the aid of fancy – yet tenderness always prevails, which inclines me to be angry with myself, when I do not animate and please those I [love].

Now will you not be a good boy, and smile upon me, I dine at half past four – you ought to come and give me an appetite for my dinner, as you deprived me of one for my breakfast.

Mary

734. According to his diary Godwin met 'Miss Hayes' at Wollstonecraft's.
735. In the first of two letters from 17 August Godwin had written: 'Upon consideration I find in you one fault, and but one. You have the feelings of nature, & you have the honesty to avow them. In all this you do well. I am sure you do. But do not let them tyrannise over you. Estimate every thing at its just value' (*G&M*, p. 17).

232. *To William Godwin*[736]

[London, August 19th, 1796]

As I was walking with Fanny this morning, before breakfast, I found a pretty little fable, directly in my path; and, now I have finished my review,[737] I will transcribe it for thee.

A poor Sycamore growing up amidst a cluster of Evergreens, every time the wind beat through her slender branches, envied her neighbours the foliage which sheltered them from each cutting blast. And the only comfort this poor trembling shrub could find in her mind (as mind is *proved* to be only thought,[738] let it be taken for granted that she had a mind, if not a soul) was to say, Well; spring will come soon, and I too shall have leaves. But so impatient was this silly plant that the sun could not glisten on the snow,[30] without her asking, of her more experienced neighbours, if this was not spring? At length the snow began to melt away, the snow-drops appeared, and the crocus did not lag long behind, the hepaticas next ventured forth, and the mezereon began to bloom.

The sun was warm – balsamic as May's own beams. Now said the sycamore, her sap mounting, as she spoke, I am sure this is spring.

Wait only for such another day, said a fading Laurel; and a weather-beaten Pine nodded, to enforce the remonstrance.

736. The entries in Godwin's diary for 18 and 19 August include the phrase 'chez elle'.
737. Wollstonecraft was once more reviewing for the *AR*.
738. Wollstonecraft added the note: 'See Godwins Political Justice'. Godwin's footnote to 'The Characters of Men Originate in their External Circumstances', *Enquiry Concerning Political Justice* (London, 1796), bk. 1, ch. 4, p. 26n., stated that, although some philosophers objected to the use of the word 'mind' and although he admitted that we remain uncertain whether the causes of sensation are similar to the ideas they produce, 'if there be any one thing that we know more certainly than another, it is the existence of our own thoughts, ideas, perceptions or sensations (by whatever term we may choose to express them), and that they are ordinarily linked together so as to produce the complex notion of unity or personal identity. Now it is this series of thoughts . . . that is most aptly expressed by the term mind.' See also 'Of the Mechanism of the Human Mind', bk. 4, ch. 7 in the first edition, and bk. 4, ch. 9 in the second edition of 1796.

The Sycamore was not headstrong, and promised, at least, to wait for the morrow, before she burst her rind.

What a to morrow came! The sun darted forth with redoubled ardour; the winds were hushed. A gentle breeze fluttered the trees; it was the sweet southern gale, which Willy Shakespear felt, and came to rouse the violets; whilst every genial zephyr gave birth to a primrose.[739]

The Sycamore no longer regarded admonition. She felt that it was spring; and her buds, fostered by the kindest beams immediately came forth to revel in existence.

Alas! Poor Sycamore! The morrow a hoar frost covered the trees, and shrivelled up thy unfolding leaves, changing, in a moment the colour of the living green – a brown, melancholy hue succeeded – and the Sycamore drooped, abashed; whilst a taunting neighbour whispered to her, bidding her, in future, learn to distinguish february from April. —

Whether the buds recovered, and expanded, when the spring actually arrived – the Fable sayeth not[740] —

[Unsigned]

739. Anemones, the shrub Daphne mezereum, violets and primroses all bloom in early spring. Shakespeare seems never to have written of 'the sweet southern gale', but it was a common phrase (with variations) in eighteenth-century poetry, e.g. James Thomson's *Summer*, (1727), l. 154; James Beattie's *The Fifth Pastoral. Menalcas, Mopsus* (1760), l. 131, and Oliver Goldsmith's *The Traveller, or a Prospect of Society* (1764), l. 139.
740. Godwin misunderstood the appeal. He wrote, 'I have no answer to make to your fable, which I acknowledge to be uncommonly ingenious & well composed. . . . Your fable of to day puts an end to all my hopes. I needed soothing, & you threaten me. Oppressed with a diffidence and uncertainty which I hate, you join the oppressors, & annihilate me' (*G&M*, p. 22).

233. *To William Godwin*[741]

[London, August 22[d], 1796]

I am sometimes painfully humble – Write me, but a line, just to assure me, that you have been thinking of me with affection, now and then – Since we parted —— [742]

[Unsigned]

234. *To William Godwin*

[London, August 24th, 1796]

As you are to dine with M[rs] Perfection[743] to day, it would be dangerous, not to remind you of my existence – perhaps – a word then in your ear – should you forget, for a moment, a possible *accident* with the most delightful woman in the world, your fealty, take care not to look over your left shoulder[744] – I shall be there — Wednesday —

[Unsigned]

---

741. After receiving the letter quoted in note 740, Wollstonecraft went to Godwin's lodgings and they spent the following evening 'chez elle' according to Godwin's diary. The next day, Sunday, Godwin wrote 'chez moi, toute'.

742. Godwin replied at once, 'Humble! for heaven's sake, be proud, be arrogant! You are – but I cannot tell what you are. I cannot yet find the circumstance about you that allies you to the frailty of our nature. I will hunt it out' (*G&M*, p. 23).

743. Inchbald, whom Godwin continued to see, sometimes alone.

744. Godwin replied, 'I will report my fealty this evening.'

235. To William Godwin

[London] Friday [August 26th, 1796]

I seem to want encouragement – I therefore send you my M.S.[745] though not all I have written. Say when – or where, I am to see you Godwin.

[Unsigned]

236. To William Godwin

[London] Saturday morning [August 27th, 1796]

The wind whistles through my trees.

What do you say to our walk?

Should the weather continue uncertain *suppose* you were to bring your tragedy[746] here – and we shall be so snug – yet, you are such a kind creature, that I am afraid to express a preference, lest you should think of pleasing me rather than yourself – and is it not the same thing? – for I am never so well pleased with myself, as when I please you – I am not sure that please is the exact word, to explain my sentiments – May I trust you to search in your own heart for the proper one?

Mary

---

745. Of *The Wrongs of Woman*.

746. Possibly Godwin's MS of *Antonio*, first produced on 13 December 1799, but which had 'occupied a considerable part of his time for at least three years' according to Brown (*Life of William Godwin*, p. 183). *CL* suggests it might have been *The Iron Chest* by George Colman the Younger, based on Godwin's *Caleb Williams* and mentioned in Letter 240. The play was first performed on Saturday, 12 March 1796 to general disapproval, partly because the lead, John Philip Kemble, had a heavy cold, which he tried to cover with opium. Later, revised and cut, the play achieved success and was one of the earliest plays Wollstonecraft saw in the new season.

237. To William Godwin

[London] Monday [August 29ᵗʰ, 1796]

I will come and dine with you to day, at half past four or five.

You shall read your tragedy to me, & drive clear out of my mind all the sensations of *disgust*, which I brought home with me last night.

Twiss put you out of conceit with women; and he led my imagination to trace the fables of the Satyrs to their source.[747]

Mary

238. To William Godwin

[London, August 30ᵗʰ, 1796]

I sent no Amulet to day; but beware of enchantments. —

Give Fanny a biscuit – I want you to love each other —

[Unsigned]

---

747. Twiss had visited Wollstonecraft with Godwin on 25 August. He cut an odd figure. George Hardinge described him at Sarah Siddons's house: 'Mr Twiss came unpowdered. . . . He is of my height, but very thin, and stoops. His face is ghastly in the paleness of it. He takes absolute clouds of snuff; and his eyes have an ill-natured cast of acuteness in them. He is a kind of thin Dr Johnson without his hard words (though he is often quaint in his phrase); very dogmatical, and spoilt as an *original*': quoted in John Nichols, *Illustrations of the Literary History of the Eighteenth Century* (London, 1818), 3, 37f.

239. *To William Godwin*

[London, August 30th, 1796]

The weather, I believe, from the present appearance will not permit me to go out to dinner – If so you will call on me in your way home – will you not? – You need not write – I shall take it for granted —

[Unsigned]

240. *To William Godwin*

[London] Wednesday [August 31st, 1796]

Since you think that I mean to cheat you I send you a family present, given me, when I was let loose in the world – Look at the first page and return it – I do not intend to let you extend your scepticism to me[748] – or you will fright away a poor weary bird who, taking refuge in your bosom, hoped to nestle there – to the end of the chapter. –

The day is dreary. The Iron Chest[749] must wait – Will you read your piece at your fire side or mine? And I will tell you in what respect I think you a little[31] unjust.

On second thoughts, I believe, I had better drink tea with you; but then I shall not stay late.

Yours Mary

748. This sounds like a religious work received in childhood. Although Godwin insisted that Wollstonecraft had lost religious feelings in her last years, there is no conclusive evidence from her letters and works.
749. See note 746.

241. *To William Godwin*

[London, August 31ˢᵗ – September 4ᵗʰ, 1796][750]

This evening, dear Godwin, we must alter our plan – I am not actuated by any thing like caprice – I mean to see you, and tell you why

[The rest of the note has been cut off]

242. *To William Godwin*

[London] Sunday morning [September 4ᵗʰ, 1796]

Labouring all the morning, in vain, to overcome an oppression of spirits, which some things you uttered yesterday, produced; I will try if I can shake it off by describing to you the nature of the feelings you excited.

I allude to what you remarked, relative to my manner of writing – that there was a radical defect in it – a worm in the bud[751] – &c What is to be done, I must either disregard your opinion, think it unjust, or throw down my pen in despair; and that would be tantamount to resigning existence; for at fifteen I resolved never to marry from inter- ested motives, or to endure a life of dependence. You know not how painfully my sensibility, call it false if you will, has been wounded by some of the steps I have [been] obliged to take for others. I have even now plans at heart, which depend on my exertions; and my entire confidence in Mʳ. Imlay plunged me into some difficulties, since we parted, that I could scarcely away with. I know that many of my cares

750. Godwin did not date this letter but his numbering suggests that it was written between 31 August (Letter 240) and 4 September (Letter 242).

751. *Twelfth Night*, II, iv, 113f.: 'But let concealment, like a worm i' the bud, / Feed on her damask cheek'. Wollstonecraft was always sensitive about her writing style and was upset by critical comments from Godwin. He must have responded tactfully since he was soon tutoring her in grammar, possibly through Latin; in a letter of 6 October 1796 he told her to bring her Latin books to his house.

have been the natural consequence of what, nine out of ten would termed folly – yet I cannot coincide in the opinion, without feeling a contempt for mankind. In short, I must reckon on doing some good, and getting the money I want, by my writings, or go to sleep for ever. I shall not be content merely to keep body and soul together – By what I have already written Johnson, I am sure, has been a gainer. And, for I would wish you to see my heart and mind just as it appears to myself, without drawing any veil of affected humility over it, though this whole letter is a proof of painful diffidence, I am compelled to think that there is something in my writings more valuable, than in the productions of some people on whom you bestow warm elogiums – I mean more mind – denominate it as you will – more of the observations of my own senses, more of the combining of my own imagination – the effusions of my own feelings and passions than the cold workings of the brain on the materials procured by the senses and imagination of other writers –

I am more out of patience with myself than you can form any idea of, when I tell you that I have scarcely written a line to please myself (and very little with respect to quantity) since you saw my M.S. I have been endeavouring all this morning; and with such dissatisfied sensations I am almost afraid to go into company – But these are idle complaints to which I ought not to give utterance, even to you – I must then have done —

Mary

243. To William Godwin

[London] Sunday night, past ten o'clock! [September 4th, 1796]

I have spent a pleasant day, *perhaps*, the pleasanter, for walking with you first, with only the family, and M^{rs}. Inch[bald.] We had less wit and more cordiality – and if I do not admire her more I love her better – She is a charming woman! – I do not like her the less, for having spoken of you with great respect, and even affection – so much so that I began to think you were not out in your conjecture[752] – you know what.

752. Perhaps that Elizabeth Inchbald had some romantic interest in Godwin.

I only write now to bid you Good Night! – I shall be asleep before you – and I would leave you a God bless you – did you care for it; but, alas! you do not, though Sterne says that it is equivalent to a – kiss[753] —

[Unsigned]

244. *To William Godwin*

[London, September 8th, 1796]

I received an apology this morning from M[rs]. Newton[754] and of course you did. I should have called on you in my way home, an hour ago, had I not taken it for granted, in spite of my fatigue – and I do not like to see you when I am not half alive.

I want to see you – and *soon* – I have a world to say to you – Pray come to your

Mary —

245. *To William Godwin*

[London] Saturday morning [September 10th, 1796]

Fanny was so importunate with her 'go this way Mama, me wants to see Man,' this morning that you would have seen us had I not had a glimpse of a blue coat at your door, when we turned down the Street – I have always a great deal to say to you, which I say to myself so kindly that 'tis pity you do not hear me –

I wanted to tell you that I felt as if I had not done justice to your essay, for it interested me extremely – and has been running in my

753. Wollstonecraft had already referred to the same passage in Sterne's *Sentimental Journey* in Letter 128 to Imlay.
754. This might refer to a relative of J. F. Newton (not to his wife Cornelia Collins whom he married only in 1799). Newton was a friend of Godwin and his colleague James Marshall; he later influenced the poet Shelley with his vegetarian, nudist and Zoroastrian beliefs.

head while other recollections were all alive in my heart – [755] You are a tender considerate creature; but, entre nous, do not make too many philosophical experiments, for when a philosopher is put on his metal, to use your own phrase, there is no knowing where he will stop – and I have not reckoned on having a wild-goose chace after a – wise man – You will ask me what I am writing about – Why, as if you had been listening to my thoughts –

I am almost afraid on reflection that an indistinct intuition of our affection produced the effect on Miss H—— that distressed me – She has owned to me that she cannot endure to see others enjoy the mutual affection from which she is debarred – I will write a kind note to her to day to ease my conscience; for when I am happy myself, I am made up of milk and honey, I would fain make every body else so —

I shall come to you to night, probably, before nine – May I ask you to be at home – I may be tired and not like to ramble farther – Should I be later – you will forgive me – It will not be my heart that will loiter — By the bye – do not tell *any* body especially yourself – it is alway on my lips at your door –

The return of the fine weather has led me to form a vague wish that we might *vagabondize* one day in the country – before the summer is clear gone. I love the country – and like to leave certain associations in my memory, which seem, as it were, the land-marks of affection – Am I very obscure?

Now I will go and write – I am in a humour to write – at least to

---

755. Probably one of Godwin's essays in *The Enquirer*. Wollstonecraft's raillery suggests a passage that reflected their own relationship, possibly 'Essay VII, Section III. *Of Personal Reputation*': '. . . it is an error to be acutely anxious about reputation, or, more accurately speaking, to suffer our conduct to be influenced in essential particulars by a consideration of the opinion of others'; or 'Essay X. *Of Cohabitation*': 'The ill humour which is so prevalent through all the different walks of life, is the result of familiarity, and consequently of cohabitation. If we did not see each other too frequently, we should accustom ourselves to act reasonably and with urbanity. . . . It is true, that genuine virtue requires of us a certain frankness and unreserve. But it is not less true, that it requires of us a quality in some degree contrasted with this . . . that we maintain a vigilant consciousness strictly animadverting and commenting upon the whole series of our actions' (*The Enquirer. Reflections on Education, Manners, and Literature. In a Series of Essays*, London, 1797, pt. 2, pp. 279f., pt. 1, pp. 91f.). The offended friend mentioned below is Mary Hays.

you – Send me one line – if it be but – Bo! to a goose[756] – Opie[757] left a card last night –

[Unsigned]

246. To Archibald Hamilton Rowan

London, September 12th, 1796

My dear friend

I wrote to you some Months since by a private hand – and though you have never acknowledged the receipt of my letter, which I think a little unkind, in spite of the affectionate remembrances that have reached me through the medium of M[r] Maxwell, I feel an inclination to avail myself of the present opportunity to inform you of the state of my mind. – It is calmer – I have been used ill, and very wretched has the cruellest of disappointments, that of discovering I was deceived by a person in whom I trusted with all the confidence of the most perfect esteem, made me. – Still the consciousness that my conduct – for I governed my thoughts as well as my actions – merited a very different return by ——. Self-respect seems to promise me satisfaction, on which alone true happiness is built. – I have sent you my last publication[758] – and I would give a more circumstantial account of my situation had I time at present, in order to induce you to be more explicit[32] with me. – I am not apt to forget those whom I esteem; and in your fate I shall

---

756. Godwin replied 'Bo! . . . I shall cork up my heart; to see whether it will fly out ce soir at sight of you' (G&M, p. 32).

757. The Cornish artist whom Wollstonecraft had known before she went to Paris. His wife Mary Bunn had committed adultery and he was now divorcing her. According to Ada Earland, *John Opie and his Circle* (London, 1911), p. 111, years later when Opie was walking with Godwin they passed the church of St Martin-in-the-Fields: 'Ah!' said Opie, 'I was married in that church.' 'Indeed,' said Godwin, 'and I was christened in it.' 'It is not a good shop, their work don't last,' replied Opie. Wollstone-craft and Opie got on so well at this time that some onlookers thought they would make a match.

758. *Letters from Sweden*. Rowan, who was living in Delaware in 1796, probably arranged for an American edition, 'Printed for, & Sold by J. Wilson, & J. Johnson, Booksellers, Wilmington, (Del.)'.

always take the most lively interest respecting the qualifications of your hand and heart.[33] – It would afford me the sincerest of pleasures to hear that there was a chance of your being restored to your family,[759] and I wish, with all my heart, that my *good* luck, if there be any in store for me, may throw me into the same quarter of the Globe, for I am sure I should like – say love Mrs Rowan, and delight to see you both in the midst of your babes. – Mine grows apace, and prattles apace. – She is a motive, as well as *a reward*, for existion.[34]

I neglected calling on Mr Maxwell for some time during my residence in the Country, and when my mind was in the most perturbed state. – I now hear with pain of his declining health. – If, therefore, you should write to me address me at Mr Johnson's, Bookseller, N° 72, St Paul's Church Yard.

The Bearer of this, Mr Cooper,[760] is a very ingenious young man, for whom an intimate friend of mine has a particular affection. – By shewing him any attention you would oblige Mr G. – as well as myself – and I much mistaken if his countenance does not prejudice you in his favour, for it is the sort of one I like to see on young shoulders

What do you think of the present state of Europe? – the English seem to have lost the common sense which used to distinguish them.[761]

Adieu! Believe me your affectionate friend

Mary Imlay

759. Rowan's wife, Sarah Anne, and his ten children were still in Ireland. He himself may have secretly returned there or have been intending to return there in 1798, since a secret intelligence report records him as one of the future five-man directory which was to govern after the '98 rebellion. By 1802, however, he had moderated his radical opinions; he supported the Act of Union between Britain and Ireland and in 1803 formally petitioned the Irish government to reverse his sentence of outlawry. He was granted a pardon but not the right to live openly in Ireland until 1806 when his father died. See Seamus Cullen, 'Archibald Hamilton Rowan', *Fugitive Warfare: 1798 in North Kildare*, ed. Seamus Cullen and Hermann Geissel (Kildare, 1998), pp. 65–77.

760. Thomas Abthorpe Cooper (1776–1849), Godwin's second cousin and ward, was an aspiring actor. He had little success in England but became quite well known in America as a tragic actor and theatre manager. A note in Godwin's diary records his and Cooper's visit to Wollstonecraft on 12 September.

761. In response to the later imperialist phase of the French Revolution and the long war, England had become more conservative and insular and Wollstonecraft's liberal opinions were less acceptable than they had been in 1790–1791. In late summer

P.S. I have repeatedly requested your opinion of Charles[762] — of his character and prospects.

247. *To William Godwin*

[London, September 13th, 1796]

You tell me, William, that you augur nothing good, when the paper has not a note, or, at least, Fanny to wish you a good morning –

Now by these presents let me assure you that you are not only in my heart, but my veins, this morning.[763] I turn from you half abashed – yet you haunt me, and some look, word or touch thrills through my whole frame – yes, at the very moment when I am labouring to think of something, if not somebody, else. Get ye gone Intruder! though I am forced to add dear – which is a call back –

When the heart and reason accord there is no flying from voluptuous sensations, I find, do what a woman can – Can a philosopher do more?

Mary –

248. *To William Godwin*

[London, September 14th, 1796]

I have no genius this morning[764] – Poor Fannikin has the chicken-pox – which I am glad of – as I now know what is the matter with her. Business takes me to M[r]. Johnson's to day – I had rather you would

---

1796 Pitt was trying to negotiate a peace with France while Nelson was blockading Mediterranean ports.

762. Charles Wollstonecraft's huge schemes for enrichment had been abandoned and he was temporarily working in Rowan's calico-printing shop. The business failed and in 1800 Charles would join the American army, in which he had a reasonably successful career.

763. Godwin's diary for the previous day records 'chez elle'.

764. Wollstonecraft was replying to a playful note in French from Godwin asking her to visit that evening: 'Je ordonne à vous que vous écrivez ce matin, et avec une génie étonnante!' (*G&M*, p. 34).

come to me this evening – I shall be at home between eight and nine; but do not make a point of interrupting any party – I like to be near Fanny till she is better.

[Unsigned]

249. To Mary Hays

[London] Thursday morning [September 15th, 1796][765]

I send you the fourth volume of T-S. there are but six, of course you have had them all.[766]

If you are not reading the Elegant Enthusiast send it by Mary,[767] and I shall soon return it.

Mr. Johnson has been invited to dine out of town on Sunday, and I requested him not to be ceremonious with us, but receive our visit the Sunday following – Thus stands the engagement.

A fever, which has tormented my little Darling for some days past, gave me no little uneasiness. I am now relieved by the sight of the Chicken-pox, and know that she will soon be well again.

I am glad to find that you are out of suspense with Robinson.[768] Say what day you will drink tea with me – I will then tell you what I think of your Sisters M.S.[769] It has merit; but displays more rectitude of mind than warmth of imagination.

Adieu! Mary

---

765. Dated through reference to Fanny's chickenpox.

766. Possibly Sterne's *The Life and Opinions of Tristram Shandy*, issued originally in nine volumes, but reproduced in six in 1772, 1775, 1777, 1782, and 1793.

767. William Beckford's *Modern Novel Writing; or, the Elegant Enthusiast; and Interesting Emotions of Anabella Bloomville. A Rhapsodical Romance; Interspersed with Poetry*, a parody of a sentimental novel, published under his pseudonym 'the Right Hon. Lady Harriet Marlow'. Mary was Wollstonecraft's general servant; Marguerite Fournée was still with her as Fanny's nurse.

768. Hays's novel *Memoirs of Emma Courtney* came out in late 1796 with the publisher Robinson.

769. This manuscript seems never to have been published. Elizabeth Hays contributed two 'Moral Tales', signed E. H., to Hays's *Letters and Essays, Moral and Miscellaneous* (1793).

250. *To William Godwin*

[London, September 15th, 1796]

The virulence of my poor Fanny's distemper begins to abate, and with it my anxiety – yet this is not, I believe, a day sufficiently to be depended on, to tempt us to set out in search of rural felicity.[770] We must then woo philosophy *chez vous* ce soir, nest-ce pas; for I do not like to lose my Philosopher even in the lover.

You are to give me a lesson this evening – And, a word in your ear, I shall not be very angry if you sweeten grammatical disquisitions after the Miltonic mode[771] – Fancy, at this moment, has turned a conjunction into a kiss; and the sensation steals o'er my senses. N'oublierez pas, I pray thee, the graceful pauses, I am alluding to; nay, anticipating – yet now you have led me to discover that I write worse, than I thought I did, there is no stopping short – I must improve, or be dissatisfied with myself –

I felt hurt, I can scarcely trace why, last night, at your wishing time to roll back. The observation wounded the delicacy of my affection, as well as my tenderness – Call me not fastidious; I want to have such a firm *throne* in your heart, that even your imagination shall not be able to hurl me from it, be it ever so active.

Mary.

---

770. Wollstonecraft and Godwin were hoping to take a trip into the country without Fanny. They had spent no extended time alone since they met.
771. Wollstonecraft had already referred to the Milton quotation, 'hee, she knew, would intermix / Grateful digressions, and solve high dispute / With conjugal Caresses, from his Lip / Not Words alone pleas'd her' (*Paradise Lost*, 8, 54f.), in Letter 123 to Imlay.

251. To William Godwin[772]

[London, September 17th, 1796]

My poor Fanny is not so well as I expected – I write with her in my arms – I have been trying to amuse her all the morning to prevent her scratching her face. I am very glad, I did not stay from her last night; for I find she did nothing, but seek for me the morning before and moan my absence, which increased her fever.

Opie called Tuesday evening – from a message, which he left, I am *almost* afraid that the *Devil*[773] will call this evening —

[Unsigned]

252. To William Godwin

[London] Monday noon [September 19th, 1796]

I am a little feverish to day. I had full employment yesterday; nay, was extremely fatigued by endeavouring to prevent Fanny from tearing herself to pieces; and afterwards she would scarcely allow me to catch half an hour, of what deserved the name of sleep.

I could have wished to have spent a long evening with you, instead of a flying visit, and I should have been myself again. Why could you not say *how do ye do* this morning? It is I who want nursing first, you perceive – are you above the feminine office? I think not, for you are above the affectation of wisdom. Fanny is much better to day.

[Unsigned]

772. Despite Fanny's illness, Wollstonecraft and Godwin had taken a trip to the village of Ilford near Barking, about seven miles from Somers Town. From there they had visited the old house near Epping in which she had lived as a young child. The pair had reduced their stay to one night only.

773. Presumably the printer's devil wanting some work from her or possibly a playful reference to one of their fierce acquaintances such as Fuseli, still working on his *Paradise Lost* illustrations.

253. To Mary Hays

[London] Tuesday morning [September 20th, 1796][774]

If this letter should not be forwarded, pray request that it may be returned.

Fanny is recovering her beauty daily. Are you quite restored to health?

I will send you the Monk[775] as soon as M[r]. Godwin returns it, to whom I have lent it. He means to call on you soon.

I return your Sister's M.S. with some observations which appear to me important.

Yours
Mary

When am I to see you and your Sister? – and your Mother, if she be not afraid to venture out.

254. To William Godwin

[London] Wednesday morning [September 21st, 1796]

Though I am not quite satisfied with myself, for acting like such a mere Girl, yesterday – yet I am better – What did you do to me? And my poor Lambkin seems to be recovering her health & spirits faster than her beauty – Say only that we are friends;[776] and, within an hour or two, the hour when I may expect to see you – I shall be wise and demure – never fear – and you must not leave the philosopher behind[777] –

[Unsigned]

---

774. The date derives from the allusion to Fanny's recovery.

775. Matthew Gregory Lewis's *Ambrosio; or, the Monk*, published in 1795, was still a literary sensation.

776. Godwin replied: 'Friends? Why not? If I thought otherwise, I should be miserable' (*G&M*, p. 37).

777. Perhaps a reference to past quarrels or perhaps to a method of birth control in which the pair avoided certain times in Wollstonecraft's menstrual cycle. St Clair speculated that the cycle was being plotted by Godwin in his diary, which also recorded sexual intercourse with a series of dots and dashes (*The Godwins and the Shelleys*, Appendix 1).

255. *To William Godwin*

[London, September 28th, 1796]

I was detained at Miss Hay's, where I met M^{rs}. Bunn,[778] as it was necessary for me to out stay her. But this is not the worst part of the story. M^{rs}. Bunn was engaged to dined at Opie's, who had promised to bring her to see me this evening –. They will not stay long of course – so do as you please I have no objection to your drinking tea with them – But should you not like it – may I request you drink tea with M. Hays, and come to me at an early hour. Nay, I wish you would call on me in your way for half an hour – as soon as you can rise from table; I will then give you the money.

[Unsigned]

256. *To William Godwin*

[London, September 29th, 1796]

It is my turn, William, to be indisposed. Every dog has his day, you know. And, as you like a moral in your heart, let me add, as one, applicable to the present occasion, whatever you may think – that there is no end to our disappointments when we reckon our chickens too soon.

I shall be with you at five, to receive, what you promised to give me *en passant* – Mais, à notre retour, rien que philosophie. Mon cher ami. Etes-vous bien fâché?[779]

Mon Bien-aimé – Moi aussi, cependant la semaine approchant,[35] do you understand me —

[Unsigned]

---

778. Wife of Benjamin and mother of Mary. The various stages of Opie's complete divorce from Mary Bunn lasted from early in 1796 to 23 December, when the bill received royal assent.

779. Again the allusion to the philosopher; Godwin's possible disappointment suggests Wollstonecraft was proposing a chaste evening.

257. To William Godwin

[London] Friday [September 30th, 1796]

When there is not a good reason to prevent it I wish you to dine with me, or, I with you, of a saturday, to enable *us* to bear the privation of sunday, with philosophie.[780] To morrow is my turn, and I shall expect you. This arrangement renders it necessary to alter the previous plan for ce soir. What say you – may I come to your house, about eight – to philosophize? You once talked of giving me one of your keys, I then could admit myself without tying you down to an hour, which I cannot alway punctually observe in the character of a woman, unless I tacked that of a wife to it.

If you go out, at two, you will, perhaps call and tell me that you thought as kindly of me last night, as I did of you; for I am glad to discover great powers of mind in you, even at my own expence. One reason, I believe, why I wish you to have a good opinion of me is a conviction that the strongest affection is the most involuntary – yet I should not like you to love, you could not tell what, though it be a french compliment of the first class, without my explanation of it: the being enamoured of some fugitive charm, that seeking somewhere, you find every where: yes; I would fain live in your heart and employ your imagination – Am I not very reasonable?

You do not know how much I admired your self-government, last night, when your voice betrayed the struggle it cost you – I am glad that you force me to love you more and more, in spite of my fear of being pierced to the heart by every one on whom I rest my mighty stock of affection. – Your tenderness was considerate, as well as kind, – Miss Hays entering, in the midst of the last sentence, I hastily laid

---

780. Godwin dined with his friend Holcroft on Sundays, sometimes to Wollstonecraft's annoyance. She had less regular dining appointments with the Twisses. Thomas Holcroft (1745–1809), son of a shoemaker, was an actor, playwright, novelist and translator. He was one of Godwin's closest friends and had possibly been in love with Wollstonecraft before her involvement with Godwin. See Todd, *Mary Wollstonecraft*, pp. 377–8.

my letter aside, without finishing, and have lost the remain – Is it sunk in the quicksand of Love?

I have now only to say that I wished you to call by two, because I go into the city round by Finsbury Square.[781]

If you send me no answer I shall expect you.

[Unsigned]

258. To William Godwin

[London, October 4th, 1796]

So I must write a line to sweeten your dinner – No; to give you a little salt for your mutton, rather; though your not partaking of a morsel, Mary was bring me up, of this dinner, as you were going out, prevented me from relishing it –

I should have liked to have dined with you to day, after finishing your essays – that my eyes, and lips, I do not exactly mean my voice, might have told you that they had raised you in my *esteem*. What a cold word! I would say love, if you will promise not to dispute about its propriety, when I want to express an increasing affection, founded on a more intimate acquaintance with your heart and understanding.[782]

I shall cork up all my kindness – yet the fine volatile essence may fly off in my walk – you know not how much tenderness for you may escape in a voluptuous sigh, should the air, as is often the case, give a pleasurable movement to the sensations, that have been clustering

781. Rebecca Christie, Thomas Christie's wife, lived part of the time in Finsbury Square.

782. Godwin had famously not included the word 'love' in the first edition of *Political Justice* (1793). The work contained a chapter 'Of the Tendency of Virtue', bk. 4, ch. 9, which described how individual virtue would gain the 'esteem' of others: 'Nothing can be more indisputable, than that the direct road to the esteem of mankind, is by doing things worthy of their esteem.' The chapter was omitted from the second edition (1796). This second edition, bk. 1, ch. 5, 'The Voluntary Actions of Men Originate in their Opinions', suggested that virtue would spark love rather than merely esteem: 'Virtue, sincerity, justice, and all those principles which are begotten and cherished in us by a due exercise of reason, will never be very strenuously espoused, till they are ardently loved.'

round my heart, as I read this morning – reminding myself, every now and then, that the writer *loved me*. – Voluptuous is often expressive of a meaning I do not now intend to give. I would describe one of those moments, when the senses are exactly tuned by the rising tenderness of the heart, and according reason entices you to live in the present moment, regardless of the past or future – It is not rapture. – It is a sublime tranquillity. I have felt it in your arms – Hush! Let not the light see, I was going to say hear it – These confessions should only be uttered – you know where, when the curtains are up – and all the world shut out –

Ah me! What shall I do to day, I anticipate the unpleasing task of repressing kindness – and I am overflowing with the kindest sympathy – I wish I may find you at home when I carry this letter, to drop it in the box, – that I may drop a kiss with it into your heart, to be embalmed, till we meet, ~~closer~~ Don't read the last word – I charge you!

[Unsigned]

259. *To William Godwin*

[London, October 6th, 1796]

I was vext, last night, to hear the rain patter, while I was undressing myself – . Did he get wet? poor fellow!

Will you give Mary the coat you mentioned, for her boy, if it be not inconvenient. And the corn plaster, for me, should it be at hand.

Are you very gay to day?[783] Gay without an effort – that is best – Fanny won't let me alone – Adieu!

[Unsigned]

---

783. Possibly a late answer to Godwin's undated note 'Adorable maitresse! J'éspère que vous étes plus gai ce matin!' (*G&M*, p. 39). Godwin replied to Wollstonecraft's note on the same day: 'Non: je ne suis pas gai sans effort. The rain fell, but did not wet me; I wore a charmed skin' (*G&M*, p. 43).

260. *To William Godwin*

[London, October 7th, 1796]

The weather has disarranged my plan to day – Will you come and spend the evening with me? – Let me see you, if you please, at an early hour, and I will tell you why you damped my spirits, last night, in spite of all my efforts – Reason may rule the conduct; but even philosophers, I find, cannot command the spirits – yet, – we are so happy, sometimes, when we least know why.

Can you solve this problem? I was endeavouring to discover last night, in bed, what it is in me, of which you are afraid. I was hurt at perceiving that you were – but no more of this – mine is a sick heart; and in a life, like this, the fortitude of patience is the most difficult to acquire.

Au revoir –
[Unsigned]

261. *To William Godwin*[784]

[London, October 26th, 1796]

I think, as *amende honorable*, you ought to read my answer to Mr. Burke.[785]

Fanny wishes to ask Man's pardon – She won't cry any more.

Are you burnt up alive?

[Unsigned]

784. Between this and the previous letter Godwin seems to have fallen ill with fever and the dashes in his diary which appear to record sexual intercourse ceased.
785. *A Vindication of the Rights of Men, in a Letter to the Right Honourable Edmund Burke* (1790). Godwin did not admire Wollstonecraft's two polemical *Vindications* as much as he did her more sentimental works such as *Mary, A Fiction* and *Letters from Sweden*.

262. To Mary Hays

[London] Wednesday morning [c. October 26th, 1796][786]

My dear friend.

I have not received a letter from M^{rs}. Cotton,[787] yet I must beg you
to excuse me, for I have unluckily been invited to dine out on thursday
where business calls me – If any day next week will be the same to
you, you would much oblige me by permitting me to be free, or I shall
not be able to wait on you till late in the evening.

your's affectionately
Mary

263. To William Godwin

[London, October 27th, 1796]

M^{rs}. Cotton comes to morrow, should it prove fine, or Saturday. She
talks of a *few* days. Mon Dieu! Heaven and Earth!

[Unsigned]

264. To William Godwin

[London] Thursday morning [November 3^{d}, 1796]

If you are not *all alive* at your Essays I will come to you in the course
of half an hour – Say the word – for I shall come to you, or read Swift.

You have almost captivated M^{rs} C—— Opie called this morning –

786. *CL*'s dating, inferred from the implication in Wollstonecraft's note to Godwin of
Thursday, 27 October (Letter 263), that she had heard from Mrs Cotton.
787. A close and valued family friend whom Wollstonecraft had visited in Sonning,
near Reading, when she was recuperating from the break-up with Imlay. She was
expecting Mrs Cotton to come to stay but was dismayed to find her arrival occurring
at the end of a period of sexual abstinence owing to Godwin's illness (see Letter 263).

But you are the man[788] – Till we meet joy be with thee – Then – what then?

Mary

265. To William Godwin

[London] Thursday [November 10th, 1796]

I send you your houshold linen – I am not sure that I did not feel a sensation of pleasure at thus acting the part of a wife, though you have so little respect for the character.[789] There is such a magic in affection that I have been more gratified by your clasping your hands round my arm, in company, than I could have been by all the admiration in the world, tho' I am a woman – and to mount a step higher in the scale of vanity, an author.

I shall call toward one o'clock not to deprive the world of your bright thoughts, this exhilarating day.

Mary

788. Rumour associated Wollstonecraft and Opie. Writing from Norwich, Amelia Alderson reported gossip that they were to marry 'Law willing' (Abinger MSS, Dep. b.210/6). Neither seems to have been intent on matrimony, however, since Joseph Farington recorded in his diary for 11 November, 'I told Opie it had been reputed that he was going to be married to Mrs Wolstencraft, but that could not be as she is already married to Mr Imlay an American. He replied that would not have been an obstacle if he had had any such intention, as Mrs Wolstencraft had herself informed him that she never was married to Imlay . . .' (Supp., p. 312). Opie married Amelia Alderson in 1798.

789. In the first edition of Political Justice, bk. 8, ch. 6, Godwin had attacked marriage as 'the worst of all laws': 'The institution of marriage is a system of fraud; and men who carefully mislead their judgments in the daily affair of their life, must always have a crippled judgment in every other concern. We ought to dismiss our mistake as soon as it is detected; but we are taught to cherish it.'

266. To William Godwin

[London] Sunday morning [November 13th, 1796]

If the felicity of last night has had the same effect on your health as on my countenance, you have no cause to lament your failure of resolution: for I have seldom seen so much live fire running about my features as this morning when recollections – very dear; called forth the blush of pleasure, as I adjusted my hair.

Send me word that all is safe – and that we are to hear no more of the hard word; though, since I have seen M[r] Allen,[790] I should not lay so much stress on it.

The place is to be taken to day There seem then something like a certainty of freedom next week – are you sorry?

Return me a line[791] – and I pray thee put this note under lock and key – and, unless you love me *very much* do not read it again.

[Unsigned]

Lend me M[rs]. Robingson's Poems.[792]

790. Possibly a reference to 'a gentleman whom I have heard called satirically Lady Holland's atheist, a Mr Allen, but better known as an elegant scholar and Edinburgh reviewer' (*Henry Crabb Robinson's Diary*, 1, 277).

791. Godwin's undated letter is probably a response: 'What can I write with Marguerite perched in a corner by my side? I know not. I am in health: I do not lament my failure of resolution: I wish I had been a spectator of the live fire you speak of: I *shall* rejoice in our freedom' (*G&M*, p. 47).

792. Mary Robinson published her first book, *Poems by Mrs Robinson*, in 1775 while she and her husband were imprisoned for debt. In 1791 a collection, *Poems*, vol. 1, was published with nearly 600 subscribers; in January 1794 *Poems*, vol. 2, appeared. *Poems, by Mrs Mary Robinson. A new edition* was possibly printed in 1795.

267. To William Godwin

[London] Friday morning [November 18th, 1796]

How do you do this morning – are you alive? It is not *wise* to be cold during such a domesticating season, I mean then to dismiss all my frigid airs before I draw near your door, this evening, and should you, in your way from Mr Carlisle's,[793] *think* of inquiring for the fourth act of Mrs Inc's comedy[794] – why it would be a pretty mark of attention – And – entre nous, *little* marks of attention are incumbent on you at present – But – don't mistake me – I do not wish to put you on your mettle. No; I only want to secure a play, of some kind or other, to rouse my torpid spirits, chez vous.[795]

Mary

793. Anthony (in 1821 Sir Anthony) Carlisle (1768–1840), surgeon at the Westminster Hospital and writer on science; later surgeon extraordinary to the Prince Regent and professor of anatomy in the Royal Academy.

794. Probably the MS of Inchbald's *Wives as They Were, and Maids as They Are*, first performed at Covent Garden on 4 March 1797. Godwin's diary entry for 17 November records: 'call on Inchbald: dine. Primitive Wife, 3 acts'. He called again the following day. An unsigned review in *AR*, vol. XXV (June 1797), p. 602, claims to praise but actually criticizes Inchbald: 'Mrs I. has fortunately succeeded in gratifying her motley and capricious audiences, without condescending to steal approbation by tricks and trappings: the incidents are rather easy and natural, than remarkably striking, and we do not find any character to be particularized for it's energy or eccentricity. Miss Dorillon reminded us of Charles Surface in the School for Scandal, and the disguise of sir William, it's cause and it's consequence, are precisely the same as those of sir Oliver. Mrs I., it is possible, might not have been aware of this similarity, striking as it is; but we are persuaded, that on the reference she will immediately recognise it.' The play was published on 4 April 1797.

795. Godwin replied: 'Yes, I am alive. Perhaps I am better . . . You spoil little attentions by anticipating them' (*G&M*, p. 67).

268. To William Godwin

[London] Saturday morning [November 19ᵗʰ, 1796]

I wish you would always take my ye for a ye; and my nay for a nay. It torments me to be obliged to guess at, or guard against, false interpretations – and, while I am wishing, I will add another – that you could distinguish between jest and earnest, to express myself elegantly. To give you a criterion. I never play with edged-tools; (I believe) for when I am really hurt or angry I am dreadfully serious. Still allow me a little more tether than is necessary for the purpose of feeding, to keep soul and body together – Let me, I pray thee! have a sort of *comparative* freedom, as you are a profound Grammarian, to run round, as good, better, best; – cheerful, gay, playful; nay even frolicksome, once a year – or so, when the whim seizes me of skipping out of bounds. Send me a *bill of rights* – to this purport, under your hand and seal, with a *Bulletin* of health.[796]

Now I have an inclination to be saucy and tell you that I kissed Fanny, not with less kindness, because she put me in mind of you this morning, when she came crowing up stairs to tell me that she did not cry when her face was washed – I leave you to make the application —

Johnson has sent to inform me that he dines out to morrow; probably with your party.

I was going to close my note without telling you to what particular circumstance the first sentence alludes. I thought of not sending Marguerite to day, because I really felt with respect to her as you imagined I did in the other case, the day before yesterday; but Mary had business for me another way, and I hate to disguise any feeling, when writing or conversing, with you, cher ami.

Voilà! my resolution —

[Unsigned]

796. Godwin replied: 'I can send you a bill of rights & a bill of health: the former *carte blanche*; the latter, much better (as I think). But to fulfil the terms of your note, you must send me a bill of understanding. How can I distinguish always between your jest & earnest, & know when your satire means too much & when it means nothing? But I will try' (*G&M*, p. 50).

269. To Mary Hays

[London] Monday morning [c. November 1796][797]

My Good friend, not receiving a line with the book, I take it for granted that you are hurt by my seeming neglect. – But let me expostulate with you, a moment, of what a slight texture must be the friendship, which could change without a cause? – and I have no cause to change my opinion of you. I have not called on you, it is true, or sent the book; but I have still the same regard for you, and was merely prevented by rain, business, and engagements. M[r]. Godwin has been ill, and as I am a tolerable nurse, and he in a little want of one, I have frequently been with him, as well to amuse as to see that the things proper for him were got. He is much better, but I believe had rather not see any company for a few days. M[rs]. Christie is likewise in Town, only for two or three days and I have had business to do for her – Thus have you a full and true account of my moments. I will call on you soon, and you will find me at home any morning, but wednesday – at least I believe so –

Yours truly
Mary

I should be glad to have the Monk, as soon as you have finished it.

797. Dated through references to Godwin's being 'much better' (see note 784) and to *The Monk*, which Wollstonecraft promised to lend Mary Hays in late September after Godwin had returned it (see Letter 253).

270. *To William Godwin*

[London, November 19th–23^d, 1796]⁷⁹⁸

I do not think myself worse to day – yet, from the appearance of the weather, must determine not to go to the play to night. The heavy clouds promise snow, and I have suffered so much that I have learnt prudence.

What will you do with yourself? ma cher ami – Is there any probability of my seeing you to day? Or, will you confine all your world of love in your own bosom to keep yourself warm? Adieu!

Mary

271. *To William Godwin*

[London, November 19th–23^d, 1796]

I am decidedly better to day; but I have suffered so much that I must be careful. I think I may venture to go with you to the play to morrow, and then I will renew my acquaintance with your kennel,⁷⁹⁹ for which, by the bye, I have *some* kindness.

I do not intended to be out late; yet, as I shall be attended, I must go home, and I cannot well go out again immediately, now I am considered as indisposed, and probably I should only come to cough with you – you may look up at my window for a sign, if you please; but I had almost *rather* you should spent the evening comme autrefois, because I do not like – may I say? to disappoint you –

Our *sober* evening was very delicious – I do believe you love me better than you imagined you should – as for me – judge for yourself —

Fanny will scarcely let me write she is so affectionate, because I

798. This and the two subsequent letters have no date but Godwin placed them in series as 70–72 between notes dated 19 and 23 November. Their allusions both to Wollstonecraft's ill-health – she seems to have caught a heavy cold – and the cold weather confirm their closeness.
799. Godwin's cramped lodgings in 25 Chalton Street.

breakfasted in bed. I am not well – for holding down my head makes it ache – yet I begin to hope –

[Unsigned]

272. *To William Godwin*

[London, November 19th–23^d, 1796]

The references were, in general, just. I have inserted the few words left out or mistaken. There were a few other observations on the first & second essay.

My pen will not allow me to add any thing kind. This is a day for friends to be together. –

[Unsigned]

273. *To William Godwin*

[London] Thursday [November 23^d, 1796]

My cough is still *very* troublesome – so that, I believe, it will be most prudent to stay at home to night – I am sorry I kept you with me last night – and insist on your going without me this evening.[800] I own, for I like to tell the truth, I was a little displeased with you for mentioning, when I was seriously indisposed, your inclination to go – and was angry with myself for not permitting you to follow your inclination – I am now quite well enough to amuse myself – and will dine with you some day next week, to day it would fatigue me, for my head aches with coughing.

[Unsigned]

---

800. On 23 November Sarah Siddons was acting Calista in Nicholas Rowe's *The Fair Penitent*; J. G. Holman's *Abroad and at Home* was playing at Covent Garden.

274. To William Godwin

[London, November 23ᵈ–28ᵗʰ, 1796][801]

Half after two.

I mean to call with this note, just to say that finding myself better, and the day clearing up, I might have been tempted to accompany you this evening had you *thought* of tempting me —

[Unsigned]

275. To William Godwin

[London] Monday morning [November 28ᵗʰ, 1796]

You tell me that 'I spoil little attentions, by anticipation.'[802] Yet to have attention, I find, that it is necessary to demand it. My faults are very inveterate – for I *did* expect you last night – But, *never mind it.* You coming would not have been worth any thing, if it must be requested.

I have just written to Mʳˢ R. to say that I cannot go to the play. I insist on my not preventing you from going this evening to see Milwood.[803] I am not such a child as I thought myself.

[Unsigned]

---

801. Undated but placed by Godwin between notes dated 23 November and 28 November.

802. See note 795.

803. The friend was probably Mary Robinson. Sarah Siddons was playing the prostitute Milwood in George Lillo's tragedy, *The London Merchant; or, the History of George Barnwell*, which opened at Drury Lane on 28 November. Godwin's diary does not record a theatre visit for this day; instead he spent the evening 'chez elle' and went to see Lillo's tragedy on 7 December.

276. To William Godwin

[London] Tuesday morning [December 6th, 1796]

I am not well, to day, yet I scarcely know what to complain of, excepting extreme lowness of spirits. I felt it creeping over me last night; but I will strive against it instead of talking of it – I hate this torpor of mind and senses.

[Unsigned]

277. To William Godwin

[London] Wednesday morning [December 7th, 1796]

I want to scold you for not having secured me a better place, because it is a mortification to me to be where I can neither see nor hear.[804] We were thrust into a corner in the third row, quite as bad as the Gallery – I had trouble enough with my companion without this circumstance; but I am determined to return to my former habits, and go by self and shift for myself – an amusement loses its name when thus conducted.

If you will call on me this morning, and allow me to spend my spite – I will admit you after the play to night.

You and M^{rs}. I—— were at your ease enjoying yourselves – while, poor I! – I was a fool not to ask Opie to go with me – had I been alone I should not have minded it – But enough for the present —

[Unsigned]

804. Godwin's diary entry for 6 December records that he and Elizabeth Inchbald saw Holcroft's *The Force of Ridicule*. Presumably Wollstonecraft also decided to go at the last minute and Godwin had had to find a seat for her and a companion – probably another woman, considering the reference to Opie.

278. To William Godwin

[London, December 12ᵗʰ, 1796]

I increased my cold, or rather cough, yesterday. The dress of women seems to be invented to render them dependent, in more senses than one. Had not Miss R—— promised to call for me, even Mʳˢ. Siddons would not have tempted me out to day, though I want winding up.[805] I do not know how you make authorship and dissipation agree, my thoughts are sometimes turned adrift.

I will take care of the two news-paper, which contain the debates,[806] if you will let me have them again, with this day's. —

[Unsigned]

279. To William Godwin

[London] Tuesday morning [December 13ᵗʰ, 1796]

I thought, after you left me, last night, that it was a *pity* we were obliged to part – just then.

I was even vext with myself for staying to supper with Mʳˢ. R.[807] But there is a manner of leaving a person free to follow their own will, that looks so like indifference, I do not like it. Your *tone* would have decided me – But, to tell you the truth, I thought, by your voice and

---

805. The caller was probably Mary Robinson's daughter; see note 816. Sarah Siddons was still playing Millwood at Drury Lane. Godwin's diary records that he went to see 'theatre, Shipwrek'.

806. The parliamentary debate concerned a subsidy of over a million pounds which the prime minister Pitt proposed to grant to the Austrian emperor Francis II to help him pursue the war against France. Charles James Fox, an opponent of the war, objected and considered 'himself a traitor to his Constituents if he voted One shilling of their Money before the transactions of the Minister's advancing this sum to the Emperor had been fully investigated . . .' (*The Times*, 9 December 1796).

807. Godwin's diary records that he, Wollstonecraft and Inchbald had supper with Mary Robinson on 12 December.

manner, that you wished to remain in society – and pride made me *wish* to gratify you.[808]

I mean to be with you, as soon as I can, this evening,[809] I thought of calling in my way, at three o'clock – Say shall you be at home; but do not stay at home on that account, unless you intend it, though I do not intend to *peck* you.

[Unsigned]

280. To Mary Hays

[London] Wednesday morning [December 14th, 1796]

Mary telling me that you could not decide, whether you could come to morrow, and M[rs]. Robinson's servant calling to day, I have fixt on friday, and shall expect you. I could not wait for your answer, so that if I receive a letter from you to day, saying you will come to morrow, I shall nevertheless expect you on Friday.

Adieu!
Mary.

281. To William Godwin

[London, December 18th, 1796]

I do not know whether you have sufficient philosophy to read this debate without indignation, I could not, and I love M[r]. Fox, for feeling and expressing it in so forcible – and so manly a manner – This is what I call humanity[810] – I will own to you that I am hurt when humanity

---

808. Godwin replied on the same day: 'I own I had the premeditated malice of making you part with me last night unwillingly, I feared Cupid had taken his final farwel' (*G&M*, p. 56).

809. Godwin's diary records 'chez moi' for the evening.

810. In the debate on General Fitzpatrick's motion on behalf of the early French revolutionary leader M. La Fayette, now imprisoned by the Austrians, Fox defended La Fayette against charges that he had not tried to prevent the massacres in France:

and cruelty are beheld with indifference, as speculative points – I could say more, but of this, however, I am certain that true eloquence is only to be produced by the embodying of virtue and vice.

Shall I see you before you go to dinner, I do not mean to stir out to day. If you intend to call say when, because I do not wish you to come, at the moment of dinner, when you do not dine with me.

[Unsigned]

282. To George Dyson[811]

[London] Tuesday morning [c. late 1796]

I received your note at the peep of dawn, consider it is a foggy morning, and cannot then get any other expressions together than the simple ones necessary, that I shall be glad to see you, may I say? because I think you have talents, or promise to have them, that are not common. –

I have not, I believe, expressed myself in the politest terms; but I mean to be more than civil when I assure you of my respect for your independence of character.

Mary Imlay

'the reason was obvious; it was not because he thought those massacres had been the causes of the war, but because he thought the war had been the occasion of those massacres, and any interference might have tended to increase them. Had it been otherwise? But, good God; has M La Fayette been the only cause of the calamities of France? Has he been the cause of as many even as the Ministers of Great Britain? Undoubtedly not' (*The Times*, 17 December 1796).

811. George Dyson (d. 1822), writer and painter, friend of Godwin and his ward Thomas Cooper. He translated *The Sorcerer* by 'Veit Weber' (Georg P. L. L. Wächter), published by Johnson in 1795, a curious Gothic tale in which a lover gains wealth by magic and murder, and, when the beloved then rejects him, tries to kill himself and dies a slow horrific death with hornets sucking at his wounds and a cormorant picking out his eyes. Both Godwin and Wollstonecraft thought Dyson gifted but he later alienated the former with his drunkenness and quarrelsome ways.

283. *To William Godwin*

[London, December 20th, 1796]

I send you the work, which M^r. Dyson says, is 'so dear to curiosity.'[812] He sent it home, this morning, he tells me, does he tell lies? that lameness prevented his bringing it himself. Fanny says, *perhaps* Man come to day – I am glad that there is no perhaps in the case. – As to other perhaps – they must rest in the womb of time.[813]

Send me some Ink.

[Unsigned]

284. *To William Godwin*

[London] Friday morning [December 23^d, 1796]

Was not yesterday a very pleasant evening?

There was a tenderness in your manner, as you seemed to be opening your heart, to a new born affection, that rendered you very dear to me.

There are other pleasures in the world, you perceive, beside those know to your philosophy.

Of myself I am still at a loss what to say.[814] —

[Unsigned]

---

812. Probably part of Wollstonecraft's novel *The Wrongs of Woman*; although his translation of *The Sorcerer* was marked by clichés, she later asked Dyson for an opinion on what she had completed.

813. The first clear mention of Wollstonecraft's suspicion that she might be pregnant for the second time.

814. On the cover of the note Wollstonecraft added: 'Send me one bottle of wine. No more, because *your* stock is almost out. – '

285. To Mary Robinson

[London] Friday evening, or rather night [c. late 1796]

Dear Madam,

I believe it is scarcely necessary to inform you that Miss Hays will accept of your invitation, and accompany me on Sunday next to dinner at your house.

As you were so obliging as to offer to send the carriage for the little *Fannikin*, I promised to call for her.[815] In the evening, if one of your servants will put Marguerite in her way, she and Fanny may return at an early hour.[36] You will smile at having so much of the womanish mother in me; but there is a little philosophy in it, *entre nous*; for I like to rouse her infant faculties by strong impressions.

I write in haste, with kind remembrance to your Mary[816] I am yours Sincerely

Mary Imlay

286. To William Godwin

[London] Wednesday [December 28th, 1796]

I am not well to day. A lowness of spirits, which I cannot conquer, leaves me at the mercy of my imagination, and only painful recollections and expectations assail me. Should it freeze to night, I believe, I

---

815. Robinson was unusual in having her own carriage, costing around £200 a year, but, since she was paralysed, it was a necessity.
816. Mary Robinson's daughter, Maria Elizabeth (1775–1818), about whom Robinson wrote tenderly: 'She was the most beautiful of infants! I thought myself the happiest of mothers; her first smile appeared like something celestial, – something ordained to irradiate my dark and dreary prospects of existence' (J. Fitzgerald Molloy (ed.), *Memoirs of Mary Robinson 'Perdita'. From the Edition Edited by her Daughter*, London, 1895, pp. 97f.).

had better have a coach – I would give, more than I ought, not to go[817]
– I dare say you are out of patience with me.

[Unsigned]

287. *To William Godwin*

[London] Friday morning [December 30th, 1796]

Unless it rains I mean to dine with Johnson to day, and will be with
you in the evening; but shall not tie myself to the hour of tea.

I spent a pleasant day, yesterday; only with Opie and Peter.

[Unsigned]

288. *To William Godwin*

[London, December 31st, 1796]

I shall dine with Johnson; but expect to be at home between seven and
eight.

If you were to get the constant Couple,[818] and bring it with you to
read, this evening – would it not be pleasant?

Looking over some of your essays, this morning, reminds me that the
one I most earnestly wished you to alter, from the most perfect conviction, was that on Public and private Education – I wanted you to recommend, *Day* Schools, it would obviate the evil, of being left with
servants, and enable children to converse with children without clashing
with the exercise of domestic affections, the foundation of virtue.[819]

[Unsigned]

817. That evening Godwin and Wollstonecraft were to attend one of the regular dinners
of the veteran radical and philologist, John Horne Tooke, in Wimbledon. Godwin's
diary records that they went as planned and that Mary Hays was also present.
818. George Farquhar's *The Constant Couple; or, a Trip to the Jubilee* was last
performed at Drury Lane on Friday, 29 May 1795, when it had to be 'put an end to
by a general condemnation of it' (*London Stage*, pt. 5, 3, 1760).
819. 'Of Public and Private Education', Essay VII of Part 1 of *The Enquirer*. As *The
Rights of Woman* suggested, Wollstonecraft favoured a universal public education

289. To William Godwin

[London] Saturday morning [December 31st, 1796]

This does not appear to me just the moment to have written me such a note as I have been perusing.[820]

I am, however, prepared for any thing. I can abide by the consequence of my own conduct, and do not wish to envolve any one in my difficulties.

[Unsigned]

290. To William Godwin

[London] Sunday morning [January 1st, 1797]

The weather is so unfavourable that I find I must have a coach, or stay at home. I was splashed up to my knees yesterday, and to sit several hours in that state is intolerable.

Will you then come to me, as soon as you can; for Mary, after leaving this with you, goes on for a coach.

I am not well – I have a fever on my spirits that has tormented me these two night's past. You do not, I think make sufficient allowance for the peculiarity of my situation. But women are born to suffer.

system; radicals who had formerly been Dissenters, such as Paine and Godwin, feared the state's control. Godwin appears to have considered Wollstonecraft's view and later added a paragraph which does not appear in the manuscript version of his essay (Pforzheimer MSS; *SC*, 1, 146f.): 'The objections to both the modes of education here discussed are of great magnitude. It is unavoidable to enquire, whether a middle way might not be selected, neither entirely public, nor entirely private, avoiding the mischiefs of each, and embracing the advantages of both. . . . There is nothing so fascinating in either, as should in reason check the further excursions of our understanding.'

820. Earlier in the day Godwin had written to Wollstonecraft: 'You treated me last night with extreme unkindness: the more so, because it was calm, melancholy, equable unkindness. You wished we had never met; you wished you could cancel all that had passed between us. Is this, – ask your own heart, – Is this compatible with the passion of love? Or, is it not the language of frigid, unalterable indifference?' (*G&M*, pp. 59f.). Despite the quarrel the pair spent New Year's Eve 'chez elle'.

I cannot bear that you should do violence to your feelings, by writing to M^r. Wedgewood.[821] No; you shall not write – I will think of some way of extricating myself.

You must have patience with me, for I am sick at heart – Dissatisfied with every body and every thing.

My depression of spirits is certainly increased by indisposition.[822]

[Unsigned]

291. To William Godwin

[London] Thursday morning [January 5th, 1797]

I was very glad that you were not with me last night, for I could not rouse myself – To say the truth, I was unwell – and out of spirits. I am better to day.

I shall take a walk before dinner, and expect to see you this evening, chez moi, about eight, if you have no objection.

[Unsigned]

292. To William Godwin

[London] Thursday morning [January 12th, 1797]

I am better this morning. But it snows, so incessantly, that I do not know how I shall be able to keep my appointment this evening. What

821. Wollstonecraft was heavily in debt, having published little since *Letters from Sweden*. Godwin offered to write to his young admirer, Thomas Wedgwood, wealthy son of the pottery manufacturer Josiah Wedgwood of Etruria. Earlier the pair had discussed patronage and the selfishness implied in giving; Godwin had written, 'If the loan or the gift of £100 would . . . be of eminent service to me in my pursuits, I think it probable that I ought to ask you for it without scruple, & that you ought to advance it', but he added 'I am not sure that I should think it my duty, when the case occurres' (Abinger MSS, Dep.b.228/3). Wollstonecraft's impecuniousness was common knowledge: through Amelia Alderson a Norfolk bachelor had offered her a gift of £5, which was indignantly refused (see Todd, *Mary Wollstonecraft*, pp. 408f.).

822. According to Godwin's diary entry, on 1 January Wollstonecraft persuaded Godwin to talk of 'children & marriage'.

say you? But you have no petticoats to dangle in the snow. Poor Women how they are beset with plagues – within – and without.

[Unsigned]

293. To William Godwin

[London] Friday morning [January 13th, 1797]

I believe I ought to beg your pardon for talking at you, last night, though it was in sheer simplicity of heart – and I have been asking myself why it so happen – Faith and troth, it. [was] because there was nobody else worth attacking, or who could converse – C——[823] had wearied me before you entered. But, be assured, when I find a man that has any thing in him, I shall let my every day dish alone.

I send you *the Emma*;[824] for M^{rs}. Inchbald supposing you have not altered your mind.

Bring Holcroft's remarks with you, and Ben Johnson[825] —

[Unsigned]

---

823. According to the diary, Godwin and Wollstonecraft had 'Tea Carr's, w. mrs. Barbauld, . . . Tookes & Woods' on 12 January. Perhaps John Carr (1772–1832), later Sir John, barrister of the Middle Temple and writer of gossipy travel books about Europe, or the Carr who was Solicitor to the Excise and a conservative acquaintance of Crabb Robinson and Wordsworth (*Henry Crabb Robinson's Diary*, 1, 390n.).

824. Probably a reference to Mary Hays's autobiographical novel of seemingly unrequited female passion, *Memoirs of Emma Courtney*. Like so many female novels of the time such as those by Charlotte Smith, Inchbald and Eliza Fenwick, it displayed the difficulties of women's lives but was far more outspoken than these about the problems of the double sexual standard and female desire. Kegan Paul, in *WG*, 1, 242, suggests that the reference is to the novel *Emma; or, the Unfortunate Attachment* (1773).

825. Possibly Thomas Holcroft's *A Narrative of Facts, Relating to a Prosecution for High Treason; Including the Address to the Jury, Which the Court refused to hear* (London, 1795) or his *Letter to the Right Honourable William Windham on the Intemperance and Dangerous Tendency of His Public Conduct* (1795). Both publications concern the charges for treason against him and Thomas Hardy, set out proposals for parliamentary reforms from the Society for Constitutional Information, describe government reprisals and his and Hardy's imprisonment and subsequent acquittal through lack of evidence. *CL* also speculates that Wollstonecraft might be referring to Holcroft's criticism of one of her or Godwin's MSS. Ben Jonson's *Every Man in his Humour*, with alterations and additions by David Garrick, had been

294. *To William Godwin*

[London] Sunday [January 15th, 1797]

I have only a moment to tell you, that I cannot call this morning, and I do not know whether I shall be able to go to Mr J. tho' I should be sorry to fail. If the weather be tolerable, or I catch a coach I shall go, and therefore cannot say when; but probably before the hour you set out, usually. I am not quite so well to day, owing to my very uncomfortable walk, Last night. I was very glad I did not promise to call on you; for I was obliged to undress immediately on my return.

To morrow, I suppose, is out of the reach of fate.

Yours truly
Mary

295. *To William Godwin*

[London] Saturday morning [January 21st, 1797]

I forgot to invite you to dine with me this present Saturday, the 21th of Jany. Still I shall expect you at half past four – so no at present from yours &c — Mary

296. *To Mary Hays*

[London, c. January 1797][826]

I have sent you the Gossips Story to review, as you wish to read it, but I would thank you if you would do it immediately, because Johnson is in want of materials for the present month. The great merit of this

---

performed at Covent Garden in 1792 and was included in Jones's *British Theatre*, 3 (1795) and Bell's *British Theatre*, 4 (1797).

826. Dating from the reference to Jane West's *A Gossips Story*, reviewed by V.V. in *AR*, vol. XXV (January 1797), pp. 25f.

work is, in my opinion, the display of the small causes which destroy matrimonial felicity & peace. In reviewing, will you pardon me? you seem to run into an errour which I have laboured to cure in myself: you allude to things in the work which can only be understood by those who have read it, instead of, by a short summary of the contents, or an account of the incident on which the interest turns, enabling a person to have a clear idea of a book, which they have never heard of before. I could explain myself better, were I not in haste.[827]

I expect M^{rs}. Robinson & daughter, to drink tea with me, on thursday, will you come to meet them. She has read your novel, and was *very much* pleased with the *main* story; but did not like the conclusion. She thinks the death of Augustus the end of the story and that the husband should have been suffered to die a natural death. Perhaps she is right. I know my sympathy ceased at the same place; but I thought that was owing to having had a peep behind the curtain.[828] I shall expect you Adieu!

[Unsigned]

297. To William Godwin

[London] Tuesday morning [January 24th, 1797]

I am still an invalid – Still have the inelegant complaint, which no novelist has yet ventured to mention as one of the consequences of

---

827. In fact the review became a defence of didactic fiction: 'It requires but little knowledge of the human mind to discover, that the most effectual method of giving instruction, is by interesting the imagination and engaging the affections . . . If novels, romances, and fables, be held as an inferiour and insignificant species of literary composition, it must be by those who have paid little attention to the human heart. . . . The writer of the present production, without attempting those higher investigations of principle and action, which exercise the understanding, and stimulate it's dormant faculties, is yet entitled to praise.'

828. The ending of *Memoirs of Emma Courtney* killed off the heroine's husband as well as the hero, Augustus Harley, openly based on William Frend. Like Robinson and Wollstonecraft, Alderson was enthusiastic about the book: 'I am delighted with Miss Hays's novel! I would give a great deal to have written it.' Since the book was much condemned in less radical circles, Alderson congratulated herself on her courage in publicly supporting it (18 December 1796, Abinger MSS, Dep.b.21).

sentimental distress. If prudence permit I shall take a walk this morning, and, perhaps, call on you, going or returning; but do not stay at home a moment for me. Should I continue unwell, I believe, I had better spend the evening alone; but you shall hear of me, or see me, in the course of the day.

[Unsigned]

298. To William Godwin

[London, January 27ᵗʰ, 1797]

I am not well this morning – It is very tormenting to be thus, neither sick nor well; especially as you scarcely imagine me indisposed.

Women are certainly great fools; but nature made them so. I have not time, or paper, else, I could draw an inference, not very illustrative of your chance-medley[829] system – But I spare the moth-like opinion, there is room enough in the world &c.

[Unsigned]

299. To William Godwin

[London] Saturday [January 28ᵗʰ, 1797]

I was glad that you were not with me last night, for the foolish woman of the house laid a trap to plague me. I have, however, I believe put an end to this nonsense, so enough of that subject.

A variety of things assail my spirits at present, and some of my endeavours to throw off, or rather to extricate myself, by failing, have only given an edge to my vexation.

I shall expect you this evening.

[Unsigned]

---

829. Most likely a reference to Godwin's theories of birth control. *CL*, however, speculates that the term refers to his materialistic philosophy.

300. To William Godwin

[London] Friday morning [February 3^d, 1797]

M^{rs}. Inchbald was gone into the City to dinner, so I had to measure back my steps.

To day I find myself better; and, as the weather is fine, mean to call on D^r. Fordyce.[830] I shall leave home about two o'clock. I tell you so lest you should call after that hour. I do not think of visiting you, in my way, because I seem inclined to be industrious. I believe I feel affectionate to you in proportion as I am in spirits; still I must not dally with you when I can do any thing else – There is a civil speech for you to chew. –

[Unsigned]

301. To William Godwin

[London] Saturday morning [February 4th, 1797]

When I promised to visit you, this morning, you forgot that you had previously mentioned your intention of calling on Fuseli. Only say what you mean to do; and whether my visit is to be to day or to morrow.

I shall, probably invite the Frenchman, to drink a glass of wine, if you say you shall not come to night[831] –

[Unsigned]

830. Dr George Fordyce; see note 410. He was a friend of Godwin as well as Johnson. Probably Wollstonecraft was consulting him on her pregnancy.
831. Possibly a man called Boisville, whom, according to his diary, Godwin met on 22 January and 2 and 4 February.

302. *To William Godwin*

[London] Monday morning [February 13th, 1797]

I intended to have called on you this morning, but for the rain, to beg your pardon, as Fanny says, for damping your spirits last night. Everina, only said, that she was so oppressed by her cold that she could not sit up any longer, but she hoped you would not think her uncivil, especially as she found herself unable to join in the conversation.[832] So you shall seal my pardon when we meet.

[Unsigned]

303. *To William Godwin*

[London, February 14th, 1797]

Unless the weather prove very tempestuous, my sister would like to go to the play this evening.[833] Will you come to early tea.

832. Everina Wollstonecraft had left her Dublin post and was staying with her sister (she was mentioned in Godwin's diary on 10 February) on her way to Etruria, the Wedgwood family home close to Stoke-on-Trent. She was to act possibly as a temporary companion and governess of the young children of Elizabeth and Josiah Wedgwood II. In a letter to his aunt Anna Laetitia Barbauld, Charles Rochemont Aikin wrote: 'Mr Jos. Wedgewood . . . has with him at Etruria a sister of Mrs Woolstonecraft (now Mrs Godwin is she not!) as governess to his children. She has much of her sister's good sense but is more reserved' (27 May 1797, in Betsey Rodgers, *Georgian Chronicle. Mrs Barbauld & her Family*, London: Methuen, 1958, p. 219). It is likely that Everina did not stay long enough to be a proper replacement for a governess since she was not mentioned in the detailed educational writings of Josiah II at this time. She seems not to have been dismissed, for she remained very fond of the Wedgwoods. Whatever its specifications, the position was probably obtained through Godwin's friendship with Tom Wedgwood or through another friend, Basil Montagu, engaged to Josiah II's sister Sarah. Wollstonecraft seems not to have divulged either her pregnancy or her relationship with Godwin to Everina during her stay.

833. She could see Rowe's *Jane Shore* with Sarah Siddons at Drury Lane, Thomas Morton's *A Cure for the Heart Ache* at Covent Garden or *Zémire et Azor* at the King's.

I intended to have called on you this morning – we were shopping and I am weary. –

[Unsigned]

304. To William Godwin

[London, February 15th, 1797]

I have been prevent by various little things from calling on you this morning – You must excuse this seeming neglect – do not say unkindness. I write now lest I should not find you at home, to say that Everina will pass to-morrow with Miss Cristall[834] and that I will dine with you – If you please.

[Unsigned]

305. To Mary Hays

[London] Wednesday morning [February 15th, 1797][835]

My Sister's cold has been so troublesome that we have remained at home; and as she wishes to pay Miss Cristall the first visit, our party must be posponed 'till next week. I have had my eye on the papers; but M[rs]. Siddons has not performed any of her best parts[836] to make me, on your account, regret the delay.

---

834. Anne Cristall, friend of both sisters from the late 1780s. She had recently published a book of poems with Johnson, to which both Mary and Everina Wollstonecraft had subscribed. The poet Robert Southey admired Anne Cristall and her work: on 13 March 1797 he wrote to Joseph Cottle, 'have you seen her poems? – a fine, artless sensible girl! . . . Her heart is alive, she loves poetry, she loves retirement, she loves the country: her verses are very incorrect, and the literary circles say she has no genius; but she has genius . . . or there is no truth in physiognomy' (*The Life and Correspondence of the late Robert Southey*, ed. Charles Cuthbert Southey, London, 1849, I, 305).

835. CL's dating, based on the connection between this letter and the previous dated one. 15 February 1797 was a Wednesday.

836. Sarah Siddons had recently played Aspasia in Rowe's *Tamerlane* (3, 6, and 8 February), Portia in *The Merchant of Venice* (11 February), and Jane Shore in Rowe's

I enclose you a letter for M^r. Brown.[837] Adieu!

Mary

306. To William Godwin

[London, February 17th, 1797]

Did I not see you friend, Godwin, at the theatre last night?[838] I thought I met a smile; but you went out without looking round.

We expect you at half past four.

If you have any business, in the city, perhaps, you will leave a letter, for me, at Johnson's, as it is not perfectly convenient to send Mary. But do not put yourself out of your way, I will try to contrive to do it *myself* should you[37] have had an intention of directing your steps in another

[Unsigned]

307. To William Godwin

[London] Tuesday [February 21st, 1797]

My Sister talks of going to Miss Cristall's tomorrow or next day, I shall not then expect you this evening – I would call on you this

---

Jane Shore (14 February). Wollstonecraft was perhaps being consolatory since certainly *Jane Shore* was considered one of Mrs Siddons's major roles; the critic in *True Briton* was intermittently enthusiastic about her performance in *Tamerlane*: 'Mrs Siddons's manner of receiving the death of Moneses, and the struggle that ended in her own, was one of the best efforts of the art we ever beheld. This effort, however, was too much for her powers; for, after her fall, her groans were so audible that the curtain was properly dropped, and it was some moments before she could be removed from the stage.'

837. Probably the Unitarian clergyman who admired Mary Hays's literary talents and tried to attract public attention to her writings. See *Love-Letters of Mary Hays*, p. 220.

838. Godwin's diary records no visit to the theatre on 16 February but one for the following day: 'Theatres; 1/2 Barnwel', presumably referring to Lillo's tragedy *The London Merchant*; see note 803.

morning, but I cannot say when – and I suppose you will dine at Johnson's. The evenings with her silent, I find very wearisome and embarrassing. It was what you said in the morning that determined her not to go to the play.[839] Well a little patience.

I am going out with Montagu[840] to day, and shall be glad by a new train of thoughts to drive my present out of my head.[841]

[Unsigned]

308. To William Godwin

[London, February 22[d], 1797]

Everina's cold is still so bad that, unless pique urges her, she will not go out to day. For to morrow, I think, I may venture to promise. I will call, if possible, this morning – I know I must come before half after one; but if you hear nothing more from me you had better come to my house this evening.

Will you send the 2[d] vol. of Caleb[842] – and pray *lend* me a bit of indian-rubber – I have lost mine.

Should you be obliged to quit home before the hour I have mention – say —

[Unsigned]

839. Everina Wollstonecraft had decided against C. Cross's *The Purse* at Drury Lane and *Abroad and at Home* at Covent Garden.
840. Basil Montagu (1770–1851), illegitimate son of the fourth earl of Sandwich. At this point he was a follower of Godwin; he later eschewed radical principles while remaining broadly liberal on political issues.
841. Wollstonecraft was much occupied by her social position, which would be affected once her pregnancy became public. As a result of her anxiety, Godwin agreed to marriage. Wollstonecraft was also anxious about money and at the end of February, preparing for their wedding, Godwin wrote an embarrassed letter to Tom Wedgwood requesting an immediate loan of £50 for 'another person' (Abinger MSS, Dep.c.513). The money was sent and used to pay Wollstonecraft's most pressing debts.
842. Godwin's novel *Things as They Are; or, the Adventures of Caleb Williams* (1794). Since there is some resemblance between motifs in Godwin's novel and her own *The Wrongs of Woman*, possibly Wollstonecraft was requesting the volume to inspire her to continue writing what she found a difficult work.

309. *To William Godwin*

[London, c. early 1797][843]

You will not forget that we are to dine at four. I wish to be exact, because I have promised to let Mary go and assist her brother, this afternoon. I have been tormented all this morning by Puss, who has had four or five fits. I could not perceive what occasioned them, and took care that she should not be terrified. But she flew up my chimney, and was so wild, that I thought it right to have her drown. Express concern to Lucas.[844] – Fanny imagines that she was sick and ran away. –

[Unsigned]

310. *To Mary Hays*

[London] Friday morning [c. early 1797][845]

I have now to request you, *as a particular favour*, to thank the persons, to whom you have applied for Mary, and request, with some *earnestness*, their interest for the next year.[846]

I have not time, at present, or I would tell you how I defended your novel yesterday – that is your character, to M[r]. Barbauld, with whom I dined, you are *stygmatized* as a Philosophess – a Godwinian – I assured him that your nove[l] would not undermine religion, &c[847]

---

843. Godwin placed this undated letter immediately after Letter 308. WG, 1, 243 printed Letters 308 and 309 as a single letter but *CL* points out that there are conflicting plans for the day ahead, that the notes were written with different pens, and that each was addressed: Mr Godwin.

844. The 'deaf and dumb' son of Godwin's housekeeper, aged 8.

845. Dating from the reference to Hays's novel and to the review probably of Peter Pindar.

846. Mary Hays had been attempting to enter Mary's son in a school (see also Letter 314).

847. The Revd Rochemont Barbauld, husband of Anna Laetitia. At the age of eighteen he went to Warrington Academy even though he was intended for the ministry of the Established Church, and became a Dissenter and schoolteacher. In 1787 he was

I send you P. P[848] – if you do not chuse to review it return it after you have perused it –

yours truly
Mary

Take no notice to Miss C.[849] that I mentioned to you her opinion of your novel –

311. To William Godwin

[London] Monday [March 6th, 1797]

Everina goes by the mail, this evening. I shall go with her to the coach and call at Johnson's in my way home. I will be with you about nine, or had you not better *try*, if you can, to while away this evening, those to come are our own. I suppose you will call this morning to say adieu! to Everina. Do not knock loud, for a child is born.

[Unsigned]

---

appointed pastor at the old Presbyterian chapel on Red Lion Hill, Hampstead, a post he held for fifteen years. Frances Burney described him as 'a very little, diminutive figure, but well bred and sensible' (Charlotte Barrett. (ed.), *Diary and Letters of Madame D'Arblay*, London, 1905, 5, 419f.); Maria Edgeworth knew him as a benevolent, amiable man and a liberal opponent of the slave trade (*A Memoir of Maria Edgeworth, with a Selection from her Letters Edited by her Children*, London, 1867, 1, 97f.). All his life Rochemont Barbauld was depressive and around 1805–6 he suffered a severe mental illness, which included violence towards his wife. He and Anna separated, and he committed suicide in 1808.

848. The satirist John Wolcot wrote pamphlets under the pseudonym Peter Pindar. An unsigned review of his *One Thousand Seven Hundred and Ninety-Six; a Satire: in four Dialogues* occurs in *AR*, vol. XXV (March 1797), pp. 281f., and another of his *An Ode to the Livery of London, on their Petition to His Majesty for kicking out his worthy ministers* in vol. XXVI (July 1797), p. 45f. A further unsigned review, less likely to be the one referred to, is of Paul Positive's *Prison Amusements, and other Trifles*, in vol. XXV (April 1797), pp. 411f.

849. Probably Anne Cristall, a friend of both Hays and the Wollstonecraft sisters.

312. To William Godwin

[London] Saturday morning [March 11th, 1797]

I must dine to day with Mrs. Christie, and mean to return as early as I can; they seldom dine before five.[850]

Should you call, and find only books, have a little patience, and I shall be with you.

Do not give Fanny a cake to day. I am afraid she staid too long with you yesterday.

You are to dine with me on Monday, – remember, the salt-beef waits your pleasure. —

[Unsigned]

313. To William Godwin

[London] Friday morning [March 17th, 1797]

And so you goose you lost your supper – and deserved to lose it for not desiring Mary to give you some beef.

There is a good boy write me a review of Vaurien. I remember there is an absurd attack on a methodist Preacher, because he denied the Eternity of future punishments.[851]

I should be glad to have the Italian,[852] were it possible, this week, because I promised to let Johnson have it this week.

[Unsigned]

---

850. Thomas Christie had gone to Surinam on business and died there in 1796.
851. *Vaurien; or Sketches of the Times*, by Isaac D'Israeli. In the novel Godwin himself is mocked as Mr Subtile, 'the coldest blooded metaphysician of the age'. Wollstonecraft appears as Miss Million, supporter of sex outside marriage. An unsigned review of *Vaurien* appeared in the April 1798 issue of *AR* criticizing the book as malicious and sarcastic. Eleanor Nicholes points out that the style of the review is Godwinian (*Romantic Rebels: Essays on Shelley and His Circle*, ed. K. N. Cameron, Cambridge, Mass., 1973, p. 43n.); Godwin's diary shows him reading the book at intervals after early March; he finished it on 16 March.
852. Ann Radcliffe's gothic novel *The Italian* (1797), reviewed by Wollstonecraft in the May 1797 issue of *AR*, vol. XXV, 516.

314. To Everina Wollstonecraft[853]

London, March 22[d] [1797]

I have just received your letter, without a date, and I am totally at a loss to guess what you mean by the parcel you speak of as to be sent to *York Street*, which street I never heard of before. You have left nothing behind you, but some powder, which you did not, or I am much mistaken, express a wish to have immediately. I may have forgotten, yet I scarcely think I have, for I have had a number of cares, since you left me. The scarcity of money makes all the tradesmen send in their bills, and I have had some sent to me which I could hardly avoid paying. The mantua maker called so often for your bill, three pound four, and seemed in such distress to pay her rent I was obliged to let her have it, and I then gave to young Cristall[854] all the money I had. I am continually getting myself into scrapes of this kind. I must get some in a day or two, Johnson teazes me, and I will then send you a guinea. My pecuniary distress I know arises from myself – or rather from my not having had the power of employing my mind and fancy, when my soul was on the rack. I was obliged to let my father have all my money; but I did imagine that M[r]. I—— would have paid, at least, the first half-year's interest of the bond given to me for Fanny. A year, however, is nearly elapsed,[38] and I hear nothing of it;[39] and have had bills sent to me which, I take it for granted, he *forgot* to pay. Had M[r]. I—— been punctual, I should, after the first year, [from] the amount of which is due to me, have put by the interest for Fanny, never expecting to receive the principal, and not chusing to be under any obligation to him. But more than enough of this subject. Johnson is either half ruined by the present public circumstances, or grown strangely mean, at any rate he torments me, and Charles' neglecting to answer his, and my request, respecting a provision for my father,

853. The letter was sent to Everina Wollstonecraft at Josiah Wedgwood's home in Etruria, Staffordshire.

854. Joshua Cristall; see note 385. After some struggling he later established himself as a watercolourist, painting mainly classic and rustic scenes. According to Samuel Redgrave's *A Dictionary of Artists of the English School* (London, 1878), p. 106: 'His

makes me very uneasy.[855] Your description of the females, of your happy family, makes me hug myself in the solitude of my fire side. I was really fatigued at only hearing of their animal spirits; and the contents of the dozen novels,[40] they devour in a week, whirled round my head till it ached again. In short when you call them an amiable set you have contrive to give me an idea of a party destitute of sentiment, fancy or feeling, taste is, of course, out of the question. I will let you have as much food for laughter as I can; but I am afraid I cannot let you have M^{rs}. Ratcliff's till it is reviewed, Johnson would not like to have two sets soiled; and, entre nous, Mrs Robinson's[41] would do just as well;[856] for as works of genius do not occur every day, I would advise you to read M^{rs}. R's Italian in your own chamber, not to lose the picturesque images with which it abounds.[857] And while I think of it let me tell you that I have not seen a scrap of your drawring. As for my Mary, I consider it as a crude production, and do not very willingly put it in the way of people whose good opinion, as a writer, I wish for; but you may have it to make up the sum of laughter – The omission

art was simple, he used no body colour, and was free from all trick. Original in manner and character, entirely without insipidity and prettiness.'

855. Charles Wollstonecraft's expected fortune had not materialized and Wollstonecraft had to make up her father's shortfall as Eliza Bishop had done from Upton while her sister had been in France.

856. Mary Robinson's three-volume novel *Angelina* (1796). Wollstonecraft reviewed it in the March 1796 issue of *AR*. She praised its didactic aims and noted that it kept the reader's attention but criticized its confused and over-complicated story, which 'will not greatly rouse or deeply agitate' (*Works*, 7, 462). *The British Critic*, vol. 7 (April 1796), p. 429, found the novel 'exceedingly entertaining' and suitable for 'our fair readers' but considered 'some characters overdrawn, some incidents beyond all probability, and, what is the great fault of many novelists, the dialogue often extended to a most tedious length'.

857. In her review of Radcliffe's *The Italian* Wollstonecraft wrote: 'The picturesque views of the varying charms of nature, drawn by an animated imagination, are less diffuse than in the former productions of this writer; and the reflections, which oftener occur, give strong proofs likewise of an improving judgement. The nature of the story obliges us to digest improbabilities, and continually to recollect that it is a romance, not a novel, we are reading; especially as the restless curiosity it excites is too often excited by something like stage trick. – We are made to wonder, only to wonder; but the spell, by which we are led, again and again, round the same magic circle, is the spell of genius. Pictures and scenes are conjured up with happy exuberance; and reason with delight resigns the reins to fancy, till forced to wipe her eyes and recollect, with a sigh, that it is but a dream' (*Works*, 7, 484f.).

was on the part of Rowland, indeed, it seems to me such an imperfect sketch that I seldom think of it.[858]

Fanny enjoys the dry weather, and is very proud of being allowed to go for the news-paper by herself, Mary was aloof. Poor Mary has been, and is unwell, the nurse will not keep the boy any longer, and I have been obliged to let him come here for a while, poor fellow! you might some time or other; but this hint I submit to you own judgment, perhaps, get Mr T. W. to do something for him. I am sure he would make a good engraver were he properly taught. I am trying to getting him into a school, but should I succeed it cannot be before christmas.[859]

Adieu! Mary.

315. To William Godwin

[London] Friday [March 31st, 1797]

I return you the volumes – will you get me the rest? I have not, perhaps, given it as careful a reading as some of the sentiments deserve. –

Pray send me, by Mary, for my luncheon, a part of the supper you announced to me last night – as I am to be a partaker of your worldly goods – you know![860]

[Unsigned]

858. *Mary, A Fiction*, which Wollstonecraft no longer valued. Roland Hunter was Joseph Johnson's adopted nephew and colleague.
859. Mary's son; Wollstonecraft was hoping for the patronage of Tom Wedgwood. See also note 846.
860. On 29 March Wollstonecraft and Godwin had married at the church of St Pancras. Godwin recorded the event in his diary as 'Panc'. Henry Fuseli revealed the marriage to William Roscoe: 'You have not, perhaps, heard that the assertrix of female rights has given her hand to the *balancier* of political justice' (*HF*, 1, 170). The Book of Common Prayer marriage service included the man's vow to the woman, 'with all my worldly goods I thee endow'.

316. To William Godwin

[London] Tuesday morning [April 4ᵗʰ, 1797]

I am certainly not at my ease to day – yet I am better – Will you send Mʳ. Marshall[861] to me and I take it for granted that you mean, and can conv[en]iently, get me my spectacles, before you go to dinner – or I will send Mary.

[Unsigned]

317. To William Godwin

[London] Saturday [April 8ᵗʰ, 1797]

I have just thought that it would be very pretty in you to call on Johnson to day – It would spare me some awkwardness, and please him; and I want you to visit him often of a Tuesday – This is quite disinterested, as I shall never be of the party[862] – Do go – you would oblige me – But when I press any thing it is always with a true *wifish* submission to your judgment and inclination.

Remember to leave the key with us of Nᵒ 25[863] – on account of the wine.

[Unsigned]

861. James Marshall, Godwin's friend since student days, shared his lodgings in Chalton Street and sometimes acted as his amanuensis and general factotum. He was the witness at Godwin's marriage to Wollstonecraft.
862. Wollstonecraft might have felt embarrassed at either revealing or hiding her marriage. She was still very much in debt to Johnson and her indebtedness would be assumed by her new husband. Wollstonecraft and Godwin had agreed not to socialize together as a conventional married couple.
863. A reference to Godwin's old lodgings at 25 Chalton Street. After their marriage Godwin and Wollstonecraft had moved into a semicircular block of newly-built, three-storeyed houses in Somers Town: 29, the Polygon, close to open country. To avoid the monopoly of marriage, Godwin also took another apartment for himself near by in 17 Evesham Buildings. He wrote in his diary for 6 April: '*sleep at Polygon*'. The new arrangement was expensive and Godwin approached Tom Wedgwood for another £50. The money was sent. In *CL* Wardle reads '25' as '29'.

318. To William Godwin

[London, April 9th, 1797]

Pray don't set me any more tasks – I am the awkwardest creature in the world at manufacturing a letter –

[Unsigned]

319. To William Godwin

[London, April 11th, 1797]

I am not well to day my spirits have been harassed. Mary will tell you about the state of the sink &c do you know you plague me (a little) by not speaking more determinately to the Landlord of whom I have a mean opinion. He tires me by his pitiful way of doing every thing – I like a man who will say yes or no at once.

[Unsigned]

320. To William Godwin

[London, April 11th, 1797]

I wish you would desire Mr. Marshall to call on me. Mr. Johnson, or somebody, has always taken the disagreeable business of settling with trades-people off my hands – I am, perhaps as unfit as yourself to do it – and my time, appears to me, as valuable as that of other persons accustomed to employ themselves. Things of this kind are easily settled with money, I know; but I am tormented by the want of money – and feel, to say the truth, as if I was not treated with respect, owing to your desire not to be disturbed —

[Unsigned]

321. To Amelia Alderson[864]

[London] Tuesday night [April 11th, 1797][865]

My dear Girl,

Endeavouring, through embarrassment, to turn the conversation from myself last night, I insensibly became too severe in my strictures on the vanity of a certain lady,[866] and my heart smote me when I raised a laugh at her expense. Pray forget it. I have now to tell you that I am very sorry I prevented you from engaging a box for M[rs]. Inchbald, whose conduct, I think, has been very rude. She wrote to M[r]. Godwin to-day, saying, that, taking it for granted he had forgotten it, she had spoken to another person. 'She would not do so the next time he was married.' Nonsense! I have now to request you to set the matter right. M[rs]. Inchbald may still get a box; I beg her pardon for misunderstanding the business, but M[r]. G. led me into the error, or I will go to the pit.[867] To have done with disagreeable subjects at once, let me allude

864. This letter has survived only in the version published in Brightwell's *Amelia Opie*, pp. 59f.

865. The date comes from Wollstonecraft's reference to Inchbald's note which is dated 11 April 1797 (a Tuesday). Inchbald had written to Godwin about securing a box for 'Reynolds's night' on 19 April, the first night of Frederick Reynolds's *The Will* at Drury Lane with Mrs Jordan. Having heard of Godwin's marriage to Wollstonecraft, Inchbald wrote to him, 'I most sincerely wish you and Mrs Godwin joy – But, assured that your joyfulness would obliterate from your memory every trifling engagement, I have entreated another person to supply your place and perform your office in securing a Box on Reynolds's night. If I have done wrong – when you next marry I will act differently' (Abinger MSS, Dep.c.509).

866. Presumably Inchbald. She had chaperoned the young Amelia Alderson when she first visited London. Wollstonecraft must have realized that her criticism of Inchbald, her friend's friend, was unwise.

867. In the end Wollstonecraft persuaded Godwin and Alderson to prevail on Inchbald to keep the theatre arrangement. The two women therefore met at the theatre on 19 April, were hostile and avoided further contact. When Wollstonecraft and Godwin returned home, they quarrelled and Godwin wrote on 20 April, 'I am pained by the recollection of our conversation last night. The sole principle of conduct of which I am conscious in my behaviour to you, has been in every thing to study your happiness. I found a wounded heart, &, as that heart cast itself upon me, it was my ambition to heal it. Do not let me be wholly disappointed.' (When he numbered his and

to another. I shall be sorry to resign the acquaintance of M^{rs}. and M^{r}. F. Twiss,[868] because I respect their characters, and feel grateful for their attention; but my conduct in life must be directed by my own judgment and moral principles: it is my wish that M^{r}. Godwin should visit and dine out as formerly, and I shall do the same; in short, I still mean to be independent, even to the cultivating sentiments and principles in my children's minds, (should I have more,) which he disavows.[869] The wound my unsuspecting heart formerly received is not healed. I found my evenings solitary; and I wished, while fulfilling the duty of a mother, to have some person with similar pursuits, bound to me by affection; and beside, I earnestly desired to resign a name which seemed to disgrace me.[870] Since I have been unfortunately the object of observation, I have had it in my power, more than once, to marry very advantageously; and of course, should have been courted by those, who at least cannot accuse me of acting an interested part, though I have not, by dazzling their eyes, rendered them blind to my faults. I am proud perhaps, conscious of my own purity and integrity; and many circumstances in my life have contributed to excite in my bosom an indignant contempt for the forms of a world I should have bade a long good night to, had I not been a mother. Condemned then, to toil my hour out, I wish to live as rationally as I can; had fortune or splendor been my aim in life, they have been within my reach, would I have paid the price. Well, enough of the subject; I do not wish to resume it. Good night! God bless you.

Mary Wollstonecraft,
femme GODWIN.[871]

Wollstonecraft's letter, also dated 20 April, Godwin put his own after Letter 323. I have adopted a reverse order since Wollstonecraft's letter seems to indicate they had made up.)

868. Wollstonecraft had been in the habit of dining with the Twisses on every third Sunday. They had believed her married to Imlay but, when they heard of her marriage to Godwin, they realized the truth and broke off their friendship.

869. Wollstonecraft was still not publicly admitting her advancing pregnancy.

870. Without having experienced the pressures on an unmarried mother, Mary Hays had been urging Wollstonecraft to revert to her own name instead of passing as 'Mary Imlay'. Wollstonecraft used her own name on her published works, such as *Letters from Sweden*.

871. Wollstonecraft was coy about using the name Mary Godwin to Amelia Alderson and Mary Hays, though she wished to remind them that she was married. She did use her married name to male correspondents like Marshall and Dyson.

322. To Mary Hays?[872]

[speculative reconstruction]

[London, c. April 1797]

Those who are bold enough to advance before the age they live in, and to throw off, by the force of their own minds, the prejudices which the maturing reason of the world will in time disavow, must learn to brave censure. We ought not to be too anxious respecting the opinion of others. – I am not fond of vindications. – Those who know me will suppose that I acted from principle. – Nay, as we in general give others credit for worth, in proportion as we possess it – I am easy with regard to the opinions of the *best* part of mankind. – I *rest* on my own.

323. To William Godwin

[London, April 20th, 1797]

Fanny is delighted with the thought of dining with you – But I wish you to eat your meat first, and let her come up with the pudding. I shall probably knock at your door in my way to Opie's;[873] but, should I not find you, let me now request you not to be too late this evening. Do not give Fanny butter with her pudding.[42]

[Unsigned]

872. The excerpt from a letter is undated. I am surmising that it might have been written after the furore that greeted Wollstonecraft's marriage in 1797. It was quoted in Hays's obituary notice for *Annual Necrology* as written to a 'friend'. Presumably she is the 'friend' but the original letter was not among the letters inherited by her great-great-grandniece, Anne F. Wedd, who deposited the correspondence in the Pforzheimer Library.

873. According to Godwin's diary, he and Wollstonecraft had supper at Opie's on 20 April, together with John Wolcòt (Peter Pindar). Possibly Wollstonecraft went earlier to the house to sit for the painting of her in her pregnant state. It is now in the National Portrait Gallery.

324. To George Dyson

Polygon N° 29, [Friday] morning [April 28th, 1797][874]

Mr. Godwin, my dear Sir, would fain persuade me that I was rude to your friend, last night, when I am sure I had no such intention, quite the contrary. I requested you, very naturally, to call on me soon, because I am more intimate with you, and with a reference to my novel,[875] which I meant to shew you, and not from the most distant thought of excluding him, whom I shall always be glad to see.

Should he have chanced to misunderstand me – pray set the matter right,

and believe me yours
Sincerely
Mary Godwin[876]

325. To George Dyson

N° 29 Polygon, Somers Town, Monday morning
[c. May 16th, 1797][877]

I have been reading your remarks and I find them a little discouraging. I mean I am not satisfied with the feelings which seem to be the result

---

874. Although the letter was headed 'Thursday Morning', the editors of SC point out (4, 886) that Wollstonecraft must actually have been writing on Friday morning, 28 April, the day recorded as postmark. Godwin's diary states that Dyson and a man called Dibbin (presumably the friend mentioned in Wollstonecraft's letter) had tea with him and Wollstonecraft on Thursday, 27 April.

875. The Wrongs of Woman; or Maria, about which Wollstonecraft later sought an opinion from Dyson.

876. This is the first occasion in the extant letters where Wollstonecraft used her married name.

877. The letter is undated though the abbreviation for the name of the month is clearly distinguishable in the postmark and reads [?16] MA [97]. The letter must have been written after Wollstonecraft and Godwin had moved into the Polygon in early April 1797 and probably after 28 April, the date of the letter in which Wollstonecraft wrote that she intended showing Dyson something concerning her novel.

of the perusal. I was perfectly aware that some of the incidents ought to be transpossed and heightened by more harmonious shading; and I wished to avail myself of yours and M^r G's criticism[878] before I began to adjust my events into a story, the outline of which I had sketched in my mind at the commencement; yet I am vexed and surprised at your not thinking the situation of Maria sufficiently important, and can only account for this want of – shall I say it? delicacy of feeling, by recollecting that you are a man – For my part I cannot suppose any situation more distressing than for a woman of sensibility with an improving mind to be bound, to such a man as I have described, for life – obliged to renounce all the humanizing affections, and to avoid cultivating her taste lest her perception of grace, and refinement of sentiment should sharpen to agony the pangs of disappointment.[879] Love, in which the imagination mingles its bewitching colouring must be fostered by delicacy – I should despise, or rather call her an ordinary woman, who could endure such a husband as I have sketched – yet you do not seem to be disgusted with him!!!

These appear to me (matrimonial despotism of heart & conduct) to be the particular wrongs of woman; because they degrade the mind. What are termed great misfortunes may more forcibly impress the mind of common readers, they have more of what might justly be termed *stage effect* but it is the delineation of finer sensations which, in my opinion, constitutes the merit of our best novels, this is what I have in view; and to shew the wrongs of different classes of women equally oppressive, though from the difference of education, necessarily various[.]

I write in haste, and, therefore, can only add that if you will drink tea with me wednesday or thursday, I should prefer wednesday, – I would converse with you on the subject. I am engaged to morrow and friday. –

I am not convinced that your remarks respecting the style of Jemima's[880] story is just; but I will reconsider it. You seem to [m]e

878. Dyson's and Godwin's criticism of *The Wrongs of Woman*.
879. Wollstonecraft's arguments here may have echoed those used over a decade before to rescue her sister Eliza from the unappreciated husband, Meredith Bishop.
880. Jemima, the illegitimate prostitute turned warder of the madhouse in which the heroine Maria is incarcerated, is the most innovative character of the novel.

to confound simplicity and vulgarity. Persons who have received a miscellaneous education, that is are educated by chance, and the energy of their own faculties, commonly display the mixture of refined and common language I have endeavoured to imitate. Besides I do not like *stalking horse* sentences.

One word more   strong Indignation in youth at injustice &c appears to me the constant attendant of superiority of understanding –

[Unsigned]

326. To William Godwin[881]

[London, c. May 16th, 1797]

Unwilling to suffer the original which I have transcribed on the opposite side of the sheet[882] to quit my own custody from a fear that if superfluous I am not inclined to consider as culpable, I have been perhaps superstitiously exact in retaining on the copy all the omissions and inaccuracies of the piece itself. I was not certain that to have made even slight alterations would not have been an unwarrantable usurpation on the rights of your judgment and there was certain charm as well as sanctity about these little negligences & rudenesses that would not permit me remove them. You receive it therefore with all its blemishes,[883] I wish you to be free of any regard to myself in your

Wollstonecraft lets her tell her own tale of working-class oppression, using educated but less sentimental and emotional language than Maria's.

881. This letter exists in a transcript owned by Burton R. Pollin and taken from the original formerly in the possession of Clinton N. Rutan. It was first published in *CL*. Although living with Godwin at the Polygon, Wollstonecraft addressed her note to him there. Perhaps she was writing it at a friend's house.

882. Wollstonecraft had copied out her reply to Dyson for Godwin.

883. Wollstonecraft retained her errors so that Godwin could properly judge the discussion. The retention also suggests that, although she submitted to Godwin's grammatical tutelage and solicited others' opinions, Wollstonecraft continued to revere her own self-expression. Godwin used part of her letter to Dyson, newly punctuated, to preface his edition of the unfinished *Wrongs of Woman* in *PW*.

use of it yet I feel as if the contents of it were of a nature that I should
be rather averse to being published *as addrest to me*.

[Unsigned]

327. *To William Godwin*

[London] Saturday morning [May 21st, 1797]

I am sorry we entered on an altercation this morning, which probably
has led us both to justify ourselves at the expence of the other. Perfect
confidence, and sincerity of action is, I am persuaded, incompatible
with the present state of reason.[884] I am sorry for the bitterness of your
expressions when you denominated, what I think a just contempt of a
false principle of action, *savage resentment, and the worst of vices*, not
because I winced under the lash; but as it led me to infer that the
coquetish candour of vanity was a much less generous motive.[885] I
know that respect is the shadow of wealth, and commonly obtained,
when that is wanted, by a criminal compliance with the prejudices of
society. Those who comply can alone tell whether they do it from
benevolence or a desire to secure their own easy. There is certainly an
original defect in my mind – for the cruelest experience will not
eradicate the foolish tendency I have to cherish, and expect to meet
with, romantic tenderness.

I should not have obtruded these remarks on you had not Montague
called me this morning, that is breakfasted with me, and invited me to
go with him and the Wedgwoods into the country tomorrow, and

884. Godwin's insistence on frankness had perhaps modified Wollstonecraft's. In *The
Rights of Woman* and in the letters to Imlay she had repeatedly promoted the quality
without any sense that it had to be limited.
885. The argument was probably over Wollstonecraft's dislike and resentment of
Godwin's friend Tom Wedgwood, who had already subsidised their marriage by £100:
£50 to settle Wollstonecraft's debts, and another to enable them, as Godwin put it, 'to
start fair'. At this time Wedgwood was staying with his brother, John, a banker, in a
grand house in Devonshire Place, Marylebone. Wollstonecraft often accused Godwin
of putting too high a value on Wedgwood's intellect because he, like others, valued
Wedgwood's wealth and status.

return the next day.[886] As I love the country and think with a poor mad woman, I knew, that there is God, or something, very consoliatory in the air,[887] I should, without hesitation, have accepted of the invitation; but for my engagement with your Sister.[888] To her even I should have made an apology, could I have seen her, or rather have stated that the circumstance would not occur again. As it is I am afraid of wounding her feelings, because an engagement often becomes important, in proportion as it has been anticipated. I began to write to ask your opinion respecting the propriety of sending to her, and feel, as I write, that I had better conquer my desire of contemplating unsophisticated nature, than give her a moments pain.

Mary –

328. To William Godwin

[London] Saturday morning [June 3ᵈ, 1797]

How glad I am that you did not go to day![889] I should have been very uneasy lest you should have pushed on in the teeth of the weather,

886. Godwin's young friend Basil Montagu was a widower, at present courting Tom Wedgwood's sister Sarah.

887. This is very much the poet William Cowper's view. Cowper was one of Wollstonecraft's favourite poets in her youth.

888. Hannah Godwin (d. 1817), William's sister, made a modest living as a dressmaker in London. She also wrote poetry.

889. Godwin and Montagu were planning a visit to the Wedgwoods in Etruria. The idea was prompted by Godwin owing to a surmised frostiness in his relations with Tom Wedgwood. The two men had not met often while Wedgwood was in London and, before returning to Etruria, Wedgwood had failed to take a promised leave of Godwin. When Godwin complained, Wedgwood replied that he had felt unwelcome and had been hurt by Montagu's report that Godwin found him cold. Godwin wanted to mollify Wedgwood, knowing both were 'inclined to a vicious reserve' and he suggested he come to visit Wedgwood in Etruria so that they could arrive at 'a mutual understanding' (Abinger MSS, Dep.b.215/5). The planned trip would be made more enticing by including visits to Godwin's sparring partner Dr Parr in Hatton, the radical novelist Robert Bage, and the evolutionary poetic botanist Erasmus Darwin. From Etruria Godwin would bring back a china mug for Fanny. Godwin had one further undivulged reason for his excursion: that he believed absence would increase his 'value' to his wife.

laying up a store of rheumatism in your bones – and who knows what effect it might have had on future generations!!!

Have you seen, or heard any thing of Montague?

[Unsigned]

329. *To William Godwin*

[London] Tuesday, June 6th [17]97

It was so kind and considerate in you to write sooner than I expected[890] that I cannot help hoping you would be disappointed at not receiving a greeting from me on your arrival at Etruria. If your heart was in your mouth, as I felt, just now at the sight of your hand, you may kiss or shake hands with the letter; and imagine with what affection it was written – If not – stand off, profane one!

I was not quite well the day after you left me; but it is past, and I am well and tranquil, excepting the disturbance produced by Master William's joy, who took it in his head to frisk a little at being informed

890. Godwin's first letter was written from Hampton Lucy. He and Montagu had spent the first night at Beaconsfield, reaching Oxford on Sunday, where, to cheer himself up, Montagu drank too much punch. He vomited it up in Hampton Lucy. Although unprepossessing, their horse had 'turned out admirably, & we were as gay as larks'. In this first letter Godwin was clearly wondering what style to adopt for his travel narrative; he decided on a jocular one, noting that at Oxford their host John Horseman had said of himself and Wollstonecraft, 'you & I are the two greatest men in the world'. Then he changed to more affectionate style: 'And now, my dear love, what do you think of me? Do not you find solitude infinitely superior to the company of a husband? Will you give me leave to return to you again, when I have finished my pilgrimage, & discharged the penance of absence? Take care of yourself, my love, & take care of William [the baby she was carrying]. Do not you be drowned, whatever I am. I remember at every moment all the accidents to which your condition subjects you, & wish I knew of some sympathy that could inform me from moment to moment, how you do, & how you feel. Tell Fanny something about me. Ask her where she thinks I am. Say I am a great way off, & going further & further, but that I shall turn round & come back again some day. Tell her I have not forgotten her little mug & that I shall chuse a very pretty one. Montagu said this morning about eight o'clock upon the road, Just now little Fanny is going to plungity plunge. Was he right? I love him very much. He is in such a hurry to see his chere adorable [Sarah Wedgwood], that, I believe, after all, we shall set forward this evening, & get to Etruria to-morrow' (*G&M*, pp. 78f.).

of your remembrance.[43] I begin to love this little creature, and to anticipate his birth as a fresh twist to a knot, which I do not wish to untie – Men are spoilt by frankness,[891] I believe, yet I must tell you that I love you better than I supposed I did, when I promised to love you for ever – and I will add what will gratify your benevolence, if not your heart, that on the whole I may be termed happy. You are a tender, affectionate creature; and I feel it thrilling through my frame giving, and promising pleasure.

Fanny wants to know 'what you are gone for,' and endeavours to pronounce Etruria. Poor papa is her word of kindness – She has been turning your letter on all sides, and has promised to play with Bobby till I have finished my answer.

I find you can write the kind of letter a friend ought to write, and give an account of your movements.[892] I hailed the sunshine, and moon-light and travelled with you scenting the fragrant gale – Enable me still to be your company, and I will allow you to peep over my shoulder, and see me under the shade of my green blind, thinking of you, and all I am to hear, and feel when you return – you may read my heart – if you will.

I have no information to give in return for yours. Holcroft is to dine with me on Saturday – So do not forget us when you drink your solitary glass; for nobody drinks wine at Etruria, I take for granted.[893] Tell me what you think of Everina's behaviour and situation;[894] and

891. Part of the ongoing debate over frankness. Conduct books for women stressed that women should not be forward in showing their love for a man. Dr Gregory in *A Father's Legacy to His Daughters* (London, 1774) advised women, even if they loved a man, 'never to discover to him the full extent of your love, no not although you marry him. That sufficiently shews your preference, which is all he is intitled to know. If he has delicacy, he will ask for no stronger proof of your affection, for your sake; if he has sense, he will not ask for his own' (pp. 87f.).

892. Godwin had begun his first letter: 'I write at this moment from Hampton Lucy in sight of the house and park of Sir Thomas Lucy, the great benefactor of mankind, who prosecuted William Shakespeare for deer stealing, & obliged him to take refuge in the metropolis. . . . Is that the right style for a letter?' (*G&M*, pp. 78f.).

893. Wollstonecraft was always irritated by the Wedgwood combination of high-mindedness and wealth. She herself was appalled at much drinking of alcohol, as can be seen from her *Letters from Sweden*, but the seemingly pretentious Wedgwood abstemiousness annoyed her.

894. See note 832.

treat her with as much kindness as you can – that is a little more than her manner, probably, will call forth – and I will repay you.[44]

I am not fatigued with solitude – yet I have not relished my solitary dinner. A husband is a convenient part of the furniture of a house, unless [he] be a clumsy fixture. I wish you, from my soul, to be riveted in my heart; but I do not desire to have you always at my elbow – though at this moment I did not care if you were. Yours truly and tenderly.

Mary.

Fanny forgets not the Mug[895]

Miss Pinkerton[896] seems content – I was amused by a letter she wrote home. She has more in her than comes out of her mouth. – My dinner is ready it is washing day – I am putting every thing in order for your return. — Adieu! —

I did not think it necessary to forward T.W.'s[897] letter to you —

330. To William Godwin

[London] Saturday, half after one o'clock [June 10th, 1797]

Your letter of wednesday, I did not receive till just now, and I have only *a half* an hour to express the kind emotions which are clustering about my heart, or my letter will have no chance of reaching Gen

---

895. On 10 June Godwin wrote, 'Tell Fanny we have chosen a mug for her, & another for Lucas. There is an F on hers, & an L on his, shaped in a garland of flowers, of green & orange-tawny alternately. With respect to their beauty, you will set it forth with such eloquence as your imagination will supply' (*G&M*, pp. 91f.).

896. This is the first mention of Miss Pinkerton, who caused Wollstonecraft such misery in her last months of life. Godwin's diary records meetings with N. and A. Pinkerton (possibly two women or more likely Ann Pinkerton sometimes called Nancy). Rather like Mary Hays before her, she had been turning emotionally to Godwin and bombarding him with letters.

897. Thomas Wedgwood. Wollstonecraft later forwarded the letter, as appears from Godwin's letter of 12 June, 'I received your letter, accompanying T W's . . .' (*G&M*, p. 97).

Tarlton[898] to day, and to-morrow being sunday, two posts would be lost. My last letter, of course you had not got, though I reckoned on its reaching you wednesday evening.

I read T. W. letter – I thought it would be affectation not to open it, as I knew the hand. It did not quite please me.[899] He appears to me to be half spoilt by living with his inferiors, in point of understanding, and to expect that homage to be paid to his abilities, which the world will readily pay to his fortune. I am afraid that all men are materially injured by inheriting wealth; and, without knowing it, become important in their own eyes, in consequence of an advantage they contemn.

I am not much surprised at Miss Parr's conduct.[900] You may remember that I did not give her credit for as much sensibility (at least the sensibility which is the mother of sentiment, and delicacy of mind) as you did, and her present conduct confirms my opinion. Could a woman of delicacy seduce and marry a fool? She will be unhappy, unless a situation in life, and a good table, to prattle at, are sufficient to fill up the void of affection.[901] This ignoble mode of rising in the world is the consequence of the present system of female education.

---

898. Godwin and Wollstonecraft had decided to use for their letters the frank of Banastre Tarleton, MP for Liverpool and unsatisfactory lover of Mary Robinson.

899. In his letter Wedgwood declared he was hurt by Godwin's attitude when he was in London and did not welcome the proposed visit. He wrote that he found Godwin's manner 'distant & cold'. Godwin had of course not received this letter when he set out to visit Etruria with Basil Montagu.

900. Sarah Ann Parr, daughter of the liberal clergyman, teacher, and scholar, Dr Samuel Parr (1747–1825) of Hatton, Warwickshire. Earlier Godwin had met the 22-year-old Sarah on a trip to her father; when she visited London she began writing flirtatiously to him, claiming she had resolved when a child 'never to marry – a wise man'. This resolve was based on her mother's advice and experience. When she heard of Godwin's marriage, so much against his principles, Sarah Parr promised him 'the most complete roasting'. On the journey to Hatton Godwin and Montagu met Dr Parr on the road. He called off their visit since on the previous night Sarah had eloped to Gretna Green with one of his pupils, the 28-year-old John Wynne of Plasnewydd, Denbigh, Wales. Since the young man was the son of a wealthy MP, Godwin suspected that, although he protested, the doctor was not utterly distraught.

901. Wollstonecraft's remarks proved correct. The marriage was unhappy and violent. Sarah produced three daughters, then sued for separate maintenance. Her health deteriorated under the strain of lawsuits, and she died at her father's house on 8 July 1810.

I have little to tell you of myself. I am very well. M^rs. Reveley[902] drank tea with me one evening and I spent a day with her, which would have been a very pleasant one, had I not been a little too much fatigued by a previous visit to M^r. Barry.[903] Fanny often talks of you and made M^rs. Reveley laugh by telling her, when she could not find the monkey to shew it to Henry, 'that it was gone into the country.'[904]

I supposed that Everina would assume some airs at seeing you[905] – She has very mistaken notions of dignity of character.[45]

Pray tell me the precise time, I mean when it is fixed – I do believe I shall be glad to see you! – of your return, and I will keep a good look out – William is all alive – and my appearance no longer doubtful – you, I dare say, will perceive the difference, what a fine thing it is to be a man![46]

You were very good to write such a long letter. Adieu! Take care of yourself – now I have ventured on you, I should not like to lose you.

Mary —

---

902. Maria Reveley (née James), later Mrs Gisborne (1770–1836), clever, pretty wife of the radical architect Willey Reveley. She was raised in Rome and Constantinople. She often met Godwin without her husband and had an assignation with him in Greenwich in January 1795. Godwin seems to have hung back from an affair but, of the women in whom he had had some interest before Wollstonecraft, she was the most significant. According to Mary Shelley, 'Two ladies . . . shed tears when he announced his marriage: Mrs Inchbald & Mrs Reveley. . . . Mrs Reveley feared to lose a kind & constant friend, but becoming intimate with Mary Wollstonecraft, she soon learned to appreciate her virtues & to love her. . . . A cordial intercourse subsisted between the parties' (Harriet Jump (ed.), *Lives of the Great Romantics III. Godwin, Wollstonecraft & Mary Shelley by their Contemporaries*, London, 1999, 2, 250, and *WG*, 1, 239).

903. James Barry (1741–1806), an historical artist and for a time before his dismissal in 1799 professor of painting at the Royal Academy. An Irish patriot and committed republican, he was a friend of Godwin. After her death he wrote of the 'eloquent, generous, amiable sensibility of the celebrated and long-to-be lamented Mary Wollstonecraft' and praised her 'honest heart' (*A Letter to the Dilettanti Society, respecting the Obtention of certain Matters essentially necessary for the Improvement of Public Taste, and for accomplishing the original Views of the Royal Academy of Great Britain*, London, 1798, p. 68).

904. Henry was Maria Reveley's young son. Godwin replied, 'Tell Fanny the green monkey has not come to Etruria' (*G&M*, p. 98).

905. Godwin had written, 'Your sister would not come down to see me last night at supper, but we met at breakfast this morning. I have nothing to say about her' (*G&M*, p. 88). Everina was slightly more forthcoming when they all visited the Wedgwood pottery.

331. To William Godwin

[London] Monday, almost twelve o'clock[906] [June 19th, 1797]

One of the pleasures you tell me, that you promised yourself from your journey was the effect your absence might produce on me[907] – Certainly at first my affection was increased; or rather was more alive – But now it is just the contrary.[908] Your latter letters might have been address to any body – and will serve to remind you w[h]ere you have been, though they resemble nothing less than mementos of affection.[909]

I wrote to you to Dr. Parr's you take no notice of my letter – Previous to your departure I requested you not to torment me by leaving the day of your return undecided. But whatever tenderness you took away with you seems to have evaporated in the journey, and new objects – and the homage of vulgar minds,[910] restored you to your icy Philosophy.

You told me that your journey could not take up less than three

906. i.e. midnight. Wollstonecraft was staying up late to await Godwin's return.
907. On 10 June Godwin had written, 'One of the pleasures I promised myself in my excursion, was to increase my value in your estimation, & I am not disappointed. What we possess without intermission, we inevitably hold light; it is a refinement in voluptuousness, to submit to voluntary privations' (G&M, p. 90).
908. Godwin had been afraid of Wollstonecraft's moodiness while he was absent. In a letter of 12 June when he had failed to receive an expected letter, he wrote, 'How many possible accidents will the anxiety of affection present to one's thoughts? What am I to think? Not serious ones I hope: in that case, I trust I should have heard. But head-aches; but sickness of the heart, a general loathing of life & of me. Do not give place to this worst of diseases! The least I can think is, that you recollect me with less tenderness & impatience than I reflect on you' (G&M, p. 97).
909. Encouraged by Wollstonecraft's appreciation of his letter of 5 June, Godwin had written five more detailed letters telling of his stay in Etruria and his progress through Warwick and Derby, his encounter with Bage, a visit to Dr Parr, to whose house the eloping daughter and new son-in-law had returned, and a detour to see Coventry Fair.
910. Wollstonecraft always imagined Godwin seduced by Tom Wedgwood's flattery. In fact the two men had had a prickly meeting and Godwin had been silent much of the time.

days,[911] therefore as you were to visit D[r]. D and P – Saturday was the probable day – you saw neither – yet you have been a week on the road – I did not wonder, but approved of your visit to M[r]. Bage[912] – But a *Shew*[913] which you waited to see & did not see, appears to have been equally attractive. I am at a loss to guess how you could have been from Saturday to sunday night travelling from C——y to C——ge – In short – your being so late to night,[914] and the chance of your not coming, shews so little consideration, that unless you suppose me a stick or a stone, you must have forgot to think – as well as to feel, since you have been on the wing. I am afraid to add what I feel – Good night. —

[Unsigned]

332. *To William Godwin*

[London, June 25th, 1797]

I know that you do not like me to go to Holcroft's. I think you right in the principle; but a little wrong in the present application.[915]

911. Godwin had written from Etruria on 12 June, 'We propose leaving Etruria at four o'clock to-morrow morning (Tuesday). Our journey cannot take less than three days . . .' He expected to arrive either 'Friday or Saturday' but added, 'Do not however count upon anything as certain respecting it, and so torment yourself with expectation' (*G&M*, pp. 97f.).

912. Robert Bage (1728–1801) was a self-educated paper-manufacturer. After the failure of an iron factory, at the age of fifty-three he began writing novels. He was prolific and his novels include *The Fair Syrian* (1787), *Man as He Is* (1792) and *Hermsprong; or, Man as He Is Not* (1796), in which he had enthusiastically used Wollstonecraft's feminist arguments. When Godwin returned to London he and Wollstonecraft read *The Fair Syrian*.

913. Godwin and Montagu planned to visit Coventry Fair to see 'a procession of all the trades, with a female, representative of lady Godiva at their head, dressed in a close dress, to represent nakedness.' However, they arrived too late: 'We saw the crowd which was not yet dispersed, & the booths in the fair, but the lady, the singularity of the scene, was retired' (17 June, *G&M*, p. 105).

914. Godwin's diary records that he travelled from Coventry to Cambridge and arrived in London on 20 June.

915. According to Godwin's diary, he and Wollstonecraft dined together at Holcroft's on Sunday, 25 June.

When I lived alone I always dined on a sunday, with company in the evening, if not at dinner, at St P's.[916] Generally also of a Tuesday, and some other day at Fuselis.

I like to see new faces, as a study – and since my return from Norway, or rather since I have accepted of invitations, I have dined every third sunday at Twiss's. Nay, oftener, for they sent for me, when they had any extraordinary company. I was glad to go, because my lodgings was noisy of a Sunday, and Mr. J——s house and spirits were so altered, that my visiting him depressed instead of exhilirated my min[d].[47]

I am then, you perceive, thrown out of my track, and have not traced another.[917] – But so far from wishing to obtrude on yours, I had written to Mrs. Jackson, and mentioned sunday – and am now sorry that I did not fix on to day – as [one] of the days for sitting for my picture.[918]

To Mr. Johnson – I would go without ceremony – but it is not convenient for me, at present to make haphazard visits.

Should Carlisle,[919] chance to call you this morning send him to me – But, by himself, for he often has a companion with him, which would defeat my purpose. —

[Unsigned]

916. 72 St Paul's Churchyard, where Joseph Johnson had his shop and where he entertained.

917. Several once hospitable acquaintances had dropped Wollstonecraft since her marriage, including the Twisses and Sarah Siddons. Wollstonecraft may have expressed her bitter feelings at social ostracism in *The Wrongs of Woman* when she wrote, 'if a woman has been practising insincerity, and neglecting her child to manage an intrigue, she would still have been visited and respected. If, instead of openly living with her lover, she could have condescended to call into play a thousand arts, which, degrading her own mind, might have allowed the people who were not deceived, to pretend to be so, she would have been caressed and treated like an honourable woman' (*Works*, 1, 176).

918. Wollstonecraft was sitting for her portrait with John Opie.

919. Carlisle was a friend of both Godwin and Wollstonecraft (see note 793). Presumably Wollstonecraft wished to consult him about her pregnancy and, since she favoured female attendance, about possible midwives.

333. *To William Godwin*

[London, June 26ᵗʰ, 1797]

The weather, I believe, will not permit me to go out to day, and I am not very sorry for I feel a little the worse for my yesterday's walk – or rather confinement at dinner – I have not been able to employ myself this morning, and have ordered my dinner early hoping to make it up in the evening – I send for the paper – and I should ask you for some novel, or tale, to while away the time 'till dinner, did I suppose you had one.[920]

[Unsigned]

334. *To Maria Reveley*

[London, Monday night, June 26ᵗʰ, 1797][921]

Will you, my dear Mʳˢ Reveley, dine with us next wednesday, to meet the same party as you did before, with the addition of Mʳ. Godwin.

He desires me to say many fine things for him to excuse his not visiting you last wednesday; but, is it not sufficient to tell you, that he only came home on tuesday.

Pray come or he will be *in despair* (that ought to have been said in French)[922] at not being able to keep his engagement with you.

Your coming with this party is not to prevent you from paying me

---

920. Godwin was not a devotee of novels although in 1784, as an impecunious writer, he had churned out three tales of seduction and betrayal: *Italian Letters, or The History of Count de St Julian*; *Damon and Delia. A Tale*; and *Imogen, a Pastoral Romance, from the Ancient British*.

921. The date of this letter derives from Wollstonecraft's statement that Godwin 'came home [from Etruria] on Tuesday' and from the diary entry noting that he and Wollstonecraft entertained a party of six, including Maria Reveley, on Wednesday, 28 June (see *SC*, 1, 182f.). As Wollstonecraft points out in her postscript, she had wrongly dated the letter 'Tuesday night'.

922. Presumably Wollstonecraft was mocking Godwin's employment of French phrases, especially in emotional or socially embarrassing situations.

a visit *hap-hazard*, alone, when I will shew you one of Mr Godwin's epistles, I mean one addressed to him, from another Fair[923] in intellectual distress – But this *entre nous*. Good night! yours Sincerely.

Mary Godwin.

Tuesday night.

I have written Tuesday but remember that it is only Monday –

335. *To Maria Reveley*

Polygon, Wednesday morning [c. spring/summer 1797][924]

Little Fanny would be very glad to have the promised Rake, in the course of a day or two, because she wishes to make Hay in the fields opposite to her house. If Henry will bring it she shall like to have a tumble with him on the Hay. The Pitchfork has been used every day.

Fanny sends her love to Henry, and wishes him to direct his next letter to herself, and she will put it up with her books, in her own closet.

Mama hopes to see Mrs. Reveley on Saturday (half after four) if not before. — She sent a note yesterday by the Post. —

[Unsigned]

923. Probably Miss Pinkerton. The other 'fair' lady might have been Mary Hays. Her intellectual involvement with Godwin had been made public in her novel *Memoirs of Emma Courtney*, which quoted some of their correspondence.
924. The letter must have been written between early April and late August when Fanny and Wollstonecraft were living at the Polygon.

336. To Maria Reveley(?)[925]

[London, c. spring/summer 1797]

Dear Madam,

Little Eliza[926] has been here two or three hours; and appears so horrified at not seeing her playmates, that I send to remind you of your promise. The day[48] is so fine it would be a pity to deprive them of the expected pleasure; nay, we hope to see Henry return with the messenger, though you should have chanced to misunderstand me.

[Unsigned]

337. To William Godwin

[London] Monday morning [July 3d, 1797]

M^{rs}. Reveley can have no doubt about to-day, so we are to stay at home. I have a design on you this evening, to keep you quite to myself (I hope then nobody will call!) and make you read the play —

I was thinking of a favourite song of my poor friend, Fanny's[927] – 'In a vacant rainy day you shall be wholly mine' – &c[928]

---

925. *CL* assumed that the letter, although lacking an address, was intended for Maria Reveley because her son Henry was one of Fanny's playmates. It is copied from a transcript of the original MS in *Supp.*, p. 316. Durant states that Frederick Locker-Lampson had inserted the note in his copy of *Mary, A Fiction*. According to *A Catalogue of the Printed Books, Autograph Letters, Drawings and Pictures, Collected by Frederick Locker-Lampson* (London, 1886) his Rowfant library included a copy of the 1788 edition of *Mary, A Fiction* with an 'Autograph note (1 page 8vo) inserted'.

926. Probably Eliza (1789–1827), daughter of John and Eliza Fenwick. She would have a difficult life. At seventeen she became an actress in private theatres, eventually moving to Barbados where she married fellow-actor Rutherford in 1812; he deserted her and their four children. In 1814 her mother joined her in running a school which failed and in 1822 they and the children moved to New Haven, Connecticut, where Eliza jr. died, leaving her mother to raise the grandchildren, two of whom drowned. For her mother Eliza Fenwick, see note 941.

927. The dead friend, Fanny Blood.

928. Allan Ramsay's poem *The Kind Reception*, sung to the tune of *Auld Lang Syne*. It opens with 'Should auld Acquaintance be forgot, / Though they return with Scars?'.

Unless the weather prevents you from taking your accustomed walk, call on me this morning, for I have something to say to you. —

[Unsigned]

338. To William Godwin

[London, July 3ᵈ, 1797]

I have been very well till just now – and hope to get rid of the present pain before I see you. I have ordered some boiled mutton, as the best thing for me, and as the weather will probably prevent you from walking out, you will, perhaps, have no objection to dining at four. Send some more of the letters; and, if you bring *more* with you, we might read them after dinner, and reserve my favourite *act* till we were sure of not being interrupted.[929]

You are to send me yesterday's as well as to day's Paper. Yours truly and kindly —

[Unsigned]

339. To William Godwin

[London, July 4ᵗʰ, 1797]

I am not well – no matter. The weather is such, I believe, as to permit us to keep our appointment – and it may as well be over.

What will you do about Addington?[930]

Let me have the remainder of Mʳˢ. V's letters, when you have finished

929. In his diary Godwin mentions reading 'Vaughan's letters' on 1, 2, 3, 4 and 5 July, a day after he had noted 'Addington calls' on 29 and 30 June (see next letter). According to his diary entry for 3 July, he and Wollstonecraft were reading act 1 of *Idomenée* together (Abinger MSS, Dep.e.503).

930. Addington, a frequent visitor to Godwin, could be either Samuel Reymer Addington (b. 1755) or Philip Addington (b. 1771), both sons of Stephen Addington (1729–96), Dissenting minister and tutor of Mile End Academy; see also note 953.

them, that I may not prevent your returning them, when Addington calls.[931]

To be frank with you, your behaviour yesterday brought on my troublesome pain.[932] But I lay no great stress on that circumstance, because, were not my health in a more delicate state than usual, it could not be so easily affected. I am absurd to look for the affection which I have only found in my own tormented heart; and how can you blame me for taken refuge in the idea of a God, when I despair of finding sincerity on earth?

I think you *wrong* – yes; with the most decided conviction I dare to say it, having still in my mind the *unswervable* principles of justice and humanity. You judge not in your own case as in that of another. You give a softer name to folly and immorality when it flatters – yes, I must say it – your vanity, than to mistaken passion, when it was extended to another – you termed Miss Hay's conduct insanity when only her own happiness was envolved[933] – I cannot forget the strength of your

931. Mrs Vaughan might be the author of the letters mentioned in Letter 338. A list of contacts at the back of one of Godwin's diaries shows that he knew several people named Vaughan: (1) 'B Vaughan' (met in 1779); (2) 'S Vaughan' (met in 1782); and (3) 'F Vaughan' (met in 1793). The third of these is Felix Vaughan, a radical lawyer and one of the defence counsel at the 1794 treason trials; the first is Benjamin Vaughan (1751–1835), Unitarian radical politician and journalist, friend of Price, Priestley, Horne Tooke and Paine. He fled to France in 1794 and then to the US but frequently visited London. Mrs V may have been Benjamin's wife Sarah Vaughan (née Manning), left behind in London during his absences and befriended by Godwin, whom she often visited. Godwin's diary states that a Mrs Vaughan arrived on 23 August and did not leave until 13 September, three days after Wollstonecraft's death. She became a friend of Mary Hays. For Thursday, 14 September, Godwin's diary entry records having supper with the Fenwicks and 'PV', possibly Benjamin's third son, Petty Vaughan, about twelve at the time (see *SC*, 1, 197). Or of course Mrs V might have been an estranged wife of an unknown Mr Vaughan. Godwin might have been helping her to publish her letters or a novel in letters since he frequently read manuscripts for his women friends. *CL* suggests the bluestocking Elizabeth Vesey (?1715–1791) but in a letter of 28 July 1769, Elizabeth Carter called her 'a very idle Correspondent' (Montagu Pennington (ed.), *A Series of Letters between Mrs Elizabeth Carter and Miss Catherine Talbot, from the Year 1741 to 1770*, London, 1809, 3, 364).
932. Wollstonecraft was upset by Godwin's indulgent attitude to Miss Pinkerton, who was writing letters to him and had often been in his company alone during the past few weeks, as his diary reveals.
933. Godwin had been occasionally sympathetic and often exasperated by Mary Hays's much-expressed misery over her unrequited love for William Frend.

expressions – and you treat with a mildness calculated to foster it, a romantic, selfishness, and pamper conceit, which will even lead the object to – I was going to say misery – but I believe her incapable of feeling it. Her want of sensibility with respect to her family first disgusted me – Then to obtrude herself on me, to see affection, and instead of feeling sympathy, to endeavour to undermined it, certainly resembles the conduct of the fictitious being, to whose dignity she aspires. Yet you, at the very moment, commenced a correspondence with her, whom you had previously almost neglected – you brought me a letter without a conclusion – and you changed countenance at the reply – My old wounds bleed afresh – What did not blind confidence, and unsuspecting truth, lead me to – my very soul trembles sooner than endure the hundred part of what I have suffer, I could wish my poor Fanny and self asleep at the bottom of the sea.

One word more – I never blamed the woman for whom I was abandoned. I offered to see; nay, even to live with her,[934] and I should have tried to improve her. But even she was deceived with respect to my character, and had her scruples when she heard the truth[49] – But enough of the effusions of a sick heart – I only intend to write a line or two[935] –

The weather looks cloudy; but it is not necessary immediately to decide.

[Unsigned]

934. In *Memoirs* (pp. 137f.), Godwin recorded Wollstonecraft's proposal to live with Imlay and his mistress. See Letter 207.
935. Godwin replied, 'I am much hurt at your note' (*G&M*, p. 112). He could not answer it at once since he had company. The pair must have talked over the matter amicably since Wollstonecraft's next letters are no longer distraught.

340. To William Godwin

[London, July 7ᵗʰ, 1797]

Opie has just been here to put me off till Sunday, papa. Should the morning prove favourable have you any objection to calling with me, by way of sparing my blushes, on Mʳˢ. Carr – & Nichcolson.[936]

Remember that I have no particular desire to interfere with your convenience – only say the word.

I have just recollected that Sir R. Smith[937] is to set out to day – Had you not better forward your letter, for Miss W——[938] under cover to him immediately. —

[Unsigned]

341. To William Godwin

[London, July 7ᵗʰ, 1797]

Don't laugh at me – I saw the letter and thought today Tuesday –

I shall be ready at half past two – Between then and three I shall expect you – Have you now sent me all Mʳˢ. V's letters? You forgot

936. William Nicholson (1753–1815), scientist and inventor, interested in phrenology. On 18 September 1797, he examined the head of the infant Mary, daughter of Wollstonecraft and Godwin, and wrote an analysis of her character based on his observations, judging that 'the outline of the forehead' was 'such as I have invariably and exclusively seen in subjects who possessed considerable memory and intelligence', while the 'eyes and eyebrows' were familiar to him 'in subjects of quick sensibility, irritable, scarcely irascible, and surely not given to rage' (*WG*, 1, 289f.). Mrs Carr might be the wife of either Carrs mentioned in note 823. Wollstonecraft's embarrassment was presumably due to her advanced pregnancy, apparent to the public rather too soon after her marriage. Godwin replied on the same day that he would obey 'with a pious & chearful obedience, & will be ready to squire you to Thornhaugh & Newman Street at any hour you shall appoint' (*G&M*, p. 113). Nicholson apparently lived in Newman Street and presumably Mrs Carr was in Thornhaugh Street.

937. Sir Robert Smith, an acquaintance of Godwin.

938. Possibly Helen Maria Williams in Paris, whom both Wollstonecraft and Godwin knew. Godwin replied on the same day: 'Sir Rob. Smyth told me he should set out on

that I wished to see the one addressed to you – I have been very much affected by her account of one scene with her husband. —

[Unsigned]

342. To William Godwin[939]

[London, July 13th, 1797]

Send me the Fair Syrian[940] – That is the first volume, if you have not finished it. I still feel a little fatigue from my walk –

[Unsigned]

343. To William Godwin

[London, July 15th, 1797]

Mr. Johnson goes to Dorking to day, of course will not dine with us to morrow.

I invited The Fenwicks[941] to drink tea with us to morrow – They had mentioned to you an intention of coming to day – and I wished to put it off. But you may be free notwithstanding.

I do not quite understand your note – I shall make no comments on the *kindness* of it, because I ought not to expect it according to my

---

Tuesday: if you will tell me how you come to know of his having delayed his journey, I should eagerly make use of his conveyance' (*G&M*, pp. 113f.).

939. On the back of Wollstonecraft's note Godwin wrote: 'We will not refuse to enjoy now, from an apprehension that we shall one day cease to enjoy. Carpe vitam.'

940. Robert Bage's third novel, published in 1787.

941. John Fenwick (d. 1820), radical editor of several short-lived journals, was a close friend of Godwin. He was also spendthrift and drunken, and inspired the character Ralph Bigod created by Charles Lamb in *Elia: The Two Races of Men* (1820). He spent much time in debtors' prison. His wife Eliza Fenwick (d. 1840), author of the novel *Secresy* (1795) and later of children's books, became a close friend of Wollstonecraft. In 1800 she separated from John and raised her children alone.

ideal – You say 'WITHOUT a determined purpose.'[942] Do you wish me to have one?

[Unsigned]

344. To William Godwin

[London, July 18th, 1797]

I have thought more of it, and think that I ought to write on the subject which, gave me some pain,[943] at first. I should only wish you so far to allude to it, as to convince her that we coincide in opinion. I am very well – and will walk to Kearsley's's[944] –

Say when?

[Unsigned]

345. To William Godwin

[London, July 23[d], 1797]

If it interfere with no previous plan will you accompany me, before dinner, the later the better, to see those Stupid Carrs?[945]

942. Earlier in the day Godwin had written: 'I thought you expressed yourself unkindly to me in the beginning last night. I am not conscious of having deserved it. But you amply made up your injustice, in what followed; & I was tranquil & easy. To day you have called on me, & said two or three grating things. Let me intreat you, not to give me pain of this sort, without a determined purpose, & not to suppose that I am philosopher enough not to feel it' (G&M, p. 115).
943. Godwin's relationship with Miss Pinkerton.
944. Godwin records in his diary a visit he and Wollstonecraft made on Kearsley – presumably a member of the family of the bookseller George Kearsley who had died in 1790. The bookshop was located at 46 Fleet Street: see Ian Maxted, The London Book Trades 1775–1800 (Old Woking, 1977), p. 127.
945. Godwin records in his diary that he and Wollstonecraft called on the Carrs on 23 July, but found them not at home.

Do not suppose it is necessary to go with me; for I only want to go, because I ought – and such a *motive* will not spoil by keeping.[946]

Fine morality!

[Unsigned]

346. *To William Godwin*[947]

[London, July 31st, 1797]

Saddlers-Wells[948] has been the breakfast [   ]
day is cool, and we may as well not wear out [   ]
If it be convenient to you – determine – and [   ]
hour we must dine to have sufficient time [   ]
slowly, and have a few minutes to rest, pre [   ]
commencement.

347. *To William Godwin*

[London, August 1st, 1797]

No – But you will remember that you have an engagement with a Dame ce soir.[949] –

[Unsigned]

946. Godwin wrote, 'I think it not right, mama, that you should walk alone in the middle of the day. Will you indulge me in the pleasure of walking with me?' He had written before he received Wollstonecraft's note.

947. The letter has been badly damaged.

948. Godwin's diary entry for 31 July notes 'Sadler's Wells; Askins, & Sadak & Kalastrade, w. M, & c'. Among the performances exhibited at Sadler's Wells during this time were 'A new Burletta, called the MAGICIAN, or, The Invisible Lover', a dance entitled 'the CUSTOM of ZURICH', a Pantomime called 'SADAK and KALASTRADE, or, the Waters of Oblivion', and Mr Askin's 'Wonderful Performances of VENTRILOQUISM'. See *The Times* for Saturday, 22 July and 3 August.

949. Wollstonecraft wrote these words at the bottom of a note from Godwin which read: 'I forgot to tell you that I intend, if the weather favour me, to dine at Johnson's to day. Do you know any reason why I should not?' (*G&M*, p. 117). Godwin's diary entry for 1 August records a supper engagement with Amelia Alderson and Opie.

348. To William Godwin

[London] Wednesday morning [August 9th, 1797]

If you find nothing *objectionable* in the enclosed note[950] put a wafer in it, and send it by Mary. I do not now feel the least resentment, and I merely write, because I expect to see her to day or tomorrow, and truth demands that I should not seem ignorant of the steps she takes to extort visits from you.

    If you have the slightest wish to prevent my writing at all – say so[951] – I shall think you actuated by humanity, though I may not coincide in opinion, with respect to the measures you take to effect your purpose.

[Unsigned]

349. To Miss Pinkerton

[London] Wednesday morning [August 9th, 1797]

Miss Pinkerton, I forbear to make any comments on your strange behaviour; but, unless you can determine to behave with propriety, you must excuse me for expressing a wish not to see you at our house.

Mary Godwin[952]

950. The subsequent note to Miss Pinkerton. Although Wollstonecraft had gained her point with Godwin over the impropriety of his relations with Miss Pinkerton, she did not think he had done sufficient to remedy the situation. Miss Pinkerton may have gone away for a short stay and, before she began 'extorting' further visits, Wollstonecraft drafted an admonitory note, Letter 349.

951. Godwin replied on the same day, 'I am fully sensible of your attention in this matter, & believe you are right. Will you comply one step further, & defer sending your note till one or two o'clock? The delay can be of no consequence, & I like to have a thing lay a little time on my mind before I judge' (*G&M*, p. 119). Godwin substituted 'incomprehensible conduct' for Wollstonecraft's phrase 'strange behaviour', then returned the note to be recopied and sent.

952. Wollstonecraft's letter prompted the reply from Miss Pinkerton, 'At length I am sensible of the impropriety of my conduct. Tears and communication afford me relief.' The note was signed 'N Pinkerton' and dated 'Saturday July 10'. The date is not correct since 10 July was a Monday and her note must follow Wollstonecraft's written

350. To William Godwin

[London, August 19th, 1797]

I send you Addington's Letters.[953] I find the melancholy ones the most interesting – There is a grossness in the raptures from which I turn – They excite no sympathy – Have no voluptuousness for me. —

Fanny promises to return at your *bidding* – and would not be said nay —

[Unsigned]

351. To James Marshall

[London] Monday morning [August 21st, 1797][954]

My Dear Sir,

I thank you for your kind enquiries; I am very well, only a little impatient to regain my activity, and to reduce to some *shapeliness* the portly shadow, which meets my eye when I take a musing walk.

I thank you for your present, and your manner of offering it.

Will you take charge of a fruit knife, which Miss Jones left behind.

Mary Godwin.

reprimand. In her confusion Miss Pinkerton probably wrote July for August, but 10 August, the day following Wollstonecraft's letter, was not a Saturday.

953. Possibly a reference to the letters of Mrs V., for which Addington seems to have been responsible.

954. The date has been calculated from a reference in Godwin's diary to a visit by Louisa Jones. She was a friend of Godwin's sister Hannah. Following the death of Wollstonecraft, for a short time she took over the duties of housekeeper for Godwin and foster mother of the two children.

352. *To William Godwin*

[London, August 30th, 1797][955]

I have no doubt of seeing the animal to day; but must wait for M[rs]. Blenkinsop[956] to guess at the hour – I have sent for her – Pray send me the news paper – I wish I had a novel, or some book of sheer amusement, to excite curiosity, and while away the time – Have you any thing of the kind?

[Unsigned]

353. *To William Godwin*

[London, August 30th, 1797]

M[rs]. Blenkensop tells me that Every thing is in a fair way, and that there is no fear of the event being put off till another day – Still, *at*

---

955. The beginning of Wollstonecraft's labour. The previous days are fully chronicled in Godwin's diary. From it one can see that on 25 August Wollstonecraft had felt a bit unwell, but the following days were uneventful, and she and Godwin continued their social life. Mary Hays called and Godwin saw Fuseli and Inchbald, but without Wollstonecraft. On Tuesday, 29 August Wollstonecraft and Godwin walked together and in the evening read Goethe's *Werther*. On the 30th after she had felt the onset of labour, Godwin left the Polygon for his separate apartment in Evesham Buildings. He was visited by a couple of friends, including Dyson, and he read *Mary, A Fiction*.

956. Possibly the midwife was called Mary Holby Blenkinsop since, although Godwin and Wollstonecraft gave her name as Blenkinsop, the registration document of their daughter Mary is signed by Mary Holby, who declared herself present at the birth. Mrs Blenkinsop was an experienced midwife and matron at the Westminster Lying-In Hospital. As such she was inferior in status to the male doctors. There was much debate at the time about the use of female midwives or male obstetricians who could use instruments such as forceps. Poorer women would have used midwives. Inchbald later remarked, '[Wollstonecraft] was attended by a woman, whether from partiality or economy I cant tell – from no affected prudery I am sure' (*Memoirs of Mrs Inchbald*, London, 1833, 2, 14; Durant, *Supp.*, p. 324). Wollstonecraft believed that 'decency' as well as policy allotted midwifery to women and she saw the earlier preference for the midwife as proof of 'the former delicacy of the sex'. In *The Rights of Woman* she wrote, 'Women might certainly study the art of healing, and be physicians as well as nurses' (*Works*, 5, 218). Mrs Blenkinsop arrived at the Polygon by 9 o'clock.

present, she thinks, I shall not immediately be freed from my load[957] –
I am very well – Call before dinner time, unless you receive another
message from me –

[Unsigned]

354. To William Godwin

[London, August 30th, 1797][958]

M[rs]. Blenkinsop tells me that I am in the most natural state, and can
promise me a safe delivery – But that I must have a little patience[959]

[Unsigned]

957. The baby was clearly in the right position, so there was no fear of a breech birth,
but a long labour was not welcomed by midwives.

958. On the top of the note, Godwin wrote 'three o'clock'.

959. In *Memoirs* (p. 28) Godwin noted that Wollstonecraft never forgot her mother's
last words: 'A little patience and all will be over.' Echoes of these words recur throughout the letters and were used as the fictional mother's last words in *The Wrongs of
Woman*, ch. 8. They are probably Wollstonecraft's last written words. The next ten
days of Wollstonecraft's slow dying are recorded in *Memoirs* as well as Godwin's
diary. When the placenta failed to follow the birth of baby Mary at 11.20 at night, the
midwife declared she 'dared not proceed any further' (p. 176) and sent Godwin for her
senior colleague Dr Louis Poignand. When Poignand arrived, he pulled out the placenta;
it broke into pieces while Wollstonecraft repeatedly fainted away with pain. In the afternoon Wollstonecraft asked for Dr Fordyce, which irritated Poignand. Fordyce came
about 3 o'clock and approved the treatment of Poignand and Blenkinsop. By Sunday
Wollstonecraft was suffering uncontrollable fits which signalled septicaemia, and
Godwin concluded that this day 'finally decided on the fate of the object dearest to my
heart that the universe contained' (p. 180). In the early hours of the following Thursday
Godwin fetched Poignand again. When he found that Fordyce had been in attendance as
well as their friend Carlisle, he declined to treat Wollstonecraft further. Maria Reveley
took Fanny and then the baby Mary to her home, while Eliza Fenwick moved into the
Polygon to help Wollstonecraft's servant Mary and Louisa Jones with the nursing. Montagu, John Fenwick, Dyson and Marshall were all present 'to be dispatched, on any
errand, to any part of the metropolis, at a moment's warning' (p. 187). On Tuesday,
5 September Fordyce brought in the skilled obstetrician Dr John Clarke, who saw that it
was too late for intervention and declared Wollstonecraft dying. He suggested Godwin
give her as much wine as she could take. Carlisle roused Godwin at 6 o'clock on Sunday
morning, 10 September, and at twenty minutes to eight Wollstonecraft died. Godwin
recorded the time in his journal, then drew three lines. Wollstonecraft was buried on
15 September in St Pancras Church. Henry Fuseli, on hearing of her death, added a
postscript to his letter to Roscoe: 'Poor Mary!' (*HF*, 1, 170).

Sources for Letters 112, 207, 218 and 322

John Knowles, The Life and Writings of Henry Fuseli
(London, 1831), 1, 163–8

'Mrs Wollstonecraft had the strongest desire to be useful to her connexions and friends, and she began her career in life by sacrificing her feelings and comforts to what she fancied purity of conduct, and the benefit of others. It was a favourite consideration with her, that "she was designed to rise superior to her earthly habitation", and that she "always thought, with some degree of horror, of falling a sacrifice to a passion which may have a mixture of dross in it."

Having a face and person which had some pretensions to beauty and comeliness, Mrs. Wollstonecraft had been frequently solicited to marry, but previously to her acquaintance with Mr. Fuseli, she had never known any man "possessed of those noble qualities, that grandeur of soul, that quickness of comprehension, and lively sympathy", which she fancied would be essential to her happiness, if she entered into the marriage state. These she found in him. . . . For some years before their acquaintance, with the view of usefulness which she had prescribed to herself Mrs. Wollstonecraft "read no book for mere amusement, not even poetry, but studied those works only which are addressed to the understanding; she scarcely tasted animal food, or allowed herself the necessaries of life that she might be able to pursue some romantic schemes of benevolence; seldom went to any amusements (being resident chiefly at Bath, and in the midst of pleasure), and her clothes were scarcely decent in her situation of life". . . . Talents such as [Fuseli's], Mrs. Wollstonecraft acknowledged she had never seen united in the same person; and they accordingly made a great impression on her mind. "For", said she, "I always catch something from the rich torrent of his conversation, worth treasuring up in my memory, to exercise my understanding". . . . She falsely reasoned with herself, and expressed to some of her intimate friends, that although Mrs. Fuseli had a right to the person of her husband, she, Mrs. Wollstonecraft, might claim, and, for congeniality of sentiments and talents, hold a place in his heart; for "she hoped", she said, "to unite herself to his mind". . . . The tumult which was raised in her mind by conflicting feelings, having love for the object, and yet the wish that her affection should be so regulated as to be strictly within the bounds which she had assigned to love, that of "strength of feeling unalloyed by passion", injured in a degree her health, and unfitted her for those literary pursuits which required a more than ordinary exertion of the mind. For more than twelve months "she wrote nothing but criticisms for the Analytical Review", and even these, which required but little exertion of the talents which she possessed, would not have been written but for her daily necessities. Fuseli reasoned with her, but without any effect, upon the impropriety of indulging in a passion that took her out of common life. Her answer was, "If I thought my passion criminal, I would conquer it, or die in the attempt. For immodesty, in my eyes, is ugliness; my soul turns with disgust from pleasure tricked out in charms which shun the light of heaven." At length Mrs. Wollstonecraft appears to have grown desperate, for she had the temerity to go to Mrs. Fuseli, and to tell her, that she wished to become an inmate in her family; and she added, as I am above deceit, it is right to say that this proposal "arises from the sincere affection which I have for your husband, for I find that I cannot live without the satisfaction of seeing and conversing with him daily". This frank avowal immediately opened the eyes of Mrs. Fuseli, who being alarmed by the declaration, not only refused her solicitation, but she instantly forbade her the house. No resource was now left for Mrs. Wollstonecraft, but to fly from the object which she regarded: her determination was instantly fixed, she wrote a letter to Fuseli, in which she begged pardon "for having disturbed the quiet tenour of his life", and on the 8th of December, 1792, left London for France. Shortly after her arrival in Paris, she again wrote to Fuseli, gave him her opinion of the state of public feeling at that important period of the revolution, and implored him to write to her occasionally. As this letter was not answered, all communication on her part during her residence abroad ceased.'

The Annual Necrology, for 1797–8 (London, 1800), pp. 424 and 451

'In the close of the year 1792 Mrs. Wollstonecraft quitted England on a tour to France, with a view, as she expressed herself to a friend on the eve of her departure, "to lose in public happiness the sense of private misery".'. . .

'In this interview [Imlay] still affected to speak of returning, after the wanderings of libertinism (with a debauched mind, and, probably, a shattered constitution) to repose on the tried faith of the only woman whom he had ever *loved with distinction*, entreating her to continue to bear his name, to which no other, he vehemently protested, should ever have a claim. "It was not for the world (said she in a letter to a friend) that I complied with this request, but I was unwilling to cut the gordian knot, or tear myself away in appearance, when I could not in reality."'

William Godwin, *Memoirs of the Author of A Vindication of the Rights of Woman* (London, 1798), ch. 8

'It is impossible to imagine a period of greater pain and mortification than Mary passed, for about seven weeks, from the sixteenth of April to the sixth of June [1795], in a furnished house that Mr Imlay had provided her.... When she saw him, all her fears were confirmed.... Her reception by Mr Imlay was cold and embarrassed.... Mary was incapable of sustaining her equanimity in this pressing emergency. "Love, dear, delusive love!" as she expressed herself to a friend some time afterwards, "rigorous reason had forced her to resign; and now her rational prospects were blasted, just as she had learned to be contented with rational enjoyments." ... [after her suicide attempt] Mr Imlay assured her that his present was merely a casual, sensual connection; and, of course, fostered in her mind the idea that it would be once more in her choice to live with him. With whatever intention the idea was suggested, it was certainly calculated to increase the agitation of her mind ... She saw the necessity of bringing the affair to a point, and not suffering months and years to roll on in uncertainty and suspence ... The language she employed, was, in effect, as follows: "If we are ever to live together again, it must be now. We meet now, or we part for ever. You say, You cannot abruptly break off the connection you have formed. It is unworthy of my courage and character, to wait the uncertain issue of that connection. I am determined to come to a decision. I consent then, for the present, to live with you, and the woman to whom you have associated yourself. I think it important that you should learn habitually to feel for your child the affection of a father. But, if you reject this proposal, here we end. You are now free. We will correspond no more. We will have no intercourse of any kind. I will be to you as a person that is dead." ... In the following month, Mr Imlay, and the woman with whom he was at present connected, went to Paris, where they remained three months. Mary had, previously to this, fixed herself in a lodging in Finsbury-place, where, for some time, she saw scarcely any one but Mrs

Christie, for the sake of whose neighbourhood she had chosen this situation; "existing", as she expressed it, "in a living tomb, and her life but an exercise of fortitude, continually on the stretch". Thus circumstanced, it was unavoidable for her thoughts to brood upon a passion, which all that she had suffered had not yet been able to extinguish. Accordingly, as soon as Mr Imlay returned to England, she could not restrain herself from making another effort, and desiring to see him once more. "During his absence, affection had led her to make numberless excuses for his conduct," and she probably wished to believe that his present connection was, as he represented it, purely of a casual nature. To this application, she observes, that "he returned no other answer, except declaring, with unjustifiable passion, that he would not see her". . . . At his particular request, she retained the name of Imlay, which, a short time before, he had seemed to dispute with her. "It was not," as she expresses herself in a letter to a friend, "for the world that she did so – not in the least – but she was unwilling to cut the Gordian knot, or tear herself away in appearance, when she could not in reality".'

Provenance of Letters

1. *To Jane Arden.* From [Beverley] Sunday afternoon, 4 o'clock [c. spring 1773]. Pforzheimer MSS, MW 12.

2. *To Jane Arden.* From [Beverley, c. spring 1773]. Pforzheimer MSS, MW 13.

3. *To Jane Arden.* From [Beverley, mid–late 1773]. Pforzheimer MSS, MW 14.

4. *To Jane Arden.* From [Beverley, c. mid–late 1773 – November 16th, 1774]. Pforzheimer MSS, MW 15.

5. *To Jane Arden.* From [Beverley, c. mid–late 1773 – November 16th, 1774]. Pforzheimer MSS, MW 16.

6. *To Jane Arden.* From [Beverley, c. mid–late 1773 – November 16th, 1774]. Pforzheimer MSS, MW 17.

7. *To Jane Arden.* From [Beverley] Wednesday noon, November 16th, 1774. Pforzheimer MSS, MW 18.

8. *To Jane Arden.* From Milson Street, Bath [?mid 1779]. Pforzheimer MSS, MW 19.

9. *To Jane Arden.* From [Bath, ?Christmas 1779]. Pforzheimer MSS, MW 22.

10. *To Jane Arden.* From [Bath, ?early 1780]. Pforzheimer MSS, MW 20.

11. *To Miss Arden /* Sir Mordant Martin's bart. / Burnham / Norfolk. From Bath, October 17th [?1780]; postmark illegible. Abinger MSS, Dep.b.210/5.

12. *To Jane Arden.* From [Windsor, ?April 1781]. Pforzheimer MSS, MW 23.

13. *To Miss Wollstonecraft /* near the Church, the Chace side / Enfield. From Windsor, August 17th [?1781]; postmarked 20 AU. Abinger MSS, Dep.b.210/1.

14. *To Jane Arden.* From [Windsor, ?late summer 1781]. Pforzheimer MSS, MW 24.

15. *To Jane Arden.* From Mr. Bloods, Walham Green, Fulham, Middlesex. [c. mid–late 1782]. Pforzheimer MSS, MW 25.

16. *To Jane Arden.* From [Walham Green, c. late 1782]. Pforzheimer MSS, MW 26.

17. *To Averina.* From [Bermondsey] Saturday afternoon [c. late 1783]; no postmark visible. Abinger MSS, Dep.b.210/2.

18. *To Miss A. Wollstonecraft.* From [Bermondsey, c. late 1783]; no postmark visible. Abinger MSS, Dep.b.210/2.

19. *To Miss Averina Wollstonecraft.* From [Bermondsey, c. December 1783]; no postmark visible. Abinger MSS, Dep.b.210/2.

20. *To Miss Wollstonecraft* / Mr Wollstonecraft's / N° 1 St Katherine's Street / Tower. From [Bermondsey] Monday morning [January 5th, 1784]; postmarked JA 8. Abinger MSS, Dep.b.210/2.

21. *To Miss A. Wollstonecraft* / Mr Wollstonecraft. / N° 1. St Katherine's Street / Tower. From Church Street, Hackney [c. January 1784]; postmark illegible. Abinger MSS, Dep.b.210/2.

22. *To Everina Wollstonecraft.* From [Hackney] Sunday afternoon [January 11th, 18th, or 25th, 1784]; no address or postmark visible. Abinger MSS, Dep.b.210/2.

23. *To Everina Wollstonecraft.* From [Hackney, c. January 1784]; no address or postmark visible. Abinger MSS, Dep.b.210/2.

24. *To Miss Averina Wollstonecraft* / Mr Wollstonecraft's Attorney / N° 1 St Katherine's Street / Tower. From [Hackney] Tuesday night [c. January 1784]; postmark illegible. Abinger MSS, Dep.b.210/2.

25. *To Mr George Blood* / Miss Delane's / N° 48 Brittain Street / Dublin. From Newington Green, July 3^d [1785]; postmarked 5 IU (London), JY 10 (Dublin). Abinger MSS, Dep.b.210/8.

26. *To Mr George Blood* / Miss Delane's / N^o, 48 Brittain Street / Dublin. From Newington Green, July 20th [1785] postmarked IY 22 (London), JY 26 (Dublin). Abinger MSS, Dep.b.210/8.

27. *To Mr George Blood* / Miss Delane's / N° 48 Brittain Street / Dublin. From Newington Green, July 25th [1785]; postmarked 26 IY (London), JY 31 (Dublin). Abinger MSS, Dep.b.210/8.

28. *To Mr George Blood* / Dublin. From Newington Green, August 14th [1785]; no postmark visible. Abinger MSS, Dep.b.210/8.

29. *To Mr George Blood* / at Mr Hughes Linen-Draper / N° 10 Bride Street / Dublin. From Newington Green, September 4th [1785]; postmarked 6 OC (London), OC 10 (Dublin). Abinger MSS, Dep.b.210/8.

30. *To Mrs Bishop* / Newington Green / London. From [Lisbon, c. late November 1785]; postmark illegible. Abinger MSS, Dep.b.210/1.

31. *To Mr George Blood* / Miss Delane's / N° 48 Brittain Street / Dublin. From Newington Green, February 4th [1786]; postmarked 6 FE (London), FE 10 (Dublin). Abinger MSS, Dep.b.210/8.

32. *To Mr George Blood* / Mr Home's N° 48 Brittain Street / Dublin. From

Newington Green, February 27th [1786]; postmarked 27 FE (London), MR 3 (Dublin). Abinger MSS, Dep.b.210/8.

33. *To George Blood.* From Newington Green, May 1st [1786]; no address or postmark visible. Abinger MSS, Dep.b.210/8.

34. *To Mr George Blood* / Brabⁿ Noble's Esqr / N° 96 Britain Street / Dublin. From Newington Green, May 22^d [1786]; postmarked 23 MY (London), MY 26 (Dublin). Abinger MSS, Dep.b.210/8.

35. *To Mr George Blood* / Brabⁿ Noble's Esqr / N° 96 Britain Street / Dublin. From Newington Green, June 18th [1786]; postmarked 20 JU (London), JU 23 (Dublin). Abinger MSS, Dep.b.210/8.

36. *To Mr George Blood* / Brabⁿ Noble's Esqr / N° 96 Britain Street / Dublin. From Newington Green, July 6th [1786]; postmarked 12 IU (London), JY 16 (Dublin). Abinger MSS, Dep.b.210/8.

37. *To Mr George Blood* / Brabⁿ, Noble's Esqr / N°, 96 Britain Street / Dublin. From Newington Green, August 25th [1786]; postmarked 28 AU. Abinger MSS, Dep.b.210/8.

38. *To Elizabeth* / Harbro. From Newington Green, September 23^d [1786]; no postmark visible. Abinger MSS, Dep.b.210/1.

39. *To Miss Everina Wollstonecraft* / Mr Wollstonecraft Attorney at Law / N° 1 St Katherines, – Tower / London. From Eton, Sunday, October 9th [1786]; postmarked 10 OC. Abinger MSS, Dep.b.210/2.

40. *To Miss Everina Wollstonecraft,* / Mr Wollstonecraft's, Attorney at Law / N° 1 St Katherine's, near the Tower / London. From the castle Mitchelstown, October 30th [1786]; postmark illegible. Abinger MSS, Dep.b.210/2.

41. *To Mrs Bishop* / Mrs Sampel's / Marketharborough / Leicestershire / England. From Mitchelstown, November 5th [1786]; no postmark visible. Abinger MSS, Dep.b.210/1.

42. *To George Blood.* From Mitchelstown, November 7th [1786]; no postmark visible. Abinger MSS, Dep.b.210/8.

43. *To Miss Everina Wollstonecraft* / Mr Wollstonecraft, Attorney at Law / St Katherines, near the Tower / London. From Mitchelstown, November 17th [1786]; postmarked [N]O 20. Abinger MSS, Dep.b.210/2.

44. *To Mr George Blood.* From [Mitchelstown] 12 o'clock night, December 4th [1786]; no postmark visible. Abinger MSS, Dep.b.210/8.

45. *To Mr Johnson,* Bookseller, / St Paul's Church-yard. / London. From Mitchelstown, December 5th [1786]; postmarked JA 8 (Dublin), 13 IA (London). Pforzheimer MSS, MW 9.

46. *To Mrs Bishop* / Mrs Tew's / Marketharborough / Leicestershire. From Mitchelstown, December 22^d [1786]; postmarked DE 25. Abinger MSS, Dep.b.210/1.

47. *To Miss Everina Wollstonecraft* /Mr Wollstonecraft's, Attorney at Law, / N° 2 King's Street / Tower-hill / London. From [Mitchelstown, c. January 15th, 1787]; postmarked JA 15 (Dublin) and 19 JA (London). Abinger MSS, Dep.b.210/2.

48. *To George.* From [Mitchelstown, c. January 1787]; no postmark visible. Abinger MSS, Dep.b.210/8.

49. *To Miss Everina Wollstonecraft,* / Mr Wollstonecraft's, attorney at Law, / N° 2. King's Street, near the Tower / London. From Dublin, February 10th 17[87]; postmarked FE 10 (Dublin), FEB 13 (London). Abinger MSS, Dep.b.210/2.

50. *To M^r, Gabell.* From [Dublin] Friday morning, two o'clock [c. early 1787]; no postmark visible. Pforzheimer MSS, MW 31.

51. *To Miss Everina Wollstonecraft* / Mr Wollstonecraft's Attorney at Law / N° 2 King's Street, Tower Hill / London. From Dublin, February 12th, 17[87]; postmarked FEBY 19. Abinger MSS, Dep.b.210/2.

52. *To Miss Everina Wollstonecraft.* / Mr Wollstonecraft's Attorney at Law / N° 2, King's Street, Tower-hill / London. From Dublin, March 3^d [1787]; postmarked MR 3 (Dublin), March 8 (London). Abinger MSS, Dep.b.210/2.

53. *To Miss Everina Wollstonecraft,* / Mr Wollstonecraft's Attorney at Law / N° 2 King's Street, Tower-hill / London. From Dublin, March 4th [1787]; postmark illegible. Abinger MSS, Dep.b.210/2.

54. *To Everina Wollstonecraft.* From Dublin, March 14th [1787]; no address or postmark visible. Abinger MSS, Dep.b.210/2.

55. *To Miss Everina Wollstonecraft* / Mr Wollstonecraft's Attorney at Law, / N° 2 King's Street, Tower-hill / London. From Dublin, March 24th [1787]; postmarked MR 30 (Dublin), APRIL 7 (London). Abinger MSS, Dep. b.210/2.

56. *To Miss Everina Wollstonecraft* / Mr Wollstonecraft's Attorney at Law, / N° 2 King's Street, Tower-hill / London. From Dublin, March 25th [1787]; postmarked AP 28 (Dublin), MA 2 87 (London). Abinger MSS, Dep.b.210/2.

57. *To Joseph Johnson.* From Dublin, April 14th [1787]. Letters to Johnson, I.

58. *To The Rev^d, M^r, Gabell* / Shanes Castle / near Antrim. From Dublin, April 16th [1787]; postmarked AP 17. Pforzheimer MSS, MW 34.

59. *To Miss Everina Wollstonecraft,* / Mr Wollstonecraft's, Attorney at Law, / N°, 2 King's Street, Tower-hill, / London –. From Dublin, May 11th, 1787; postmarked MA 16 87. Pforzheimer MSS, MW 10.

60. *To Everina Wollstonecraft.* From Dublin, May 15th [1787]; no address or postmark visible. Abinger MSS, Dep.b.210/2.

61. *To Mrs Bishop* / Mrs Tew's / Marketharborough / Leicestershire. From Bristol, June 27th [1787]; postmarked JU 28 87. Abinger MSS, Dep.b.210/1.

62. *To Mr George Blood*, / M^r, Noble's Mer^t, / Britain Street, / Dublin. From Henley, September 11th [1787]; postmarked SE 12 87 (London), SE 15 (Dublin). Abinger MSS, Dep.b.210/8.

63. *To Joseph Johnson*. From Henley, Thursday, September 13th [1787]. Letters to Johnson, II.

64. *To The Rev^d, M^r. Gabell* / The R^t. Hon. John O'Neill's, / Shanes Castle, / near Antrim, / Ireland. From Henley, September 13th [1787]; postmarked SE 14 87. Pforzheimer MSS, MW 32.

65. *To Joseph Johnson*. From Market Harborough, September 20th [1787]. Letters to Johnson, III.

66. *To The Rev^d. M^r. Gabell*, / The R^t. Hon. John O'Neill's, / Shanes Castle, / near Antrim, / Ireland. From [London, October 9th–19th, 1787]; postmarked OC 1[ ]. Pforzheimer MSS, MW 33.

67. *To Miss Everina Wollstonecraft* / Miss Rowden's / Henley / Oxfordshire. From London, November 7th [1787]; postmarked NO 9 87. Abinger MSS, Dep.b.210/2.

68. *To Everina Wollstonecraft*. From [London, c. mid November 1787]; no address or postmark visible. Abinger MSS, Dep.b.210/2.

69. *To Joseph Johnson*. From [London] Friday night [c. late 1787 – early 1788]. Letters to Johnson, IV.

70. *To Mr George Blood*. / Mr Noble's / Britain Street. / Dublin. From London, January 1st [1788]; postmarked JA 6. Abinger MSS, Dep.b.210/8.

71. *To Mr George Blood*. / Mr Noble's Britain Street / Dublin. From London, January 17th [1788]; postmarked JA 17 88 (London), JA 22 (Dublin). Abinger MSS, Dep.b.210/8.

72. *To Joseph Johnson*. From [London, ?early 1788]. Letters to Johnson, V.

73. *To Mr George Blood* / Mr Noble's. Britain Street. / Dublin. From London, March 3^d [1788]; postmark illegible. Abinger MSS, Dep.b.210/8.

74. *A Mad^{elle} Wollstonecraft*. / chez Mad^{elle} Henry, Rue de Tournon Faubourg Germaine / vis à vis L'Hotel de Laval. / A Paris. From [London] March 22^d [1788]; postmark illegible. Abinger MSS, Dep.b.210/2.

75. *To Mr George Blood*. / Mr Noble's. / Britain Street. / Dublin. From London May 16th [1788]; postmarked [ ] [ ] 88 (London), M [ ] 2[ ] (Dublin). Abinger MSS, Dep.b.210/8.

76. *To Mr George Blood* / Mr Noble's. / Britain Street / Dublin. From [London] May 26th or 27th [1788]; postmarked MA 28 88 (London), MY 31 (Dublin). Abinger MSS, Dep.b.210/8.

77. *To Joseph Johnson*. From [London, c. July 1788]. Letters to Johnson, XIV.

78. *To Joseph Johnson*. From [London, ?late 1788 – early 1789]. Letters to Johnson, VII.

79. *To Joseph Johnson.* From [London, ?late 1788 – early 1789]. Letters to Johnson, XV.

80. *To Joseph Johnson.* From [London] Monday morning [?early 1789]. Letters to Johnson, X.

81. *To Mr George Blood.* / Mr Noble's. / Britain Street. / Dublin. From London, February 28th [1789]; postmarked FE 28 89 (London), MR 4 (Dublin). Abinger MSS, Dep.b.210/8.

82. *To Mr George Blood.* / Mr Noble's. / Britain Street. / Dublin. From [London] April 16th [1789]; postmarked AP 16 89 (London), AP 20 (Dublin). Abinger MSS, Dep.b.210/8.

83. *To Mr George Blood.* / Mr Noble's Britain Street. / Dublin. From London, September 15th [1789]; postmarked SE 16 89 (London), SE 20 (Dublin). Abinger MSS, Dep.b.210/8.

84. *To Mr George Blood* / Mr Nobles / Britain Street / Dublin. From [London] November 19th [1789]; postmarked NO 20 89 (London), NO 25 (Dublin). Abinger MSS, Dep.b.210/8.

85. *To Joseph Johnson.* From [London, ?1790]. Letters to Johnson, VIII.

86. *To Mr George Blood* / Mr Noble's. / Britain Street / Dublin. From London, March 10th [1790]; postmarked MR [ ] 90 (London), MR 15 (Dublin). Abinger MSS, Dep.210/8.

87. *To M^r. Cristall,* / Mr Turners China Manufacture / near Brosely Salop. From London, March 19th [?1790]; no postmark visible. Henry E. Huntington Library and Art Gallery.

88. *To Joseph Johnson.* From [London] Friday morning [?early 1790]. Letters to Johnson, VI.

89. *To Mrs Bishop* / Mrs Bregantz's Boarding School / Putney. From [London] Thursday noon [c. mid 1790]; postmark illegible. Abinger MSS, Dep. b.210/1.

90. *To Joseph Johnson.* From [London, ?summer 1790]. Letters to Johnson, XI.

91. *To* ——. From [London] Tuesday evening [?summer 1790]. Letters to Johnson, XII.

92. *To* ——. From [London] Wednesday, 3 o'clock [?summer 1790]. Letters to Johnson, XIII.

93. *To Miss Everina Wollstonecraft* / Mrs Bregantz's / Putney / Surry. From The Revd Mr Gabell's, Warminster, Wiltshire, Saturday morning [August 21st, 1790]; postmarked AU 23 90. Abinger MSS, Dep.b.210/2.

94. *To Miss Everina Wollstonecraft.* / Mrs Bregantz's. / Putney. Surry. From [Warminster] Saturday night, September 4th [17]90; postmarked SE 7 90. Abinger MSS, Dep.b.210/2.

95. *To Miss E. Wollstonecraft.* / Mrs Bregantz's. / Putney. / Surry. From [Warminster] Friday, September 10th [17]90; postmarked SE 11 90. Abinger MSS, Dep.b.210/2.

96. *To Mrs Bishop* / Mrs Bregantz's Boarding School / Putney. From [London] Thursday night [?autumn 1790]; postmark illegible. Abinger MSS, Dep.b.210/1.

97. *To Mrs Bishop* / Mrs Bregantz's Boarding-School / Putney. From [London] Saturday [c. late 1790]; postmark illegible. Abinger MSS, Dep.b.210/1.

98. *To Mr Cristall* / Caughley, near Brosely, Salop. From [London] December 9th [?1790]. Royal Watercolour Society, Bankside.

99. *To Mrs Macaulay.* From [London] Thursday morning [December 1790]; no postmark visible. Pforzheimer MSS, MW 47.

100. *To Mr George Blood* / Mr Skeys's Britain St / Dublin. From London, February 4th [17]91; postmarked FE 5 (91) (London), FE 9 (Dublin). Abinger MSS, Dep.b.210/8.

101. *To Mr George Blood.* / Britain Street. / Dublin. From New Store Street, October 6th [17]91; postmarked OC 6 (91) (London), OC 9 (Dublin). Abinger MSS, Dep.b.210/8.

102. *To William Roscoe.* From [London] October 6th [17]91; no address or postmark visible. Liverpool Central Libraries.

103. *To George Blood.* From [London] January 2^{d} [17]92; no address or postmark visible. Abinger MSS, Dep.b.210/8.

104. *To M^{r}. Willm Roscoe* Attorney at Law / Liverpool. From Store Street, January 3^{d} [17]92; postmarked JA 4 92. Liverpool Public Libraries, MSS 5329.

105. *To Mr Willm Roscoe* Attorney at Law / Liverpool. From Store Street, Bedford Square, February 14th [17]92; postmarked FE [ ] 92. Liverpool Central Libraries.

106. *To Miss Wollstonecraft.* / Saml Boyse's Esqr / Waterford / Ireland. From [London] February 23^{d} [1792]; postmarked FE 23 92. Abinger MSS, Dep.b.210/2.

107. *To William Roscoe.* From [London, c. 1792]; no address or postmark visible. Liverpool Central Libraries.

108. *To Miss Wollstonecraft.* / Saml Boyse's Esqr. / Bishop's Hall. / near Waterford. From London, June 20th [17]92; postmarked JU 21 92. Abinger MSS, Dep.b.210/2.

109. *To Miss Hays.* / Gainsford Street. / Southwark. From Store Street, Bedford Square, August 11th [1792]; postmark illegible. Pforzheimer MSS, MW 37.

110. *To Miss Wollstonecraft* / Saml Boyse's Esqr/ Bishop's Hall / near Water-

ford. / Ireland. From London, September 14th [17]92; postmarked SE 15 92. Abinger MSS, Dep.b.210/2.

111. *To William Roscoe*. From London, October 2[d] [17]92; no address or postmark visible. Liverpool Public Libraries.

112. *To Henry Fuseli*. Speculative reconstruction. From [London, ?late 1792].

113. *To Joseph Johnson*. From [London] Saturday night [?October 1792]. Letters to Johnson, IX.

114. *To William Roscoe*. From London, November 12th [17]92; no address or postmark visible. Liverpool Central Libraries.

115. *To Mary Hays*. From Store Street, November 25th [17]92; no address or postmark visible. Pforzheimer MSS, MW 35.

116. *To Miss Hays*. / Gainsford Street, / Southwark. From Store Street, Saturday morning [c. late 1792]; postmark illegible. Pforzheimer MSS, MW 46.

117. *To [Miss] Wollstonecraft* / [Saml] Boyse's Esqr / Waterford / Ireland. From [London, c. early December 1792]: DE 9 / DE 10. Abinger MSS, Dep.b.210/2.

118. *To Miss Wollstonecraft*. / Saml Boyse's Esqr Bishop's-Hall / near Waterford. / Ireland. From Monsr. Filliettaz, Rue Meslée N°. 22, Paris, December 24th [17]92; postmarked DE 31. Abinger MSS, Dep.b.210/2.

119. *To Joseph Johnson*. From Paris, December 26th, 1792. Letters to Johnson, XVI.

120. *To Eliza Bishop*. From [Paris] January 20th [1793]. Abinger MSS, Dep.b.210/7.

121. *To Mrs Barlow*. From Rue Meslée, Paris, February [1st – 14th, 1793]; no postmark visible. Pforzheimer MSS, MW 28.

122. *To M[r] Jos. Johnson* / n°72 S[t] Paul's Church y[d] London. From Paris, May 2[d], 1793; no postmark visible. Pforzheimer MSS, MW 1.

123. *To Gilbert Imlay*. From [?Paris] Wednesday morning [c. April/May 1793]. Letters to Imlay, III.

124. *To Gilbert Imlay*. From [Neuilly-sur-Seine] Two o'clock [c. June 1793]. Letters to Imlay, I.

125. *To Eliza Bishop*. From [Neuilly-sur-Seine] June 13th [1793]. Abinger MSS, Dep.b.210/7.

126. *To Eliza Bishop*. From Neuilly-sur-Seine, June 24th [1793]. Abinger MSS, Dep.b.210/7.

127. *To Joseph Johnson*. From Paris, July 13th, 1792; no address or postmark visible. Pforzheimer MSS, MW 3.

128. *To Gilbert Imlay*. From [Neuilly-sur-Seine] Monday night, past twelve o'clock [c. August 1793]. Letters to Imlay, II.

129. *A la Citoyenne Barlow.* / Hotel de la Grande Bretagne. / Rue Jacob. / Faubourg S^r. Germain. From [?Neuilly-sur-Seine] Friday afternoon [c. mid 1793]; no postmark visible. Historical Society of Pennsylvania.

130. *To Gilbert Imlay.* From [Paris] Friday morning [c. September 1793]. Letters to Imlay, IV.

131. *To Gilbert Imlay.* From [Paris] Sunday night [c. November 1793]. Letters to Imlay, V.

132. *To Gilbert Imlay.* From [Paris] Friday morning [c. December 1793]. Letters to Imlay, VI.

133. *To Gilbert Imlay.* From [Paris] Sunday morning [December 29th, 1793]. Letters to Imlay, VII.

134. *To Gilbert Imlay.* [Paris] Monday night [December 30th, 1793]. Letters to Imlay, VIII.

135. *To Gilbert Imlay.* From [Paris] Tuesday morning [December 31st, 1793]. Letters to Imlay, IX.

136. *To Gilbert Imlay.* From [Paris] Wednesday night [January 1st, 1794]. Letters to Imlay, X.

137. *To Gilbert Imlay.* From [Paris] Monday night [January 6th, 1794]. Letters to Imlay, XI.

138. *To Gilbert Imlay.* From [Paris] Wednesday morning [January 8th, 1794]. Letters to Imlay, XII.

139. *To Gilbert Imlay.* From [Paris] Thursday night [January 9th, 1794]. Letters to Imlay, XIII.

140. *To Gilbert Imlay.* From [Paris] Saturday morning [January 11th, 1794]. Letters to Imlay, XIV.

141. *To Gilbert Imlay.* From [Paris] Sunday morning [January 12th, 1794]. Letters to Imlay, XV.

142. *To Gilbert Imlay.* From [Paris] Tuesday morning [January 14th, 1794]. Letters to Imlay, XVI.

143. *To Gilbert Imlay.* From [Paris] Wednesday morning [c. January 15th, 1794]. Letters to Imlay, XVII.

144. *To Mrs Barlow.* From [?Le Havre] February 3^d [1794]; no postmark visible. Bancroft Library, University of California, Berkeley.

145. *To Miss Wollstonecraft.* From [Le] Havre, March 10th [17]94; no postmark visible. Abinger MSS, Dep.b.210/2.

146. *To Gilbert Imlay.* From [Le] H[avre], Thursday morning, March [13th, 1794]. Letters to Imlay, XVIII.

147. *To Gilbert Imlay.* From [Le Havre, c. March 1794]. Letters to Imlay, XIX.

148. *To Mrs Barlow.* From [Le] Havre, April 27th [17]94; no postmark visible. Bancroft Library, University of California, Berkeley.

149. *To Mrs Barlow.* From [Le] Havre, May 20th [17]94; no postmark visible. Bancroft Library, University of California, Berkeley.

150. *To Mrs Barlow.* From [Le] Havre, July 8th [17]94; no postmark visible. Boston Public Library.

151. *To Gilbert Imlay.* From [Le Havre] Sunday, August 17th [1794]. Letters to Imlay, XX.

152. *To Gilbert Imlay.* From [Le] H[avre], Tuesday, August 19th [1794]. Letters to Imlay, XXI.

153. *To Gilbert Imlay.* From [Le] H[avre], August 20th [1794]. Letters to Imlay, XXII.

154. *To Miss Wollstonecraft* / Miss Moore and C° / Finsbury Square / London. From Paris, September 20th [1794]; no postmark visible. Abinger MSS, Dep.b.210/2.

155. *To Gilbert Imlay.* From [Paris] September 22^d [1794]. Letters to Imlay, XXIII.

156. *To Gilbert Imlay.* From [Paris] Evening, September 23^d [1794]. Letters to Imlay, XXIV.

157. *To Gilbert Imlay.* From Paris, September 28th [1794]. Letters to Imlay, XXV.

158. *To Gilbert Imlay.* From [Paris] October 1st [1794]. Letters to Imlay, XXVI.

159. *To Gilbert Imlay.* From [Paris] October 26th [1794]. Letters to Imlay, XXVII.

160. *To Gilbert Imlay.* From [Paris] December 26th [1794]. Letters to Imlay, XXVIII.

161. *To Gilbert Imlay.* From [Paris] December 28th [1794]. Letters to Imlay, XXIX.

162. *To Gilbert Imlay.* From [Paris] December 29th [1794]. Letters to Imlay, XXX.

163. *To Gilbert Imlay.* From [Paris] December 30th [1794]. Letters to Imlay, XXXI.

164. *To Gilbert Imlay.* From [Paris] January 9th [1795]. Letters to Imlay, XXXII.

165. *To Gilbert Imlay.* From [Paris] January 15th [1795]. Letters to Imlay, XXXIII.

166. *To Gilbert Imlay.* From [Paris] January 30th [1795]. Letters to Imlay, XXXIV.

167. *To Gilbert Imlay.* From [Paris] February 9th [1795]. Letters to Imlay, XXXV.

168. *To Gilbert Imlay.* From [Paris] February 10th [1795]. Letters to Imlay, XXXVI.

169. *To Gilbert Imlay.* From [Paris] February 19th [1795]. Letters to Imlay, XXXVII.

170. *To Gilbert Imlay.* From [Le Havre] April 7th [1795]. Letters to Imlay, XXXVIII.

171. *To Archibald Hamilton Rowan.* From [Le Havre] April 9th [1795]; no postmark visible. Beinecke Rare Book and Manuscript Library, Yale University.

172. *To Archibald Hamilton Rowan.* From [Le] Havre, April, 1795. Abinger MSS, Dep.b.210/5.

173. *To Gilbert Imlay.* From Brighthelmstone, Saturday, April 11th [1795]. Letters to Imlay, XXXIX.

174. *To Eliza Bishop.* From Nº 26 Charlotte S^t, Rathbone Place, London [c. April 23^d, 1795]. Abinger MSS, Dep.b.210/7.

175. *To Miss Wollstonecraft* / Mr Skey's / Britain Street / Dublin. From Nº 26 Charlotte Street, Rathbone Place, April 27th [1795]; postmark illegible. Abinger MSS, Dep.b.210/2.

176. *To Gilbert Imlay.* From London, Friday, May 22^d [1795]. Letters to Imlay, XL.

177. *To Gilbert Imlay.* From [London] Wednesday [May 27th, 1795]. Letters to Imlay, XLI.

178. *To Gilbert Imlay.* From [Hull] Wednesday, two o'clock [June 10th, 1795]. Letters to Imlay, XLII.

179. *To Gilbert Imlay.* From [Hull] Thursday [June 11th, 1795]. Letters to Imlay, XLIII.

180. *To Gilbert Imlay.* From [Hull] Friday, June 12th, [1795]. Letters to Imlay, XLIV.

181. *To Gilbert Imlay.* From [Hull] Sunday, June 14th [1795]. Letters to Imlay, XLV.

182. *To Gilbert Imlay.* From [Hull] June 15th [1795]. Letters to Imlay, XLVI.

183. *To Gilbert Imlay.* From [Hull] Tuesday morning [June 16th, 1795]. Letters to Imlay, XLVII.

184. *To Gilbert Imlay.* From [Hull] Wednesday morning [June 17th, 1795]. Letters to Imlay, XLVIII.

185. *To Gilbert Imlay.* From [Hull] Thursday [June 18th, 1795]. Letters to Imlay, XLIX.

186. *To Gilbert Imlay.* From [Hull] Saturday [June 20th, 1795]. Letters to Imlay, L.

187. *To Gilbert Imlay.* From [Hull] Sunday morning [June 21st, 1795]. Letters to Imlay, LI.

188. *To Gilbert Imlay.* From [Gothenburg] Saturday, June 27th [1795]. Letters to Imlay, LII.

189. *To Gilbert Imlay.* From [Gothenburg] June 29th [1795]. Letters to Imlay, LIII.

190. *To Gilbert Imlay.* From [Gothenburg] July 1st [1795]. Letters to Imlay, LIV.

191. *To Gilbert Imlay.* From [Gothenburg] July 3^{d} [1795]. Letters to Imlay, LV.

192. *To Gilbert Imlay.* From [Gothenburg] July 4th [1795]. Letters to Imlay, LVI.

193. *To Gilbert Imlay.* From [Strömstad] July 7th [1795]. Letters to Imlay, LVII.

194. *To Gilbert Imlay.* From [Larvik] July 14th [1795]. Letters to Imlay, LVIII.

195. *To Gilbert Imlay.* From [Tönsberg] July 18th [1795]. Letters to Imlay, LIX.

196. *To Gilbert Imlay.* From [Tönsberg] July 30th [1795]. Letters to Imlay, LX.

197. *To Gilbert Imlay.* From [Tönsberg] August 5th [1795]. Letters to Imlay, LXI.

198. *To Gilbert Imlay.* From [Tönsberg] August 7th [1795]. Letters to Imlay, LXII.

199. *To Gilbert Imlay.* From [Tönsberg] August 9th [1795]. Letters to Imlay, LXIII.

200. *To Gilbert Imlay.* From [Gothenburg] August 26th [1795]. Letters to Imlay, LXIV.

201. *To Gilbert Imlay.* From [Copenhagen] September 6th [1795]. Letters to Imlay, LXV.

202. *To Gilbert Imlay.* From [Hamburg] September 25th [1795]. Letters to Imlay, LXVI.

203. *To Gilbert Imlay.* From [Hamburg] September 27th [1795]. Letters to Imlay, LXVII.

204. *To Gilbert Imlay.* From [Dover] Sunday, October 4th [1795]. Letters to Imlay, LXVIII.

205. *To Gilbert Imlay.* From [London, c. October 10th, 1795]. Letters to Imlay, LXIX.

206. *To Gilbert Imlay.* From [London] Sunday Morning [c. October 1795]. Letters to Imlay, LXX.

207. *To Gilbert Imlay.* Speculative reconstruction. From [London, c. October 1795].

208. *To Gilbert Imlay.* From [London] Monday morning [c. October 1795]. Letters to Imlay, LXXI.

209. *To Gilbert Imlay.* From [London] Saturday night [c. November 1795]. Letters to Imlay, LXXIII.

210. *To Gilbert Imlay.* From [London] Thursday afternoon [c. November 1795]. Letters to Imlay, LXXIV.

211. *To Gilbert Imlay.* From London, November 27th [1795]. Letters to Imlay, LXXV.

212. *To Gilbert Imlay.* From London, December 8th [1795]. Letters to Imlay, LXXVI.

213. *To Gilbert Imlay.* From [London, c. December 1795]. Letters to Imlay, LXXVII.

214. *To M^r. Fuseli.* From [London] Monday morning [c. late 1795].

215. *To Miss Hays.* From [London] Saturday evening [c. late 1795]; no postmark visible. Pforzheimer MSS, MW 36.

216. *To Hamilton Rowan Esqr.* From London, January 26th [1796]; no postmark visible.

217. *To Gilbert Imlay.* From [London, c. March 1796]. Letters to Imlay, LXXVIII.

218. *To Mary Hays(?).* Speculative reconstruction. From [London, c. April – May 1796].

219. *To Gustav, Graf von Schlabrendorf.* From London, May 13th, 1796.

220. *To William Godwin.* From [London] July 1st, 1796.

221. *To Mr Godwin. / N° 25 Chalton Street.* From Judd Place West, Thursday [July 21st, 1796]; no postmark visible. Abinger MSS, Dep.b.210/4, no. 3.

222. *To William Godwin.* From [London] Tuesday [July 26th, 1796]; no address or postmark visible. Abinger MSS, Dep.b.210/4, no. 4.

223. *To Mary Hays.* From [London] Sunday morning [1796]; no address or postmark visible. Pforzheimer MSS, MW 44.

224. *To William Godwin.* From [London, August 2^d, 1796]; no address or postmark visible. Abinger MSS, Dep.b.210/4, no. 5.

225. *To William Godwin.* From [London, August 4th, 1796]; no address or postmark visible. Abinger MSS, Dep.b.210/4, no. 6.

226. *To Willm Godwin Philosopher.* From [London, August 6th, 1796]; no postmark visible. Abinger MSS, Dep.b.210/4, no. 7.

227. *To William Godwin.* From [London, August 7th, 1796]; no address or postmark visible. Abinger MSS, Dep.b.210/4, no. 8.

228. *To William Godwin.* From [London, August 11th, 1796]; no address or postmark visible. Abinger MSS, Dep.b.210/4, no. 9.

229. *To William Godwin.* From [London, August 16th, 1796]; no address or postmark visible. Abinger MSS, Dep.b.210/4, no. 11.

230. *To William Godwin.* From [London] Wednesday morning [August 17th, 1796]; no address or postmark visible. Abinger MSS, Dep.b.210/4, no. 12.

231. *To William Godwin.* From [London] Two o'clock [August 17th, 1796]; no address or postmark visible. Abinger MSS, Dep.b.210/4, no. 14.

232. *To William Godwin.* From [London, August 19th, 1796]; no address or postmark visible. Abinger MSS, Dep.b.210/4, no. 17.

233. *To William Godwin.* From [London, August 22^d, 1796]; no address or postmark visible. Abinger MSS, Dep.b.210/4, no. 19.

234. *To William Godwin.* From [London, August 24th, 1796]; no address or postmark visible. Abinger MSS, Dep.b.210/4, no. 21.

235. *To William Godwin.* From [London] Friday [August 26th, 1796]; no address or postmark visible. Abinger MSS, Dep.b.210/4, no. 23.

236. *To William Godwin.* From [London] Saturday morning [August 27th, 1796]; no address or postmark visible. Abinger MSS, Dep.b.210/4, no. 24.

237. *To William Godwin.* From [London] Monday [August 29th, 1796]; no address or postmark visible. Abinger MSS, Dep.b.210/4, no. 25.

238. *To William Godwin.* From [London, August 30th, 1796]; no address or postmark visible. Abinger MSS, Dep.b.210/4, no. 27.

239. *To William Godwin.* From [London, August 30th, 1796]; no address or postmark visible. Abinger MSS, Dep.b.210/4, no. 28.

240. *To William Godwin.* From [London] Wednesday [August 31st, 1796]; no address or postmark visible. Abinger MSS, Dep.b.210/4, no. 29.

241. *To William Godwin.* From [London, August 31st – September 4th, 1796]; no address or postmark visible. Abinger MSS, Dep.b.210/4, no. 30.

242. *To William Godwin.* From [London] Sunday morning [September 4th, 1796]; no address or postmark visible. Abinger MSS, Dep.b.210/4, no. 31.

243. *To William Godwin.* From [London] Sunday night, past ten o'clock! [September 4th, 1796]; no address or postmark visible. Abinger MSS, Dep.b.210/4, no. 32.

244. *To William Godwin.* From [London, September 8th, 1796]; no address or postmark visible. Abinger MSS, Dep.b.210/4, no. 33.

245. *To William Godwin.* From [London] Saturday morning [September 10th, 1796]; no address or postmark visible. Abinger MSS, Dep.b.210/4, no. 34.

246. *To Archibald Hamilton Rowan.* From London, September 12th, 1796; no address or postmark visible. Abinger MSS, Dep.b.210/5.

247. *To William Godwin.* From [London, September 13th, 1796]; no address or postmark visible. Abinger MSS, Dep.b.210/4, no. 36.

248. *To William Godwin.* From [London, September 14th, 1796]; no address or postmark visible. Abinger MSS, Dep.b.210/4, no. 39.

249. *To Miss Hays.* From [London] Thursday morning [September 15th, 1796]; no postmark visible. Pforzheimer MSS, MW 2.

250. *To William Godwin.* From [London, September 15th, 1796]; no address or postmark visible. Abinger MSS, Dep.b.210/4, no. 40.

251. *To William Godwin.* From [London, September 17th, 1796]; no address or postmark visible. Abinger MSS, Dep.b.210/4, no. 42.

252. *To William Godwin.* From [London] Monday noon [September 19th, 1796]; no address or postmark visible. Abinger MSS, Dep.b.210/4, no. 44.

253. *To Miss Hays.* From [London] Tuesday morning [September 20th, 1796]; no postmark visible. Pforzheimer MSS, MW 42.

254. *To William Godwin.* From [London] Wednesday morning [September 21st, 1796]; no address or postmark visible. Abinger MSS, Dep.b.210/4, no. 45.

255. *To William Godwin.* From [London, September 28th, 1796]; no address or postmark visible. Abinger MSS, Dep.b.210/4, no. 47.

256. *To William Godwin.* From [London, September 29th, 1796]; no address or postmark visible. Abinger MSS, Dep.b.210/4, no. 48.

257. *To William Godwin.* From [London] Friday [September 30th, 1796]; no address or postmark visible. Abinger MSS, Dep.b.210/4, no. 52.

258. *To William Godwin.* From [London, October 4th, 1796]; no address or postmark visible. Abinger MSS, Dep.b.210/4, no. 53.

259. *To William Godwin.* From [London, October 6th, 1796]; no address or postmark visible. Abinger MSS, Dep.b.210/4, no. 54.

260. *To William Godwin.* From [London, October 7th, 1796]; no address or postmark visible. Abinger MSS, Dep.b.210/4, no. 56.

261. *To William Godwin.* From [London, October 26th, 1796]; no address or postmark visible. Abinger MSS, Dep.b.210/4, no. 58.

262. *To Miss Hays.* From [London] Wednesday morning [c. October 26th, 1796]; no postmark visible. Pforzheimer MSS, MW 45.

263. *To William Godwin.* From [London, October 27th, 1796]; no address or postmark visible. Abinger MSS, Dep.b.210/4, no. 59.

264. *To William Godwin.* From [London] Thursday morning [November 3d, 1796]; no address or postmark visible. Abinger MSS, Dep.b.210/4, no. 61.

265. *To William Godwin.* From [London] Thursday [November 10th, 1796]; no address or postmark visible. Abinger MSS, Dep.b.210/4, no. 63.

266. *To William Godwin.* From [London] Sunday morning [November 13th, 1796]; no address or postmark visible. Abinger MSS, Dep.b.210/4, no. 64.

267. *To William Godwin.* From [London] Friday morning [November 18th, 1796]; no address or postmark visible. Abinger MSS, Dep.b.210/4, no. 66.

268. *To William Godwin.* From [London] Saturday morning [November 19th, 1796]; no address or postmark visible. Abinger MSS, Dep.b.210/4, no. 68.

269. *To Miss Hays.* From [London] Monday morning [c. November 1796]; no postmark visible. Pforzheimer MSS, MW 40.

270. *To William Godwin.* From [London, November 19th – 23[d], 1796]; no address or postmark visible. Abinger MSS, Dep.b.210/4, no. 70.

271. *To William Godwin.* From [London, November 19th – 23[d], 1796]; no address or postmark visible. Abinger MSS, Dep.b.210/4, no. 71.

272. *To William Godwin.* From [London, November 19th – 23[d], 1796]; no address or postmark visible. Abinger MSS, Dep.b.210/4, no. 72.

273. *To William Godwin.* From [London] Thursday [November 23[d], 1796]; no address or postmark visible. Abinger MSS, Dep.b.210/4, no. 73.

274. *To William Godwin.* From [London, November 23[d] – 28th, 1796]; no address or postmark visible. Abinger MSS, Dep.b.210/4, no. 74.

275. *To William Godwin.* From [London] Monday morning [November 28th, 1796]; no address or postmark visible. Abinger MSS, Dep.b.210/4, no. 75.

276. *To William Godwin.* From [London] Tuesday morning [December 6th, 1796]; no address or postmark visible. Abinger MSS, Dep.b.210/4, no. 76.

277. *To William Godwin.* From [London] Wednesday morning [December 7th, 1796]; no address or postmark visible. Abinger MSS, Dep.b.210/4, no. 77.

278. *To William Godwin.* From [London, December 12th, 1796]; no address or postmark visible. Abinger MSS, Dep.b.210/4, no. 78.

279. *To William Godwin.* From [London] Tuesday morning [December 13th, 1796]; no address or postmark visible. Abinger MSS, Dep.b.210/4, no. 79.

280. *To Miss Hays.* / Corner of Little John Street. / Gray's Inn-Lane. From [London] Wednesday morning [December 14th, 1796]; postmarked 4 o'Clock 14 DE 96. Pforzheimer MSS, MW 36.

281. *To William Godwin.* From [London, December 18th, 1796]; no address or postmark visible. Abinger MSS, Dep.b.210/4, no. 81.

282. *To M[r] Dyson.* From [London] Tuesday morning [c. late 1796]; no postmark visible. Pforzheimer MSS, MW 11.

283. *To William Godwin.* From [London, December 20th, 1796]; no address or postmark visible. Abinger MSS, Dep.b.210/4, no. 82.

284. *To William Godwin.* From [London] Friday morning [December 23[d], 1796]; no address or postmark visible. Abinger MSS, Dep.b.210/4, no. 83.

285. *To Mary Robinson.* From [London] Friday evening, or rather night [c. late 1796]; no address or postmark visible. Pforzheimer MSS, MW 27.

286. *To William Godwin.* From [London] Wednesday [December 28th, 1796]; no address or postmark visible. Abinger MSS, Dep.b.210/4, no. 84.

287. *To William Godwin.* From [London] Friday morning [December 30th, 1796]; no address or postmark visible. Abinger MSS, Dep.b.210/4, no. 85.

288. *To William Godwin.* From [London, December 31st, 1796]; no address or postmark visible. Abinger MSS, Dep.b.210/4, no. 86.

289. *To William Godwin.* From [London] Saturday morning [December 31st, 1796]; no address or postmark visible. Abinger MSS, Dep.b.210/4, no. 88.

290. *To William Godwin.* From [London] Sunday morning [January 1st, 1797]; no address or postmark visible. Abinger MSS, Dep.b.210/4, no. 89.

291. *To William Godwin.* From [London] Thursday morning [January 5th, 1797]; no address or postmark visible. Abinger MSS, Dep.b.210/4, no. 90.

292. *To William Godwin.* From [London] Thursday morning [January 12th, 1797]; no address or postmark visible. Abinger MSS, Dep.b.210/4, no. 91.

293. *To William Godwin.* From [London] Friday morning [January 13th, 1797]; no address or postmark visible. Abinger MSS, Dep.b.210/4, no. 92.

294. *To Mr Godwin* / Nº 25 Chalton Street. From [London] Sunday [January 15th, 1797]; no postmark visible. Abinger MSS, Dep.b.210/4, no. 93.

295. *To William Godwin.* From [London] Saturday morning [January 21st, 1797]; no address or postmark visible. Abinger MSS, Dep.b.210/4, no. 94.

296. *To Miss Hays.* From [London, c. January 1797]; no postmark visible. Pforzheimer MSS, MW 43.

297. *To William Godwin.* From [London] Tuesday morning [January 24th, 1797]; no address or postmark visible. Abinger MSS, Dep.b.210/4, no. 95.

298. *To William Godwin.* From [London, January 27th, 1797]; no address or postmark visible. Abinger MSS, Dep.b.210/4, no. 96.

299. *To William Godwin.* From [London] Saturday [January 28th, 1797]; no address or postmark visible. Abinger MSS, Dep.b.210/4, no. 97.

300. *To William Godwin.* From [London] Friday morning [February 3d, 1797]; no address or postmark visible. Abinger MSS, Dep.b.210/4, no. 98.

301. *To William Godwin.* From [London] Saturday morning [February 4th, 1797]; no address or postmark visible. Abinger MSS, Dep.b.210/4, no. 99.

302. *To William Godwin.* From [London] Monday morning [February 13th, 1797]; no address or postmark visible. Abinger MSS, Dep.b.210/4, no. 101.

303. *To William Godwin.* From [London, February 14th, 1797]; no address or postmark visible. Abinger MSS, Dep.b.210/4, no. 102.

304. *To William Godwin.* From [London, February 15th, 1797]; no address or postmark visible. Abinger MSS, Dep.b.210/4, no. 103.

305. *To Miss Hays.* From [London] Wednesday morning [February 15th, 1797]; no postmark visible. Pforzheimer MSS, MW 39.

306. *To William Godwin*. From [London, February 17th, 1797]; no address or postmark visible. Abinger MSS, Dep.b.210/4, no. 104.

307. *To William Godwin*. From [London] Tuesday [February 21st, 1797]; no address or postmark visible. Abinger MSS, Dep.b.210/4, no. 105.

308. *To William Godwin*. From [London, February 22[d], 1797]; no address or postmark visible. Abinger MSS, Dep.b.210/4, no. 106.

309. *To William Godwin*. From [London, c. early 1797]; no address or postmark visible. Abinger MSS, Dep.b.210/4, not numbered.

310. *To Miss Hays*. From [London] Friday morning [c. early 1797]; no postmark visible. Pforzheimer MSS, MW 41.

311. *To William Godwin*. From [London] Monday [March 6th, 1797]; no address or postmark visible. Abinger MSS, Dep.b.210/4, no. 107.

312. *To William Godwin*. From [London] Saturday morning [March 11th, 1797]; no address or postmark visible. Abinger MSS, Dep.b.210/4, no. 108.

313. *To William Godwin*. From [London] Friday morning [March 17th, 1797]; no address or postmark visible. Abinger MSS, Dep.b.210/4, no. 109.

314. *To Miss Wollstonecraft* / Josiah Wedgwood Esq / Etruria / Staffordshire. From London, March 22[d] [1797]; postmarked M[ ]23 [97]. Abinger MSS, Dep.b.210/2.

315. *To William Godwin*. From [London] Friday [March 31st, 1797]; no address or postmark visible. Abinger MSS, Dep.b.210/4, no. 114.

316. *To William Godwin*. From [London] Tuesday morning [April 4th, 1797]; no address or postmark visible. Abinger MSS, Dep.b.210/4, no. 115.

317. *To William Godwin*. From [London] Saturday [April 8th, 1797]; no address or postmark visible. Abinger MSS, Dep.b.210/4, no. 116.

318. *To William Godwin*. From [London, April 9th, 1797]; no address or postmark visible. Abinger MSS, Dep.b.210/4, no. 117.

319. *To William Godwin*. From [London, April 11th, 1797]; no address or postmark visible. Abinger MSS, Dep.b.210/4, no. 118.

320. *To William Godwin*. From [London, April 11th, 1797]; no address or postmark visible. Abinger MSS, Dep.b.210/4, no. 119.

321. *To Amelia Alderson*. From [London] Tuesday night, [April 11th, 1797].

322. *To Mary Hays(?)*. Speculative reconstruction. From [London, c. April 1797].

323. *To William Godwin*. From [London, April 20th, 1797]; no address or postmark visible. Abinger MSS, Dep.b.210/4, no. 120.

324. *To M[r] Geo. Dyson* / Ironmonger's Hall / Fenchurch Street. From Polygon N[o] 29, [Friday] morning [April 28th, 1797]; postmarked 28 AP 97 NIGHT. Pforzheimer MSS, MW 29.

325. *To M[r] Geo. Dyson* / Ironmonger's Hall / Fenchurch Street. From N[o] 29

Polygon, Somers Town, Monday morning [c. May 16th, 1797]; postmarked 4 o'Clock, [?16] MA [97] EVEN. Pforzheimer MSS, MW 30.

326. *To M[r] Godwin.* / Polygon / Somers Town. From [London, c. May 16th, 1797]; no postmark visible.

327. *To William Godwin.* From [London] Saturday morning [May 21st, 1797]; no address or postmark visible. Abinger MSS, Dep.b.210/4, no. 123.

328. *To William Godwin.* From [London] Saturday morning [June 3[d], 1797]; no address or postmark visible. Abinger MSS, Dep.b.210/4, no. 125.

329. *To M[r] Godwin* / Josiah Wedgwood Esq / Etruria / Staffordshire. From [London] Tuesday, June 6th [17]97; postmarked JU 6 97. Abinger MSS, Dep.b.210/4, no. 128.

330. *To William Godwin.* From [London] Saturday, half after one o'clock [June 10th, 1797]; no address or postmark visible. Abinger MSS, Dep.b.210/4, no. 131.

331. *To William Godwin.* From [London] Monday, almost twelve o'clock [June 19th, 1797]; no address or postmark visible. Abinger MSS, Dep.b.210/4, no. 135.

332. *To William Godwin.* From [London, June 25th, 1797]; no address or postmark visible. Abinger MSS, Dep.b.210/4, no. 136.

333. *To William Godwin.* From [London, June 26th, 1797]; no address or postmark visible. Abinger MSS, Dep.b.210/4, no. 137.

334. *To M[rs] Reveley.* From [London, Monday night, June 26th, 1797]; no postmark visible. Pforzheimer MSS, MW 8.

335. *To Maria Reveley.* From Polygon, Wednesday morning [c. spring/summer 1797]; no address or postmark visible. Henry E. Huntington Library MSS.

336. *To Maria Reveley(?).* From [London, c. spring/summer 1797]; no address or postmark visible.

337. *To William Godwin.* From [London] Monday morning [July 3[d], 1797]; no address or postmark visible. Abinger MSS, Dep.b.210/4, no. 138.

338. *To William Godwin.* From [London, July 3[d], 1797]; no address or postmark visible. Abinger MSS, Dep.b.210/4, no. 139.

339. *To William Godwin.* From [London, July 4th, 1797]; no address or postmark visible. Abinger MSS, Dep.b.210/4, no. 140.

340. *To William Godwin.* From [London, July 7th, 1797]; no address or postmark visible. Abinger MSS, Dep.b.210/4, no. 142.

341. *To William Godwin.* From [London, July 7th, 1797]; no address or postmark visible. Abinger MSS, Dep.b.210/4, no. 144.

342. *To William Godwin.* From [London, July 13th, 1797]; no address or postmark visible. Abinger MSS, Dep.b.210/4, no. 145.

343. *To William Godwin.* From [London, July 15th, 1797]; no address or postmark visible. Abinger MSS, Dep.b.210/4, no. 147.

344. *To William Godwin.* From [London, July 18th, 1797]; no address or postmark visible. Abinger MSS, Dep.b.210/4, no. 148.

345. *To William Godwin.* From [London, July 23d, 1797]; no address or postmark visible. Abinger MSS, Dep.b.210/4, no. 149.

346. *To William Godwin.* From [London, July 31st, 1797]; no address or postmark visible. Abinger MSS, Dep.b.210/4, no. 151.

347. *To William Godwin.* From [London, August 1st, 1797]; no address or postmark visible. Abinger MSS, Dep.b.210/4, no. 152.

348. *To William Godwin.* From [London] Wednesday morning [August 9th, 1797]; no address or postmark visible. Abinger MSS, Dep.b.210/4, no. 153.

349. *To Miss Pinkerton.* From [London] Wednesday morning [August 9th, 1797]; no address or postmark visible. Abinger MSS, Dep.b.210/4, not numbered.

350. *To William Godwin.* From [London, August 19th, 1797]; no address or postmark visible. Abinger MSS, Dep.b.210/4, no. 157.

351. *To Mr. Marshall.* From [London] Monday morning [August 21st, 1797]; no address or postmark visible. Pforzheimer MSS, MW 48.

352. *To William Godwin.* From [London, August 30th, 1797]; no address or postmark visible. Abinger MSS, Dep.b.210/4, no. 158.

353. *To William Godwin.* From [London, August 30th, 1797]; no address or postmark visible. Abinger MSS, Dep.b.210/4, no. 159.

354. *To William Godwin.* From [London, August 30th, 1797]; no address or postmark visible. Abinger MSS, Dep.b.210/4, no. 160.

Endnotes

1. In the transcript the words 'so well' have been crossed out.
2. In the transcript the word 'uneasiness' has been crossed out and replaced with 'misery'.
3. In the transcript the word 'entertaining' has been crossed out and replaced with 'improving'.
4. In the transcript the word 'power' has been crossed out and replaced with 'purse'.
5. In the transcript the word 'character' has been crossed out and replaced with 'man'.
6. In the transcript the words 'sort of thing' have been crossed out.
7. *CL* reads 'they'.
8. *CL* reads 'wife'.
9. Above 'your' Wollstonecraft (henceforth M.W.) wrote 'our'.
10. M.W. added 'and well' but then crossed it out.
11. M.W. transposed the figures of the date, writing '78' for '87'.
12. M.W. again reverses the numbers in the date, writing '78' for '87'.
13. The passage 'I am afraid . . .

present thoughtless' has been defaced.
14. The letter is unclear. Wardle read it as 'Mr. N'.
15. M.W. wrote 'ought'.
16. M.W. wrote 'Accepting'.
17. The passage 'and it is not easy . . . recommend him' has been defaced.
18. M.W. probably meant to write 'he'.
19. The lower part of the sheet has been cut off, and the signature is written on the next sheet in another hand.
20. On the back of the sheet, written in another hand: 'Pay the within to Messrs. Turnbull Forbes & Co / *Thos* Christie / Turnbull Forbes & Co / Reed for / J Martin Esq & Co / G *Bull*'.
21. M.W. wrote 'be'.
22. In his autobiography Rowan omitted this sentence.
23. The transcript reads 'and will and will'.
24. In his autobiography Rowan added 'your country'.

463

25. Wardle reads this as 'Jones' but it seems closer to James.

26. M.W. first wrote 'state', then crossed it out.

27. In his autobiography Rowan omitted the postscript relating to Imlay's clerk.

28. The transcript reads 'illness'.

29. The transcript reads 'Ethild'.

30. The comma is written in pencil, not in the ink which M.W. was using, and is thus most probably Godwin's.

31. 'Little' was underlined in the original letter but not in the ink M.W. was using.

32. In his autobiography Rowan wrote 'equally explicit'.

33. In his autobiography Rowan wrote 'respecting as I do the qualities of your head and heart'.

34. In his autobiography, Rowan wrote 'exertion'.

35. M.W. misspelt it as 'approachant' and then she, or more likely Godwin, crossed out the 'a'.

36. M.W. wrote 'house'.

37. 'You' was very likely inserted by Godwin.

38. The comma is written in pencil, not in the ink M.W. was using.

39. The semi-colon, amending a comma, was again made in pencil.

40. Once again, the comma is in pencil.

41. ''s' was added in pencil.

42. On the back of M.W.'s note Godwin wrote a list of names: Inchbald, Debret, Dealtry, Lawrence, and Northcote. Inchbald's name was crossed out.

43. Pencil brackets around the sentence 'excepting . . . remembrance' in the original.

44. Pencil brackets around the sentence 'Tell me . . . repay you' in the original.

45. Pencil brackets around the sentence.

46. Pencil brackets around the two sentences 'William . . . to be a man!'

47. M.W. wrote 'mine'.

48. Durant's transcript of the original MS in *Supp*. reads 'boy'.

49. Pencil brackets around the sentences 'One word . . . the truth'.

Index

465